The British Courts and Extra-territoriality in Japan, 1859–1899

The British Courts and Extra-territoriality in Japan, 1859–1899

By

Christopher Roberts

GLOBAL ORIENTAL

LEIDEN · BOSTON
2014

Library of Congress Cataloging-in-Publication Data

Roberts, Christopher, (lawyer)
The British courts and extra-territoriality in Japan, 1859-1899 / By Christopher Roberts.
p. cm.
Includes bibliographical references and index.
ISBN 9789004257566 (hardback : alk. paper) 1. Courts--Great Britain--History. 2. Jurisdiction--Great Britain--History. 3. Exterritoriality. 4. Consular jurisdiction. 5. Great Britain--Foreign relations--Japan 6. Japan--Foreign relations--Great Britain. 7. Great Britain--Commerce--Japan--History. 8. Japan--Commerce--Great Britain--History I. Title.

KD7261.J37R63 2013
347.41'04--dc23

2013033815

This publication has been typeset in the multilingual "Brill" typeface. With over 5,100 characters covering Latin, IPA, Greek, and Cyrillic, this typeface is especially suitable for use in the humanities. For more information, please see www.brill.com/brill-typeface.

ISBN 978-90-04-25756-6 (hardback)
ISBN 978-90-04-25855-6 (e-book)

Koninklijke Brill NV incorporates the imprints Brill, Global Oriental, Hotei Publishing, IDC Publishers and Martinus Nijhoff Publishers.

This book is printed on acid-free paper.

This book is dedicated to my mother

CONTENTS

List of Tables and Note on Sources xi
Note on Place-names xiii
Note on Currency xv
Abbreviations xvii
Preface xxi
Acknowledgement xxxi

1. British Extra-territoriality 1
   - Why Extra-territoriality? 1
   - The Treaty 7
   - British Legal Basis for Extra-territorial Regime 10
   - China and Japan Order in Council, 1865 15
   - The Yokohama Court 20
   - Later Orders in Council 27
   - British Regulations and Japanese Law 31
   - The Courts 39

2. The Players in the Legal System 47
   - The Judges 48
   - Legal Profession 58
   - Crown Advocates 72
   - The Consuls 75
   - Interpreters, Clerks, Constables and Ushers 84
   - Remuneration 87

3. Criminal Jurisdiction 93
   - Defendants 99
   - Prosecutors 103
   - Prosecutions by the Japanese Authorities 110
   - Convictions and Possible Bias 126
   - Punishments 135
   - Gaols 139
   - Deportations from Japan 144
   - Removal to Hong Kong for Trial 147
   - Conclusion 148

4. The Sea 151
Jurisdiction 152
The Impact of War 162
The Sealing Cases 165
Shipping Offences 167
Civil Matters 176
Inquiries and Naval Courts 179

5. Civil Jurisdiction 191
Jurisdiction 191
Case-load and the Litigants 194
Claims 200
Results and Possible Bias 214
Court Procedures 219
Reconciliation and Arbitration 223
Civil Status 227
Probate and Administration 236
Kaleidoscope of Regimes 241

6. Appeals 253
Criminal Offences 253
Civil Cases 261

7. The *Chishima-Ravenna* Collision 283
The Naval Court 284
The Legal Battle 288
The Drowned Sailors 300
Settlement 302
What the *Chishima Cases* Show 303

8. The End of Extra-Territoriality 315
The Iwakura Mission 316
The Tokyo Treaty Revision Conferences 319
Discussions in London 328
Implementation of the 1894 Treaty 334

9. Conclusion 339

Epilogue 349

Appendices
I Legal Officers, Ministers and Foreign Secretaries, 1859–1899 353
II Orders in Council Applicable to Japan 355
III British Lawyers in Japan 356
IV Foreign Population in Japan 358
V Tables Relating to Cases 359
VI List of Deportations from Japan, 1866–1899 407
VII *Chishima Cases*: Time-line of Events 410

Sources and Bibliography 415
Primary Sources 415
Statutes 415
Orders in Council 415
Official Records 415
Collections of Primary Sources 415
Law Reports 416
Secondary Sources 416
Newspapers 416
Bibliography 417

Index 423

LIST OF TABLES AND NOTE ON SOURCES

Shipping movements and British populations (1883–1884) 168

Note on Sources 359

1. Japan-wide, 1859–1899. Summary of Court case-load by year. 362
2. All Ports, 1859–1899. Criminal Offences—shipping offences and criminal cases: summary case-load. 364
3. All Ports, 1859–1899. Criminal Offences—shipping offences and criminal cases: annual case-load. 366
4. Criminal Cases, 1862–1899: Offences classified by defendants. 370
5. Criminal Cases, 1862–1899: Prosecutors. 375
6. Nagasaki, 1866–1899. Criminal cases: Prosecutors. 376
7. Criminal Cases, 1862–1899: Prosecutors and defendants' residence. 378
8. Criminal Cases, 1862–1899. Breakdown of offences by prosecutor. 379
9. Criminal Cases, 1862–1899: Acquittals. 381
10. Criminal Cases, 1862–1899: Pleas and acquittals by prosecutor. 382
11. Nagasaki, 1875–1899. Criminal Cases Acquittals: time-sliced by numbers and percentages. 383
12. Hakodate, 1863–1878. Criminal Cases: Convictions. 383
13. Criminal Cases, 1862–1899: Punishments. 384
14. Shipping Offences, 1862–1899: Nationality, charges and results. 386
15. Shipping Offences, 1862–1899: Punishments. 388
16. Naval Courts of Enquiry, 1864–1899. 389
17. All Ports, 1859–1899. Civil Cases: case-load. 390
18. Civil Cases, 1859–1899. Summary and annual averages. 393
19. Civil Cases, 1862–1899. Classification. 394
20. Civil Cases, 1862–1899. Amounts of claims (where available). 395
21. Civil Cases, 1862–1899. Results. 397
22. Appeals, 1859–1899. 399
23. Appeals in Civil Cases: Classification. 402

24. Appellants in Civil Cases: Identities. 403
25. Appeals in Civil Cases: Results. 404
26. Use of counsel in appeals and results (civil cases). 405
27. Nagasaki, 1878–1899. Fees in civil and criminal cases. 406

NOTE ON PLACE-NAMES

For Japan and China, the current naming and spelling of place names is used with one exception. That exception is in relation to Kanagawa and Yokohama. Although the British consulate was physically located at Yokohama, it was usually described, in official documents, as being at Kanagawa—the place mentioned in the Anglo-Japanese Treaty of Yedo 1858 as the location for a consulate. All references in this book are to Yokohama except to distinguish that consulate's consular court (which is referred to as the Kanagawa Court) from the Yokohama Court (see Chapter 1) and when referring to the Japanese prefecture of Kanagawa.

NOTE ON CURRENCY

A confusing factor in all records and reports is currency. Four currencies were relevant: Sterling (£), Yen (¥) (which, itself, replaced the older categories of *bu*, *mon*, *shu* and *ryo* in 1870), the silver Mexican Dollar ($) (which was the effective currency in much of the Asia-Pacific region), and silver taels (Ts),[1] which were used concurrently in China. With no consistency, all four were referred to in contemporary records and newspapers. Currency is irrelevant when distinguishing between types of case, acquittals and convictions, and success or failure in civil cases; but, it is relevant when considering the level of claims and fines. The problem is that the Yen and the silver-based tael and Dollar depreciated significantly during the period: for instance, from $3:£1 in 1863[2] and $5:£1 in 1865,[3] the Dollar dropped to $10:£1 in March 1894,[4] whilst the Yen had dropped from ¥5: £1 in 1870 when the Yen was introduced at parity with the Dollar[5] to ¥10:£1 by 1899.[6] Except for certain analytical purposes (when other currencies have been converted to Dollars) the text refers to the currency referred to in the relevant records.

1 Approximately Ts1.33: $1; FO276/2, page 32.

2 For instance, the 1863 indemnity paid by Japan to Britain was calculated at five shillings per Mexican Dollar: Neale to Russell, 26 June 1863; FO410/7.

3 Foreign Office Circular, 8 July 1865; FO276/9.

4 Various Circulars from the Legation to Consuls, FO798/51.

5 Grace Fox, *Britain and Japan, 1858–1883* (Oxford: Clarendon, 1969), page 403.

6 Certificate from the Hong Kong and Shanghai Banking Corporation (HSBC), 30 September 1899; FO276/59.

ABBREVIATIONS

$	Mexican Dollars
£	Pounds Sterling
¥	Yen
1894 Treaty	Treaty of Commerce and Navigation, 1894 between Japan and the United Kingdom
AWOL	Absent without leave
Chief Justice	from 1879 onwards, Chief Justice of the Supreme Court. (Note: in cited correspondence, usage is often inaccurate and this term is used occasionally in correspondence after 1870 but, before 1879, when it describes the Judge of the Supreme Court)
Chishima case	The Japanese government's suit against P&O in respect of the collision between the *Chishima* and the *Ravenna* which culminated in the reported case, *IJG v. P&O*
Chishima cases	The *Chishima case* and the *Tsune Kijima case*
Consular Courts	Courts held by British Consuls as part of the extra-territorial system
Courts	All the courts: Consular Courts, the Yokohama Court and HMCJ
Criminal case	A criminal offence committed within Japanese territory (i.e. in Japan or on a ship within Japanese territorial waters)
Criminal offence	A criminal offence wherever committed
Directory	*Japan Directory* (and others of a similar nature)
EW	*The Eastern World*
FO	Foreign Office series of papers in the British National Archives
HMCJ	Her Britannic Majesty's Court for Japan
HN	*The Hiogo News*
HSBC	The Hong Kong and Shanghai Banking Corporation Limited (and all predecessor organizations)
HSW 1882 Memorandum	Memorandum to Sir Thomas Wade (British Minister in Beijing) enclosed with Wilkinson to Parkes, 27 July 1882; FO656/31

HSW 1894 Memorandum	Wilkinson to unknown addressee, 15 November 1894; FO656/31
HSW 1882 Letter	Wilkinson to Parkes, 30 November 1882; FO83/885
IJG v. P&O	*The Imperial Japanese Government v. Peninsular and Oriental Steam Navigation Company* [1895] AC 644
Inquiry	An Inquiry into a Death at Sea on board a British flagged merchant vessel
JDH	*Japan Daily Herald*
JG	*Japan Gazette*
JTOM	*The Japan Times Overland Mail*
Judge	1865–1878, Judge of Supreme Court; thereafter, Judge of HMCJ
JWC	*Japan Weekly Chronicle*
JWM	*Japan Weekly Mail*
Kanagawa Court	The Consular Court of the Kanagawa (Yokohama) consulate as distinct from the Yokohama Court
KWC	*Kobe Weekly Chronicle*
MSA1854	Merchant Shipping Act, 1854
MSA1894	Merchant Shipping Act, 1894
MSA	MSA1854 and MSA1894
MT	Transport Ministries' series of papers in the British National Archives
Naval Court	A Naval Court of Enquiry
NCH	*North China Herald*
NCHLR	Law reports contained in NCH
OC1859	Japan Order in Council, 1859
OC1860	Japan Order in Council, 1860
OC1861	Japan Order in Council, 1861
OC1865	China and Japan Order in Council, 1865
OC1878	China and Japan Order in Council, 1878
OC1881	China and Japan Order in Council, 1881
OC1884	China, Japan and Corea Order in Council, 1884
OC1886	China, Japan and Corea Order in Council, 1886
OC1899	Suspension of Jurisdiction in Japan Order in Council, 1899
OC1904	China and Corea Order in Council, 1904
P&O	Peninsular and Oriental Steam Navigation Company

P&O Memorandum	Memorandum prepared by P&O for use in settlement negotiations
PC	Privy Council series of papers in the British National Archives
PCO	Privy Council Office
PJS	Transactions and Proceedings of the Japan Society 1892–1941; The Bulletin of the Japan Society from 1950 to 1985; and Proceedings of the Japan Society thereafter
Privy Council	The Judicial Committee of the Privy Council
PRO	Public Record Office series of papers in the British National Archives
Rennie's Circular	Circular No. 1 of 4 March 1884, Supreme Court to Consuls; FO796/10
SCHK	Supreme Court of Hong Kong
Shanghai Returns	Annual returns of cases heard by the Supreme Court in Shanghai, 1867–1870
Shipping offence	A criminal offence committed on board a British flagged merchant vessel justiciable pursuant to the MSA or OC1865
Spring-Rice Memorandum	Memorandum prepared by Cecil Arthur Spring-Rice (Second Secretary at the Legation) enclosed with de Bunsen to Rosebery, 13 July 1893; FO46/480
Supreme Court	Her Britannic Majesty's Supreme Court for China and Japan
TJH	*The Japan Herald*
Treaty	Treaty of Yedo, 1858 between Japan and the United Kingdom
TRS&NE	*The Rising Sun & Nagasaki Express*
Ts	Taels
TS	Treasury Solicitor's series of papers in the British National Archives
Tsune Kijima case	*Tsune Kijima and Others v. Peninsular and Oriental Steam Navigation Company* reported as *Peninsular and Oriental Steam Navigation Company v. Tsune Kijima and Others* [1895] AC 661
Yokohama Court	The court based in Yokohama 1871–1878 and presided over by an officer detached from the Supreme Court (see Chapter 1)

PREFACE

Since Japan was 'opened up' to the West by the *Ansei* treaties in the 1850s, three waves of foreign lawyers have 'invaded' Japan and each has impacted upon Japanese legal and commercial life out of proportion to its size. The first, predominantly British, wave followed the *Ansei* treaties.[1] In the Treaty of Yedo 1858 (**Treaty**), the British, along with the other Western powers who signed similar treaties, demanded extra-territorial rights. The Treaty and the other *Ansei* treaties provided for Hakodate, Yokohama and Nagasaki to be opened for foreign residence and trade from 1859 and Kobe, Niigata, Osaka and Tokyo followed in 1868 and 1869; but, foreigners were banned from travelling to, living in or trading with any other part of Japan.

In any discussion of life and business within the Treaty Ports one often finds a degree of confusion about just what is meant by 'extra-territoriality'. The term requires explanation as it is a somewhat uncommon concept in the twenty-first century outside the military area and 'status of forces agreements'. 'Extra-territoriality' does not cover the establishment or existence of the Treaty Ports as such or many of the other aspects of the *Ansei* treaties such as the Western imposed regulation of Japanese customs duties and tariffs or the restriction of the Westerners' residence rights to just the Treaty Ports. It was a creature of custom and usage or, by the nineteenth century, treaty and, in the Anglo-Japanese context, a system whereby a British subject in Japan was subject not to the territorial jurisdiction of Japan's courts and sovereign but to the jurisdiction of his own sovereign.

Extra-territoriality amounted to an exception to the contemporary international order which recognized a sovereign's jurisdiction over all within his own territories and looked, instead, to a personal jurisdiction. Extra-territoriality must be distinguished from immunity, where a person is not amenable to suit; extra-territoriality confers no such immunity but speaks to the courts having jurisdiction. If a Briton committed any crime or incurred any civil liability, the complainant was obliged to bring him

[1] The second, predominantly American, group of foreign lawyers arrived with, and stayed on after, the Occupation in 1945 whilst the most recent arrival of foreign lawyers occurred after 1987 with the growing internationalization of legal practice in Japan.

exclusively before the British Consuls who operated a court system similar to that back in Britain. In Japan, British defendants were amenable to no other jurisdiction regardless of whether the crimes were committed against, or liabilities incurred towards, a fellow Briton, a Japanese or another Westerner.[2]

A discussion of extra-territoriality does not, strictly, extend to a consideration of British claims against Japanese subjects for, although such claims were referred to in the Treaty, they remained within the ambit of Japanese jurisdiction—albeit that British Consuls were involved in providing consular assistance in relation to such claims in the early years. This book looks at how British jurisdiction operated within Japan from its inception in 1859 until its abolition in 1899 and what extra-territoriality meant for the small British community there and transient visitors to Japan; particularly sailors crewing British vessels.

Niigata never developed as a port[3] and no cases were reported there; and Osaka became, principally, a residential base for missionaries during most of the period under consideration so that, after the early years, consular business for Osaka was handled at Kobe. Thus, neither Niigata nor Osaka plays much part in the story of the British Courts in Japan. This is equally true of Taiwan. After the Japanese occupation of Taiwan in 1895, Japan applied the Treaty to Taiwan with effect from 22 January 1896[4] and the British consulates there came under the Minister in Tokyo.[5] However, no cases came before the British consuls at Tainan (including its adjacent settlements of Anping and Kaohsiung (then Takow)) or Tamsui in the period 1896–1899.[6]

---

[2] The terms 'Western' and 'Westerners' encompass Europeans and North Americans. The only non-Western states with extra-territoriality in Japan were China, Peru and Hawai'i but none impacts upon this story.

[3] J.F. Lowder opened the Niigata Consulate in February 1869. James Troup replaced him later that year but Niigata never attracted a large foreign body or took off as a port due to the treacherous bar off the harbour entrance. During Winter months it was an unsafe anchorage and the Japanese agreed that Western ships could use the nearby anchorage at Ebisu-Minato at this time of year. The Consulate was closed down in 1872 but re-opened in 1877 and 1878 for the summer season, when shipping might be expected. It was finally closed in 1878 due to lack of activity and staffing constraints which meant that the Niigata Consul could be better deployed elsewhere.

[4] Hurst (Consul, Tainan) to Satow, 29 February 1896; FO262/735.

[5] Hurst to Satow, 13 December 1895; FO262/735. Hurst and the other Consul in Taiwan asked to be re-located to China and J.H. Longford was sent from Japan as Consul in Tainan.

[6] Taiwan was not a centre of litigation—only one civil dispute in the preceding five years had been recorded and even this had settled before hearing.

Although extra-territoriality was a key feature of Japan's changing relations with Britain for forty years, most English language literature on Japan and Anglo-Japanese relations of the period treats extra-territoriality as a fixture—usually, a thorn—in Anglo-Japanese relations, without any discussion of its practical workings. By examining the underlying bedrock of court cases and the individuals who operated the system, this book uses the available English language source materials to evaluate the workings of the British regime and its practical consequences for the British community in Japan. Although it re-assesses criticisms of the regime made by earlier studies, it does not examine the conceptual merits or history of extra-territoriality as such or aim to cover the impact of foreign extra-territoriality upon Japanese society apart from noting how disputed cases helped to form and mirror changes in the overall Anglo-Japanese relationship during the period. Equally, it does not seek to draw any comparisons with how other states exercised their extra-territorial rights in Japan or how British extra-territorial rights were exercised elsewhere.

The Japanese authorities faced a balancing exercise between not buttressing a system which the Japanese came to regard as demeaning and insulting to their dignity and whose abolition they sought whilst, concurrently, ensuring that order was maintained in the seaports and Japanese nationals had effective remedies against British subjects. This book examines how the Courts regulated the British community's dealings with the Japanese and the other foreign communities resident in Japan and how the Japanese authorities dealt with the Courts and the nature of prosecutions and suits brought against British subjects by Japanese and other foreign, businesses and individuals.

The general assumption has always been that the Courts were biased in favour of British defendants and Japanese could obtain no justice there; but, is this assumption justified? Chang[7] demonstrated that the Japanese belief that the Courts were biased is not sustained by a review of five well-known cases involving Japanese claimants which he argues were correctly decided in the light of contemporary English legal and sentencing practice. This book compares the success rates of Japanese and non-Japanese litigants in a far broader range of cases before, largely, confirming Chang's conclusions.

---

[7] Richard T. Chang, *The Justice of the Western Consular Courts in Nineteenth-Century Japan*, (Westport and London: Greenwich Press, 1984).

Whilst several weighty tomes on extra-territoriality in China exist and Eileen Scully's bibliography on the subject is extensive,[8] no great body of English language literature exists directly on the subject of British extra-territoriality in Japan and the Courts' daily work has not been covered in detail before in the English language literature. Previous writings have tended to consider the background to the *Ansei* treaties, the court structure and the negotiations leading to extra-territoriality's abolition; but, when discussing the system itself, authors have tended to confine themselves to describing, somewhat formulaically, the court structure and highlighting the more notorious cases without examining the range of cases heard by the Courts or the Courts' decisions as a whole. Given the emotion to which extra-territoriality gave rise on all sides, this is a strange omission for, without understanding the Courts' daily work, it is impossible to assess whether such emotion was just hot air (and a cover for something else). For British subjects, the consequences of extra-territoriality went beyond amenability to suit in the Courts: such as personal status (e.g. nationality and procedures for marriage—particularly to Japanese subjects; protection of lunatics and their property), bankruptcies, insolvencies and inheritance—all of which had a direct and practical personal relevance to individual Britons resident in Japan.

F.C. Jones provided the first survey of extra-territoriality in Japan from an historical perspective in 1931.[9] Although his work founds the small body of literature that deals specifically with extra-territoriality in Japan, he does not consider the great mass of the Consuls' work and, the *Chishima case*[10] apart, discusses only a handful of the earlier cases. Much the greatest examination of the extra-territorial system in Japan to date came in 1971 when Hoare placed the system within the overall context of the expatriate experience of life within the Treaty Ports.[11] He described how successive Japanese governments sought to push back, and limit, the boundaries of British extra-territoriality by insisting upon a strict observance of the Treaty's terms. Various of the more famous incidents and

[8] Eileen P. Scully, *Bargaining with the State from Afar* (New York: Columbia University Press, 2001).

[9] F.C. Jones, *Extraterritoriality in Japan* (Yale and Oxford: Yale University Press, 1931).

[10] The subject of Chapter 7 (The *Chishima-Ravenna* collision). It arose from the collision between the Japanese warship, *Chishima kan*, and the P&O steamer, ss *Ravenna*, and involved the Japanese government taking an appeal to the Privy Council over the extent of extra-territoriality.

[11] J.E. Hoare, 'The Japanese Treaty Ports' (PhD diss, Queen Mary College, London, 1971) which formed the basis for J.E. Hoare, *Japan's Treaty Ports and Foreign Settlements* (Folkstone: Japan Library, 1994).

cases have been written up or commented upon over the years—often in an isolated context. Although these are referred to within the body of this book, I have not sought, except for aspects of the *Chishima case*, to repeat the case descriptions—although readers are referred to these other accounts.

The principal sources used in this book are original and contemporary English language sources. Treaties, legislation (primary and secondary) and reported cases are accessible in the general statute books and law reports. Other key sources are correspondence in the British National Archives and the Court records including many of the semi-annual returns of cases which the Consuls were required to make after 1865. These semi-annual returns are a key base for a quantitative analysis of the Consular Courts' work. However, they vary in quality and are incomplete: for instance, they were not always completed, which prompted admonitory demands for them from the Judge to Consul, nor were they always completed in a consistent manner—even within the same Consulate from one year to the next let alone between Consulates.

The Nagasaki Court records are the most detailed. They include the Register of Civil Cases (1878–1899), the Register of Criminal Cases (1878–1899) and the Charge Book (1885–1899). The court minute books for 25 of extra-territoriality's 40 years (1875–1899) provide a wealth of detail and allow for a detailed analysis of that Court's workload. The Hakodate semi-annual returns[12] and Court correspondence for the period 1863 to 1878 also enable us to build up a good picture and analysis of the cases tried there during that period. The other Courts' semi-annual returns are, largely, missing and, save for occasional transcripts relating to appealed cases, contain no records of individual cases. The Tokyo Vice-Consulate's semi-annual returns summarize case results from 1871 to 1897 (apart from 1892 and 1893) but provide no description of the cases or explanation for the judgments.

The biggest gap in the official records is the absence of any detailed case records for Her Britannic Majesty's Court for Japan (HMCJ) which, from 1879, heard almost all the major cases in Japan and supervised the other Courts. Its archives and other property were all transferred to the Yokohama Consulate-General when HMCJ closed. None of these records—nor any of the Tokyo Vice-Consulate's archives, which were also transferred to the Yokohama Consulate-General in 1897 when that

[12] Each Court was required to submit semi-annual returns to the Judge listing the criminal and civil cases before that Court during the half year in question.

Vice-Consulate was abolished[13]—are available. It is quite possible that these were destroyed along with the Yokohama Consulate during the earthquake and subsequent fire of 1923. These records' absence is not replaced effectively by the other Courts' correspondence records (the busiest of which, Kobe, are also missing—presumably destroyed along with that consulate's other records during the Second World War[14]). Statistical analysis of the official records is, thus, dependent largely on the Nagasaki and Hakodate cases.

Where there are no official records, we are compelled to rely upon the case reports in the newspapers. Newspaper coverage was of two types: first, verbatim reports of court proceedings which, although not categorized as Law Reports, may be treated as original sources on a par with them; and, second, journalistic accounts of cases and editorials. In Japan, no single English language newspaper covered the whole period and, in the newspapers' early days, they were often unaware of when cases were due to come before the Consuls because there were no regular court sitting days and newspaper editors were unlikely to be favoured by the court clerk with the relevant information. This led the first newspapers, *The Nagasaki Shipping List and Advertiser* and *The Japan Herald*, to encourage their readers to inform them of any cases coming before the Courts.[15] The most consistent coverage is to be obtained from the *Japan Weekly Mail*, the *Japan Daily Herald* and the *Japan Gazette* which were published in Yokohama. Although the *Eastern World* was published in Yokohama from the late 1880s, the only extant copies date from 1899. Unsurprisingly, they all tended to concentrate on cases heard in Yokohama and reported only the more journalistically important cases elsewhere. The *Japan Weekly Mail* provided the best law report style case reports but, from the late 1870s, it focused on what it regarded as major cases and not run-of-the-mill cases whereas the *Japan Daily Herald* and the *Japan Gazette*, being published daily, provided greater coverage of the daily case-load.

However, the quality of factual reporting of this latter case-load varied considerably and there appears little difference between then and now as to what determined which cases were reported: shortage of other news, public standing of the litigants, salaciousness and journalistic whimsy

---

[13] Arthur Hyde Lay to Gerald Lowther, 16 November 1897; FO262/662.

[14] Kobe Consul to Hereward Hook (19 June 1952; FO1045/1) explains that the Kobe consulate's records—without detailing them—had been destroyed during the War.

[15] Editorial, 17 August 1861; *The Nagasaki Shipping List and Advertiser*; and 17 October 1863; *The Japan Herald* (**TJH**).

being the deciding factors. Editorials cannot be relied upon for dispassionate accounts and, almost always, reflected the editor's views—or, in the case of the *Japan Weekly Mail*, a general pro-Japanese stance as it was supported financially by the Japanese authorities and often questioned the stance taken by the British authorities in Japan and China. Despite these drawbacks, the contemporary English language press does provide a substantial basis for covering the official records' lacuna relating to the Kanagawa Court, the Yokohama Court and HMCJ.

In Kobe, we are, again, largely reliant upon newspaper reports for coverage of proceedings in that Court. As with Yokohama, no newspaper covers the entire period but *The Hiogo & Osaka Herald*, *The Hiogo News* and *The Kobe Chronicle* cover the periods 1868–1870, 1869–1888 and 1897 onwards respectively. Although the quality and frequency of case reports in all three newspapers varies from time to time, they do provide a fair insight into legal life in the Kobe Court.

Likewise, there is no complete set of records relating to appeals from Japan to Her Britannic Majesty's Supreme Court for China and Japan (**Supreme Court**) in Shanghai but, for those cases which were reported, the Law Reports (**NCHLR**) in the *North China Herald*, published in Shanghai, are an adequate substitute—certainly more so than the Chief Justice and Assistant Judge's minute books, which are skimpy. However, only 16 out of a total of 66 appeals were reported in NCHLR. For the other appeals, we are dependent upon the correspondence records between the Courts and the Supreme Court, referring to cases remitted for appeal and decisions received. Except for the *Chishima case*, no separate file exists in the National Archives for any appeal case. Therefore, assembling the history of any appeal is an exercise in fitting together pieces from each of the above-mentioned sources: an exercise which becomes easier after 1881 when the Supreme Court usually printed copies of its judgments for remission to HMCJ and distribution to the litigants.[16]

Until 1878, correspondence records exist between the Supreme Court and the Courts. These illustrate the Supreme Court's supervision of the Courts and the development of the Yokohama Court and HMCJ and provide insights into the legal profession. However, I have been unable to trace similar correspondence records been HMCJ and the Courts (other than Nagasaki) arising out of HMCJ's supervision of such Courts after January 1879. Additionally, the Nagasaki and Tokyo general

[16] The first being three cases sent by Hannen to Robertson on 21 November 1881; FO656/39.

correspondence files, covering 1869 to 1897, provide insights into other aspects of consular legal work over the years.

Although the source material for this book has been restricted to English language sources, I do not believe that non-consideration of Japanese language sources affects materially the analysis given this book's focus on the British community and its experiences of the Courts.

The first two chapters consider the background to, and legal basis for, British extra-territoriality in Japan and the court structure developed by Britain in Japan before identifying the key players within the system. It becomes clear very rapidly from even a cursory consideration of the case statistics that the bulk of cases—at least numerically—concerned criminal offences; and the vast majority of these concerned sailors on British flagged vessels rather than British subjects resident in Japan. Chapters 3 and 4 consider the Courts' criminal jurisdiction and divide all criminal offences into those which consisted of crimes committed within Japan and those which related to, or arose in connection with, British shipping trading with Japan. The chapters consider the nature of the offences which came before the Courts and who tended to prosecute which types of offences before looking at the proportion of convictions and the range of sentences which tended to be handed down. Chapter 4 also looks at the Naval Courts of Enquiry held in Japan under the British Merchant Shipping Acts.

Chapter 5 looks at the nature of the civil cases which came before the Courts. Although less numerous, they often involved large sums of money and occupied more of the Courts' time. It also considers the complexities to which the multiplicity of jurisdictions extant in Japan at that time gave rise. Chapter 6 reviews the appeals process—a process which related more to civil cases than criminal cases. All four chapters consider the extent to which allegations of a pro-British bias and partiality against the Courts and the judges can be substantiated on the basis of a numerical analysis of the case results. Each chapter also considers the extent to which the interplay between Britain and Japan in relation to the day-to-day operation of British extra-territoriality may be taken as a proxy for the changing diplomatic and power relationships between the two countries.

Chapter 7 examines in detail the court cases which resulted from the collision between the Japanese warship, the *Chishima kan*, and the P&O steamer, *ss Ravenna* in 1892. The case dragged on for nearly three years and overlapped the final negotiations for the 1894 Treaty which brought an end to British extra-territoriality in Japan. It also highlighted—and crystallized—many of the practical issues surrounding civil litigation between the subjects of different countries under a general regime of extra-territoriality. Then, chapter 8 reviews the history of the negotiations which led to that treaty.

Christopher K. Roberts
London
May 2013

ACKNOWLEDGEMENT

I wish to acknowledge: the support and guidance given to me by Dr Angus Lockyer of SOAS for his encouraging me to write this book and his perceptive comments on the issues covered; Dr Jocelyn Chatterton of SOAS for her insightful review of early drafts; the staff at the National Archives at Kew who traced numerous record files for me; the staff at the Yokohama Archives of History, the Kobe City Archives and the Nagasaki Prefectural Library in Nagasaki who allowed me to access many of the English language newspapers published in Japan during the period; and Alison Evans, Stefan Gross and Brian Harrison for reading and commenting upon earlier drafts of sections of the work. My thanks are also due to Paul Norbury and his team at Global Oriental for keeping me to deadlines and for publishing this book. Of course, I alone remain responsible for the ultimate product and any errors in it are entirely down to me.

CHAPTER ONE

BRITISH EXTRA-TERRITORIALITY

Why Extra-territoriality?

Following the Westphalian settlement of 1648, territorial jurisdiction became an accepted tenet of Western international dealing and no country could exercise jurisdiction over its subjects in another country without that other country's consent;[1] so, why was extra-territoriality—a 'system of law'[2] which was described as 'exceptional'[3]—adopted by Britain to oust Japan's territorial jurisdiction? Without an understanding of the background, we cannot assess the extent to which the British regime in Japan met the original aims behind its imposition or appreciate several areas of difficulty which arose during its course.

Whilst historians point to the *Saris* agreement[4] and Admiral Stirling's treaty[5] as precursors to British extra-territorial rights in Japan, the Treaty of Yedo 1858 (the **Treaty**) was the post-1859 basis for these rights. Japan's explicit consent was a non-negotiable *sine qua non* to British trade and residence in Japan[6] and, despite later Japanese fulminations against the perceived insult occasioned by Western extra-territoriality, the Treaty's extra-territorial provisions, which largely followed the Treaty of Tianjin 1858, were uncontentious at the time the Treaty was negotiated.

Given how little debate these provisions occasioned at the time and the fact that none of the contemporaneous accounts by participants in the

---

1 W.E. Hall, *A Treatise on the Foreign Powers and Jurisdiction of the British Crown* (Oxford: The Clarendon Press, 1894), page 3.

2 Russell's instructions to Hornby, May 1865; FO17/433.

3 Ibid.

4 A grant of privileges from Japan to the East India Company, 1610.

5 Exchanged between Admiral Stirling and the Governor of Nagasaki in 1854. This provided that 'inferior persons' should be 'delivered over to the commanders of their ships for punishment' if they broke Japanese laws. It was not a general commercial treaty but negotiated in the context of the Admiral's desire for a naval base and naval help to counter the Russians. See William McOmie, *The Opening of Japan 1853–1858* (Folkestone: Global Oriental, 2006), chapters 12 and 13.

6 See Hugh Cortazzi, *Britain and the 'Re-opening' of Japan: The Treaty of Yedo 1858 and the Elgin Mission* (Dorchester: The Japan Society, 2008), pages 51–53. Cortazzi describes Elgin's instructions from the Foreign Office which required that the extra-territoriality provisions be drawn in clear and explicit language.

negotiations of the *Ansei* treaties addresses extra-territoriality in detail, there is no contemporary evidence as to either side's motivations. Equally, none of these accounts suggests that extra-territoriality caused any problem in the negotiations. Michael Auslin reviewed, from both sides, the *Ansei* treaties' negotiation.[7] Although considering the treaties as a whole without focusing upon extra-territoriality, he demonstrates that extra-territoriality was a non-issue for the Japanese. The *bakufu* (the Shogunate government) were content to treat foreigners as another *han* (feudal domain) and leave administration of justice over them to their leaders.[8] This is explicable when we appreciate that there was no single legal regime in Tokugawa Japan: in somewhat simplistic terms, it was not unlike feudal Europe or the mediaeval Welsh Marches with a multiplicity of overlapping regimes where each lordship or *han* had its own laws but within a wider overlordship context.

Auslin contends that the Japanese authorities (*bakufu* and Meiji) focused upon extra-territoriality only after 1865 when they accepted the impracticality of assuaging domestic xenophobic elements by ejecting the foreigners and, so, determined upon a course of proving to the Japanese nation that it was the equal of the Westerners—and one way to do this was by eliminating the one-sided nature of the *Ansei* treaties (including extra-territoriality).

Therefore, we must look to *ex post facto* rationalizations and justifications for British extra-territoriality in Japan. Extra-territoriality is sometimes presented in Christian versus non-Christian terms and some contemporary Westerners did talk in terms of the superiority of Christian moral values. When Winchester reached a tentative agreement with the Japanese authorities regarding the desirability of their including assessors from the Western Powers when trying any Westerner who was not protected by his own extra-territoriality, the Law Officers,[9] whilst conceding

[7] Michael Robert Auslin, *Negotiating with Imperialism: The Unequal Treaties and the Culture of Japanese Diplomacy* (Harvard: Harvard University Press, 2004), based upon 'Negotiating with Imperialism: Japan and the unequal treaty regime 1858–72' (PhD diss., University of Illinois, 2000).

[8] Cortazzi, 2008, page 74 footnote 96 also cites comments from Professor Nakasuga Tetsuro to this effect.

[9] The English Law Officers (as distinct from the Scottish and Irish Law Officers) also advised the British government on public and private international law matters. They consisted of the Attorney General and the Solicitor General (both of whom were politicians and changed with each government) and, until 1875, the Admiralty Advocate who represented the Crown in the Admiralty Courts (Robert Joseph Phillimore, 1855–1862; Travers Twiss, 1862–1867 and Dr James Parker Deane, 1867–1875) and, until 1877, the Queen's Advocate who represented the Crown in the Ecclesiastical Courts

that the Japanese had jurisdiction, said that it seemed 'most expedient ... that... this jurisdiction should be tempered (if possible) by the advice, and moral control, of Christian Assessors'.[10] In this, they were merely reiterating the standard view of the time. Two years earlier, Dr Lushington, when delivering the Privy Council's judgment in the *Laconia* on appeal from the British court in Constantinople, said that 'in almost all transactions, whether political or mercantile, a wide difference subsists in the dealings between an Oriental and a Christian State and the intercourse between two Christian nations'.[11]

On the other hand, Hinckley stated any perception of Christian versus non-Christian was mere coincidence and simply reflected the relative dominance of the Western (Christian) Powers; it had no theological imperative.[12] Whatever the historical derivation—or dressing-up—of Britain's practice of extra-territoriality by the 1850s, it was simply how matters were handled from the Levant eastwards[13] and, as British influence expanded eastwards, so extra-territoriality followed. As can be seen from Britain's fundamental negotiating position about the later abolition of extra-territoriality, Britain—and its traders—required a settled system of law, based on generally accepted international precepts, which was publicly available and administered—and enforced—by an independent judiciary.

It is unclear what, if anything, Britain knew or understood about Japanese law before it negotiated the Treaty: it certainly had no reason to depart from its recent demands for extra-territoriality in China where extra-territoriality had been specifically demanded in the Foreign Office's negotiating instructions for the Treaty of Humen, the provisions of which

(Sir John Dorney Harding, 1852–1862; Sir Robert Joseph Phillimore and Sir Travers Twiss, 1867–1877). Practitioners in both the Admiralty Courts and the Ecclesiastical Courts were usually the same. The Admiralty Advocate and the Queen's Advocate advised on public international law matters until both positions were abolished. The Admiralty Advocate and the Queen's Advocate were apolitical appointments and did not change as governments changed.

10 Law Officers to Russell, 26 March 1865; FO83/2299.

11 *Papayanni v. The Russian Steam Navigation Company* 15 Eng Rep 862, 889 (2 Moo. P.C. (N.S.) 1863).

12 '...the religions of the Far East have had no direct bearing upon the rights of foreigners sojourning in those countries..,' Frank E. Hinckley, *American Consular Jurisdiction in the Orient*, (Washington DC: W.H. Loudermilk, 1906), page 115.

13 The East is a region 'in which custom and necessity have set up relations between Western and Oriental countries differing widely from anything which now exists' among Western powers with extensive judicial privileges and correlative derogations of sovereignty; Hall 1894, page 132.

had been expanded upon in the recent Treaty of Tianjin.[14] Its concerns were, to its own mind, soon justified for the British found the Japanese system to be an opaque, secret, arbitrary and barbaric one with torture commonplace[15] and a bias against foreigners. Even the USA, the Power most inclined to favour Japan on the subject, considered that 'the utter incompatibility of habits of thought on all legal and moral questions made it impossible to trust the person, the property and the lives of our own people to such a jurisdiction'.[16]

Such complaints lingered. In 1872, Sir Harry Parkes, the Minister to Tokyo,[17] argued that abolition was impossible until the Japanese 'possess and are able to apply a criminal code of a humane character, and until they acquire an adequate knowledge of Civil law and procedure'.[18] A decade later, when Britain was preparing for Treaty revision negotiations, Richard Rennie, then the British Judge at Yokohama, repeated concerns about secrecy surrounding Japanese criminal proceedings, the absence of trained judges in the Japanese courts and said that such criminal codes as existed (which had been taken from Chinese precedents) were 'totally unsuited to Western ideas',[19] both as regards the definition of crimes and punishments meted out. Martin Dohmen, a British Consul, complained of defective interpretation in the Japanese courts and such courts' failure to call British witnesses;[20] complaints which were echoed by the US consul at Yokohama.[21]

Despite improvements over time, the expatriate's jaundiced view of the Japanese legal system, derived from the earlier days, never left him. British communities felt that 'they would be exposed to frequent and vexatious police interference on frivolous pretexts and to constant petty

---

[14] The Treaty of Nanjing, 1842's omission of any extra-territorial provisions was remedied, at the Foreign Office's direction, by the Treaty of Humen (The Bogue), 1843; the provisions of which were confirmed, and extended, by the Treaty of Tianjin, 1858. (G.W. Keeton, *The Development of Extraterritoriality in China* (New York: Longmans Green and Co., 1928), Vol. I, pages 174–176.)

[15] Alcock to Japanese Ministers for Foreign Affairs, 31 December 1861; FO881/1135.

[16] James Blaine (Department of State) to Sir Edward Thornton (British Minister, Washington) 3 June 1881; FO656/31.

[17] Britain was represented by Ministers at Legations in Beijing and Tokyo. The early Ministers to Tokyo also held the position of Consul-General to Japan. The Tokyo Legation was upgraded to an Embassy in 1905, when the Minister was designated an Ambassador.

[18] Memorandum, Parkes to Granville, 13 December 1872, of Parkes's interview with Iwakura Tomomi (a leading Japanese statesman of the period) on 27 November 1872; FO46/263.

[19] Rennie's memorandum 21 August 1880; FO46/268.

[20] Dohmen to Parkes, 6 December 1878; FO798/20.

[21] US consul at Kanagawa to Dohmen, 21 August 1876; FO798/24.

annoyances'[22] and diplomats feared the result would be frequent representations to consular authorities involving them in 'troublesome correspondence with the Japanese Government'.[23] Corruption was also an issue amongst the lower judiciary and Joseph H. Longford, a British Consul, bemoaned that, where foreigners were concerned, the Japanese judges were 'grossly partial and that not one ... is capable of dealing with many of the intricate questions that must arise among foreigners'.[24]

From the Meiji Restoration onwards, as John McMaster showed,[25] the British trading community's complaints centred less around the criminal code than on the lack of a Japanese bankruptcy law, which made debt collection difficult, and the difficulties of having justice administered—and judgments enforced—impartially. Some of these complaints may have been exaggerated and Russell Robertson (Yokohama Consul, with a reputation for having cordial relations with local Governors) provides a counter-balancing view when writing that Britons' just claims within the Governor's jurisdiction met with a ready settlement.[26] The problematic cases were those involving larger amounts and defendants outside the Governor's jurisdiction when delays often occurred—but he found that these were not all unreasonable and a settlement was usually concluded. He also highlighted instances where Japanese chances of obtaining payment for just claims against some Britons were remote due to financial exigencies. Allyson Honjo, whilst describing the trading environment between Western and Japanese traders as 'one of mutual distrust',[27] also cautions that 'one must not overstate the degree of mistrust which existed between the merchants'[28] because the newspaper reports and court cases reflected, inevitably, relationships that had broken down and not the daily details of smooth running operations.

Japanese nationalists, during their campaigns for the abolition of extra-territoriality, implied that the *bakufu* had not appreciated the nature of

22 Kennedy to Granville, 21 September 1880; FO46/268.

23 Ibid.

24 Longford to Satow, 14 September 1896, Ian Ruxton, *The Correspondence of Sir Ernest Satow, British Minister in Japan, 1895–1900* (Ian Ruxton, 2005), page 170. Satow regarded Longford as 'very anti-Japanese'; Satow to Bertie, 24 March 1898; Ian Ruxton, *The Semi-Official Letters of British Envoy Sir Ernest Satow from Japan and China (1895–1906)* (North Carolina: Lulu Press. Inc., 2007), page 109.

25 John McMaster, 'British Trade and Traders in Japan, 1859–69' (PhD diss., SOAS, 1962).

26 Robertson to Wilkinson, 25 February 1872; FO881/2315.

27 Yuki Allyson Honjo, *Japan's Early Experience of Contract Management in the Treaty Ports* (London: Japan Library, 2003), page 147.

28 Ibid, page 203.

the extra-territorial provisions. However, this argument is unsustainable: the Japanese had exercised effective control over the Dutch at Deshima for over 200 years and must have been cognizant of the issue for both their agreement with Admiral Stirling and the Russian treaty, 1855 addressed it. They were also familiar with extra-territoriality's workings in China after 1843 and the negotiation of the Treaty of Tianjin. Hinckley stated that neither Townsend Harris nor the Japanese authorities at the time regarded extra-territoriality as a marked disparagement to Japanese sovereignty[29] and Auslin, who examined the drivers on both sides for the negotiation of the *Ansei* treaties, concurred that the Treaty provisions relating to extra-territoriality were not disputed by the Japanese.

The practical consideration, for both sides, was that leaving each country responsible for its own citizens removed potential areas for dispute. Had the Japanese retained power over British subjects in the early days, it is easy to imagine that those troubles which did arise from attacks on British and other foreigners, and disputes between them and Japanese, would have multiplied the pressures on the British authorities to take even stronger action against Japan. This argument is supported by the explanation of the Japanese Foreign Minister, Mutsu Munemitsu, to the Diet in 1893 that 'the *bakufu*, in pursuit of their policy of isolating foreigners, endeavoured as far as possible to avoid all contact with them, ... accordingly made arrangements by which foreign consuls were authorized to exercise more or less jurisdiction over'[30] foreigners. This could be justified on the basis that, within Japan, *daimyo* exercised jurisdiction within their own *han* and foreigners were being treated almost as another *han* subject to their own authorities.[31] It was only when the impossibility of expelling the foreigners was recognized and Japan embarked upon a policy of seeking equality with Westerners that extra-territoriality became a political issue.

Earl Granville, the British Foreign Secretary, recognized this when, following the Iwakura Mission,[32] he stated that Britain desired the most

---

[29] Hinckley 1906, pages 37–38.

[30] Translation of Mutsu's speech of 29 December 1893 accompanying de Bunsen to Rosebery, 31 December 1893; FO881/6582.

[31] See Pär Cassel, *Grounds of Judgment* (New York: Oxford University press, 2012), chapter 1 for a discussion of legal pluralism in Japan before the Meiji period.

[32] A major diplomatic mission in 1871–1872 led by Iwakura Tomomi to the USA and Europe which raised Japan's desire to end the *Ansei* treaties' extra-territorial provisions. See Chapter 8 (Ending of Extra-territoriality) and, for a fuller description of the Mission, Ian Nish, ed, *The Iwakura Mission in America and Europe: A new Assessment* (Richmond: Japan Library, 1998).

friendly relations with Japan but was not prepared to expose the maintenance of these relations to risk by 'removing the security for British life and property which the extra-territoriality now enjoyed by Great Britain in Japan is calculated to secure'.[33] The British view was that it was not in Japan's interests to undertake responsibilities in this respect which it could not discharge and, by neglecting to discharge them, would bring Japan into collision with Britain. This concern about sources of dispute was real for, when extra-territoriality ended, Sir Ernest Mason Satow[34] considered that the Consulates might need to devote additional consular assistance facilities to British subjects enmeshed in Japanese criminal courts.[35]

Western concerns about secret laws enforced in a partial manner by an untrained judiciary are confirmed by the arrangements surrounding the implementation of the Anglo-Japanese Treaty of Commerce and Navigation of 1894 (**1894 Treaty**) which abolished extra-territoriality. Its implementation was postponed for five years to allow Japan time to meet essential Western concerns by establishing a trained independent judiciary and completing work on drafting and publishing a comprehensive set of legal codes based upon Western legal principles.

The implicit *quid pro quo* for extra-territoriality (which the Japanese articulated more explicitly over time) was that Britain would provide effective recourse for Japanese subjects against, and maintain peace and order amongst, British subjects. Chapters 3 and 5 (Criminal Jurisdiction and Civil Jurisdiction, respectively) consider Japanese criminal prosecutions of, and the pursuit of civil claims against, British subjects to see whether the system met these requirements and whether British fears of vexatious prosecutions and frivolous claims were justified.

The Treaty

The Treaty 'opened up' Japan to Britons from 1859 but trade and residence were restricted to just the Treaty Ports. Other than diplomatic agents, no Westerner could travel outside the Treaty Ports without the consent of the Japanese government. The Treaty and associated trade regulations also

---

33 Granville to Parkes, 13 January 1873; FO881/2159.

34 Then, Minister in Tokyo. He had come to Japan as a Student Interpreter in 1862 and spent the next 20 years in Japan rising to be Japanese Secretary at the Legation. After a 13 year absence, he returned as Minister in 1895.

35 Satow to Cockerell, 24 February 1898; Ruxton 2007, page 100.

specified the Customs duties which the Japanese government could charge on imports. It also went on to establish the legal basis, as between Britain and Japan, for Britain to exercise jurisdiction over British subjects within Japanese territory. It included separate provisions dealing with each of property and personal rights, criminal complaints, civil disputes and debt claims. It provided that:

> IV. All questions in regard to rights, whether of property or person, arising between British subjects ..., shall be subject to the jurisdiction of the British authorities.
>
> V. ... British subjects who may commit any crime against Japanese subjects, or the subjects or citizens of any other country, shall be tried and punished by the Consul ... according to the laws of Great Britain.
>
> Justice shall be equitably and impartially administered on both sides.
>
> VI. A British subject having reason to complain of a Japanese must proceed to the Consulate and state his grievance.
>
> The Consul shall enquire into the merits of the case, and do his utmost to arrange it amicably. In like manner, if a Japanese have reason to complain of a British subject, the Consul shall no less listen to his complaint, and endeavour to settle it in a friendly manner. If disputes take place of such a nature that the Consul cannot arrange them amicably, then he shall request the assistance of the Japanese authorities, that they may together examine into the merits of the case, and decide it equitably.

Article VII dealt with debts and provided that neither government was responsible for the debts contracted by its subjects but that the authorities of each would do their utmost to bring the defendant to justice, and to enforce recovery of the debts.

Article XXIII's 'most favoured nation' provision was to prove important in two areas. First, Article IV provided only for extra-territoriality in relation to civil disputes between British subjects and, unlike Article V in relation to crimes, was silent about disputes between British subjects and third country nationals. Therefore, on a strict reading of the Treaty, Japan retained jurisdiction over such disputes. This was never the Western intention for, from the beginning, the British—and other Western Powers—operated as they did elsewhere where extra-territoriality applied and treated the defendant's consul as having jurisdiction. Although the most favoured nation provision created practical difficulties when it came to treaty renegotiation, it was—and is—a common treaty provision and was not the insult to Japan that some commentators have claimed.

During the early period of a weak *bakufu*, this probably mattered little as the *bakufu* was not in a position to take the point. However, lawyers must have been aware of the lacuna for the 1869 Austro-Hungary treaty gave Austro-Hungarian consuls jurisdiction over all claims against that empire's subjects whereupon the British claimed similar rights by virtue of Article XXIII. Thereby, the Austria-Hungary treaty enlarged 'the jurisdictional privileges of all the treaty powers beyond those granted in the [treaties]'.[36]

Given that the Japanese authorities were already employing Western legal advisers at this time, it is unlikely that they were unaware of the lacuna so one must speculate why the Japanese conceded this point to the Austro-Hungarians (or, more accurately, Parkes, who led in the treaty's negotiation for the Austro-Hungarians[37]). Auslin evidenced changed Japanese attitudes after 1868 and Hoare showed several examples of Japan using various legal means at its disposal to qualify and resist Western encroachments on its jurisdiction, but neither addresses this point.

It may be that, whilst Meiji authorities were moving towards seeking the abolition of extra-territoriality, no definitive position had been taken or they may have viewed it as not worth creating a breach with all foreign Powers on this point; particularly as this was how extra-territoriality then operated and the Japanese, perhaps, recognized that they were not in a position to administer such disputes alone.[38] Whilst, from a domestic political perspective, no new (or amending) treaty with an existing Treaty Power could have been agreed to clarify the matter, all concerned may have accepted the sleight of hand involved in negotiating the Austro-Hungarian treaty and other Powers' utilizing their 'most favoured nation' rights to regularize the existing position. The only hint in the British archives to answer the point are comments by Parkes that the negotiations for the Austro-Hungarian treaty had proved 'most satisfactory ...

---

[36] Hinckley 1906, page 17. Unlike section XXI of the Treaty which stipulated that the Dutch version was to be treated as the original version, the Austro-Hungarian treaty (section XXIII) provided for the English language version to be the original version in case of dispute between the German and the Japanese versions.

[37] The Austro-Hungarian plenipotentiary accepted the treaty draft with which Parkes provided him in place of his own; (Parkes to Foreign Office, 8 October 1869; FO391/15, page 196).

[38] In the *Saadkia* case, which, as it concerned a Tunisian vessel, fell under Japanese jurisdiction as the Sublime Porte had no treaty with Japan, all the counsel were British and the Japanese judge was advised by a foreign legal adviser to the Japanese government; 22 July 1872, *Japan Weekly Mail* (JWM).

throughout'[39] and that all the Japanese government had done in relation to the treaty was 'in complement to ourselves ... their new friends.'[40] The only points which the Japanese government took on Parkes's draft were unrelated to extra-territoriality; namely, its insistence that Austria-Hungary appoint a resident Diplomatic Agent and not appoint trading consuls.

Another provision of the Austro-Hungarian treaty where the British availed themselves of 'most favoured nation' rights was that which provided that goods subject to a Customs dispute were to be held by the Consul and not the Japanese Customs.[41] These legal points are important because, just as we shall see that the Law Officers looked to the Treaty's exact terms when advising successive British governments of their rights so, as time went on, the Japanese looked to the Treaty's narrow terms as part of their campaign for extra-territoriality's abolition.

British Legal Basis for Extra-territorial Regime

Despite the Crown's purported exercise of jurisdiction over British subjects abroad through British consuls since at least Richard III's time,[42] doubts existed as to its prerogatives in this area. These doubts were confirmed by the Law Officers in 1826, and the position was regularized by the Foreign Jurisdiction Act, 1843[43] pursuant to which the various Orders in Council establishing the Courts[44] were made—although this did not prevent lawyers continuing to quibble.[45]

The early Orders in Council for Japan underwent frequent revision between 1859 and 1865 when the China and Japan Order in Council of 9 March 1865 (**OC1865**) was made. With only few modifications, OC1865 governed the arrangements for the remainder of the period.

The first Japan Order in Council regulating British jurisdiction in Japan was made on 3 March 1859 (**OC1859**). It authorized Consuls to perform 'any act of administration or jurisdiction ... which British consuls within

39 Parkes to Foreign Office, 23 October 1869; FO391/15.
40 Ibid.
41 See page 257 and the *Hiogo Treasure case*; 10 December 1881; JWM.
42 Keeton 1928, Vol. II, page 160.
43 Superseded by the Foreign Jurisdiction Act 1890.
44 The term 'Courts' is used to encompass each of the Consular Courts (later, and more properly, called Provincial Courts), the Kanagawa Court, the Yokohama Court, HMCJ and the Supreme Court.
45 See pages 42–43.

other states in amity with Her Majesty are, by law, usage or sufferance, enabled to perform'[46] and to grant Probate and Letters of Administration or, where none was taken out, to administer the estates themselves and receive a commission not exceeding 2.5%.[47] Anticipating large numbers of seamen coming under their jurisdiction, it empowered them to exercise a magistrate's powers over merchant seamen.[48] Additional powers included the right of deportation.[49] All fees and fines were payable to HM Treasury except for those which the Treaty provided were payable to the Japanese authorities.[50]

The litigious nature of many traders on the China Coast and their antipathy to British officialdom was recognized by providing that suits against Consuls in relation to their exercise of jurisdiction should be brought within six months of the matter in dispute and allowed Consuls the various protections afforded them by the Foreign Jurisdiction Act 1843. In practice, this appeared to be of little relevance in Japan for the only suit against an official was *Moss v. Alcock* heard before the Supreme Court of Hong Kong (**SCHK**).[51]

OC1859 had been prepared by the Law Officers on the basis of precedents for China and Thailand, especially the latter as the Foreign Secretary, the Earl of Malmesbury, had indicated that the situation in Japan was closer to that in Thailand. The Law Officers were aware of their lack of local knowledge, however, for they advised that somebody with more local experience review it as to its practical working—especially as regards providing that SCHK should be the appropriate court for certain matters.[52] OC1859 came into force only when ratifications of the Treaty had been exchanged. Until then, the Minister, Sir Rutherford Alcock,[53] advised Pemberton Hodgson, the temporary Consul in Nagasaki at its opening, that he had no legal jurisdiction within Japan and should be careful not to exercise judicial authority until the exchange of ratifications.[54]

After OC1859's promulgation, Alcock suggested that it should be more closely assimilated to the Orders in Council for China as regards appeals

---

46 Section XXXVIII.
47 Section XXXV.
48 Section XXXVII.
49 Section XIX. This reflected Article XIX of the Treaty.
50 Section XXXIV.
51 See pages 14–15 and 117–119.
52 Law Officers to Malmesbury, 11 and 31 January 1859; FO83/2298.
53 First British Consul-General and Minister to Tokyo, 1859–1865 when he went as Minister to Beijing.
54 Alcock to Hodgson, 16 June 1859; FO410/1.

and the enforcement of consular decisions in civil claims[55]—which, presumably, led to the subsequent Order in Council. This was prepared by the Treasury and approved by the Law Officers later that year,[56] although there were further amendments so it was not until January 1860 that the Law Officers signed off on the final draft of the Japan Order in Council of 23 January 1860 (**OC1860**)[57] which revoked and replaced OC1859.

Whilst, broadly, continuing OC1859's regime, OC1860 addressed the Consuls' jurisdiction in more detail and empowered the Consul-General to establish rules of practice in the Courts[58] and gave Consuls explicit power to enforce the Treaty and to make and enforce regulations 'for the peace, order, and good governance of Her Majesty's subjects within ... Japan'.[59] It provided for a Consul to hear civil suits between British subjects and for appeals from Court decisions—in both criminal and civil matters—to be made to the Secretary of State. Its principal innovation was the introduction of lay members of the British community as Assessors into certain civil and criminal hearings.[60]

Admiralty and Matrimonial jurisdiction were reserved to SCHK whilst both OC1859 and OC1860 conferred a concurrent jurisdiction upon SCHK for all other civil disputes between British subjects—but no others. The Law Officers advised that, whilst SCHK had sufficient authority to deal with the criminal cases allocated to it by OC1859, it did not have the authority to hear those appeals in civil cases which were to go to it under these Orders in Council.[61] Therefore, specific Letters Patent were issued in 1860 empowering SCHK to hear civil cases originating in Japan.[62] OC1860

[55] Law Officers to Russell, 25 July 1859; FO83/2298.

[56] Edmund Hammond (later Baron Hammond, Permanent Under Secretary at the Foreign Office, 1854–1873) to Law Officers 16 September 1859; FO83/2298.

[57] Law Officers to Russell, 3 January 1860; FO83/2298.

[58] On 15 November 1860, the Legation issued Rules of Practice in Judicial Cases brought before HM Consuls to deal with procedural matters and fees.

[59] Section IV.

[60] Sections XIV and XX.

[61] Law Officers to the Duke of Newcastle (Secretary of State for the Colonies), 13 October 1859; FO83/2298.

[62] Alcock to Consuls, 20 June 1860; FO796/20. The original Letters Patent of 30 January 1860 purported to confer concurrent jurisdiction upon SCHK, alongside the Consular Courts in Japan, over civil matters arising in Japan together with an appellate jurisdiction over decisions of such Courts in civil matters. However, when Moss commenced legal proceedings in Hong Kong, the Chief Justice of Hong Kong realized that the Letters Patent referred to OC1859 which had itself been revoked and cancelled by OC1860 which had been made a week before the Letters Patent were issued; Adams CJ to Hercules Robinson (Governor of Hong Kong); FO46/30 page 189. Thus, these Letters Patent were of no effect and new ones needed to be issued.

allowed for British subjects to be sent to Hong Kong for criminal trial and persons convicted in Japan to be held in gaol in Hong Kong.[63] It continued British subjects' obligation to register—at no cost—with the Consul but provided that anyone failing to register was not entitled to protection as a British subject.[64]

It would appear that Alcock had not been consulted in advance about OC1860's provision for appeals to the Foreign Secretary for he drew the attention of Earl Russell[65] (the Foreign Secretary) to the 'injurious results likely to arise' from the practicalities surrounding such appeals and suggested that they should be within the remit of the Minister. The Foreign Office accepted that the point was deserving of attention and asked the Law Officers for advice. They pointed to the peculiar circumstances in Japan where Consuls had the power to make, interpret and enforce their own Regulations and said that it was obvious that 'without any efficient appeal or control, serious hardship and even irreparable injury may be inflicted upon British subjects' and, in framing OC1860, they had tried to guard against this.

However, they conceded that, given the practicalities and the fact that Alcock 'will in no case act judicially "in first instance" but only on appeals,' the Minister could be substituted for the Foreign Secretary as the person to whom appeals should lie from the Consuls—subject to the Minister's being required to report periodically to the Foreign Secretary on all appeals decided by him.[66] A draft Order in Council amending the appeal provisions was then prepared within the Foreign Office and submitted to the Law Officers for their approval before being promulgated as the Japan Order in Council on 4 February 1861 (**OC1861**).[67]

This further amended a Consul's jurisdiction so that, sitting alone, he could try breaches of the Treaty and related Trade Regulations and other charges punishable by a fine or imprisonment of less than $200 and one month respectively. Otherwise, he was required to hear the case with Assessors. All decisions in Treaty and Trade Regulation cases and those in other cases where an Assessor dissented were to be reported to the Consul-General who could confirm, vary or reverse them.[68]

---

63 Sections XXVII and XXVI.

64 Section XXXVIII.

65 Formerly Lord John Russell until 1860.

66 Hammond to Law Officers and their response 8 September and 16 October 1860 respectively; FO83/2298.

67 Hammond to Law Officers and their response 22 November and 18 December 1860 respectively; FO83/2298.

68 Section II and III.

In 1861, Alcock drafted Rules of Procedure for the Courts and Port Regulations based on pre-existing ones in China which had been sanctioned by the Hong Kong Colonial Government's legal advisers. When he submitted them to London for approval, the Law Officers said they had no comments to make save to suggest that Alcock be supplied with a copy of the Consular Rules for Turkey which Hornby had prepared.[69]

In what must have been a response to a specific incident (although the details are not mentioned in the sources), the question arose, in 1861, about a Consul's power to re-deport someone who, having been convicted of two offences, had been deported but returned to Japan. Alcock sought advice from the Attorney General in Hong Kong who advised that a Consul had power to re-deport someone under section 21 of OC1861 and forwarded drafts of the necessary Warrants to be used.[70] Ultimately, the Japan Order in Council of 1863 (**OC1863**) made it a specific offence for a deportee to return to Japan without permission; the offence was to be punishable by a fine of $200 or one month's imprisonment.

The Japan Order in Council made on 7 January 1864 (**OC1864**) empowered the Consul-General to make rules regulating the navigation by British vessels in Japanese waters enforceable by a fine of up to $5,000 or three months imprisonment and allowed offending vessels to be seized by British naval officers.

These constant amendments all suggest a government reacting to events and circumstances as they happened. Given growing British involvement in China and Japan, a general belief that Consuls in both were legally uneducated and inexperienced, and SCHK's alleged deficiencies in *Moss v. Alcock*, which discredited it from an ongoing supervisory role over justice outside Hong Kong[71] (besides costing the British government over £1,145

[69] Law Officers to Russell, 6 March 1861; FO83/2298.

[70] John Smale (Attorney General, Hong Kong) to Alcock, 29 October 1861; FO796/23. Interestingly, Smale suggested that the Consul should also disclaim responsibility for protecting the offender and so inform the Japanese authorities in the hope that they might arrest him and imprison him—the threat of which would be sufficient alone to encourage the malefactor to leave Japan. Someone—presumably the Nagasaki Consul—has annotated a copy of this despatch with the pencilled comment that not only would the Japanese authorities not imprison such a person but they would also find such a course of conduct by the Consul to be inexplicable. Smale's suggestion certainly runs counter to the general views of the British community in Japan with its insistence upon the privileges of extra-territoriality.

[71] After this case, *The Times* famously described SCHK as 'the greatest nuisance in the East' with verdicts 'fitter for a jest book than for a grave discussion;' 13 July 1863. These comments are, to be fair, more attributable to the Hong Kong jury rather than to the judges in the case.

in damages and costs to Moss[72] and a further £416 in costs to Alcock's counsel[73]), the government must have seen a need to re-order the whole justice regime. Another difficulty with the current system was highlighted when Browning was sent to Hong Kong to face trial for murder in 1864.[74] It was impossible to send the Japanese witnesses to Hong Kong for the trial and, but for the recently enacted Hong Kong Ordinance which allowed for evidence to be given by written deposition, it would have been impracticable to hold the trial. Winchester suggested that this difficulty could be overcome if a judge from SCHK were based permanently in Shanghai with power to visit Japan on circuit—a suggestion which the Law Officers agreed was workable.[75] Thoughts to enhance consular jurisdiction along these lines were clearly in common circulation amongst British officials in Asia for Alcock, after being sued by Moss in *Moss v. Alcock*, made similar suggestions in his book describing his time in Japan. He said that Consuls in Japan and China would welcome the introduction of a legally qualified judicial element so as to address the problems which they incurred by having judicial duties imposed upon them in addition to their other duties.[76]

Despite the cases of Moss and Browning, one must suspect that, given that jurisdiction in Japan was very recent, the principal causes for this overhaul came from China where 'rough and ready decisions of the Consuls were held up to the ridicule of an ever-increasing Bar'.[77]

China and Japan Order in Council, 1865

Instead of following through on the suggestions of a greater role for SCHK in the administration of British justice throughout East Asia, the government induced Sir Edmund Hornby, then Judge of the consular court in Constantinople, to leave Constantinople in 1864, assume responsibility for establishing a new court system in China and Japan, draft the legislative

72 Invoice from Moss's Hong Kong counsel; FO276/8, page 155.

73 Invoice; FO276/9, page 43.

74 See pages 147 and 258–259.

75 Correspondence between Russell and the Law Officers, 4 and 25 June 1864; FO83/2298.

76 Sir Rutherford Alcock, *The Capital of the Tycoon: A Narrative of a Three Years' Residence in Japan*, vol. 2 (London: Longman, Green, Longman, Roberts & Green, 1863; reprinted by ULAN Press).

77 Editorial, 10 August 1877; *Japan Daily Herald* (**JDH**). Platt 1971, pages 189–190 suggests that Parkes, as consul-general in Shanghai, was a prime mover in the need to establish a regular judicial officer there.

framework and associated rules of procedure and proceed to Shanghai to supervise its implementation. OC1865, which replaced the extant Orders in Council, ran to 141 sections and created a separate jurisdiction for China and Japan supervised by the Supreme Court based in Shanghai and presided over by a Judge[78] who was required to be a barrister of at least seven years' call.[79] It also extended the Courts' jurisdiction to offences committed on board British vessels within 100 miles of the Japanese coast[80] whilst creating new offences for British subjects deriding publicly the established religion of Japan,[81] making war against the Tycoon or trading at unopen ports (for which the offending vessel could be seized).[82] It also granted the Courts jurisdiction over all bankruptcy cases.[83] Prior to Hornby's taking up his position as Judge, he, together with Charles Wycliffe Goodwin (the Assistant Judge) and Sir Francis Savage Reilly,[84] drafted, in London, Rules of Her British Majesty's Supreme Court and other Courts in China and Japan (**Rules**) to regulate the conduct of proceedings within the Courts. Replacing the rules previously issued by Alcock, they comprised 344 paragraphs, plus relevant forms, and were promulgated[85] on 4 May 1865.[86]

The 'supervisory team' included an Assistant Judge and a Law Secretary, who also acted as the Supreme Court's Registrar. The Assistant Judge was required to be legally qualified but the Law Secretary could be unqualified—and often was in the early years—especially when acting Law Secretaries were drawn from the Consular Service in China to stand in during the absence of the post's substantive holder. Substantive appointments were to be made by the Secretary of State but acting appointments could be made by the Minister in Beijing. Unlike judicial appointments at home and in most colonies,[87] all such appointments were held 'during the pleasure of Her Majesty'.[88]

---

[78] Initially styled the Judge, but between 1879 and 1905, styled the Chief Justice to distinguish him from the head of HMCJ who was styled Judge. Note, however that, before 1879, the Judge was often referred to, erroneously, as the Chief Judge or Chief Justice—even in official correspondence.

[79] Section 9.

[80] Section 101.

[81] Section 100.

[82] Section 92.

[83] Section 52.

[84] An English barrister who was frequently consulted by the Foreign Office in relation to the drafting of Orders in Council relating to extra-territorial jurisdiction.

[85] Pursuant to Section 127.

[86] Sir Edmund Hornby, *Sir Edmund Hornby, An Autobiography* (London, 1929), page 193.

[87] Judges at Home and in most colonies had security of tenure for life for so long as they displayed 'good behaviour'.

[88] Section 23.

The Judge could appoint a deputy,[89] with the same powers who could go on circuit or remain in Shanghai whilst the Judge was on circuit or who would deputize for the Judge whilst he was absent. Usually, but not exclusively, the deputy would be the Assistant Judge. With absences on leave back in England or on circuit, it was not unusual to find a Deputy Judge acting as such for over a year and we even see acting Deputy Judges.

As for the Consuls and their Courts, despite a change of official nomenclature whereby their consular courts became Provincial Courts,[90] there was no substantive change in that each Consul continued to exercise jurisdiction over British subjects within his consulate's 'province' subject to the Supreme Court's concurrent extra-ordinary jurisdiction over all matters (not just civil as had been the case with SCHK) and provision for the Judge to go on circuit.[91] In the vernacular, most people continued to refer to the Provincial Courts as 'consular courts'.

That each Consul's jurisdiction was limited to his own Province was a practical drawback for everyone as defendants could avoid prosecutions, claims and judgments by leaving one port and fleeing to another. In 1866, a Japanese plaintiff, Kakichi, obtained a judgment in Nagasaki against Pounds who absconded from Nagasaki to Yokohama without satisfying the judgment. Marcus Flowers, the Nagasaki Consul, was then compelled to seek assistance from Myburgh, the Consul in Yokohama, to arrest Pounds in order to obtain settlement for the judgment.[92] However, this does not appear to have been as big a problem as it might have been: partly because of the Supreme Court's, and later HMCJ's, extraordinary jurisdiction and partly because consular jurisdictions were not contiguous and each port was like an island and, usually, required sea travel between them. Departure from a port was only effected easily by ship; so, when Jardine Matheson heard that C.P. Jones, master of *Oxfordshire*, whom they had sued successfully in the Yokohama Court for $2,500, was about to leave Yokohama for Kobe, Jardine Matheson had him arrested and held pending his settlement of the judgment debt.[93] When the Japanese authorities sought to prosecute Abdul Kader for running a gaming house in Tokyo, he fled the Tokyo Vice-Consul's jurisdiction to Yokohama but they were still able to effect his prosecution in HMCJ by means of its extraordinary jurisdiction.[94]

89 Section 10.
90 Section 36.
91 Sections 37 and 38.
92 Flowers to Myburgh, 20 April 1866; FO796/29.
93 1 July 1876, NCH.
94 Tokyo Vice-Consul to General Kabayama, Chief Superintendent of Police, Tokyo, 7 and 11 November 1882; FO798/11.

OC1865 removed the Consul-General's previous supervisory involvement in the Courts and transferred administrative supervision to the Judge. Consuls were placed under his control 'for all judicial and magisterial purposes'[95] and required to file semi-annual reports with him regarding proceedings in their courts and to account to the Supreme Court for financial matters (costs, fees and fines). The Judge's supervisory function was emphasized when the Assistant Judge at the Supreme Court, Charles Goodwin, declined to advise Adolphus Annersley, the Consul in Kobe, on a case because it might come before Goodwin on appeal. When Annersley made the wrong decision and imprisoned the *Cathaya*'s master, the Foreign Secretary, the Earl of Derby,[96] absolved Annersley but rejected Goodwin's excuses. Derby said this exceptional system of justice was only justified by the appointment of a Chief Judge whose duty it was to watch and supervise the proceedings of the legally unqualified consular judges under him and to assist and advise them on the discharge of their judicial functions; Goodwin should have either heard the case himself or given Annersley the necessary advice to obviate the mistake.[97]

OC1865 removed the Consul-General's appellate and sentencing functions. Henceforth, appeals from the Courts lay to the Supreme Court thence to the Privy Council. The Minister (*qua* the Executive in Britain) remained involved in only three aspects of the Courts and their administration of extra-territorial jurisdiction. First, he retained the executive power to make Regulations 'as seem fit for the peace, order and good Government of British Subjects resident in or resorting to Japan and for the observance of the Treaty'.[98] Second, he remained responsible for appointing acting Judges and for the deployment of consular staff where he needed to balance seniority and ability. In practice after 1879, a legal qualification was desirable for the Yokohama Consul (who was, *ex officio*, Assistant Judge) but not for appointment as acting Consul there. Elsewhere, although desirable for appointment as a Consul, a legal qualification was not essential. Finally, with sentences, if the circumstances of any case made it 'just or expedient,' the Judge could recommend the Minister to mitigate or remit the punishment awarded by the Court and the Minister had a discretion to act upon such recommendation[99] whilst a

[95] Russell to Hornby, May 1865; FO17/433.
[96] He had been Foreign Secretary previously as Lord Stanley.
[97] Derby to Goodwin, 12 December 1877; FO17/766.
[98] Section 91.
[99] Section 77.

death sentence was to be referred to him to determine whether to sanction it or to exercise his powers of pardon or commutation.[100]

SCHK lost all its previous roles in the administration of justice in Japan except where it was involved by the Judge. OC1865 included a permissive power whereby persons charged with a criminal offence could, with the Judge's sanction, be sent for trial in Hong Kong;[101] and convicted criminals could be sent to gaol in Hong Kong.[102] The only jurisdictional connection remaining as of right for SCHK was that the Courts were obliged to execute its warrants and orders without re-investigation.[103] After the Supreme Court and SCHK (neither being binding precedentially upon the other) reached different conclusions in bankruptcy cases in 1867, the Chief Justice of SCHK suggested unifying them and creating a single appellate court for British interests in East Asia but nothing came of this (or a further suggestion along these lines in 1878). Why the government did not follow the local suggestions for an enhanced role for SCHK is not clear: quite possibly, because Hong Kong was a colony under the Colonial Office whereas relations with Japan and China were handled by the Foreign Office and British jurisdiction in those countries arose by treaty. Another reason may have been that the whole Moss affair showed just how uncoordinated administrative matters appeared to be as between Foreign Office, the Colonial Office and the administration in Hong Kong with the latter two seeming to have been unaware of OC1860 before Moss arrived in Hong Kong.[104]

The new scheme, described by *The Times* as very comprehensive and well drawn up,[105] began on 4 September 1865, when the Supreme Court opened for business,[106] and formed the bedrock of British judicial administration in Japan until the ending of extra-territoriality when it was

---

[100] Section 69. The Minister's discretion was personal and not subject to Foreign Office direction. When Satow commuted Edith Carew's death sentence (after she had been convicted of murdering her husband by arsenic poisoning), he acted on his own initiative with no formal approval forthcoming—or considered apposite—from Salisbury (Davidson to Satow, 16 March 1897; Ruxton 2005, page 13). For a good description of the Carew trial and its surroundings, see Molly Whittington-Egan, *Murder on the Bluff* (Glasgow: Neil Wilson Publishing, 1996).

[101] Section 67 and section 4, Foreign Jurisdiction Act 1843.

[102] Section 79.

[103] Section 42.

[104] That said, nothing had prevented SCHK's original involvement with China and Japan or the Supreme Court in Singapore being made the immediate appellate body for the British court in Bangkok.

[105] Norton-Kyshe 1898, page 79.

[106] Hornby to Russell, 4 August 1865; FO17/433.

reviewed comprehensively and replaced by the China and Korea Order in Council, 1904 (**OC1904**).

The China and Japan Order in Council 1869 replaced all references in OC1865 to the Tycoon by references to the Mikado. This substitution was necessary when the British at last appreciated the relationship between the Shogun and the Emperor. The Law Officers said the references to the Tycoon in OC1865 raised questions as to that Order in Council's effectiveness and validity but went on to suggest that 'as the courts have existed for some time in Japan and jurisdiction has been exercised by Her Majesty we think Her Majesty may be considered as having jurisdiction by usage or sufferance within Japanese Dominions'. Nevertheless, they recommended the position be made clear by a new Order in Council.[107]

The Yokohama Court

Hornby had developed the court structure in the abstract without any sure knowledge of how court business in Japan would develop. Russell instructed him to visit the Treaty Ports to determine whether 'it is necessary that you visit them periodically on fixed circuit or only ... as the state of business may seem to require'[108] and Hornby visited all the Treaty Ports at some stage although there is no evidence that he held formal hearings of the Supreme Court anywhere other than at Yokohama and Nagasaki.[109]

His first report on Japan provides an early indication of the level of Japanese work and he flagged, right from the new regime's start, that it might require modification. Work at Yokohama was of a greater volume and more important nature than Hornby had expected and he advised that 'as the trade with Japan increases it will become a matter of great consideration whether it will not be necessary to appoint an Assistant Judge of the Supreme Court to reside at Yokohama to take charge under the superintendency of the Supreme Court ... of the different consulates in Japan'.[110] Meanwhile, he was not above telling the Consuls how to handle,

---

[107] Law Officers to Stanley 9 April 1868; FO83/2299.

[108] Russell to Hornby, May 1865; FO17/433.

[109] We have records of Hornby's visiting Japan in 1865/66 (perhaps on a tour of inspection rather than on circuit as such); in September/October 1867; and in 1869 (Parkes recorded in 1869 that Hornby had only been able to visit Japan twice on circuit up until then: Parkes to Foreign Office, 6 November 1869; FO391/15, page 209) and, again, in 1872. See also pages 49–51.

[110] Hornby to Russell, 11 September 1865; FO17/433.

and the fines to levy in, the individual cases which came before them during his visits.

The volume of judicial work in Japan—or, more precisely, at Yokohama—made him contemplate spending three months a year in Yokohama on a travelling assize.[111] Even if this were partly an exaggeration in an attempt to obtain decent accommodation for himself locally (and Hornby's correspondence does exhibit a tendency to use exaggeration to make a point), it shows an early recognition of the need in Yokohama for alterations to the basic structure established by OC1865. The British in Yokohama were a trading community[112] where many legal disputes derived considerable importance from their commercial nature.[113] The situation was exacerbated by the development of a Yokohama Bar from 1868 which was wont to try to overawe the legally uneducated Consuls such as when 'an impudent barrister, a feeble judge and some prevaricating witnesses combined to make a jest of justice'.[114] By 1868, Hornby was telling the community there that he recognized the need for a branch of the Supreme Court to be established permanently in Yokohama.[115]

Matters came to a head in 1869 when Fletcher, the Yokohama Consul, died suddenly and Robertson, the acting Consul, was absent. Judicial business came to a standstill and Parkes asked Hornby to visit Yokohama urgently to deal with the considerable arrears of pending cases.[116] Hornby was in Yokohama from August to December 1869 which gave him and Parkes the opportunity to propose the establishment of a Japanese court. Even discounting an advocacy element in Hornby's despatches on the matter, they confirm the growth of judicial work at Yokohama. He wrote of the press of judicial and magisterial work at Yokohama[117] and the Consular staff's inability to cope with it. Several pending civil cases involved difficult points of law and most were, pecuniarily at least, of considerable importance to the parties involved.[118] There was also a great deal of work on the criminal side.

---

[111] Major Crossman (Office of Works in Shanghai) to HM Treasury, 24 November 1866; FO656/22.

[112] Editorial, 5 February 1876; JWM. The 1863 Trade Returns showed British trade with Japan at over $11 million out of total foreign trade for Japan of nearly $14 million; Inclosure No 100 with Alcock to Russell, 27 June 1864; FO410/8.

[113] Editorial, 28 October 1871; JWM.

[114] Unidentified case, 19 September 1868; *The Japan Times Overland Mail* (**JTOM**).

[115] 2 May 1868; JTOM.

[116] Hornby to Clarendon, 10 August 1869; FO17/530.

[117] Ibid: 'nine tenths of the work in the Yokohama Consulate is judicial.'

[118] Hornby to Clarendon, 23 October 1869; FO881/1749.

This growing, and increasingly complex, work was all 'done by HM Consular Officers who have no legal education, and who are besides very young and inexperienced'.[119] Whilst, conceding that they endeavoured conscientiously to do the work, he said 'the hearing of cases occupies a great deal of time and the result is often as unsatisfactory to themselves as it is to the public ... as they have neither the necessary education or experience'.[120] This caused the local Press to complain of 'the imbecility of the Consular Courts ... a corrupt and utterly inefficient system of administration of the laws'.[121]

The key proposal which Parkes and Hornby made was 'the appointment of a permanent judicial officer for Japan'[122] by detaching the Assistant Judge and a Court Clerk from Shanghai to Yokohama. Budget was an issue so they proposed restructuring positions in the Yokohama Consulate and the Supreme Court to obviate any cost increase. The Judge in Japan would remain subordinate to the Chief Justice in China so far as Yokohama was concerned but they proposed that he should hear appeals from the other Consulates.[123]

Parkes supported the proposals as 'the need of professional control is also greatly felt to enable the principal Consular Court in Japan to check the vexatious litigation which is fostered by pettifogging practitioners.'[124] He also urged the 'material advantage that would also be derived by his Legation if the Minister had at hand a competent law adviser to give occasional advice in international questions and to sift ... claims of British subjects on Japan and which have frequently to be adjusted or recovered through the Minister'[125] so he and Hornby proposed that the Judge at Yokohama should act as Law Officer to the Legation and sift merchants' claims against the Japanese authorities before they were taken up by the Minister.[126]

Establishing a branch of the Supreme Court in Yokohama would deal with another, growing issue. OC1865's reservation of Admiralty jurisdiction

119 Ibid.

120 Ibid.

121 Editorial 2 May 1868; JTOM. This was the only (unsubstantiated) accusation of corruption against the Courts. Presumably, the word 'corruption' was used in the sense of the Courts not being good or competent rather than their being dishonest.

122 Hornby to Clarendon, 23 October 1869; FO881/1749.

123 Ibid.

124 Parkes to Clarendon, 5 November 1869; FO881/1750.

125 Ibid. This reflected Article VI of the Treaty which provided for Consuls to try to arrange British claims against Japanese subjects with the Japanese authorities. It was also a time when many British traders were pursuing claims against the old *han*.

126 Hornby to Clarendon, 23 October 1869; FO881/1749.

to the Supreme Court had caused problems in Japan, where many cases involved shipping. In 1868, Fletcher had triggered diplomatic complaints from the Prussian Minister about the absence of British courts with Admiralty jurisdiction[127] when Fletcher misread Hornby's warrant and instructions about arresting the *Bolivar* and its cargo and sought to arrest the cargo which had passed already into Prussian and Swiss hands.[128] It would seem that the possibility of conferring Admiralty jurisdiction on the Courts in Japan was raised after this incident because correspondence from the Law Officers suggests that they supported Hornby's view that it would not be appropriate to do so (presumably, because it was a technical legal area) but they raised the possibility of confiding a limited Admiralty jurisdiction to a particular court in Japan in matters of immediate pressure such as Bottomry Bonds and salvage claims.[129] Parkes said that the appointment of a Judge-consul would meet the question of Admiralty jurisdiction.[130]

Hornby and Parkes's proposals were partially implemented in 1870 during Hornby's absence in England. Goodwin, then Deputy Judge, appointed Nicholas John Hannen 'as Acting Assistant Judge of the Japan Branch of the Supreme Court empowered under section 38 OC1865 to hear civil and criminal (except capital) cases arising at Yokohama'[131] (such branch being referred to as the **Yokohama Court**—as distinct from the **Kanagawa Court** which was the consular court of the Yokohama Consulate) and sent from Shanghai to Yokohama. This *ad hoc* arrangement had no legislative backing and created a jurisdictional and procedural morass for OC1865 and the Rules did not contemplate the Assistant Judge's being resident permanently in Japan.[132] Hannen quickly identified a number of issues affecting both criminal and civil matters and argued that 'a jurisdiction almost co-extensive with that of the Chief Judge of the Supreme Court should rest upon more solid grounds than the mere inference to be derived from

[127] Parkes to von Brandt (Minister for Prussia to Tokyo), 10 June 1868 acknowledging his complaint and explaining that Admiralty cases could have been brought in September/October 1867 and in February 1868 when Hornby and Goodwin respectively sat in Yokohama on circuit as a branch of the Supreme Court; FO656/19.

[128] Hornby to Fletcher, 12 May 1868; FO656/18. Hornby had, on Messrs Louis Kniffler & Co.'s application, issued an arrest warrant and carefully instructed Fletcher, against the plaintiff's executing a bottomry bond and providing security for costs, to arrest the vessel and, if necessary, trace its cargo and the cargo's proceeds but Fletcher misread the warrant, which had been limited to cargo found in British hands.

[129] Law Officers to Stanley, 12 September 1868; FO83/2299.

[130] Parkes to Granville, 26 February 1870; to FO391/15.

[131] Wilkinson to French, 21 November 1879; FO656/53.

[132] Hornby to Granville, 17 September 1872; FO17/637.

the wording of the OC1865 interpreted by the light of analogy with a case which when tried could certainly not have suggested to the mind of the Chief Judge the conclusions which I would have considered follow from it'.[133] However, until Hornby returned to Asia in 1872, nothing was resolved. The problem appears to have been his absence and the domination which he exercised over the Supreme Court and the British jurisdictional edifice in East Asia so that no major decision could be taken without him.

The Rules meant that Hannen was powerless to try prisoners on indictable offences without having depositions completed and sent to Shanghai for the Law Secretary to issue indictments and nominate a prosecutor. Of course, the Consul with Assessors could try cases where a sentence of twelve months or a fine of $1,000 would be adequate; but, as Hannen said, such a course would be anomalous as the Yokohama Court's object was to relieve the Consul of most of his judicial duties.[134] Robert Anderson Mowat, the Law Secretary at the Supreme Court, solved this temporarily by sending blank instructions for Hannen to complete with the name of the consular assistant who would prosecute; but Goodwin was reluctant to appoint someone to represent the Law Secretary permanently because communications between Shanghai and Yokohama were so regular.[135]

Despite shipping cases being a reason for the Yokohama Court's establishment, it was unclear whether Hannen could hear Admiralty cases although he assumed he could as Hornby had decided the *Julie* at Yokohama in 1870, thereby implying that the Judge had Vice-Admiralty jurisdiction even when on circuit—and, as acting Assistant Judge on circuit, Hannen had the same powers as the Judge.[136] Equally important was the question of appeals. Hannen had sought advice from Goodwin on the subject almost from the moment of his appointment but without resolution. Hornby's correspondence with the Foreign Office on the subject had been lost in a fire that engulfed the Supreme Court in 1870[137] which meant that Goodwin did not know the answer. He recollected that, although appeals from the Yokohama Court to the Privy Council had not been considered desirable, nothing had been settled and supposed that, in small

133 Hannen to Goodwin 29 April 1871; FO656/37.

134 Hannen to Goodwin, 4 January 1872; FO656/37.

135 Goodwin to Hannen, 17 January 1872; FO656/39. See pages 103–104 for a description of the prosecution process.

136 Hannen to Goodwin, 29 April 1871; FO656/37.

137 Following the fire, new Supreme Court buildings were constructed in 1871. These new buildings, on Yuanmingyuan Road, housed the Supreme Court until its end.

cases, the parties would not run the risk of the expenses attendant upon a re-hearing in Shanghai and suggested that parties simply appeal as they would from a Provincial Court.[138]

The matter came to a head in 1872 in *Findlay Richardson & Co. v. Pitman & Co.* Hannen awarded the plaintiff $1,500 in a dispute over the non-delivery of copper whereupon Frederick Victor Dickins, counsel for the defendant, applied to appeal to the Judge. Hannen gave judgment on this application extemporaneously because, as he explained, he had considered the matter over many months and there was no need for him to consider the point further and reserve his judgment. As the Yokohama Court was a branch of the Supreme Court, he held that no appeal to the Judge was possible: the defendant could either appeal to the Privy Council—with the inconvenience and expense involved—or proceed to a re-hearing *de novo* before the Judge (and hope that the Judge treated it as an appeal).[139]

His ruling triggered editorials in the local Press which complained of the loss of an effective right of appeal.[140] When Dickins appealed to Hornby, on circuit in Yokohama, against Hannen's ruling, Hornby upheld Hannen's judgment and ruled that re-hearings were only applicable where the Assistant Judge was temporarily assigned to a case and did not cover the permanent Yokohama Court so the only right of appeal was one which lay to the Privy Council.[141]

Everyone recognized that this was an unsatisfactory mode of reviewing the Yokohama Court's decisions so, in order that appeals might lie to the Supreme Court, Hornby patched-up a workable solution by re-designating Hannen as hearing all cases—except Admiralty cases—within the Kanagawa Provincial Court[142] and, for prosecutions, attaching Robertson to the Supreme Court as Law Secretary for the district of his Consulate at Yokohama.[143] Thus, there would be no delays for prosecutions; and appeals would lie, as from the other Courts, to the Supreme

138 Goodwin to Hannen, 30 January 1872; FO656/39. OC1865 distinguished (a) an *appeal* from a Consul to the Judge (with the usual procedural limitations of appeals) and (b) a *re-hearing* of a case heard originally by the Assistant Judge or the Law Secretary (which involved a completely new hearing and was not subject to such procedural limitations); Chapter 6 (Appeals).

139 29 June 1872; JWM.

140 20 July 1872; JWM. Until then, appeals had been either considered in Shanghai on the basis of paper pleadings or heard by Hornby on circuit in Yokohama—see Chapter 6 (Appeals).

141 17 August 1872; JWM.

142 Wilkinson to French, 21 November 1879; FO656/53.

143 Hornby to Hannen, 13 September 1872; FO656/39.

Court (and not, as Hornby and Parkes had proposed originally, from the out-ports to the Yokohama Court and thence to the Supreme Court). In Admiralty matters, where jurisdiction was reserved by OC1865 to the Supreme Court, Hannen continued to sit as acting Assistant Judge of the Supreme Court thereby giving the Yokohama Court Admiralty jurisdiction; but, here, appeals would lie direct to the Privy Council.

On this basis, the Yokohama Court staggered on until the China and Japan Order in Council of 14 August 1878 (**OC1878**); but, as Hornby recognized when he prepared and circulated a draft new Order in Council for consideration by the Foreign Office and the Law Officers,[144] this structural 'patch-up' was not an entirely satisfactory solution. Continuing problems with the Rules included those for juries which were more applicable to Shanghai and those for Assessors which were more applicable to Consular Courts whereas the Yokohama Court fell between them.[145] Even a Consul was required to hear civil claims over $1,500 with Assessors[146] which proved inconvenient when Assessors refused to sit or the parties or the Judge wanted a jury trial. Hannen suggested extending the provisions of section 62 OC1865 (which allowed the Supreme Court to hear civil suits exceeding $1,500—with or without a jury) to the Yokohama Court.[147] Both Hornby and the Law Officers supported this recommendation and agreed that there was no reason why the Foreign Secretary should not exercise his power to effect such an extension.[148]

On the criminal side, problems continued over indictments and prosecutors (with increasing numbers of blank Appointments of Prosecutors being sent from Shanghai to Yokohama for completion on an as needs basis) so that, when Hiram Shaw Wilkinson returned to Yokohama from Shanghai in 1876, he was appointed acting Law Secretary with power to dispatch all summary criminal offences, to appoint prosecutors and even exercise the Supreme Court's authority to dispense with a jury where it would ordinarily be required.[149]

It is not clear that anyone in London understood fully the Yokohama Court arrangements for, when the Japanese government challenged

---

144 Hammond to Goodwin seeking comments on it, 30 May 1875; FO17/660.

145 Hannen to Goodwin, 29 April 1871; FO656/37.

146 Section 63 OC1865.

147 Hannen to Hornby, September 1872; FO656/37.

148 Hammond to Law Officers and Law Officers to Granville 3 and 6 December 1872 respectively; FO83/2299.

149 Goodwin (then acting Judge in Yokohama) to Wilkinson, 20 December 1876; FO656/39.

Wilkinson's interpretation of the Treaty in the *Hartley cases*,[150] the Law Officers questioned his authority to hear them.[151] As Wilkinson explained, this depended upon the validity of Hornby's arrangements for the Yokohama Court from September 1872 onwards.[152] Although the Japanese government never raised publicly the issue of his authority, it is clear that the Law Officers' doubts became more widely known for the Japanese Minister in London, Wooyeno, argued that, if Wilkinson had not been appointed properly, then all decisions since 1870 except those rendered by the Consul were invalid.[153]

Later Orders in Council

So matters continued until 1 January 1879 when OC1878 'placed the administration of justice in Japan on a new footing'[154] by creating Her Britannic Majesty's Court for Japan (**HMCJ**) at Yokohama with a Judge and an Assistant Judge[155] whilst the Judge of the Supreme Court was re-styled the Chief Justice.[156] HMCJ replaced both the Yokohama Court (which, of course, had no legislative foundation) and the Kanagawa Court. As such it was similar to the Supreme Court which had similarly supplanted the Shanghai consulate's court.

The Judge was to be a barrister of at least seven years' call[157] and, unless otherwise appointed, the Yokohama Consul was, *ex officio*, the Assistant Judge[158] but ceased to hold a separate Consular Court. In practice, the Consul, *qua* Assistant Judge, continued to hear the more minor cases that he had heard previously as Consul in the Kanagawa Court. If the Judge or the Assistant Judge were absent, the Minister could appoint a fit person as

150 Involving the Japanese government's prosecution of Hartley for opium smuggling which led to a dispute whether the Treaty prohibited the importation of medicinal opium. See pages 123 and 256 and Chang chapter 3.

151 The Law Officers (or, perhaps, the Foreign Office's permanent officials) thought that he had heard them *qua* Supreme Court on circuit which led Parkes to comment that 'there is some confusion and uncertainty as to the precise capacity and as to the particular authority under which Mr Wilkinson tried the above cases and generally discharged judicial duties.' (Parkes to French, 12 August 1879; FO656/37).

152 Wilkinson to French, 21 November 1879; FO656/53.

153 Wilkinson to Parkes, 20 February 1879; FO656/19.

154 Julian Pauncefote (then a Foreign Office official, later Lord Pauncefote and Permanent Under-Secretary of State for Foreign Affairs, 1882–1889) to French, 28 November 1879; FO46/361.

155 Section 5.

156 Section 4(1).

157 Section 9(2).

158 Section 6(2).

acting Judge or acting Assistant Judge;[159] but, unlike the Assistant Judge in Shanghai's right to be appointed acting Chief Justice,[160] the Assistant Judge had no inherent right to be appointed acting Judge because, whilst the Assistant Judge of the Supreme Court would always be legally qualified, the Yokohama Consul need not be. The only Yokohama Consul (as opposed to acting Consul) who was not legally qualified was James Troup in the 1890s; this meant that he could not be appointed acting Judge whilst the Judge took a lengthy Home furlough.

OC1878 effected wholesale substitutions in OC1865 of references to HMCJ and the Judge[161] for references to the Supreme Court and the Chief Justice respectively so that they replaced the Supreme Court and the Chief Justice in all matters relating to the administration and supervision of the Consular Courts and HMCJ assumed the Supreme Court's previous extraordinary jurisdiction over the whole of Japan which enabled it to hear cases not suitable for hearing in the Consular Courts.[162] HMCJ was created a vice-admiralty court and granted Admiralty jurisdiction.[163]

Appeals from the Consular Courts in the out-ports lay now to HMCJ[164] whilst parties to cases in HMCJ heard by the Assistant Judge alone[165] were entitled to a re-hearing before the Judge, as of right.[166] Appeals from HMCJ (including cases heard on appeal from the other Courts) lay to the Supreme Court.[167] In a clear establishment of a regional judicial hierarchy, such appeals were to be heard by the Chief Justice and the Assistant Judge of the Supreme Court or, in the case of the latter's unavoidable absence, the Chief Justice alone.[168] Save where the Assistant Judge sat as acting Chief Justice, they could not be heard by the Assistant Judge sitting alone. In the case of a disagreement, the decision of the Chief Justice was to prevail.[169]

Japan was, from 1879, a separate jurisdiction from China—linked only by a common appellate body. The only change 'adverse' to the jurisdiction's

159 Section 10(2).
160 Section 10(1).
161 After 1 January 1879, references to the Judge are to the Judge of HMCJ.
162 Section 6(5).
163 Section 11.
164 Section 6.
165 This did not apply where the Assistant Judge sat as acting Judge.
166 Section 5(6).
167 Theoretically, this added another layer of appeal from the Consular Courts before the Privy Council was reached; but, in practice, it was not an issue because any case which might justify such an appeal would almost certainly be commenced in HMCJ under its extraordinary jurisdiction.
168 Section 8(1).
169 Section 8(2).

independent status was that appeals in Admiralty now lay from HMCJ to the Supreme Court whereas those from the Yokohama Court had lain direct to the Privy Council. It was, however, the previous position that had been anomalous—but the only practical way to create Admiralty jurisdiction in Yokohama. As there had been no such appeals in Admiralty before 1878, it may be regarded as both a minor change and not disadvantageous to the jurisdiction's independence.

Whereas the earlier correspondence of Hornby and Parkes explains the thinking and reasoning behind the 1870 changes, we have no clear explanations for OC1878. Given that a *modus operandi* had been established by Hornby in 1872, it is unclear what triggered OC1878—especially as Hornby's draft amending Order in Council had been ignored. There were, probably, two causes: Hornby's sudden retirement in 1876 led to a hiatus during which 'there has been an interregnum over the whole Court. Every office has been filled by an acting appointee or deputy'[170] and rumours circulated of changes in the Supreme Court's constitution.[171] This presaged a wholesale personnel re-organization of judicial staff;[172] but the more immediate trigger was, probably, the *Hartley cases* which raised questions as to the Yokohama Court's jurisdiction and the Foreign Office's wish to avoid such embarrassing questions for the future.

Unilateral and sudden action by London was not unknown as evidenced by the China and Japan Order in Council 1881 (**OC1881**) which was promulgated without warning or discussion with HMCJ or the Supreme Court and caused many diplomatic problems surrounding suits by foreigners in the Courts until adjusted by the equally unannounced China, Japan and Korea Order in Council 1884 (**OC1884**) and China, Japan and Korea Order in Council 1886 (**OC1886**). None of these altered the Courts' structure but dealt either with the position of foreign plaintiffs (which is examined in Chapter 5 (Civil Jurisdiction)) or routine matters concerning bills of sale and mortgages.

Later, internal, Foreign Office comments suggest that delays in dealing with new Orders in Council in the mid-1870s arose due to a combination of pressure of work, retirements and deaths of the individuals responsible for such matters. Francis Henry Thomas Streatfield, the Foreign Office Counsel, said that OC1881, which replicated the Ottoman Empire Order in Council 1873 with appropriate name changes, was shown

170 Editorial, 21 September 1878; *Japan Gazette* (**JG**).
171 Editorial, 10 August 1877; *Japan Daily Herald* (**JDH**).
172 See Chapter 2 (The Players in the legal system).

to the Law Officers in advance for their comments but the others were not.[173]

This somewhat cavalier attitude in London applied not just to Orders in Council. Officials frequently did not keep Consular officials abreast of statutory developments and, in 1873, Hornby requested that copies of all Acts be sent immediately to Consuls as no one in Japan had been told of the Consular Marriage Act, 1868.[174] Even after the *Hartley cases*, Parliamentary Counsel ignored the legal niceties of the Courts' basis and structure and, in the 1890s, the government failed in its attempt to confer jurisdiction upon HMCJ to arrest sealing vessels which were operating illegally in Russian waters through drafting slips in primary legislation.[175]

Despite the questions over Wilkinson's appointment, even the Foreign Office still missed technicalities over consular and judicial appointments as shown when Satow complained that James Troup (Consul-General in Yokohama), Mowat (then Judge) and Wilkinson had found 'a choice collection of mare's nests'[176] because Troup, having been gazetted Consul-General for Yokohama, was no longer Consul there and, consequently, incapable of discharging the duties of sheriff. More seriously, as OC1878 provided for the Consul, *ex officio*, to be Assistant Judge, Troup could not have held that position from the time of his appointment as Consul-General without a new warrant—which raised concerns that all proceedings over which he had purported to preside as Assistant Judge were void. As in the *Hartley cases*, the Foreign Office ignored the difficulty and adopted a course of silence: it did not wish to issue a new warrant for Troup to act as consul for this would have required a Japanese *exequatur*[177] and alerted the Japanese authorities to the issue.

---

173 Streatfield to Law Officers, 31 August 1893; FO46/480. The problem with this was that extra-territoriality in the Ottoman Empire was based upon Capitulations, custom and usage whereas in Japan it was based upon treaty rights.

174 Hornby to Granville, 25 June 1873; FO17/660.

175 See pages 166–167.

176 Satow to Davidson 5 February 1897; Ruxton 2007, pages 70–71.

177 An official recognition by, and consent from, the Japanese government allowing a consul to exercise his position. Whilst *exequaturs* may not have been required originally in 1859, practice now required them as seen by Satow writing that a commission conferring the rank of Consul-General upon Troup 'will have to be sent to the Japanese Foreign Office for exequatur...' (Satow to Davidson (private), 9 June 1897; PRO30/33/5/2) and Davidson's (private) response (undated 1897; PRO30/33/5/2 page 46) asking Satow 'perhaps to allude [presumably, formally] to the point about the exequatur. It will be wise to have it on record...' As a result of this concern, when Bonar, the Yokohama Consul-General, was appointed as HMCJ's last Assistant Judge, the Foreign Office sent him a formal Warrant appointing him to that position; Foreign Office to Bonar, 4 August 1898; FO46/506.

British Regulations and Japanese Law

From OC1860 until OC1865, Consuls, subject to the Minister's approval, could issue regulations in respect of their Province and the Minister—as Consul-General—was empowered, subject to the Foreign Secretary's approval, to make regulations binding upon British subjects in Japan. By OC1865, the power was reserved solely to the Minister—although still subject to the Foreign Secretary's approval.

The authority to issue Regulations was limited to those necessary 'for the peace, order and good behaviour' of British subjects. There was a clear concern by the Minister to act *intra vires* in issuing Regulations—otherwise, he could be criticized or, even worse, sued by Britons in Japan for wrongful restriction of their rights. It was, therefore, usual for drafts to be submitted, prior to promulgation, to the Law Officers and/or the Attorney General in Hong Kong until 1865 after which time, his advisory role was undertaken by the Judge.

In 1860, when Alcock questioned whether he had power to frame Port regulations to suppress disturbances caused by unruly seamen ashore as the Treaty—unlike the treaty of Nanjing—contained no provision on the subject, the Law Officers advised that Consuls had this power under OC1860.[178] However, on the whole, the lawyers construed the Consuls' and the Minister's authority to make regulations narrowly. On several occasions, they either ruled that the Minister could not issue the Regulations which he had proposed or, even, advised that Regulations already issued and approved by the Foreign Secretary were *ultra vires* and, so, of no effect.

In 1861, Alcock prepared draft Regulations which would not only ban Britons from residing in Tokyo but provide for those in breach to be handed over to the Japanese authorities to be dealt with according to the laws of Japan. The Law Officers and the Foreign Office were quick to advise that not only was it *ultra vires* for Alcock to ban Britons from residing in Tokyo as they had a right to do so under the Treaty but it would be wrong to hand Britons over to the Japanese for punishment. Instead, Alcock should issue Regulations—which would need to be approved by the Foreign Secretary—prohibiting resort to Tokyo without his approval and providing for penalties for breach enforced by the Courts.[179] Later that

178 Law Officers to Russell, 29 March 1860—in response to Hammond to Law Officers, 2 March 1860; FO83/2298.

179 Russell to Alcock, 26 February 1862; FO410/1.

year, when Alcock submitted for approval draft Port Regulations for Kanagawa and Hakodate, which had been prepared by the Consuls there, the Law Officers urged that an attempt be made for uniformity between the two as the draft Port Regulations for Kanagawa seemed 'vague and imperfect' whereas those for Hakodate were 'much superior, both in structure and in form.'[180]

In 1863, the Law Officers advised that Regulations issued by Neale, the *Chargé d'Affaires*, to control vagrants and already approved provisionally by Russell were *ultra vires* the Consuls because, by defining vagrancy as the failure to give security when required for good behaviour, the Regulations sought to create an offence which was not an offence in England.[181] Then, in 1864, the Law Officers said the Minister had no power to issue Regulations to prevent British steamers going through the Inland Sea to test various batteries established by *daimyos* at Shimonoseki as such regulations were not for the 'peace, order and good government' of British subjects.[182] On the other hand, the Minister did have power under section 85 OC1865 (which replaced the Consuls' powers in the earlier Orders in Council) to issue Regulations prohibiting Britons from sending arms to enemies of the Japanese government.[183]

When, after the *Moss case*, Alcock was ordered by Russell to frame Regulations binding upon Britons in Japan, Alcock instructed Francis Howard Vyse, Consul in Yokohama, to frame appropriate rules and regulations for the enforcement of the Treaty. Alcock advised Vyse that 'when these Rules and Regulations have been fully framed I will then come to some understanding with the Japanese Government as to the circumstances under which British Subjects shall be held liable to arrest by Japanese Officials, for what specific offences and in what manner this power may be exercised'.[184] The preparation of these regulations proceeded slowly. Alcock justified this delay by the need to obtain some preliminary knowledge of Japanese laws and customs and to determine those which it was most important to respect and those which it would be bad policy to enforce (such as the need to render obeisance to Japanese governmental officers and *daimyos*). He also sought the input of the

[180] Law Officers to Russell, 6 March 1861; FO83/2298.

[181] Law Officers to Russell, 30 November 1863; FO83/2298.

[182] Law Officers to Russell, 6 January 1864; FO83/2298.

[183] Law Officers to Russell, 10 April 1865; FO83/2299.

[184] Letter from Alcock to Vyse reported on 21 December 1861; *North China Herald* (**NCH**).

Attorney General in Hong Kong before sending a copy of the Regulations he had issued for Russell's approval.[185]

It was not until 19 November 1861 that, after some further to-ing and fro-ing between Alcock, Russell and the Law Officers, these first Regulations[186] were issued by Alcock. For the most part, they only prohibited 'such acts as are forbidden absolutely or conditionally in every country for the peace, order and good government of all'[187] such as furious riding and the discharge of firearms. More contentious, however, were the bans on the pursuit of game, sleeping away from home and mounting Chinese servants on horseback except in attendance upon their masters. These, Alcock argued, were rendered necessary by Japanese complaints about such matters and the passing of cortèges or processions without due regard and the need to '...keep the exercise of Treaty rights within such bounds of discretion and good judgment as may be compatible with the security of those concerned...'[188]

Other regulations concerned the slaughtering of animals for food. The Law Officers confirmed that the Yokohama Consul could issue such regulations (which Alcock had approved) but condemned the 'peculiarity' of the actual Regulations themselves as the Law Officers advised that they did not promulgate any practical Regulations at all and so should not be approved by the Foreign Secretary.[189] Subsequently, Parkes, on Hornby's advice, made Regulations relating to the opening of abbatoirs, pubs and boarding houses by British subjects; and specific port regulations were issued in Nagasaki and Yokohama regulating the movement of British vessels in those ports. The Law Officers also signed off on the Minister's Regulations for Kobe and Osaka when those places were opened to Westerners.[190]

Other regulations, made by Parkes, governed the registration of mortgages and bills of sale[191] under sections 85 and 90 of OC1865 but, despite their having been based upon similar Regulations for China and the

---

185 Alcock to Russell, 20 November 1861; FO410/1.

186 23 November 1861; TJH—which was banner headlined 'Official organ for Publication in Japan of Notifications from HBM Legation'.

187 Alcock to Consuls, 1 December 1861; FO881/1135.

188 Alcock's Circular to British residents in Japan, 1 December 1861; FO410/1 and Alcock to Harris (USA Minister to Tokyo), 24 December 1861; FO881/1135.

189 Law Officers to Russell, 17 November 1864; FO83/2298.

190 Law Officers to Stanley, 29 February 1868; FO83/2299.

191 FO656/28. Regulations approved by Stanley on 10 January 1867 and later subsumed into OC1881.

Foreign Secretary of the time having approved them, Hannen[192] said that they were *ultra vires* and, therefore, invalid. When the matter was raised with the Law Officers, they concurred with Hannen as the Regulations were not, strictly, 'for the peace, order and good government' of British subjects in Japan.[193] Sir Francis Reilly was then instructed to prepare OC1881 to give retrospective validity to the Regulations.[194] Reilly, when submitting the draft Order in Council to the Foreign Office, said he had dealt not only with this point but had also included section 47—which he had taken substantially from the Ottoman Orders in Council[195]—which, as we see in Chapter 5 (Civil Jurisdiction) was to cause so many problems for the Courts and legal practitioners in Japan.

The narrow, legalistic approach adopted by the Law Officers back in London can be seen as early as 1859 when, in response to a Foreign Office suggestion that, mirroring the senior appointment in China, Alcock should be appointed 'Envoy, Minister Plenipotentiary and Superintendent of Trade in Japan', the Law Officers advised the Foreign Secretary that Alcock needed to continue as Consul-General for the jurisdiction granted by the Treaty was vested in 'Consuls' and, without a consular commission, a Superintendent of Trade would not be a Consul for the purposes of the Treaty and, so, would have no jurisdiction.[196] The Foreign Office quibbled and said that Article IV of the Treaty spoke of 'the British Authorities' without specifying them but accepted that, as Article VI, which dealt with British-Japanese disputes, referred specifically to consular officers, Russell would give up on his plan to appoint Alcock as Superintendent of Trade in Japan.

The constructionist approach to both the Treaty and Orders in Council and the Ministers' and Consuls' powers thereunder taken by the Law Officers sitting in London drew comment locally from the beginning. In 1861, Smale suggested that the Law Officers appeared 'not fully to appreciate the difficult circumstances in which Consular Officials in Japan are placed'.[197] An extreme example of this narrow approach may be seen

---

192 At that time, he was acting Chief Justice. See Chapter 2 (The Players in the legal system).

193 Law Officers and Dr J. Parker Deane (Admiralty Advocate) to Granville 3 August 1881; FO17/945 page 122.

194 Reilly to Pauncefote, 24 March 1881; FO17/945, page 123. Section 5 of OC1881 dealt with this.

195 Reilly to Charles Abbott Tenterden (Lord Tenterden, 1870, and Permanent Under-Secretary of State for Foreign Affairs, 1873–1882); FO17/945, page 267.

196 Law Officers to Russell, 22 November 1859. FO83/2298.

197 Smale to Alcock, 24 October 1861; FO410/1.

in 1868 when, as conflicts grew between the *bakufu* and those Japanese pressing for an imperial Restoration, the Law Officers, as we have already seen, went so far as to suggest that the Treaty appeared to be worthless because it referred to the Tycoon—and not the Mikado, or Emperor; although they did concede that then may not have been the moment 'to throw doubt on the appointment of Consular Officers or upon their rights and jurisdiction'.[198]

Almost from the beginning the question arose of whose rules and laws should British subjects follow in Japan. Were they:

a. Subject to Japanese laws—but simply tried for breach of those laws in the Courts; or
b. Obliged only to obey British laws and rules made by the Minister?

In the latter case, they could only be required to obey Japanese criminal and administrative laws and rules if such laws and rules were intermediated by the Minister and made into British regulations. Whereas the Japanese viewpoint was clear from the beginning: namely the former—and the Americans quickly accepted the Japanese position—the British response to the question involved inconsistencies and changes over time, depending upon the background. Admiral Stirling's treaty had clearly contemplated British observance of Japanese laws and Michael Moss had been charged with violating Japanese laws—besides breaching consular regulations—on shooting game. When Vyse, Consul in Yokohama, issued a Consular Notification after the *Moss case*, he said 'that residence in a foreign country carries with it by the common polity of nations the obligations to obey its laws—this obligation holds good in Japan no less than in other countries ... The right to disregard any Japanese laws is not a privilege conceded by the Treaty.'[199] However, when instructing Vyse to frame formal regulations after the *Moss case*, Alcock, although recognizing the need to prevent Britons violating 'the municipal laws of Japan',[200] qualified this by adding the proviso that any such Japanese law should 'be not in itself either unjust or unreasonable',[201] thereby adopting a selective approach as to those Japanese laws which Britons should obey.

---

198 Law Officers to Stanley, 12 May 1868; FO83/2299. The question was overcome by the Emperor's adoption of the Treaty and the substitution of references to the Emperor for references to the Tycoon in OC1865 by the China and Japan Order in Council, 1869.

199 Consular Notification by Vyse, 5 January 1861.

200 21 December 1861; NCH.

201 Ibid.

Moss had argued that, as section XXX of OC1860 provided that a British subject could not be convicted of an offence by a Court unless it was also a crime in England, British subjects in Japan could not be prosecuted for breaches of Japanese law alone. Both Vyse, at Moss's trial, and Alcock, when reviewing the trial and sentence, had dismissed this argument (although Alcock suggested a need to comply only with 'reasonable' Japanese laws); but, the Law Officers disagreed with them and upheld Moss's interpretation of OC1860 when they reviewed the *Moss case*.[202] The Law Officers advised that, although shooting game was a violation of Japanese municipal law, it was not a crime under English law—and, as such, could not be prosecuted in the Courts. In order to convict Britons in Japan of such an offence, the Minister should have availed himself of his power under OC1860 to make and to publish rules and regulations for the peace, order and good government of British subjects in Japan and to include, within such rules and regulations, a regulation which prohibited shooting game.[203]

Despite Vyse and Alcock's statements about the need to obey Japanese laws, the British authorities in Japan subsequently took a narrower approach. After the *Moss case*, the first occasion on which the issue of new Japanese government regulations and their applicability to British subjects arose on an inter-governmental basis was in 1872 in relation to proposed regulations for safety on Japanese railways. Parkes insisted that Japanese laws—and these regulations—could only be applied to Westerners through the intermediation of regulations issued by representatives of the Western Powers. The Law Officers agreed that the Japanese government needed to communicate such regulations to R.G. Watson, the then *Chargé d'Affaires*, who, if he thought them reasonable, should sanction their enforcement so far as British subjects were concerned. They subsequently advised that Watson's Notification to enforce them could be sanctioned by the Foreign Secretary.[204] The Law Officers' advice was the same in 1874 when the Japanese authorities proposed to

---

[202] FO46/30. Section XXX of OC1860 was continued into section 6 of OC1865.

[203] Law Officers to Russell 26 April 1861; FO83/2298. As to the Consuls' sentencing powers, the sentence imposed by Vyse would have been a legal sentence assuming the conviction to have been proper in the first place—but Vyse had no power to include costs. Alcock, as Consul-General, had no power to couple imprisonment with a fine (or vice versa). The Consul-General could vary a sentence—so long as it did not exceed the maximum punishment (which was 12 months *or* a fine of $1,000)—but he could not couple them.

[204] Law Officers to Granville, 20 September 1872 and 30 May 1873 respectively, FO83/2299.

issue quarantine regulations; the Japanese draft was fine but, as regards British subjects, it must be promulgated by the Minister.[205]

The question arose again regarding regulations proposed by the Japanese government in relation to shooting when Parkes explained that the Japanese authorities 'appear to have conceived an idea that in public and municipal matters they would make their own laws binding also upon foreigners'.[206] After much discussion, agreement was reached between the Japanese and the foreign Ministers as to the terms of regulations which the Ministers would issue whereupon the Japanese demanded that any fines imposed by the Courts for breach should be remitted to them in the same manner as with fines levied under the Treaty for breach of the Customs Regulations annexed to the Treaty.

Parkes contended that the cases were not analogous and the fines should accrue, in the usual manner, to the foreign courts. The precedent was important for the Japanese government acknowledged that it might demand the fines not only for breach of the shooting regulations but also any other regulations it required to be issued. He explained this was the key to the Japanese government's opposition to the foreign Ministers' proposals and argued against conceding this unless Britain was prepared for an early renunciation of extra-territoriality: 'trivial as it may first appear, the question at issue ... [was] ... who is to make laws for foreigners in Japan?'[207]

When the Foreign Office asked the Law Officers their views on the question, the Law Officers agreed that it was for Parkes to promulgate the necessary Regulations but as to whom the fines should be payable, they said it was a policy matter rather than a legal matter; but suggested that, as it could constitute a precedent if it were agreed that they should be paid to the Japanese government, Britain should only acquiesce if the other foreign Powers did likewise.[208] Derby, advised by the Law Officers, approved Parkes's stance.[209] Eventually, in 1877, Parkes issued Regulations which required British subjects to obtain shooting licences from the Japanese government, failure to obtain which would result in a fine of up to $100,[210] but, as with other fines generally, any fines imposed accrued to the British government.

---

205 Law Officers to Granville, 14 January 1874; FO83/2299.

206 Parkes to Derby, 7 February 1876; FO881/2847.

207 Ibid.

208 Law Officers to Derby, 22 March 1875; FO83/2299.

209 Derby to Parkes, 25 May 1876; FO881/2847 and Derby/Wooyeno Kagenori (Japanese Minister in London) correspondence July and August 1876; FO881/2924.

210 Regulation, 2 January 1877; FO798/26.

It had proved so difficult to resolve the exact terms of the shooting regulations that the next regulations promulgated by the Minister at the Japanese government's request were those made by Parkes in 1876 to prevent British subjects publishing Japanese language newspapers thereby avoiding the Japanese language Press censorship laws.[211]

Opium imports were seen by Japan as a better battleground upon which to win this battle; but it was only with the *Hartley cases* that the Foreign Office realized that, without its knowledge, Parkes had been engaged in a form of diplomatic warfare with the Japanese government since 1872 on the opium question.[212] When considering the *Hartley cases*, the Law Officers re-affirmed the earlier advice that Japan could frame regulations binding on British subjects provided that the Minister made mirroring regulations with fines, which themselves would accrue to the British government. Salisbury not only accepted this advice but, unlike Derby, accepted that, in future, the Minister would promulgate the necessary regulations upon formal Japanese requests; i.e. the Minister lost his discretion to refuse.

If one compares the Treaty with the Orders in Council, it becomes apparent quickly that the latter go beyond the former as the Treaty was not as comprehensive or as detailed a document as the latter. Successive Japanese governments were able increasingly to insist upon the Treaty's strict terms as its eagle-eyed foreign advisers came to understand its deficiencies in later years, particularly during discussions surrounding Treaty revision.[213]

A problem identified early on was the Treaty's not covering disputes with third party nationals although the Orders in Council did—but this had been finessed by the Austro-Hungarian treaty. Another aspect was that it did not require Japanese subjects to bring actions in the Courts—but rather to involve the Consuls who, with the Japanese authorities, would decide matters equitably; but, over time, this was ignored because the Courts provided effective remedies. Japan also left unpursued its argument that the Treaty applied only to crimes against individuals

---

[211] The aim was to stop the publication of J.R. Black's *Bankoku Shimbun*. For a fuller description of the incident, see J.E. Hoare, 'The 'Bankoku Shimbun' Affair: Foreigners, the Japanese Press and Extraterritoriality in Early Meiji Japan', *Modern Asian Studies*, Vol. 9, No.3 (Cambridge University Press, 1975).

[212] Pauncefote to Salisbury; FO46/361, pages 82–87.

[213] Sir Francis Piggott, *Extraterritoriality, The Law relating to the Consular Jurisdiction and to Residence in Oriental Countries* (London: William Clowes & Sons Ltd, first edition 1892; second edition 1907), page 1.

and not those against the state itself or its administrative laws[214]—apart from insisting upon compliance with Japanese laws and regulations. However, the clash between the Treaty and Orders in Council came into increasing focus in the 1880s with extradition where Japan construed the Treaty as limiting its cession of jurisdiction to offences committed within Japanese territory only but not over foreigners within Japan in respect of crimes committed in third countries.[215] Japan was to use this particular discrepancy as part of its campaign to secure the abolition of extra-territoriality.[216]

The Courts

The Courts were courts of record and English courts were to treat their determinations of fact as conclusive, but it remained an undecided question whether they were to be treated as foreign courts for other matters.[217] In 1880, when the *Japan Gazette* published a derogatory report about Dohmen (then acting Assistant Judge), the question arose whether HMCJ was a superior court and entitled to punish contempts committed outside its precincts or whether, as an inferior court of record, it was restricted to punishing only contempts committed within its precincts.[218] After discussions between Rennie, who opined that it was superior court, and defence counsel, who argued for a narrow construction of section 65 OC1865, the prosecution was dropped. The defence appears to have had the better view for the matter was put beyond question by OC1904 which clarified the point in favour of the consular courts in China and Korea.

Formal hearings were in court and, in both HMCJ, the Supreme Court and the other Courts when the Judge travelled on circuit and exercised the extraordinary jurisdiction of HMCJ or the Supreme Court, the judges wore wigs and robes[219] and donned the black cap when passing a death sentence. Counsel also wore gowns. Interlocutory matters were usually heard in chambers but, reports suggest, with no formal dress.

---

214 Parkes to Salisbury, 14 January 1880; FO46/267.

215 Fraser Memorandum, 28 November 1892; FO881/6417.

216 See Chapter 8 (The ending of extra-territoriality).

217 *Barber v. Lamb* in relation to a Constantinople case; 141 Eng Rep, 1100.

218 *Reg v. Talbot & Anglin*, 13 December 1880; JDH.

219 Hornby claimed six guineas (£6.30) and nine guineas (£9.45) for his wig and gown respectively which had been lost in the Supreme Court fire (Hornby to Granville, 19 February 1872; FO17/637). *Japan Punch* had several cartoons over the years of lawyers in Yokohama bewigged and gowned. See Jozef Rogala, *The Genius of Mr. Punch* (Yokohama: Yurindo Co., Ltd, 2004), page 146.

In the smaller consulates, the Consuls held their Courts in their offices or, in Kobe and Yokohama, a special room set aside as the courtroom.[220] The state of the Yokohama Court, however, called for Hannen to complain in 1872 about the unfurnished state of the offices and Judge's room and to urge that a proper residence and facilities be constructed for the state of affairs was not proper 'to the dignity of the Court, or just to the Officers'.[221] Security was also an issue for even the court buildings were not immune from theft as seen when the Yokohama Court's registry was burgled in 1872 and a sum of about $300 stolen therefrom together with a silver watch and a gold chain belonging to an intestate estate.[222] Nothing happened until, in another tirade, Hannen claimed that the cold had contributed to Clifford Bate, the clerk, needing to take home leave.[223] Eventually, proper facilities were constructed for HMCJ[224] with formal courtrooms and Judges' private chambers. They were part of the British Consulate complex in Yokohama—all of which was destroyed in the 1923 earthquake. Besides the cold, the courtrooms lacked lighting as seen when defence counsel left the courtroom before the Judge even realized because 'in the thick darkness, the Bench alone was illuminated by a glimmering candle'.[225]

The Courts depended upon supplies from home for their law books, record books and even their stationery and we see Robertson complaining about the 'inferior quality' of the blotting paper supplied to the Kanagawa Court[226] by HMSO—a complaint that was simply passed on to HMSO by the Foreign Office. Each Court was meant to have a separate seal but, in practice, they did not have one and simply used the consulate's seal. However, although the Yokohama consulate's seal was used for the Kanagawa Court this meant there was no court seal for the Yokohama Court. When Hannen raised this point, Goodwin adopted a robust practical view and responded that 'in the present state of things, it does not matter a fig what the Yokohama seal is'.[227]

---

[220] Hornby considered that consular offices would be adequate for judicial purposes when travelling on circuit; Crosse to Hornby, 24 November 1866; FO656/22.

[221] Hannen to Hornby, 20 September 1872; FO656/37.

[222] Hannen to Hornby, 3 November 1872; FO656/37.

[223] Hannen to Hornby, 10 March 1873; FO656/37.

[224] Cowan (an official in the Office of Works based in Shanghai) to Satow dealing with the alteration of the court-house after extra-territoriality's end, 20 March 1899; Ruxton 2005, page 40.

[225] *Japanese Police v. H.C. Gullard*, 18 November 1893; JWM.

[226] Robertson to Granville, 31 March 1885; FO46/339.

[227] Goodwin to Hannen, 11 April 1871; FO656/96.

The Courts in the out-ports could face practical problems with securing the accused and keeping witnesses available for a trial. These problems, which continued until the end of extra-territoriality, can be seen when William Cuthbert was accused of murder in Nagasaki in 1897. The Consul was most anxious to be rid of the accused as early as possible as he had no proper means of looking after him and, if he did not send the witnesses—nationals of France, Germany and Sweden—to Yokohama immediately control over them might be lost. Therefore, as no trial on indictment could take place in Nagasaki on account of the state of the jury list, he telegraphed to HMCJ that: 'Accused committed for trial wilful murder. Ship sails today with 5 witnesses recognizances completed 2 medical witnesses and surgeon *Immortalite* about proceed Yokohama 1 US citizen resident practitioner last most important witness Forward depositions as soon as possible.'[228]

Community involvement in the judicial process—criminal and civil—was introduced into the more important cases through Assessors and juries by OC1861 and OC1865. Assessors were to be British subjects 'of good repute'[229] within the relevant Consular district. A Consul was required to sit with between two and four Assessors depending upon the size of the claim or gravity of the offence; although, if no Assessor were available, he could sit without them and record his reasons for so doing.[230] He was required to consult them and take account of their opinion; but, they were not a jury and it was the Consul alone who decided the case and, in criminal trials, the applicable punishment.

Every January, each Court was obliged to compile a jury list of every British male over 21 with an annual income exceeding $250 capable of speaking and reading (but not, necessarily, writing) English within its Province before convening a special court in February to revise the list after which it came into force on 1 March for the ensuing year.[231] Individuals could claim exemption from a jury list on grounds of age or infirmity or because they were already included on another jury list within Japan.[232] Outside Yokohama and Kobe, settling the jury list was, largely, a symbolic exercise for there are no recorded jury trials elsewhere—although juries were required for inquests. In the smaller consulates, the

228 Nagasaki Consul to HMCJ, 24 and 27 October 1897; FO796/10.

229 Section II, OC1861.

230 Section 34, OC1865.

231 Sections 26 and 28, OC1865.

232 In 1899, two in Kobe were excused on the former ground and one on the latter ground—he was listed in Taiwan; 15 February 1899; *Kobe Weekly Chronicle* (**KWC**).

lists were not always compiled—even in Yokohama there was no extant list when Hannen arrived in 1871; but Goodwin confirmed that attendance upon juries was enforceable even without a list.[233]

Unlike Assessors, juries played a decisive part in proceedings and were arbiters of fact in criminal and civil trials and, in the latter, often determined the damages as a factual question. In civil cases, the parties could opt for trial by judge alone. Inquests required a jury of just three;[234] but, for jury trials, usually 15 potential jurors would be summoned from the jury list from whom a panel of five would be selected with each party having three peremptory challenges in addition to challenges for cause.

Jury service was unpopular as it could be an onerous and time-consuming business, which tended to fall upon the leading members of the British community in each Treaty Port. It was not unusual for potential jurors to challenge their inclusion on the jury list due to infirmity, etc. and, when a trial came along, it was common to find a number who had been summoned for potential service to be absent. The *Carew case* provides the most extreme example of potential jurors seeking to avoid being called. 20 jurors were summoned but half failed to appear: two had left the port, one was deaf and three produced medical certificates to exempt them from service whilst four failed to appear and were 'fined the usual $50'[235]—presumably deciding that either they could not afford the time commitment involved in what promised to be a lengthy trial or they wished to avoid the embarrassment of being involved in the trial. Eventually, a jury of five was empanelled but only after four potential jurors had been challenged peremptorily by the defence or the Crown.

From the beginning, the legitimacy of a five-man jury was queried. Hannen argued before the Supreme Court that the Crown had no power to make laws and regulations at variance with the laws of England and limiting jury numbers to five was unconstitutional. Hornby rejected this contention and refused to declare the point a fit one for appeal to the Privy Council;[236] but the point was not forgotten. When Edith Carew sought leave direct from the Privy Council to appeal, besides arguing that the evidence did not support her conviction, she took up Hannen's argument that, under English law, no native born British subject could be convicted except by the verdict of 12 men. The twist on this argument relevant to Japan was that the Treaty provided for criminal trials to be 'according

[233] Goodwin to Hannen, 25 May 1871; FO656/39.
[234] Section 53, OC1865.
[235] Account of first day's proceedings, TS36/104.
[236] Hornby to Clarendon 29 July 1869; FO17/530.

to the laws of Great Britain'[237] whereas a five man jury was not British law: in other words, much of the OC1865 criminal system in Japan was—and had been—illegal. As the *Japan Weekly Mail* recognized, this argument was unlikely to achieve much in her interests and the Lord Chancellor, in delivering the panel's rejection of her application, declared simply that 'Her Majesty had full jurisdiction to constitute the Court ... with a jury of five.'[238]

We cannot assess fully the cost of administering justice under the extra-territorial regime as, although the Legation's accounts contained line items for 'Administration of Justice' and 'Fines levied', they were never completed and there are no extant records of an individual Court's costs. The only—somewhat uninformative—expense entries against the Administration of Justice headings in consular reports to the Legation are entries for the financial year April 1859 to March 1860 when Nagasaki recorded a total of £5/2/9 (£5.14) and Hakodate recorded £6/9/2 (£6.46) for the final quarter.[239] Nothing is recorded against Kanagawa for that year.

Only in Yokohama and Shanghai was any distinction made between the Courts and the consulates; elsewhere, it would seem that Court costs were part of the consular establishments' general funding. The volume of judicial business at consulates (other than Yokohama before 1879) was not so great that it would not be regarded as part of a consulate's running costs—particularly as a Consul would be *in situ* in any event. In Tokyo, the Vice-Consul, in later years, operated from the Legation's chancery and fulfilled functions there so the Vice-Consular Court's costs would be marginal—indeed, in Tokyo, the case-load had almost disappeared before that Vice-Consulate's abolition just before the end of the century. In Hakodate, the bulk of the later years' consular work was shipping related with few Court cases.

The initial hope that the Supreme Court's fees would cover not only current expenditure but also part of the judicial salaries was justified by its first year's figures and Hornby reported that there was every prospect of the fees defraying all its expenses except for his own and Goodwin's

---

237 Article V.

238 *Ex Parte* Edith Mary Hallowell Carew [1897] AC 719,720. Initial surprise at a six member panel of the Privy Council considering Carew's application and the judgment's being delivered by the Lord Chancellor is probably explained by the principal grounds for appeal which raised the fundamental issue of the Crown's jurisdiction over British subjects abroad—and not just in Japan.

239 Alcock to Russell, 13 July 1860; FO881/942.

salaries.[240] It is unclear whether this was also the case with the Yokohama Court or HMCJ, the only full-time Courts in Japan. For the other Courts, however, the administration of criminal justice could hardly have been a money spinner as the fees were usually $1.50 per prosecution: a level which did not increase during the period despite the Dollar's depreciation. Civil suits incurred higher costs, not least because they were set at a percentage of the amount claimed and additional fees were levied in connection with most of the procedural steps. Even so, they would hardly have made significant contributions to the Courts' costs outside the Kanagawa Court, the Yokohama Court and HMCJ. In Nagasaki, the total fees in respect of initial criminal and civil claims from 1878 to 1899 was $1,547 or an annual average of $70[241]—albeit that there would have been additional fixed fees in relation to various filings, etc. in civil cases. In most years, the fees for criminal cases exceeded the fees in civil cases although, over the period as a whole, the fees in Nagasaki arose almost evenly from civil cases at $798 and from criminal cases at $749. Apart from the first two years, when the fees exceeded $100, fees in criminal matters were within $15 of the annual average of $34; but the level of civil fees fluctuated widely from one year to the next. This wide variation is reflected in the only Tokyo figures we have where $59 was collected in fees in 1871 but $331 in 1872;[242] and it is reasonable to assume that the difference was caused by the different values in the civil claims.

Some idea of the costs of running the Supreme Court and the Yokohama Court may be derived from Treasury regulations in 1876 which provided for funds to be supplied by the Treasury Chest in Hong Kong and prescribed the maximum drawing allowable each quarter and the maximum that could be held at the quarter's end.[243] The figures are given in Sterling although the drawings and balances were to be remitted in Dollars. The Supreme Court and the Yokohama Court would both have had a substantial income from fees and fines which would have reduced the need for cash drawings:

	Quarterly supply £	Maximum Quarter-end balance £
Supreme Court	1,300	400
Yokohama Court	650	200

[240] Hornby to Clarendon, 8 February 1866; FO17/453.
[241] Table 27.
[242] FO262/501.
[243] FO881/4339.

The Yokohama figure gives annual drawings of up to £2,600 for the Yokohama Court—which is in line with Satow's estimate, in 1899, that HMCJ was costing some '£2,400 a year besides the wages of the constable and 2 turnkeys'.[244] With the Judge's annual salary being £1,500 and the costs of clerks and a partial contribution to the Assistant Judge's salary being taken into account (given that he was also the Consul in Yokohama), we must assume that the balance of the running costs was met by the HMCJ's fee and fine income.

Waste was not permitted and the Legation's accounting files reveal Foreign Office auditors questioning all perceived extravagances or items additional to the Estimates. They reprimanded Wilkinson for spending £18 on law books which he needed for the Tokyo Vice-Consulate but which had not been contemplated by the original estimates and for which he had paid by making savings elsewhere.[245]

It was unusual for the Courts to pay the costs of witnesses; but, this could be done in exceptional cases such as when Wilkinson ordered that a witness who was a *jinrikisha* drawer be paid 50 cents expenses as he had lost earnings by coming to court and the costs were irrecoverable from the defendant.[246]

Many of the costs and expenses were handled through accounting entries in the general governmental accounts with specie being provided from the Treasury Chest in Hong Kong. Local banking accounts were also used. In the early days, the Yokohama Court's bank accounts were in Hornby's personal name and, when Hannen arrived in 1871, only Robertson and Bate were authorized signatories on the accounts.[247] Such arrangements continued even after Hornby's departure in 1876 and, when appointing Wilkinson to the Yokohama Court in 1876, Goodwin authorized Wilkinson to draw on his and Hornby's accounts in respect of the Yokohama Court at the Oriental Banking Corporation in Yokohama.[248]

---

[244] Satow to Gosselein, 22 February 1899; Ruxton 2007, page 153.

[245] Wilkinson to Parkes, 23 November 1877; FO278/25.

[246] Wilkinson to Salisbury, 18 July 1878; FO46/234.

[247] Goodwin to Hannen, 11 April 1871; FO656/39 responding to Hannen to Goodwin, 29 April 1871; FO656/37.

[248] Goodwin to Wilkinson, 20 December 1876; FO656/39. The British government subsequently lost most of the court funds held by that bank when it became insolvent in the 1880s.

CHAPTER TWO

THE PLAYERS IN THE LEGAL SYSTEM

The extra-territorial edifice was run by government employees with independent lawyers playing a participatory role. For their first six years, the Courts were subject to oversight by the Executive before legally trained judges assumed this responsibility. Over the remaining 34 years, six judges were responsible for the administration of British justice in Japan. This chapter reviews the Courts' staffing, the Consuls' legal training and the role of the independent Bar and looks at various criticisms that have been made about the Consuls' legal inexperience and training.

During the first six years, Alcock, as Consul-General and, during his absence in England, his deputy, Lt. Col. St. J. Neale as *Chargé d'Affaires*, were at the apex of the edifice with Consuls in Nagasaki, Hakodate and Yokohama[1] although provision was made for the more complex cases to be handled by SCHK—a court not without its own problems in terms of respect and competence. Immediate legal input was provided by the Attorney General in Hong Kong with ultimate supervision the responsibility of the Foreign Secretary who, in turn, looked to the Law Officers for advice.

Alcock appreciated that the judicial powers granted to a consul in Japan were 'extensive and such as under ordinary circumstances would not be placed in the hands of persons not professionally educated.'[2] When he appointed Myburgh as Consul at Nagasaki, he adjured him 'in the execution of the magisterial duties ... to combine the firm administration of justice with temperate and considerate indulgence ...[and to]... order the proceedings in your Consular Court as to earn for it the confidence of all who may come within its jurisdiction...'[3] It is somewhat ironic, therefore, that the most notorious case concerning the consular exercise of judicial power during this early period arose from Alcock's own handling of the *Moss case*. Despite the furore surrounding that case, the case-load until 1862–1863 was, in fact, relatively low and most of the consular focus was

---

[1] See page 75 et seq. for a discussion on the Consuls.

[2] Alcock to Myburgh, 10 February 1864; FO796/26.

[3] Ibid. These adjurations of Alcock to Myburgh followed similar language used by Alcock in the case of other consular appointments.

upon the general security situation for foreigners in Japan. We have already seen that much time, initially, was taken up with the question of initial regulations. With OC1865, came the more immediate judicial supervision of the extra-territorial edifice in the person of the Judge of the Supreme Court in Shanghai.

The Judges

For Sir Edmund Grimani Hornby, the first of the judges, Japan was just part of his responsibilities as he also supervised the Supreme Court and the consular courts in China. He established the OC1865 regime in Asia and, under him, Hannen, in his first tour of duty in Japan, established the Yokohama Court as Britain's principal judicial and legal centre in Japan. Goodwin and Wilkinson, who successively followed Hannen in running the Yokohama Court, likewise had no responsibility for the outlying Courts which remained the Judge's responsibility. Between the three of them, they laid the groundwork for HMCJ's establishment, with the Judge ranking second only to the Chief Justice in the British legal establishment in Asia. Richard Temple Rennie was the first Judge of HMCJ under the OC1878 regime but he stayed only a short time in Japan before being replaced by Hannen, on his second tour of duty in Japan, Mowat and, finally, Wilkinson who wound up and closed HMCJ during his final tour of duty in Japan. These last four operated and supervised the entire Court structure in Japan subject only to general instructions from the Foreign Office and appeals to the Supreme Court.

Apart from Goodwin, all exemplified Hornby's idea of a career ladder of judicial service in Asia;[4] but only Rennie, Hannen and Wilkinson became Chief Justice after being Judge, which, at the end of the nineteenth century, had come to be seen as an essential stepping stone to the Chief Justice-ship—a point which George Jamieson highlighted when, as Assistant Judge in Shanghai, he, unsuccessfully, pushed his claims to the Chief Justice-ship.[5]

---

[4] The Yokohama Court 'would greatly benefit the judicial branch of the service by creating a series of steps by which … the lowest judicial officer might rise to the position of Chief Justice through the offices of a senior Law Secretary, Judge in Japan &c…': Hornby to Clarendon, 23 October 1869; FO17/453.

[5] Jamieson implicitly recognized this hierarchy when applying to replace Mowat at HMCJ in 1897 'not because he wanted to go to Japan but to pre-empt another person being appointed in Shanghai as Sir Nicholas Hannen transferred from Japan … and if Sir Nicholas Hannen retires, the applicant from Japan would have a better claim'. (Jamieson to Salisbury,

Sir George French, who was Judge from mid-1878 (and Chief Justice from 1 January 1879) until he died in 1881 after a long illness, was the only person apart from Hornby with no East Asian experience before appointment. He had been Chief Justice of Sierra Leone[6] before accepting the Supreme Court on Hornby's resignation. French had responsibility for Japan for only half a year as OC1878 came into force shortly after his appointment and, consequently, he had little impact upon the legal structure in Japan.

All the Judges brought different characteristics to play. Hannen and Rennie had both been practitioners in Shanghai whilst Hornby, Mowat and Goodwin were judicial administrators and judges. Only Wilkinson combined experience of government service, independent practice, judicial experience and fluency in the Japanese language.

Although not based in Japan, Hornby alone of the Chief Justices had substantial immediate oversight of Japan and visited on circuit. He was 40 years old when he was plucked from Constantinople to become midwife to the OC1865 regime, as its draftsman and first administrator. His previous experience in Constantinople well-fitted him for the task of 'dealing with an imperfectly established judicial system and for eliciting order out of chaos'.[7] He was also legal guide to the Consuls, judge on circuit in Japan, appeal judge for cases from Japan and a leading British official in East Asia in terms of stature and influence—in Japan, perhaps, second only to the Minister, whose legal adviser he was. Described by Dr Willis, the Legation's doctor, as a 'jolly card,'[8] his letters to junior Consuls suggest an individual who brooked no nonsense or questions: very different from Goodwin with his almost avuncular approach. Of course, Hornby came with an established reputation and was very much a senior figure whereas, Goodwin apart, the other Judges were younger and contemporaries who worked together over the years and so a different tone in their mutual correspondence was only to be expected.

---

23 April 1897; FO17/1324.) In the event, the Chief Justice-ship and the Consul-Generalship in Shanghai, which had been united in the person of Hannen from the time of his appointment in 1891, were separated in 1897 (as the union had never worked) and Jamieson was appointed Consul-General and ceased to have any judicial involvement whilst Hannen surrendered all consular responsibilities but retained his full salary—and precedence—as Chief Justice (Salisbury to Hannen, telegram, 30 December 1897; FO17/1324).

6 1867–1875 before being pensioned off due to the lack of work in the impoverished colony: 5 April 1878; *Japan Gazette* (**JG**).

7 17 June 1876; NCH.

8 Hugh Cortazzi, 'The First British Legation in Japan', *PJS* Vol. 102 (1986), 38.

Hornby's robust approach to administering the law may be seen when, before visiting Japan in 1870, he wrote 'I can dispose of all pending cases—and the mere fact of my being there will precipitate all those that are hatching. There is always a lull in litigation after I have been in a place, because I talk people out of their absurd grounds and settle those amicably which really have any points in them without fighting—and, in criminal matters, I generally manage to inspire a wholesome respect for the law, that the Rowdy chaps keep in order for at least three months after I leave.'[9] On the other hand, he was conscious of many fellow Europeans' shortcomings for 'so often foreigners who have been long resident in China and Japan refuse to look upon Chinese and Japanese as human beings entitled to the same protection they claim for themselves. They appear incapable of understanding why a coolie is not to be treated worse than a dog.'[10]

He introduced two features of great assistance to the legal community. First, as directed by Russell,[11] he wrote and, in 1867, published his Instructions to Consuls.[12] Based upon his similar work in Constantinople, they were a set of practical instructions, guidance notes and the necessary forms for untrained Consuls. As with OC1865, they stood the test of time and were not revised until 1885 when Rennie, assisted by Mowat and Wilkinson, updated them.[13]

Second, he established the *Supreme Court and Consular Gazette* as the official organ of the Supreme Court and the British authorities in China and Japan.[14] It included accurate case reports—described as having been 'officially vetted' by the presiding judge—in the nature of Law Reports which could be cited in argument and enabled practitioners throughout Japan and China to follow local legal developments. Whilst only covering those cases of legal importance, they report many of the cases taken on appeal from Japan to the Supreme Court and several others heard in Japan (before both the Courts and Hornby on circuit).

Hornby visited Japan several times on circuit between his appointment in 1865 and 1870 and again in 1872 when he settled the Yokohama

[9] Hornby to Foreign Office, 21 March 1870; FO17/557.

[10] Hornby to Watson, 22 September 1872; FO656/19.

[11] Russell to Hornby, May 1865; FO17/433.

[12] Instructions to Her Majesty's Consular officers in China and Japan on the mode of Conducting Judicial Business.

[13] Rennie to Salisbury, 10 October 1885; FO17/997.

[14] This publication was not a commercial success and, in 1870, was folded into the NCH.

Court's status.[15] There is no evidence that he came to Japan on circuit after that before his retirement in 1876—thereby reinforcing the growing independence of Japan as a jurisdiction separate from China. French never visited Japan on circuit. To complete his team at the Supreme Court, Hornby selected Goodwin, then aged 48 and practising in the Temple, as Assistant Judge and John Fraser, then Law Secretary at Izmir, as Law Secretary.[16]

Nicholas John Hannen was, in 1871, the first judge specifically selected for Japan. When Parkes and Hornby, in 1869, proposed the Yokohama Court's establishment, Hornby recognized that 'the chief difficulty' would be 'in the working of it;'[17] a difficulty exacerbated by his own impending return on leave to Europe on health grounds. For Japan, Hornby first considered Goodwin, but questioned whether Goodwin would want the post or be as fitted for it as a younger man whilst he considered Mowat[18] too young. He wanted someone about 35 who was a thorough practical commercial lawyer for he viewed Japan as going ahead in government and, to be useful as an adviser, the Judge needed to be an able lawyer: 'To send out a *nisi prius* lawyer would do immense mischief at this juncture.'[19]

Without further discussion, the Foreign Office gave Goodwin no choice and simply notified him that the growing importance of British commercial interests in Japan rendered it necessary that a branch of the Supreme Court be established in that country and he, as Assistant Judge, should henceforth reside at Yokohama. One of the Supreme Courts' Clerks would be attached to his Establishment and he should use some of the office servants from the Yokohama Consulate as ushers and messengers.[20] However, for the moment, he remained in Shanghai as Deputy Judge during Hornby's leave.

As interim acting Assistant Judge, the Foreign Office now raised Hannen's name or, if not him, enquired whether 'Mowat be fit ... if he were ordered to return?'[21] Hannen was then practising at Shanghai but

---

15 If only to avoid the summer heat in China as he admitted when reporting on his six weeks on circuit in Nagasaki and Yokohama in 1866; Hornby to Clarendon, 1 September 1866; FO17/453. See footnote 109 on page 20.

16 Foreign Office to Hornby, 10 February 1865; FO17/414.

17 Hornby to Clarendon, 23 October 1869; FO881/1749.

18 Mowat had succeeded Fraser as Law Secretary in 1868 upon the latter's death. At the time Hornby wrote, Mowat was in London reading for the Bar. Interestingly, Hornby argues against Mowat on grounds of age—not because he was still unqualified.

19 Hornby to Foreign Office, 21 March 1870; FO17/557.

20 Clarendon to Goodwin, 8 April 1870; FO17/557.

21 Hammond to Hornby 11 March 1870; FO17/557.

had been called only in 1866.[22] We do not know why he was preferred for this appointment over Rennie, who was of nine years' call and had practised in Shanghai since shortly after the Supreme Court's establishment. Possibly, the Earl of Clarendon, then Foreign Secretary, had picked up on an earlier suggestion of Hannen's name by Hornby,[23] who was friendly with Hannen's brother[24] (then a judge of the Queen's Bench Division)[25] or, as must have been conceivable in an age of patronage, Hannen's brother, or others, had lobbied on his behalf in London. In any event, Hannen was appointed acting Assistant Judge and sent to Yokohama where he remained until 1874, when he returned to private practice in Shanghai upon Goodwin's returning from leave and taking over the Yokohama Court.

Despite voluminous correspondence in the British National Archives involving Hannen in Yokohama and both Hornby and Parkes's comments beforehand, the local newspapers considered that the amount of judicial business thrown onto Hannen had not been large before conceding that 'his advice and assistance have been sought under a variety of circumstances which have not come under the public eye and thus the law reports which are daily published afford no full indication of the actual work he has had to do'.[26] This view was not shared by the Legation; R.G. Watson, the *Chargé d'Affaires*, declared the business 'sufficiently large to fully engage the attention of both Judge and Consul'[27] and that Hannen's detachment to Yokohama had benefitted both the community and the Consulate there and allowed the Consul to concentrate more on consular affairs.

Hannen's standing may also be seen by his involvement by other countries such as when, in 1873, he tried a case in the Dutch consular court in Yokohama.[28] In the diplomatic sphere, his work included the *Maria Luz* affair where he was consulted privately by the Japanese authorities anxious not to incur 'the censure of the civilized world or any liability to the Peruvian government'.[29] He also assisted Parkes in relation to British

[22] List of barristers called to the Hong Kong bar in Norton-Kyshe 1898, Appendix III.
[23] Hornby to Clarendon, 23 October 1869; FO881/1749.
[24] 9 January 1897; JWM.
[25] Hornby to Clarendon, 23 October 1869; FO881/1749.
[26] 25 April 1874; NCH.
[27] Watson to Hornby, 6 June 1872; FO656/19.
[28] *Takeshima Colliery case*, 27 March 1873; NCH.
[29] Hannen to Watson, 9 September 1872; FO656/21.

claims against the old *han* and sat with a Japanese assessor in an arbitration involving several of them.[30]

On his return to Shanghai in 1874, he re-entered private practice but retained links with officialdom and was appointed Crown Advocate in the OC1878 reorganization. Upon French's death during Rennie's absence on furlough, Hannen became acting Chief Justice[31] until January 1883 when he relocated to Yokohama to assume the Judge-ship to which he had been appointed formally in December 1881 and which had been filled by Robertson, the Yokohama Consul, as acting Judge in the interim.

Hannen's second tour of duty in Japan lasted until 1891 when, upon Rennie's retirement as Chief Justice and the amalgamation of the two positions in 1891, he became Chief Justice and Consul-General in Shanghai. In Japan, besides overseeing the Consuls' judicial work, he assumed an advisory role to the Ministers—particularly in connection with the Treaty revision discussions which occupied much of the 1880s and, when Plunkett required additional support, Hannen was appointed the UK's second Delegate to the International Treaty Revision Conference in Tokyo in December 1886 to July 1887. Due to retire as Chief Justice in May 1900, he died, aged 58, in post—in April 1900.

Before assuming charge of the Yokohama Court in 1874, Charles Wycliffe Goodwin had had little experience of Japan save visiting once on circuit and having supervised the Courts in his position as Deputy Judge. In Yokohama, he continued the system established by Hannen and made no innovations. His sojourn in Japan was, probably, an unhappy one—marred by disputes over housing and other allowances, which left him worse off than in Shanghai, and increasing ill-health—so that, upon Hornby's somewhat precipitate retirement and departure in 1876, he transferred back to Shanghai early in 1877 as acting Judge.

He might have expected to succeed Hornby as Judge; but it was not to be and, upon learning of French's appointment over his head at the end of 1877, he immediately sought home leave rather than return from Shanghai to Japan.[32] Before he could set out for Britain, he died in January 1878, whereupon Mowat became acting Judge until French's arrival in Shanghai in mid-1878.

---

30 15 August 1874; NCH.

31 He immediately 'set to work ... to dispose of the cases of appeal left to his jurisdiction through the long illness of his predecessor;' 20 December 1881; JWM.

32 Goodwin to Derby, 13 December 1877; FO17/766.

Upon the re-arrangement of the judicial establishment consequent upon OC1878, the HMCJ Judge-ship was offered to Richard Temple Rennie, by then a leading Shanghai barrister. His only prior relationship with Japan seems to have been in 1869 when he appeared in Yokohama both before the American consular court and in number of cases over which Hornby presided on circuit. He spent barely two years *in situ* as Judge before taking leave in mid-1881 during which he was promoted Chief Justice in December 1881 following French's death. He had little noticeable impact upon judicial administration in Japan during his short tenure at HMCJ.

Robert Anderson Mowat joined the Consular Service in the same year as Wilkinson. His being made Law Secretary upon Fraser's death in 1868[33] demonstrated that, in the early days, non-legally qualified personnel could have a responsible input into the administration of justice in China and Japan; but, he obviously felt the lack of a formal qualification for, when requesting leave in 1869, he explained that his chief purpose was to read law in order to qualify himself for his duties[34] and he was permitted a year's extension of leave in London in order to be called to the Bar.[35]

Until appointed Judge in 1891, he, like Goodwin, had had no direct dealing with Japan apart from his involvement in the supervision of the Courts' affairs to a greater or lesser extent since 1868: as Law Secretary, Assistant Judge and acting Judge/Chief Justice. Unlike Hannen, he played no role in the Treaty revision negotiations—because they were suspended between 1891 and 1893 whereafter their locus moved to London. Whilst Court administration may have been fairly routine during his tenure, he presided over two of the (if not the two) biggest cases of the entire extra-territoriality period: the *Chishima case* and the *Carew* murder trial—both of which went to the Privy Council. The latter case left Mowat entirely exhausted and caused his nervous breakdown and early retirement in 1897.[36]

---

[33] Stanley to Hornby, 25 March 1868; FO17/502.

[34] Mowat to Hornby, 15 January 1869; FO17/530.

[35] Mowat to Hammond, 20 December 1870. Alcock, then Minister at Beijing, supported his application and urged that 'this system should be encouraged because of benefit to the public service'; Alcock to Granville, 23 December 1870; FO17/563.

[36] Hannen urged that Mowat be allowed to retire as 'this beastly *Carew case* has completely broken him up'; Hannen to Thomas Henry Sanderson (Foreign Office official and Permanent Under-Secretary of State for Foreign Affairs, 1894–1906 when he was elevated to the peerage), private, 4 March 1897; FO17/1324.

After passing his student interpretership examinations in 1864, Hiram Shaw Wilkinson[37] worked in Japan until the end of the decade when he went on home leave where he read for the Bar. Until then, there is no evidence that he had been involved in the judicial work of the consulates but, in 1872, he became the first member of the Japan Consular Service to be called to the Bar. After his return to Japan later that year, his consular career focused principally on the legal side of consular work. After being based in Kobe as a consular assistant for a short period, he acted as prosecutor at Yokohama before transferring to the Supreme Court in Shanghai for a tour of duty. In October 1876, upon Goodwin's return to Shanghai, he was given charge of the Yokohama Court as acting Law Secretary. Besides running the Yokohama Court, he also had charge from time to time of the Tokyo Vice-Consulate and, when Robertson went on leave, the Kanagawa Court.

Upon HMCJ's establishment, he was not entitled to be considered for appointment as its Judge—and so continue in the role he had been performing for the last two years—because he was still just under seven years' call at that time. Nevertheless, as Robertson was still on leave, he was appointed acting Assistant Judge under Rennie until he left for Shanghai in April 1879. Wilkinson spent the next 15 years in Shanghai: first as acting Assistant Judge of the Supreme Court whilst Mowat went on furlough.[38] Then, in 1882, when Mowat returned from leave and Hannen became acting Chief Justice, Wilkinson left the Japan Consular Service, was admitted to practise before the Supreme Court, entered, and built up, a thriving private practice and succeeded Hannen as Crown Advocate.[39]

In 1894, Wilkinson was appointed acting Judge of HMCJ whilst Mowat went on Home leave.[40] Usually the Yokohama Consul—who was also the Assistant Judge—would have been appointed as the acting Judge but, on this occasion Mowat was to be away for at least a year and Troup, the Yokohama Consul was not legally qualified. Dohmen, as acting Consul and acting Assistant Judge, had been appointed acting Judge during short periods of absence by Rennie, but the more complex cases could not be held over for the whole of Mowat's furlough—hence the need to appoint an experienced lawyer as acting Judge. When Mowat resigned

[37] See also Chris Roberts, 'Sir Hiram Shaw Wilkinson' in *Biographical Portraits, Vol. VIII* ed. Hugh Cortazzi (Leiden-Boston, Global Oriental, 2013) pages 147–163).

[38] 15 April 1879; NCH.

[39] Hannen to Granville, 20 April 1882; FO17/908.

[40] Wilkinson to Hannen, 20 January 1894; FO656/76.

in 1897, the issue of his successor as Judge arose and whether the post should be merely a temporary position given the impending end of extra-territoriality. Hannen argued that it would be unfair to the community in Japan not to fill the post and that Wilkinson was 'the best man to fill the post. He has been very good in filling the Acting Post to the detriment of his private practice here and has a kind of claim to the permanent appointment'.[41] Satow, then Minister in Tokyo, also supported Wilkinson's appointment and envisaged his likely succession to the Chief Justice-ship,[42] and advised that he was the only available man to take Mowat's place, would be a very efficient judge and, on Hannen's retirement, would be the obvious successor at Shanghai so the issue of a termination pension would not arise.[43]

Perhaps because of the press of Hannen's other duties and Mowat's increasing nervous illness, it had become the practice for the Judge to take the important cases only—leaving much of the work to be done by the Yokohama Consul (as Assistant Judge) which interfered with his consular duties.[44] Upon Mowat's retirement, James Troup, then Consul-General at Yokohama, lobbied for what he saw as a fairer division of the work and Satow enquired of the Foreign Office whether it would be possible to limit the Assistant Judge's judicial work to purely magisterial functions except during the Judge's absence from Yokohama and, conversely, that, whenever the Consul was absent, the Judge should assume magisterial work unless the appointment of an acting Assistant Judge was otherwise imperative.[45] Whatever Troup's wishes may have been, there was little change in work responsibilities—even as extra-territoriality drew to a close—for, in 1898, Satow again reported that, at Yokohama (as distinct from Kobe), the Consulate did the greater part of the judicial work[46] and Henry Bonar who succeeded Troup as Consul-General in Yokohama, was appointed Assistant Judge and, in time, acting Judge.

In January 1898, Wilkinson's acting appointment was made substantive and he became HMCJ's last Judge, with responsibility for clearing up the Courts' affairs and ending Britain's first legal foray into Japan. Upon the

[41] Hannen to (private), 4 March 1897; FO17/1324.
[42] Exchange of letters Cockerell and Satow, 5 and 6 July 1897; Ruxton 2005, page 16.
[43] Satow to Bertie, 11 March 1897; Ruxton 2007, pages 73–74.
[44] Satow to Cockerell, 2 July 1897; Ruxton 2007, page 82.
[45] Ibid.
[46] Satow to Cockerell, 24 February 1898; Ruxton 2007, page 100. (In 1896, Enslie had written that there was a great deal of routine judicial work at the Kobe Consulate; Enslie to Satow, 12 March 1896; Ruxton 2005, page 301.)

closure of HMCJ, Wilkinson was appointed Chief Justice in Shanghai where he remained until he retired in 1905.

There were close links between Japan and China at judicial staffing levels both before 1878, when the Courts were supervised from Shanghai, and afterwards. In 1879, when Mowat went on leave, French was constrained to appoint Wilkinson in Mowat's place because 'there is no Consular Officer in China who could take his place as a judge of appeal and the remuneration which would be paid to Mr Mowat's substitute would not be sufficient to induce any legal practitioner here to give up his practice'.[47]

The constant merry-go-round of appointments caused by death and the sensitivities of service personnel to hierarchy and their positions was highlighted in 1888 when Robertson died suddenly during Hannen's absence on leave and Wilkinson declined the offer of the acting Judgeship in Japan.[48] Jamieson was transferred from Shanghai to HMCJ as acting Judge whilst John Carey Hall of the Japan Consular Service re-located to Shanghai as acting Assistant Judge[49] because Hall was too junior to be made acting Judge over the heads of James Joseph Enslie[50] and other Consuls whereas he was merely the acting Assistant Judge in Shanghai.[51]

This incident and French's comments in 1879 when Wilkinson transferred to Shanghai suggest that the Japan Consular Service had more legally qualified officers with judicial experience than the China Consular Service for the only China Consular Service contender for the acting Shanghai appointment in 1879 was Bullock, who could not be spared. Again, when Jamieson became Consul-General in Shanghai in 1897, only one member of the China Consular Service, Frederick S.A. Bourne, was legally qualified and eligible to be appointed Assistant Judge.[52] However, without a deeper analysis of the China Consular Service, it is impossible to be definitive about this suggestion.

Wilkinson certainly had a reputation for industriousness and provided officials with lengthy detailed memoranda on various matters from foreign sailors on British vessels through a draft Order in Council for Parkes in relation to the extension of British jurisdiction in Korea. A number

---

47 French to Parkes, 12 December 1878:FO656/50.

48 See page 71.

49 Telegram, Mowat to Salisbury, 17 April 1888; FO17/1072.

50 Enslie had applied to replace Robertson (Telegram, Mowat to Salisbury, 25 April 1888; FO17/1051).

51 Mowat to Bertie, undated; FO17/1051.

52 Bertie to Hannen, 6 December 1897; FO656/58.

of his judgments showed an imaginative reading of the law in order to achieve the result he desired. Both characteristics were reflected when W.E. Davison[53] wrote that Wilkinson's memorandum on domicile for Britons who continued to reside in Japan after the end of extra-territoriality displayed 'great industry and care' but, perhaps, lacked practicality.[54]

Legal Profession[55]

As trade followed the flag, so lawyers followed trade and OC1865 made provision for the legal profession with the Judge authorized to admit 'fit persons' to practise in the Supreme Court as barristers, attorneys and solicitors.[56] As in Singapore and the Straits Settlements—but not Hong Kong where the fused profession split in 1864,[57] the legal profession in the Supreme Court and Japan was fused with barristers and solicitors both having rights of audience. It was, presumably, because legal numbers were so small that the profession remained fused.

It was customary for the Judge to admit suitable applicants upon their submitting evidence of admission or call in another appropriate jurisdiction; the only restriction being that Hornby would not 'sanction the admission of persons to practise in the Provincial Courts at any Port unless there are two or more fit persons at such Port'[58] to prevent a situation whereby only one side could be represented.

Practice varied: a lawyer could simply write, with his relevant certificates and papers, to the Consul or Judge requesting permission to practise in the relevant Court and written permission would be granted. Otherwise, a person already admitted to practise before that Court would move the admission of the newcomer who would then sign the Court Roll[59] as a record of his admission and evidence of his acceptance of the Rules.

[53] Later Sir Edward Davison, Legal Adviser in the Foreign Office.

[54] Davison to Satow (private) 16 January 1899; PRO30/33/5/2, page 64.

[55] See also Chris Roberts, 'British Lawyers in Japan, 1859–1899' in *Biographical Portraits, Vol. VIII* ed. Hugh Cortazzi, pages 164–183.

[56] Section 41 (the power under which was, by Section 7(2) OC1878, transferred to the Judge).

[57] Amalgamation/Legal Practitioners Ordinance, 1862, cap 13.

[58] Hornby to Marks, 15 April 1868; FO656/21.

[59] Traditionally, the Roll was parchment; but, absent parchment (which had not been destroyed in the Supreme Court fire of 1870), Goodwin recommended Hannen to use a paper Roll but keep it secure in an iron chest; Goodwin to Hannen, 29 September 1871; FO656/39.

Hornby considered that anyone admitted as a practitioner in the Supreme Court was entitled to practise in a Court but allowed that, if a motion for permission to practise in a Court were necessary, that Court's judicial officer was to decide the applicant's fitness and not the Judge.[60] The latter practice may have grown up as counsel liked its attendant publicity; certainly, in the later period, this route was usually followed in Japan.

Admission was not always straightforward and a pragmatic approach tended to be adopted. In 1871, when John H. Wilkins, an unqualified clerk who claimed to have served under Articles for over two years and worked in several lawyers' offices in London and New Zealand and was currently employed by Ross Johnson, a barrister in Yokohama, sought permission to practise as a solicitor in the Yokohama Court,[61] Goodwin was prepared to permit this provided Wilkins passed a satisfactory examination in legal knowledge before a board of examiners appointed by Goodwin at Shanghai despite the period of his Articles not complying strictly with the applicable statute.[62]

As in England, only independent lawyers could represent third parties. British lawyers employed by the Japanese authorities were admitted to practise but only upon undertaking to appear solely for their employer; as when John Frederick Lowder undertook only to appear for the Japanese Customs.[63] British officials who were qualified lawyers appeared *ex officio* such as when acting as prosecutor but did not otherwise represent the British authorities in the Courts. Foreign lawyers holding official positions elsewhere were not admitted to practise. Denison, an American, was refused permission to practise whilst he held a vice-consulship for the USA; but, upon his resignation from that position, 'the difficulty in the way of Mr Denison's practising in our Courts being thus removed,' he was admitted.[64]

Although there was no rank of Queen's Counsel amongst the Japan Bar, and so no obligation for senior barristers to take a junior counsel, it was not unusual—particularly by the 1890s—for two counsel to be instructed in a matter. Whilst this may reflect clashing commitments and/or general work convenience (or, where Henry Charles Litchfield led, perhaps

60 Hornby to Goodwin, 6 May 1874; FO656/39.

61 Wilkins (possibly, Williams) to Goodwin, 26 May 1871; FO656/22.

62 Goodwin to Wilkins, 22 June 1871; FO656/21. Despite Goodwin's flexibility, there is no evidence that Wilkins took up this proposal.

63 Lowder to Hornby, 17 September 1872; FO656/22.

64 Mowat to Wilkinson, September 1878; FO656/39.

concerns about the impact of his deafness on his abilities in court), it also suggests there was a significant number of more complex cases.

Obtaining accurate details of which lawyers were based where and when they were first admitted to practise in Japan is difficult. There are three principal sources: first, Court documentation and correspondence; second, newspaper and law reports of cases and, finally, a scouring of the Directories.[65] The first two sources are not comprehensive for their focus is contentious legal work—and, with newspaper reports, only where the case was of reportable interest. The Directories—whilst overcoming this problem—depended upon individuals putting forward the relevant information in a timely manner and they are not always complete. Further, when an individual left Japan, it was not unusual for his entry to continue for a year or two subsequently. Thus, whilst a useful guide, they cannot be taken as conclusive.

Another difficulty in preparing a list of lawyers in Japan[66] is that civil litigants could appear by counsel or 'by an attorney'.[67] This reference to 'attorney' is not to a lawyer but to an agent appointed by power of attorney under Rule 12 which required the power to be presented to the Court as evidence of authority. The intention must have been to allow a firm to be represented by one of its partners or by an employee or, on occasion, an individual to be represented by a friend or associate: it was not intended as a means whereby unqualified individuals could, in effect, carry on a legal business. However, this is what happened; William Cruchley, who made his first appearance in the Kanagawa Court in 1862, was one who carried on such a business—and described himself as a 'solicitor' in the Directories. In an 1869 advertisement in *The Hiogo & Osaka Herald*, he claimed to be a 'Law, Land, House and Property and General Business Agent and Auctioneer' and to attend to 'all legal business.'[68]

The Courts were somewhat grudging in their tolerance of such practice. In 1862, the Kanagawa Court refused to allow Cruchley to represent the defendant on the technical ground that he had not lodged his authority to do so with the Court.[69] In 1867, Hornby, who disapproved of such practice,

[65] 'Directory' means the various directories published in Asia whose name varied slightly over the years from *The Chronicle and Directory for China, Japan and Philippines* in 1864, to *Japan Directory* from 1872 onwards.

[66] See Appendix IV.

[67] OC1865. Criminal defendants were obliged to appear in person, but could be represented by counsel.

[68] 12 June 1869; *The Hiogo & Osaka Herald.*

[69] *Cook v. Frey*, 14 June 1862; *The Japan Herald* (TJH).

instructed Myburgh not to allow Cruchley to appear for others but Cruchley referred Hornby to Rule 12 which allowed for litigants to be represented by attorneys.[70] No outcome to Cruchley's complaint is apparent but he continued in business although, whether as a consequence of the arrival of lawyers in Yokohama in 1868 is unclear, he relocated to Kobe in the late 1860s where he continued to appear as an 'attorney' until the early 1880s—as a side-line to his newspaper publishing business.[71] We see a number of reports in the Kobe newspapers where Cruchley acted not only for the plaintiff or defendant in civil cases (both in the Courts, the USA consular courts and the Japanese courts) but also for defendants and, very occasionally, the prosecutor (but never the Crown as prosecutor) in criminal cases. Although the Courts did enforce civil claims by Cruchley for the payment of his fees for advising clients, they refused to allow successful litigants to reclaim fees they had paid to Cruchley from the losing party on the grounds that he was not a legal practitioner and, so, those fees were not allowable legal costs.[72]

Cruchley was not unique as is reflected by the exchange between Hannen, counsel for the respondent, and Hornby in *Chaya Yakichi v. Mourilyan & Co.* on appeal. Hannen said it was 'not an ordinary case in which a Japanese had left everything to the Court for the plaintiff was represented by a Mr Cruchley, who practised as an attorney though not admitted to the Courts but who represented the plaintiff by virtue of a power of attorney.'[73] Hornby said that he had questioned more than once whether an unadmitted person should be allowed to conduct a case merely by a power of attorney to which Hannen responded: 'it was certainly an abuse, but it was done'.[74] In 1878, Robert John Beadon, who appeared to represent the Imperial Japanese Railways, objected even to Cruchley's appearing for the plaintiff as no grounds had been shown as to why the plaintiff was unable to appear personally—and so needed to be represented under a power of attorney.[75]

In time, the Supreme Court made it more difficult for such unqualified attorneys by ruling that they could neither cross-examine witnesses nor address Courts on a point of law.[76] It is impossible to assess such practice's

70 Cruchley to Hornby, 18 January 1867; FO656/22.
71 He published *The Hiogo and Osaka Herald*.
72 See *Albert Morris v. James Norton Lock*; 19 July 1876; *The Hiogo News* (**HN**).
73 24 December 1874; NCHLR.
74 Ibid.
75 *Henry Seymour v. Walter F. Page*, 1 June 1878; HN.
76 Rennie in *Busch Schraub & Co. v. C. Hyver*, 14 January 1879; *Japan Daily Herald* (**JDH**).

prevalence. There is no evidence that it occurred in the Supreme Court, the Yokohama Court or HMCJ and the practice appears to have been confined to the lower Courts where litigants, presumably, sought cheaper advice or, in many cases, some advice from someone who had some familiarity with the law and legal processes.

The term 'solicitor' throws up the same difficulties as the term 'attorney' did in the earlier days. Besides referring to someone who had qualified as a solicitor, the term was also used in relation to individuals—legally qualified or not—who operated as scriveners or clerks in relation to legal documents or handled land transfers within the foreign settlements. Cruchley was not the only one so to describe himself. F. Schroeder, the owner and editor of *The Eastern World* in Yokohama from the late 1880s until 1908,[77] was another who advertised himself as a solicitor and adviser on legal matters.[78] However, while he may well have advised individual clients on legal matters or handled conveyancing transactions for them, there is no evidence that he followed Cruchley and appeared as an advocate in the Courts—although he conducted the last case reported in the German consular court in Yokohama. In 1900, he was described as the 'manager' of 'The "Eastern World" Law and Patent Office' which office included Dr Koide Ryutara, a Japanese barrister. My suspicion is that, although knowledgeable about legal affairs—he published a detailed commentary on the new Commercial Code of Japan—he was not an English qualified solicitor: certainly, he was never reported as having appeared in the Courts.

Most British lawyers were English qualified although three were called to the Scots Bar (Dickins, Gavin Parker Ness and John Richard Davidson). While many Shanghai counsel were called first in Hong Kong, only Frederick James Barnard and H.A.C. Brushfield of those in Japan were called first in Hong Kong (in 1866 and 1890 respectively)[79] and only Litchfield, who had practised in Shanghai before moving to Japan in 1878, was called in Shanghai before practising in Japan.[80]

The first reference to a lawyer appearing before a Court was to Cooper Turner from Hong Kong who appeared to defend Michael Moss at his trial before Vyse—although he had not appeared at the committal proceedings.[81] This was a one-off appearance for the next reference to a

[77] Editorial, 14 November 1908; EW.

[78] In 1900, he advertised, in *The Eastern World*, that the office advised on 'arbitrations and companies arranged under the provisions of Japanese, English and German law'.

[79] See list of Hong Kong lawyers in Norton-Kyshe 1898, Appendix III.

[80] Shanghai Directory, 1873.

[81] FO46/30, page 75.

lawyer advising in relation to a Japan based case was in *Sanders v. Alt & Co.* in 1865 when Abel Gower (then, Consul in Nagasaki) wrote to Edward Lawrence who was described as 'legal advisers [*sic*] to the plaintiff.'[82] Lawrence was based in Shanghai where the Directories had listed him as a 'Notary and Practitioner at Law' from 1862. The first qualified lawyer based in Japan was Francis Walker Marks in 1867 followed soon by Barnard whereupon Marks was admitted to practise in Court.[83] By 1872, three lawyers were listed[84] and the Yokohama Bar ranged from two to a maximum of six lawyers practising independently in Japan at any one time, compared with the Shanghai Bar which grew from just one in 1861 to six in 1866,[85] nine in 1891[86] and 13 in 1900.[87]

Counsel admitted to practise must be distinguished from those practising independently. In 1874, nine admitted counsel welcomed Goodwin to the Yokohama Court[88] but only four practised privately;[89] another four were employed by the Japanese authorities[90] and Wilkinson was in the Consular Service. Private practitioners peaked around 1876 with six independent practitioners; Litchfield and William Montague Hammett Kirkwood also having been admitted to practise. From then, despite the establishment of HMCJ, independent practitioner numbers declined so that only three or four practised regularly before it. The coming end of extra-territoriality must have discouraged new practitioners coming to Japan and, sometimes, there were difficulties in avoiding conflicts of interest for, in the late 1890s, Professor Henry Terry, professor of English Law at the Imperial University (now, Tokyo University), appeared occasionally on behalf of defendants.

Most counsel were based in Yokohama but also travelled to the outports and, from Dickins' defence of Archibald King onwards,[91] we see

---

82 Gower to Lawrence, 22 September 1865; FO796/29.

83 'The objection which previously existed … being now removed by the arrival of Mr Barnard, you are at liberty to plead.' Goodwin to Marks, 29 August 1868; FO656/21.

84 Marks, Dickins and the American, G.W. Hill.

85 Shanghai Directory, 1876.

86 Chief Clerk to Joseph A. Shearwood; 8 June 1891; FO656/76.

87 Circular from acting Crown Advocate, A.C. Platt, to Members of the Bar for HBM Supreme Court, 3 August 1900; FO656/93.

88 11 April 1874; JWM.

89 Ness, Marks, Dickins and Andrew Duncan. Duncan may have been an American citizen—see footnote 108.

90 Lowder (Japanese Customs), Hill (*Saibansho*: he had been employed previously by the *Kobusho* (Japanese Public Works Department)), W.W. Cargill (Japanese Railways and Telegraphs) and Davidson (Japanese Public Works Department).

91 King was charged with the rape of a teenage Japanese girl in Tokyo—a case which caused emotions in both the Japanese and the British community to run high. See page 134 and also Chang chapter 2 for a fuller discussion of the case.

references to lawyers in, or dealing with, the Tokyo Court, which is unsurprising given its proximity to Yokohama. Whilst the Nagasaki Court's correspondence files mention lawyers as advising litigants, there is only one reported instance of any appearing before that Court. Likewise, there was only one occasion on which lawyers appeared before the Hakodate Court (when Kirkwood acted for Porter in the cross actions in *Henson v. Porter*—and was shipwrecked along with Robertson, the Assistant Judge, on his journey there for the case).[92]

Kobe was the other centre for lawyers' operations. In 1873, the plaintiff, in *Reynell v. E.C. Kirby for Hall & Holtz* sought to recover his costs for travelling 'to consult counsel at Yokohama, there being none available at Kobe';[93] but, by the next year, lawyers were appearing on circuit in Kobe[94] and a newspaper report of a case brought by Duncan personally to enforce a judgment suggests that he was practising regularly there by 1877[95] and the inclusion of his name in the 1876 List of Electors for the Kobe Municipal Council suggests he was resident there as well. The 1890 Directory lists H.J. Pearce and J. Laufenberg as solicitors in Kobe and John Creagh as a 'solicitor and conveyancer'.

Although not certain, it would seem that Creagh was almost certainly a legally qualified practitioner for he signed himself as a 'solicitor of Her Britannic Majesty's Court for Japan' when he witnessed a Lunacy Petition in relation to George Harvey Whymark, a Kobe based pilot.[96] He would scarcely have done this (and gone on to appear in HMCJ on circuit in Kobe in this case) had he not been qualified and have signed HMCJ's roll of practitioners. He had also represented the Japanese Customs in the *Hiogo Treasure case*.[97] It is probable that Laufenberg was not legally qualified: there is certainly no evidence of his having appeared in court. With Pearce, the position is less clear-cut: in 1893, he was described as a 'solicitor in Kobe' (which could, of course, cover his not being a qualified practitioner) when *The Rising Sun and Nagasaki Express* reported that the *Kobe Weekly Chronicle* had accused him of professional malpractice for receiving $600 for disclosing confidential information about an American client but the

92 4 August 1882; NCH.

93 Gower to Hornby, 17 March 1873; FO656/41.

94 Duncan for the defendants in *Yamamoto Hempei v. Lucas & Walters* (with Cruchley as attorney for the plaintiff); Annersley to Hornby, 5 December 1874; FO656/41.

95 *Andrew Duncan and N.N. Nordenfeldt v. C.J. Strome*, 16 June 1877; JWM. The 1876 Directory also records Duncan under Kobe.

96 4 December 1886; *The Kobe Weekly Chronicle* (**KWC**).

97 5 December 1881; HN.

newspaper went on to call for the British authorities to investigate the matter 'with a view to striking him off the roll of solicitors'[98]—which suggests that he was legally qualified. Another possible Kobe lawyer was P. Mackenzie Skinner who had been an editor of *The Hiogo News* but, in 1899, was described by the *Kobe Weekly Chronicle* as a barrister.[99] He was not listed as such in the Directories and, apart from representing the Sowters in their claim against Mr & Mrs Rowe—which he could easily have done under a power of attorney, there is no other reported occasion on which he appeared in Court. Thus, it is unclear whether he was actually qualified or engaged generally in legal practice or whether, as with other newspapermen, he turned his hand to legal advice from time to time.

By 1893 at the latest, Charles Neville Crosse, a barrister, was based in Kobe but Creagh, Pearce and Laufenberg had all disappeared from the Directories by 1894 when Brushfield first appears as a barrister in the Kobe Directory. The Kobe lawyers did not have a monopoly of legal work there for Yokohama counsel are reported frequently as appearing before the Kobe Court. When Mowat went there on circuit for the *Hiogo Hotel case*—a corporate dispute, described as 'stirring and exciting'[100] involving allegations of fraudulent misrepresentation surrounding the hotel's sale—counsel were Lowder and Tison, a US lawyer admitted in Yokohama.

Despite the number of names of lawyers (qualified and unqualified) that appear in the Kobe Directories, there are two suggestions in newspaper reports that, even by the late 1880s, it was not always easy to obtain legal representation in Kobe. The most significant case was in relation to Captain Drake's committal proceedings.[101] When Lowder appeared on behalf of the Governor of Hiogo *ken* and the Japanese government to prosecute Drake and seek his committal to trial for manslaughter, Drake sought to have the committal proceedings adjourned so he could obtain advice from Shanghai 'as no legal assistance was obtainable in Japan'. Lowder objected to any adjournment on the grounds that legal advice was available in Yokohama—an objection which was sustained by the Court.

---

98 4 January 1893; *The Rising Sun and Nagasaki Express* (**TRS&NE**). Pearce denied the accusations—see 11 January 1891—but there is no report as to the result of any investigations.

99 19 July 1899; KWC.

100 17 June 1892; NCH.

101 17 November 1886; H.N. Drake was prosecuted by the Japanese authorities for manslaughter when he abandoned his ship, the ss *Normanton*, and left many Japanese passengers to drown; see pages 186–188. Chang, chapter 4, provides a fuller background to the case and discusses the extent to which the three month prison sentence given to Captain Drake was in conformity with contemporary sentencing practices.

In 1898, Remegio Perez, a Spanish plaintiff, sought permission, and was allowed, to have his interpreter read out a statement on his behalf to the Kobe Court as 'he was unable to obtain legal representation in Kobe because of the absence of the other barrister [Brushfield] practising' in Kobe when Crosse was acting for the defendant.[102] This suggestion that Crosse and Brushfield were the only lawyers in Kobe would support the view that Mackenzie Skinner was not, in fact, legally qualified.

Unlike the judicial level, with its regular exchange between Shanghai and Japan, there seems to have been little cross-over amongst the lawyers. Although Shanghai had the larger Bar, Shanghai counsel were not instructed regularly to appear in Japan—even in Nagasaki which was relatively close. Rennie and Robinson appeared in several Yokohama cases when they followed Hornby on circuit in 1869; but, presumably, with the Yokohama Bar then established and the Yokohama Court following in 1871, it became economically unviable—and unnecessary—for Japan based litigants to instruct Shanghai counsel. The only other exceptions of Shanghai counsel appearing before HMCJ in Yokohama were when Alfred Robinson defended Drake in the *Normanton case*; Edward Robinson defended Woodward in 1887 and Wilkinson led Litchfield, the Crown Prosecutor for Japan, in the *Carew case.* The last was a true exception: besides being a *cause célèbre* in the foreign community, the trial lasted 26 days and involved J.C. Hall, who, as Coroner, had conducted the inquest, being called to give evidence and an attempt by the defence to call the Minister to give evidence. Satow reported that Mowat had urged privately that Wilkinson should be retained which Satow felt was 'absolutely necessary'[103] not least because he had doubts about Litchfield, who was deaf 'and quite unable to conduct a cross-examination or to hear the speeches of Counsel'.[104] When Edward Robinson came from Shanghai to defend Edward Daniel Woodward in 1887, Woodward had been arrested in Shanghai and brought back to Kobe by a Shanghai constable to face the first of three linked cases brought against him by H. McGregor of Kobe, represented by Creagh and Litchfield, for forgery and embezzlement.[105]

---

[102] *Remegio Perez v. Imperial Insurance Company of London*, 2 July 1898; KWC.

[103] Satow to Francis Leveson Bertie (later Viscount Bertie, a Foreign Office official and later Ambassador to France 1905–1918) (private), 24 November 1896; Ruxton 2007, pages 57–58.

[104] Ibid. From the moment of Edith Carew's arrest, rumours swirled around the Yokohama foreign community that an external prosecutor would be brought in. Initial rumours suggested that Francis QC would come from Hong Kong for the purpose but these were soon scotched: 18 November 1896; TRS&NE.

[105] See also pages 95–96.

It may have been his own connections with Shanghai that meant he employed Shanghai counsel to defend him.

Conversely, Japan based barristers seem to have appeared equally rarely in Shanghai—even in appeals where they had conducted the case at first instance. Exceptions included Kirkwood in *E.C. Kirby v. Howles* and Lowder when he appeared for the appellants and defendants in *Owners of William H. Macy v. Owners of the Isis*.[106] The Supreme Court roll cannot be taken as conclusive of counsel who practised before the Supreme Court for, when Kirkwood and Lowder took the *Chishima case* to the Supreme Court, Wilkinson moved their formal admission to the court and they signed the roll—despite Kirkwood, at least, having appeared previously before it.[107] Despite Kirkwood and Lowder having argued the *Chishima case* at first instance, both parties instructed additional counsel: the Japanese government instructed Wilkinson and his son, Hiram Parkes Wilkinson who was then a junior barrister in Shanghai practising in Wilkinson's chambers, and P&O instructed A.P. Stokes and Francis Q.C. from Hong Kong, which suggests that clients considered the capabilities of the Shanghai and Hong Kong Bars to be superior to that in Japan.

Rights of audience were not confined to British lawyers and Hornby expressed the view that 'gentlemen who are admitted to practise in the US Courts are entitled to practise in Provincial Courts'.[108] Internationalization of legal representation was not confined to the Courts for British lawyers also appeared before other nations' consular courts and, into the early 1880s, before the Japanese courts. The most famous (but neither the first nor the only) instance of the latter was the *Maria Luz* where the vessel's Peruvian master and Spanish owner sought to enforce the coolie contracts before the Kanagawa *Kencho*. Two British barristers (Dickins, for the plaintiffs, and Davidson, for the coolies) represented the litigants and the American, Hill, the Japanese authorities. The Japanese presiding officer delivered a judgment for the defendants in English, relying upon British authorities, texts and maritime Acts.[109]

Despite this internationalization, the majority of counsel appearing before the Courts were British although Alexander Tison, an American

---

[106] 1 May 1896; NCHLR.

[107] 13 October 1893; NCHLR. Similarly, Stokes, P&O's counsel from Hong Kong, was formally admitted—despite having appeared previously before the Supreme Court.

[108] Supreme Court to Duncan, 7 May 1874; FO656/21. This letter suggests that Duncan was an American but a case commentary in 16 June 1877 JWM (see footnote 95) suggests he was a British subject.

[109] 17 October 1872; NCH.

Professor of Law at Imperial University, Tokyo, was a popular choice of counsel and appeared frequently after 1891—not solely for American or other foreign litigants in the Courts. Another American lawyer of note was Scidmore who represented the American owners in *Owners of William H. Macy v. Owners of the Isis*[110] and Miss Jacob, the Carew nanny. Non-British practitioners in the Courts were, usually, American although, in 1875, a French advocate, P. Gross, prosecuted in *Reg. v. Archibald King;*[111] but, whether he was an independent advocate appointed by the Japanese authorities or their employee is unclear.

For completeness, one should mention the Japanese who qualified, in London, as English barristers. These Japanese barristers qualified not to practise in the Courts but to broaden their horizons and study foreign legal systems. English law was widely studied in Japan at the time as can be seen by contemporary complaints about the reprinting of English legal works in breach of copyright.[112] At the HMCJ hearing of the *Chishima case*, one of the Japanese government's counsel was Okamura Teruhiko who, when he appeared with Kirkwood, was welcomed by the court with the words: 'you are not the first Japanese barrister to sign the roll but you are ... the first to appear in this court'.[113] Numbers were sufficient that, in 1899, an Anglo-Japanese Inns of Court Association was founded.[114]

The Japanese authorities employed a number of foreign legal advisers to advise as regards their dealings with foreigners and to assist in drawing up the new Codes and the Constitution. Many were American or Europeans—partly because Europeans were cheaper to employ than British or American lawyers. Among the first so employed was Lowder, who left the Consular Service soon after qualifying to become Legal Adviser to the Japanese Imperial Customs until 1874/75 when he began to practise independently in Yokohama. The number of lawyers employed by the Japanese authorities reduced after the 1870s as successive Japanese governments sought to reduce Japan's reliance upon foreign advisers in all fields. Hill, who represented the Japanese Authorities in the *Maria Luz* affair was legal adviser to, in 1873, the *Kobusho* (Public Works Department) and, in 1874, the *Saibansho,* which also had two Western interpreters.

---

[110] Mowat to Hannen enclosing Record of Appeal, 23 March 1896; FO656/49.

[111] Court Minutes accompanying Dohmen to Hornby, 19 June 1875; FO656/40. Gross was assisted by a Japanese interpreter, Motu.

[112] The Law Quarterly Review noted, in 1893, that 'a school of English law flourishes in Japan' before complaining of works being reprinted without the authors' consent: LQR ix.113.

[113] Japan Weekly Advertiser, report 25 May 1893; pasted into FO46/480.

[114] 20 May 1899; JWM.

In 1877, when Beadon, an English barrister, was admitted to practise in the Yokohama Court, it was noted that he was attached to the *Kobusho*.[115]

Two leading British legal advisers to the Japanese government were Kirkwood and Francis Taylor Piggott. Kirkwood was approached, while Crown Advocate for Japan, to become legal adviser to the Minister of Justice and filled that position from 1885 to 1901. Besides acting for the Japanese government in litigation, he assisted in revising the Criminal Code and the Code of Criminal Procedure and was associated with Satow in translating them into English.[116] He also played a major role in contributing to Japan's legal policies in Taiwan after its occupation by Japan. Piggott, meanwhile, was recruited in London to act, from 1888 until 1891, as special legal adviser to the Prime Minister in connection with the new constitution.

Outside the law, we find lawyers (widely defined) engaged in commerce and general professional activities. Barnard was also a ship-owner whilst Dickins, Creagh, Skinner, Cruchley and Schroeder owned and/or edited various of the English language newspapers from time to time in Yokohama and Kobe. It was not uncommon for leading companies to include a lawyer amongst their directors. For instance, in Yokohama, Litchfield was a director of The Club Hotel in Yokohama and Crosse was a director of The Oriental Hotel in Kobe whilst Lowder and Brushfield sat on the boards of directors of their rivals.

The first lawyers were part of the rough and tumble of frontiersmen and not above trying to bully the Consuls with talk of connections back home and adopting a superior attitude. *The Hiogo News* suggested there was no respect for the Consul judges for 'the conducting of a case too often degenerates into an unseemly wrangle'.[117] Parkes reflected this when he argued the need for a legally-qualified judge to control the litigious nature of 'pettifogging practitioners'.[118]

Two early instances highlight the disciplinary problems. The first was Barnard who was a bully in court and a trouble-maker outside. After numerous warnings, and extreme patience on the part of Lowder, the Yokohama Consul, and Hornby,[119] the former suspended Barnard from

115 The only record of Beadon's appearing was when he defended a claim against the Imperial Japanese Railways.

116 Le Poer Trench to Salisbury, 11 November 1887; FO881/5697.

117 31 August 1870; HN.

118 See page 22.

119 Hornby admitted that he would be glad to suspend Barnard 'but preventing a Barrister practising is a very delicate matter' before authorizing Lowder to suspend him

appearing in court in 1870, a decision with which Hornby concurred.[120] Barnard was re-admitted the next year,[121] but not before being tried for assault and warned that he faced deportation if convicted a second time.[122]

The following year, Marks incurred Campbell's wrath by agreeing to represent the defendant in *Campbell v. Davison* (*qua Administrator of the estate of R.B. Scotland*) after Campbell had tentatively discussed the matter with him—Marks said by way of seeking friendly advice rather than his formal services. Campbell's resulting prosecution of Marks for wilful and corrupt perjury was dismissed by Hannen. When Campbell pressed for Marks to be struck off the Roll, Goodwin urged leniency as Marks had expressed regret and was motivated by nothing other than the desire to earn fees from the defendant which he knew he could not obtain from Campbell.[123]

From the beginning, legal fees in Japan were regarded as being very high—higher even than in Shanghai and Hong Kong where, in 1868, fees had been described as 'exorbitantly high as compared with the fees paid to counsel and solicitors in England of the highest position. Nor are legal expenses more moderate in places where the professions are united as at Shanghai and Yokohama...; on the contrary, ...the luxury of going to law is more costly.'[124]

None of the lawyers was embarrassed at their fee levels for two brought libel actions on the subject. In 1870, when the *Japan Times* described lawyers' fees as exorbitant, Johnson sued for libel, claiming that, as the only barrister then in Yokohama, the remark was directed against him.[125] The next year, Marks contended that he was individually pointed out in a *Japan Gazette* editorial commenting upon lawyers' charges in Yokohama and successfully sued it for libel.[126] The Court (including the two Assessors) awarded him $250 damages (against $1,050 claimed). Even though a merchant had, anonymously, paid the damages, the newspaper appealed.[127]

---

should he again be guilty of 'misconduct such as calling witnesses "liars", using insulting remarks to the Court, refusing to obey an order of the Court or being guilty of wilful falsehood in any statement appertaining to business in Court.' Hornby to Lowder, 11 April 1870; FO656/18.

[120] Hornby to Flowers, 28 June 1870; FO656/18.

[121] 29 March 1871; NCH.

[122] 18 October 1870; NCH.

[123] Hannen to Goodwin, 29 November 1871; FO656/37.

[124] Chief Justice, Hong Kong to Colonial Secretary, Hong Kong, 27 August 1878; Norton-Kyshe 1898, Vol. 2, page 280.

[125] 13 December 1870; NCH.

[126] 29 March 1871; NCH.

[127] 8 February 1871; NCH.

Goodwin considered the appeal on papers and, although indisposed to interfere in the Court's judgment, considered the libel to be 'a very general one'[128] and ordered a new trial before a jury—but sense appears to have prevailed for there is no evidence that such a re-trial occurred.

Similar complaints were echoed as the decade ended when *The Japan Herald* declared that the 'limbs of the law in Yokohama are in clover just now and making a good thing of it. Litigation is rampant ... All the lawyers are busy and the courts occupied. The newspapers are full of law reports to the exclusion of more interesting reading ... law charges are abnormally high and lawyers naturally wax rich, whilst their clients become poor.'[129] The comments about the lawyers' fees even provoked a cartoon in the *Japan Punch* of four begging lawyers entitled 'Don't you pity the poor Lawyers.'[130]

It is impossible to guess the incomes of individual lawyers but Hornby reckoned that, in the late 1860s, leading lawyers in Shanghai were earning around £4,000 due to the boom in bankruptcy work.[131] His total remuneration package was £4,500 and this may be simply slightly envious reminiscences. However, we may assume that the more successful lawyers' earnings were higher than they could expect on the Bench. This has generally been true in England and seems also to have been true in Japan and China for the Foreign Office recognized that Rennie might prefer to remain in Shanghai and take the Crown Advocate-ship rather than the HMCJ Judge-ship 'as he has a very important and lucrative practice at the Bar'.[132] Likewise, Wilkinson declined the acting Judge-ship in 1888 because 'the pecuniary sacrifice which would follow from his acceptance of a merely temporary appointment [would be] too great to warrant his incurring it'.[133]

Salisbury called for a report on the scale of professional remuneration in the Supreme Court in 1879, but there is no evidence that a similar request was made of HMCJ.[134] In response, French described the Supreme Court's taxation system which had applied since its establishment: it was broadly similar to that operating in England today with provision, in

128 Ibid.

129 21 December 1878; NCH.

130 Rogala 2004, page 146.

131 Sir Edmund Hornby, *An autobiography* (London: Constable & Co. Ltd., 1929), page 255.

132 Internal memorandum, initialled by Salisbury, 12 October 1878; FO17/791.

133 Mowat to le Poer Trench, 16 April 1888; FO656/50.

134 Perhaps, because officials in London treated them as one and the same or, perhaps, the documentation has not survived.

disputed cases, for costs to be taxed by a taxing master subject to appeal to the Judge. There was no set scale of practitioners' costs; that which existed for taxation purposes was an *ad valorem* one prepared by Hornby.[135] There is no reason to believe that HMCJ operated any differently.

Newspaper reports suggest the minimum legal costs awarded to a successful litigant were a standard $25 (as claimed by Kirkwood in *Lane Crawford v. Charles Gabriel*) when it was justified to instruct counsel because a point of law was at issue.[136] Otherwise, reported awards of costs range from $150 for a two day trial[137] through $350[138] to $1,000 for a three day trial[139] (and these examples ignore the major shipping cases where we may imagine that the costs were considerably higher).

French's only specific recommendation was a fee of $60 (about £11) for counsel to defend a prisoner on a capital charge—to be paid by HM Treasury.[140] Against this, the 500 guineas brief fee[141] and £59 expenses (at £1 *per diem*[142]) paid to Wilkinson for two months' work for the *Carew* trial were substantial but in line with Hornby's estimates of senior Shanghai counsel's earnings—especially given the usually lower levels of remuneration for Crown prosecution work compared with commercial work. Litchfield received ¥3,012 and ¥1,237 in fees and expenses for the *Carew* and *Cuthbert* trials respectively. (By comparison, Dr Barrie received fees of $1,000 in connection with attending at the Cuthbert murder trial.)[143] Lesser criminal charges would involve much lower fees such as $50 awarded (against the $75 claimed) to the innocent defendant in *Mary C. Bohm v. Abbott* on a theft charge.[144]

Crown Advocates

British possessions all had Law Officers—usually, an attorney general and, sometimes, a solicitor general—whose role encompassed being the

135 French to Salisbury, 10 January 1879; FO656/53.
136 6 September 1884; JWM.
137 *The Coventry Machinists Company v. S. Cocking* involving a claim for $500; 18 April 1885; JWM.
138 *Peter Bishop v. Macarthur* involving a claim for $3,758; 4 July 1885; JWM.
139 Editorial 26 November 1870; JWM.
140 French to Salisbury, 31 January 1879; FO656/53.
141 Satow to Salisbury, 4 January 1898; FO46/510.
142 Invoice, 31 March 1898; FO276/59.
143 Receipts 2 November 1897, and 31 March and 4 May 1898; FO276/59.
144 22 August 1885; JWM.

government's legal advisers and acting as prosecutors for serious criminal offences; but Japan was not a possession and from the very 'opening' of Japan in 1859, the lack of legal knowledge amongst the consular establishment in Japan was a concern to policy makers. The Law Officers advised Russell that, if it were impracticable to select a Consul-General for Japan with legal knowledge, Alcock's proposal for the appointment of legal advisers to assist the Consul-General 'may be adopted with advantage' but that it was, ultimately, a policy question for the government.[145] In the meantime, the Minister relied, initially, upon the Attorney General in Hong Kong for immediate advice or, where matters could wait, upon advice from the Foreign Office back in London which, in turn, frequently consulted the Law Officers.

Although neither Japan nor China was a British possession, the OC1865 regime contemplated that the Law Secretary would act as prosecutor for the Courts in Japan and China. As for more general advice, Hornby was instructed, as regards the Minsters to China and Japan, to act in the same capacity as the Law Officers and to advise on legal questions.[146] After OC1865 had been promulgated, the Attorney General in Hong Kong ceased to be consulted by Ministers in Japan. Even the Law Officers declined to comment on questions raised about municipal regulations governing the Western Settlements in the Treaty Ports. They advised Russell that the Supreme Court's establishment gave the government the opportunity of obtaining competent advice on the best course to adopt on the subject from the Judge, who would know the local conditions. Accordingly, they advised awaiting Hornby's advice on the subject.[147]

Going forward, although the Law Officers were still consulted, the Minister looked increasingly to the Judge, and after him, the Judge of HMCJ for advice on immediate legal matters rather than referring back to London. However, it was a gradual process and in 1865 and 1866 we still see the Law Officers being consulted—particularly where Japan or other Powers were or could be involved—over Municipal regulations, Parkes's handling of the *Ainu* bones affair and the use of the British municipal lock-up in Yokohama by other nations. For example, 52 enclosures (including Hornby's advice) accompanied Parkes's report to the Foreign Secretary on

145 Law Officers to Russell, 25 July 1859; FO83/2298.

146 Russell to Hornby, May 1865; FO17/433.

147 Law Officers to Russell, 4 August 1865; FO83/2299.

the *McKechnie v. Glackmeyer* litigation and the actions of the US Consul in Yokohama.[148]

Hornby's reputation and influence was such that not only did he advise the Minister in dealings with the Japanese government but Japanese officials also sought his views—particularly in the *Maria Luz* affair when he influenced the Japanese government to take the lead.

The OC1878 re-organization abolished the Law Secretary's position and Hannen was appointed as the first Crown Advocate for China and Japan[149] on an annual retainer of £500. His formal appointment stated that he was to act both as legal adviser to the Minister and other British officials in Japan (and China) and as prosecutor in serious criminal matters and the Rules were amended to impose the Law Secretary's former duties in relation to criminal prosecutions upon the Crown Advocate.[150]

The post of Crown Advocate was not a full-time appointment and he remained in private practice with liberty to retain his private practice in cases in which the Crown was not involved and, where the Crown instructed him in civil cases, he could charge separately. As with the judicial appointments in Japan, the position was held 'during Her Majesty's pleasure'. Upon Hannen's becoming Judge in 1881, Wilkinson was appointed his successor. The formal terms of his appointment were identical, but it was recognized that his role in relation to criminal prosecutions was limited to China.[151]

Despite the terms of Hannen's appointment—which envisaged his advising also in relation to Japan, soon after OC1878 became operational, it appears to have been decided to appoint a separate Crown Prosecutor for Japan and, in 1880, John Joseph Enslie was appointed acting Crown Prosecutor, thus reverting to the previous practice of an official having charge of prosecutions. Around this time, Parkes (who had urged the need for an adviser to be on hand for the Minister when proposing the Yokohama Court arrangements) determined that he needed local advice and appointed Kirkwood as acting Crown Advocate for Japan on an annual retainer of £60[152] (increased to £300 when his appointment was

[148] Hammond to Law Officers and Law Officers to Clarendon, 21 April and 15 May 1866 respectively; FO83/2299. With one minor exception, the Law Officers approved the conduct of all the British officials in the affair and confirmed Hornby's advice.

[149] Although the Directories from 1873 onwards list Rennie as 'Counsel to HMG', this may have been an informal appointment. There is no evidence that he advised in relation to Japan.

[150] Foreign Office to French, 7 November 1878; FO17/791.

[151] Foreign Office to Wilkinson, 1 June 1882; FO17/908.

[152] Income Tax Returns; FO276/45.

formalized in October 1882[153]) and Wilkinson's role was wholly restricted to China—albeit with no change to his retainer.[154]

Kirkwood's appointment was on the standard terms and involved responsibility for criminal prosecutions in Japan besides advising the Minister. When Kirkwood resigned in 1885, Litchfield was appointed as acting Crown Prosecutor and held the position until extra-territoriality's end. Despite the change in title, Litchfield appears also to have been appointed formally to advise the Consuls upon such points as they referred to him.[155] However, in practice, his functions seem to have been restricted to prosecutions for Ministers reverted to the immediate post-OC1865 position of relying upon the Judge as legal adviser.[156] Why Litchfield never advised more generally outside the criminal sphere is unclear: it may have been that the Ministers simply felt more comfortable with Hannen and Wilkinson or because Litchfield was made Crown Prosecutor at a time when nobody else was available. Satow thought him 'exceedingly dull and slow'.[157]

The Consuls

The first Consuls in Japan were established consular or governmental officials and appointed from those with experience in China or from Europe in the case of those, such as Richard Eusden and Marcus Flowers, who were fluent in Dutch, being the early language of communication with the *bakufu*. From 1860, the government aimed to build up a cadre of linguistically trained consular officers and the Civil Service Commissioners held competitive examinations on an irregular basis as needs arose and budgets permitted to recruit Student Interpreters for the Japan Consular Service.

At that time, appointment to any consular position involved patronage and was usually through candidates, aged 18 to 24, being recommended to the Foreign Secretary who then nominated those of whom he approved for examination.[158] Besides the unsolicited recommendations, he sought

153 Foreign Office to Kirkwood, 24 October 1882; FO46/293.

154 Pauncefote to Wilkinson, 24 October 1882; FO656/67.

155 Litchfield to Longford, 22 April 1885; FO278/44.

156 There is no record of Litchfield's advising Ministers whereas there is ample evidence of the Judges' doing so.

157 Satow to Bertie, 24 November 1896; Ruxton 2007, page 57.

158 Alcock recommended Lowder, the 'orphan son aged 17 of the late chaplain of Shanghai, as student interpreter'. (Alcock to Russell, 24 September 1859; FO881/864.)

recommendations from the leading universities.[159] After 1872, the examinations were open to all.[160] Student Interpreters were needed for China, Japan and Thailand and successful examinees were offered their choice of location—depending upon vacancies and prior selections. In 1864 there were five vacancies (two in each of China and Japan and one in Thailand)[161] and four successful candidates played roles in administering extra-territoriality in Japan: William George Aston (recommended by Queen's College, Dublin) topped the list, followed by Mowat (recommended by London University), Wilkinson (sponsored by Lord Lurgan), and Jamieson (recommended by Aberdeen University).

When considering the various complaints about Consuls' legal skills, we must appreciate that their role was wider than merely administering the Courts: they were also political agents, trade officials and handled shipping registration matters and the full range of consular activities. Although the examination system resulted in the Far East consular service generally being 'staffed by men of a higher calibre than those employed by any other power',[162] they were not lawyers and had no prior experience of legal matters and law was not one of the subjects examined—at least in the early days. Complaints were made about various Consuls' conduct of their judicial functions—principally arising out of their being legally inexperienced. Norton-Kyshe said they 'frequently based their decisions upon common sense grounds without paying any attention to the technicalities'[163] so 'their decisions were repeatedly reversed on appeal and more than once they were condemned in damages for false imprisonment'.[164] Several commentators have subsequently highlighted the lack of legal training as a problem with extra-territoriality.

Norton-Kyshe's comments may be more apposite to China and are, perhaps, exaggerated so far as Japan is concerned where the evidence is that the Consuls did try to grapple with the law's technical requirements. Relatively few Consuls' decisions from Japan were reversed on appeal[165] and the only damages claim against an official arising from Japan was

---

159 In 1864, Cambridge, Oxford, Dublin, Queen's Belfast, Aberdeen, Glasgow and London were asked for nominations (12 April 1864; FO17/617).

160 Hoare 1997, page 99.

161 Foreign Office to Civil Service Commissioners, 12 March 1864; FO17/617.

162 Ian Nish and David Steeds, *China, Japan and Nineteenth Century Britain*, (Dublin: Irish University Press, 1977), page 14.

163 Norton-Kyshe 1898, page 59.

164 Ibid.

165 See Chapter 6 (Appeals).

that of Moss—against Alcock, the Consul-General.[166] On the Yokohama Court's creation, Consuls were praised for the 'painstaking and impartial spirit' in which they had hitherto generally performed their duties.[167]

Doubtless, some complaints were justified at the beginning. *The Japan Herald* complained of Vyse's indecision and his inability to handle *Schoyer v. Hope, Ashing & Asow*, a complicated case involving cross-actions in different courts.[168] It criticized him again when he allowed the US Consul to sit alongside him on the Bench and cross-examine and harangue witnesses.[169] Such Press criticism found an echo in Hornby's admonishing Vyse for attempting to refer cases to the Supreme Court for decision instead of deciding them himself.[170] Hornby's arguments to the Foreign Office in favour of establishing the Yokohama Court and his comments on several early appeals are often cited as evidence for the early Consuls' inexperience.[171] We should, however, be slightly cautious of relying—without question or qualification—upon Hornby on this point for his correspondence often displays touches of exaggeration in order to make a point. Even as 1870 drew to a close, Parkes wrote that Robertson, who was left running the Kanagawa Court until Hannen appeared, '...acquits himself of it succeedingly well...'[172]

Hornby was clearly aware of the issues for he supported training junior staff in the Courts' business and he recommended that 'there should always be at least two supernumerary members of the Judicial Branch of the Service attached to the Court'.[173] He suggested to Parkes that Vyse be temporarily attached to the Supreme Court to familiarize himself with the conduct of judicial duties.[174] Whilst this suggestion disappeared along with the Ainu Bones,[175] Parkes accepted the principle and Eusden, then Consul in Hakodate, spent three months attached to the Supreme Court in 1866/67 'to enable him to obtain sufficient insight into legal practice'.[176]

---

166 Although Annersley's wrongly imprisoning a merchant caused Derby to admonish Goodwin, it appears not to have resulted in any claim.
167 Editorial, 28 January 1871; JWM.
168 2 August 1862; TJH.
169 30 September 1862; TJH.
170 Hornby to Vyse, 28 December 1865 and 12 January 1866; FO656/18.
171 See pages 20–22.
172 Parkes to Granville, 17 December 1870; FO391/15.
173 Hornby to Clarendon, 8 February 1866; FO17/453.
174 Ibid.
175 See pages 112–113.
176 Parkes to Hornby, 15 December 1866; FO656/19.

Platt refers to this suggested arrangement as something of more general application,[177] but Eusden, then Consul in Hakodate, was the only example of an official from Japan being clearly seconded for this purpose. It is unclear why no other unqualified consular official from Japan was so attached after Eusden: probably, a combination of budgetary and staffing constraints[178] and the reality that, after 1871, Japan became increasingly detached from the Supreme Court's day-to-day supervision. Both the Yokohama Court and HMCJ were headed by legally qualified judges so the Student Interpreters could obtain legal experience by an attachment to those Courts without the need to travel abroad to the Supreme Court. Such attachments to the Supreme Court for training purposes as may have occurred after Eusden's attachment may have been from the Shanghai Consulate-General with less cost and disruption as when Jamieson temporarily replaced Mowat as acting Law Secretary when he went home to read for the Bar before Jamieson himself took leave 'with a view ... [to] ... pursuing the study of the law and being called to the Bar'.[179]

One other member of the Japan Consular Service who went on attachment to the Supreme Court was Wilkinson, who spent time there in 1876; but, as a barrister, he may well have been assisting Mowat in the running of the Supreme Court during Hornby and Goodwin's absence rather than being there for any training purposes. The only other member of the Japan Consular Service who spent time at the Supreme Court was Hall in 1888 when he changed places with Jamieson[180]—but this transfer was driven by personnel considerations and was not for training purposes.

Another reason why attachments to the Supreme Court may have become viewed as unnecessary is that, from 1870 onwards, it became increasingly common for members of the Japan Consular Service to take advantage of another of Hornby's suggestions,[181] where they were encouraged to read for the Bar[182] during home leaves. Some seized this opportunity more enthusiastically than others, particularly those who saw their career more on the consular side of the Service whereas others—especially where the principal focus of their work was not

---

[177] Platt 1971, page 19.

[178] Parkes acknowledged that 'the time allowed to Mr Eusden was way too short to ensure proficiency as a lawyer' but he needed him back because of pressure of work; Parkes to Hornby, 14 June 1867; FO656/19.

[179] Goodwin to Granville, 21 September 1871; FO17/593.

[180] See page 57.

[181] Hornby to Clarendon, 8 February 1866; FO17/453.

[182] None became a solicitor—presumably because of the longer qualification process.

judicial—adopted a more leisurely approach and spread their studies over several home leaves.

Satow complained that the Foreign Office did not seem to be concerned about officials getting called to the Bar and would neither provide the necessary leave nor ask the Inns for the keeping of terms to be dispensed with.[183] However, his complaints were not justified because leaves were granted and extended—Wilkinson, Enslie, Mowat and Robertson all had their leaves extended to enable them to read for the Bar and to keep terms at an Inn—and Granville interceded to allow Wilkinson to be called after keeping just seven terms at Inner Temple instead of the normal eight terms for overseas based students—itself a concession from the 12 terms that Home-based students were required to keep. In Satow's case, one must bear in mind that, although a member of the Consular Service, his work was very much focused on the political and diplomatic side in Japan where it was unnecessary to have a legal qualification. He also showed little inclination to forego leisurely trips around Europe in order to concentrate on reading for the Bar.[184]

Robertson did not complete his studies until he had been Consul at Yokohama for a number of years. His complaint to the Foreign Office was not that he was not allowed the necessary leave but that the Foreign Office refused to allow him to read for the Bar on his Consul's full salary of £900 per annum because there was no precedent for allowing a Consul—as opposed to a more junior officer—to extend his leave for such a purpose. Robertson's attempts to call in aid the examples of Satow and Enslie were dismissed when the Foreign Office said that Satow's salary had been subject to the normal deductions in 1875/1876 whilst Enslie had been merely an Assistant at the time of his leave.[185] Eventually, Regulations respecting training and Examination in Law dated 1 March 1883 were issued to cover such study leave, which could be extended for a further year.[186]

The practical result of OC1878 and the increasing numbers of legally qualified Consuls was that, after 1879, the Yokohama consul-ship was usually filled by a qualified lawyer (because he was, *ex officio*, the Assistant Judge); although, as Dohmen showed, from 1880 to 1881, non-qualified individuals were occasionally appointed in an acting capacity—both as acting Consul and as acting Assistant Judge. The principal exception to

---

183 Satow to Aston, 16 May 1875; PRO30/33/11/2, page 13.

184 Ibid.

185 Hervey to Robertson and draft (initialled by Salisbury) Foreign Office to Robertson, 8 March and 25 July 1878 respectively; FO46/234.

186 The Regulations are mentioned in Bourne to Rennie, 28 June 1890; FO656/76.

this was Troup, who was Yokohama Consul and Assistant Judge for most of the 1890s.

By the mid-1880s, Consuls at Kobe (where most other cases were heard) and Nagasaki were also, usually, legally qualified—although, on Enslie's death in 1896, Satow, despite the heavy judicial work-load in Kobe, was, initially, reluctant to depart from the principle of seniority determining appointments and not appoint the legally unqualified John James Quin there.[187] However, the Foreign office appointed J.C. Hall. Thus, the early complaints about unqualified Consuls had been largely addressed.

Simple shortage of experienced staff (often exacerbated by leaves) also caused problems, as in 1871 when Dohmen had not returned from his furlough to take up the Tokyo Vice-Consulate and J.C. Hall, then a Student Interpreter, acted as locum Vice-Consul until Dohmen's return. Francis Ottiwell Adams, the *Chargé d'Affaires*, wrote that 'it would not do to keep Hall [there], a man without jurisdiction'[188] for the place was 'full of loafers living from hand to mouth'.[189] After Hannen had complained to Adams several times about the problems caused by Hall's lacking jurisdiction, Adams appointed Robertson temporarily as formal acting Vice-Consul and Robertson came from Yokohama from time to time to hold Courts in Tokyo.[190]

This case highlights another point that is sometimes missed when commentators seek to tarnish the exercise of British extra-territorial jurisdiction by pointing to junior staff who were left in charge of consulates as locums. Whilst it may have been true that junior staff acted as temporary locums whilst the office holder was away for short periods, such junior staff never exercised any judicial authority or held any Courts. This was for the simple reason that only formally appointed Consuls or acting Consuls[191] had the authority to exercise judicial powers: had an unauthorized temporary locum attempted to exercise such powers, he would have been acting *ultra vires* and, so, have opened himself up to a personal liability in damages to any litigant brought before him. Thus, it was never the

187 Mowat had supported Hall's application for the post because of his legal qualification. After protesting at being passed over, Quin retired on a pension due to ill-health. See FO46/476 papers on Hall, Mowat and Quin.

188 Adams to Hammond (private), 3 July 1871; FO391/26.

189 Ibid.

190 Adams to Hammond (private) 23 July 1871; FO391/26.

191 Or Vice-Consuls. Kobe often had a Vice-Consul formally appointed to its consulate in addition to the Consul. As a formal appointee, such Vice-Consul held full consular and judicial powers.

case that the exercise of consular judicial duties was delegated down to wholly inexperienced juniors.

Even where a presiding consul judge was unqualified, he would have a maturity and experience—as in the case of Dohmen and Troup. As for these non-legally qualified Consuls, Rennie, agreed with Hornby's views that they could reasonably be expected to know where to find the law on matters most likely to come under their notice and to apply it fairly.[192] In practice, after 1880, few cases (certainly of any significance) were heard in the Hakodate or Tokyo Courts and the Hakodate Consuls were usually experienced men, whilst the Tokyo Consuls could easily refer to HMCJ for advice in those few cases that arose in Tokyo. That said, unqualified Consuls were not immune from press criticism for their handling of judicial cases. Upon Troup's appointment as Yokohama Consul, *The Rising Sun and Nagasaki Express* commented that the trouble with Troup was that he had never been called to the Bar[193] whilst the same newspaper, picking up a comment from *The Hiogo News*, said of Annersley that he was 'not what a lawyer would call a good judge—he always entered into the feelings of both parties ... too much to satisfy either of them entirely'.[194]

Although Satow's writing to his friend, Dickins, of his fear of being compelled to sit in judgment when appointed, in place of another of their friends—John Harrington Gubbins—who was on leave, as acting Vice-Consul in Tokyo in July 1880 and of his 'complete ignorance of the law',[195] is sometimes[196] taken as evidence to show the continued deficiencies caused by the Consuls' lack of legal training, it is not clear that Satow ever did sit judicially.[197] His comments to Dickins and his exclamation 'Fancy me a Judge'[198] were probably somewhat tongue in cheek and self-deprecatory: his claimed ignorance of the law was certainly an exaggeration for he had been admitted to Lincoln's Inn in 1875 and had already started reading for the Bar. The greater surprise is that he felt the need to comment in this manner to Dickins as he had already acted as Vice-Consul in Tokyo—and been authorized to hold a Court—two years earlier when McClatchie had been away.[199]

---

192 Rennie to Salisbury, 10 October 1885; FO17/997.
193 12 September 1888; TRS&NE.
194 24 November 1877; TRS&NE.
195 Satow to Dickins (private), 22 August 1880; PRO30/33/11/5.
196 See J.E. Hoare, 1994, pages 73–74 and Honjo, 2003, pages 101–102.
197 Only one civil case and one criminal case are recorded as having been heard in Tokyo during that half year for part of which Satow was Vice-Consul and the records do not show whether or not he presided over them.
198 Satow to Dickins (private), 22 August 1880; PRO30/33/11/5.
199 Parkes to Satow, 1 July 1878; FO262/521.

Satow went on to act again as Vice-Consul for eight months from October 1880[200] when Gubbins took further leave due to ill-health.[201] During this tenure, Satow wrote that the 'Vice-Consulate has been almost a sinecure for years past'[202] and the Vice-Consul had 'very little to do and one morning a week'[203] was sufficient to enable him to discharge his duties there. More practically, he said that he hoped to have most of the Vice-Consulate's judicial business handled by HMCJ as he conceded the constable knew more about it than he did and that it might be better if he did not attempt to 'play the judge' so as to avoid a miscarriage of justice upon the several ruffianly British subjects whom he should have liked to deport.[204]

In any event, Satow handled the Campbell oil exchange affair,[205] which arose in Tokyo during his acting Vice-Consulship, with diplomatic skill and had obviously acquitted himself well for Kennedy, the *Chargé d'Affaires*, informed Satow of his satisfaction with the way Satow had performed duties 'outside the sphere of your position in the Service'.[206] Satow was again appointed temporarily as Vice-Consul when Longford was absent the next year.[207]

Tokyo—and Osaka—were very much Vice-Consulates apart from the norm. When both cities were opened for residence, Parkes was of the view that just a Vice-Consul with no assistants could be stationed at them 'as any judicial work might be reserved for the Courts at Kanagawa and Kobe'.[208] This expectation of Tokyo not needing a full-time Consul was reflected when Dohmen, in addition to the Vice-Consular role at Tokyo, was appointed as *Cancellier* and Archivist at Legation in 1871.[209]

A general re-organization of the consular establishments in 1882 resulted in wholesale movements, but death, illness or retirement were the more usual precipitators of changes in consular posts—all compounded by lengthy leaves, themselves exacerbated by a general desire to

---

[200] Kennedy to Satow, 5 October 1880; FO262/531.
[201] Gubbins to Kennedy, 5 October 1880; FO262/531.
[202] Satow to Aston (private) 14 November 1880; PRO30/33/11/2.
[203] Satow to Aston (private) 26 November 1880; PRO30/33/11/2.
[204] Satow to Aston, 12 October 1880; PRO30/33/11/2, page 98. This letter, which is later than the letter to Dickins, implies that Satow had not, in fact, sat judicially.
[205] See page 120.
[206] Kennedy to Satow, 1 June 1881; FO262/536.
[207] Legation to Satow, September 1882; FO262/536.
[208] Parkes to Foreign Office, 21 January 1867; FO391/14, page 83.
[209] Parkes to Dohmen, 26 October 1871; FO262/498.

avoid travelling during the hot season.[210] The result was frequent movement around the various positions and it was common for positions to be filled by acting officers—often for months at a time.

The first half of Enslie's career encapsulates this constant movement. He joined the Japan Consular Service in 1861 but his career suffered under Parkes from his association with Vyse and the Ainu Bones[211] and he was shunted from post to post and served in each of the Consulates before complaining to the Foreign Office. Having qualified as a barrister in 1877, he became acting Registrar of HMCJ and Crown Prosecutor in 1880 and, in 1882, acting Consul at Yokohama and acting Assistant Judge upon Dohmen's going on leave before being offered the Vice-Consulship of Hakodate as a permanent posting upon Eusden's retirement in the 1882 re-organization when Hakodate was downgraded to a vice-consulate.[212] From Hakodate, Enslie moved, as Consul, to Nagasaki before ending his career in Kobe, then the senior posting in Japan, where he died in June 1896 when he was the oldest British official in Japan, doyen of the consular body and President of the Kobe Foreign Settlement's Municipal Council.[213]

Ill-health was a feature of nineteenth century life in Asia and the climates of China and Japan were 'considered to be more or less trying to English constitutions',[214] so the Foreign Office, when seeking nominations from the universities, was clear that 'the health of candidates [needed to] be such as to bear existence in those climates'.[215] When computing superannuation payments, two years' service in an 'unhealthy place' counted as three years and, except Hakodate, all ports were considered 'unhealthy'.[216] Relatively few Consuls lived to retirement and death in post was not uncommon. Goodwin, French, Robertson, Enslie and Hannen were among those who died in post, whilst Dohmen died in 1882 off Aden on a voyage home on leave. Lawyers also became ill and Dickins returned home in 1878 to recover (before moving to Alexandria to practise for a short time before returning to England).

---

210 When Goodwin went home on leave in 1872 upon Hornby's return, Hannen stayed running the Yokohama Court until 1874 to enable both Hornby and Goodwin to avoid the unpleasant travelling season: Hornby to Granville, 19 February 1872; FO17/637.

211 J.E. Hoare, 'Mr. Enslie's Grievance: the Consul, the Ainu and the Bones' *PJS* Vol. 78 (1976), page 14.

212 Foreign Office to Enslie, 22 April 1882; FO46/293.

213 26 June 1896; JWM.

214 Foreign Office to universities, 12 April 1864; FO17/617.

215 Ibid.

216 Charles James Tarring, *British Consular Jurisdiction in the East* (London: Stevens and Haynes 1887), page 122.

On the other hand, a few enjoyed a long retirement: Hornby, despite frequent complaints of ill health whilst in Shanghai, lived another 20 years to die in 1896. Wilkinson, another judge with good health, retired in 1905 and died only in 1926 whilst Troup and Mowat, who both retired on health grounds in the late 1890s, also had long retirements and died only in 1925. The 1920s also saw the deaths of Longford (1925), Kirkwood (1926) and Satow (1929).

Ill health of Judges could cause delays and problems in the administration of justice. French's ill-health caused serious delays in the dispatch of appeal cases in 1879–1881. In January 1896, Playfair needed to persuade Enslie, who rather enjoyed his judicial duties, that he was too ill to hear *Reynell v. Cameron* and to summon Mowat to Kobe at short notice to hear the case for which counsel had already been arranged.[217] The next year, it was Mowat's turn to collapse when he went to Nagasaki to deal with Norman's lunacy shortly after the *Carew* trial, so Wilkinson was summoned from Shanghai to conclude the matter as Troup, the Assistant Judge, was also unwell and unable to leave Yokohama.[218]

Interpreters, Clerks, Constables and Ushers

In the British Empire—particularly India and Africa—interpreters played an important role in court procedure. This was less the case in Japan for, by the nature of the jurisdiction, most defendants (apart from a few sailors and Chinese and Indian subjects of the Crown) spoke English; so, interpretation was only an issue in relation to some plaintiffs and witnesses. Often, the Student Interpreters acted as interpreters and combined the role with a more junior role in the Consulate or, in Tokyo, the Legation. Thus, only when no Student Interpreter was attached to a Consulate or was unavailable might the Consul need to use his Japanese language skills. With the Yokohama Court and HMCJ, it was common for the positions of Registrar and Interpreter to be combined. This arrangement would sometimes be substantive and sometimes, perhaps, a means of increasing the individual's salary within the constraints of the Budget.

Other Western witnesses who spoke English would be sworn just as if they were British whilst, in the Woodward trials, Fung Dong, a shroff (or cashier) at the local branch of HSBC, was sworn 'in Chinese fashion'.[219]

---

[217] Playfair to Satow, 8 and 9 May 1896; Ruxton 2005, page 303.
[218] Satow to Salisbury, 25 February 1897; Ruxton 2007, page 73.
[219] 22 October 1887; HN.

Japanese witnesses were treated in the same way as other non-British witnesses who could not speak English. They were usually deposed after being warned, through the Interpreter,[220] to speak the truth after which they would sign their deposition in *kanji* or, if illiterate, with a cross (under which would be written, 'his mark') followed by the interpreter's signature. The exception was Japanese police officers where the record simply says they 'state' something without any warning to speak the truth.[221] From 1896, Japanese witnesses were sworn in the manner observed for witnesses in the Japanese tribunals.[222]

Most Consuls were fluent in Japanese (so, could intervene if necessary)[223] and, despite occasional problems with interpretation involving Japanese litigants and witnesses, it does not appear to have been a significant issue (at least there is no evidence of reported complaints)—despite Longford's stating that 'interpretation in our courts is now anything but perfect'.[224] There could be greater practical difficulties when third country nationals were involved—particularly sailors: but, this was not a consequence of extra-territoriality.

With the Yokohama Court's establishment, it required an experienced staff and Bate was despatched from the Supreme Court in July 1870 as Clerk to the Judicial Department of the Yokohama Consulate,[225] later to be replaced by Bishop, the Chief Clerk of the Supreme Court, who accepted the post of Registrar at Yokohama because the salary was higher.[226] When Bishop went on leave in 1878, Hall, then a Student Interpreter, acted in his place.[227] On Bishop's retirement in 1882, Hall was replaced by Enslie as acting Registrar before being replaced permanently by C.D. Moss.[228]

---

220 Where the interpreter was not a Consular official, he would declare that he would 'interpret faithfully and truly' (Record of Hearing in *Groenewort v. Pritchard*, 11 June 1866; FO656/14).

221 Newspaper report enclosed with Flowers to Hornby, 12 November 1872; FO656/34, which showed the different approaches to policemen and ordinary Japanese witnesses.

222 Mowat's Circular to Consuls, 15 December 1896; FO796/10.

223 Although, when Dohmen discussed matters in German with one plaintiff, he was roundly criticized in the Press for doing so; *Louise Wehrun v. Ellen Walker*, 6 July 1880; JDH. This criticism may have stemmed more from journalistic antipathy towards Dohmen than anything else.

224 Longford to Satow, 14 September 1896, Ruxton 2005, page 170. Longford's complaint reflected upon the competence of the Student Interpreters then attached to his Kobe Consulate.

225 Hornby to Parkes, 19 July 1870; FO656/19.

226 Supreme Court to Goodwin, 7 July 1876; FO656/39.

227 French to Wilkinson, 13 December 1877; FO656/39.

228 Foreign Office to Robertson, 22 April 1882; FO46/293.

Most Consulates had a British constable attached to them. The first reference to a constable was Morrison, in Nagasaki, writing 'to Shanghai for a constable (European)';[229] and he found one in Kettle whom he employed for $45 per month. At the same time, he engaged a gaol cook and coolie at $10 a month.[230] The Constables' original function was to support the Consul in enforcing his jurisdiction over, and maintaining order amongst, British subjects; but, in time, they became used as general factotums—particularly in relation to shipping registrations and keepers of the Births and Deaths registers. Besides such 'constabulary' duties (which, occasionally—especially outside Yokohama—included acting as prosecutor of minor criminal offences), they also acted as Court clerks, messengers, ushers and process servers and had charge of consular gaols outside Yokohama. By 1882, at least three constables were attached to the Yokohama Consulate, for George Hodges described himself as 'third constable'. He also acted as Usher at HMCJ.[231]

Constables tended to have a longevity of their own and all seemed to be retained until death or a new posting removed them.[232] They were often ex-servicemen, although the Legation's military Escort was replaced, in 1867,[233] by 12 Metropolitan policemen, one or two of whom were used by the Tokyo Vice-Consulate in relation to its judicial functions. Although, Parkes had considered that the Tokyo Vice-Consulate could be run by just a Vice-Consul, Adams authorized the appointment of a constable at Tokyo in 1872 during Parkes's absence. Adams had been pushed into authorizing the appointment by Hannen and Hornby as the judicial work there was increasing at that time. Adams explained that 'there are between 30 and 40 British subjects in the jurisdiction and there are more cases in the Court than there were—thus necessitating the serving of a number of summons, petitions, etc. This and the registering of British subjects give work to the Constable...'[234] As court work in Tokyo dropped off during the 1870s, it was, as seen by Satow's letter to Dickins, the Constable who came to handle most of the routine administrative work at that Vice-Consulate.

[229] Morrison to Alcock, 15 August 1859; FO881/864.
[230] Morrison to Alcock, 31 August 1859; FO262/6.
[231] Hodges to Foreign Office, 3 August 1882; FO46/293.
[232] Peter Peacock, who arrived as Inspector with the Metropolitan policemen in 1867, was still on the Legation's books in 1900 at the same daily pay of 12/- (60p). When Longford arrived in Taiwan, he found a Constable, aged 70, whom he described as 'useless,' being paid $20 per month; Longford to Satow, 25 June 1896; FO262/735.
[233] Stanley to Parkes, 11 February 1867; FO276/13.
[234] Adams to Foreign Office, 5 February 1872; FO391/26, page 168.

Remuneration

The 'General Regulations for the Establishment of the Superintendency and Consulates of China and Japan Consular Service' published in 1862[235] (supplemented from time to time by HM Treasury guidance) detailed the terms and conditions of service of the consular and the judicial establishments throughout China and Japan, including travel, holiday and outfit allowances.

The Chief Justice commanded a substantial salary. Hornby's salary of £3,500 plus £1,000 housing allowance was generous even by the standards of the time[236] but it dropped with each new Chief Justice. French and Rennie were paid £2,500 (plus £500 housing allowance[237]) but Hannen was paid just £2,100 (plus accommodation) for the combined posts of Chief Justice and Consul-General in Shanghai[238] (which remuneration he retained even after the separation of the two offices in 1897[239]) whilst Wilkinson received only £1,800 upon appointment as Chief Justice in 1900 (plus a £450 housing allowance): barely more than the £1,500 he had received as Judge. The reductions in the Chief Justice's salary after French reflect the halving in the Dollar's value against Sterling more than real salary reductions and, after Rennie complained about the Dollar's 12% depreciation during 1886,[240] HM Treasury agreed to pay a fixed proportion of salaries in Sterling.[241]

When the Yokohama Court was established, there was much discussion regarding Hannen's terms; he initially declined £1,200 (equal to the Assistant Judge's salary in Shanghai) and Hornby doubted whether he would accept less than £2,000 'so well are lawyers paid out here'[242] and he had an improving business. Given that Hannen eventually accepted £1,200, this may have been another of Hornby's tactical negotiating letters. Goodwin was transferred to Yokohama on the same £1,200 he received in Shanghai as Assistant Judge but lost the £450 he saved annually out of his

---

235 FO881/1926.

236 As was his pension at over £2,300 (Derby to Hornby, 15 March 1876; FO17/735). Rennie's pension was £1,361 when he retired in 1891 (Salisbury to Rennie, 3 March 1891; FO656/58). Wilkinson received a pension of £1,350 upon his retirement (Foreign Office telegram to Wilkinson, 5 January 1905; FO17/1682).

237 Derby to French, 11 October 1877; FO17/766.

238 Salisbury to Hannen, 1 April 1891; FO656/58.

239 Telegram, Salisbury to Hannen, 6 December 1897; FO656/58.

240 Rennie to Iddesleigh, 15 September 1886; FO17/997.

241 Iddesleigh to Rennie, 5 January 1887; FO656/58.

242 Hornby to Foreign Office, 21 March 1870; FO17/557.

housing allowance and the allowance for acting as Judge (worth about £120). In trying to obtain better terms for Goodwin, Hornby pointed out that even County Court judges in England were paid £1,500 whereas, in Japan, 'the cost of living is so much greater than in England'.[243] The Foreign Office conceded that no one had asked Goodwin if he would move and he was the poorer because of it but still refused to recommend to the Treasury an increase in Goodwin's salary unless Hornby could find savings elsewhere.[244]

Upon HMCJ's creation, the post of Judge was offered to Rennie at £1,500 (plus £250 housing allowance in lieu of accommodation)[245] whilst Mowat received £1,200 as Assistant Judge in the Supreme Court[246] thus establishing a clear hierarchy of judicial positions—at least in remunerative terms. The Consuls' annual remuneration remained fairly static over the whole period and was:[247]

Yokohama	Kobe	Nagasaki	Hakodate £	Osaka	Tokyo	Niigata
1,000	1,000	900	800 (650)	600	600	500

Student Interpreters started on salaries of £200 rising to £400 per annum.[248] They, the Judges and Consuls also received an Outfit Allowance of two-ninths of their salary upon initial appointment to each new post.[249] The HMCJ clerk received £400 but no outfit or travel allowances. The Constables and Yokohama gaolers' wages were $50–60 per month.

At all levels, 'extras' could increase basic salaries, such as Enslie's receiving an additional £150 as acting Registrar of HMCJ in 1881[250] and £60 as Post Office Agent when acting Consul in Kobe in 1869.[251] Copying

243 Hornby to Derby, 11 June 1875; FO17/709.

244 Foreign Office endorsement on above, initialled by Derby.

245 Foreign Office telegram to French, October 1878; FO17/791.

246 Ibid.

247 Inclosure No. 4 with Report on Living Expenses: Parkes to Clarendon, 5 November 1869; FO881/1750. The 1882 consular re-organization closed the Niigata Vice-Consulate and reduced Hakodate to a Vice-Consulate at a lower salary; FO46/293.

248 Foreign Office to various universities, 12 April 1864; FO17/617.

249 Foreign Office to Hornby, 13 March 1865; FO17/433.

250 Income Tax Returns; FO276/44.

251 Postmaster-General, Hong Kong to Parkes, 13 October 1869; FO276/28.

documents[252] proved to be a 'nice little earner' sideline for the Court and consular clerks as the fees ($2.50 for the first page and $0.50 per subsequent page) were divided with one half going to the Court and one half to the copyist[253] although the work was always meant to be done outside office hours. Peacock was even paid a standing £30 annual gratuity for copying public documents for the Legation. Several Consuls sought to benefit from OC1865 which allowed Consuls to charge 2.5% *ad valorem* for administering an intestate's estate. Myburgh received $470 for administering John Macdonald's estate in Yokohama in 1866;[254] but, subsequently, Hornby generally refused to allow Consuls to take this allowance.[255]

Salaries in Japan were higher than in Europe and Shanghai (as seen by R.G. Watson's salary dropping from £800 as *Chargé d'Affaires* in Tokyo to £500 on moving to Copenhagen in 1873[256] and the Clerk's £400 (plus accommodation[257]) in HMCJ exceeding the £306 paid to him in Shanghai[258]); but this did not prevent gripes about the higher cost of living, housing and relocation allowances and adverse currency movements. From the beginning, Consuls complained about pay and allowances. In 1859, Morrison lamented that the remuneration scale was fixed under an impression that Japan was an inexpensive country whereas a month's experience proved the contrary, with all articles of necessity or comfort being proportionately dearer than in Shanghai.[259]

HM Treasury nibbled away at what it saw as generous salaries and allowances and this became a frequent source of friction—as when Goodwin, on moving to Yokohama, was provided with a house at the Legation and lost his separate housing allowance.[260] Hannen could look after his own interests and, when appointed Crown Advocate, he enquired if it was a superannuated post[261] only to be rebutted by HM Treasury as it was a part-time post. In 1882, voluminous correspondence ensued between

---

252 For example, in *Groenewort v Pritchard*, the Record of Appeal consisted of at least 49 pages making a total of $25 (Petition, $4.5; Answer, $3.5; Record of Hearing, $26; Judgment $2; Answer to Appeal Petition $6.5, Reply $6); Flowers to Hornby, 11 November 1866; FO656/14.

253 Hannen to Granville, 16 January 1884 and Granville approved the arrangement on 22 March 1884; FO656/49.

254 Income Tax Returns; FO276/10.

255 Goodwin to Lowder, 8 October 1868; FO656/18.

256 FO276/35, page 88.

257 Hornby to Clarendon, 21 March 1870; FO17/557.

258 Hornby to Clarendon, 8 February 1866; FO17/453.

259 Morrison to Alcock, 2 September 1859; FO881/864.

260 Clarendon to Goodwin, 8 April 1870; FO17/557.

261 Hannen to Parkes, September 1879; FO656/28.

him and the Foreign Office about his pay and allowances (acting and housing) as acting Chief Justice during Rennie's absence.[262] In 1897, he offered to retire if given a Compensation Allowance—an offer side-stepped by Salisbury who was 'unwilling that your services as Chief Justice should be prematurely lost'.[263]

Retirement was compulsory at 70 but the Foreign Secretary could allow staff to retire earlier if ill or upon their post's abolition, when they would be entitled to a pension. On a post's abolition, the official concerned was entitled to an enhanced retirement annuity of an additional 10 years deemed service. The pensions could be generous—especially for long serving officials.[264]

Arguments were continuous over acting allowances (usually, a quarter of the substantive holder's salary in addition to the locum's current salary) and HM Treasury and the Foreign Office were skinflints in this area. Generally, acting allowances were allowed only when the substantive holder was on leave for over three months and, therefore, on half pay.[265] The only exception to the half pay rule for officers on long leaves was that Student Interpreters and junior consular staff who were reading for the Bar during their leaves (and any extension of leave) did not see their pay reduced.

When Wilkinson agreed to Mowat's request to act as Judge when Mowat went on home leave from 1 April 1894 to 31 May 1895, he had, obviously, not agreed his remuneration in advance for, in early 1895, he was forced to write to the Earl of Kimberley, the Foreign Secretary, for a 'suitable salary'.[266] He pointed to the precedent of Hannen in 1871 who was paid the same of the Assistant Judge in Shanghai. Initially, the Foreign Office suggested he be paid just a quarter of the usual salary (i.e. £375) for an acting position—notwithstanding that Wilkinson had to pay half his Crown Advocate's fees (£200) to his acting replacement and had foregone his lucrative private practice in Shanghai! Eventually, the Foreign Office conceded the whole of the half salary (i.e. £750) saved because Mowat was on home leave and, so, on half pay—but refused to approach HM Treasury to sanction any more.

---

262 FO17/908.

263 Bertie to Hannen, 6 December 1897; FO656/58.

264 Eusden and Flowers retired in 1882 on pensions of £611 and £602 respectively (against prior salaries of £850 and £900).

265 Derby to Goodwin; 13 November 1876; FO17/735.

266 Wilkinson to Kimberley, 12 January 1895 plus internal Foreign Office notes thereon; FO46/458.

Judges and Consuls were fortunate to be paid their passage money for home leaves and contributions (but not the full cost) to their family members' travel costs—but only after five years' continuous service whereas clerks and other staff, not being covered by the regulations, were denied such benefits and depended upon the government's generosity or otherwise. When Bate needed to go on leave in 1872, it was only at Hornby's intercession that the government paid his passage money and allowed him his full salary whilst on leave.[267] However, Bishop was refused both an outfit allowance and passage money for his family from Shanghai on becoming Registrar of the Yokohama Court because these were restricted to consular officers.[268]

The Treasury also took a hard line with regard to losses of personal possessions—even from natural disasters—when on official business as illustrated by its refusal to compensate Robertson and Moss for their losses on route to Hakodate to hear two cases on circuit when the *Kokonoye maru* foundered and their possessions were 'plundered by local fishermen and the crew'.[269]

267 Hornby to Granville, 8 April 1873—approved by Granville; FO17/660.
268 Derby to Hornby, 8 May 1876; FO17/735.
269 Robertson to Granville, 13 October 1882; FO46/293.

CHAPTER THREE

CRIMINAL JURISDICTION

This chapter assesses the extent to which Britain's exercise of criminal jurisdiction in Japan affected the British community. British criminal jurisdiction may be divided into two parts: offences committed within Japan or its territorial waters (for convenience, called '**criminal cases**') and offences committed upon British flagged merchant vessels (for convenience, called '**shipping offences**'). This chapter focuses upon criminal cases with shipping offences covered in Chapter 4 (The Sea).

Criminal cases were triable summarily or on indictment. Most cases were tried summarily where anyone (British, Japanese, foreign, official or individual) could institute the prosecution and there were three gradations of a Consul's power—all linked to his sentencing powers. First, authority to try cases alone for breaches of general laws, rules and regulations where a Consul was limited to imposing a maximum fine of $200 or one month's imprisonment. Second, he could try cases with two Assessors whereupon his sentencing limits were increased to $500 or three months' imprisonment or, if he brought in a third or fourth Assessor, to $1,000 and twelve months' imprisonment.[1] A Consul sitting alone could also try cases for breach of the Treaty where punishment did not exceed fines of $500 or three months' imprisonment; the only Treaty breach not covered by a Consul's summary jurisdiction was trading at closed ports which was subject to a fine of $1,000 and the forfeiture of the goods concerned.

This jurisdiction proved adequate for the bulk of criminal cases. More serious cases were tried upon indictment—usually before the Supreme Court on circuit and before a jury or in the Yokohama Court under the Supreme Court's extraordinary jurisdiction.[2] After OC1878, HMCJ took the place of both the Supreme Court and the Yokohama Court and serious criminal cases were usually heard in Yokohama before HMCJ; although we do find occasional reports of HMCJ travelling on circuit to hear more serious criminal cases at Kobe under its extraordinary jurisdiction. The first

---

1 Sections VI, VII and XX, OC1860.

2 Prior to OC1865, the accused was sent to SCHK for trial (Section XXVII, OC1860).

reported instance was when Wilkinson, as acting Assistant Judge, and a jury tried Masefield at Kobe for manslaughter.[3]

Where the Assistant Judge was a lawyer, he often travelled on circuit for criminal trials as when Marston was tried in Kobe for rape in 1881[4]—although we also see instances of the Judge travelling on circuit for criminal trials. For instance, Hannen went to Kobe for a manslaughter trial in 1888 and, during Troup's tenure as Assistant Judge, it was, of necessity, the Judge who travelled.

Unlike summary cases, only the Crown could bring prosecutions on indictment following committal proceedings before the Consul; no private prosecutions were permissible—although an individual could initiate committal proceedings by laying information before the Consul and retain counsel to assist in the prosecution.[5] With these more serious cases, the charge would be laid before the Consul who, like magistrates today, would hold an initial committal hearing to assess whether or not a *prima facie* case had been established to go to trial. If yes, the defendant would be committed for trial—either before the Consul and Assessors or, more usually (but not always) after the Yokohama Court's establishment, before the Yokohama Court or HMCJ. Following committal, depositions of the facts and evidence would be prepared and delivered to the Law Secretary (or, after OC1878, the Crown Advocate or Crown Prosecutor) who would either prosecute or delegate the role to another official.[6]

Pending the trial itself, the defendant would either be held in custody in the consular gaol or sent to the Yokohama gaol or be allowed bail. In order to be allowed bail, a defendant would need to post not insubstantial bail bonds—often $250 or $500—in his own recognizances and/or those of two other sureties.[7] Instances were reported—but not many—of defendants failing to surrender to their bail bonds at the hearing. After the mate and second officer of the *Hing Sang* had been charged by the Japanese

---

[3] NCH 21 March 1879. Masefield was convicted and sentenced to 2 years in Kobe gaol. See also page 126.

[4] 27 September 1881; NCH.

[5] Rules for Courts in Japan and China, prepared by Hannen and approved by Granville: 23 March 1882; FO656/53.

[6] Rule 309.

[7] When Nickel & Co. prosecuted Frederick da Sylva for embezzlement in Kobe, Frank Playfair, the Acting Consul, presided over two days of committal proceedings where Crosse appeared for the prosecutor and Brushfield for the defence. Playfair committed da Sylva for trial in the Kobe Court before the Consul and two Assessors. Meanwhile, Brushfield reserved da Sylva's defence and da Sylva was allowed bail on a third party surety of $500: 25 September 1897; KWC. The result of the trial was not reported.

water police with assault, they were remanded on bail of $200 each in their own recognizances but both failed to appear at the hearing whereupon the Court ordered their bail to be forfeit and the consular constable to locate and arrest them.[8]

The Crown, as in England, retained rights to take over private prosecutions and of *nolle prosequi* so, after indictment, the individual at whose instance the prosecution had been brought could not drop the prosecution unilaterally. As seen in Chapter 1 (British Extra-territoriality), the Law Secretary's involvement in cases prosecuted before the Yokohama Court became something of a fiction given that, in time for administrative convenience, he sent to the Yokohama Court pre-signed blank indictments for completion by the British authorities in Japan.

In Shanghai, Hornby reported that 'Jury trials are not frequent—most cases being determined summarily'[9] and, in 1867–1870, only 1% of cases there were tried by a jury;[10] being a mixture of murder/manslaughter cases, fraud, aggravated assaults and piracy. Although there are no precise figures for jury trials in Japan, newspaper reports suggest the position was similar. From 1860 to 1899, just 32 criminal jury trials are mentioned—overall, not even averaging one a year—and, except piracy (for which there were no trials in Japan), covering similar offences. Use of Assessors is scarcely more frequent with just five cases reported for Yokohama in the newspapers before 1871 and only a handful in the out-ports. With the Yokohama Court's establishment—and, more so, with HMCJ and its extraordinary jurisdiction—most serious cases were tried in the Yokohama Court or HMCJ so the need for Assessors in the out-ports almost disappeared; although we see five cases being tried in the Kobe Court with Assessors after 1878. Occasionally, as when Enslie tried *Reg. v. Hering* in Kobe in 1889 with Assessors, it is unclear why Assessors were involved in these cases as the sentence he imposed was well within his limits when trying the case alone).[11]

The three fraud/embezzlement cases in Kobe against Edward Daniel Woodward in 1887 are an example of the interplay between summary charges and charges tried on indictment.[12] Woodward was accused by his employer, McGregor, of having embezzled $100 from the latter's business

8 19 and 26 March 1898; KWC.

9 Hornby to Clarendon 15 April 1866; FO17/502.

10 Reports attached to Hornby to Clarendon in FO17/502, 17/530 and 17/557 and Goodwin to Granville in FO17/593 (such Reports being, together, referred to as the **Shanghai Returns**).

11 3 October 1889, JG.

12 17 September to 23 October 1887; HN.

and was arrested in Shanghai and returned to Kobe under a police escort to face prosecution. In Kobe, he was bailed (in his own recognizances of $500 and those of two sureties of $250 each) to appear four days later for the trial which was heard in the Kobe Court by Troup, the Consul, and two Assessors. The prosecution was a summary one and the local solicitor, Creagh, prosecuted on behalf of McGregor but Woodward was defended by Edward Robinson, a barrister from Shanghai.

When the prosecution opened, Robinson highlighted another difference in practice between Japan and China by enquiring why the Crown was not represented—as would have been the case in Shanghai. Despite Robinson's citing *Archbold on Pleading* on the subject, Troup informed him that it was not the practice in Japan for the Crown to be represented in summary cases before Provincial Courts and ruled that it was unnecessary.

After a four day trial, Troup (with the Assessors' concurrence) found Woodward not guilty and went on to say that the charge of embezzlement had been frivolous and vexatious. Therefore, he ordered the prosecution to pay all the court costs and the costs of finding and transporting Woodward back from Shanghai to Kobe. The next day, McGregor submitted a new charge against Woodward of forging McGregor's signature on a cheque for $1,850 and a further charge of embezzling $67.61 by alleging that Woodward had made fraudulent entries in the books of McGregor's business. The following day (29 September), Woodward was committed by Troup at the Kobe Court to stand charge on indictment for these offences and Troup announced that Hannen would try them before a jury. Meanwhile, Woodward was again released on bail—this time against two sureties of $500 each.

On 15 October the trial date was fixed for 21 October and Hannen travelled to Kobe with Moss, the clerk of HMCJ, to hear the charges. Unlike in the summary case, Litchfield, the Crown Prosecutor, prosecuted as this was a trial on indictment. Edward Robinson again acted for the defence. First, the charge of forgery was tried over two days before the jury acquitted Woodward whereupon Litchfield announced that he had decided not to proceed with the embezzlement charge—which was then dismissed formally.

The official returns often divided criminal offences into criminal cases and police cases. Without exception, police cases were minor offences and tried summarily. They were so called because similar offences in England at that time were tried in Magistrates Courts or 'Police Courts'. The majority of such police cases consisted of shipping offences. Even criminal offences identified as criminal cases were usually heard summarily by the Consul without Assessors. As the records are inconsistent in their treatment of criminal cases and police cases and there is no substantive practical difference between them, they are all treated as criminal offences for analytical purposes in this book.

The first reported criminal case was *Bassett v. Charles Munroe*, which was heard shortly after Nagasaki was opened to trade. Munroe, described as a native of Jamaica, was convicted by the Nagasaki Consul and two Assessors (K.R. Mackenzie and J.H. Evans) of having made 'a fierce and repeated assault with a knife' on Bassett for which he was sentenced to 12 months' imprisonment with hard labour followed by deportation.[13] However, it is the period from 1875 to 1899 in Nagasaki which lends itself to the deepest—and surest—statistical analysis because of the availability of its Court records whereas there are no similarly detailed records for any other Court (except Hakodate until 1878). Even where some figures are available for other ports, the overlap is for only a short period thus making any useful comparative analysis difficult. Although the newspaper reports also allow for an analysis of criminal cases in Yokohama and Kobe—particularly, the more serious criminal cases heard in each of those ports—in later periods, we must be aware of the limitations of such reports which are not comprehensive whilst the available semi-annual returns for those—and other—ports often provide little scope for in-depth analysis.

Table 2 summarizes the numbers of criminal offences found in the available semi-annual returns, the Nagasaki Court records, the correspondence records of the consulates and newspaper reports. Three characteristics are immediately noticeable from these records and reports: the dominance of shipping offences, the key role of Yokohama, and a drop in the case-load after 1880.[14] The split of cases between the ports is as we should expect and, with the largest foreign population of any port, Yokohama saw the largest criminal case-load followed by Kobe and Nagasaki. Yokohama's dominance is clear from both the few semi-annual returns available for that port and the newspaper reports. Most of Japan's foreign trade (and, consequently, sailors) passed through these three ports so it is unsurprising that the other ports saw fewer cases. Only in two years (1874 and 1875) did the Tokyo Court's case-load even enter double figures (19 and 12 respectively)—and this was a blip for its case-load tails off

[13] Morrison to Alcock, 31 August 1859; FO262/6.
[14] Tables 2 and 3.

rapidly thereafter to almost nothing—and Hakodate's British population was only about 20 for the entire period; although, at both the beginning and end of the extra-territoriality period, Hakodate saw large movements of British flagged vessels.

An initial flurry of criminal cases followed by a levelling off or near complete disappearance is most evident in Tokyo but we also see it elsewhere. In Nagasaki, the peak years, with 29 defendants, were 1866 and 1878. After 1878, the number of defendants dropped to the low teens or single figures thereafter (albeit with a sudden upsurge in assaults from brawls, largely involving sailors, in the late 1890s). In both Yokohama and Kobe, the newspaper reports suggest a peak in the 1870s with a fall thereafter—although it is important to acknowledge that reporting trends changed and, generally, the newspapers reported on fewer cases after the late 1870s. The total number of annual cases in Table 3 for Kobe shows such a variation from 1870 to 1899 (and rather greater fluctuations than for Yokohama) that the most likely explanation is indeed down to the sifting of cases worthy of report by the newspapers rather than showing a reliable trend.

There is no clear reason for the declining case-loads and none of the figures offers any explanation. The near complete fall-off of criminal cases in Tokyo over the longer term may reflect that, being the capital and diplomatic centre and not a port, the foreign residents were of a more peaceable disposition—although, clearly, there had been problems with 'loafers' in Tokyo just after its opening as seen by the need to appoint Robertson formally as Vice-Consul with judicial authority over them. Although Hakodate provides a superficial contrast of a more stable case-load over the period for which there are records, a closer examination of the case details reveals that just three incidents distort the numbers so it is not possible to draw any general trends from Hakodate.

We must assume that the late 1860s' increasing case-load in Yokohama reflects the settlement's growth; but, the period covered by the official returns is too short to yield a clear trend. The apparent decline from the peak in the late 1870s suggested by newspaper reports could well result solely from changed reporting practices where the newspapers covered fewer cases—but may also reflect reality as the *Japan Weekly Mail* reported that cases had been fewer over the Christmas/New Year holidays in 1878/79.[15] Rather than seeking to explain the decline in case-load, it may be more appropriate to seek an explanation for the high case-loads

---

[15] 4 January 1879; JWM.

initially. A simple explanation would be that, as newly established communities, the foreign communities were in a state of flux; but, as they settled down, the ports became calmer. This then raises questions about the defendants' make-up and the charges prosecuted.

Defendants

The Nagasaki Court minutes from 1875 and the newspaper reports on the Yokohama and Kobe cases from 1862 and 1869, respectively, usually contain sufficient information to determine the precise nature of the offence and the defendant's habitual abode—details which are usually missing elsewhere in the court and related records except Hakodate where its small population, low case-load and correspondence records permit us to make a similar analysis. Elsewhere, a judgmental approach to the returns is often needed to determine the defendant's abode: usually from the nature of the offence or the sentence. Some offences (e.g. being absent without leave (**AWOL**)) can only be shipping offences. Likewise, a sentence to be 'imprisoned until departure' indicates a sailor being tried. Most Treaty breaches (except breaching the Treaty limits) were (by their nature) committed by sailors. Descriptions of most other offences and sentences are unspecific so the defendant could be a sailor or a port resident—and how should a discharged sailor living ashore be classified? Thus, except with those minutes and newspaper reports, the number of sailors identified amongst defendants in criminal cases is almost certainly an underestimate.

From 1875 to 1899, two thirds of all defendants in Nagasaki were transient visitors.[16] For Yokohama and Kobe, the proportions—on the basis of the newspaper reports—were just over a half and nearly three-fifths respectively. Most visitors were sailors on board ships (merchant or naval) but also including a small number of soldiers and other visitors. The 'Rowdy' element was certainly a source of trouble-makers and an early editorial in *The Hiogo News* lamented of the need to contend with the greater evil of the very large numbers of 'unemployed and loafing' foreigners with which Kobe had become infected within a couple of years of its opening.[17] Setting aside shipping offences and defendants who were

[16] Table 2. The Yokohama figures, almost certainly, underestimate the proportion of sailors due to insufficient information in the newspaper reports. This is less of an issue with the Kobe figures based upon newspaper reports.

[17] 19 January 1870; HN.

sailors, we find, on average, at most six British residents a year in Yokohama, and three in each of Kobe and Nagasaki, being prosecuted out of populations which averaged around 600, 250–300 and 100 respectively over the period. Thus, for all the resident British community's brouhaha surrounding the abolition of extra-territoriality, no more than ten to twelve resident members a year (perhaps, some 400—450 over the entire 40 year period) faced prosecution for criminal offences.

In Nagasaki, the proportion of defendants constituted by sailors was fairly constant over the whole period—except for Japanese initiated prosecutions from 1881 to 1890 when the drop in sailors prosecuted and a smaller rise in residents prosecuted resulted in a noticeable change.[18] Although this was a decade with fewer prosecutions than other periods, a review of the cases provides no obvious explanation for this variation or any significance in this temporary different make-up of defendants.

The Hakodate figures are amenable to analysis for the 15 year period from 1863 to 1878. They show 25 charges being brought against Britons in Hakodate. Of course, that community was much smaller: in 1870, there were just 14 registered Britons there (plus families)[19] and it never subsequently rose above 20 registered individuals. This bare prosecution statistic would support the concerns of the British community in Japan that it faced a serious threat of harassment in the event of extra-territoriality being abandoned. However, a closer examination of the cases suggests otherwise: just three incidents gave rise to 13 charges: five charges against three defendants in the *Ainu bones case*; Blakiston faced four charges connected with his assaulting, and imprisoning, a Japanese employee, Kiroku, who then committed suicide;[20] whilst John Will faced four separate charges arising out of what was, essentially, a domestic, or personal, squabble between him and Blakiston over the affections of a local woman.[21]

These last charges, and Connor's two charges against Berwick (possibly, Barwick), are more reflective of the quarrelsome nature of a small, somewhat cut-off and inward looking community in an outpost in northern Japan rather than aggressive Japanese police harassment of the wider British community. As it would be difficult to criticize the charge brought by the British authorities in Hakodate against Berwick for sending the

---

[18] Table 7.

[19] Eusden to Hornby, 14 January 1870, FO656/35.

[20] See pages 113–115.

[21] When Eusden acquitted Will of burglary, Blakiston was so annoyed, he went around around making scurrilous statements about Eusden (Eusden to French, 19 November 1878; FO17/791).

Wanja to sea in an unseaworthy condition, this leaves just three other criminal prosecutions in Hakodate over a 14 year period: hardly a serious threat to that community's liberty.

In all ports, the defendants were almost exclusively male. No women were prosecuted in Hakodate, Tokyo[22] or, during the period covered by the semi-annual returns, Kobe; and none is mentioned in the newspaper reports as a defendant in Kobe. In the later days of extra-territoriality, three women in Nagasaki were charged with assault and/or using abusive language (including one case where both prosecutor and defendant were women)[23] and women defendants were scarcely more common in Yokohama with just eight listed or reported. They included Edith Carew who was prosecuted, in 1897, for poisoning her husband in the most celebrated trial of the entire period; Edith Labain who was charged, in 1876, with keeping a house of ill-fame;[24] and Elizabeth Scarfield who was prosecuted for concealing the birth of a child on the *Annie W. Weston* from Cardiff to Yokohama and throwing the body into the sea.[25]

It is understandable that few women were prosecuted when we consider the offences usually brought. Generally, the charges preferred are those one would expect in a seaport with two-thirds or more of cases being, broadly, public order offences (breach of the peace, drunkenness and disorderly conduct degenerating into assault and battery) with a broad consistency over time, between ports and as between sailors and residents.[26] Of the remainder, approximately 10% of cases involved theft or some fraudulent element whilst the remainder constituted a miscellaneous category.

Assaults were usually at the trivial end and arose when the police were trying to arrest an offender for drunkenness or another other breach of the peace; but, a handful involved serious batteries and several knife stabbings, which often resulted in murder or manslaughter prosecutions. The 1890s saw a spate of such prosecutions arising from incidents in the Arctic sealing trade.[27] In all, there were some 12 prosecutions for murder or manslaughter and similar number for rape or indecent assault.

---

22 Bridget Blockley avoided prosecution in Tokyo for assaulting a Japanese woman only because of a dispute between Dohmen and the Japanese officials over whether her civil claim against the complainant had been handled properly; Dohmen to Toshinazu, 28 August 1876; FO798/5.

23 *Reg. ats Rebecca Reich v. Rosa Zanzulicht* (December 1897); and *Joseph Tannenbaum v. Anne Grand and Adela Schwartz* (cases 3 and 4 of 1896); FO796/7.

24 10 July 1875; NCH.

25 29 March 1877; NCH.

26 Table 4.

27 For example, the prosecutions of Carozzi and Hallinan of the *Nemo* in 1889.

Most thefts involved petty thieving by sailors taking goods from hawkers or market stalls; or vagrants stealing food, as when Masefield was convicted of the theft of a goose.[28] More serious cases included the embezzlement of $6,000 from Comptoir d'Escompte de Paris,[29] the *Leopold case*[30] involving the fraudulent negotiation of ¥80,000 bills of lading, the Yokohama Consulate's chief constable's theft of $1,288 of charitable donations destined for the smallpox hospital[31] and a second mate's theft of $2,000 from the *Saikyo maru*'s mailroom.[32] Other theft prosecutions arose from wider-ranging disputes. In *Katsuki v. Richard A. Ford,*[33] Ford was convicted (and sentenced to a day's imprisonment) for stealing Katsuki's licence and refusing to return it during a dispute over Ford's allegations that Katsuki had undercut him on the sale of provisions to the *Hildon*. As *Kaneko Suikichi v. James F. Mitchell* showed, Japanese individuals were as adept as *gaijin* at the litigation game for Suikichi accused Mitchell of stealing some papers which he, Suikichi, required for his concurrent civil case against Mitchell.[34] In Hakodate, as one might expect in a smaller, more stable community, theft by residents was non-existent and the two theft cases involving a resident were mere devices to allow a Japanese individual to seek recovery of property detained by the local consular constable.

'Miscellaneous' is a mixed bag: politically, the most important were the Japanese authorities' prosecutions for breach of trade and quarantine regulations (16 in Kobe and six in each of Nagasaki and Hakodate and, according to newspaper reports, 10 in Yokohama). This category includes seven prosecutions by Japanese and British authorities in Nagasaki and four in Kobe for passing alcohol into, or escaping from, the consular gaol, obstructing, or escaping from, arrest. More individual prosecutions included those for having a dog which bit, vagrancy, firearms offences, four 'misconduct in employment' cases (three in Nagasaki and one in Kobe), a Japanese prosecution of a Singaporean Chinese for collecting and selling bones from a Nagasaki cemetery housing the remains of soldiers who had died in the Taiwan Campaign of 1875 and a prosecution of a British curio trader in Kobe for taking curios on board a ship for sale

---

[28] *Reg. ats. Ward v. W.J. Masefield*, 26 April 1876; HN.
[29] *Reg. v. Adds*, 1 May and 19 June 1875; JDH.
[30] *Reg. v. C.E. Leopold*, 17 December 1898; JWM Supplement.
[31] *Reg. v. Smith*, 15 April 1868; TJH.
[32] *Reg. (ats. Nippon Yusen Kaisha) v. Ryder*, 29 August 1896; JWM.
[33] Case 6 of 1885; FO796/7.
[34] Case 21 of 1881; FO796/7.

without permission. The Municipal Council in Kobe also prosecuted one of its Municipal policemen for ill-treating a prisoner whilst in his charge on the way to the police station.[35] Creagh, the Kobe solicitor, took defamation claims to a new level by instituting a private prosecution for criminal libel against a fellow resident, J. Blackmore, who was alleged to have published a 'false, scandalous, malicious and defamatory libel in the form of a drawing, sketch of caricature' about Creagh. Blackmore was committed for trial before Troup and three Assessors but, when the trial opened, Montague Kirkwood, who appeared for the defence, demurred to the indictment and argued that Creagh had not established the technical requirements for the offence whereupon the indictment was quashed and Creagh was saddled with the Court and defence costs.[36]

Prosecutors

The first step in any prosecution was for the complainant to lay a complaint or charge at the consulate. The Charge Book for the Nagasaki Court for 1885–1899[37] shows the standard format of a charge as being along the following lines:

> In HBM Court of Nagasaki on 20 January 1885, Takeshita Ichitaro of 272 buramachi Nagasaki charges Alexander Macpherson of Nagasaki with having a dog to bite him on 31 December 1884.[38]

The complainant would then sign his name and the charge would be witnessed by, usually, the Constable or the Assistant Consul or, more rarely, the Consul. Japanese complainants usually signed in *kanji*. Even though recorded in the official Charge Book, the charge was then, usually—but not always, chopped with the Consulate's seal. The more serious or unusual charges were attended with a greater degree of formality: on 30 July 1886, a consular official charged Beltram with larceny of $30,000 on the basis of 'telegraphic communications received from the Secretary of the Hong Kong government which I verily believe to be

[35] *Reg (ats. T. Lenz representing the Police Committee of the Hiogo Municipal Council) v. Alvum Hazlett, constable of the Municipal Police Force*, 9 November 1878; HN. Although convicted of using too much force, Hazlett was let off with a reprimand as it was his first offence.

[36] 25 November and 2 December 1885; HN.

[37] FO796/13.

[38] 20 January 1885; FO796/13.

[39] 30 July 1886; FO796/13.

correct',[39] before the charge was recorded as having been 'sworn before J.J. Enslie, Judge'[40] and chopped. When, Morimoto Yoshimatsu, a coal-heaver, charged George Bungay, a sailor from the *Pembrokeshire*, with having seized and ravished Fujita Hiro, another coal-coolie, it was specifically noted that Morimoto had been 'duly cautioned'[41]—a procedure not recorded in other cases. The formulation of some of the charges must have seemed slightly incongruous to those Japanese who were involved such as when Yeguchi, a Police Inspector, charged Oscar Olin, the *Sinkolga*'s master, with having fired a gun within the Nagasaki anchorage to kill a bird to the danger of the public 'against the Peace of Our Lady the Queen, her Crown and Dignity'.[42] Whilst British officials and lawyers may well have treated this formulation as just standard verbiage, it must have rubbed salt into the wound of extra-territoriality for the Japanese. Even the Governor of Hiogo *ken* was obliged to use this formulation when charging Captain Drake with the manslaughter of his Japanese passengers.[43]

Occasionally—but only in the case of Japanese complainants, a claim for damages against the defendant was added by either the complainant or others. When Yeijuchi Minseki, an Inspector on behalf of the Japanese police, charged Ernest Jacobs, seaman of HMS *Champion*, with assault on Yoshida Mitsu, three claims for damages were added against Jacobs. The first, by Sasaki Otajiro for 42 *sen* in respect of an iron rake which Jacobs had seized and thrown into the dock; the second by Sentake Seijiro who claimed 16 *sen* in respect of a broken lantern whilst Muta Masujiro claimed 16 *sen* in respect of Jacobs' hire of a *jinrikisha*.[44]

All indictable—and some summary—offences were prosecuted in the name of the Crown (as opposed to the individual most immediately affected or who laid the complaint). This makes it difficult to identify the underlying prosecutor from the semi-annual returns alone where the case is described as *Reg. v. X* with no further information. The Nagasaki Court minutes and, usually, newspaper reports allow us to look behind this; but, without this underlying information, categorization of prosecutors from the returns alone must be more approximate.

As the bulk of prosecutions involved public order offences it is reasonable to expect that prosecutions were usually at the instance of those responsible for the maintenance of public order and, as this responsibility

40 Ibid.

41 23 January 1885; FO796/13.

42 21 September 1893; FO796/13.

43 17 November 1886; HN.

44 26 June 1885; FO796/13.

shifted over time, so too did the prosecutors. The early part of the period covered by the Yokohama returns (1867–1872) was when the foreign settlement was trying to run itself and had its own Municipal Police who were responsible for nearly three-quarters of all prosecutions where we can identify the prosecuting agency (and almost two-fifths of all prosecutions). However, with the collapse of Westerners' attempts to run the Yokohama and Nagasaki settlements by 1867 and 1876 respectively[45] and the growing sophistication, organization and administration of the Japanese police and criminal justice following the adoption of a Criminal Code in 1880 (which led Sir Francis Plunkett, Minister 1884–1887, to agree that the Japanese need not replace European police constables in the Yokohama police force after 1884[46]), we see a fall in the proportion of British prosecutions in Nagasaki after 1890 and an increase in prosecutions by the Japanese authorities.[47] This change is also reflected in newspaper reports of criminal cases in Yokohama where, after the mid-1880s, most public order charges are at the instance of Japanese authorities—even where no Japanese individual was involved. This is unlike Kobe, where the (limited) newspaper reports suggest a similar decline in British inspired prosecutions in the 1890s but, instead of British inspired prosecutions being replaced by those by the Japanese authorities, Japanese individuals appear to have played a larger role in bringing the prosecutions. Of course, this conclusion—which is at odds with Nagasaki and Yokohama—may simply reflect the reported cases.

Over the period 1875–1899, under a third of Nagasaki cases were prosecuted by the British authorities or fellow Britons and most of the remainder were prosecuted at the instance of the Japanese authorities or Japanese individuals. Even the 1866–74 figures, which show British prosecutions predominating, probably understate the number of prosecutions brought at the behest of Japanese individuals or where they were the victims.[48]

The British authorities instigated just 14 prosecutions (8% of the total) in Nagasaki in the period 1875–1899; the remainder of the prosecutions brought in their name arose from complaints laid by others. Enforcement

---

[45] See Hoare 1994, pages 106–126. The Yokohama Municipal Council collapsed in 1867 (although the Japanese employed a Western Municipal Director to assist in the Settlement's running until 1877) and the Nagasaki arrangements collapsed in 1876.

[46] An experiment which he pronounced 'an entire success'; Plunkett to Rosebery, 10 July 1886; FO881/5380. Prior to this, the Japanese authorities in Yokohama had employed a number of Western policemen to deal with cases involving foreigners.

[47] Tables 5, 6 and 8.

[48] Table 5.

of laws arising from diplomatic engagements was an obvious area for official interest, although the nature of such prosecutions changed over time. Initially, it involved enforcing restrictions against trading at unopen ports and the supply of weapons. By the 1890s, the British authorities were enforcing restrictions on seal fishing in northern waters following Anglo-Russian agreements on this subject—although it is unclear whether the British took independent action in these cases or acted only when prompted by the Russian authorities.

From the beginning, the British authorities were aware that provocation was frequently given to Japanese individuals by 'the rudeness and violence of foreigners themselves'[49] and Alcock ordered Morrison to take action in such cases. Alcock advised that he would view 'no penalty within the assigned limits of [OC1859] for such offence too severe'.[50] An egregious case was when Winchester, then Consul in Nagasaki, fined Edward Harrison $10 for taking the law into his own hands and painting the faces of some coolies who had stolen a quantity of silk from Glover & Co. Unusually, the fine was paid over to the Japanese Police—but whether or not as compensation to the coolies is unclear.[51]

British officialdom was also concerned with the administration of justice and officially inspired prosecutions included perjury cases, prosecutions for defacing jury lists, gaol escapes, attempted gaol break-ins to free prisoners and passing alcohol into consular gaols, breaches of deportation orders and several contempt charges. A perennial issue was the enforcement of the registration obligations and, although the *North China Herald* decried 'Britons paying up like willing slaves',[52] many cases were brought to enforce this obligation with several cases referred to in Kobe in 1871[53] and another 16 in 1873 alone. Thefts from the stores of the British Garrison at Yokohama led to several prosecutions in the early 1870s.

The protection of British lives was the responsibility of the British authorities who initiated two prosecutions for attempted suicide and, in *Reg. v. Browning*, *Reg. v. Carew* and *Reg. v. Cuthbert*, murder cases at both ends of the period. Otherwise, British official prosecutions were something of a mixed bag and ranged from prosecutions for running an abattoir or pub without a licence to keeping a disorderly house or a brothel

---

[49] Alcock to Morrison, 24 September 1859; FO410/1.

[50] Ibid.

[51] Nagasaki Consulate to Chief of Police, 3 November 1863; FO796/25.

[52] 8 February 1871; NCH.

[53] 18 February 1871; HN. None was fined but all were ordered to register and pay the court costs.

(two of which prosecutions were brought by the British Admiral because so many of his sailors contracted venereal disease following visits to these establishments).

When it comes to prosecutions by individual prosecutors, a difference in approach between Japanese and British prosecutors may be seen. Most individual Western prosecutors had genuine cases arising from injuries they had suffered—although, some can only be described as the continuation of personal disputes. Two charges brought in Hakodate by Connor against Berwick were retaliation for Berwick's civil suit against Connor for defamation and all actions were subsequently withdrawn. A more modern use of the Courts was *Reg. v. Bevill*[54] when an individual sought, in effect, a declaration that the hawking exhibition at the Bluff Gardens (which involved hawking wild pigeons) constituted cruelty to animals and should be proscribed for the future.

Whilst not suggesting that prosecutions brought by Japanese individuals (and, often, the more minor prosecutions by the Japanese authorities on behalf of individuals) did not stem from genuine causes, a large number seem to have been more concerned with the recovery of damages for property destroyed, goods or services provided, goods stolen or personal injury.[55] In two Nagasaki cases, the defendant, even though acquitted, was ordered to pay compensatory damages to the injured Japanese. Most damages in these cases were minor and ranged from a few *sen* to a few Dollars—usually 10–30 cents for the hire of a *jinrikisha* or a couple of Dollars or Yen for food and drink consumed. *Jinrikisha* men were regarded by the Western community as a 'great nuisance and [giving] great provocation to foreigners'[56] and, throughout the period, we see innumerable scrummages arising from their touting for fares and endless disputes and claims at the end of the journey. *The Rising Sun and Nagasaki Express* described the assault case against a stoker from HMS *Narcissus* as arising from 'the usual squabble over the fare'.[57] In Nagasaki, none of the associated claims exceeded a claim for $3 damages.

---

54 15 June 1872; JWM.

55 This mixing of purposes is seen in *Reg. ats. Kawada Usaburo through the Japanese Police v. Perkins* (of *HMS Lily*) when Perkins was charged with assault and battery of a brothel keeper. In convicting Perkins, the Court stated that, as the property damages were not substantiated, it would deal solely with the criminal charge (and not consider damages). Case 63 of 1878; FO796/2.

56 Editorial commentary on *Reg. ats. Okada Sakichi v. William Harris*; 27 May 1876; TRS&NE.

57 18 August 1898; TRS&NE. The stoker was convicted and fined ¥20.

Similarly in Kobe, with one exception, the highest amount awarded was $3. A sailor was ordered to pay $2 to a Japanese policeman for damaging his uniform whilst trying to avoid arrest whilst a Japanese curio dealer was reported as having 'looked disgusted' when awarded just ¥2 compensation for a broken tooth against the ¥115 he had claimed when his assailant was convicted of assault and fined ¥3.[58] The exception involved another sailor from HMS *Narcissus*, Alfred Brown, who was charged with furious riding through the town.[59] He had originally pleaded not guilty but changed his plea in court and offered to pay the medical expenses for a young Japanese woman who had been injured by his horse as she was crossing the street. In view of this, and the fact that one witness said that Brown had tried to pull up when he saw the woman—who had stopped in the middle of the street as the horse was riding along, Consul Hall fined him only $5 and ordered the payment of the woman's medical expenses for a month—and commented that $80 for a month looked to be a moderate amount. The newspaper reported subsequently that, due to the exemplary behaviour of men from *HMS Narcissus* during its stay in port, $90 was raised by public subscription for Brown to defray these costs and the court costs; otherwise, it would have been his wife and young family (who received half his pay) who would have suffered. Reports from Yokohama showed a similar pattern—generally very small amounts awarded but, again, with one exception where four offenders in an assault were required to pay a total of $74 as compensation for medical expenses (in addition to serving short periods of imprisonment).[60]

The mixing of criminal prosecutions and civil claims is seen even more clearly in those cases where, despite having pleaded guilty or admitted the factual background of the case, the defendant is discharged or acquitted. John Scott pleaded guilty to a charge of wounding Japanese man with a shot but claimed it was accidental. After hearing all the evidence, the Consul acquitted him of the offence (despite Scott's guilty plea) and said it was a 'pure accident'. However, as the prosecutor was incapacitated from working through a want of proper care on Scott's part, it was only right that Scott should compensate the Japanese man for 20 days' loss of pay plus his medical expenses.[61]

---

[58] *Reg. ats Japanese Police v. Eli Knowles* of *HMS Lily* 28 December 1878; HN and *Oka Jutaro v. William Cox* 15 October 1898; KWC, respectively.

[59] 10 July 1897; KWC.

[60] 13 August 1889; JWM.

[61] *Reg. ats. Japanese government v. John Scott*; 13 May 1876; TRS&NE.

Unlike such 'compensation claims' brought by Japanese individuals, no Westerner appears to have instituted a prosecution as an alternative to civil proceedings to obtain damages. It is unclear why the Japanese brought such cases as criminal prosecutions as opposed to civil actions. Possibly, the reasons were procedural—although none is obvious. Fees were remitted for Japanese plaintiffs as well as prosecutors and smaller civil cases were also tried summarily and subject to no greater delays than summary criminal cases, which were usually heard within a few days (if not the same, or immediately succeeding, day) of the charge; so, neither fees nor timing should have been the reason. Nor should it have been the burden of proof, for this was higher in criminal cases.

A technical justification would have been OC1860 which required the Consul to 'promote reconcilement in cases of assaults'[62] but this is never suggested anywhere. It may have been that, in civil cases, the logistical burden of the proceedings and documentation was solely upon the plaintiff whereas, in a criminal action, the authorities played a greater role. Another possible procedural explanation on the Japanese side is that, until 1876, all civil and criminal actions brought by Japanese subjects against foreigners were processed by the *Fu* or *Ken* office before submission to the Consul and the local Japanese officials may have made little distinction between the two—particularly where the primary aim was to obtain compensation. After 1876, purely civil actions continued to processed by the *Fu* or *Ken* with criminal actions being handled by the *Kenji* or other Japanese police officials and not processed separately.[63] However, the conflation of criminal and civil actions continued as criminal cases which also involved a civil action were also handled by the Japanese police.

The different handling of claims may also reflect the economic status of the two groups. Japanese who pursued compensation claims via the criminal process were all small stall-keepers, *jinrikisha* coolies and tea-house *mama-san* whereas, the Chinese apart, none of the foreign settlers operated at that low an economic level and, therefore, might be expected to follow the proper claims routes—and even the Chinese prosecutors were shop-keepers or traders of a slightly higher economic echelon than the Japanese individual traders mentioned.

An area of common interest to a specific class of individual Japanese and Western prosecutors was the enforcement of the 1878 Japanese

---

62 Section XXIX, OC1860.

63 Terashima Munenori (Japanese Foreign Minister) to Parkes, 30 November 1876; FO798/26.

Pilotage Regulations (which the *Chargé d'Affaires* published in 1879) which restricted pilotage rights to pilots licensed by the Japanese authorities. Carter was fined $5 and $10 in January and June 1881 for piloting a ship in the Inland Sea whilst unlicensed. HMCJ held itself unable to enforce Hodnett's civil claim for ¥17 against the *Cyclops* for declining his pilotage offer because the Regulations allowed no civil remedy; but, the Court suggested that he bring a criminal prosecution against the master.[64]

Women are almost as scarce amongst prosecutrices as amongst defendants—certainly below 5% overall. Their infrequent involvement reflected that they were not sailors, the smaller female British population,[65] and the times' social mores where the dictates of 'gentlemanly conduct' meant that Bush's prosecution for assaulting Mrs Tannenbaum and her Japanese servant was brought in Mr Tannenbaum's name.[66]

With Western prosecutrices, the charges involved a fracas or minor assault, as when Louise Wehrun prosecuted Ellen Walker for criminal damage and breach of the peace in Yokohama in 1880. Ignoring cases involving injuries caused by furious riding[67] (which was more a general public order offence), prosecutions involving Japanese women arose out of disputes at tea-houses which either led to a fracas (and, one must suspect, were brought principally to recover compensation for the damage caused) or arose in respect of non-payment. Other charges included those for indecent assaults or rape. Rapes were usually heard on indictment before the Supreme Court or HMCJ following committal proceedings before the Consul; but, as in *Reg. v Archibald King*,[68] perhaps the most notorious rape case, a Consul could try such cases with Assessors—but without the full sentencing powers available to the higher court.

Prosecutions by the Japanese Authorities

Of greater importance to the British community was the Japanese authorities' prosecution practice which gave rise to Westerners' long memories

64 *Reg. v. Carter*, 17 January 1881; *Deguchi v. Carter*, 22 June 1881; and *Hodnett v. Butler* (*Master of Cyclops*), 20 May 1881; JWM.

65 For example, the Hakodate registration return of 1870 lists no women independently and has just two references to 'and family' (Eusden to Hornby, 14 January 1870; FO656/35); thus, there were only two adult British females as against 14 males.

66 *Reg. ats. J. Tannenbaum v. A.F. Augustus Walsh Bush*, case 26, 1898; FO796/7. (Bush was convicted and imprisoned for four weeks with hard labour.)

67 For example, *Reg. v. Ekins and Verrall*, cases 10 and 11, 1878; FO796/2 and *Reg. ats. Japanese Police v. G. Davey*, case 3, 1886; FO796/7.

68 May 1875; FO656/46. See also page 134.

of the alleged arbitrary nature of the Japanese criminal system when first encountered and a general nervousness of over-zealous policemen with their books of regulations upon extra-territoriality's ending in 1899.[69] Without considering the Japanese archives, it is impossible to determine whether any particular policy influenced official Japanese prosecution practice. Nevertheless, certain consistent strands are identifiable from the cases, which strands change to some extent as the Japanese assumed greater responsibility for the maintenance of law and order in the settlements.

First, and least contentious, was the maintenance of public order. Here, Japanese interests were little different from those of the British authorities where controlling the 'rowdy class' was a concern to British officialdom throughout East Asia. Over four-fifths of official Japanese prosecutions in Nagasaki concerned public order offences:[70] a proportion that was nearly a third higher than with British prosecutions. The court minutes reflect this community of interest and reveal considerable co-operation between the Japanese police and the consular constables in maintaining public order and bringing appropriate prosecutions.[71] This need to maintain public order generated no controversy amongst the Western communities and, in 1867, the Japanese government asked Parkes to name someone to assist the Governor of Kanagawa in arresting and prosecuting foreigners (not just Britons) for trespass and disorder on the streets.[72]

Linked to public order, was the support that the Japanese police gave to the 'small' Japanese individuals dealing with the British (*jinrikisha* coolies, tea-house *mama-san,* et al.) where the underlying reason for the prosecution was to enforce a proper settlement or compensation for goods and services provided or damage done as when Robert Miller, a sailor, was prosecuted in 1866 for refusing to pay for breakfast.[73] In this sense, the local police (and authorities), presumably, saw themselves as defending their fellow-countrymen's interests in appropriate circumstances. British officialdom's awareness that it was being observed as to its protection of

69 Hoare 1971, page 224.

70 Table 8. Where residents alone were concerned, the proportions were the same at two-thirds.

71 The Nagasaki authorities employed Peter Doel as a police inspector to assist in controlling foreigners. He had been employed previously by the Osaka Municipal Council: 7 November 1879; NCH.

72 Parkes to Hornby, 7 November 1867; FO391/14, page 208.

73 6 April 1866; *Japan Times*. He was convicted, fined 50 cents and ordered to pay for the breakfast.

Japanese interests and control of the more unruly elements of the British community is clear from the *Cousens case*.[74]

A counter-argument may be seen by a small number of cases such as the prosecutions for assault in *Yatsugoro v. Denny*[75] and *Japanese Government on behalf of Yamtoya Sayoske v. Pai-Yokusan* (chief steward on HMS *Hunt*).[76] The Consul described the first as involving 'trumped up charges' and exaggerated claims (although he convicted the defendant and fined him $1) whilst, in the second, he allowed that the evidence was 'so conflicting as to render it difficult to decide which party had been the aggressor in the quarrel'[77] but called the Japanese authorities' attention to the 'shameful imposture'[78] which had been attempted by the complainant's petition, backed up by a Japanese doctor's certificate, in an attempt to mulct the defendant. He criticized the Japanese policeman conducting the case for not ascertaining fully beforehand its merits, as such claims could seriously prejudice the value placed on similar claims in future.

There was no objection to the latter prosecution itself: the evidence was conflicting and, after hearing it, the defendant was acquitted. The Court's objection was to the patently exaggerated damages claim ($58); an attempt which went beyond the usual exaggerations and, more seriously, appeared to be sanctioned by the Japanese authorities. This case was noteworthy in that the Consul felt compelled to criticize the Japanese police for lack of diligence in assessing the damages claim. Such admonition must have been effective for we see no subsequent prosecutions by the Japanese authorities in Nagasaki involving obviously exaggerated damages claims.

Another strand of cases was those that appear to have been brought to assuage local public sentiment (possibly, xenophobia)—particularly where a foreigner was involved in the death of a Japanese—even in circumstances where prosecutions could not succeed. They may have been brought to show the authorities as defenders of the national interest or simply to deflect local concerns and, despite being hopeless on legal grounds, may have been used by contemporary local opinion formers to support arguments that extra-territoriality was unfair and biased against the Japanese. Alternatively, some may have reflected cultural differences.

The earliest case reflecting local anger and antipathy to foreigners was the *Ainu bones case* when the Japanese authorities prosecuted three

[74] See pages 138 and 261.
[75] 29 August 1874; JWM.
[76] 20 September 1876; FO796/2.
[77] Ibid.
[78] Ibid.

Britons for the theft of Ainu bones from an Ainu burial site in Hokkaido. The incident, described by Hoare,[79] embarrassed the British authorities as the defendants included the local British constable and gaoler and Vyse, the Consul, was clearly involved (and, ultimately, resigned as a result). The defendants were convicted and sentenced (by Vyse) to twelve months hard labour for the theft. After they had been conveyed to the British gaol in Yokohama, Parkes and Hornby removed the embarrassment of their presence in Japan by commuting their sentence to one of deportation to Hong Kong.[80]

Later that year, the Governor of Nagasaki sought to prosecute Captain Anderson over the death of his servant, Sanski. Anderson's watch had been stolen and, believing that Sanski was party to the theft (a matter unproved either way), Anderson hit Sanski with his hands. Later, Sanski jumped overboard and, six days later, his body was found dead in the water. When the Governor pressed for Anderson's prosecution, Hornby explained that, as Sanski's death was not the direct consequence of any act of Anderson's, he could not be held guilty of it. Anderson had been wrong in beating Sanski; but, in an example of Hornby's occasional 'rough and ready' approach, Hornby considered that he had already been punished amply for that by not being allowed to leave Japan about his own business thereby incurring loss of time and money. Hornby added that he had commented at length on the Governor's letter 'as a mark of respect to him personally since it is not customary for a Judge of my rank to discuss the reasons of his judgment with anyone'.[81]

In 1873, Thomas Wright Blakiston, the leading British merchant in Hakodate, berated and beat his employee, Kiroku, before confining him in a godown where Kiroku hanged himself. The local Governor complained that if Blakiston 'had a complaint against a Japanese, he should have complained to the *saibansho*'[82] and not taken the law into his own hands before seeking to charge Blakiston with Kiroku's manslaughter. After a preliminary examination in Court, Troup, then acting Consul in Hakodate, applied to Hornby for directions.[83] Hornby advised that there was insufficient causal link evidence to support a manslaughter charge and suggested Blakiston be charged with Kiroku's assault and battery and

79 Hoare 1976.
80 Parkes to Hornby, 29 May 1866; FO656/19.
81 Hornby to Flowers, 1 September 1866; FO656/37.
82 Governor of Hakodate to Troup, 28 February 1873; FO656/35.
83 Troup to Hornby, 5 March 1873; FO656/35.

fined $400.[84] It is unclear in what depth the Japanese authorities considered the manslaughter charge; but, it is clear that local feeling against Blakiston ran high which the Governor sought to assuage by a manslaughter prosecution.

The Japanese government complained that the $400 fine on Blakiston was too light a punishment and raised the matter to a diplomatic level with Parkes. They claimed that Troup appeared to treat Blakiston's complaints against the Japanese authorities' indifference to offences committed against Westerners as justifying the 'lenient' sentence.[85] They demanded that either Blakiston be re-tried or his sentence increased. This complaint was an example of where, even after the Supreme Court's establishment, the Law Officers became involved in advising the British government in relation to the international legal and diplomatic side of extra-territoriality for, when Parkes referred the Japanese complaint back to the Foreign Office, it consulted them. The Law Officers rejected both suggestions made by the Japanese authorities as both would be contrary to the spirit of the criminal law as administered in England.[86]

Both cases involved the death of a Japanese individual after a beating by a Briton and the Japanese authorities highlighted the embarrassment allegedly suffered by the victims as a result of the assault which caused them to commit suicide. It is unclear whether Japanese jurisprudence at the time (or subsequently) would have imputed any culpability to Anderson or Blakiston; but, in neither case, was there a sufficient causal link to establish a charge of manslaughter under English law. The time gap between the two incidents illustrates a changed British approach. In the *Anderson case*, Hornby assumed a somewhat lofty attitude and

---

[84] Hornby to Troup, 8 April 1873; FO656/18.

[85] This attitude by Britons was not new. Just after the opening of Nagasaki to trade in 1859, Pemberton Hodgson, the acting Consul, was compelled to complain about British residents occasionally taking the law into their own hands and striking coolies whom they considered to be guilty of theft or other misdemeanours. Hodgson reminded Britons that it was contrary to the law that they should do so and that they should desist. The Japanese authorities had told him that, if the British complained to them, they would punish the Japanese offenders—and have them flogged in the complainant's presence. Circular from Hodgson to the British community in Nagasaki, 5 August 1859; FO796/19.

[86] Law Officers to Derby, 15 January 1875; FO83/2299. The Blakiston trial also highlighted the contemporary practical communications difficulties between the different ports for we see Hannen reporting from Yokohama to Hornby that Parkes had informed him that Hornby's original instructions to Troup with regard to Blakiston's trial, which Hannen confirmed had been duly posted by the Consular constable in time for the Hakodate steamer, had miscarried and not reached Troup in Hakodate and asking Hornby to send duplicate despatches immediately: Hannen to Hornby, 14 May 1873 FO656/37.

implied that the Japanese needed to follow a 'civilized' approach to jurisprudence[87] whereas, in the *Blakiston case*, he was alert to the impropriety of Troup's holding an inquest into Kiroku's death and advised a trial and what he regarded as a substantial fine for the assault. Presumably, the Meiji Restoration, its Westernizing approach and known hostility to extra-territoriality was having an impact upon British officialdom's handling of such incidents.

This impact can be seen in two other well-known cases of alleged bias: the *Archibald King* and the *Normanton* cases, which are described in Chang. In the former case, arising from King's rape of a Japanese girl in Tokyo, local feeling was so strong in Tokyo that Dohmen tried the case summarily rather than delay matters by communicating with Shanghai to obtain an indictment against King (which would have allowed a longer sentence than the twelve months within Dohmen's immediate power when sitting with three Assessors).[88] The *Normanton* case, again, shows a Japanese desire for some recognition of culpability for loss of life. When the *Normanton* sank in 1886 on route from Yokohama to Kobe with the loss of 23 Japanese lives, the Kobe Naval Court's finding that Captain Drake was not responsible for their deaths caused outrage in the Japanese Press, which demanded his prosecution for manslaughter and one of the drowned victim's relatives brought a civil action for damages.[89] The Japanese authorities initiated a prosecution of Drake for manslaughter and he was convicted by a jury in HMCJ and sentenced to three months' imprisonment (described as 'an ample sentence' by the Japanese supported *Japan Weekly Mail*) following which the civil claim was dropped—the plaintiff saying that Captain Drake and his wife had been punished sufficiently.[90]

Cases to enforce the Treaty divide into three broad categories: first, the *bakufu*'s efforts to prevent trading at unopen ports and related gun-running; second, the Japanese government's use of the Treaty in its wider battle against extra-territoriality,[91] which overlapped with the third area, namely enforcement of the Customs and Trade Regulations. Foreigners and foreign trade were concentrated in just three ports so co-ordination between Japanese officials—even informally—would have been relatively

87 Hornby to Flowers, 1 September 1866; FO656/37.
88 Dohmen to Hornby, 19 June 1875; FO656/40.
89 6 and 20 November 1886; JWM.
90 18 December 1886; JWM. See also pages 186–188.
91 Its pressure and activity were not constants but fluctuated—presumably depending upon domestic pressures and priorities.

easy. Whilst the Court records would not evidence Japanese governmental co-ordination of prosecutions to enforce the Treaty, it is difficult to believe that there was no central government involvement for, although prosecutions may have been initiated by local officials, central government became involved when matters were raised to the diplomatic plane.

The British authorities fought a losing battle to prevent Britons breaching the Treaty by gun-running and supporting the insurgency against the *bakufu*. In 1866, Parkes prohibited Britons' aiding and abetting insurgents against the Tycoon by conveying arms supplies and provisions,[92] but this did not stop them. The Meiji government, equally, insisted upon no trading at unopen ports. When, in 1869, the *Helen Black*'s master was charged with trading unlawfully at a port not opened to trade, his defence that everyone else was doing it availed him nought for Hornby convicted him, fined him $1,000 and forfeited his cargo worth $9,000.[93] Of course, what constituted 'trading' was an open question. When the Japanese government prosecuted Scott in 1876 for trading at an Inland town not open to foreign trade, Annersley acquitted him because, although Scott had clearly been at that town and discussed business there, all the evidence showed that the contract had been concluded in Kobe—i.e. within the Treaty limits.[94]

Travel beyond the port limits was another problem area. The *Ansei* treaties prohibited foreigners from travelling within Japan beyond 10 *ri* (approximately 25 miles) from the Treaty Ports themselves. The only exceptions were that consular agents were not subject to this limitation—which led many of the leading traders to seek appointment as honorary consuls for the smaller Powers so as to avail themselves of this exception—and the Japanese government would grant permissions on an individual basis where a foreigner applied through his consulate for permission to travel to the interior. The Treaty stipulated no penalties for breach of the relevant provisions and, usually, defendants were simply ordered back to the ports, admonished not to breach the Treaty in future or fined a nominal fine. In time, a system developed whereby the Japanese authorities granted passports allowing foreigners to travel in the interior and Parkes promulgated regulations in 1868 (updated in 1893 by Maurice

[92] Order made by Parkes in September 1866 applying sections 81 and 94 OC1865 to prevent trading with rebels and to allow the Royal Navy to seize British ships given the state of war which existed between the *bakufu* and the *daimyo* of Nagato and Suwo; FO656/19.

[93] *Japanese Government v. Master and Owner of the Helen Black*, 4 September 1869; JTOM.

[94] *Japanese Government v. John Marshall Scott*, 3 June 1876; HN.

de Bunsen, then *Chargé d'Affaires*, when annual passports became possible) requiring British subjects to produce these passports upon request by Japanese officials and imposing fines of up to $200 for failure. Prosecutions were occasional, inconsistent and, usually, tied into some other objective as when Blakiston and Batchelor were charged with breaching the Treaty limits; in neither case, one suspects, because of the breach *per se*, but for extraneous reasons: in Blakiston's case, his assault on Kiroku and, in Batchelor's case, his support for the Ainus and their culture.[95]

Firearms offences were an issue of public order and, from the beginning, the Japanese attempted to restrict foreigners shooting game or carrrying firearms; attempts which were resented by foreigners who enjoyed shooting and, in the early days, viewed possession of firearms as a protection against attacks by Japanese. Nevertheless, the British authorities attempted to impose some control only to incur the odium of the Press and 'the first important trial in a British Consular Court in Japan'[96] and, it seems, the first prosecution instituted at the instance of the Japanese authorities was *Reg. v. Moss* in 1860 when Moss was prosecuted, at the instance of the Governor of Kanagawa *ken*, for violating Japanese laws and consular regulations by shooting game, resisting Japanese officers in lawful execution of their duty and wounding one of them.[97] This case set the tone for the entire period of a British community antagonistic to control and wishing to carry on as it pleased in defiance of Japanese laws.

In shooting game in November 1860, Moss was following the general practice of many Westerners. In 1859, the Japanese government had objected to the killing of game and the use of firearms within the environs of the Shogun's palace and Britons were ordered[98] to desist pending negotiations between the foreign Ministers and the Japanese government. These negotiations reached no conclusion and, in the Autumn of 1860, Westerners resumed shooting. The Japanese government complained; but its

---

[95] See Hugh Cortazzi, 'Dr. John Batchelor: British Scholar and Friend of the Natives of Hokkaido', *PJS* Vol. 105 (1986), page 20.

[96] 22 December 1860 to 12 December 1861, NCH.

[97] See FO46/30 (which is devoted to just this case) and Alcock, 1863 vol 2, pages 14–17. In the records of the committal proceedings, the case was listed as 'Cause No. 14.' It is unclear whether this was the fourteenth criminal case in Yokohama in 1860 or since the port opened in 1859 or whether it was the fourteenth case—civil and criminal—in 1860 or since 1859. Lowder's report referred to in the Notes on sources in Appendix V would be consistent with its being the fourteenth case—civil or criminal—heard in Yokohama since 1859.

[98] The Consular Notice was framed in the terms of a 'request' but Vyse and Alcock claimed that this was merely a formulation and, in effect, the Notice should be construed as an order; FO46/30, page 101.

remonstrances were lightly regarded and Vyse, then Consul at Yokohama, told the Governor of Kanagawa that he could do nothing unless a defendant and the gun were produced. The insinuation is that Vyse assumed that the Governor would be unable to do so; but, the Governor arranged for 20 police to lie in wait and they arrested Moss as he returned from a day's shooting. In the ensuing scuffle, his gun was fired and wounded a Japanese officer before Moss was detained by the police and prosecuted in the Kanagawa Court presided over by Vyse sitting with three Assessors. The British community sided with Moss; but, despite all three Assessors dissenting,[99] Vyse convicted him, fined him $1,000 (plus costs) and ordered that he be deported.[100] When, as required by OC1860, the sentence went to Alcock for confirmation, he upheld Vyse's decision and punishments but also added three months' imprisonment in Hong Kong to the $1,000 fine—which he ordered be paid to the wounded officer as compensation for his injury.

On arrival in custody in Hong Kong, Moss had a writ of *Habeas Corpus* moved in SCHK which held that Moss must be released because the Hong Kong Magistrates' clerk, when endorsing Vyse's Warrant, had endorsed it by reference to OC1859—which had been repealed—rather than OC1860 (a copy of which had never been received, or published, in Hong Kong). Therefore, the gaol had no authority to hold Moss. Moss then sued Alcock in SCHK and claimed $30,000 in damages for false imprisonment in Japan and Hong Kong. After lengthy debate as to SCHK's jurisdiction to hear the matter, the Chief Justice ruled that, as OC1860 had never been published in Hong Kong, he had no jurisdiction to hear Moss's claim in relation to his imprisonment in Japan or on the ship but only for the 120 hours which Moss had spent incarcerated in the Hong Kong gaol. The jury displayed the traditional attitude of juries on the China Coast when faced with someone in authority and awarded Moss $2,000 damages. In response to a

99 The Assessors' dissents were all slightly different. Edward Clarke agreed that Moss had been shooting and that he had obstructed the Japanese police officers but said that Moss did not know the Japanese law or know that the Japanese were police officers. He also found that Moss had not discharged the shot which had wounded the police officer. Whilst dissenting from the $1,000 fine, he agreed that the deportation order 'though severe was justifiable under the circumstances'. Macpherson took a similar position except that he also dissented from the deportation order whereas the third Assessor, John Ross, was not convinced that there was a Japanese law which forbade shooting game—and said that Moss was only doing what other Westerners were doing. He also disbelieved the Japanese officers' account of the scuffle. FO46/30 pages 96–98.

100 Both Vyse's judgment and Alcock's review were silent as to the place to which Moss should be deported but Vyse's Warrant conveying Moss to Hong Kong specified England as the place of deportation following his gaol term. FO46/30.

question from the Chief Justice, the jury declared that they would have awarded a further $15,000–$20,000 had SCHK also had the jurisdiction to try the claim for Moss's imprisonment in Japan.[101]

The *Moss case* shows the British community in East Asia as something of an 'awkward squad' uncowed by authority and prepared to go to law to defend what it saw as its own interests and subject British officialdom to a barrage of Press criticism. However, the Consuls and local governmental officials needed to tread a line to balance the demands and interests of both sides so that, often, one or other community was affronted and accused the Consuls of favouring the other.

The case was also a precursor to the strict interpretative approach which the Law Officers were to adopt whenever legal questions arose from Japan. When they reviewed the proceedings, the Law Officers advised that the conviction was illegal due to Alcock's failure to have issued Regulations for the Treaty's observance. Therefore, Alcock was obliged to rescind the deportation order and remit the fine.[102] After this, he issued the first Regulations binding upon British subjects, which included $200 fines for firing revolvers.[103]

Britons and guns were a sensitive combination for, in 1873, a repeat of the *Moss case* nearly occurred when Swabey and Cousens were arrested and bound by Japanese policemen for shooting in breach of regulations and pointing their guns at the police. However, this time, after discussions between Dohmen and the local police, the police recognized that they had been wrong to bind the malfeasants and agreed to punish the policemen for doing so but, nevertheless, required the two to be prosecuted.[104]

Unlike China with its 'lie *hongs*',[105] there are only a few instances of Japanese subjects seeking, in co-operation with Britons, to avoid Japanese laws by utilizing the extra-territorial rights of British subjects and the Japanese government resisted all such attempts. The press was the first area. In 1876, John Reddie Black published the *Bankoku Shimbun* in Japanese. As a Briton, he could not be prosecuted by the Japanese authorities for failing to comply with the censorship requirements of the Japanese

101 Smale to Alcock; FO46/30 page 355.

102 It is unclear whether Moss had ever paid the fine or, if he had, whether it had been paid over to the wounded Japanese officer. If it had, there is no report of any amount being reclaimed from that officer.

103 Editorial, 21 December 1861, NCH.

104 Daito Yoshito to Dohmen; FO798/2, page 122.

105 For a discussion on 'lie *hongs*', see Robert Bickers, *The Scramble for China*, (London: Penguin Books, 2011), pages 188–189 and 293.

Press laws. Equally, the British authorities could not prevent him publishing the newspaper or prosecute him because it was not illegal under British law to publish a newspaper—in English or in Japanese. The Japanese authorities adopted a practical approach to prevent circulation of Black's newspaper by making it illegal for Japanese subjects to distribute the newspaper.[106] In order to support the Japanese authorities and prevent extra-territoriality being used to undermine the local authorities, Parkes issued Regulations in support of Japanese laws and prohibited British subjects from publishing newspapers other than in English.[107] In 1890, the Japanese government complained of abuse of extra-territorial privileges when a British owned newspaper published a translation of a long article by a Japanese politician when publication of the original article in a Japanese newspaper had been prohibited by the Japanese authorities. However, its complaint appears not to have been pursued. Another instance was Campbell's oil exchange in 1880. Japanese laws prohibited oil trading exchanges but Campbell established one in his Tokyo premises where the only traders were Japanese. When the Japanese authorities sought to close it down, Satow, as acting Vice-Consul in Tokyo, declined to prosecute as no British law had been broken but he informed Campbell that the Treaty should not be used to aid Japanese subjects in evading Japanese laws[108] and refused to assist Campbell when the Japanese authorities took practical steps to close down the exchange by surrounding his premises and preventing Japanese subjects entering them.[109]

Enforcement of the Customs' and Trade Regulations caused particular difficulty for the British authorities and is an area where accusations of bias or prejudice on the part of the consular judges may be more justified as Consuls often applied their perception of 'fairness' to some prosecutions and tried interpreting the Treaty and Trade Regulations as they wished they had been written. Many of these prosecutions may have been driven by more local considerations or, perhaps, a desire by the local officials to impose their will upon the foreigner; but, even here, some central Japanese government involvement may be seen. The Japanese were

---

[106] Tokyo Vice-Consul to Parkes, 20 January 1876; FO798/25.

[107] Official Notification 8 February 1876; FO798/26. Compare the Japanese authorities' treatment of Black with their apparent lack of action against earlier foreigners who published Japanese language newspapers—presumably because such editors had adopted a pro-regime (*bakufu* or Meiji) attitudes. See Todd S. Munson, *The Periodical Press in Treaty Port Japan: Conflicting Reports from Yokohama, 1861–1870* (Leiden: Global Oriental, 2013) chapters 1 and 2.

[108] Satow to Campbell 26 July 1880; FO798/37.

[109] Campbell to Gubbins 28 August 1880; FO798/9.

perceived to enforce the Trade Regulations rigidly and there are records of over 30 cases. The Trade Regulations allowed the Customs to seal hatches overnight to prevent smuggling and breaking the seals incurred a fixed penalty of $60.[110] On the one hand, Consuls were supportive of Japanese prosecutions of flagrant breaches and enforced the Treaty in clear cases of fraud and potential smuggling as seen by *Reg. ats. Japanese Authorities v. William Ramsey Kennedy*[111] and *Custom House v. Oscar Vidre*[112] when the masters were fined $60 for failing to enter the ship at the Customs within 48 hours of arrival and *Custom House v. Peterson*[113] where the master was fined $60 in respect of broken Customs' seals.

However, where the Courts considered the Customs were being over-zealous in bringing a prosecution, there was a tendency for the Consuls to interpret the Treaty to say what the British wished it had said rather than adopting the Japanese narrow, constructionist approach or, even, to override the Treaty's language by adopting a consideration of 'fairness'. Whilst the Customs' seals cases may have been initiated by local prosecutors, central government must have been, at the least, informed if not consulted (even if it did not take a directing role) in cases of difficulty and may have possibly exercised a degree of central direction in the *Hartley cases*.

The first reported case involving broken Customs' seals was in December 1863 in Nagasaki. Consul Myburgh fined the master of a British schooner $60 and sent the money to the Japanese Customs, all as stipulated in the Treaty. However, the schooner's mate said he had only opened the hatches because, although still dark at 7.00 a.m., boats were alongside and he wanted to trans-ship the cargo without wasting time. He also claimed that Customs officials often did not come on board to unseal the hatches and that no previous complaints had been made. Myburgh asked the Customs to investigate this claim and said it was negligent of the Customs' Officers not to attend promptly to unseal the hatches as the Treaty only authorized their sealing between dusk and dawn.[114]

This was an ongoing source of friction with British complaints that the Customs officers were occasionally slow in going around the ships at dawn to remove the seals. To the British, this was a question of business efficiency. In 1872, when the Japanese authorities at Nagasaki prosecuted the master of the *Oregonian* for landing goods prior to their having been

---

110 Regulation II.

111 Case 23 of 1898; FO796/14.

112 Hakodate, 1878; FO656/49.

113 Hakodate, 1875; FO656/35.

114 Myburgh to Nagasaki Governor, 19 December 1863; FO796/25.

inspected, the master admitted that he had done so but claimed that the Japanese Customs were over four hours late in arriving to inspect the goods. The Consul said that this delay was contrary to Article VII of the Treaty and urged the Customs to use greater efforts to ease business instead of impeding it.[115] On the other hand, there were also clear examples of Britons flouting the rules. James Taylor was convicted by the Nagasaki Consul of landing timber in front of his own house contrary to the local Customs' regulations—despite having been told not to do so by the Japanese Customs. When he said he had been doing this for the last fourteen months, the Consul told him that once he had been told by the Customs not to do so, he should have desisted.[116]

The next year in Kobe, Wilkinson held a master justified in removing the seals when the Customs did not arrive in time to do so. Wilkinson based his decision on the grounds that the Customs' authority under the Trade Regulations to seal the hatches ended at dawn and a master could break the seals after that time. However, in Yokohama, Hannen, despite being satisfied there was no fraudulent intention on the ships' masters' part, decided the contrary and that a master's remedy for the delay in the Customs' unsealing the hatches was an action—in the Japanese courts—against the Customs in negligence. The Japanese government sought to reverse Wilkinson's decisions by raising the matter diplomatically with Parkes who suggested to Hornby that the Consuls needed clear guidance on the Trade Regulations.[117] Hornby—despite Wilkinson's writing him a lengthy memorandum justifying his decision—concurred with Hannen.[118]

This did not end the matter for cases regarding broken customs seals over the hatches continued. A particular problem was that the seals were somewhat flimsy paper seals and were easily broken—even without any ill-will on the part of the ships' crews. In three Nagasaki cases,[119] the result was always the same: the master of the ship was acquitted of having broken the customs seal when the Consul found no fraudulent intention or allegation of smuggling. The Consul urged the need for bigger and stronger seals and suggested that they always be affixed in the presence of the

---

[115] 28 December 1872; *The Nagasaki Express* (**NE**).

[116] *Japanese Customs v. James K. Taylor*; 8 February 1873; NE. Taylor was bound over to keep the Peace for six months in his own surety of $100 and that of another for $100.

[117] Parkes to Hornby, 13 March 1874; FO656/19.

[118] Hornby to Parkes, 26 May 1874; FO656/19.

[119] *Reg. at instance of Japanese authorities v. Master of Induna* 12 March 1875; FO796/28; *Reg. v. captain of Hopewell*, criminal case 1 of 1878; FO796/2 and *Reg. ats. Japanese authorities*, case 16 of 1880; FO796/7.

master. When the *Forward Ho*'s master was prosecuted for having broken the seals, he admitted that they were broken but said he was not amenable to paying any fine because the Lloyds surveyor had told him to break open the hatches to dry the cargo of rice and it was 0930 and long after sunrise. Despite Hornby's earlier interpretation, Annersley acquitted the master and refused to levy a fine because he said the Customs' right to seal the hatches ceased at sunrise, the hatches had been opened due to necessity and no cargo had been removed.[120]

Although many cases suggest an over pedantic application of the rules by local Japanese officials, this was not always the case. In *Japanese Customs House v. Dobson, master of Sunbeam*,[121] the Kobe Consul, when convicting the master, recorded that the Customs had conceded they would not have prosecuted had he produced satisfactory evidence that he had not broken the seals. When Lowder, on behalf of the Customs, prosecuted Captain Crighton of the *Gaucho* for failing to enter his ship with the Customs within the prescribed time, he said the Customs had sent a messenger on board to remind Crighton to do so; but, he had responded that he was too busy.[122]

One avenue which the Japanese authorities followed as they sought to abolish extra-territoriality was a stricter implementation of the *Ansei* treaties: in particular, they sought to tackle opium imports. At the end of 1877, they prosecuted a Yokohama chemist, John Hartley, for illegally importing opium. Wilkinson interpreted the Treaty as not prohibiting the importation of medicinal opium—because, he said, that this must have been the original intention and he noted that the Japanese had included medicinal opium in the list of dutiable goods and allowed its import for several years.[123] However, when Hartley was prosecuted a second time, Wilkinson convicted Hartley of attempted smuggling of 'smoking' or 'non-medicinal' opium and fined him $165 (being $15 a catty as provided in the Trade Regulations).[124]

From the Treaty Ports' first days, anxieties were voiced by the British community about Japanese attempts to restrict what they regarded as normal activities which led the British to fear that extra-territoriality's abolition would lead to unrestricted prosecutions and they pointed to the disputes over shooting and opium. However, other cases which could be

120 *Imperial Japanese Customs v. Edward Ward*; 2 August 1878; HN.
121 6 September 1879; HN.
122 *Imperial Japanese Customs v. Captain Crighton*, 9 September 1876; JDH.
123 Wilkinson to Parkes, 30 March 1878; FO656/49.
124 See also pages 256–257.

argued to support their anxieties do not, on closer examination, do so—particularly after the Meiji restoration and Japanese acceptance of Japan's opening to the wider world. Some arose from simple cultural misunderstandings—or, often, arrogance on the British part. An example of the former was the Japanese wanting to prosecute Dr Faulds, a British medical doctor practising in Tokyo, for dissecting a body;[125] all was resolved when it was found that he had simply conducted a post-mortem on a Japanese and himself paid for the deceased's burial in a Japanese temple.[126] A case of cavalier British action was a Mr Hall's slaughtering a calf at home instead of at the public slaughterhouse; again, the Japanese request for a prosecution was resolved amicably when Hall undertook not to repeat the incident.[127]

The two *Norman* cases[128] in Nagasaki might be argued to support these British anxieties—but, equally, may be cited as examples of Western arrogance towards the Japanese authorities. In both, the Japanese authorities appear to have sought to make a point rather than impose a punishment. In the first, they sought no fine but only a judicial order requiring Norman not to obstruct the police in enforcing Japanese laws and regulations regarding the registration of Japanese subjects—including those working for foreigners.[129] A year later, Norman repeated his contempt for the Japanese authorities by demolishing a notice closing a road pending roadworks. Pleading not guilty to a charge of criminal damage, he claimed that the notice-board was dangerously sited, should have been lit and, somewhat perversely, contained no evidence that it had been authorized by the proper authorities. This case was trivial enough on its facts and a symbolic \$1 fine imposed; but, the Japanese police had made their point. When, in *Japanese Government v. Mansfield*, HMCJ asked the Japanese prosecutor if he wanted a heavy fine imposed on Mansfield for shooting without a licence, the prosecutor left it to the Judge to decide[130]—again suggesting that the principle of compliance was more important than the fine.

The early cases concerning the anti-*bakufu* insurgencies apart, the only case which shows the Japanese prosecuting a Briton for purely domestic

---

[125] Tokyo Vice-Consul to Chiji of Tokio-fu, 29 June 1876; FO798/28.

[126] Tokyo Vice-Consul to Chiji of Tokio-fu, 5 July 1876; FO798/28.

[127] Tokyo Vice-Consul to Kawaji Toshinazu, 16 October 1877; FO798/5.

[128] *Nomaguchi Kenichi v. Arthur Norman* (case 10 of 1883) and *Reg. on the prosecution of the Japanese Authorities v. Arthur Norman* (case 17 of 1884); FO796/7.

[129] When the Japanese had called at Norman's house in order to register his Japanese servants, Norman refused admittance to the police.

[130] 19 January 1881; JG.

Japanese concerns was their 1884 prosecution of Dr John Batchelor,[131] a missionary in Hokkaido, on three charges arising out of a trip beyond the Treaty limits. First, building a house (in reality a temporary hut), second shooting game (to live on) and, finally, having remained outside the limits over the time granted in his passport. All three charges were fig-leaves for, when pressed by the Hakodate Consul, the Japanese prosecutor conceded that the prosecution was brought because of Batchelor's support for the Ainu culture which the Japanese wished to suppress.[132]

British officials ascribed a sinister motive to several Japanese prosecutions in the mid-1870s when it was well-known that the Japanese authorities were seeking to reduce Japan's dependence upon foreign technical instructors. The British suspected them of bringing prosecutions in order to have the defendants deported. When indicting N.A. Smyth for rape, the Supreme Court commented that, but for the known Japanese anxiety to get rid of all Europeans who acted as teachers and supervisors in their public works, little doubt would have been entertained over his guilt.[133] This concern was deep enough for the *Chargé d'Affaires* to try, the following year, to have the Railway Department pay the costs of Westmoreland's deportation after he had been charged with misconduct in employment.[134]

Where a foreigner was involved, the complainant would complain either direct to the Consul or to their own consul and have their consul file a complaint with the British Consul. In practice, though, a complainant often had no choice for Britain was the only country represented in all the ports and many other countries were not represented by their own consul outside Yokohama and, often, the Consul represented several other countries—particularly in Nagasaki. France was represented by Britain in Kobe in 1879 when John Masefield, a sailor from the *John Milton*, killed Aristide Victorin Eugene Desaunais of the French corvette, *Cosmao*. The first step was for Marcus Flowers, as acting French consul, to preside over an official enquiry in Desaunais's death at the British consulate after which Duman-Vence, the *Cosmao*'s commander, charged Masefield with killing Desaunais. At Masefield's committal hearing before Flowers in his capacity as Consul, he admitted having done so but claimed to have acted

131 Cortazzi 1986, page 20.

132 When the Japanese procured an efficient interpreter, Batchelor's reading of the passport was confirmed and he was acquitted of all charges.

133 Supreme Court to Hannen, 2 February 1874; FO656/39.

134 See page 146.

in self-defence. Flowers committed Masefield to stand trial and, meanwhile, removed him to the Municipal goal in Kobe.

Three weeks later, Masefield stood trial on indictment in HMCJ on circuit in Kobe before Wilkinson and a jury. The French consul-general from Yokohama sat on the Bench with Wilkinson and Quin prosecuted on behalf of the Crown. Masefield was unrepresented. It took the jury just ten minutes to convict him of manslaughter for which Wilkinson committed him to two years' gaol in Kobe. However, due to Masefield's youth and a degree of concern for his safety, Wilkinson said he would not be subject to penal servitude.[135]

Convictions and Possible Bias

The semi-annual returns enable us to calculate the proportions of defendants who were wholly acquitted or pleaded (or were found) guilty whereas the Court records and newspaper reports enable us, usually, to ascertain the proportions of guilty and not guilty pleas and divide the latter into convictions and acquittals. Broadly, around a fifth to a quarter of defendants were acquitted of all charges although deviations from this pattern can be seen at different times, in different ports and between different classes of prosecutor.[136] The Yokohama acquittal rate rose from 15% when looking at the semi-annual returns to 18% when considering those cases reported in the newspapers, whereas the Nagasaki acquittal rate of 26% was fairly consistent over time except in 1878—itself the peak year for prosecutions—when over half of all defendants were acquitted.[137] Just as there is no explanation for this peaking of prosecutions, so there is no obvious explanation for the aberration in the acquittal rate. However, within these acquittal rates, we see differences between classes of prosecutor.

Defendants in Nagasaki pleaded guilty to at least one charge in similar proportions when prosecuted by Britons (whether the British authorities or individuals) or the Japanese authorities and the acquittal rates for such prosecutions were also similar (at just under 20%). The striking characteristic is the tendency of defendants to plead not guilty when prosecuted by an individual Japanese or other foreigner—presumably in the hope

[135] 12 and 15 February and 5 March 1879; HN.

[136] Table 9.

[137] Table 11.

(or expectation) that they would win in court, a hope for which the acquittal figures provide some substance as prosecutions by Japanese individuals resulted in a 32% acquittal rate and an even higher 48% acquittal rate for prosecutions by foreigners.[138] In Kobe, the overall acquittal rate dropped from 34% in 1870–1875 (on the basis of the semi-annual returns) to 21% from 1869 to 1899 (on the basis of the newspaper reports). Within the latter figure, the most noticeable characteristic was that just 12% of defendants were acquitted of all charges brought by Japanese individuals.[139]

The greater tendency to plead not guilty when prosecuted by Japanese individuals would seem to support the view that the British community considered itself almost above the law and assumed that they would win against an individual Japanese in court—despite nothing being said in the Courts' judgments that provides any encouragement for this assumption. However, when we consider the results in greater detail, it is difficult to argue that the acquittals were the result of systemic bias.

In Nagasaki, all four prosecutions by Chinese individuals for assault or damage to property were successful. As to prosecutions by other Westerners, the results may simply reflect the nature of the offences (11 prosecutions for drunkenness and disorderly behaviour and 15 for assaults) where the evidence was often conflicting. We must also wonder whether the Kobe figures from the semi-annual returns are exceptional (and reflective of that port's early days). The high acquittal rate partly reflects the large number of individuals' prosecutions which were not pursued[140]—which would support the notion that some prosecutions were merely a means to seek compensation or part of a wider dispute or personal quarrel with less focus on the chances of success. The newspaper reports would suggest that these early figures were an aberration.

A closer examination of the Kobe cases suggests that its results were not out of line with those of other ports. In Kobe, Japanese officials, generally, succeeded in their prosecutions. Five prosecutions involved enforcement of the Trade Regulations in respect of Customs' seals on hatches but all failed due to the Consuls' resistance to what they considered to be an over-zealous enforcement of the rules. Four other prosecutions for breach of Treaty Regulations also failed (albeit another four were successful and

[138] Table 10.
[139] Tables 9 and 10.
[140] Five assault charges were withdrawn, two for misconduct in employment and one each of trespass, breaking down the prison door and making a false declaration.

resulted in heavy fines): again suggesting a British resistance to over-zealous application of the Treaty's restrictive provisions. Leaving these cases aside, only one of the remaining defendants prosecuted by a Japanese was acquitted—after a three day trial.[141] Thus, while the Kobe figures support the view that Consuls reacted against a perceived over-zealous enforcement of the Customs' regulations, they do not support suggestions of a more general anti-Japanese prejudice on the part of the Courts. Further, if we exclude the 14 convictions for non-registration and the two contempt convictions reversed by Hornby, the proportional differences between British and Japanese prosecutions would disappear—although the overall proportion of acquittals in Kobe would be even higher. Conversely, in Hakodate with its much smaller number of criminal cases, the conviction rates show the opposite trend with only four out of 30 defendants prosecuted by the Japanese authorities and Japanese individuals being acquitted;[142]—on a par with the outcome of individual Japanese prosecutions in Kobe as reported in the newspapers.

If we accept a reluctance by the Consuls to convict for technical breaches of the Trade Regulations in the Customs' seals cases and their attitude to medicinal opium as shown in the first *Hartley case*, an examination of the other criminal cases prosecuted by the Japanese authorities or Japanese individuals where the defendants were acquitted of all charges suggests that this reluctance to convict was very much confined to the former cases.

Outside the Customs cases, there were, essentially, three common grounds for acquittals with Japanese inspired prosecutions—and none suggests a more general bias on the Courts' part. The first was that the prosecutor or principal prosecution witness—in most cases, a Japanese individual—did not appear when the case came on before the Court. These cases involved relatively minor assaults or damage and it is fair to assume that a settlement had been reached outside the court; indeed, occasionally, the records record the fact of an agreement and the plaintiff's withdrawing the case. Although there may have been some exaggeration of the damages suffered, most had a genuine basis and may be argued to be little more than compliance with the Treaty whereby 'if a Japanese have reason to complain of a British Subject, the Consul shall no less listen to his complaint, and endeavour to settle it in a friendly manner'.[143]

---

[141] *Reg v. Morris* for issuing counterfeit *kinsatsensu;* FO656/34 (1871 returns).
[142] Table 12.
[143] Article VI.

In a few cases—particularly in the earlier years—it was not a case of the matter having been settled outside the court: the conduct of the Japanese complainants was itself to blame for an acquittal. In 1864 in Nagasaki, Gower arrested a British master for intimidating and assaulting Torikusa, a Japanese Customs Officer, on board his vessel. When Gower convened a Court with two Assessors to hear the case, Torikusa failed to show up until a messenger was sent for him. Then, he failed to bring his witnesses or a proper interpreter despite having been warned to do so. Gower had no option but to discharge the master whereupon Torikusa claimed he was unable to obtain justice. It is unclear whether Torikusa's handling of the matter was due to his ignorance of the procedures for bringing complaints or otherwise. However, the end result was that Gower was so offended by his conduct that he complained to the Governor that he could not allow the lowest coolie to insult him as Torikusa had done and demanded that the Governor punish Torikusa and ensure that Torikusa never appeared at the Consulate again![144]

Another common cause of acquittals was lack of reliable identification. There are a number of cases—usually involving general scrummages and/or assaults on *jinrikisha* coolies or damage to their *jinrikisha*—where there is total confusion over which foreigners were involved and the coolies all swore that the defendant was the guilty party only for the relevant warship's log book to show the defendant was on board at the relevant time.[145] An extreme case of mis-identification was the prosecution of F.H. Sanders in Kobe where all four Japanese witnesses gave different evidence: the prosecutor identified the defendant, the second said it was a ginger-haired man and the other two agreed but said it was not the defendant, who then produced evidence that he had been at a meeting with the former Governor of Kobe at the time of the alleged incident.[146]

Another form of mis-identification was nationality. This was a continual problem for both the Japanese and the British authorities. Dohmen explained[147] that the Japanese authorities often lodged a complaint with

144 Gower to Nagasaki Governor, 3 November 1864; FO796/25.

145 *Hirota Omakichi v. John Woodward*, case 21 of 1879; FO796/2 and *Reg. v. Cooper and Jenkins* (both of *HMS Leander*), cases 16 and 17, 1895; FO796/14 are examples of this.

146 *Reg. v. F.H. Sanders*, 23 July 1870; HN. The case was brought by Sanders' landlord who, it transpired, wanted Sanders imprisoned so he could terminate the lease which prohibited the landlord from building in front of the property rented by Sanders. In Court, Gower expressed disapprobriation of the Japanese land officer who had appeared in support of the prosecutor's attempt to cancel the land lease.

147 Dohmen to Daito Yoshito, 16 April 1873; FO798/1.

him only for him to find that the alleged miscreant had been identified as British when he was American or neither. Such cases would not appear in the Court figures as they would never proceed beyond the initial complaint.

Finally (and equally applicable to British prosecutions), the evidence could be conflicting and contradictory or certain witnesses were stated to be preferable to other witnesses. There is nothing strange about this and there is no evidence that the Courts had an anti-Japanese bias in this regard. For instance, when two Japanese small boat owners claimed for damage caused by HMS *Daphne*'s crashing into their boats, the Court recorded the evidence as being conflicting but found for the plaintiffs.[148] When Aston convicted the first and second engineers from the *Kokonoye-maru* of assaulting a Japanese oiler on board that vessel, he said that there could no doubt that a very serious assault had been committed but conceded that the evidence was very contradictory. In view of this, he refused to allow the Japanese witnesses their expenses or the prosecutor his hospital costs.[149] However, in another case, Playfair, as Vice-Consul in Kobe, considered the prosecution's evidence to be too contradictory 'to induce one to believe that the affair could have happened as the Japanese prosecution had claimed.' The first prosecution witness had been vague whilst the evidence of the next two was diametrically opposed to that of the first.[150] Another example of the Japanese prosecution's witnesses failing to back up the claim occurred when a Japanese policeman accused a sailor from HMS *Frolic* of assaulting him by seizing his sword and slashing his legs. It was agreed that the sailor had, for some unknown reason, tried to draw the sword but had not used it as alleged and there was no evidence of malice on his part.[151]

A scrummage on the *Pathan* led to cases in both the Kobe Court and the local Japanese court. Four Japanese sailors prosecuted the mate, the third engineer, the bosun and two Chinese quartermasters for assault. Whilst Hall concluded that there had been a scrummage he acquitted all five defendants after a two day trial: the two Chinese had been acting under

---

[148] *Murakami Shujiro and Okano Otomatsu v. George MacArthur R.N., commanding HMS Daphne*, case 2 of 1883; FO796/8.

[149] *Kumitaro Yataro v. Mathews and Scott*; 14 June 1880; HN.

[150] Frederick da Sylva and Victor Thompson were acquitted whilst the third defendant had fled the port. Interestingly, da Sylva was represented by Crosse whereas Thompson was unrepresented; 24 July 1897; KWC.

[151] The sailor was sentenced to 10 days imprisonment for trying to draw the sword: *Reg.* (*ats. Arima Gunzi v. John Luke*; 8 May 1878; HN.

orders and the mate acted entirely in self-defence. He said that the Chief Engineer had really been responsible for the scrimmage but he had not been prosecuted. In noting that one of the Japanese prosecutors had been acquitted by the local Japanese court in relation to the same affray, he observed that if everyone stood on their legal rights Society could not carry on. Hall had clearly been striving for a practical result.[152]

With British official prosecutions, acquittals usually came down to a question of evidence and we see Wilkinson directing the jury to acquit in a charge of obtaining goods by false pretences in *Reg. v. Edwards.*[153]

There is no explanation for the generally higher acquittal rate in the case of individual Japanese prosecutions as against those by the Japanese authorities; it may be that the authorities only prosecuted those cases where they considered there was a reasonable chance of conviction. The similarity in acquittal rates for Japanese official and British prosecutions suggests that Japanese official prosecutions were not brought on an unwarranted basis or on an overly aggressive approach and the actuality of prosecutions and associated conviction rates did not support the British community's fears of an over-zealous Japanese prosecution policy. A further point (but one which cannot be proved) to mitigate these fears would have been any inhibition felt by the Japanese police over the need to prove their cases in a foreign court so they only prosecuted those cases where the evidence was clear. Whilst Consuls had a reciprocal disdain for many of the merchant class and little sympathy for the 'rowdy class', they did not shy away from criticism of what they perceived to be unmeritorious prosecutions as seen in the Customs' seals cases or where damages claims were patently exaggerated or when Troup criticized a Japanese prosecution for being badly prepared.[154]

The Consuls were attuned to the need for strict impartiality and resisted pressures from the British community for acquittals even when the Assessors wished to acquit, as in the *Moss* and the *Archibald King* cases. They were also sensitive to Japanese concerns of the need to protect Japanese subjects—as the *Cousens* case shows.[155] In *Japanese Police v.*

152 16 April 1898; HN. A Japanese procurator had watched the proceedings on behalf of the Japanese prosecutors and through Hobart Hampden (the Student Interpreter) had cross-examined various witnesses on their behalf. Crosse had appeared for the defendants but Hall encouraged him not to address the Court at the end of the hearing as none of the prosecutors could speak English and would be unable to do so.

153 1 October 1898; JWM.

154 *Japanese Police v. Gullard*, 18 November 1893; JWM.

155 See page 138.

Barber Field, when the Crown Prosecutor entered a *nolle prosequi* on a charge of arson, Jamieson, the acting Judge, made a point of explaining to the many Japanese officials in court that he agreed with this action as the technical requirements of the charge could not be proved but, despite acquitting Field of assaulting a policeman following a two day trial, he bound Field over in his own bond of $2,000 and two bonds from sureties for $1,000, saying it was the least he could do for the Japanese.[156] As Field was unable to produce the security, he was gaoled for six months.

Consuls were also scrupulous towards the Japanese in procedural terms and Court minutes of cases involving Japanese—particularly cases brought by the Japanese authorities—tend to be more extensive than in other cases. One may surmise that this arose from a concern about possible appeals and/or diplomatic complaints where the need to demonstrate due process would be important. It is clear, however, that complaints about court procedures were not confined to the Japanese for Captain Hewett of HMS *Argus* complained to the Minister in 1866 about the proceedings at the trial in the Nagasaki Court of several sailors from that ship. Annersley wrote a lengthy memorandum to the Minister to refute the complaints and added that he had exercised the utmost patience in not convicting the sailors' defending Lieutenant of contempt.[157]

As for jury trials, all were conducted by the Judge or the Assistant Judge and prosecuted by British officials or barristers appointed by the Law Secretary (or, from 1879, the Crown Advocate or Crown Prosecutor). If anything, jurors exhibited a wish to avoid decisions and tried returning verdicts such as 'not proven' or 'guilty but provoked' only to be directed that such verdicts were unknown to English law and they must decide guilty or not guilty.[158] They also showed the same tendency as juries in England not to convict in murder cases: only Edith Carew was convicted of murder; other defendants were always acquitted of the murder charge and, where applicable, convicted of manslaughter. The 32 reported criminal jury trials between 1871 and 1898 had the same 20% acquittal rate as non-jury trials in Yokohama. Although three out of seven defendants prosecuted at the instance of Japanese were acquitted as against just two out of fourteen prosecuted at the instance of Britons and one out of seven in the case of prosecutions by foreigners, the small numbers involved

156 23 June 1888; JWM.

157 Annersley to Legation, 8 December 1866; FO796/27.

158 *Reg. v. Suliman*, 10 November 1877; JDH and *Reg. v. Mariano Blanco*, 11 April 1885; JWM.

magnify the apparent proportional differences. A reading of the case reports, however, suggests no general, inherent bias by juries against the Japanese in these cases. In *Reg. v. Bolton, Moor & Hobbs*, only one of three defendants was acquitted on a charge of burglary and assault—which suggests that the jury's split decision reflected the evidence.[159] The only two Japanese instigated prosecutions which raise questions about the juries' impartiality were the two rape trials, *Reg. v. Smyth*[160] and *Sono v. Daniel Robertson*,[161] where Wilkinson acted as prosecutor in both.

Smyth, accused of raping a lighthouse-keeper's wife, was acquitted after a two day trial. Dickins, defence counsel, attacked the character of the victim and the chief female witness before appealing to the jury's 'experience of the Japanese character and customs for the measure of the offence charged'[162] but Hannen disagreed and directed the jury 'to act more wisely in referring the question to their experience of human nature generally'.[163] In the other case, after the jury acquitted on the rape charge, Wilkinson withdrew the associated assault charge—with which Hannen concurred, therefore suggesting that the jury did not acquit without some justification. Rapes are often difficult cases involving uncorroborated evidence on both sides where much depends upon intention and subjective belief. It is, therefore, difficult to express a clear view on the justice of either acquittal. However, it was not for want of the British authorities prosecuting them or taking the allegations seriously for Parkes and Satow were accommodated on the Bench in the *Smyth case*.[164]

Dickins' attack on the witnesses's credibility was not unique and there is evidence of a racial stereotyping amongst Westerners which seemed to favour Western witnesses.[165] In *Reg. v. Chun Pat*, even the Crown Prosecutor, Litchfield, told the jury that it 'would have to take into consideration European officers' evidence and what reliance to place upon Chinese witnesses' evidence';[166] but, the jury nonetheless accepted Chun Pat's claim that he acted in self-defence and acquitted him of manslaughter. Although individual jurors may have wished to avoid convicting someone they

[159] 24 August 1872; JWM.
[160] 24 January 1874; *Japan Mail*.
[161] 4 April 1874; JWM.
[162] Ibid.
[163] Ibid.
[164] 20 December 1873 and 21 February 1874; JWM.
[165] In reverse, a leading Japanese barrister argued in a Tokyo court that foreigners outside the Settlements could claim no protection under Japanese law because 'beasts and hairy animals were not provided for under Japanese laws'. 14 March 1894; TRS&NE.
[166] 11 January 1896; JWM.

might have known—and failed to appear to answer the jury summons (and paid the $50 fine for doing so)—one must assume that the juries acted impartially for there is no evidence of any Press criticisms or any complaints from the Japanese authorities about these acquittals.

Although the Kobe figures appear not to raise any questions as to the Assessors' impartiality, this cannot always be said of all cases involving Assessors. Only a small number of cases involved Assessors so any assessment of their partiality must be based, necessarily, on this small sample. Of the seven Kobe cases heard with Assessors and reported in the newspapers, four were heard with just two Assessors, two with three and one—very unusually—with four. In no case was any note of dissent by an Assessor recorded and the results are evenly balanced. Three cases resulted in convictions, three in acquittals and the seventh[167] in a conviction on one charge and an acquittal on the other. Of the two prosecutions at the instance of a Japanese, one resulted in a conviction and the other in an acquittal.

Elsewhere, in the *Moss* and the *Archibald King* cases, both of which involved Japanese victims, all the Assessors disagreed with the Consul's conviction and clearly suggest partiality on the Assessors' part.[168] The Assessors' disagreement in these cases contrasts with their complete agreement with the Consul in convicting a Briton in two other cases. Only one reported case involving Assessors led to divided opinions amongst the Assessors. This was *Reg. v. Oastler & Mighton*[169] where one Assessor wished to convict the defendant of assault upon a Chinese when the other two and the Consul were for acquittal.

In only two cases involving a Japanese prosecution did the Consul agree with the Assessors upon an acquittal. The first was the Japanese prosecution, before Winchester and two Assessors, of three Britons for wounding a Japanese.[170] One defendant objected to an Assessor but Winchester held that he had no right to do so as Assessors were not jurors. Much evidence

[167] Captain Drummond of the *Kumamoto maru* prosecuted his freight clerk for stealing two bags of sugar and several slabs of copper. The defendant was convicted of the former but not the latter. Aston, when sentencing the defendant to two months' imprisonment in the Municipal Gaol said the sentence would have been heavier but for the loose way in which all dealings with the vessel's cargo seemed to have been handled. 8 August 1888; HN.

[168] In the *Archibald King case*, one Assessor even agreed that the chief defence witness was 'totally untrustworthy'. but, nevertheless, wished to acquit; Dohmen to Hornby, 19 June 1875; FO656/40.

[169] 23 August 1869; JTOM.

[170] *Reg. ats. Governor of Kanagawa v. Tatham, Davies and Davies*; 12 September 1863; TJH.

was submitted but the Japanese evidence was uncorroborated so the defendants were acquitted. The case turned much upon language difficulties, cultural misunderstandings and the defendants' seemingly genuine belief that they were acting in self-defence. Afterwards, Winchester made it clear that every opportunity had been give to the Japanese authorities to bring forward evidence because it was important that the Japanese could obtain justice in the Courts as the British authorities had been making demands upon them for satisfaction of injuries suffered by Britons. The second case involved the prosecution of Albert Morris before Gower and two Assessors in Kobe for forgery and passing false *kinsatsensu*. Cruchley appeared for the defendant and the Consul and the two Assessors all agreed to acquit the defendant.[171]

Thus, even where inconsistent figures in conviction rates could raise questions about possible bias, we find other explanations for the differences and, certain Customs cases apart, there is little evidence to support more generalized claims of institutional bias by the Courts in criminal cases.

Punishments

Fines were the most common punishment followed by varying terms of imprisonment and both—particularly where the prosecutor was Japanese—were often linked to the payment of damages to the injured Japanese individual.[172] Occasionally, offenders in public order cases were bound over (usually in their own recognizances and those of two others) or deportation would be included in the overall sentence. Fines and confiscations ordered for breaches of the Treaty or Trade Regulations belonged to the Japanese government,[173] but, otherwise, accrued to the Crown. The following analysis ignores the fixed fines under the Treaty.

In Nagasaki, of the 166 guilty pleas or findings from 1875 to 1899, 88 resulted in fines, 42 in imprisonment and 25 in a binding over, an order to pay damages or to serve the remainder of the sentence in solitary confinement

---

171 *Reg. v. Albert Morris*; 16 September 1871:HN.

172 Table 13.

173 Article XIX, Treaty. The fines specified were: $60 for neglecting to register a ship with the Customs and $15 for any error in the manifest (Regulation I), $1,000 for trading at an unopen port (plus forfeiture of all illegally landed goods), $15 per catty (approximately 22 ounces) for smuggled opium and $60 for breaking the Customs seals (Regulation II); $125 for a false declaration to defraud the Japanese Revenue (Regulation V); and the forfeiture of all unrecorded exported goods (Regulation III).

or re-deportation.[174] The 23 fines imposed on defendants where the prosecutor was British ranged from $1 to $30 with the most usual fine being $5 although an exceptional $100 fine was imposed in lieu of a heavy prison sentence upon an offender after being convicted for the third time of keeping a disorderly house and harbouring prostitutes but who was known to be dying.[175] The 53 fines levied in Japanese prosecutions show a similar range with 42 in the $1–5 range,[176] although Chisholm was fined $100 in 1873 for a 'brutal assault' on a Japanese but half was 'to go as compensation to the sufferer'.[177] Where a defendant had no means to pay the fine, prison terms were often set as an alternative (roughly, at the rate of one day for each $1) and, in Nagasaki, a third (28 out of 87) of fined offenders faced this alternative.

When Gower convicted James Mackintosh, a lighthouse-keeper in the employ of the Japanese government, of assault and being drunk on duty, he fined him $50 and explained to the Japanese government representatives in Court that, although the fine was 'relatively light', Mackintosh's loss of his employment was a heavy penalty which he must suffer. Gower went on to admonish him for placing everyone at the Board of Trade and the British government—who had placed him in his job—in an 'unpleasant position'.[178]

Occasionally, fines that would otherwise have accrued to the British government were appropriated for the benefit of the defendant—especially where serious injury had been occasioned. When Joseph Mooney, the master of the *Hellespont*, injured a Japanese boy by shooting him in the knee in 1863, he was fined $500. Alcock authorized the Consul to appropriate the fine for the boy's benefit but, instead of paying the monies to the boy's parents 'who would probably spend it,' Myburgh invested the sum with a British merchant at Ora on 12% per annum to yield $5 per month for the boy's maintenance until he came of age when the whole sum would be transferred to him.[179]

54 prison terms were imposed in Nagasaki, 20 following British prosecutions and 32 Japanese—of the latter, all but one were awarded in

[174] Some defendants faced several charges but punishments were not attributed to particular charges.

[175] *Reg. v. Thomas Bozer*, criminal case 11, 1880; FO796/2.

[176] For assaults, drunken behaviour and trying to spring a friend from the Japanese prison.

[177] 3 April 1874; NCH.

[178] *Reg. v. James Mackintosh*; 9 August 1875; HN.

[179] Myburgh to Governor of Nagasaki, 5 March 1864; FO796/25.

response to official prosecutions and reflected the trend where the more serious Japanese prosecutions were handled by the Japanese authorities. Of the prison sentences imposed where the prosecutor was British, sentences ranged from seven terms of seven days or less through six of 14–28 days and just two terms of three months. Unlike a number of the shipping offences, none was ordered to be served in the Japanese prison and only three (one of three months, one of a month and one of seven days) were ordered to be with hard labour. Prison sentences following Japanese prosecutions followed a similar pattern with seven for seven days or less, and nine for 15–28 days (including in the case of the individual prosecution).

A feature that is not uncommon in the newspaper reports of prison sentences in Kobe is that the first week (or couple of days if the sentence were under a week) was expressed to be 'on bread and water' or a 'low diet'. In Nagasaki a similar restriction limiting the prisoner's diet to 'rice and water'[180] was only mentioned in a couple of shipping offence cases and in no criminal cases. Nothing in the reports of cases in Yokohama suggests a similarly restricted diet there but *The Hiogo News*, in an editorial comment in relation to a shipping offence, mentioned 'so as to remove the not uncommon view that the municipal gaol is a kind of luxurious retreat ... that offenders imprisoned from the British Court pass the first 10 days of their sentence on bread and water.'[181] It is unclear whether such a standard regime was applied to all British prisoners in Japan or only to those in Kobe.

These sentences are consistent with those seen elsewhere and the short prison terms reflect the Consuls' limited sentencing powers in summary cases. With the smaller fines and shorter gaol terms, an order to pay damages and responsibility to pay the court costs (usually $1.50) represented a significant additional burden upon convicted defendants—and two in Nagasaki were also required to pay the costs of their imprisonment. In Kobe, the requirement to pay for their own prison costs appears, from the newspaper reports, to have been a more common requirement—particularly in relation to shipping offences where it was easy (and practical) for the Courts to order that these costs be deducted from the sailors' future wages. Even at this lower level of offences, the Courts took account of a defendant's means to determine the punishment particularly when balancing the conflicting pressures on them from a foreign community which assumed that Westerners could treat the locals with impunity

180 Case heard 15 October 1877; FO796/2.
181 Editorial comment on *Master of ss Birker v. Edward Edmond*; 3 March 1885; HN.

against the need to demonstrate to the Japanese authorities—and local population—that the British judicial system would control the British population and prevent (and punish) abuse of local Japanese inhabitants. A case in point was Arthur Cousens's conviction for assaulting a Japanese *scindo* (boatman) in 1872.[182]

As Cousens's boat was approaching the Kobe to Yokohama steamer, the consular launch (carrying R.G. Watson, Gower, the Kobe Consul, and Wilkinson) nosed ahead whereupon Cousens struck its *scindo* twice in the face with a piece of matting (despite having been warned by Wilkinson to desist after the first blow) for which Wilkinson charged him with assault and Gower awarded two days' imprisonment because he felt that Cousens's friends would simply pay any fine for him and Cousens would laugh it off—as he showed when, in Court, he admitted the assault but still pleaded not guilty.[183] The imprisonment of Cousens outraged the Western community which memorialized Watson, to complain. Watson, in dismissing the memorial, made the point that it was the Queen who prosecuted—not the *scindo*—and this was not the first occasion on which Cousens had laid himself open to arrest by his violent conduct towards Japanese.[184] Hornby confirmed that, where a defendant's friends were likely to pay the fine, he never provided the option of a fine but always gaoled the offender. Had Wilkinson ignored Cousens's conduct, Hornby doubted 'whether it would have raised the Consular character either in the estimation of the Boatman or of his countrymen or of his native authorities who would certainly have been informed'.[185]

Although the Yokohama Court and HMCJ had greater sentencing powers, the majority of their sentences reflected the relatively minor nature of most cases before them with only 64 offenders in total (about two a year on average) sentenced to over a month's imprisonment and only 12 to over a year.[186] Especially where sailors were involved, the majority of gaol

---

[182] *Reg. v. Cousens*; FO656/41.

[183] Although Gower had witnessed the incident, the prosecution was brought by Wilkinson. Gower relied only upon the evidence adduced by Wilkinson in order to convict Cousens and did not take account of his own witnessing the incident: Watson to Hornby, 6 October 1872; FO656/19.

[184] Ibid. See page 119 for when Cousens was charged, along with Swabey, for breach of the shooting regulations.

[185] Hornby to Watson, 30 October 1872; FO656/19. Alcock said that he had imposed the prison sentence upon Moss for the same reason: namely, the Western community had announced that it would raise a subscription to pay Moss's $1,000 fine and so, effectively, Moss would be going unpunished; Alcock, 1863, page 16.

[186] Table 13.

terms longer than a week given in Yokohama involved hard labour, which seems to have involved chores such as cleaning the prison and consulate, and only one sentence was recorded as being 'on a low diet'.[187] In Kobe and Nagasaki, just under half of prison sentences were expressed to be with hard labour. The only death sentence imposed was that imposed upon Edith Carew. The longest prison sentences were five years given to Joseph Hardnett and Cuthbert for manslaughter of the *Sakata maru*'s Japanese quartermaster[188] and a shipmate respectively.[189] In 1875, following fraud and robbery at the Yokohama branch of the Comptoir d'Escompte de Paris, Adds was sentenced to two years with hard labour[190] and, in 1881, Marston received the same sentence for rape.[191]

Although it might appear that a defendant who was merely bound over had escaped lightly, this was not always the case. The sentence was a guard for the defendant's future good behaviour. When James Budd was convicted of assault and battery upon a Japanese, he was not only sentenced to one month in prison but the Consul forfeited the sureties which he had been obliged to put up just a month earlier in relation to a similar offence.[192] Even defendants who were acquitted were warned as to their future behaviour—even if not bound over formally. Johnson was acquitted of stabbing a Portuguese subject (because the prosecutor's story was not borne out by the witnesses), but the Court nonetheless warned him that, as it was the second time he had appeared before it, he should be careful not to be summoned a third time.[193]

Gaols

Four classes of gaol were available to the Courts: the local consulate gaols, the British gaol at Yokohama, local Japanese gaols and Victoria Gaol in Hong Kong.

Except in Yokohama, the consular gaol was little more than a lock-up facility under the consular constable's supervision. Longford described the Tokyo Vice-Consulate's gaol as a small lock-up in the corner of the

---

187 22 September 1865; *Japan Times*.

188 *Japanese Police v. Hardnett*. September and October 1889; JG.

189 24 December 1897; NCH.

190 3 March 1875; NCH.

191 27 September 1881; NCH.

192 Budd had put up ¥50 and two others had put up ¥25 each. All were forfeit: *Katashiro v. James John Budd*; 23 April 1898; KWC.

193 11 March 1871; HN.

stables which should never be used for more than one night in any one individual case.[194] He believed that the Tokyo lock-up had never been used as a gaol and that prisoners were always transferred from Tokyo to the British gaol at Yokohama under the Judge's Warrant—although the Tokyo Vice-Consulate was charged their costs. The consular gaols were suitable for short sentences but Hornby considered their great fault was that 'they are not places of punishment and that consequently they are by no means unpopular places of retreat'.[195] They certainly were not secure given that several prosecutions were for passing alcohol to friends inside them and/or escapes. In the more minor cases, class attitudes came into play with several instances of prisoners of a 'better class' outside Yokohama being lodged within the consulate instead of the consular gaol[196]—although Dr Kerr 'went into a violent fit' when sentenced to a week's imprisonment in Yokohama for breaking into a rival doctor's home.[197] Convicted defendants in the out-ports with longer sentences were transferred to Yokohama or held in the local Japanese gaols.

Yokohama had the only purpose-built European style British gaol in Japan and other countries also used it on payment of a fee. We have little information about this gaol but a glimpse as to its running costs can be seen by Wilkinson's report for the last quarter of 1878 when he reported direct costs in relation to the prisoners of nearly £32 ($173) for the quarter—broken down into the following expenses:[198]

	£		$
	(£sd)	£p	
Subsistence for prisoners	20/-/3	20.01	102.30
Clothing for prisoners	1/15/8	1.78	19.10
Medicine for prisoners	2/4/8	2.23	11.35
Contingencies	7/18/10	7.94	40.50

194 Longford to Plunkett, 1 July 1885; FO262/536.

195 Hornby to Gower, 3 October 1872; FO656/18.

196 For example, Fawcett's being allowed his liberty in Nagasaki pending his return to Yantai. Even though Cousens was gaoled for two days in Kobe (see page 138), the consular constable resigned rather than carry out the sentence by confining Cousens to the local Japanese prison. When the Consul sent for a Western doctor, the doctor certified that the local Japanese prison was unfit for the reception of a foreigner so that, as the Kobe Municipal Council refused to have Cousens in its lock-up, he was confined within a room at the Consulate; 14 September 1872, NCH.

197 14 October 1871; JWM.

198 Wilkinson to Salisbury, 18 July 1878; FO46/234.

Imprisoning British subjects in Japanese gaols was controversial but had been undertaken from the beginning. In Nagasaki, different Japanese gaols were used for different purposes: the gaol at Sagaramatsu for imprisonment overnight; the gaol at Kinbauscio for terms of up to ten days and Nakuramatsu gaol for longer periods of imprisonment.[199] Of course, the British were obliged to re-imburse the Japanese authorities the costs of housing British prisoners. In 1863, the Nagasaki Consul refused a Japanese request to pay a fixed fee of 12 *tempos* per day in respect of maintenance expenses of every Briton held in a Japanese gaol. He agreed to reimburse the Japanese the actual expenses—which should be not more than ten or 11 *tempos* a day except in unusual circumstances when they might be up to 12 *tempos* a day.[200]

The British community disliked the idea of Westerners being incarcerated in Japanese gaols for they were often unhealthy and dirty places but the Foreign Office[201] supported Hornby when he argued that if British subjects, despite repeated warnings and punishments, continued to maltreat Japanese subjects, they could not expect the government to build prisons for them or employ constables to watch over them in local prisons.[202] Noble's death in the Japanese gaol at Osaka resulted in official consideration (and a good description) of Japanese gaols. In August 1872, after being sentenced to seven days imprisonment—to be served in the Japanese gaol in Osaka—for his second offence of assault that year, he died there. Although the Inquest attributed his death to apoplexy,[203] the Western community complained about the confinement of a European in a Japanese gaol. Gower reported that nothing had led him or the Inquest jury to think that Noble had suffered from ill treatment or neglect.

Hornby subsequently described the Osaka gaol facility for Europeans as consisting of two cells placed within an ordinary Japanese house built in a compound abutting the main road within the Foreign Settlement. Like all Japanese prisons, the cells were built like cages of wood—but had ample accommodation and the drainage was good. They were so clean that no one could object to having his dinner or bed laid down on the bare boards and prisoners were allowed Japanese mats, similar to those in country

199 Gower to Governor of Nagasaki, 9 August 1865; FO796/25.

200 Schmid (a Dutch Interpreter at the Nagasaki consulate) to Chief of Police, 30 October 1863; FO796/25.

201 Granville to Hornby, 7 January 1873; FO17/660.

202 Hornby to Gower, 3 October 1872; FO656/18.

203 Gower to Hornby, 19 August 1872; FO656/34.

tea-houses, on which to sleep.[204] This was clearly the exception for Gower compared it with Japanese gaols at the other ports and said he had 'never seen one better kept'.[205] Hornby described the Nagasaki gaol as 'utterly unfit to confine a dog in'[206] before suggesting the Japanese authorities replace it with a new prison and three or four rooms like Osaka for foreigners.[207] There is no evidence that any immediate steps were taken by the Japanese for Japanese gaols remained an issue right to the end of extra-territoriality—although, in 1893, Hugh Fraser, the Minister, reported that no exception could be taken to the treatment of prisoners in Japan.[208] Hall described the new Himeji gaol in 1898 as having solid wall partitions instead of the usual bamboo cages and said it was to be warmed in Winter by hot water pipes. Without greater explanation, he described its cloacal arrangements as an improvement on those generally in use. Nevertheless, the gaol governor conceded that changes to prisoners' clothing and diet would be indispensible to suit the needs of foreigners, who also could not be expected to be confined five to a cell—Hall said three would be more reasonable. Unconvicted prisoners had a cell to themselves.[209]

Consuls had no powers to order the removal of a prisoner outside of their consular provinces. Prior to HMCJ's establishment, prisoners from Japan could be transferred to China or Hong Kong with the Judge's authority; but, after HMCJ's establishment, this was no longer possible as OC1878 removed the Chief Justice's power in relation to prisoners in Japan and restricted the Judge's power to removal of prisoners within Japan or to Hong Kong (but not to China). This was highlighted in 1879 when Troup, the Nagasaki Consul, removed George Wilson from Nagasaki to Shanghai to serve the remainder of his 12 weeks sentence after Troup discovered that the Japanese authorities were using the Japanese gaol in which Wilson was incarcerated as a cholera hospital and all British prisoners there were in danger of infection.[210] Wilkinson (then acting Assistant Judge in Shanghai), despite recognizing the difficult position in which Troup had been placed, freed Wilson upon arrival at Shanghai because his removal

204 Hornby to Watson, 30 October 1872; FO656/19.
205 Gower to Hornby, 19 August 1872; FO656/34.
206 Hornby to Watson, 30 October 1872; FO656/19.
207 Ibid.
208 Memorandum, 17 July 1893; FO881/6417.
209 Hall to Satow, 26 February 1898; FO262/786.
210 Troup to French, 19 August 1879; FO656/42.

had no legal basis.[211] Apart from these unusual circumstances, there is no evidence that the power to remove prisoners from Japan to China had been exercised previously and the change in OC1878 was of no practical significance.

The only instance where a removal within Japan is referred to was when Hall and two Assessors convicted Edward Mackay of obtaining ¥150 of cash and goods by false pretences and sentenced him to 12 months with hard labour. Hall, when pronouncing sentence in Kobe, said that in view of its length, he would apply to Wilkinson for Mackay's transfer to Yokohama.[212] This does suggest that the consular gaols in the out-ports were usually used for shorter sentences—although as mentioned earlier Wilkinson ordered Masefield's incarceration in the Kobe Municipal gaol for two years.

Transfers from Japan to the Victoria Gaol had several motivations. Mere convenience was not an adequate reason for Hornby refused Myburgh's application to transfer three prisoners to Hong Kong in 1867 because the Hong Kong authorities had no wish to be burdened with prisoners except in case of 'urgent necessity'[213] such as those arising 'from the absence of prison accommodation for those of a dangerous character'.[214] Some transfers were to remove individuals whose presence had become an embarrassment to the British authorities or whose presence offended the Japanese authorities as when Moss and the convicted defendants in the *Ainu bones* case were transferred to Hong Kong.[215] O-Sing was transferred in 1870[216] but whether because he was a Hong Kong native, for security reasons or as a means, other than deportation, of removing a trouble-maker from Japan is unclear. Edith Carew was another prisoner removed to Hong Kong; in her case, three factors came into play: embarrassment and a desire to remove her from Japan; the absence of facilities

---

211 Wilkinson to Troup, 3 September 1879; FO656/18. Presumably, Troup sent Wilson to Shanghai because he wanted Wilson removed from Japan in any event or shipping may have been more immediately available.

212 *Inouye Mankichi of the Yaomi Hotel v. Edward Allan Wallace Mackay*; 25 April 1898; KWC.

213 Hornby to Myburgh, 14 December 1867; FO656/34.

214 Ibid.

215 Alcock had also highlighted the question of Moss's safety as a reason for his deportation. Alcock had wished both to protect Moss from any possible assault by Japanese officials and to remove a source of potential trouble to the British community from Japanese anger should Moss remain in Japan. Alcock, 1863, page 16.

216 Hornby to Lowder, 19 April 1870; FO656/18.

for female prisoners in the Yokohama Gaol;[217] and the forthcoming end of extra-territoriality (which also meant that other offenders, such as Cuthbert and Leopold, whose gaol terms would not expire before August 1899, were also ordered to serve their sentences in Hong Kong). Prisoners removed from Japan to Victoria Gaol, nevertheless, remained the Minister's responsibility: not only were their associated costs attributed to the Tokyo Legation[218] but he retained the power to remit their sentences.

Effecting a transfer from Japan to Hong Kong was sometimes easier ordered than implemented. In 1865, Gower wished to transfer 11 prisoners to the gaol in Hong Kong as there was 'no consular gaol' in Nagasaki. He tried to arrange for the master of the *Mary Mildred*, Capt. Fine, to convey the prisoners to Hong Kong and authorized him to claim reimbursement for the costs of feeding them from the Chief Magistrate in Hong Kong. After agreeing the arrangements, Capt. Fine changed his mind and sought to resile from his commitment whereupon Gower refused to issue sailing papers to the *Mary Mildred* and ordered HMS *Barrosa* to arrest the vessel if it tried to leave Nagasaki without them. Gower's actions had the desired effect and Capt. Fine eventually agreed to sail with the prisoners.[219]

Deportations from Japan

British subjects could be deported from Japan if convicted of two minor crimes or a single serious crime;[220] but, although a Consul could order deportation as part of a sentence, it could be carried out only with a Warrant[221] from the Judge who was required to report to the Minister and the Foreign Secretary on all deportations.[222] Deportations were usually to the person's last principal place of residence and were a final resort as they were a costly business (approximately $75 from Japan to Britain). Judges

[217] Only Mrs Carew and Elizabeth Scarfield were sentenced to imprisonment. The only other woman reported to have been detained in prison was Miss Jacob, the Carews' nanny, pending her trial.

[218] Parkes to Auditor-General, Hong Kong, approving hospital expenses for a prisoner; 3 November 1869; FO276/27.

[219] Gower to Fine, 11 August 1865 and Gower to Capt. Boys, 12 and 14 August 1865; FO796/29.

[220] Articles XXI and XXII, OC1860.

[221] Warrants were addressed to a ship's master to transport the convict to the relevant destination and, with deportations to Hong Kong, to the Chief Magistrate of Police there to receive the deportee.

[222] Section 3, OC1865.

were ever-mindful of public expenditure and Hornby had John Andrews shipped to Madras as a sailor by P&O to save the deportation costs[223] and ordered Lowder to give Alfred Hatten a year in which to find sureties for good behaviour as, if deported, his wife and children left behind might become a charge on British government funds.[224]

Where deportation formed part of a sentence, the deportation order came into effect only upon the offender's failure to provide security. The Shanghai practice was to consider giving effect to the order only upon completion of any prison sentence; but, as Hannen explained after the Yokohama Court was established, such practice was inconvenient in Japan as it meant delaying application to the Judge until the prison sentence had expired and detaining the offender in custody beyond his sentence with the additional detention costs falling upon the government.[225] Goodwin, initially, insisted upon the Shanghai practice being followed;[226] but, in 1874, the Supreme Court sent a bundle of pre-signed blank Warrants to the Yokohama Court to avoid these delays—delays which disappeared with HMCJ's creation when the necessary authority to order deportations from Japan was transferred to the Judge.

The Judges needed to ensure that a particular deportation was legally justified and to guard against Consuls' too easily ordering deportations. Hannen was reluctant to ratify John Davis's deportation in 1888 after Davis had been prosecuted by the Japanese police for a Breach of the Peace. He cited standing instructions which provided that deportations should be confined to cases where the frequency and gravity of the crimes had become a source of danger or serious discomfort and alarm to the community and said that Davis had not been convicted of a very serious offence and he had not seen much evidence to support deportation.[227] Once the Consul had supplied all the trial evidence to show what a nuisance Davis had been[228] together with a letter from the Japanese authorities complaining about his drunkenness and violent conduct towards Japanese and urging his immediate removal,[229] Hannen ratified the deportation order.[230]

---

223 FO656/19.
224 Hornby to Lowder, 28 March 1870; FO656/18.
225 Hannen to Goodwin, 27 October 1871; FO656/37.
226 Goodwin to Hannen, 17 October 1871; FO656/39.
227 Hannen to Nagasaki Consul, 7 November 1888; FO796/10.
228 Case 13, 1888; FO796/7.
229 Nagasaki Consul to Hannen, 15 November 1888; FO796/10.
230 Hannen to Nagasaki Consul, 23 November 1888; FO796/10.

In all, we see 22 deportations to Hong Kong, four to the UK and one to Madras.[231] In time, the Hong Kong authorities refused to accept prisoners with no connection to the colony which meant increased expenses for deportations to the UK and, therefore, increased official reluctance to order deportation. However, Consuls tended to adopt a practical approach. In 1878, when French overturned Daniel O'Farrell's conviction by Troup in Nagasaki, ordered his release and refused to ratify Troup's deportation order,[232] Troup shipped O'Farrell, as a distressed seaman, to Shanghai to search for employment. It is likely that the local Japanese authorities applied pressure for the removal of obvious trouble-makers and Consuls must have looked for ways to accommodate them such as by requiring security for good behaviour of such high amounts that the offender could not meet the requirement and would be deported upon such failure. Likewise, one must suspect that, as with Davis, the Japanese authorities locally assisted the Consul by providing the necessary written supporting evidence as when Annersley's request for Henry Trone's deportation from Kobe to Hong Kong on the grounds that he had been imprisoned 14 times in 1875 was supported by affidavits from a British Inspector in the Japanese Police.[233]

The costs issue was highlighted in 1872 when Westmoreland was convicted of breaching the peace and sentenced to deportation. A month earlier, he had been charged with 'misconduct in employment', but the Japanese Railway Department, which had brought him out from England two years earlier, dismissed him and withdrew the case.[234] When seeking Hornby's consent to the deportation, Wilkinson (cognizant of the cost issue) said he would ask the Japanese Railway Department to pay the costs;[235] but it refused to pay them, even after the *Chargé d'Affaires* had raised the matter with it, because Westmoreland had been dismissed for misconduct.[236]

---

[231] Appendix VI contains a list of deportations compiled from various Court records. It is, almost certainly, incomplete because there is no record of the Yokohama Court's completion of the blank Warrants sent to it or any of HMCJ's deportations.

[232] French to Troup, 19 December 1878; FO796/42. French said that failure to pay for food gave rise to civil remedies not criminal penalties. French may have been right; but this did prevent other convictions in similar circumstances.

[233] Annersley to Hornby 29 July 1875; FO656/41. In fact, Trone (who could be the same Henry Trone who had been consular constable in Hakodate and convicted, and deported, in the *Ainu bones* case) is listed as appearing in the Kobe Court only five times over 1873–1875 (for larceny and drunkenness).

[234] FO656/41.

[235] Wilkinson to Hornby, 24 October 1872; FO656/34.

[236] Gower to Hornby, 17 March 1873; FO656/41.

Removal to Hong Kong for Trial

Before OC1865, the most serious cases were removed to SCHK for trial; but, after OC1865, such removal was intended as an extraordinary step and required the Judge's sanction.[237]

The pre-1865 problems were seen in *Reg. v. Browning* when Browning was tried in Hong Kong in 1864 for murdering his landlord at Yokohama. The prosecution, conducted by the Hong Kong Attorney General, could not obtain the witnesses' presence as they were all in Japan and relied upon a recent Hong Kong Ordinance allowing trial on deposition alone to obtain Browning's conviction (for manslaughter) despite Browning's counsel, Pollard, addressing the jury on the unsatisfactory nature of deposition evidence in a murder trial. Even reliance upon deposition evidence was not straightforward for Pollard successfully resisted the admission of the Japanese witnesses' depositions as they had not been sworn whilst those from US, Portuguese, Dutch and British witnesses, being sworn, were admitted.[238]

Witness availability and the related cost issues (particularly, upon which governmental department they were to fall) were seen in 1869 when the Kanagawa Court committed Albert Muller to face trial in Hong Kong for murder on the high seas. The three prosecution witnesses—who had also been sent to Hong Kong so they could provide evidence at the trial—applied to the Governor for support during their detention and compensation for loss of employment pending the trial because the acting Attorney General (Pollard, who had been Browning's defence counsel) refused to conduct a murder charge on depositions alone and insisted upon their detention to allow Muller the opportunity to cross-examine them in the interests of justice. Parkes, advised by Hornby, suggested the colony should claim reimbursement of these costs from the Home government and not the Legation because the committal to Hong Kong occurred because the Courts had no jurisdiction in the case.[239]

Occasionally, costs and inconvenience could be saved by an accused's removal to Hong Kong as when Hornby authorized a defendant's removal to Hong Kong on a murder indictment in 1867 'as the deceased, the

237 Section 67, OC1865.

238 Memorial from the British residents of Izmir to Hornby, 3 July 1865; FO656/22.

239 Auditor-General to Parkes, 11 September 1869; FO276/26. It is unclear why Hornby declined jurisdiction—presumably either because Muller (as his name suggests) was a foreign national or the crime was committed beyond 100 miles from the Japanese coast.

prisoner and all the witnesses belong to the Regiment stationed at Yokohama and as the Regiment is almost leaving for Hong Kong'.[240]

Conclusion

Overall, the available semi-annual returns record the trial of some 3,500 defendants over the entire period. The many missing returns for Yokohama and Kobe mean this figure must underestimate significantly the total as the newspaper reports (which record the prosecution of some 1,250 criminal offences) are not a complete substitute for looking at the Court records. However, whilst recognizing that we must look to Yokohama in relation to the more serious offences, the broad consistency of the analytical breakdown of the criminal offences reported in the newspapers and those recorded in the Nagasaki Court records suggests that the Nagasaki Court records are a reliable basis from which to draw wider conclusions about the operation and exercise of British criminal jurisdiction under extraterritoriality in Japan as a whole.

A clear majority of criminal offences involved shipping offences with no relationship with Japan and, in criminal cases, the majority of defendants were sailors or other transient visitors to Japan so that individual members of the resident British population were only marginally affected. There was a broad consistency between sailors and residents in the nature of offences committed with about two-thirds being public order offences and, judging by the preponderance of punishments comprising fines of $5 or less, goal terms of seven days or less and the number of defendants being simply bound over, relatively minor offences at that. It was in the third of offences which did not fall into the category of public order offences that the nature of offences diverged between sailors and residents. By their very nature, most Treaty breaches were applicable only to ships' masters and non-registration charges to residents. Otherwise, residents faced a wider range of charges in the miscellaneous category and perpetrated the few serious thefts. They were also more likely to use court processes to establish a point of general principle or to continue a personal squabble.

As the Japanese authorities assumed greater responsibility for the maintenance of public order in the ports so they came to predominate as prosecutors, although British officials or barristers prosecuted the more

---

240 Hornby to Myburgh, 23 December 1867; FO656/18.

serious cases—even those instigated by the Japanese authorities. There is some evidence, on a pure statistical basis, to raise questions as to possible bias on the Courts' part against Japanese prosecutors or witnesses; but, a closer examination of the cases shows that bias was unlikely to have been the reason for the disparity in conviction rates. That said, two or three cases tried with Assessors *may* show that Assessors had an anti-Japanese bias or arrogance reflective of the wider community; but, Assessors were never the decisive voice in the decisions and the number of cases in which Assessors sat is too small to draw meaningful conclusions. Even though the British community—in the form of Assessors—may have displayed a bias or anti-Japanese prejudice, such bias and prejudice appears not to have fed through into the few jury trials involving Japanese prosecutors. Again, when it came to punishments, there is a broad consistency in the sentences imposed on convicted defendants regardless of the prosecutor's nationality.

A justification—at least in the eyes of the British community—for extra-territoriality would have been if the Japanese authorities had adopted too aggressive an approach to prosecutions. The cases show two arguments which could support this view: their prosecutions for Treaty breaches often appeared over-zealous and, in Nagasaki, the Japanese authorities preferred a greater number of charges against individual defendants.

On the first point, it must be recognized that the Japanese authorities were not above using the Treaty's strict enforcement as a weapon in their campaign to abolish extra-territoriality; but, even here, it seems that they were judicious in their prosecutions. For instance, Hartley was not the only pharmacist in Yokohama yet no other pharmacist there was prosecuted. Even when the British agreed in principle, after this case, to make regulations allowing the enforcement of Japanese opium regulations, there were no subsequent reported opium-related prosecutions. This suggests that, whilst the Japanese authorities tolerated medicinal opium use amongst Westerners, they were not prepared to countenance a flagrant case of smuggling. Likewise, with the Customs' seals cases, if the seals were as flimsy as suggested, it is difficult to believe that there were not more breaches—which suggests Customs officers exercised a benevolent discretion absent other reasons—a point reinforced by prosecution statements in the *Sunbeam* and *Gaucho* cases. As to the second point, this is easily explained away as reflecting distortions arising from the nature of the incidents—usually drunken brawls which generated multiple defendants and several charges against each.

Despite obvious conflicts about extra-territoriality on a wider, political level from around 1870 onwards and the Japanese authorities' using certain issues as pawns in their battle for its abolition, the case reports show a high degree of co-operation on a practical day to day level between the Japanese and British authorities when it came to controlling the rowdier elements and elsewhere to obtain satisfactory outcomes for both. Lyne was convicted of embezzling the British Garrison's stores in Yokohama upon the evidence of many Japanese traders to whom he had sold the goods.[241] Such a prosecution could not have been mounted without the Japanese authorities' support; for only they could compel the attendance of Japanese witnesses.

Other incidents were resolved through negotiation, communication and compromise such as the Faulds' post-mortem case or by an acceptance of some responsibility by the payment of compensation. In 1873, Dohmen declined to prosecute Gilbert for killing a Japanese child because the evidence showed that the death was accidental and this was accepted when Gilbert offered compensation, fixed by Dohmen at 100 *Rios*.[242] Where, presumably, the British authorities preferred to avoid a public trial, the Japanese authorities could be accommodating as when a midshipman from HMS *Ocean*, whilst furiously riding through Nagasaki, knocked down an elderly Japanese who died shortly thereafter. No prosecution was brought but the midshipman was punished by a ship's court, stripped of six months' seniority and ordered to pay £100 to the deceased's friends.[243] This co-operation and sensitivity to the pressures on the other also meant the British authorities took action in response to Japanese pressure or to protect Japanese subjects as when they prosecuted Moss, Blakiston and Cousens.

---

[241] *Reg. v. Lyne*, 4 July 1874; JWM.

[242] Dohmen to Kusada Hideyo and Watanabe Ki, 11 March 1873; FO798/1.

[243] 16 June 1871; NCH.

CHAPTER FOUR

THE SEA

In the second half of the nineteenth century, the British mercantile marine was by far the largest in the world and as we have already seen, shipping offences committed aboard British vessels dominated the court lists in Japan. In addition, as part of their consular function, the Consuls administered the Merchant Shipping Acts for British vessels trading with Japan. These Acts added two additional features to the judicial scene although, strictly, these features had nothing to do with extra-territoriality as such: Naval Courts of Enquiry (**Naval Courts**) and Inquiries into Deaths at Sea on board British vessels (**Inquiries**). Nothing in the Treaty provided for these two administrative bodies which were creatures of the Board of Trade. Whilst consuls in other ports and countries where extra-territoriality did not apply also had responsibilities under the Merchant Shipping Acts towards British vessels, the existence of a British judicial edifice in Japan meant that powers granted to courts and authorities elsewhere within the formal Empire were, as a matter of convenience, often—but not always—extended to the Consuls and the Courts.

Britain's jurisdiction in these areas was largely uncontested and its handling of shipping offences and administration of the Merchant Shipping Acts had little immediate impact upon Japan. It must be arguable that discussion of shipping offences, the Naval Courts and Inquiries is outside the scope of a discussion of the Courts and extra-territoriality. However, the numerical importance of shipping offences in the Courts' work-load and the interplay at the margins, where it exercised a punitive jurisdiction over foreign sailors on British vessels, between British and foreign jurisdictions which provided scope for challenge from other nations—including Japan—suggests that they should not be ignored when considering the work of the Courts and the role of British lawyers during the period of extra-territoriality.

The exercise of this punitive jurisdiction reveals changing practice over time, with people on the spot adopting a practical approach (where, one cannot but feel, 'might is right' had a role) whereas, back in London, the government—or, at least, its legal advisers—followed a more legalistic approach. In the confusion, Japan became mindful to prevent others extending extra-territoriality beyond its strict treaty terms and, in time, insisted that, in relation to shipping offences, it be treated in accordance with standard international law and not subject to usages common in China which had grown up alongside extra-territoriality there. The working and findings of the Naval Courts and Inquiries also reveal much Anglo-Japanese co-operation at a working level and highlight the changing attitudes of the two communities.

Jurisdiction

Consular jurisdiction over shipping offences had three strands. First, under international law, Consuls had a jurisdiction distinct from extra-territoriality which jurisdiction was derived from European maritime customs, which left shipboard matters to the nation of the vessel's flag. These customs were codified within the Merchant Shipping Acts and conferred jurisdiction on the Consuls over shipboard matters. The Merchant Shipping Act 1894 created several criminal offences ranging from a general offence against discipline through desertion, being AWOL, drunkenness, damage, embezzlement to assaulting the master or mate; all punishable by loss of wages or imprisonment (with or without hard labour) for terms up to 12 weeks.[1] The Merchant Shipping Acts also regulated the running of British flagged merchant vessels and imposed obligations upon shipmasters for the protection of sailors on those vessels.

Second, OC1860 conferred the powers of a Justice of the Peace upon Consuls in relation to sailors abroad.[2] Third, OC1865 established jurisdiction in respect of offences committed by British subjects within 100 miles of the Japanese coastline—not just within Japan or its territorial waters.[3] The first two bases explain why we find Consuls sitting alone imposing prison terms in excess of a month for shipping offences—something they could do in criminal cases only when sitting with Assessors. These bases

[1] Sections 220–225 of the Merchant Shipping Act 1894 (**MSA1894**) (which replaced similar provisions in the Merchant Shipping Act 1854 (**MSA1854**, the two Acts being together referred to as **MSA**)).

[2] Section XXXIX. Although not followed through into section 5, OC1865 and notwithstanding that OC1865 repealed OC1860, Rennie stated that jurisdiction under this section continued to be exercised (Rennie to Salisbury, 10 October 1885; FO17/997). The Foreign Office, when justifying the China Estimates for 1869/1870, also made it clear that 'control of British seamen resorting to the ports rests with the Consular officer...' (Hammond to HM Treasury, 26 February 1869; FO881/1643).

[3] Section 101.

also explain why the Yokohama Consul—*qua* Consul, and not, after 1879, *qua* Assistant Judge—tried all but the most serious shipping offences in the Kanagawa Court and, after 1879, in HMCJ. The Judge, not being a consul, had jurisdiction under only OC1865.

Contemporary writers distinguished between two aspects of jurisdiction in relation to extra-territoriality and both came into play with crews of British vessels and led to conflicts between Britain and both Japan and other foreign Powers, principally the USA. By punitive jurisdiction, Britain exercised jurisdiction over, and punished, its own subjects—and certain other categories of individual; whereas, by protective jurisdiction, it protected its subjects and certain other individuals as against the Japanese authorities. The two were not co-extensive and the exercise of punitive jurisdiction over foreign seamen on British vessels was a question of 'difficulty and delicacy'[4] with the potential to embroil Britain in conflict with Japan and other nations.

Traditional European practice distinguished between offences against a ship's discipline, which were subject to the punitive jurisdiction of that vessel's flag, and more serious offences where territorial jurisdiction applied save when offences occurred on the High Seas where, in Britain's case, the Merchant Shipping Acts provided that the offenders—of whatever nationality—could be sent to British territory for trial. In 1877, Derby suggested that the Supreme Court's jurisdiction should be extended to cover that exercised by Colonial courts under section 11 of the Merchant Shipping Act 1867 in respect of crimes and offences committed by British subjects on any British ship and that a general power be granted to the Foreign Secretary to extend such jurisdiction[5] but there is no evidence that this suggestion was acted upon.

Japan—and other countries—accepted that offences against discipline on British flagged vessels were subject to the Consuls' jurisdiction. The problems arose with more serious offences committed ashore or within Japanese waters—where Japan's territorial jurisdiction would, ordinarily, apply (subject to its other treaty engagements). By international law, neither the Consuls nor the Courts had any power to try foreign sailors for such offences: they were the responsibility of the Japanese or, for those sailors who benefitted from extra-territoriality, their own consular authorities; but, as Wilkinson admitted, although the distinction between ship's

[4] Circular No. 1 of 4 March 1884, Supreme Court to Consuls; FO796/10 (**Rennie's Circular**).

[5] Pauncefote to Reilly, 22 November 1877; FO97/489.

discipline matters and other matters was well-recognized, 'the limits between these categories have never been clearly defined'.[6]

Further, when the *Ansei* treaties were made, he believed that it had been 'contemplated that all the men on board the ships of the Treaty Powers should be considered as the subjects of that Power for all purposes so far as regards the Japanese authorities';[7] but, the treaties did not so provide. Over the years, practice varied (between different countries, ports and individual consuls) and was not in conformity with that in European or American waters or, in the British case, always consistent with Foreign Office guidance. The question concerned principally Britain, Japan and America for the majority of foreign ships trading in Japanese waters were British followed by American. Britain was compelled to review the exercise of punitive jurisdiction over sailors in East Asian waters on three separate occasions. First, in 1868/1869; second, at the 1882 Treaty Revision Conference (when the Japanese government pushed unsuccessfully for the adoption of a common position based on jurisdiction accruing to the vessel's flag);[8] and, third, in the context of the Sino-Japanese War of 1894–95.

Mid-nineteenth century China Coast practice was for the 'consul of the nationality of the vessel to assume and exercise jurisdiction over all members of the ship's crew, even in case of offences committed onshore'[9] (although Hornby must have recognized that this was a local practice for he conceded that the cases concerned had 'usually been of trifling importance').[10] In 1868, the US consul-general in Shanghai disputed this practice. Both Clarendon and Derby recognized the strict international legal position. Derby advised that 'however convenient a practice of exercising such jurisdiction may be, [Consuls] must be warned not to assume it'[11] whilst Clarendon advised that, where a foreign consul claimed jurisdiction over a foreign sailor, British consuls should decline jurisdiction before allowing that, if there were no challenge, they could rely on the current practice.[12]

---

[6] Wilkinson to Parkes, 27 July 1882, enclosing memorandum to Sir Thomas Wade (Minister to Beijing); FO656/31 (**HSW 1882 Memorandum**).

[7] Wilkinson to unknown addressee, 15 November 1894; FO656/31 (**HSW 1894 Memorandum**).

[8] Except for Japanese subjects when in Japan or Japanese waters.

[9] Hornby to Fittock (consul, Ningbo) 28 June 1869; FO17/681.

[10] Ibid.

[11] Derby's manuscript indorsement on Hornby to Derby, 5 November 1874; FO17/681.

[12] Clarendon to Hornby, 30 October 1869; FO656/31.

The theoretical British position may be summarized as one where Consuls would exercise jurisdiction over offences against discipline but, in more serious cases, 'decline to try the offender and:

a. where the offender's consul was willing to exercise jurisdiction, to hand him over to such consuls; and
b. where the offender's consul declined to exercise jurisdiction, to send the offender to Hong Kong for trial under section 268 [MSA1854].'[13]

Until OC1884 extended the definition of 'British subject' to include a 'British protected person' (interpreted to include a foreign seaman serving on a British ship), even the limited jurisdiction which the Courts had exercised for many years in respect to offences ashore was *ultra vires*—although no one had ever taken the point.[14]

The case of Gen-ga-so[15] exemplifies the problems of sailors and jurisdiction. He was prosecuted in Hakodate for desertion, being drunk and disorderly and assaulting a Japanese policeman. The Consul assumed jurisdiction because he was a sailor on board a British flagged vessel; but, being Chinese, he was not, strictly, subject to British jurisdiction for offences committed ashore (i.e. certainly the last and possibly also the middle offence) and would have been subject to either Japanese territorial jurisdiction or Chinese consular jurisdiction. However, absent a Chinese consul in Hakodate, all concerned—local authorities and the Consul, simply took the practical way forward and the Consul assumed jurisdiction even for the offence committed ashore.

The foreign sailors themselves, even if aware of the issue, may well have preferred trial in the British courts to the local Japanese courts or even other consular courts and so did not take the point. *Chinese Consul v. Wong Pun Dzu*[16] shows the multifaceted nature of the extra-territorial regime. The defendant, a Chinese sailor on board a British vessel, was arrested by the Japanese police in Nagasaki for passing counterfeit Chinese currency in the market-place. This case came before the Court only because he was on a British vessel's articles and, so, was treated by all as being subject to British jurisdiction. The case proved, the Consul simply discharged him from the vessel's books and ordered that he be handed over to the Chinese authorities.

---

13 HSW 1894 Memorandum.
14 Ibid.
15 Hakodate semi-annual returns, second half 1872; FO 656/35.
16 Nagasaki, Case no. 1 of 1891; FO796/7.

The problem with simply handing offenders over to their own authorities was, as Rennie recognized, a total failure of justice in many cases. Consequently, he advised Consuls to assume jurisdiction where it seemed expedient to do so over all foreigners on British merchant vessels in respect of 'trifling offences committed ashore such as drunkenness and common assault'[17] and also when it seemed expedient in respect of more serious offences although, with these, it meant conveying such offenders to Hong Kong for trial. He side-stepped nationality issues by introducing a rebuttable presumption that, unless the question of jurisdiction was raised by the accused or otherwise brought formally before the Court, Consuls should presume that the master and crew were British subjects.[18]

Rennie's concern was genuine; other consuls were often unprepared, unable or unwilling to deal with criminal offences committed by their fellow citizens. In 1879, Linstroom and Caroe wounded Frederick Barnes in a fight ashore. All three were sailors on a British ship but Linstroom was Swedish and Caroe Danish.[19] They were exempt from Japanese territorial jurisdiction but their consuls were unwilling to handle the case and wished the Courts to do so. However, given Derby's instructions of 1875, the Courts could not try them, even with such consent. Therefore, either they would go free or it was necessary to send them to Hong Kong which Wilkinson did with their consuls' consent (although, he complained of the great inconvenience and expense in sending them there).[20] The result was that intermediate offences committed by foreigners on British ships ashore or in Japanese waters went unpunished as their own consuls would not exercise jurisdiction whilst the British in Japan could not and the offences were insufficiently serious to justify shipping the offender to Hong Kong for trial. In 1884, a Norwegian master assaulted a British sailor at sea but went free because Aston had no jurisdiction—even though the consul for Sweden and Norway wanted him to try the case.[21]

Wilkinson accepted that exceptions could be pointed to his general statements. Troup tried Chinese crewmen for offences committed ashore in Kobe even though the Chinese consul had requested that they be surrendered to him. This may have stemmed from an anti-Chinese bias, doubts as to whether the Chinese consul would punish them or, even, to protect them from the Chinese consul's seeking an opportunity for

[17] Rennie's Circular.
[18] Ibid.
[19] Wilkinson to Parkes, 13 February 1879; FO656/19.
[20] Ibid.
[21] Aston to Wilkinson, 6 February 1884; FO656/70.

squeeze. More seriously, USA consuls sought an enlarged jurisdiction to try all sailors on USA flagged vessels.

Despite the US Shanghai consul-general's 1868 circular precipitating the first British official correspondence trail, the USA was, by 1880 at the latest, claiming jurisdiction over everybody on its vessels.[22] When John Ross, a British subject on the US merchant vessel *Bullion*, murdered the second mate whilst she lay at anchor in Yokohama, he was tried for murder by the US consul at Yokohama despite British challenges to the US jurisdiction and subsequent complaints by Britain to Washington.[23] Britain argued that the 1868 circular had distinguished properly between breaches of discipline on a merchant ship and serious offences whether committed ashore or on board ships; a seaman did not become a citizen of another country merely by serving in its merchant service, and Japan, by its treaty with the USA, had waived its territorial jurisdiction over only USA citizens.[24]

The USA, despite the earlier circular, rejected British complaints and hoped that Britain would 'recognize the advantages to both ... of maintaining the principle of consular jurisdiction as it has been heretofore applied'.[25] Its argument was that, otherwise, sailors of nationalities without consuls, or with less energetic consuls, in Japan could evade punishment for serious offences.[26] Although there is no evidence that the Japanese, at the time, argued against the American position, they subsequently claimed that the USA had been wrong to assert jurisdiction over Ross.[27] Discussions between Britain and the USA petered out as both recognized that a murder had been committed and Ross would remain in prison (or be executed) whoever exercised jurisdiction.[28]

The Courts' handling of Japanese crewmen is a confused picture; even Wilkinson is inconsistent in his reports on practice. At one point in 1882, he said that the Courts did not consider charges against Japanese subjects—for offences against discipline or otherwise[29] whilst, at another, he said the Courts acted as regards discipline but not otherwise.[30] In 1894,

---

22 Wilkinson to Parkes, 30 November 1882; FO83/885 (**HSW 1882 Letter**).
23 Blaine to Thornton, 3 June 1881; FO656/31.
24 HSW 1882 Letter.
25 Blaine to Thornton 3 June 1881; FO656/31.
26 Ibid.
27 Editorial, 2 October 1897; JWM.
28 Ross's application for *Habeas Corpus* in the USA reached the US Supreme Court which, in October 1890, upheld the Department of State's views (case report in FO656/31).
29 HSW 1882 Memorandum.
30 HSW 1882 Letter.

he refined the latter statement by saying that Consuls handled breaches of discipline by deductions from wages in the nature of fines and not by a Court hearing whilst, for serious offences, Japanese crew were handed over to the Japanese authorities.[31] Given Japanese proposals in 1882 to give jurisdiction to the vessel's flag, it would be surprising if the Japanese authorities objected to the Courts hearing disciplinary matters; but, even here, Hannen recalled that Parkes believed the Courts should waive their right to try Japanese sailors in favour of a competent Japanese tribunal except where the Japanese authorities declined to interfere.[32] It is possible that practice varied from port to port. The Nagasaki Court minutes record cases against Japanese crewmen until 1890,[33] and there is no indication that the more informal means of proceeding was adopted or that the hearings were other than formal Court cases.[34] After 1890, there are no records of Japanese crewmen being prosecuted in the Court—even for disciplinary offences; it is unclear whether this was because none were committed after that date or whether, by then, the Japanese merchant marine had grown to such an extent that few Japanese still served on British vessels or whether different arrangements were operated with the local authorities.

As to offences committed ashore by Japanese, although Japanese offenders were usually handed over to the Japanese authorities, some were prosecuted in the Courts which led to Japanese complaints to Parkes.[35] Even in Yokohama, Robertson sentenced a Japanese sailor, Hosoi, to seven days' imprisonment for desertion; but, when Hosoi was being taken away to prison, he drew his knife and attempted to stab the vessel's master. After he had completed his sentence for desertion in the British gaol, Hosoi was handed over to the Japanese authorities to be prosecuted for the attempted stabbing.[36] Britons serving on Japanese vessels benefitted from extra-territoriality so, even if Japan would otherwise have had jurisdiction, they were tri-able by the Courts as evidenced by *John Wareham, first mate of Japanese barque Kinipponmaru charged by Macfarlane, master*

[31] HSW 1894 Memorandum.

[32] Hannen to Nagasaki Consul, 25 July 1885; FO796/10.

[33] The *Hedwig*'s Captain prosecuted three Japanese sailors for refusal of duty, criminal cases 1–3, 1890; FO796/7.

[34] The record of *Master of G.H. Wappens v. Hashimoto Yokichi and Matsumoto Nijiro* was chopped with the Court seal, which suggests a formal hearing, 4 May 1885; FO796/7.

[35] Inouye Kaoru (Japanese Foreign Minister) to Parkes protesting against Consuls' trying Japanese seamen for offences committed ashore, 15 May 1883; FO83/885.

[36] 6 March 1883; HN.

when the master prosecuted successfully the mate for being drunk and disorderly, assault and threatening behaviour.[37]

An exception to a foreign sailor being subject to his own consul's jurisdiction was in relation to ships' masters where the Courts exercised jurisdiction over foreign masters of British vessels under the Merchant Shipping Acts for breaches of their provisions. In Hakodate, Sclavo, the master of the *Thompson*, was convicted and fined £15 in 1868 for harbouring a deserter from another ship and not entering him on the *Thompson*'s books.[38] The next year, the *Jolly*'s master prosecuted Petersen, the Norwegian master of the *Runnymede*—again in Hakodate—for harbouring a deserter from the *Jolly*.[39]

A further complication (especially in the 1860s), from the perspective of Consular jurisdiction, was in relation to foreign merchant vessels which were chartered by British Naval and Commissariat authorities in China and carried a British flag on voyages to, and around, the coast of Japan—without being British registered vessels; and the reverse where British registered vessels were chartered by other Powers. Alcock avoided being definitive and simply advised Consuls to exercise 'great caution and discretion' in such cases; Consuls should not go out of their way to question a ship's nationality avowedly in the employ of another government and flying its colours.[40] Thus, Consuls should not seek to enforce the administrative and reporting provisions of the Merchant Shipping Act 1854 on British ships which were flying foreign flags. However, he was definitive that every British subject—except the master—could claim to be under the jurisdiction of a Consul and amenable only to British laws as a master could not 'denationalize his crew. They cannot be transferred like cattle.'[41] The crew, thus retained the benefits of British extra-territoriality even if the Consuls did not enforce the administrative provisions of the Merchant Shipping Act 1854 due to the vessel's being chartered by a foreign government and flying that government's flag.

We see a similar inconsistent approach with sailors on men-of-war. Under international law, naval crew were subject to the laws of the ship's nation as regards ship-board matters; but, ashore, had no additional protection and were subject to the local territory's jurisdiction. However, in China and Japan, most nations treated warships' crews as protected by

37 Criminal case 1 of 1882; FO796/7.
38 Hakodate semi-annual returns 1868; FO656/34.
39 Hakodate semi-annual returns 1869; FO656/35.
40 Alcock's Circular No.16 of 1860 to Consuls, 12 July 1860; FO796/20.
41 Ibid.

(and subject to) the warship's country for offences on board—and ashore; thereby derogating from the host nation's territorial jurisdiction. In most cases, the crew benefitted from extra-territoriality anyway so few practical consequences for Japan or the crewmen themselves arose from this distinction. All European seamen on British vessels would be protected by their own country's extra-territoriality treaty with Japan even if not protected by Britain; so the question arose only with those seamen unprotected by any treaty Power or when the crew's nationality was different from that of the vessel.[42] The few British seamen on Japanese men-of-war benefitted from extra-territoriality because, though they might, generally, be viewed as being subject to Japanese jurisdiction, Japan had waived its jurisdiction by the Treaty as instanced when a British crewman on a Japanese man-of-war was prosecuted in the Yokohama Court for stabbing a Russian sailor ashore.[43]

The USA claimed jurisdiction over all seamen aboard USA vessels. Despite this, when McCondville, a British subject on a US warship, committed a crime ashore in Yokohama in 1875, the US consul refused to try him[44] and the Yokohama Court, rather than allowing him to go unpunished, tried, convicted and fined him. His commanding officer then refused to deduct the fine from his pay arguing that, as a sailor on a USA man-of-war, he was not amenable to British jurisdiction. When asked to advise, the Law Officers both adopted the traditional view that British jurisdiction prevailed but Dr Deane, who had also been instructed, disagreed and argued that all sailors on men-of-war were subject to that ship's jurisdiction even for offences committed ashore.[45]

In the event, Lord Tenterden (Permanent Under Secretary at the Foreign Office, 1873–1882) and Derby suggested that Sir Edward Thornton (British Minister in Washington) ascertain unofficially the US government's views. Discussions in Washington ensued during which the USA suggested that the two countries agree formally to treat jurisdiction as

[42] Only Portuguese, amongst Europeans, lost extra-territoriality when Japan denounced the Portuguese treaty in the 1890s. Most non-British crew on British vessels trading in Japanese waters were Europeans, Javanese (protected by Holland), Malays, Lascars and other Indians (protected by Britain), Thai (without the benefit of an extra-territoriality but none appears as defendant in any reports) and Chinese (who, until 1894, benefitted from their own extra-territoriality).

[43] *H.I.R.M's consul v. Howard* (*aka Keily*); 10 June 1878; TJH.

[44] Ostensibly because he was British; but also because the US Consul had previously fined him for another offence only for McCondville's commanding officer to dispute the civilian jurisdiction and refuse to deduct the fine from his pay.

[45] Law Officers and Dr Deane to Derby, 21 April 1875; FO83/2299.

following the flag in East Asian waters.[46] The Law Officers advised that this was not possible under the Treaty or the Austro-Hungarian treaty so the Admiralty and the US government agreed, for the future, to treat this as the *de facto* position as regards sailors on warships in Japan and China.[47]

Neither Britain nor the USA was dissatisfied with this outcome but the Prefect of Kanagawa used the outbreak of the Sino-Japanese War, 1894–95 to contest it and assert that Japan had not ceded its territorial jurisdiction as regards Japanese or other non-protected seamen on USA vessels. The Prefect's letter, despite its general language, was aimed at Chinese crews on British and USA vessels[48] because the war's outbreak abrogated automatically the Sino-Japanese treaty conferring mutual extra-territoriality thereby leaving Chinese seamen on foreign ships without the privilege of extra-territoriality and Japan disputed any other nation's claim to protect them.

Wilkinson advised resisting the Prefect's instructions as the question of jurisdiction over Chinese seamen in the Royal Navy was 'of most importance to us'.[49] The US Consul had informed him that the Japanese authorities' attitude reflected their understanding of the British position. Wilkinson conceded that the British would not support the USA as regards Japanese seamen but would resist strenuously any Japanese claim to jurisdiction over Chinese seamen serving in British warships.[50] The matter was unresolved when the Sino-Japanese War ended in 1895: presumably, neither side, each having made its point, wished—or had cause—to push the matter to a conclusion. This was confirmed by the US Minister's reports of discussions with Mutsu Munemitsu who said that, while Japan could not accept the USA position, he 'did not want to discuss the matter until a case arose and had told the Governor of Yokohama not to cause trouble'.[51]

The matter blew up, however, in 1897 when the Japanese arrested six Chinese from British warships for gambling ashore at Hakodate. Consul Layard protested and Gerald Lowther, the *Chargé d'Affaires*, was instructed to 'make representations'[52] to the Japanese government; all to no avail for

---

[46] Thornton to Derby, 24 May 1875; FO17/945.

[47] Admiralty to Foreign Office, 31 July 1875, and Derby to Thornton, 4 September 1875; FO17/945.

[48] HSW 1894 Memorandum.

[49] Ibid.

[50] Ibid.

[51] Edwin Dunn to le Poer Trench 27 October 1894; FO656/70.

[52] Salisbury to Lowther 24 August 1897; FO881/7037.

the Chinese crewmen were gaoled for 15 days with hard labour. The result was much editorializing in newspapers in London and Yokohama; but Japan maintained that it was applying international law no differently from Britain (i.e. that, once ashore, sailors from warships were subject to territorial jurisdiction and the Chinese had lost their extra-territorial rights in Japan by the treaty of Shimonoseki which ended the Sino-Japanese War). Japan having made its point with a 15 day sentence (against a potential two year maximum), the matter dropped. The affair showed a Japan flexing its muscles and, having agreed the abolition of extra-territoriality in two years' time, Japan was not prepared to allow any exceptions and Britain was no longer prepared—or in a position—to resist.

The Impact of War

International maritime law came into play when Britain blockaded the Satsuma *daimyo* during 1862/1863 following murderous attacks on Britons in Japan. The Queen's Advocate, Robert Phillimore, advised that it would be necessary to establish a Prize Court—at Hong Kong—to deal with any Japanese or neutral vessels intercepted by the blockade as delicate and serious questions of international law could arise—particularly with the neutral commerce of France and the USA. Accordingly, he prepared the necessary Order in Council (made on 9 January 1863) to institute the blockade. In the event, the only claim against the British government that appears to have arisen out of this blockade was one by Jardine Matheson & Co. for damages which it claimed to have suffered as a result of the blockade; but this claim was later rejected on the advice of the Queen's Advocate.[53]

Two wars had the potential to threaten British extra-territoriality in Japan. The Japanese civil war of 1868/1869 caused a fluttering in the British legal dovecotes but no disputes, whilst the issues it raised of British immunity from Japanese belligerents re-echoed in the Sino-Japanese War where three incidents raised diplomatic protests—but all were contained: doubtless because, with the 1894 Treaty signed and Japan seeking British

[53] Correspondence 24 December 1862, 1 and 6 January 1863 and 5 November 1863 between the Foreign Office and the Queen's Advocate; FO83/2298 and FO410/1. (Presumably, Phillimore was advising because, until 1862, he had been Admiralty Advocate and may well have been involved in advising earlier on the matter so the Foreign Office continued to instruct him on this and not Travers Twiss, the new Admiralty Advocate).

support against (or, at the very least, for Britain not to support) the Triple Intervention,[54] neither sought an escalation.

When the civil war erupted in 1868, Parkes declared neutrality and ordered Consuls to have the Royal Navy detain any contraband of war because 'all sorts of foreign vessels have been conveying troops to both sides'.[55] Nonetheless, he allowed that either belligerent was entitled to seize such contraband as 'extra-territoriality cannot be claimed when the subjects violate rights of nations at war'.[56] Consuls were instructed, if either belligerent seized British property, to arrange that 'the proceedings of the Japanese Court shall be constituted, as far as possible in accordance with the principles of our own Prize Courts' and to alert him should either belligerent issue Letters of Marque, so that the Foreign Representatives could intervene 'to prevent if possible the adoption by the Japanese of a practice that may be attended with very pernicious results'.[57] The British authorities also considered whether or not the British troops stationed in the foreign settlement at Yokohama could occupy the native town there in order to defend the foreign settlement. The Law Officers adopted a cautious position on this. They advised that, strictly speaking, it would be difficult to justify such an occupation before conceding that 'possibly, however, expediency, rather than strict law, should ... regulate the actions of the British authorities in Japan' and if Yokohama were 'threatened by either or both of the belligerent parties ... use of force might be justified for the protection of lives and property and for the maintenance of British rights within the settlement'. Nevertheless, the British authorities in Japan should take only those steps 'which the exigencies of the case manifestly render necessary'.[58] Fortunately, the conflict concluded speedily without any diplomatic incident.

Similar issues arose in the second conflict; but, here, the Japanese instituted a naval blockade and enforced belligerent rights by stopping

---

54 By the Treaty of Shimonoseki (April 1895), which ended the Sino-Japanese War, China ceded the Liaodong peninsula to Japan but Russia, supported by France and Germany, objected and applied pressure on Japan to retrocede the territory which it did by the Treaty of Yantai (November 1895).

55 Parkes to Stanley, 22 May 1868; FO656/19. The Law Officers advised that Parkes had no power to make a declaration of neutrality because OC1865, under which he purported to make the declaration, referred to the Tycoon as the ruler of Japan and not to the Mikado, or Emperor. Accordingly, the Law Officers prepared a separate Order in Council to declare neutrality. Law Officers to Stanley, 9 April 1868; FO83/2299.

56 Hornby to Parkes, 21 March 1868; FO656/19.

57 Parkes' Circular to Consuls, 18 February 1868; FO656/19.

58 Law Officers to Stanley, 9 April 1868; FO83/2299.

and searching neutral—including British—shipping and establishing a Prize Court at Sasebo. Three incidents emphasized Hornby's earlier advice that war created rights in belligerents of a higher character than extra-territoriality secured by treaty.[59] On 25 July 1894, the *Kowshing* (or *Gaosheng*), a British vessel owned by Jardine Matheson but chartered by the Imperial Chinese government, was on passage from Dagu to Asan with 1,100 Chinese troops and ammunition when sunk by the *Naniwa* (under Captain—later Admiral—Togo Hachihiro) after the Chinese troops on board the *Kowshing* prevented its British crew from complying with the *Naniwa*'s instructions to put into Sasebo for inspection.[60] Although accepting that extra-territoriality did not protect the *Kowshing* and that the *Naniwa* was entitled to stop it, Britain insisted upon compensation[61] to which the Japanese government agreed.[62] Similarly when, with echoes of the *Trent* incident, the *Yazeyama* stopped the *Thales* at sea carrying Chinese evacuees from Taiwan to Xiamen and sought to take off seven men, the matter was viewed as one of belligerent rights versus neutrals' rights at sea, not one of extra-territoriality.[63]

Given Britain's general support for a belligerent's rights at sea, the surprise is that the British consul in Nagasaki joined his USA and French colleagues in protesting against a perceived breach of French extra-territoriality when the Japanese stopped the French ship, *Sydney*, at Nagasaki and took off contraband and Chinese sailors who had trans-shipped to it at Yokohama from the *Gaelic*, a US ship. The reason may have been the concern mentioned earlier about protecting Chinese crews on British ships or, possibly, the local Consul's acting without instructions and without considering Britain's wider position. In any event, Japan

---

59 Hornby to Parkes, 21 March 1868; FO656/19.

60 Despite the background being common knowledge, a Naval Court at Nagasaki was held on 7 August 1894 under Quin to inquire into the sinking. It exonerated the officers and crew from blame; 7 August 1894; NCH. The incident generated many newspaper articles: those in London and China tending to condemn the Japanese for sinking the vessel whilst the English language Press in Japan adopted the opposite position. For a fuller description of the stand-off over the *Kowshing*, see S.C.M. Paine, *The Sino-Japanese War of 1894–1895* (New York, Cambridge University Press, 2005), pages 132–134.

61 Kimberley to Aoki, 3 August 1894; FO46/444.

62 Mutsu to Aoki, 31 July 1894; FO46/444.

63 The *Yazeyama* was persuaded to put two officers on board the *Thales* whose master would hold the men to the order of the Japanese consul in Xiamen. Following protests by the British consul there, they were released. Eventually, the Japanese government admitted that the *Yazeyama* was in the wrong and apologized to Britain for the *Thales*'s detention and Admiral Arichi, who had ordered the *Thales*'s detention, was relieved of his command; 18 December 1895; TRS&NE.

argued that a belligerent's right was 'too clear for discussion' even 'where the right of extra-territoriality exists';[64] and the matter was not pursued.

The Sasebo Prize Court[65] operated under Japanese law, and extra-territoriality was irrelevant. This was shown when a Japanese cruiser, the *Tsukuba kan*, stopped and searched the British owned *Yiksang* off the Dagu bar and discovered 220 cases of rifle cartridges concealed amongst cargo from Shanghai to Tianjin labelled 'Chinese books' and 'bamboo steel'. The *Yiksang* was taken to Sasebo for a prize hearing. Jardine Matheson, the ship's agents, denied any knowledge of the contraband and asked the Legation to lobby the Japanese government to delay the Prize Court hearing until its Japanese lawyer could reach Sasebo. As this was the first Japanese Prize Court hearing, Lowther instructed Quin, Nagasaki Consul, to seek permission to attend the hearing. The Prize Court condemned the contraband but released the *Yiksang* as the contraband had been only a small part of its cargo.[66]

The Sealing Cases

Another source of diplomatic problems on the margins of extra-territoriality was British seal-hunting ships operating in Russian waters towards the end of the nineteenth century as Russia sought to enforce its authority in its north-eastern lands. Sealing ships tended to be crewed by the 'refuse of the ... population'.[67] In 1888, Russian troops fired upon the crew of the *Nemo*, which was otter hunting at Copper Island in the Behring Strait, and killed three Japanese sailors and injured the master, Snow. A Naval Court held before Quin, with a Japanese official present, enquired formally into their deaths but merely found that the Japanese sailors had died from wounds when their boats were fired upon.[68] The Japanese government sought to hold Britain responsible for their deaths and, for the future, prohibited Japanese from signing on sealing vessels. Britain denied responsibility,[69] but the Minister, Power Henry le Poer Trench, nonetheless issued

---

64 Professor Takahashi Sakiye (of the Tokyo Naval University and legal adviser to the Japanese Commander-in-Chief), 'Applications of International Law during the Chinese-Japanese War' (talk to the Japan Society in London), *PJS* Vol. V (1898), page 2.

65 Established on 21 August 1894 by a new Japanese Prize Court law.

66 Lowther to Kimberley, 16 May 1895; FO46/452. It should be noted that the Chinese also sought to prevent British vessels carrying contraband bound for Japan but China's enforcement of its blockade is outside the scope of this book.

67 Fraser to Salisbury, 2 May 1892; FO881/6348.

68 Printed report, 26 June 1888; FO881/5697.

69 Salisbury to Okabe (Japanese Minister in London), 4 December 1888; FO881/5697.

a Regulation (approved by Salisbury) prohibiting British sealing vessels from taking on Japanese crew and he instructed Consuls to prevent their hiring Japanese sailors. Meanwhile, the British ambassador to St Petersburg was instructed to seek recompense from the Russian government[70]—without success.

Three years later, the Russians captured the *Arctic* fishing for seals but it escaped and Russia asked the Japanese government for her restitution if she arrived in Japan.[71] Salisbury instructed Hugh Fraser, the Minister, to 'protest against the Japanese government interfering with the schooner'[72] and HMS *Leander* was dispatched to bring her into Yokohama. Matters looked as though they might escalate when Fraser telegraphed that a Russian squadron was expected at Yokohama to join its flagship;[73] but the Japanese government refused to accede to Russia's request to hand over the *Arctic*.[74]

The case took a twist when the US partner in the sealing venture sued the *Arctic*'s owner in HMCJ for his share of the profits.[75] The Russian Minister protested about HMCJ's hearing the case[76] which caused Mowat to expostulate that the Russians had no business to interfere in a case before HMCJ.[77] After the Behring Sea Award at an international arbitration, Russia was obliged, in future, to deliver captured British vessels to Yokohama where Britain should enforce the Behring Sea Award Act, 1894. In July 1893, the Legation warned the sealing ships not to approach Robben Island or the Commander Islands as Anglo-Russian agreements prohibited British vessels from sealing there.[78] However, Parliamentary Counsel's inattention to HMCJ's status meant that HMCJ was unable to act for want of jurisdiction.[79] The Act, together with the Seal Fishery (Behrings Sea) Act, 1891 and the Seal Fishery (North Pacific) Act 1893, intended that HMCJ could order a vessel's confiscation, but the necessary authority was given only to 'courts having Admiralty jurisdiction within Her Majesty's

[70] Salisbury to Morier (British ambassador to St. Petersburg), 30 November 1888; FO881/5889.

[71] Fraser to Salisbury, 13 November 1891; FO881/6348.

[72] Salisbury to Fraser, 17 November 1891; FO881/6348.

[73] Fraser to Salisbury, 23 November 1891; FO881/6348.

[74] Fraser to Salisbury, 14 December 1891; FO881/6348.

[75] *Curtis & Carey v. W.E. Pyne*; 30 April 1892; JWM. Mowat found for the defendant as 'the evidence is all on one side'.

[76] Fraser to Salisbury, 2 May 1892; FO881/6348.

[77] Mowat to Fraser, 3 May 1892; FO881/6348.

[78] 19 July 1893; TRS&NE.

[79] Mowat to Sanderson, 4 June 1894; FO656/70.

dominions'[80] whereas HMCJ was not within a British dominion and, in *Reg.* (*ats. H.I.R.M.*) *v. The Maud*[81] (the only case reported under these Acts), Mowat declined to order the *Maud*'s forfeiture when it was brought into Yokohama by a Russian cruiser.

Shipping Offences

Not only were sailors the greatest source of trouble when ashore but a Consuls' jurisdiction under the Merchant Shipping Acts created the greater part of his criminal offence case-load with some 540 prosecutions for shipping offences brought before the Nagasaki Consul over the 25 year period for which we have the Court Minutes (some 70% of all criminal offences in Nagasaki) against 217 prosecutions in criminal cases—which themselves involved 147 sailors and other visitors and just 70 prosecutions involving permanent residents for offences committed ashore.[82]

The Nagasaki Court minute books and other records allow a detailed break-down of the cases there from 1866 to 1899 but both the Yokohama and Kobe official reports are incomplete. While the newspaper reports for Yokohama and Kobe cover cases from 1862–1899, they are incomplete and, we should assume, cover either the more sensational cases or those with a local interest. Thus, the non-reporting of minor cases in these two ports needs to be borne in mind when comparing their figures with those of Nagasaki. There were no shipping offences in Tokyo or Osaka as neither city was an open port. The domination of the Courts' criminal work-load by shipping offences (and the large numbers of sailors as offenders in criminal cases) was to be expected when 25,262 sailors on British vessels (two thirds of all foreign sailors) passed through Japan in 1883[83] compared with a registered resident British population of just 1,127 in 1881.

Whilst there was *a* decline in the number of shipping offences over time from a peak in the mid-1870s, the decline was not as marked as for criminal cases and in only two years (1882 and 1886) were case numbers in Nagasaki in single figures.[84] In Yokohama and Kobe half the reported criminal

[80] The customary rider added in other legislation where there was a wish to allow for the extension of jurisdiction to courts—not just in Japan—operating under extra-territoriality was 'or where Her Majesty is accustomed to exercise jurisdiction'. However, such rider had been omitted in this piece of legislation.

[81] 25 November 1893; JWM.

[82] Tables 2 and 3.

[83] Plunkett to Granville, 22 July 1884; FO881/5072.

[84] Table 3.

offences involved shipping offences against approximately two-fifths in Hakodate.[85] Judging by the newspaper reports, the case-load appeared to come in waves with some quiet periods followed by busier periods. *The Hiogo News*, in an 1874 editorial commenting upon the number of pending cases against sailors from the *Lord Wolseley*, said the vessel 'would soon earn the reputation of being the rowdiest Kobe had experienced for a long time'[86] whilst, in 1898, the *Kobe Weekly Chronicle* commented[87] that men on British vessels had been causing a lot of trouble recently.

The higher proportion of shipping offences in Nagasaki is explicable by the higher proportion of shipping movements through the port relative to its British population as it was 'the greatest naval port in the East and ... a port of call for all mail steamers'.[88] In Yokohama and Kobe, the probable under-reporting of shipping offences in the newspapers means that their proportion of all cases reported in the newspapers appears to be lower than the reality; and it must be probable that the proportion of shipping offences of all criminal offences in Yokohama and Kobe exceeded half and was closer to the Nagasaki proportion of 70%. After 1882, in only three years (1888, 1889 and 1898) were over ten shipping offences reported in the Yokohama newspapers and in many years none at all was reported.[89] The reporting trends for shipping offences in the Kobe newspapers was similar. After 1870, Hakodate's importance fell and few merchant ships called there: it was mainly a base for whaling fleets and became the summer port for the Royal Navy in East Asian waters. Its sailors would have been subject to naval discipline. Shipping movements relative to the ports' British populations are shown below:

Shipping movements and British populations (1883–1884)

Port	Shipping Movements[90] (annual)	British Population (registered)[91]
Hakodate	25	29
Nagasaki	165	98
Kobe	115	248
Yokohama	173	594

[85] Tables 2 and 3.
[86] 21 October 1874; HN.
[87] 15 January 1898; KWC.
[88] Longford to Satow, 21 June 1899; Ruxton 2005, page 539.
[89] Table 3.
[90] Parkes to Granville, 22 July 1884; FO881/5072.
[91] Plunkett Memorandum, 31 October 1883; FO881/4870.

In nationality terms, over three-quarters of defendants in Nagasaki were British, nearly a fifth other foreigners (mainly European) and under five per cent. Japanese.[92] In status terms, the large majority of cases were brought against crewmen and involved offences against discipline (widely encompassing: AWOL, disobedience, refusal of duty or drunkenness) where the prosecutor was, usually, the master or, occasionally, the mate or another officer. Official prosecutions for breaches of the Merchant Shipping Acts were, by their nature, brought against the master or, occasionally, the mate. Although the Consul was, formally, the shipping officer, the consular constable usually handled the work and many official prosecutions are brought in the constable's name—particularly routine charges, such as failing to keep logs in order.

A third group of cases—usually involving an assault of some kind—produced a mixed bag of defendants and prosecutors from officers down to cabin boys. In Nagasaki, 20 cases were brought against officers or other crewmen by Japanese sailors, who were not slow to complain to the Consul without involving the Japanese authorities.[93] Cases were occasionally, brought by masters against officers for being drunk or abusive.[94] The charge of 'assault' covers a wide range of cases: many little more than a scuffle; but others were more serious: Chang Kai, the captain's boy on the *Columbia*, was convicted of a 'savage assault' on the ship's steward and sentenced to six weeks imprisonment.

Some prosecutions brought by sailors may have emanated from a genuine grievance or, perhaps, frustrations on board such as when Captain Saris was prosecuted for ill-treatment (and acquitted) in Kobe;[95] others arose from vindictiveness. We see several instances where, one day, a master prosecutes a crewman only, in turn, to be prosecuted for assault by that, or another, crewman a few days later or vice versa.[96] When two crewmen sued the *Lady Belona*'s master for not providing fresh provisions and medical treatment in harbour, their suit was dismissed; but, later, the master prosecuted them for assaulting his steward.[97] A Chinese sailor on

92 Table 14. In Yokohama, the proportion of British defendants in the newspaper reports was nearer nine-tenths.

93 Robertson to Parkes, 28 May 1883; FO881/4938.

94 The *Staley*'s master prosecuted the mate in Hakodate for being 'drunk and abusive' in 1867; FO656/34.

95 Semi-annual returns 1870; FO656/34.

96 In cross-actions in Nagasaki involving the *Serpent*'s master and mate and four Japanese sailors, the latter prosecuted the former for assault (the master was acquitted but the mate convicted and fined $5) whilst the Japanese were convicted for refusal of duty and AWOL and imprisoned until the ship sailed (12 June 1876; FO796/2).

97 Semi-annual returns, second half 1873; FO656/35.

the *Nemo*, a sealing ship, accused Carozzi, its master, of failing to record his injuries in the log but Carozzi was acquitted because the Chinese was believed to have waited deliberately until all the European crew had left Yokohama before laying his plaint.[98] It was not only crewmen who may have fabricated cases, for the *Oceana*'s master, after being prosecuted by the crew for failing to supply lime juice, prosecuted them for embezzling cargo; but, it transpired that this was his second attempt and the consul in Madeira had already dismissed this charge.[99]

Some ships were clearly 'unhappy ships' as shown by *criminal cases 2–4 and 6–8* in Nagasaki, 1878[100] where two Chinese sailors were accused of refusal of duty but acquitted with costs against the master, before they prosecuted him, successfully, for assault and serving short rations. A week later, he prosecuted them for desertion and they were sentenced to six weeks' imprisonment. Five crewmen from the *Annie Muriel* were sentenced to 30 days each for being in a state of mutiny and threatening the ship's master.[101] Four sailors from the *Carrier Dove*, who had been convicted of refusal of duty and sentenced to 10 days' imprisonment, were waiting on the verandah outside the courtroom to be taken off to gaol when they attacked and severely beat up the master. For this assault they were each given a further 12 weeks' imprisonment.[102]

Offences against discipline (e.g. refusal of duty and being AWOL) constituted over two-thirds of shipping offences although, within this total, there were differences in the category's precise make-up between the different ports. In Nagasaki, refusal of duty formed the bulk of cases in the early years whilst being AWOL did in the later years.[103] In Yokohama and Kobe, the level of AWOL and desertion cases appears, on the basis of the semi-annual returns, to be nearly on a par with refusal of duty cases; but AWOL cases form a much lower proportion when we consider just the newspaper reports. Some differences may be down to classification—particularly as regards drunkenness which played its part in both AWOL and refusal of duty cases. Sailors accused of these offences frequently sought, at trial, to be discharged from the ship—something that was, generally, resisted by the Consuls (because discharged sailors ashore would be unlikely to have any gainful employment and would join the ranks of

98 *Reg. (ats. Yu Sow Chow) v. Carozzi*, 5 October 1889; JWM.
99 3 August 1872; JWM.
100 FO796/2.
101 15 February 1873; NE.
102 30 April 1886; HN.
103 Table 14.

Western loafers—and trouble-makers—in the Treaty Ports and/or become a burden on government funds). Whereas assaults tried in Nagasaki declined as a proportion over time, newspaper reports of shipping offences tried in Yokohama show them to have increased—but, this difference may be a reflection of the newspapers reporting only the more serious cases.

'Others' was a mixed bag of, on the whole, very individual cases and included thefts, harbouring deserters, criminal damage, and breaches of the Merchant Shipping Acts—usually a failure to complete the various logs and records required[104] or to register sailors upon the ship's articles[105] but also included serious charges of sending ships to sea in an unseaworthy condition.[106] A number involved the master's sailing and leaving a sailor onshore (allegedly, to avoid paying his wages[107] or, with sealing ships, to avoid a return to Russian waters where the ship, when loaded with sealskins, faced capture[108]). The newspapers reported a handful of murder or manslaughter cases arising from stabbings. Two defendants were acquitted but the others were convicted of manslaughter and sentenced to between one and five years' imprisonment with hard labour.

Cases were usually heard the same day as the complaint was lodged or the next day. Only in the most serious cases, where the defendant was committed for trial on indictment, was there a time-lag—usually a couple of months—before the trial. The swift action, the evidence from the cases of a close co-operation between the local police and the consular constables and the numbers charged with being onshore without leave who were promptly sent back on board suggests (although admittedly a supposition) that many cases were instances of the local police rounding-up troublesome sailors and the British authorities removing them swiftly so as to maintain peace and order in the ports.

Reg. v. Capt. Hutchison of the *Caleban* is an example of close co-operation between the authorities. Wilkinson praised the Japanese police for alerting

---

[104] Sections 240 et seq. MSA1894; and Section 425 relating to collisions.

[105] Criminal case 13, 17 February 1879 in Nagasaki where the Master was fined $10 plus $2.50 costs; FO796/4.

[106] *Board of Trade v. Thomas Berwick* and *Reg. v. Cocking and Singleton* in respect of the *Wanja* and *Snowflake* respectively. All defendants were acquitted; Hakodate semi-annual returns, 1873; FO656/35, and 17 December 1874; NCH, respectively.

[107] Angus Croal was convicted, and fined $25, for leaving a Japanese sailor at Vladivostok; *Reg. ats. Playfair v. Angus Croal, master of the Dorothy*, 15 January 1885; FO796/7.

[108] Gierow was fined £50 for marooning two sailors on Robben Island in the Sea of Okhotsk (5 October 1889; JWM) and Pyne of the *Arctic* was fined $25 for a similar offence (23 November 1889; JWM).

the British authorities when the ship's mate took two Chinese ship's boys to the police and accused them of theft as, but for the police's good sense, 'much more serious results might have accrued'.[109] The boys were subject to British or Chinese jurisdiction—but not Japanese, and so the mate had no business taking them before the Japanese police.

A noticeable aspect of shipping offences is the high conviction rate. Over 90% of defendants in Nagasaki were convicted compared with 75% in criminal cases.[110] This is largely the result of guilty pleas as over three-quarters of defendants pleaded guilty (against only a quarter in criminal cases). The Yokohama figures are slightly lower with 85% of defendants convicted of at least one charge and just under 60% pleading guilty; but, again, this may be due to the selection of reported cases which would favour reporting disputed cases. However, acquittal rates for contested cases in both ports was the same as for criminal cases, at about a third.

Despite the view expressed by the *Teviot*'s captain that 'a master of a British ship has no chance against his crew',[111] the cases show that Consuls felt constrained to uphold discipline on ships for Robertson said he 'would uphold discipline'[112] even though not entirely happy with the circumstances surrounding the *Strathleven*'s chief engineer's prosecution of a stoker for assault. Except in the most egregious cases, the Courts tended to back up a master and officers who charged sailors for offences against discipline and to acquit masters when prosecuted by the crew. That is not to say that the Courts disregarded the crew's welfare for Wilkinson reprimanded the *Teviot*'s master for his conduct and adjured him to look after his men despite convicting three sailors of refusal of duty. In clear cases, the Courts would sanction officers and a master was fined $15 for assaulting a crewman sent back on board after being AWOL. The Court complained of the 'aggravated nature of the offence' and the master's 'disregard for the Court' by assaulting the crewman immediately after his punishment by the Court.[113] Even when convicting crewmen, Consuls took notice of their complaints and, occasionally, ordered a Naval Court or other inspection into shipboard conditions, as when Robertson ordered an

---

109 5 June 1875; JWM. The master was prosecuted for carrying them without their having signed articles contrary to section 157 MSA1854 which Wilkinson held to be a strict liability offence when dismissing his pleas of ignorance and the regional custom for such boys to be shipped privately as servants.

110 Tables 9 and 14.

111 29 March 1879; JWM. (At Wilkinson's order, he withdrew, and apologized for, the statement.)

112 7 April 1888; JWM.

113 Criminal case 58 of 1878; FO796/4.

enquiry into complaints of nine sailors from the *Thomas Perry* whom he had convicted of refusal of duty.[114]

The prosecution of two sailors from the *Cyprus* highlights the brutal conditions under which sailors served on some vessels. When Adam Olsen and Louis de Daeker were prosecuted in Kobe for being AWOL and refusal of duty, it transpired that the master, Cereno Johnson, had already imprisoned them on board the vessel and starved them into trying to force them to work—allegedly on the advice of the shipping officer at the Yokohama consulate. In view of this, Aston offered the defendants the chance to avoid further punishment provided they returned to work. When they refused, he sentenced them to one week's imprisonment. Meanwhile, he expressed his strong disapproval of the master's starvation method of trying to enforce discipline before censuring the master for not logging the punishment. In a sequel, de Daeker sued Johnson for $99 damages for deprivation of food and water. Although Aston held that the master had acted harshly and improperly and exceeded his authority and the wide powers conferred upon him by the Merchant Shipping Acts, he nonetheless awarded de Daeker just $1 in damages (and costs of $25).[115]

Mates were more likely to be convicted in assault cases than the masters, although, even here, the Courts occasionally found that the defendant, although technically guilty, was 'not to be blamed' because the assault had been provoked by the prosecutor.[116] The reverse occurred in *Lancing v. Young*, when the *Chanticleer*'s mate prosecuted a steward for assault. The Court acquitted the defendant as it found he had been beaten and ill-used by the mate whom it promptly fined $25 for such assault and criticized the master for allowing such abuse on his ship.[117] Masters were almost always convicted when charged with breaches of the Merchant Shipping Acts; particularly when accused of failing to maintain their logs—usually, the omission was patent so there could be no denial: only a plea in mitigation.

Although the Courts' punitive jurisdiction covered foreigners, the cases do not suggest any bias by the Courts against foreign—including Japanese—sailors. Such bias as may have existed lay in the Consuls' tendency to support a master where maintenance of discipline was an issue.

---

114 7 April 1888; JWM.

115 *Reg. ats. Cereno Johnson v. Adam Olsen and Louis de Daeker* and *Louis de Daeker v. Cereno Johnson*; 8 and 23 August 1883; HN.

116 Criminal case 13 of 1878; FO 796/4. A seaman on *Sir Charles Napier* prosecuted, for assault, the second mate who was convicted but fined just 10 cents 'because the prosecutor started the fight' and both were ordered to pay $2.75 costs.

117 2 March 1866; *Japan Times*.

As in criminal cases, defendants facing multiple charges were usually either found guilty or acquitted of all charges; very few cases resulted in split decisions. John Kelly, the *Riversdale*'s steward, was an example of a split decision when he was acquitted in Nagasaki of having connived at Japanese women being brought on board the vessel for passage to Hong Kong but convicted at the same hearing of wilful disobedience of other orders for which he was sentenced to one month's hard labour.[118] Punishments were awarded in respect of the overall result and—at least in the semi-annual returns—not allocated to individual charges. The range of punishments was similar to that in criminal cases but we also see sailors either being returned immediately to their ship (particularly in refusal of duty or AWOL cases) or being held in prison until their ship sailed, when they would be put back on board their ship. There was no wish to keep sailors imprisoned—at government expense—after their ship had sailed except for the most serious offences and many fixed term prison sentences were qualified by the rider that the sailor was to be returned to his ship in the event of its being ready to leave before the sentence was completed. There were no deportations, and orders to pay compensatory damages were uncommon; but deductions from wages in lieu of fines were a feature with shipping offences that was unknown with criminal cases.

A not uncommon request of sailors convicted of a shipping offence was to be discharged from the vessel; but such requests were only rarely granted. Again, the British authorities had no wish to become responsible for those sailors in the event of their being unable to find another vessel. When Joseph Paris and George da Salvo were put back on board the *Abbey Cowper* for refusal of duty, the Court allowed that they could be discharged from the vessel if they could find a berth on another ship. However, reports of several follow up cases against them for mutinous conduct and continued refusal of duty suggests that no other vessel in the port was prepared to take them and, after his third appearance before the Court, da Salvo was gaoled for 12 weeks and ordered to pay the costs of his imprisonment.[119]

No subjective assessment can be made of many sentences—even from the Nagasaki Court minutes let alone the semi-annual returns—because the information is insufficient to assess why some punishments for the same stated offence are minor (such as a mere admonishment or simply

[118] Cases 16 and 17 of 1891; Register of Criminal Cases; FO796/6.
[119] 26 February 8 and 29 March 1876; TRS&NE.

being sent back on board) when others more severe. Why, for instance, was a mutineer ordered to pay damages and eight deserters just the costs of their apprehension[120] when others convicted of similar offences were imprisoned?

If one ignores indeterminate imprisonment until departure, treats being sent back on board, fines under $6 (or the loss of up to six days' pay) and prison terms up to seven days as signifying 'minor offences', shipping offences involved a greater proportion of serious offences than in relation to criminal cases. Just under half of the sentences in Nagasaki and Kobe and just over a half in Yokohama were minor offences compared with nearly two-thirds of criminal cases.[121] As time progressed, the number of gaol terms in Nagasaki increased and, in later years, nearly two-thirds of convicted defendants were gaoled—albeit for shorter periods; most subject to hard labour. In Yokohama and Kobe (and, in later years, Nagasaki), hard labour was imposed in a significant number of prison sentences. A number of prison terms in Kobe were also ordered to be served on 'bread and water' for the first week of the sentence. In Nagasaki only seven British sailors were ordered 'to be kept on rice and water' when they were gaoled for six weeks each.[122]

Masters usually suffered higher fines, with fines of over $20 (often expressed in Sterling) common, particularly for breaches of the provisions of the Merchant Shipping Acts—which often specified the maximum fines. The *Morvern*'s master was fined £5 for not logging its collision with the *Yuzao*,[123] and the *Thompson*'s master, £15 for harbouring a deserter from the *Grasmere* in Hakodate.[124] When two deserters from HMS *Vulcan* were found concealed on board the *Imogen* in Nagasaki in 1861, its captain and mate were each fined $25 for taking insufficient measures to ensure deserters were not on board and the Consul warned them that, had complicity been proved, the fines would have been $100.[125] No master, apart from the *Normanton*'s Captain Drake, was imprisoned.[126]

As with criminal cases, court costs added significantly to the lesser punishments.[127] Consuls often imposed a deduction of wages on sailors to

120 Semi-annual return first half 1871; FO656/37.
121 Tables 13 and 15.
122 October 1877; FO796/2.
123 *S.F. Lawrence v. master of the ss. Morvern*, 31 December 1896; FO796/14.
124 Nagasaki semi-annual return 1868; FO656/34.
125 21 September 1861; *The Nagasaki Shipping List and Advertiser*.
126 See pages 186–188.
127 See the *Sir Charles Napier* case; footnote 116.

pay for the costs of their imprisonment thus increasing the effective penalty and, unlike criminal case offenders, who often hadn't the means to pay these costs, they could be deducted easily from sailors' future wages. Sailors in AWOL and desertion cases often suffered further from the British authorities' practice of charging the ship's master for constables to find and arrest missing seamen and deserters. Hornby had ruled that such charges were illegal and Mowat had described them as 'robbery',[128] but Consuls continued to levy them and masters opted to pay them and deduct the amounts from sailors' wages on the basis that the deduction would not be challenged.[129]

Sailors were usually only charged such costs when they were prosecuted by a vessel's master—who would be paying the court fees in the first instance. Where their vessel had already sailed, the records frequently show no costs entered in respect of the case and the phrase 'no funds' is found written against the case.[130] Presumably, the British authorities had no option but to charge the deserters when they were picked up by the local authorities and bear the prosecution costs themselves as the deserters had no funds and were without a vessel on which they could earn wages from which the costs could be deducted. Similarly, with deserters (or 'stragglers') from Royal Naval vessels, no court costs were charged but the 'straggler' would be detained in custody until he could be forwarded by Naval vessel to Shanghai or Hong Kong.[131]

Civil Matters

None of the Treaty Ports was a Port of Registry for British vessels. The Merchant Shipping Act 1854 provided that only British registered vessels

---

[128] Parkes to Hornby, 25 March 1873; FO656/19. Parkes demanded that 'Mowat not make such remarks from the Bench which adversely adduces the Consular Service in Japan.'

[129] Shanghai case of *C.H. Coster v. W.H. Tapp*, 10 March 1873; NCH. Coster, master of the *Washi*, had discharged a seaman at Shanghai and sought to deduct, from his wages, $14.50 that he had paid to the Kobe consular constable to find and return him to the ship. Tapp, a clerk in the Shanghai Consulate's shipping section, refused to allow the deduction; but, allegedly, retained the sum pending Coster's obtaining a confirmation of the payment from the Kobe consulate. Tapp denied making any such promise and sought to have the summons dismissed because he was merely following instructions. Mowat, presiding, found no evidence that Tapp had agreed to make the payment and dismissed the summons.

[130] See Nagasaki Register of Criminal Cases; FO796/6.

[131] See the case of George Stevens in 1899 in the Register of Civil Cases; FO796/6.

could fly the flag so the question arose as to whether British owned vessels constructed in British shipyards in Nagasaki could be registered and fly the flag so as to avail themselves of British protection. Alcock said that no one in Japan could register the vessel; but, as a practical solution, he authorized Consuls to issue the master with provisional sailing letters strictly for the purposes of proceeding to Hong Kong to register the vessel.[132] The acting Attorney General in Hong Kong concurred with this approach but suggested that, besides Hong Kong, vessels also be permitted to proceed to Sydney—or, in exceptional circumstances, another port in the British Dominions—for registration and that the sailing letters be time limited to a reasonable time for completion of the voyage.[133]

Very few civil claims arose out of purely onboard concerns. Where claimants sought a lien over the vessel or its sale to meet their claims, suits needed to be brought in Admiralty and could be brought only in the Yokohama Court or HMCJ, although Consuls could hear claims for wages under £50 under the Merchant Shipping Acts. In 1876, the Yokohama Court, sitting in Admiralty, ordered the *Rupek*'s sale to pay its sailors and return them to their ports of engagement in Singapore and the South Pacific Islands,[134] whilst, in 1895, HMCJ arrested and sold the *Arctic* to pay three sailors' claims totalling $7,634 and costs of $300.[135] Claims for unpaid wages (and other matters) could be brought as personal actions against the master and owners before a Consul—but, not being a claim in Admiralty, without having the remedy of selling the ship to meet the claim. A Japanese sailor successfully sued the *Serpent*'s master for $14.90 arrears of wages before the Nagasaki Consul,[136] whilst the Yokohama Court awarded Ah Qui $26 in unpaid wages against the *Washi*'s master who had left him behind in Hakodate so forcing him to work his passage back to Yokohama.[137]

Other cases involved disputes over terms of employment,[138] or sought to compel the master's compliance with his obligations under the

132 Alcock to Morrison, 9 September 1861; FO796/21.

133 Alcock to Consuls, 17 March 1862 enclosing a copy of Smale's Opinion of 24 October 1861; FO796/23.

134 30 December 1876; JWM.

135 7 December 1894; JWM.

136 4 November 1875; FO 796/2.

137 *Ah Qui v. Hescroft*, 7 November 1874; JWM.

138 In *Carl Beato Klante v. Captain James* of the *Omi maru*, Hannen dismissed Klante's claim for $48 because there were no signed articles—although, because Hannen considered the captain had engaged in sharp practice, he denied him costs; 27 September 1884; JWM.

Merchant Shipping Acts. Seamen were to be allowed ashore to see the Consul for such purposes; otherwise the master was liable to a fine of £10.[139] Following such a visit to the Hakodate Consul in 1873, the *Lady Belona*'s crew sought to enforce the master's obligations under the Merchant Shipping Acts.

In *Ianguro v. William Cotton*,[140] *master of the Hideyoshimaru,* the plaintiff was compelled to sue the British master in the Consular Court for payment for stores supplied despite both the plaintiff and ship's owners being Japanese and the vessel being Japanese flagged.

That civil and criminal cases could become conflated is shown by *Chief Engineer of Osaka v Fletcher, Master of Osaka* heard by Goodwin in the Shanghai Police Court in 1868.[141] Although heard in Shanghai, the case arose entirely out of Japan based facts. It was also one of the first cases heard in Shanghai involving Japan based facts where the prosecutor was represented by counsel—Hannen.[142] Fletcher was charged with assault and refusing to allow the engineer to go ashore at Hakodate to see the Consul, which, under the Merchant Shipping Act 1854, all sailors had a right to do. Initially, Fletcher had instructed that sufficient fuel be taken on board to take the ship to Yokohama but then announced the vessel would proceed direct to Shanghai. All the engineers protested at this decision because they all had outstanding civil cases against the master in Yokohama and the master was seeking to avoid the cases. When the chief engineer asked the master's permission to see the Consul in Hakodate, Fletcher replied 'damn the Consul, he is nobody' and that he would take care to see nobody left the ship on any pretence. The Captain then struck the engineer. Fletcher was convicted by the Shanghai court on all counts and fined £5 plus costs.[143]

This case shows how criminal cases could be brought in Shanghai even for crimes committed in Japan if it was convenient for the parties. It also highlights the near dictatorial powers a ship's master had at that time and how, in this case, he sought to deprive these officers of such protection as the Hakodate Consul might have afforded them and,

139 Section 211 MSA1894.

140 Civil case no. 26 of 1879, FO796/4.

141 17 October 1868; NCH.

142 This was not unusual in Shanghai by this time. Fletcher was, however, unrepresented.

143 There is no report of the conclusions of the engineers' cases against Fletcher in Yokohama.

by sailing for Shanghai, to avoid the civil case which they had laid against him in Yokohama.

Inquiries and Naval Courts

Where a death (regardless of the deceased's nationality) occurred on the High Seas on a British vessel, the Consul at the next port, sitting alone, was required to inquire into it and report to the Board of Trade.[144] These inquiries were an administrative application of the Merchant Shipping Acts to British vessels and were, in essence, a consular—not a judicial—function and unrelated to extra-territoriality. Where the death occurred whilst the vessel was in harbour, such death was usually the subject of an Inquest although we do see a couple of cases where a Board of Trade inquiry was held. Wileman, the Vice-Consul in Kobe in 1899, held such an Inquiry into the death of Kwok Ching of the *Airlie* who was washed overboard when cleaning the gangway ladder in harbour.[145]

There are 22 newspaper reports of Inquiries in Yokohama and five in Kobe; but, the only official records are the somewhat formalistic minutes of 31 Nagasaki Inquiries over a 20 year period.[146] The minutes usually started 'An Enquiry into the death of X on board *ss*...' and included signed statements from relevant people on the ship. Causes of death ranged from ship-board accidents such as falling from the topgallants into the sea,[147] falling into the harbour whilst drunk,[148] falling down the hatch,[149] through advanced syphilis,[150] to natural causes. These Inquiries also tended to look into the treatment given to the deceased by the ship's officers during any illness if only to record 'everything possible was done for him'.[151] Only one Inquiry, into the death of Lee Fong following a quarrel over a 20 cent. gambling debt, found foul play which led to the assailant's prosecution for manslaughter in 1895.

---

144 Section 690 MSA1894 provided that a shipping superintendent should carry out the role but Section 737 provided that, 'in any place outside Her Majesty's dominions in which Her Majesty has jurisdiction', Her Majesty could extend the power to the consul.

145 14 June 1899; KWC.

146 Minutes of Enquiry into Deaths on board Ships, 1883–1903, Nagasaki; FO796/9.

147 Hirata Yosuke of the *Satsuma*, 26 December 1884; FO796/9.

148 A sailor from the *Ardgowan*, 24 March 1891; FO796/9.

149 Death of John Wilkie Pant; 22 February 1899; KWC.

150 Hamada Takejiro of the *Dorothy*, 29 December 1889; FO796/9.

151 For example, the Inquiry into the death of Gustave Carlson a sailor on the *Castle Rock* whilst on passage from New York to Kobe; 26 March 1898; KWC.

The Merchant Shipping Acts also provided for Naval Courts to be convened by a Naval Officer or, in his absence, the Consul whenever a British vessel was 'wrecked, abandoned, or otherwise lost' on the High Seas or abroad or otherwise 'whenever desirable'.[152] Despite being called a 'court', a Naval Court was, like the Inquiry, not a judicial body but an administrative tribunal which enquired into, and reported to the Board of Trade, on the relevant event. As such, its processes were inquisitorial, not adversarial,[153] and the subject of the enquiry had no right to object to its composition as, although it investigated questions of fact, it was not a jury.[154]

Naval Courts were not standing bodies; but convened *ad hoc* and consisted of three to five members including a Naval and a Consular officer, the senior of whom presided, plus a master of a British vessel. In practice, they were usually convened by the senior Naval Officer on the station, who appointed the members and the Consul presided with a Commander or Lieutenant representing the Navy; but a Captain, who outranked a Consul, would preside if a member of the Naval Court. We see only two instances of a Captain presiding: the Naval Court into the *Yetchiu maru*'s sinking, where no consular representative was included on the panel (but, for the only time, we see two Japanese mercantile masters sitting as two of the four assessors); and the Naval Court into the *Chishima-Ravenna* collision. In the Naval Court into the *Argyll*'s stranding there was no consular member of the Court which was presided over by a Lieutenant.

Although Naval Courts were formal administrative hearings which could lead to sanctions against a vessel's officers and even criminal or civil proceedings, it was rare for any party to be represented before them by counsel. The first instance of counsel—Lowder—being reported as present was the Naval Court in 1884 enquiring into the loss of the *Dilsberg* and one of its lady passengers. It is unclear for whom Lowder appeared; but, when the master was held responsible for the vessel's loss as it was lying too low in the water and his certificate was suspended for two months, Lowder's request for his costs was rejected. Russell Robertson, who was presiding, said there was no precedent for counsel who appeared at a Naval Court to be entitled to costs—it was an investigation, not a court

[152] Sections 480–484, MSA1894.

[153] However, where everyone knew civil litigation would ensue, the process—although still investigative—is pervaded by this knowledge. See Chapter 7 (The *Chishima-Ravenna* collision) for a description of the Naval Court proceedings in the *Chishima case*.

[154] Captain Morton of the *Oneiza* wanted a Naval Officer replaced by a merchant seaman but Robertson dismissed his objection as the senior Naval Officer had selected the Naval Court, 23 December 1871; JWM.

case.[155] In the Naval Court into the collision between the *Ravenna* and the *Chishima kan*, Lowder appeared to represent the master and owners of the *Ravenna* while Montague Kirkwood was present in court to keep an eye on the proceedings for the Japanese government. At a Naval Court in Kobe before HMS *Iphigenia's* Lieutenant and two mercantile masters to enquire into the *Argyll's* loss, the Vice-Consul, Wileman represented the Crown in the enquiry whilst Brushfield appeared for the master. No one appeared on behalf of the mate who had been left in charge of the vessel and was censured—and his certificate suspended for three months—for not having veered the ship's cable or used its engine to prevent its stranding in the harbour during a typhoon. The master was expressly exonerated from all blame as he could not have foreseen the typhoon when he left the vessel.[156]

A Naval Court's principal remedy was to clear, or reprimand, the officers concerned and, in serious cases, remove their competency certificates. Apart from administrative appeals within the Board of Trade—judicial review not then being a general proceeding—no appeals lay from its findings. A Naval Court had no judicial enforcement powers.

The issue of blame was important for the reputation (and possible civil liability) of the officers involved. Naval Courts would often express an opinion such as freeing 'the master from all blame'[157] as when a Naval Court in Hakodate enquired into the loss of the *Siam*. However, in appropriate circumstances such as an officer not displaying adequate nautical skills, a Naval Court would recommend the suspension or removal of an officer's certificate. The Naval Court into the loss of the *Ella Beatrice* off Hokkaido suspended the master's certificate for 12 months because it found that all on board apart from him had realized that the vessel was too close to a lee shore long before she struck.[158] Similarly, Robertson suspended the *Sattara*'s master's certificate when she was lost off Cape Omaezaki because the master had not been sounding the lead and had failed to wear the ship in time.[159] When the *Yetchiu maru* sank, the Naval Court found the captain 'solely to blame for the loss'[160] and recommended the suspension of his certificate for nine months and 'severely reprimanded

155 25 November 1884; HN.
156 27 September 1899; KWC.
157 6 March 1873; NCH.
158 2 April 1881; TRS&NE.
159 21 February 1884; HN.
160 3 April 1890; NCH.

and cautioned' the second mate.[161] We also see different decisions about different aspects of an incident: when the *Belgic* was stranded at Sunosaki with the loss of 20 men, the Naval Court severely reprimanded the master but commended the mate.[162] When the P&O steamer *Bombay* collided with the USS *Oneida*, the Naval Court exonerated the master from blame for the collision but suspended his certificate for six months for failing to stand by and render assistance to the USS *Oneida*.[163] The Naval Court into the *Queen Elizabeth*'s sinking off Ikishima resulted in the mate's being commended for having warned the master that he was too close to land and should haul off. The master was censured for not having done so—and his master's certificate was suspended for six months.[164]

The only available official records are the minutes from 1884 to 1896 of Naval Courts in Nagasaki.[165] Otherwise, we are left with newspaper accounts which, in total, reported 40 Naval Courts in Yokohama; 19 in Nagasaki; 12 in Kobe and four in Hakodate. The earliest reports of Naval Courts were in Yokohama in 1864 into the loss of *Star of Peace* with 15 men off Cape Omaezaki[166] and Nagasaki in 1865 into the wreck of the *Satsuma*. The latter Naval Court determined that no blame attached to the master or officers who had missed the harbour entrance in bad weather and the Consul minuted that he was asking the local authorities to erect a lighthouse to the Nagasaki harbour entrance.[167]

Whilst most Naval Courts revolved around the loss, collision or stranding of vessels, the general power to convene one 'whenever desirable' was also utilized. A Nagasaki Naval Court cancelled the *Snap*'s master's certificate and removed him from command because, during its passage from Kobe to Shimonoseki, he 'constantly abused his authority and acted in a most tyrannical manner ... to prolong the voyage with a view to the increase of his own wages ... [and was] guilty of repeated drunkenness'.[168] This general power was also available if, during a criminal trial, crewmen complained about a vessel's condition. When several crew from the *Thomas Perry* were convicted of refusal of duty, the Court nevertheless took up their complaints, warned the master and mate to use better

---

161 Ibid.
162 26 October 1895; JWM.
163 23 February 1872; HN.
164 1 April 1891; TRS&NE.
165 FO796/11.
166 27 February 1864; TJH.
167 Gower to Board of Trade, 18 July 1865; FO796/29.
168 24 May 1873; NCH.

language to the crew and ordered a Naval Court into their complaints at which the master was fined £25 for not carrying lime juice and proper medicines.[169]

When the *Macedon* arrived in Kobe from Philadelphia with a number of crew suffering from scurvy and five others having died on passage a Naval Court was held to enquire into the background. The mate and the bosun were reprimanded for their ill-treatment of the crew whilst the master was fined £5 for doing nothing to prevent such ill-treatment. He was fined a further £5 for failing to provide lime juice to the crew and yet another £5 for not entering the sickness in the ship's log.[170]

The Chinese crew of the *Sinkolga* demanded a Naval Court to investigate their claim that the ship's master, Captain Wates, and mate, Lami Bang, had not done enough to save a sailor who had fallen overboard. The Naval Court unanimously dismissed the complaint and absolved them from blame for this incident; but, the enquiry revealed that the *de facto* positions of the master and the mate were reversed—and the Naval Court expressed its disapproval of such arrangements.[171] With the *Marcia*, it was the owners who demanded a Naval Court to investigate the master's conduct; but, after examining many witnesses, the Naval Court found all the allegations to be false and honourably discharged the master and ordered the owners to pay the costs of the enquiry.[172]

The costs of a Naval Court hearing were, usually, specified in Sterling and ranged from £4/8/- (£4.40) for the enquiry into the *Mount Lebanon*'s stranding on the No. 2 Fort at the entrance to Tokyo Bay to £26/19/8 (£26.98) in the *Ravenna*'s case; but, averaged around £10–£12. The costs were to be met by the relevant ship's master or the subjects of the enquiry and, thus, acted as an incentive towards good conduct. The £19/5/- (£19.25) costs of the Naval Court into the *Macedon* were ordered to be paid by the master, the mate and the bosun.

The Japanese equivalent was the Marine Court of Enquiry and, where Britons needed a Japanese licence, as when officering a Japanese vessel or acting as a pilot, they were subject to its administrative oversight in relation to that licence. This was not a breach of extra-territoriality for the Marine Court of Enquiry was an administrative body applying administrative provisions in relation only to the relevant Japanese permission.

169 7 April 1888; JWM.
170 11 January 1888; TRS&NE.
171 15 March 1884; TRS&NE.
172 31 August 1887; TRS&NE.

For instance, it revoked Hardnett's Japanese navigation certificate after his manslaughter conviction of the *Sakata maru*'s quartermaster.[173] Another example of practical Anglo-Japanese co-operation was the Marine Court of Enquiry into the sinking of Mitsubishi's *Sekiro maru* conducted by a British president and two merchant navy captains (who suspended the master's certificate for three months).[174] In several other cases, the Marine Court of Enquiry was presided over by a Japanese officer but the additional assessors were British mercantile marine masters. However, where a British certificate was involved, as when, Mitsubishi's *Kiinokuni maru* was lost, a Naval Court investigated the master's culpability.[175]

Of the 67 reported Naval Courts where we have a result which can be broadly categorized into 'exoneration' and 'censure'—the other cases either not being such as to avail themselves of such a classification or the results being unknown—the master or other officer was censured in just over half the cases;[176] and an officer's certificate was suspended or revoked in ten cases. Of course, there were instances when there were no survivors from the loss of a vessel so that the Naval Court was left largely with surmise. When the *Plainsmeller* bound for Yokohama was lost with all hands, the Naval Court could only conclude that the loss was probably down to the overloading of the vessel.[177] Similarly, when the *Theseus* was lost during a typhoon along with its master and mate, the Naval Court was unable to decide how the vessel had got itself into that position as the second officer, who survived, was not a navigator.[178]

The principal function of the Naval Courts was to enquire into the relevant circumstances—especially with a view to the crew's competence at sea—not to allocate blame or to allocate damages as between two vessels involved in a collision. This distinction is important when we consider accusations of inherent bias on the part of Naval Courts. Given that the results of the criminal cases and civil cases do not support any accusations of a pro-British (or anti-Japanese or other foreigner) bias on the part of the Courts and the Consuls, it would be somewhat surprising to find them sustained in the case of the Naval Courts.

---

173 See page 139.

174 11 July 1885; JWM.

175 11 October 1882; NCH. It exonerated the British master from all blame but suspended the second mate's certificate for three months.

176 Table 16.

177 15 December 1886; TRS&NE.

178 11 October 1876; HN. The Naval Court went on to record its appreciation for the kind and humane treatment of the survivors by the local Japanese authorities.

The issue comes into focus most clearly in the case of collisions, where there was always the threat of a civil action in damages, or where the loss of a vessel also involved the loss of life which could arouse Press comment. The Japanese Press condemned the findings of the Naval Courts into the loss of the *Normanton* and the *Ravenna* collision but the English language Press also criticized the Naval Court's conclusions in the loss of the *Thibet*, a P&O vessel, where the Press claimed that the findings were so completely wrong and contrary to the evidence as to make it unlikely that P&O would ever apply for another Naval Court in Japan—but would prefer to apply in Hong Kong or elsewhere.[179]

Of course, we must remember that Naval Courts were, usually, a somewhat one-sided investigatory affair and not an adversarial battle as in the Courts with two opposing sides adducing evidence in support of their cases. A Naval Court sitting at Yokohama exonerated the P&O's *Borneo* from any blame for its collision with the *Woyomaru* but the Marine Court of Enquiry in Tokyo reached the opposite conclusion and said the *Woyomaru* was not to blame and the collision was all down to the *Borneo*.[180] As Chapter 7 (The *Chishima-Ravenna* collision) will show, the same happened in the case of the *Ravenna* and the *Chishima*. A susbsequent newspaper report suggested that the *Woyomaru*'s owners were resolved upon bringing a claim against P&O—but there is no report of any such action so any dispute was, presumably, settled privately; and, of course, there never was a civil court determination of responsibility for the *Chishima-Ravenna* collision.

It was certainly possible for a Naval Court to reach one conclusion and a civil court to reach another. The Naval Court into the collision between the *Glamorganshire* and the *Clarissa B. Carver* found that no blame could be attached to the *Glamorganshire*'s master or mate for the collision and that its lights were in working order. Further, the *Glamorganshire*'s master had acted in a seamanlike manner and would have endangered his own vessel had he stood by the *Clarissa B. Carver*. Therefore, their certificates were returned to them.[181] However, the subsequent civil actions were decided conclusively in favour of the *Clarissa B. Carver* and against the *Glamorganshire*.[182]

This suggests that, while there may be no issues of bias, one might question the thoroughness with which some Naval Courts were conducted.

---

179 Editorial, 22 July 1887; TRS&NE.
180 23 April 1898; KWC.
181 20 June 1885; TRS&NE.
182 See pages 277–282.

Certainly, the findings of the Naval Court into the loss of the *Normanton*—and the loss of its Japanese passengers—which exonerated Captain Drake from blame sit at odds with Drake's conviction for manslaughter by a jury in HMCJ for allowing his Japanese passengers to drown.[183]

In late October 1886, the *Normanton* under Drake left Yokohama bound for Kobe. At Yokohama, despite the *Normanton*'s not being licensed to carry passengers, he had taken on board 23 Japanese passengers (mainly elderly men and some women) who travelled steerage: essentially, sleeping and living in a couple of the lower internal passageways. Off Cape Omaezaki, the *Normanton* grazed a rock which tore open its bottom and water flooded into its engine room. Drake ordered three lifeboats to be readied and everybody into the boats. However, the Japanese passengers refused to leave their passageways. Drake ordered the bosun to try once more to get them to abandon the vessel but they still refused and the ship sank so quickly that the bosun and six firemen—all Lascars—were left on board along with the passengers as she went down. The bosun was picked up by the lifeboats the next morning.

Of the 38 crew and one Chinese boy—who, as we have already seen, tended to be carried as a supernumerary—and 23 Japanese passengers, just 26 made it ashore: all the officers, 18 crewmen and the Chinese boy. One British sailor had died trying to lower a boat, three Lascars had died overnight of exposure in the boats, three Lascars had committed suicide and all six who had been left on board perished—along with all the Japanese passengers.

When the Naval Court, presided over by Troup along with two merchant navy masters, opened in Kobe, Troup said that the focus of the Naval Court was into the causes of the wreck and the conduct of the vessel's master, officers and crew. Note: there was no specific focus on the loss of the passengers. No lawyers were present. It was first established that Drake had not engaged a pilot and an experienced pilot, who was called to give evidence, said that the current off Cape Omaezaki was very unpredictable and much affected by the wind. The mate, who said he was the last to leave the ship, said there were seven lifeboats on board but just three were launched although if the Japanese passengers had done as they were ordered, a fourth could have been launched and there would have been sufficient room for them; essentially, had they done as they were ordered, they would not have drowned. None of the crew spoke Japanese.

[183] The description of the Kobe Naval Court and subsequent HMCJ hearing is taken from 2, 5, 17, 18, 20 and 22 November and 11, 15, 16, 20 and 23 December 1886; HN.

Drake claimed that two of the passengers were midshipmen who had helped lower the boats but they had not attempted to evacuate the passengers. His explanation for the Japanese passengers' not obeying his orders to abandon ship was that the Japanese people were fatalistic by nature and resigned to death; and, as the ship went down, they simply clung together. Before he got into a boat himself he had sent the bosun back to try again to get the passengers to abandon ship.

When the Naval Court cleared Drake of blame for the *Normanton*'s loss, Japanese public reaction was immediate and furious. The *Japan Daily Mail* argued that it was not their death that caused such indignation—for the Japanese were used to death—but the fact that the master and officers had got off in boats and left the passengers behind to their fate: it was clear that the Britons were looking after themselves first. The Naval Court was criticized for its narrow focus and for not enquiring as to why no serious attempt had been made to evacuate the passengers.

The Japanese government, through the Governor of Hiogo *ken*, immediately laid a charge with Troup at the Kobe Consulate against Drake that he 'did feloniously kill and slay' the Japanese passengers 'against the Peace of Our Lady the Queen, Her Crown and Dignity'. Troup—who, of course, had presided at the Naval Court—now presided over the committal proceedings where Lowder appeared to prosecute on behalf of the Japanese government. He called as witnesses everyone who had been on the vessel and was still in Kobe. The bosun was the first witness and he explained that no safety drill had been carried out after leaving Yokohama—his experience was that one was always carried out on passenger ships but he did not know the procedure on cargo vessels. Drake subsequently confirmed that no instructions had ever been given to the passengers as to what to do in the case of an emergency.

The bosun then claimed that not all the lifeboats were seaworthy but that there had been sufficient for all the passengers; although if they had had to force the passengers into the lifeboats he thought perhaps only 15–18 would have made it—the others being too elderly. He had been ordered by Drake to persuade them all into the lifeboats but had then been left behind when the vessel went down. Another crewman claimed that no effort had been made to save the passengers but the mate said he had tried to push several of them from their passageway but they simply refused to leave. He then admitted that it looked like a case of every man for himself.

To rebut the suggestion that Japanese were naturally fatalistic towards death and that the Japanese passengers were simply resigned to their fate,

Lowder adduced an affidavit from Russell Robertson stating that, based on his experience along with C.D. Moss when the *Kokonoye maru* went down as they travelled to Hakodate on circuit, the Japanese were not fatalists and would try to survive. In that case, the ship's crew had got off all the passengers—including those in steerage—and that the master had been the last man to leave the vessel.

After a two day committal hearing, Troup committed Drake for trial on indictment before HMCJ but allowed him bail on two sureties of $2,000 each. One must wonder whether Troup now considered himself to be in an embarrassing position. He was reported as having given $25 to a fund which had been established for the relief of the Japanese dead. We must certainly assume that the British authorities were embarrassed at the Naval Court's conclusions for it is difficult to imagine that Robertson, as Consul in Yokohama, would have sworn the affidavit he did without, at the very least, the acquiescence of higher authority.

Just three weeks later, Drake's trial opened before Hannen in HMCJ at Yokohama. As he had been indicted, Litchfield, the Crown Prosecutor, assumed the responsibility for the direction of the prosecution but Lowder also appeared to assist him. At the trial, Robinson, Drake's counsel, suggested that it should be noted that a Naval Court had been held and that it had exonerated Drake from blame but Hannen dismissed this suggestion—which, along with *Glamorganshire* and *Chishima* cases confirms the Courts' view that they were in no way bound by the factual findings of a Naval Court. Robinson then attempted a technical defence that the requirements of a manslaughter charge had not been established but the jury convicted Drake of manslaughter and he was sentenced to three months' imprisonment. Immediately afterwards, Robinson said he would appeal to the Supreme Court but there is no evidence that any appeal was taken. *The Japan Herald* reported that the verdict had given 'unbounded satisfaction' in the Japanese journals.

Thus, it can be seen that the findings of Naval Courts were certainly open to challenge. By their very nature, they were one-sided instruments looking just at the British vessel involved and its compliance with British regulations. Such criticisms as there may be of them should not be that they were biased but that they lacked the forensic skill of a Court where two opposing sides battled it out and ensured that all relevant evidence was produced.

The *Normanton* case also reflects the interplay between cases in the Courts and wider Anglo-Japanese relations: particularly in the context of Treaty revision. Immediately after the *Normanton*'s loss, the Legation, was concerned at the 'unseemly attitude displayed by the Japanese Press'[184] which launched 'a violent attack on the way in which justice is travestied in the consular courts and the "Oriental" was sacrificed to the cupidity and inefficiency of the "Occidental"'.[185] Plunkett recognized that the saving of all but one of the European lives while all others, except the China boy, were lost was to be 'deplored no less on political than on humanitarian grounds',[186] but was concerned at the way public opinion was 'whipped up into a state of frenzy from which a slight accident could have evolved most lamentable results'.[187] In an attempt to calm the situation, he used Kirkwood, by then adviser to the Ministry of Justice, as an intermediary to convey to Inouye that the British government would hold Japan responsible if any British subject were injured as a result of the tumult whipped up by the Japanese Press. This was because the Japanese Press laws gave the Japanese government absolute control over the content of the Japanese Press.[188] Plunkett's intervention was sufficient for the Japanese government to issue a circular to Japanese editors to calm the tumult, although he feared a fresh outburst if Drake were acquitted.[189]

Plunkett suspected that the tumult had been encouraged by the Japanese Foreign Ministry in the first place—and reported that one of the offensive letters published in the Japanese Press was written immediately after a dinner at the Prime Minister's house. He suggested two influences on the Japanese government: first, a desire to impress upon the foreign representatives at the current Conference on Treaty revision the grave dangers to the foreign communities if Japan's legitimate aspirations with regard to Treaty revision were neglected; and, second—not related directly to Britain—the popular excitement over the recent Nagasaki riots between Chinese sailors and Japanese police which the Japanese government hoped to divert onto the *Normanton* affair.[190] With Drake's conviction and sentence, the excitement subsided.

---

184 Plunkett to Iddesleigh, 23 November 1886; FO262/556.
185 Plunkett to Iddesleigh, 21 November 1886; FO262/556.
186 Ibid.
187 Ibid.
188 Ibid.
189 Plunkett to Iddesleigh, 1 December 1886; FO262/556.
190 Ibid.

CHAPTER FIVE

CIVIL JURISDICTION

The importance of extra-territoriality to the British commercial community was that it was able to trade using rules and a justice system that it understood. This was of critical importance in connection with the import trade where most imports were trade financed with financiers needing to be assured that they could enforce their security and traders enforce payment of debts and other contractual obligations. This factor was of no less importance to the early traders than immunity from arrest and subjection to what they perceived to be an arbitrary criminal justice system. This chapter examines the nature of the civil disputes that came before the Courts and assesses whether the general absence of bias against Japanese litigants seen in criminal matters applied equally in civil cases.

Jurisdiction

We saw, in Chapter 1 (British Extra-territoriality), that, until 1879 and HMCJ's establishment, the Courts had no Admiralty or Matrimonial jurisdiction both of which were reserved to SCHK until 1865 when such jurisdiction was transferred to the Supreme Court (although, from 1871, the Yokohama Court sat as a branch of the Supreme Court for Admiralty cases). By OC1878, both Admiralty and Matrimonial jurisdiction were vested in HMCJ. Until 1865, SCHK also had an extraordinary concurrent civil jurisdiction with the Consular Courts but this concurrent jurisdiction passed to the Supreme Court in 1865 and on to HMCJ in 1879.

As for the Courts, Articles IV and VI of the Treaty did not specify the substantive law applicable to civil disputes—unlike Article V for criminal matters—but OC1859, OC1860 and the rules made under them decreed that Consuls should apply English law and give judgment upon the substantial merits and facts of the case. In suits involving $500 or more, the Consul was obliged to summon between two and four Assessors and could do so of his own motion in other cases. However, as with criminal offences, the Consul alone decided the case[1] and could enforce his

[1] Section XIV, OC1860.

decision by distress or imprisonment 'in like manner as a decision of SCHK in a civil suit'.[2] OC1865 continued or amplified certain aspects of the existing civil regime and varied others. Now, a Consul could hear suits up to $1,500 and it was only claims over this figure that he needed to hear with between one and four Assessors—unless, again, he was unable to find Assessors (in which case his judgment must explain why he sat without them).[3]

It is not possible to identify separately the cases taken by SCHK, the Supreme Court and HMCJ under their extraordinary concurrent civil jurisdiction as opposed to their exclusive jurisdiction. The only reported case taken by SCHK under its exclusive jurisdiction before 1865 was the *Nepaul* salvage case when the master and owners of the *Island Queen* rejected P&O's offer of $14,400 salvage and sought $200,000 for salvage. Although the factual locus of the vessel's stranding—and salvage—was the Japanese coast, it fell within SCHK's exclusive jurisdiction as an Admiralty case.[4]

Hornby and Goodwin came to Japan on circuit between 1865 and 1870 and Hornby visited again in 1872 when they heard cases as judges of the Supreme Court under both its exclusive and extraordinary jurisdiction so, during this period, it is impossible to distinguish in the official records between cases heard in the Kanagawa Court or the Yokohama Court and those before Hornby or Goodwin in the Supreme Court on circuit. The Supreme Court's most important exclusive jurisdiction was Admiralty jurisdiction given the number of shipping disputes. When Hornby visited Japan in 1872, he also visited Nagasaki to hear *The Pacific Mail Steamship Company by Walter Thompson v. Henry Gribble & Co.*, a shipping dispute. He also exercised the Supreme Court's exclusive jurisdiction in the Greens' matrimonial dispute in 1866 in Nagasaki.

The Supreme Court's extraordinary jurisdiction could be invoked where the Consul or one of the parties considered the dispute suitable for trial by the Supreme Court under section 39 OC1865. Hornby was leery of Consuls seeking to abuse section 39 by passing to him decisions which they ought, in the first place, to make. When Vyse attempted to pass *Porter v. Duus* to the Supreme Court in 1865, Hornby rebuked Vyse and observed that he appeared already to have heard the case and

[2] Section V, OC1860.
[3] Sections 33 and 63, OC1865.
[4] 1 April 1865; TJH. (The plaintiffs lost.)

should, therefore, determine it[5] and not decide it subject to his approval.[6]

With the Yokohama Court's establishment, the Supreme Court's extraordinary jurisdiction became, in practice, relevant only to the out-ports; but, there is no evidence that it took any cases from them under this jurisdiction after Hornby's final visit in 1872. With HMCJ, the only cases clearly taken under its exclusive jurisdiction in the out-ports were the Norman, Lees and Berwick lunacy cases.[7] It is less easy to identify cases taken under its extraordinary jurisdiction because there is, often, confusion in the correspondence records as to the matter. In *Kniffler v. Ringer* and *Kniffler v. Stoddart*, both of which involved Nagasaki based defendants, the initial suggestion is that HMCJ accepted the reference of the cases to it[8] but Kniffler's subsequent complaints about Enslie's handling of them suggest that they ended up being tried by the Nagasaki Court.[9] Also, cases could be initiated before HMCJ without having been referred to it by a Consul in one of the out-ports. Mowat exercised HMCJ's extraordinary jurisdiction in Kobe in the *Hiogo Hotel case*[10] but when he went to Kobe in 1896, during to Enslie's last illness, to hear in *Reynell v. Cameron* it was in response to a referral by Enslie.[11] The latter involved Reynell's attempt to enforce a restrictive covenant and claim $5,000 when his former employee, Cameron, set up a competing business, but Mowat ruled the covenant to be unenforceable.

One of the last cases referred to HMCJ by a Consul was *Kate Banff v. James Stuart Clark* where the Nagasaki Consul asked Wilkinson to hear the case, which involved a claim for ¥2,000 because, although the case was easy enough, the Consul was the plaintiff's tenant and one party might object in an offensive manner to an adverse verdict which would be unfortunate if, when the Courts were near to abolition, 'even the smallest ground should be afforded for any public reflection on the most absolute disinterestedness ... of the judges of the court'.[12]

5 Hornby to Vyse, 16 November 1865; FO656/18.
6 Hornby to Vyse, 28 December 1865; FO656/18.
7 See pages 232–234.
8 Hannen to Enslie, 31 July 1886; FO796/1.
9 See FO796/8 and FO796/10.
10 See page 65.
11 16 May 1896; JWM.
12 Nagasaki Consul to Wilkinson, 21 April 1899; FO796/10. In the event, the Register of Civil Cases for Nagasaki shows that Kate Banff withdrew her claim (but, whether as a result of an agreed settlement or not is unclear); FO796/5.

Case-load and the Litigants

The striking feature of the Courts' civil case-load is how, after an initial flurry of cases, it seemed to subside in each of the Courts.[13] Apart from a two year flurry of cases in Nagasaki in 1879 and 1880 (for which there is no obvious explanation), the Nagasaki, Hakodate and Tokyo figures all show a falling off of cases whilst the official Yokohama figures indicate stability—as in Shanghai (where 356 civil cases were reported in 1867 against 292, 290 and 279 in 1868, 1869 and 1870 respectively—ignoring interlocutory matters).[14] The Kobe records cover too short a period and the absence of more official figures from there, the Yokohama Court and HMCJ—and reduced newspaper coverage of cases in both the Yokohama and Kobe newspapers after around 1880—leaves a residual uncertainty about this in relation to these Courts, although support for this proposition may be taken from the stability in the Yokohama Bar's size after about 1880.

As with the reduction in the number of criminal cases, we can only speculate on the reasons for the falling case-load. Two principal reasons may be postulated. First, the establishment of the Yokohama Court followed, in 1879, by HMCJ, with its extraordinary jurisdiction covering the out-ports, must have decreased the out-ports' case-load and—at least as regards the more major cases—concentrated cases in Yokohama with its legally trained judiciary. Second, as in the criminal context, we should, perhaps, treat the later years as revealing a more standard case-load and ask why the early years generated the level of cases they did. The initial flurries of Western enthusiasm at each port reflected the buccaneering and somewhat speculative nature of the initial advances. Closer examination of the earlier disputes suggests that debt—or the lack of access to ready cash—was behind many cases[15] and the late 1860s saw several large bankruptcies of British trading houses in China and Japan;[16] which, in itself, led to a higher case-load with disputes over security in relation to those bankruptcy cases. As the communities settled down, businesses

[13] Table 17.

[14] Shanghai Returns.

[15] In *Won-Sing t/a Campseang v. John Davis*, the defendant admitted the claim for $123 but needed time to pay as he had on-sold the goods on credit, 16 January 1878; FO796/2.

[16] The Shanghai Returns report 44 and 42 bankruptcy actions in 1867 and 1868 respectively but just nine and four in 1869 and 1870. See also pages 201–203.

became more established and stable (the weaker ones having been bankrupted) and everyone learned to live with each other so the element of vexatious personal animus based litigation subsided. This 'calming down' is also reflected in the criminal case-load figures and is supported by general commentators who talk of a dramatic change to a more stable community by the 1870s.[17]

Unlike criminal cases, where a high proportion of defendants were visiting sailors, the litigants in civil cases were, almost by definition, usually resident in the Treaty Ports: the exceptions being owners and masters of ships (in shipping cases, in relation to the supply of goods and services or when seamen claimed against them for wages). Very occasionally, we find overseas plaintiffs bringing an action as when Messrs. Dessandier & Cie. of Jarrae, France successfully claimed $1,125 against HSBC for converting 150 cases of brandy. The consignee was insolvent and HSBC, which had financed the brandy, had seized it, sold it and retained the sale proceeds. The case revolved entirely around whose interest in the brandy prevailed: the seller or the financier.[18]

Between 1865 and 1874, British plaintiffs dominated the Nagasaki Court with, on average, ten cases a year against just three for Japanese and foreign plaintiffs combined.[19] However, from around 1872, Japanese plaintiffs became increasingly noticeable in the Nagasaki Court and, from 1875 onwards, constituted the largest number, by plurality, of plaintiffs. We see a similar change in Tokyo and Hakodate; but this shift is not reflected in Yokohama and Kobe by either the limited official figures or the newspaper reports after 1870 which, despite showing greater Japanese participation, suggest they remained a minority of plaintiffs and at the same level as other foreign plaintiffs. It is unclear whether this is a real difference between Yokohama and Kobe and the other ports or a reflection of newspaper reporting policies targeted at, primarily, a non-Japanese readership. Whatever is the explanation, there is little other evidence from the case lists or in the case reports to suggest that potential Japanese plaintiffs were dissuaded from bringing suits except in the closing months of extraterritoriality when the *Eastern World* reported that some Japanese were

---

[17] Lane Earns, 'British Influence in the Foreign Settlement at Nagasaki', *PJS* vol 125 (1995), page 48.

[18] *Messrs. Dessandier & Cie. v. HSBC*; 6 and 12 October 1881; HN.

[19] Tables 17 and 18.

waiting until the expiry of extra-territoriality when they could bring their claims against Britons in the Japanese courts.

Although Hakodate had a higher proportion of litigation per head of the British population than any other port, the disputes were nearly all commercially related with only two defamation cases betraying the squabbling nature of the British communities which was seen elsewhere in Japan. Over the period for which semi-annual returns exist for Hakodate, six individuals out of just 14 listed on the 1870 Registration List accounted for 31 out of 52 litigation positions (10 as plaintiff and 21 as defendant) with Thomas Blakiston being plaintiff on five occasions and defendant on four. The other litigants were the Japanese authorities and individuals on four occasions each, three European sailors, two other Britons resident in Hakodate, one Chinese and four ships.

Amongst foreign plaintiffs in the Courts, Chinese plaintiffs were, by far, the largest group.[20] In Nagasaki, they ranged from almost one-fifth of foreign plaintiffs in 1860–1874 to just over half in 1875–1899 whilst, in Yokohama, they ranged from a quarter in the official records to a fifth in cases reported in the newspapers. Their comparative absence from Hakodate and Tokyo probably reflects Hakodate's small foreign community and Tokyo's not being a trading settlement—only a residential one with a high proportion of professional classes employed by the Japanese government as engineers or advisers. In Kobe, whereas 37 out of 104 foreign plaintiffs were Chinese in the period 1870–1875 according to the semi-annual returns, only one out of 373 was Chinese according to the newspapers reports which covered a far longer period. The difference is so noticeable that it suggests that the Kobe newspapers under-reported cases brought by Chinese plaintiffs.

The remaining foreigner plaintiffs were a mixture of European (principally, Dutch, French and German with the occasional Dane, Italian, Portuguese or Spaniard) and USA citizens although French plaintiffs predominated in Tokyo (25 out of 30 foreign plaintiffs). This is strange given that Tokyo's French population was smaller than its American and

[20]

Nagasaki:	1866–1874: four of 25 non-British plaintiffs.
	1875–1899: 22 of 39. Eight were German and the remainder American or European.
Kobe:	1870–1875 (semi-annual returns): 37 of 104.
	1869–1899 (newspaper reports): 1 of 18.
Yokohama:	1871–1872 (semi-annual returns): 22 of 89.
	1862–1899 (newspaper reports): 19 of 101.
Hakodate:	1865–1878: one of eight.
Tokyo:	1871–1897: three of 42.

German populations (and barely a fifth of the British population).[21] Only in Nagasaki, with Germans being over half the non-Chinese foreign plaintiffs, was there a similar concentration of one other nationality amongst the plaintiffs. The newspaper reports seem to concentrate principally on cases brought by Dutch and German traders which suggests that these groups were involved in the larger commercial transactions.

Women appeared in around 5% of cases—with four cases involving women on both sides—but a quarter of all civil jury trials. Apart from shipping cases (in which they had no involvement), they were involved in the same range of cases as male litigants. Bridget Blockley, a hotel-keeper, was involved in five of the 22 reported cases involving female litigants, including a jury trial over her claims against an insurance company for fire damage to her hotel.[22] Her other claim involved a suit to recover the cost of refreshments provided; otherwise, she was a defendant in claims for wages or the provision of services. She lost only one case—against a Japanese plaintiff who claimed ¥6 in respect of unpaid wages.[23] Other claims by female claimants included an illegitimate daughter seeking maintenance from her deceased father's estate,[24] applications for Probate and two slander actions. A ship-master's daughter sued the Consular constable in Yokohama and his wife for $10,000 for a slander 'too foul for publication' (but not so foul as to prevent newspapers reporting the trial) which caused her fiancé to break-off the engagement[25] and, in Kobe, the Misses Sowter sued a fellow school-teacher over his accusations of their fiddling the books.[26] Wilhelmina Carrea, a Portuguese subject, was awarded ¥20.60 out of a ¥45.60 claim for board and lodging which she brought against J.A. Montaltado de Jesus[27] whilst Mrs D'Arcy of the Occidental Hotel in Kobe sued S. Reich for ¥117 due on bills and chits incurred at the hotel by a Mr Beauchamp for whom Reich had previously held himself responsible. The defendant claimed that, although the bills were acceptable, the chits were excessive whereupon Hall, who heard the

21 In 1871, 42 Britons out of 88 Westerners lived in Tokyo rising, by 1874, to 154 out of a total of 350; FO798/20.

22 *Blockley v. Staffordshire Fire Insurance Company*, 22 March 1879; JWM.

23 18 March 1881; JWM.

24 *Mary Oastler Burdiss v. James Johnstone (Ex'or of George Burdiss)*, 12 December 1896; JWM.

25 *Ruth Farnsworth v. C.W. White and F.E. White*, 20 October 1883; JWM. The jury was unable to reach a verdict so the suit was dismissed.

26 *Misses Sowter v. Mr & Mrs Rowe*, 2 September 1897; JWM; 11 and 25 September 9 and 16 October 1897; KWC.

27 22 February 1899; KWC.

case, said that whereas chits in a pub were frequently disallowed by the Courts, those in an hotel never were.[28]

Why did Japanese plaintiff numbers increase after around 1872? No structural reason had ever prevented Japanese plaintiffs from suing in the Courts previously; yet few did, and the change after around 1872 is noticeable. Japanese litigants fell into three groups: the authorities; small traders and individuals; and Japanese businessmen.

Two, linked, explanations may be posited. First, a recognition, after the Iwakura Mission in 1871–1872, that foreigners were in Japan to stay and, probably, a greater acquiescence or recognition amongst Japanese businessmen that they needed to utilize established processes to protect their commercial position against the British. Second, with Japan settling down from the disturbed 1860s, Japanese merchants took an increasing part in the economic development of Japan and ousted Chinese merchants as the principal counterparties for Western trade. The inevitable disputes arising from trade needed to be resolved and the only place the Japanese could pursue their claims against British subjects was in the Courts—just as this period produced increasing numbers of British actions in the Japanese courts. A possible, separate, explanation is that, beforehand, Japanese claimants used the Consuls' good offices to exert pressure on British defendants to settle their obligations. The Tokyo Vice-Consulate's correspondence files contain numerous requests from Japanese for remedies in matters (usually, unpaid debts) which never approached the Courts but where the Vice-Consul encouraged Britons to honour their contractual obligations or tried to mediate compromises.

Nothing removed the right of the Japanese under Article VI of the Treaty to approach the Consuls for redress if they objected to the Court procedures and fees.[29] This suggestion may be regarded as disingenuous but for the fact that the idea was in contemporary official consideration as seen by Japanese government pressing the Legation concerning appeals from Hakodate in *Ichinosuke Sempachi v. Alexander Porter* and *Akita Han v. Blakiston Marr*.[30] Parkes asked Goodwin to inform him of the result in the former because it was '... an international case...' where he was in communications with the Japanese government.[31] In the second case, the

[28] *Mrs D'Arcy v. S. Reich*; 3 May 1899; KWC. The case was adjourned and no result reported. Presumably, given Hall's statement, the parties reached a resolution between themselves.

[29] Hannen to Adams, 17 August 1871; FO656/37.

[30] A charter-party dispute involving complicated accounting and demurrage claims.

[31] Parkes to Goodwin, 28 October 1870; FO656/19.

plaintiff was really the Japanese government, and Goodwin recognized that it could decline to appeal to the Supreme Court but look instead to Parkes for resolution. Goodwin, reluctant to embroil the Supreme Court in a dispute with the Japanese government, instructed the Consul to refer to the *Chargé d'Affaires* rather than himself as Japanese parties preferred to refer the matter to the Minister 'rather than to a Judge in Shanghai of whom they know nothing'.[32] Goodwin then remitted the case to Hakodate for further evidence and a re-hearing where the plaintiffs largely won their case—apart from one or two points of accounting.

Examination of the semi-annual returns reveals that, at least in the early periods, there were concentrations of defendants. In Kobe and Osaka, in 1871, over half the cases involved just four out of a total of 20 defendants: J.H. Wignall, Alexander Ross, Hollman and Matthews as defendants in 11, 10, four and three cases respectively. The first half of 1872 was similar and the timing of most suits suggests that they were debt claims where creditors had either determined upon concerted action or reacted simultaneously to rumours of the defendant's financial difficulties. In 1871, five Chinese plaintiffs lodged claims—which were admitted—all on the same day against Alexander Ross whilst 1873 saw the largest number of plaints issued against a single defendant on the same day when ten Chinese lodged debt claims against Philip S. Cabeldu in Kobe.

Tokyo and Nagasaki, until 1874, reveal similar—although not so pronounced—concentrations of defendants. After 1875, such concentrations in Nagasaki were fewer although we see the same names re-appearing over time: James F. Mitchell (a local shipbuilder), Richard Ford (a local doctor), Alt & Co (another trading house) and Gribble. Many of these plaints were commercially driven disputes, although all five suits against Richard Lewis in 1879 resulted from his cash-flow difficulties and he admitted the claims but had no money to meet the claims. Among plaintiffs, the concentration was much less pronounced and, only rarely, did any plaintiff pursue more than two cases at any one time—although we do see two plaintiffs bringing five[33] (and one, four[34]) cases in a single year. In all ports, we see trading concerns appearing as litigants on both sides over the years, which is unsurprising as many civil cases involved the

32 Goodwin to Parkes, 11 February 1871; FO656/19.

33 Clataud and Hall brought five cases in Tokyo in 1874 and 1875 respectively; semi-annual returns; FO656/40.

34 Hart in Kobe in 1874, semi-annual returns; FO656/41.

commercial and trading community at all levels (as opposed to disputes simply between individuals) and traders acted frequently as agents for others (particularly, insurance and shipping companies) and would be cited *in lieu* of their principals.

Claims

Claims may be classified into broad categories of Debts (including bankruptcy related proceedings); Goods and Services; Wages and Employment disputes; Shipping; and Others.[35] Inevitably, not all claims fit neatly into one or other category: for instance, most breach of contract claims come most neatly under Others, whilst others are better classified as Debt claims; likewise, claims for unpaid rent I have usually categorized as Debt claims rather than land disputes under Others. Whilst it is always possible to quibble over the allocations at the margins, the broad thrusts of the allocations are valid to reflect the balance of the different types of claim brought before the Courts.

The justification for a specific Treaty provision dealing with debt recovery[36] is easily understood when we see that debt related claims constituted a significant proportion of all claims and claims for money owed were often at the root of claims of other descriptions. Some debt related claims arose out of pure lending relationships; but, more often, out of the supply of goods and services where the purchaser had not paid (or could not pay). From 1875 to 1899, a quarter of claims in Nagasaki related to straightforward debts whilst a further two-fifths of claims arose from the supply of goods or services—although there was, sometimes, a genuine dispute as to liability or quantum with such claims. Employment claims usually related to claims for arrears of wages whilst rent disputes and ejectment actions usually arose from an inability to pay the rent. Newspaper reports suggest a similar breakdown of claims in Yokohama and Kobe.

Such breakdown as is possible of the pre-1875 Nagasaki figures suggests an even greater prevalence of debt claims. In Hakodate, similarly, half the known claims related to debt, the supply of goods and services or unpaid wages. The Tokyo and Kobe and Osaka figures derived from the semi-annual returns are not susceptible to analysis on the point, but nothing in

---

[35] See Table 19.
[36] Article VII.

the correspondence files (or the newspaper reports) suggests that the picture painted by the breakdown of the claims in Nagasaki gives a false picture about the preponderance of debt claims—a position also seen in the Shanghai Returns.

The Japanese authorities' debt claims were usually for unpaid ground rents whereas most Japanese individuals' debt claims arose from the supply of goods and services, unpaid wages and small loans. The Chinese, who outnumbered the British in Nagasaki, Kobe and Yokohama, frequently performed the *petit bourgeoisie* trading roles of general suppliers to Westerners and appear to have been subject to attempts by Britons to obtain extended credit. Whilst the combined proportion of their debt and goods and services claims was only slightly greater than that of British plaintiffs, the make-up was very different with a fifth being debt claims and the balance relating to goods and services in Nagasaki (and a quarter and three-quarters, respectively, in Yokohama). One of the more unusual claims was Sophie Witt's claim for repayment of $50 lent to Greenberg to unload two elephants at Yokohama which he hope to exhibit or sell to the Japanese.[37]

Frequently, debt claims were uncontested or admitted with the only issue being how the defendant could effect settlement: often the Courts sanctioned a compromise whereby the debt was paid in instalments.[38] Given debt claims' preponderance, it is unsurprising that there were several bankruptcies. Of the eight bankruptcies involving over $5,000, half occurred before 1872[39] and several involved individuals who played a major part in 'opening-up' Japan to British trade and/or appear elsewhere in the case history of British extra-territoriality in Japan.

Apart from the Leopold case, which was associated with his fraud, these bankruptcies were business failures; but, the process was a personal

37 *Sophie Witt v. Greenberg*, 2 October 1880; JWM. The newspaper gives no further details of what happened to the elephants.

38 In *Campseang v. W.I. Graham*, Graham admitted owing $196 for goods supplied but asked for time to pay. After an argument over his means, judgment was entered for the full amount plus costs with his paying $67 immediately and the balance at $10 or $20 per month—depending upon his earnings; 2 August 1876; FO796/2. When Moritani Denzaburo claimed ¥55 from A.R. Collins for meat which he had supplied, Collins admitted the claim but pleaded a lack of ready cash and was ordered to pay off the debt in instalments of ¥5 per month: 17 June 1899; KWC.

39 The principal ones are: S. Clifton (Kanagawa, 1866), Dent & Co. (Nagasaki, 1867); J.R. Black and Alex McKechnie (Kanagawa, 1868), Gye (Nagasaki, 1868), Rainbow Lewis & Co. (1869/1870), Thomas Glover (Nagasaki, 1870/1871), Malcolmsen (Nagasaki, 1875); Grigor (Yokohama, 1879); and Leopold (Yokohama 1899).

bankruptcy of each individual partner[40] as few businesses were carried on through joint-stock companies. The process involved the filing of an application (by the bankrupt himself or a creditor) with the Court, official notification to all creditors[41]—followed by a creditors' meeting,[42] the appointment of an official administrator, the liquidation of the bankrupt's affairs and a public bankruptcy examination in the Court. Bankruptcies were handled by Consuls under the supervision of the Supreme Court or HMCJ. After the Bankruptcy Act 1883, the Board of Trade had a key role to play in bankruptcies in England and Wales but, as Hannen explained, there was no official body in Japan corresponding to the Board of Trade so the Act would be unworkable unless HMCJ disregarded its wording and substituted itself for the Board of Trade. He was concerned that this was, in effect, 'making a new Act of it' and he worried that, were the point taken to the Privy Council, the substitution of HMCJ for the Board of Trade would be held bad form. Granville subsequently ordered the substitution[43]—but only after Hannen had complained privately to Sir Philip Currie (then, Assistant Permanent Under-Secretary at the Foreign Office) that nothing had been done in relation to his raising the point officially with the Foreign Office or writing privately to Sir Julian Pauncefote (Permanent Under Secretary at the Foreign Office, 1882–1889) on the matter.[44]

Bankruptcy gave rise to practical problems (in collecting and distributing the bankrupt's assets) and legal issues. Where no creditor was prepared to act, the Law Secretary (or, after 1879, the Registrar of HMCJ) was usually appointed as the Official Assignee of the bankrupt's property but

---

40 In the *Bankruptcy of J.R. Black and Alex McKechnie*, Hornby criticized Myburgh for holding a joint creditors' meeting for 'the fact is there are two separate bankruptcies ... Therefore there should have been two separate meetings...'; Hornby to Myburgh, 23 January 1868; FO656/18.

41 By publication in a prominent newspaper in the port concerned and in the *Supreme Court and Consular Gazette* (later, NCH).

42 Usually in the bankrupt's port; although, in the Gye bankruptcy, Flowers suggested that, as all the creditors lived in Shanghai and debts of $6,737 arose from a bad investment there, the case and creditors' meeting be transferred to the Supreme Court (Flowers to Hornby, 18 April 1868; FO656/14) but Hornby ruled that the petition and meeting should proceed in Nagasaki although the creditors could apply for its transfer to Shanghai; Hornby to Flowers, 5 May 1868; FO656/18.

43 Granville to Hannen, 20 April 1885; FO46/339.

44 Hannen to Currie (private), 2 March 1885; FO46/339. Hannen did concede, alluding to the government's current domestic and international problems, that he realized '...that at such a time as present interests of far greater moment than the difficulties which this Court may experience in the administration of an English Act of Parliament will be occupying [Granville's] and everybody else's attention...'.

he would invoke the local Consul's assistance to collect in the assets. Where creditors reached agreement with the bankrupt—under a liquidation scheme of arrangement—they would appoint an assignee and administrator of the bankrupt's property and, often, a book-keeper to go through his financial affairs. In the Glover bankruptcy, Tombrink (a locally based accountant) was appointed as assignee and administrator by the creditors under a scheme of arrangement, which avoided the personal bankruptcy of Thomas Glover and his partner, K.R. Mackenzie.[45] Nevertheless, the arrangements remained under the Court's supervision but Tombrink, as a subject of, and consul in Nagasaki for, the Netherlands, was allowed to act only if he accepted British jurisdiction in the matter.[46] Another consequence of bankruptcy was that the bankrupt's legal claims devolved upon his creditors so, in *Hall & Holtz v. Rainbow Lewis & Co,* the latter's bankruptcy trustee assumed the prosecution of the appeal against Hall & Holtz.[47]

There was never enough money available to meet all the claims in a bankruptcy so recourse was often had to the Courts to resolve competing claims to the bankrupt's assets. In Rainbow Lewis & Co.'s bankruptcy, Annersley sought Hornby's advice in relation to preferential claims by Hall & Holtz and Tombrink for $2,000 and $1,000 respectively which they claimed were secured by equitable mortgages over land (they held the deeds but the mortgages were unregistered) and HSBC's claim that a trade finance debt for Ts716 was hypothecated to a bill of exchange for £190 but where the trustee in bankruptcy argued that that HSBC had voluntarily relinquished its lien by allowing the firm to take possession of the bills of lading.[48] Hornby responded rather tersely that it was Annersley's duty to reach a decision but a dissatisfied party could appeal to him—before advising that the security in the first two cases was effective whilst, if, as he had been led to believe, HSBC had parted with the goods on the understanding that the proceeds were to be put against the London draft, HSBC had a clear right to re-delivery.[49]

---

45 The creditors discharged Mackenzie 'on account of his great age and his inability to do anything that might assist in furthering the interests of the creditors'; Annersely to Hornby, 4 July 1871; FO656/34.

46 Annersley to Hornby, 23 September 1870; FO656/34.

47 Hornby to Annersley, 8 January 1870; FO656/18.

48 Annersley to Hornby, 1 February 1870; FO656/34.

49 Hornby to Annersley, 24 February 1870; FO656/18.

Many goods and services claims revolved around the supply of food and drink or minor services, were small in size and usually involved defendants either unable to pay or quibbling about the amounts charged: for instance, Roderic claimed $5 for providing board and lodging[50] while Carl Seitz claimed just $4.12 for unloading cases of wine.[51] Larger claims included Charles Phillips claiming $50 from the *Galley of Lorne*'s master for lifting its anchor[52] and Aymonin's demand that Butterfield & Swire repair an engine piston which had been damaged when it was dropped into the sea during unloading[53] and two Japanese builders claimed $633 for building No. 40 Yokohama.[54] Professional fees were also the subject of claims as when the architect, J.W. Hart, sued successfully Lucas & Walters for $100 for designing a drainage system for their land.[55] Cruchley also recovered $75 outstanding on a $225 fee he had charged J.M. Scott for assisting him in prosecuting a case against some Chinese defendants before Japanese officials. The next year, he sued T. Wooton for $120 for services in connection with an arbitration between Wooton and the Japanese Railway Department.[56]

The smaller wage claims were, usually, by Japanese and ranged from under ¥10 to around $50 but newspaper employee disputes accounted for several reported cases—which may reflect journalistic introspection. These latter cases involved a mixture of claims for unpaid wages and claims for wrongful dismissal. The first, in 1868,[57] saw Filomeno Braga successfully sue his former employers for $80 unpaid wages after being encouraged to move from Yokohama to Kobe to start a newspaper. The *Japan Gazette* was engaged in two wrongful dismissal disputes in 1891 when a previous manager successfully sued the current manager for $1,082[58] only for the second manager, Dening, to sue the newspaper later for $11,000.[59] Dening, who had been recruited a year earlier 'to free the residents of Yokohama from the baleful pro-revision influence of the *Japan Mail*',[60] was dismissed for refusing to provide more column inches

50 *Roderic v. Wheeler*, 2 December 1871; JWM.

51 *Carl Seitz v. H. McArthur, master of the Undine*, 22 February 1879; TJH.

52 23 February 1878; HN.

53 29 November 1873; TJH. At that time, most shipping anchored offshore in the bay and cargo was offloaded into lighters for trans-shipment ashore.

54 *Sakai Takakichi and Suzuki Matsugoro v. Mrs Blockley*, 13 June 1881; JDH.

55 3 August 1870; HN.

56 14 September 1870 and 4 October 1871 respectively; HN.

57 *Filomeno Braga v. Watkins & Hansard*, 23 April 1868; HN.

58 *Nutall v. Anglin*, 20 February 1891; NCH.

59 *Dening v. Japan Gazette*, 10 July 1891; NCH.

60 Ibid.

for the sub-editoress whose style was perceived to be more exciting. Reading between the lines, Hannen brokered a settlement whereby the newspaper paid Dening his damages and costs in instalments.

Most remaining Nagasaki cases (and a large proportion of the Yokohama and Kobe cases) were shipping related disputes. For smaller claims, where it was otiose to proceed *in rem*[61] against large vessels, shipping claims could be pursued as personal actions in the Courts. Examples include claims for damages done by the steamer ferries running between Kobe and Osaka where Mowat confirmed that Admiralty procedure did not prevent such claims being pursued as personal actions against the master and owner of vessels for damage done by vessels, and not in Admiralty.[62] *Moggs v. Master and Owners of Norfolk*, in 1866, illustrated the problems with larger claims. The plaintiff's claim for £305/5/4 (£305.27) could not be brought against the vessel in the Kanagawa Court (because it lacked Admiralty jurisdiction) and, if brought against the defendants personally, would be pointless as they were neither resident nor had goods in Japan against which judgment could be levied; so the only remedy was to sue the owners in England.[63] These practical issues surrounding such claims resulted in the Yokohama Court being established with Admiralty jurisdiction in 1871 and OC1878's transferring Admiralty jurisdiction for Japan from the Supreme Court to HMCJ.

Shipping claims fell into two principal categories, arising out of: first, the carriage of goods involving the non-delivery of, or damage to, cargo and general charter-party disputes; and, second, accidents between boats colliding with each other. An early carriage of goods case was *P&O v. John Scott* where P&O won £99 for damage caused to its ship, the *Cadiz*, when an explosive package shipped by the defendant from Shanghai to Yokohama exploded on board.[64] Most cases involved damage to, or non-delivery of, shipped goods and turned on the bill of lading—and, usually, its exclusion of liability clause which, despite always being construed *contra proferentem*, succeeded to exclude the shipper's liability in several cases.

---

61 That is an action which involves and attaches to the object concerned—as opposed to a personal (or *in personam* action) which results only in a personal liability of the defendant with the plaintiff having no automatic right to attach any particular object or possession of the defendant.

62 Mowat to Gower, 12 January 1874 in response to Gower to Hornby, 2 January 1874; FO656/41.

63 Supreme Court to Myburgh, 23 August 1866; FO656/18.

64 26 August 1865; TJH.

Collisions were another source of dispute. *Iwasaki Yataro v. Capt. Philip Colomb R.N.*[65] involved a collision between HMS *Audacious* and Mitsubishi's *Chiri maru* where Mitsubishi originally claimed $7,400 for damage to its vessel and related demurrage (but reduced the claim before the first hearing). The case was heavily reported over two years without reaching a conclusion and was the basis for an amusing small article on the collision in the *Japan Punch*.[66] Its principal legal interest stemmed from Colomb's challenging the Yokohama Court's jurisdiction over service personnel. After over-ruling this challenge, Wilkinson set the jury several questions to resolve in relation to the dispute, but the jury failed to reach a verdict and a second trial was ordered.[67] Colomb—deliberately or due to naval requirements—failed to appear for the second trial and the case tailed off with a final newspaper report that the Japanese Minister in London had taken up the matter with the Admiralty.

A smaller category involved the running of vessels and their related trading accounts. Captains Hill and Norris fought for possession of the *Fair Leander*. Its owner had authorized Hill to take possession but Norris refused to yield up the vessel, alleging unpaid accounts. Despite Wilkinson's encouraging the parties to settle the matter themselves, Norris refused obstinately to do so until possession was ordered for Hill.[68] The cross-actions between Abbott and Cook (which led to Abbott's conviction for perjury) arose from disputes over a vessel's trading accounts and were settled only after exhaustive investigations by the Registrar of HMCJ when most evidence was described 'as meagre and unsatisfactory'.[69]

'Others' includes a cluster of small claims brought by Japanese individuals for damages arising from assaults, disorderly behaviour or bites from unruly dogs with the balance made up of claims ranging from general breach of contract to claims by bailors against bailees for delivery up of goods and land boundary disputes. Another source of disputes over the years was the auction rooms with claims for goods knocked down to one bidder but delivered to another or the winning bids not being recognized. Pilotage disputes were another source of litigation: W. Lees sued the *Cathaya*'s master for $63 for detaining him on board for two days and not

[65] Reported from June 1877 to December 1878; NCH.

[66] Rogala, page 87.

[67] Wilkinson held that he had jurisdiction–and cited his ruling here when, as Chief Justice, he heard a dispute involving British troops in Tianjin (Wilkinson to the Marquis of Lansdowne (Foreign Secretary), 27 November 1901; FO17/1496).

[68] 26 September 1878; TJH.

[69] 27 July 1881; JG.

using him as a pilot.[70] It would seem that racial prejudice was clearly behind Suzuki Ichigo's claim against the *Viceroy*'s master. Ichigo was a pilot and when he boarded the vessel his offer to pilot it through the Inland Sea was accepted until the vessel stopped shortly afterwards and picked up a Western pilot who the master then used. Rennie said the pilotage regulations were clear: the first pilot on board was entitled to be engaged and he awarded Suzuki his claim in full plus costs.[71]

We see just one negligence claim when a dockworker sued successfully before a jury for $1,500 damages suffered by falling down an uncovered hatch on the ss *Victoria*.[72] A case brought to determine a matter of general community interest was *Smith v. Escombe*. Framed as a claim for a refund on a season ticket, the underlying question was whether Escombe could charge an additional evening entry fee to the Bluff Gardens to holders of a season ticket—which Escombe argued allowed only day-time access. Hannen ruled against Escombe.[73]

A claim with modern echoes was *Horie Giske v. L. Horsley* where Giske, a banker, claimed ¥1,726 for Horsley's breach of a foreign exchange contract. Horsley claimed that he did not understand the contract and, when the markets moved against him, he refused to pay. Giske had hedged himself with a guild in Osaka and, so, was exposed to the guild on his hedging contract. The Court said that Horsley was clearly in breach of contract so the only question was that of quantum and, here, it held that the defendant could not reasonably be expected to have known that Giske would hedge the contract with the guild. Thus, whilst Horsley was unable to reclaim monies he had already paid to Giske, he was not liable to compensate Giske for his exposure to the guild.[74]

Just as the early Western communities in Japan were quick to initiate criminal charges against each other as part of their personal squabbles, so they brought civil actions. Libel actions were characterized by large claims but never substantial awards and the Courts did their best to discourage such suits. 1865 alone saw three actual or potential suits. First, Parkes, when sitting as Consul-General in Shanghai in *In re Esplen*, dissuaded Dr Baudouin of Nagasaki from pursuing Prideaux Selby for defamation[75]

[70] 27 May 1876; HN.
[71] 19 May 1881; HN.
[72] *Henry Clarke v. The Northern Pacific Steamship Company*, 30 November 1895; JWM.
[73] 27 July 1872; JWM.
[74] 8 June 1880; HN.
[75] The case was an investigation into the death of Esplen, mate of the *Ocean Gem* as a result of medicines administered by Selby, its master, who claimed that they had been

for suggesting that Dr Baudouin had mis-sold drugs. Then, Vyse, in Hakodate, referred *Alexander Porter v. Duus* to Hornby under section 39 OC1865 when Duus allegedly defamed Porter by saying he was not a master mariner or competent to give a survey report[76] before the Yokohama farce of *Glackmeyer v. McKechnie*. McKechnie, a consular constable, had arrested Glackmeyer, a US citizen, for creating a disturbance during proceedings in the Kanagawa Court in *US Court v Searle*. Glackmeyer then sued McKechnie for false imprisonment and defamation of character but lost on both counts and was ordered to pay McKechnie's costs before successfully appealing the costs order.[77] The sequel was that Glackmeyer assaulted, and threatened to horsewhip Ricker, the local newspaper editor, for his comments on the cases resulting in *Ricker v. Glackmeyer* in the US consular court in Kanagawa where the editor sued Glackmeyer for damages. Despite Ricker's counsel's citing cases from the reign of William III and Mary II to justify substantial damages, he was awarded derisory damages of US$0.065 and the same in costs so Ricker had to bear the balance of his costs.[78]

When James W. Dixon of the Naval Yard sued the *Japan Gazette* for alleged libel by saying he had driven his pony disrespectfully close to the Emperor on the racecourse, Hannen told both parties after the first morning's hearing that they should settle the case and, 'after tiffin, the parties announced a settlement'[79] whereby the newspaper apologized and paid Dixon's costs. In 1874, the *Japan Mail* sued the *Japan Gazette* in the Yokohama Court for libel but the jury awarded only nominal damages of $1;[80] whilst, in *Livingston v. Lewis*, Goodwin awarded Livingston just $25 instead of the $2,000 claimed because the libel was not very serious.[81] In 1875, Dr A. Goertz sued Cruchley, the editor of the *Hiogo and Osaka Herald* for libel—presumably for an article in that newspaper, and claimed $5,000 damages. Cruchley, represented by Duncan, exercised his right to demand

---

supplied by Baudouin. Baudouin said that his compradore had obtained them from a Japanese druggist in Nagasaki. 27 May 1865; NCH.

[76] Vyse to Hornby, 26 October 1865; FO656/34. There is nothing to suggest the case's eventual outcome—which suggests that it may have been dropped.

[77] Description given in Hornby to Flowers, 24 November 1865 and 13 January 1866; FO656/18. Whilst Hornby upbraided Flowers for his procedural handling of the case, he held there was nothing to justify Glackmeyer's allegations that the Court interfered with his cross-examination of the defence witnesses.

[78] Report, 24 November 1865; *Japan Times*, included in FO656/49. See also pages 242–248 and Munson 2013, chapter 5.

[79] *James W. Dixon v. James R. Anglin*, 17 December 1887; JWM.

[80] 19 November 1874; NCH.

[81] 22 May 1875; TJH.

a jury trial and to have the matter heard by the Supreme Court[82]—but there is no record of any conclusion which, again, suggests that the matter was dropped (or settled) before trial. *G. Jaffray v. J. Wickers & J.J. Keswick* was another long-running case which arose from the Yokohama Race Club's barring Jaffray from the racecourse, but the case settled privately and we do not know the outcome.[83] There were also several linked suits in the civil and criminal lists which could only be personal squabbles—where both actions often settled either before the hearing or very shortly after the court hearing had opened.[84]

Matrimonial jurisdiction was reserved to the Supreme Court until transferred to HMCJ by OC1878. Whilst some writers have suggested that this was a failure of the system, contemporary mores meant that, in actuality, few people brought such cases. The only matrimonial case that proceeded to a hearing was in 1866 when Mrs Green prosecuted her husband for assault and prayed for Judicial Separation. Flowers, the Nagasaki Consul, had attempted to effect an amicable reconciliation but without success before referring the case to Hornby who heard it on circuit in Nagasaki.[85] Hornby then persuaded Mrs Green to withdraw her application if Mr Green sent his sister away. In addition, Hornby ordered Mr Green to find security for his good behaviour for the next five years in the sum of £1,000.[86]

The next year in Nagasaki, Mrs Tabor petitioned for Judicial Separation on grounds of cruelty and ill-treatment but Flowers told her that if he forwarded her complaint to Hornby officially he must also communicate it to her husband—which she did not wish. Therefore, he merely sent it privately to Hornby and sought instructions.[87] No outcome is given but it reflects how litigants recoiled from matrimonial disputes and preferred an informal approach;[88] a desire also seen with the Blockleys (who were no strangers to litigation generally) when the Tokyo Vice-Consul arranged a conference with Mrs Blockley's counsel, Montague Kirkwood, so as to

82 Annersley to Hornby, 10 July 1875; FO656/41.

83 1 March 1877; NCH.

84 Berwick's defamation claim in *Berwick v. J.P. Connor* was linked to Connor's contemporaneous criminal actions for assault and criminal damage against him—that everything was a mountain made out of a molehill was demonstrated when all actions were withdrawn; Hakodate semi-annual return, 1871; FO656/35.

85 Flowers to Hornby, 16 June 1866; FO656/14.

86 Flowers to Goodwin, 14 August 1866; FO656/14.

87 Flowers to Hornby, 1 March 1867; FO656/14.

88 Mrs Tabor was Alt's sister and Alt had told Flowers that he would raise the matter privately with Hornby.

avoid public litigation.[89] Most parties adopted the practical solution of living apart; although, this could give rise to problems such as the need to enforce any formal maintenance agreement as when Mrs Diack sued her husband for payment of agreed annual maintenance contributions of £60.[90]

Until the Married Women's Property Act, 1882, married British women were not regarded as having independent property. This meant that claimants against the wife often looked to the husband to pay her debts but the Married Women's Property Act 1870 meant that, when the couple were living apart, the husband was not liable. When Yamamoto Hikotaro sued Thomas Bell for $26 for goods supplied to his separated wife, Bell relied successfully upon this Act for his defence.[91] However, when the Temperance Hall sued him for $56 in respect of Mrs Bell's lodging, Rennie suggested he reach a settlement and not seek to rely upon this legislation.[92] The Act worked both ways; and when Mrs Blockley sued Mills for $12.25 for food and drinks supplied, she was able to defeat his claim to set-off a debt of $14.87 due to him from Mr Blockley because she was carrying on a separate business from her husband.[93]

Litigation was also used—particularly by the larger commercial concerns (of all nationalities)—as a continuation of commercial negotiation by other means as seen by those cases which settled or where the basic facts were undisputed. One of the first cases heard in Nagasaki indicated this trait: when sued for $20 for repairing two printing presses, the defendant admitted the work had been done to his satisfaction but claimed the sum demanded amounted to overcharging. However, the Court said the factory was known for its high charges and ordered the defendant to pay the demand with costs.[94] In another Nagasaki case, involving James Mitchell, after four days of argument, the record states baldly 'Case withdrawn. Settled amicably out of court.'[95]

Claims[96] were denominated variously in Dollars, Yen and, occasionally, Sterling. Prior to 1875, the amounts of most claims are unstated in the Nagasaki semi-annual returns but the 1875–1899 Nagasaki Court minutes

---

89 Tokyo Vice-Consul to Kirkwood, 1876; FO 798/23.

90 *Elizbeth Diack v. John Diack*, 17 October 1896; JWM.

91 4 June 1879; JDH.

92 20 June 1879; JDH.

93 4 April 1877; JDH.

94 *Lasschuit v. Hansard*, 17 August 1861; *The Nagasaki Shipping List and Advertiser*.

95 *Mitsumizo Teizo v. J.F. Mitchell*, 1877; FO796/2. The dispute centred on the fitness for purpose of stones supplied by the plaintiff for constructing a dry-dock.

96 Table 20.

often contain these details as does the Nagasaki Register of Civil Claims. Most newspaper reports give the amount in dispute; but, elsewhere, it is often not possible to ascertain the sums in dispute from the available records or reports.

In interpreting the Nagasaki figures for 1875–1899, we might expect a bias towards smaller value claims because plaintiffs with higher value claims would probably have commenced proceedings in HMCJ after 1879. Nearly one-third the known claims in this period involved claims for less than $25 and a further two-fifths amounts ranging from $26 to $100; but, within these figures, wide variations exist between different categories of plaintiff which may reflect the different economic roles of the various communities. For instance, over half of Japanese (and a third of Chinese) individuals' quantified claims were below $25 and a quarter of Japanese claims under $5—usually for goods and services supplied or, occasionally, wages. Whilst such small claims existed amongst other groups of plaintiff, the wider spread of claims amongst other groups reflects roles across the economic spectrum played by British and other Western firms and individuals although some Japanese claimants were also significant commercial counterparts. The Japanese authorities' claims for ground rents were usually around $60–80.

The newspaper reports suggest that between a quarter and a third of cases in Yokohama and Kobe involved claims of over $250 (and around a third of these involved amounts in excess of $5,000 in Yokohama and $2,000 in Kobe). Whilst British and foreign plaintiffs dominated these larger cases, about a third of Japanese plaintiffs also claimed such amounts. Under a fifth of Chinese claims in Yokohama exceeded $250—which reinforces the suggestion the Chinese traders often filled a *petit bourgeois* economic position. Even though we might expect newspapers to concentrate on the larger claims, HMCJ was not the preserve of large claims as shown by newspaper reports of several disputes involving amounts of less than $5. This is not to be unexpected given that HMCJ replaced the Kanagawa Court—which had previously dealt with the smaller local claims whilst the Yokohama Court had handled the larger ones.

Until 1879, Yokohama had no monopoly on large cases and we see a $45,000 insurance claim litigated in Kobe[97] and the Glover bankruptcy with debts exceeding $30,000 in Nagasaki; but, after HMCJ's

97 *Kirby v. China Fire Insurance*, which was immediately appealed to Shanghai when decided in favour of the plaintiff but settled before the appeal was progressed. Interest was allowed at 10% on the claim. 5 and 21 December 1878; NCH.

establishment, we see few reports of 'big-money' cases heard in the out-ports. One of the few was the *Hiogo Hotel case*[98] heard by Mowat on circuit in Kobe over six days before a jury which found for the defendants. This involved the alleged sale of the hotel at an under-value but none of the reports indicates the amount claimed. Despite the absence of newspaper reports, some larger claims were pursued in the out-ports. For instance, the Nagasaki Register of Civil Claims 1878–1899 includes seven cases with claims of over $1,000 but none was reported in the Yokohama newspapers.[99]

Most civil cases were heard by the Judge alone but the newspapers recorded 11 jury trials in the Yokohama Court and six in HMCJ. They included a mixture of categories with four debt/bankruptcy cases, three disputes over payment for goods and services, one involving a claim for disputed wages, three defamation cases and five others. With the larger claims and also defamation claims, the parties could opt for a jury trial or the Judge could order one where the facts were in significant dispute. No civil jury trials were reported as having taken place in Kobe.

Jury trials mostly involved larger sums of money; but, this was not always the case: for instance, *Edgar Abbott v. John Baikie, master of Ching Too* in 1877 was a dispute over just $100 charter-party commission,[100] and *Nomi Daisuki v. J.W. Sutherland* involved a claim for just ¥262 for the supply of goods.[101] *Barnard v. Wilkin* was an action for the recovery of land before Hornby in Yokohama where the evidence was so conflicting that he said one side must have committed perjury and he was inclined to order a jury trial. Nevertheless, he ordered Bate, the Registrar, and Constable White to investigate the factual background.[102]

The jury's role was to decide factual questions put to it while the Judge determined the law and applied it to the found facts. In *Beato v. Rickett, as agent for P&O*, a carriage of goods case where Felix Beato claimed $11,000 in respect of goods, the question was whether they had been damaged on board the ship or as a result of being badly packed. The jury found the

98 22 July 1892; NCH.

99 The two Kniffler defamation cases where $7,500 was claimed in each, the Kate Banff claim for ¥2,000 (all withdrawn); two debt claims for £1,000 and $4,000 respectively and an unspecified claim by Jardines against Brown & Co. for ¥9,706 (all of which recorded decisions for the plaintiff) and a charter-party dispute for $5,000 (where no result is recorded); FO796/5.

100 12 May 1877; JWM.

101 17 February 1877; JWM.

102 24 September 1870; JWM. No result is indicated.

former whereupon Wilkinson applied the terms of the bill of lading to determine liability.[103] Jury trials could be over in a day but, often, lasted longer; and *Davison & Co. v. Oriental Banking Corporation* lasted six days.[104] In consequence, as with criminal trials, we see several examples of potential jurors who had been summoned to appear for jury service being fined when they failed to appear for duty.

Just five cases with two Assessors (and one with three) were reported in the Kanagawa Court before 1865 but none afterwards. With Hornby's subsequent frequent visits on circuit, the larger cases were reserved for him and, after the Yokohama Court's establishment, there was no need for Assessors in Yokohama, although we continue to see limited references to Assessors in the out-ports. In the Kobe newspaper reports, we see ten cases heard with Assessors before 1878 but only two afterwards. Of the claims heard with Assessors in Kobe, amounts ranged from $600 to $5,524 with six cases involving claims in excess of $2,000 and apart from one case heard by the Vice-Consul, Frank Playfair, which involved four Assessors,[105] all involved just two Assessors.

Playfair presumably heard the claim with four Assessors as a display of additional community involvement and independence because the claim arose out of an arbitration award in the same matter by Hall, the Consul. The claim was an insurance claim by a Spaniard, Remegio Perez, for goods lost in a fire. For the court case, Perez was unrepresented as he claimed he could find no legal representation in Kobe as Brushfield was absent and Crosse was acting for the defence. Thus, as his English was limited, he was aided by Danenberg as an interpreter. Hobart-Hampden, a junior consular official, read out his statement of claim to the Court. During the two day hearing Hall was called to give evidence as to the arbitration proceedings and award. The insurance company's defence was that Perez had not paid his insurance premia and so the insurance contract was terminated for non-payment—but Perez said he had not been chased for them. After an adjournment, Playfair, with the concurrence of the Assessors found for Perez—just as Hall had done in the arbitration and a later newspaper editorial attacked the insurance company for fighting the case and not having accepted the arbitration award.

---

103 4 November 1876; JWM.

104 Davison won $16,086 for customs duties and storage charges for 2,000 packages hypothecated by Felix Beato to the defendant; but the defendant appealed and the Supreme Court found the jury was wrong on one aspect and halved the damages; 5 November 1874; NCH.

105 *Remegio Perez v. Imperial Insurance Company of London*; 2, 9 and 16 July 1898; KWC.

Insurance claims were a particular area which raised suggestions of fraud. When Joseph Sylva claimed $3,000 for goods lost in a godown fire, it transpired that the insurance companies in Kobe had taken to commissioning confidential reports on every fire in the city. In this case, they instructed Brushfield to defend Sylva's claim. When, after a four day hearing, Hall and two Assessors dismissed the claim with costs, they said all the evidence pointed to a corrupt and fraudulent claim and the *Kobe Weekly Chronicle* said that there had been no more severe a denunciation of one of the parties to a suit before the Court before suggesting a prosecution be brought for perjury.[106]

Results and Possible Bias[107]

By focusing on the proportion of cases won by the defendant, we exclude those settled and admitted cases which were not fought to a conclusion and so can examine arguments of bias in the Courts. The Nagasaki case records 1875–1899, unlike other records, enable us to distinguish cases where the claims were admitted when the case reached Court from claims which settled. Admitted claims were usually debt claims which the defendant lacked the wherewithal to meet. Those cases which settled usually did so prior to the hearing (in which case they would benefit from the rebate of one-half of the court fees) or, more occasionally, during the course of the hearing—particularly with the larger, more complicated, claims.

In Nagasaki 1875–1899, on average, 71% of cases were fought and a quarter of all defendants defeated the claims brought against them, although this increased to 36% in contested cases. However, there were wide variations from this average between different plaintiff groups. Two-thirds of cases brought by the Japanese authorities were admitted or settled before trial: usually, ground rent claims were settled, admitted or uncontested whilst commercial cases were fought. Only Alfred Glover, of a leading Nagasaki commercial family, fought a ground-rent claim, and his purpose seems to have been to provide a platform from which to complain about the state of the roads locally and the Japanese authorities' failure to repair them.[108] At the other extreme, 86% of cases brought by

[106] *Joseph August Sylva v. Henry Lucas & Co. as agents for the Union Assurance Society*; 17 and 24 July 1897; KWC.

[107] Table 21.

[108] *Nakao Masahiro, officer of Nagasaki kencho on behalf of the Japanese Government v. Alfred Glover*, case 17 of 1880; FO798/8.

Japanese individuals went to trial and, with just over half of such plaintiffs winning in such trials, they were noticeably less successful than British or Chinese plaintiffs—although more successful than other foreigners.

If we look at all claims brought—and not just those that were fought out in the Nagasaki Court—Japanese individuals, in losing over a third of cases, were twice as unsuccessful as British plaintiffs and the Japanese authorities—although slightly more successful than other foreigners. Although the small numbers involved can exaggerate the differences, the proportions of successful defendants across the size range of claims are consistent with their overall averages, so it is not possible to point to a particular section within a group of claimants which was more successful than others within that group. Similarly, breaking down the results by time shows little difference save during the unexplained spike in cases in 1879–1880 when British plaintiffs, as a group, were the most unsuccessful group.

Between 1860–1874 and 1875–1899, the proportion of settled/admitted cases in Nagasaki increased by almost half from 21% to 29% whilst the proportion of successful defendants more than doubled (from 12% to 26%, with a similar increase—from 16% to 36%—in contested cases). This reflects the greater proportion of debt related cases in the earlier period. With commercial cases, which formed a greater proportion in the later period, there were, usually, genuine issues at dispute. In the earlier period, Japanese individuals were more successful than in the later period and, proportionately, more successful than Chinese and foreign plaintiffs—although, still, much less successful than British claimants.

In Yokohama, except with Chinese plaintiffs, where just a fifth of defendants were successful in contested cases, differences between groups of plaintiff were slight and all were close to the average of a third of defendants winning and there was little variation by different time periods. The biggest divergences in Yokohama and Nagasaki were with the handful of claims for amounts of under $5, where Japanese individual plaintiffs were less successful than other groups.

Of the other Courts' figures, only the semi-annual returns in Kobe might suggest a bias in favour of British plaintiffs as British plaintiffs failed in just a tenth of cases as opposed to Japanese and Chinese plaintiffs, who failed in nearly a third of claims—and, in the Japanese case, almost half of fought cases. On the other hand, the newspaper reports for Kobe from 1869 to 1899 show that nearly half of all defendants defeating claims brought by British and Japanese plaintiffs against just over a tenth doing so in cases brought by other foreigners. In Hakodate, Japanese plaintiffs were marginally more successful than other groups whilst, in Tokyo, the proportions of successful British and Japanese plaintiffs were similar.

Thus, there is no consistent trend of quantitative evidence to support claims of bias by the Courts in relation to civil claims: the figures vary as between the different ports and over time and, so far as the reports contained in newspapers are concerned, are dependent upon journalistic selection from time to time. The only quantitative evidence to support claims of possible bias against Japanese plaintiffs (or bias in favour of Britons) are the Nagasaki figures for 1875–1899 and the limited official Yokohama and Kobe figures in their semi-annual returns. In Yokohama, the semi-annual returns for 1867–1872 show that both Japanese and foreign plaintiffs were less successful than British plaintiffs (about 70% against 80% winning in fought cases). In Kobe, the semi-annual returns show that 45% of defendants in contested cases brought by Japanese plaintiffs from 1870 to 1875 were successful against a third with foreigner plaintiffs and only a sixth with British plaintiffs whereas the Kobe newspaper reports for 1869–1899 suggest that British and Japanese plaintiffs achieved similar results.

Whether cases settled or not has an impact on the figures. Except for cases reported in the Kobe newspapers, the proportion of settled/admitted claims by Japanese individuals tends to be much lower than for other groups.

Even where the underlying facts were broadly undisputed, cases still ended up in Court over disputes as to the quantum of damages. In *Ikushima Gohei v. Mourilyan, Heimann & Co*,[109] the plaintiff claimed ¥90 ground rent and ¥1,543 for damages done to a godwon which he had rented to the defendants and which they had damaged. The defendants admitted damaging the godown but claimed it was worth only ¥85. The Court said all the available evidence showed that godowns were worth around ¥3 per *tsubo* against the ¥90 per *tsubo* claimed by Gohei and also that the lease had terminated so no ground rent was payable. Therefore, the Court awarded Gohei just ¥138.50.

Against these possible suggestions of bias, we must remember that no category of plaintiffs was as successful as the Japanese authorities who lost only one out of 20 cases brought by them in Nagasaki and Hakodate and two out of five in Yokohama.[110] At the least, the Courts treated the

[109] 26 June 1878; HN.

[110] In the first hearing of *Akita han v. Blakiston Marr & Co.*, the Hakodate Court found for the defendants on 9 February 1871—but, at a re-hearing on 25 March 1872 following an appeal by the Japanese authorities, the plaintiff won on most points; FO656/35.

Japanese authorities with scrupulous fairness and may even have leant over backwards to ensure that there could be no criticism of their handling of such claims.[111] On the other hand, it may be argued that the Japanese authorities only brought cases where they were confident of success. Nothing suggests any bias against Chinese plaintiffs: merely a tendency on the part of many such traders—along with Japanese *jinrikisha* coolies—to exaggerate their claims for, in the vast majority of cases involving Chinese plaintiffs, the claim is admitted or judgment is given for the plaintiff so that, overall, they were as successful as British plaintiffs.

Of course, Japanese plaintiffs faced a novel and unfamiliar court system. Robertson acknowledged that, often, Japanese had, to their own mind, good reason to complain about English procedure but he took great pains to explain the intricacies of bills of sale, rights of mortgagees and the court machinery.[112] Robertson was regarded as sympathetic to Japanese concerns whereas Dohmen tended to be tetchier in response to Japanese authorities' complaints and questions but still maintained that he explained the differences between the two systems to Japanese litigants[113] and exhibited greater patience and forbearance towards Japanese plaintiffs than he would towards Westerners.[114] In *Benjiro v. Houseal*, Hannen explained that he had great sympathy for the plaintiff but, as the plaintiff had been the victim of fraud, he could see no way to assist him against the defendant, who was an agent for a disclosed principal.[115] Again, in HMCJ, he adjourned a case twice to enable a Japanese plaintiff to assemble and bring his witnesses to court but warned him that the case would be dismissed if he failed to present them a third time—which it was when nobody appeared on the third occasion.[116] In an earlier case in Kobe, Flowers said the Court had given the Japanese plaintiff every opportunity to establish his case but, despite the 'voluminous evidence' which he had presented, he had failed to do so. Therefore, Flowers had no alternative but to dismiss his substantive claim.[117]

The case of *The Japanese Government v. George Anderson,* a Maltese who was the late mate on the *Otento Sama*, was heard by Hornby at Nagasaki in

[111] Goodwin's comments in *Akita han v. Blakiston Marr & Co.* suggest a cautious approach when Japanese authorities were parties to a dispute. See page 267.

[112] Robertson to Wilkinson, 25 February 1872; FO881/2135.

[113] Dohmen to Honda Takahonda 5 March 1872; FO798/1.

[114] Dohmen to Honda Takahonda, 29 April 1874; FO798/1.

[115] 2 August 1873; TJH.

[116] 28 May and 4 June 1887; JWM.

[117] *Shimidzu Chiubi v. William Warburton*; 26 January 1878; HN.

the presence of Japanese officials. It is unclear what the case concerned—but the correspondence suggests that it was possibly a civil case under the Supreme Court's extraordinary jurisdiction. Perhaps irregularly but certainly showing consideration for the Japanese, Hornby deferred his judgment for a few days whilst he sent a copy of the evidence to the Governor for his remarks.[118]

The figures *may* support an argument that the British community assumed that it would be favourably treated by the Courts which, in turn, may have led to a tendency by some Britons to try to brow-beat individual Japanese by hiding behind the Courts—just as they tended to fight a higher proportion of criminal prosecutions brought by Japanese individuals. As civil cases were decided on the balance of probabilities, decisions came down very much to whether or not a Court considered a plaintiff had proved his case on this basis. A subjective reading of the cases shows the Consuls seeking to act reasonably and independently in their examination of the facts which, all too often, depended on which party was the more credible witness. In *Kaneko Suikichi v. James F. Mitchell,*[119] the Consul, after eight pages of evidence, concluded, when dismissing the claim, that the facts were complex and it all came down to the say so of the parties because such documents as there were 'do not assist the court in any way at arriving at a decision'.[120] Prejudice could, of course, work both ways for British litigants' reputations were well-known to the Courts and, when a Japanese sued Bridget Blockley for ¥5 wages, the Court found for her only after Dohmen had submitted her story 'to an exhaustive analysis'.[121] Often, as in criminal cases, oral evidence was contradictory. When Nakamura Shimsuke sued Henry Cross, who was a member of a mess where Shimsuke was the cook, for $15 paid by Shimsuke to Man Cheong, a Chinese storekeeper, for Cross's account, there was no written evidence at all regarding the alleged payment and Man Cheong had disappeared.[122]

As with criminal cases, there is no reason to believe that juries were biased against Japanese plaintiffs in the few civil cases that went before a jury. Of 17 reported jury cases, 11 involved British plaintiffs and three each Japanese and other foreigners as plaintiffs. Although British plaintiffs succeeded in two-thirds of cases whereas Japanese and foreign plaintiffs succeeded in just a third, the numbers are too small to be statistical

[118] Flowers to Governor of Nagasaki, 11 April 1866; FO796/25.
[119] Civil cases 3 and 4 of 1881; FO796/8.
[120] Ibid.
[121] 18 March 1881; JDH.
[122] 6 December 1876; HN.

evidence of bias. Likewise, trials involving Assessors provide no evidence of bias as the plaintiffs—including the sole Japanese plaintiff—won in all bar one of the cases heard with Assessors outside Kobe. Of the 12 Kobe cases heard with Assessors, six involved British plaintiffs, five foreign plaintiffs and just one a Japanese plaintiff. The Japanese plaintiff won his suit as did four of the foreign plaintiffs against just three of the British plaintiffs. The only Kobe case where the Assessors dissented from the Consul's decision involved a British plaintiff claiming the repayment of $1,000 bargain money paid in connection with the purchase of a Japanese steamer, the *Orphan* for the plaintiff's principal, George Murray of Shanghai. As the defendant was now insolvent, the question was, in effect, whether the plaintiff could recover the sum ahead of the defendant's other creditors. Enslie held for the defendant against the opinion of the two Assessors; but his judgment was reversed on appeal to the Supreme Court.[123]

Court Procedures

The Rules set out the fees. They were charged *ad valorem* in relation to the plaints, hearings and appeal petitions and on a fixed fee basis for other procedural steps. Plaint fees were 1% of the sum claimed;[124] but, to encourage settlements, half would be returned if the case settled before the hearing. Fixed fees, ranging from of $1 or $0.50, applied to the Courts' serving petitions or issuing orders and $0.50 for each page of any copy document.[125] The fee table had been denominated in Sterling until 1868 when it was changed to Dollars but, over succeeding years, the real value of the fixed fees fell due to the devaluation of the silver based Dollar as against both Sterling and, when it became gold based, the Yen.[126] However, it was not until the after the abolition of extra-territoriality that the fee table was changed (for China and Korea).

Plaintiffs were not averse to seeking recovery of their fees for 'wasted' cases. Mrs Wilkie sought to recover her 'wasted' fees in bringing an ejectment action against Alexander Porter in Hakodate in 1871 when it transpired that she could not succeed because he had already granted

123 *John Waters v. Wallworth & Co.*; 13 August and 12 October 1870 and 12 April 1871; HN.

124 1% on plaints up to a maximum fee of $100 and 2% on appeals up to a maximum fee of $200; FO17/1072 pages 58–62.

125 Rules, Schedule B.

126 Foreign Office to HM Treasury, 8 November 1897; FO83/1788.

Blakiston an (unregistered) equitable mortgage over the property.[127] Eusden referred the question to the Supreme Court—but its response is not in the files.[128]

By concession, Japanese and British litigants were excused payment of court fees in each other's courts. Hornby sanctioned these arrangements but appears not to have briefed his staff in Shanghai for, when Hannen established the Yokohama Court, Hannen sought to levy court fees upon the Japanese. This attempt triggered a swift response from the *Chikenji* of Kanagawa who threatened reciprocal fees on British claims before the Japanese courts. Adams, the *Chargé d'Affaires*, persuaded Hannen to drop his attempt but not before Hannen sought to justify his actions by explaining that there was no reason why Japanese suitors should be treated differently from other plaintiffs and the beneficiaries of this concession were certain Yokohama merchants with large claims against Japanese defendants whereas the taxpayers at home would bear the costs. He worried that, if no fees were charged, the Courts would be flooded with Japanese claims before admitting that his '...experience of Chinese claimants may not be applicable to the Japanese'.[129] As a result of these exchanges, the arrangement was formalized by Parkes, the Japanese Foreign Minister and the Foreign Secretary.[130]

The exchange is revealing. First, it shows the close day-to-day working relationship between the Consuls and the local Japanese government officials, most of whom were eager to avoid difficulties and make 'the system' work whilst having regard to what they perceived as their national interest. Second, it displays a different approach between practice in China and Japan for fees continued to be levied upon Chinese suitors in China—who, evidently, had a reputation for bringing unmeritorious claims.

Despite this formal agreement, Dohmen, when he took up his position as Vice-Consul in Tokyo, tried again to levy fees upon Japanese plaintiffs. He argued that the objection to the fees came not from the plaintiffs, who, he said, were always happy to pay them (as they could recover them when they won their case), but from the Japanese government itself. He saw no reason why Japanese litigants should be treated any differently from other litigants and, furthermore, he had no right under the Rules to change the position. He urged that 'the arrangement made between Sawa, Terashima

[127] *Estate of Frederick Wilkie v. A.P. Porter;* 20 August 1871; FO656/35.
[128] Eusden to Goodwin, 20 August 1871; FO656/35. See also page 224.
[129] Hannen to Adams, 17 August 1871; FO656/37.
[130] Robertson to Watson, 29 January 1873; FO656/19.

and Mr Adams ... be reconsidered'.[131] In response to the Japanese government's complaints, Parkes simply ordered Dohmen to observe the agreement that Japanese and British litigants were not charged in each other's courts and to desist from charging such fees as 'it is not desirable that the course followed in your Court should differ from that which obtains in all the other Provincial Courts...'[132] Despite the concerns expressed by Hannen about the potential for abuse, none of the case figures suggests any material abuse by Japanese plaintiffs of the system as a result of their being exempt from court fees.

Further attempts to ameliorate difficulties faced by Japanese plaintiffs being obliged to take legal proceedings, within their own country, in a foreign language and under, for them, a novel legal system included the convention whereby, unlike other foreign plaintiffs, unrepresented Japanese plaintiffs were not required to find security for costs (but if they employed Counsel subsequently such security was required).[133] This convention appears to have developed around 1873/1874 for, in 1872, there is a report of Hannen's ordering a Japanese plaintiff to provide $50 security for costs;[134] but, two years later, Goodwin refused Marks' application for security 'in view of the plaintiff being Japanese, he could not call upon him to furnish security'[135] before reminding Marks that, under the Treaty, the Japanese were entitled to receive every assistance in obtaining justice.

Most cases were heard by the Courts within days of the plaint being issued. For small claims, the records suggest that justice was swift with few lengthy delays between a Summons being taken out and its being heard: a number even being heard on the same day and the majority within the week.[136] Such delays as occurred were almost always down to delays by one party or another or, occasionally, the defendant's need to assemble papers or witnesses such as when the Yokohama Court adjourned a case for a fortnight to allow the defendant to fetch papers from Kobe.[137] In 1876, Lock, who had been imprisoned for assaulting Albert Morris, succeeded in applying for a postponement of Morris's civil case against him

131 Dohmen to Parkes, 7 May 1873; FO262/501.

132 Parkes to Dohmen, 3 June 1873; FO262/498.

133 Hannen in *Hirose Sima v. Blakeney*, heard on 26 June 1883; FO656/69.

134 *Hanjiro v. Jaquemot*, 23 November 1872; JWM.

135 *Kawaguchi Kamakitchi v. W. Wallace*, 5 December 1874; JWM.

136 In Kobe, of 17 cases in 1870, nine were heard within the week (one on the same day as the Summons, three the next day and four within two days). Of the other eight cases, one was heard within 14 days, three within a month, one in six weeks and three after a gap of two months. Kobe semi-annual returns; FO656/34.

137 *E. Rothmund v. T.W. Mercer*, 18 October 1871; NCH.

for damages arising out of the incident. Lock said he could not afford counsel and, being in prison, was unable to prepare his defence.[138]

Other delays were caused by the inevitable need to schedule cases to avoid conflicts between hearings and pre-existing bookings of counsel. The situation could be especially difficult in Kobe where, for much of the time, there were just two counsel, who often appeared on opposite sides of contested cases. A claim by Messrs Isaacs Bros for $991 arising out of damage to 826 kegs of nails was adjourned for three days after the first day's hearing because other cases were already scheduled for the following two days. When the case resumed, it went on for a further two days.[139]

The Courts accommodated the reality of a community which travelled frequently and allowed witnesses who were about to leave a port to be examined ahead of the main hearing[140] or held over cases to allow litigants to appear personally as when *Ishi Senzo v. Cocking & Singleton* was postponed for a fortnight as Cocking was expected in Yokohama on the next English Mail.[141] Other delays often reflected attempts at settlement.

The larger commercial cases sometimes provided an exception to this rule of swift justice. The two *Kniffler* cases dragged on for over a year with all parties playing procedural games so the substantive issues never came to trial; but, even these were speedy compared with the *Glamorganshire*[142] where the plaintiffs waited over four years before a final judgment. Japanese litigants also used the courts as an additional limb of their commercial negotiations or in an attempt to avoid contractual obligations. *Shoya Johichi v. James F. Mitchell* concerned a claim for ¥1,000 in relation to the construction of a dock at Nagasaki but, after four months of frequent procedural hearings, the parties suddenly informed the Court that 'they had come to a mutual understanding about the Plaintiff's resuming work'[143] and discontinued the case.

Around 1877–1878, when Wilkinson alone ran both the Yokohama Court and the Tokyo Court, substantial delays occurred in several cases—particularly in his handing down reserved judgments: over two months in two cases. This was so unusual that a newspaper editorial commented

[138] 17 June 1876; HN. At the eventual hearing, the Court awarded $35 against Lock as against $530 claimed; 19 July 1876; HN.

[139] *Messrs Isaacs Bros. v. Northern Pacific Steamship Company*; 16 October 1897; KWC.

[140] *James Davison v. Oriental Banking Corporation*, 3 October 1874; TJH.

[141] 1 March 1873; TJH.

[142] See pages 277–282.

[143] Civil case 19 of 1879; FO796/4.

that no blame could attach to the Yokohama Court as the delays were due to pressure of business.[144]

Reconciliation and Arbitration

By OC1865, every Court was to 'promote reconcilement and encourage and facilitate the settlement in an amicable way of any suit or proceedings'[145] but there is little evidence of the Courts doing so outside the field of matrimonial disputes and some of the more obviously personal animus motivated cases. One exception is the early 1870s when the Tokyo Vice-Consulate's correspondence files show the Vice-Consul encouraging Britons to honour their debts to Japanese applicants.

There is more evidence for the use of arbitration in dispute resolution. OC1865[146] permitted the Consuls to refer cases to arbitration and Hornby printed and distributed standard arbitration agreement forms which he encouraged Consuls to sell and explain to litigants how they could use the process.[147] This followed on from his public address in Yokohama urging parties either to use arbitration or to proceed direct to Shanghai under the Supreme Court's extraordinary jurisdiction pending the establishment of the Yokohama Court.[148] Technically, arbitration was not a matter of jurisdiction but a private arrangement and there are few instances in the records or the newspapers so it is not possible to estimate its prevalence. It was useful where the dispute involved technical matters as in the dispute between Mitchell and the Japanese government concerning the technical standards of a steam boiler and ship's engine.[149]

Consuls could, and did, sit as arbitrators. The earliest reported instance was Robertson's sitting as arbitrator in the *New York v. Ocean Queen* dispute in 1869 when he awarded $10,000 against the defendant;[150] but, this case—and several others—show that arbitration did not remove the Courts' involvement. Here, the defendant appealed to Hornby who refused to enforce the award saying that Robertson had no jurisdiction to sit as an

144 21 September 1878; JWM.
145 Section 48.
146 Section 49.
147 Hornby to Annersley, 2 March 1870; FO656/18.
148 1 November 1869; JTOM.
149 *F. Store, acting for the Japanese Government v. J.F. Mitchell*, 1875; FO796/2.
150 13 October 1869; *Japan Times*.

arbitration court—which prompted newspaper complaints given Hornby's recent advocacy of arbitration to the community in Yokohama.[151] In 1871, Hannen arbitrated a dispute between Campbell and Davison (*qua* Administrator of R.B. Scotland's estate) and, unusually—but both parties requested it—the arbitration proceedings were held in public.[152] In what was probably a case of the parties seeking the good offices of a legally qualified arbitrator, Hannen sat as arbitrator between the Japanese government and Tombrink (*qua* Trustee of Glover & Co.'s estate) in 1873.[153]

Nothing prevented individual merchants from sitting as arbitrators but, as arbitration was a private affair, examples of non-lawyers sitting alone as arbitrators rarely entered the public domain although it did happen as when Flowers sat with two merchants as arbitrators in Nagasaki in a dispute between Robert Chesterman and J.H. Wignall, owner of the *Snap*, over interrelated claims between the two. On Wignall's application, a Naval Court had found that Chesterman had deliberately delayed the *Snap*'s passage so as to increase his own wages and dismissed him from the ship and cancelled his master's certificate. The following week, Flowers and two other arbitrators conducted an arbitration between the two in relation to Chesterman's claim for $155 wages which Wignall argued were all due to him (plus a further $45 in respect of the delays). The arbitration found entirely for Wignall.[154]

Britons also used foreigners as arbitrators and H.I.R.M.'s consul in Hakodate arbitrated a dispute between Frederick Wilkie and Alexander Porter in 1871 (and Porter's refusal to implement the award led to Wilkie's estate seeking to enforce it in Hakodate Court).[155]

There are two problems inherent in arbitration: first, where one party wishes to appeal and, second, there there is no automatic judicial procedure for the enforcement of the arbitration awards. In *Wilkie & Laufenberg v. E.C. Kirby*, the disappointed party appealed to Hornby against the arbitrator's award only for Hornby to say that both parties had handled their case so badly that all he could do was effect an equitable adjustment of their claims.[156]

Even where a Consul sat as arbitrator, he could not use his judicial powers *qua* Consul to implement any award he may have given as arbitrator

151 Ibid.
152 Hannen to Goodwin, 29 November 1871; FO656/37.
153 Hannen to Hornby, 1873; FO656/37.
154 19 and 26 April 1873; NE.
155 *Estate of Frederick Wilkie v. A.P. Porter*, 20 August 1871; FO656/35.
156 3 July 1872; JWM.

for, as arbitrator, he was sitting as a private individual. In several cases, the winning party was compelled to apply to the Courts to enforce the arbitration award. The first occasion was a dispute between Kent and Stand in Yokohama in 1872 when Kent went to Court to enforce the arbitration award in his favour.[157] We have already seen that Remegio Perez was compelled to re-litigate his claim against his insurers when they refused to abide by Hall's award as arbitrator. Where the losing party to an arbitration was Japanese, the successful party would be obliged to go before the Japanese Courts to seek to enforce the award. This happened in the '*Antimony case*' where the Ichinokawa Antimony Mining Corporation refused to pay the ¥50,000 awarded to the successful party, Morf.[158] There was also the issue of responsibility for the arbitrator's fees and, in *J.W. Hall v. Frischling*, Wilkinson was obliged to enforce payment of a court-appointed arbitrator's fees of $850.[159]

One of the stranger sets of proceedings to arise out of an arbitration concerned the dispute between the Misses Sowter and Mr & Mrs Rowe in Kobe in 1897 over Mr Rowe's allegations that the sisters had been fiddling the books at the private school they ran. The dispute started off in the Kobe Court but went to arbitration when Crosse, who acted for the Sowters, suggested that it be settled by arbitration rather than by a full, public court hearing. However, when the arbitration went against the Rowes and the arbitrator ordered Mr Rowe to apologize publicly to the Misses Sowter for his allegations, he refused to do so and the Rowes applied to Playfair to set aside the arbitration award.[160]

In these subsequent proceedings—which, in one sense, could be said to be all about whether or not Mr Rowe should apologize but, in another sense, amounted to a re-trial of the underlying issues—Mr Rowe claimed to be unable any more to afford Crosse's services and represented himself whilst the editor of *The Hiogo News*, P. Mackenzie Skinner, appeared for the Misses Sowter. Crosse was called as a witness by the Sowters and deposed that he thought that Whymark had conducted the arbitration in a very fair way. After hearings lasting two days, Playfair said that, although he had bent over backwards to allow Mr Rowe to introduce new evidence, it was clear that Whymark had acted fairly in conducting the arbitration. When Mr Rowe still refused to apologize, the Court gave him two days to

[157] 13 April 1872; JWM.
[158] 2 November and 14 December 1892; KWC.
[159] 4 January 1879; JWM.
[160] 11 and 25 September and 9 and 16 October 1897; KWC.

do so—otherwise, he would be committed to prison for contempt. When Mr Rowe continued in his refusal, Playfair committed him to prison for contempt—which provoked Mrs Rowe to rail loudly in Court against 'British justice' only for Playfair to threaten to commit her as well! The *Kobe Weekly Chronicle* condemned the Court for imprisoning a 60 year old man but Rowe was released after 24 hours when a medical certificate was produced to the effect that his health would suffer from such a confinement. When the Sowters' costs in the court case came to be taxed, Mr Rowe claimed that he could not pay and applied to file for bankruptcy. At his examination in bankruptcy conducted before the Consul, Hall, he again tried to re-open the underlying issues only for Hall to refuse to allow him to do so.

Use of arbitration was not confined to Britons: Mitsubishi's standard bill of lading required all disputes to be referred to the arbitration of the Supreme Court or the Yokohama Court or an arbitrator appointed by one of them,[161] and, in *Oki Mohei v. Taylor* (a building dispute), the defendant successfully used a contractual arbitration clause to prevent the plaintiff's initiating court proceedings.[162] That arbitration was seen as a private arrangement outside extra-territoriality is demonstrated by a suit brought on 30 July 1899 against Reynell in Kobe. The case dragged on and the Japanese authorities complained about HMCJ's continued existence to hear it as a pre-existing claim so Wilkinson persuaded the parties to withdraw the case and opt for arbitration with him as arbitrator.[163]

We must wonder how extensive arbitration became amongst Westerners after 1899 for, as extra-territoriality came to a close, foreign Chambers of Commerce in Yokohama and Kobe drew up sets of arbitration regulations for members to use in order to avoid recourse to the Japanese courts. These rules were distinct from rules set by the local Japanese Chamber of Commerce due to a perception amongst the foreign community that some Japanese commercial entities viewed arbitration merely as a continuation of negotiation—with arbitrators appointed by the Japanese parties there to represent their interests and not in a neutral capacity.[164]

---

[161] 6 April 1876; NCH.
[162] 26 April 1890; JWM.
[163] Ruxton 2005, page 210.
[164] 1 April 1899; EW.

Civil Status

Extra-territoriality revolved around nationality. Nationality's importance was shown by John Duus who had been registered by the Hakodate Consul (and even prosecuted in the Hakodate Court for breaching the Treaty's customs regulations in 1863). However, when he lost a civil case in the Hakodate Court and on appeal to the Supreme Court, he used his original—and continuing—Danish nationality to avoid liability on the judgment as no Court had any jurisdiction to enforce its orders against him: only a Danish court could do so.[165]

A means of reducing potential arguments (with Japanese and other authorities) was the requirement that all adult British subjects in Japan register with their Consulate annually in January and obtain a Certificate of Registration.[166] Initially, there was no charge for registration but, in 1864, Alcock instructed Consuls to charge $1 to each British subject for registration.[167] OC1865 continued the regime and provided that the fees should be set by the Foreign Secretary.[168] Initially, he set them at $5 or, for artisans, $1 and waived them for the indigent. The levying of such fees was greeted with outrage by the British community in Japan and many denunciatory letters to the local press. Wirgman even satirized the Certificates of Registration as 'Certificates of Demoralization' in the *Japan Punch*.[169] A reverse snobbery came into play with many seeking artisan status to avoid the higher fee until Rosebery introduced a single fee of $2 from January 1894. In 1875, when two telegraphic operators employed by the Japanese government claimed that they were artisans and, thus, liable only to the $1 fee,[170] the Nagasaki Consul referred the question to the Minister. Regrettably, there is no record of the Minister's response. Even members of the British Naval Mission to Japan in 1874 sought to avoid registering and paying the registration fees but Granville ordered that they were required to register—and pay the registration fees—because they were not on the muster of a British ship.[171] In some places, the registration process operated smoothly; but, in the larger ports, many sought to avoid the

---

165 Hornby to Eusden, December 1869; FO656/18. Duus subsequently became the Danish consul at Hakodate.

166 Section 114 OC1865 (which replaced section XXXVIII OC1860).

167 Alcock to Consuls, Circular 18 May 1864; FO796/26.

168 Section 115 OC1865.

169 Munson, 2013; pages 109–110.

170 *Reg v. McLure and Mason*, 22 July 1875; FO796/2.

171 Parkes to Dohmen, 2 February 1874; FO262/509.

fees and we see frequent criminal prosecutions for failure to register,[172] which resulted in fines of up to $10.[173]

Many defendants—or, rather, their counsel—sought to use the Rules and section 47 of OC1881[174] as procedural obstacles for foreign plaintiffs. Dickins, in *Ah Chong v. J. Grigor and J. Pitman (ex'ors of Rangan)*, sought to derail Rangan's Chinese mistress's claims against his estate by claiming she was not a British subject and must, therefore, provide security. She was unable to do and would have been obliged to let her claims lapse had she been obliged to put up such security. Dickins argued that, as she was not registered, the onus of proof was on her; but Wilkinson interviewed her and said he was 'not convinced that she was not a British subject' and refused Dickins' demand.[175]

Registration was of British subjects (by birth or naturalization) only; it did not extend to individuals of other nationalities who might be 'protected' by Britain as Hornby made clear in 1867 when his review of the returns revealed that Certificates of Registration had been issued to non-Britons who, from want of their own consul in Nagasaki, were temporarily under British protection.[176] This was not an isolated case as, in the early days, foreigners sought protection by a Western power and Consuls had registered them. Hornby also complained that several Chinese in Hakodate had been registered by Gower without explaining the basis on which they claimed British protection.[177] This issue of foreigners seeking British protection and the willingness of Consuls to provide such protection seems to have dropped away after 1869—by when the Meiji Restoration had brought about greater stability within Japan and most Western nations had obtained extra-territorial rights—for there are no further references to it in the official records.

The registration of illegitimate children of British men by Japanese women was a common issue. By private international law, the child took its mother's nationality and domicile; but, with the more established liaisons, the father often wished to register the children as British and it seems that, in the early days at least, effect was given to the fathers' wishes.

---

172 In 1870, Eusden noted that he had experienced no difficulty in getting British subjects to register (Eusden to Hornby, 14 January 1870; FO656/35)—doubtless explained by Hakodate's small foreign population. Contrast this with Kobe which saw 16 prosecutions for failure to register in 1873; semi-annual returns; FO656/41.

173 Section 114 OC1865.

174 See pages 249–251.

175 6 October 1877; JWM.

176 Hornby to Flowers, 17 June 1867; FO65/18.

177 Hornby to Gower, 4 April 1868; FO656/18.

The question was certainly addressed in 1872/73 because Watson, the *Chargé d'Affaires*, referred to Hornby an application by one Osborn to register his natural son by a Japanese mother as a British subject. Watson distinguished the Ottoman dominions, where the children were automatically regarded as British, from Japan because extra-territoriality extended throughout the Sultan's possessions whereas, in Japan, foreign consular jurisdiction was restricted, in practical terms, to the Treaty limits with obvious difficulties about conferring British nationality upon (and, consequently, protecting) a child whose mother retired into the interior before its birth.[178] Osborn claimed that Hall in Kobe had informed him that a number of children similarly situated were registered in Kobe[179] and Gower, when raising a similar request, mentioned he had registered such children following a discussion with Parkes who, he believed, had consulted Hornby.[180] Hornby answered the matter in detail, but there is no record of his advice.[181]

Although section 114 OC1865 provided that anyone failing to register would not be entitled to recognition or protection as a British subject in Japan, this does not appear to have prevented such recognition of protection being granted in practice. Registration was not always conclusive as shown by the case of *Apcar v. Martin* in the Japanese courts. Apcar, a Persian trader, sued Martin for breach of contract. When Martin claimed he was from Calcutta and disputed the court's jurisdiction, the Kobe District Court accepted his demurrer but, on appeal, the Japanese courts investigated Martin's position more closely. Troup certified that Martin had been neither born nor naturalized as a British subject but went on to suggest that, as he was domiciled in India and had been registered as a British protected person, nationality should be treated as following domicile. Apcar objected and produced an affidavit from Crosse, as an expert witness as to English law, to the effect that mere registration did not confer nationality and that Martin was not a British subject. On this basis, the Japanese courts heard the case.[182]

---

178 Watson to Hornby, 5 December 1872; FO656/19.

179 Osborn to Robertson, 29 November 1872; FO656/19.

180 Gower to Hornby, 28 February 1872; FO656/41.

181 Mowat responded to Gower by enclosing a copy of Hornby's dispatch to the *Chargé d'Affaires* of 18 December 1872, 17 March 1873; FO656/41—but no copy of Hornby's dispatch is available.

182 30 October and 6 November 1897; KWC. The next we hear of the affair was Martin's detention at the Customs as he tried to leave Japan without having settled the judgment debt where he was relieved of all his possessions—bar the clothes in which he stood up plus one other suit—in order to settle the debt; 9 August 1899; KWC.

Marriage—or its formation—also proved problematic and Hornby enjoyed describing the Consular Marriage Act, 1849 (passed as an 'Act for facilitating marriages abroad') as 'An Act to impede and render doubtful marriages solemnized abroad'[183] because marriages were only valid under it if both parties were British and all its conditions were met. Instead, he suggested relying upon section 21 of that Act which provided that nothing in it affected the validity of marriages solemnized abroad otherwise than under the Act. Therefore, as the Clandestine Marriages Act 1754 did not apply overseas, he advised that the Consular Marriage Act, 1849 could be ignored if another legal marriage route could be found. He suggested relying upon either the Common Law, by which any marriage celebrated by a priest in holy orders, Anglican or Catholic, or, even, *per verba di praesenti* was valid, or the Marriage Confirmation Act 1825 which recognized marriages celebrated by an English clergyman in an Ambassador or Minister's residence.[184] However, reliance upon the Common Law could operate only if the Common Law were the applicable law in Japan. It patently was not the domestic law of Japan; however, a fiction would seem to have developed—not just in relation to Japan—whereby countries in which Britain had extra-territorial rights were deemed to be part of England for the purposes of giving effect to the recognition of marriages conducted in Anglican churches.[185]

Under the Consular Marriage Act 1849, only Consuls could perform marriages. As no Consul could appoint a locum,[186] questions—not just in Japan—arose over the validity of marriages purportedly performed by informal locums or irregularly appointed acting Consuls.[187] The Consular Marriage Act, 1868[188] remedied this defect and validated hitherto doubtful marriages. Notwithstanding these technical issues, marriages were performed frequently in the consulates[189] and 1873 saw the first marriage in Japan of a Japanese woman according to a European ceremony where the

---

183 Hornby 1929, page 292.

184 Hornby to Rev. M. Buckworth Bailey, 6 June 1868; FO656/21.

185 20 February 1908; *Japan Weekly Chronicle* (**JWC**).

186 I.e. someone appointed officially (by the Minister or the Secretary of State) as opposed to being left in charge informally by the Consul.

187 Alcock to Consuls, 7 September 1867; FO17/478. Whilst no informal locum held any Court, it would seem from this correspondence that such locums may have officiated at marriages in Japan.

188 Amended by the Foreign Marriage Act, 1891.

189 NCH records a marriage at the Nagasaki consulate on 14 July 1871.

bride had obtained the Japanese government's permission for the marriage to proceed.[190]

As time progressed, mixed marriages became more common—and even marriages by a Japanese ceremony, which raised the issue of their recognition in England. When, in 1873, the Japanese government planned to introduce a marriage law applicable to marriages conducted in Japan, Hannen questioned whether the Japanese government could enact such a law—which also allowed for marriages with foreigners resident in Japan. The Law Officers advised that such law—if confined to individuals resident in Japan (which it should be)—was not beyond 'the competency of a civilized country' and Treaty rights were not inconsistent with the Japanese right to enact such a law.[191] That said, they expressed no opinion on the 'character of such marriages if they came to be adjudicated upon in England'.[192]

Hornby suggested, from the beginning, that such marriages were lawful (as satisfying the Common Law requirements of marriages *per verba di praesenti*) and he implied the existence of many bigamous Pinkertons; but, he never decided the point judicially.[193] In 1890, the matter came before the Probate, Admiralty and Divorce division of the English High Court when Captain Brinkley, who had married a Japanese woman by a Japanese ceremony in 1886, sought a declaration of his son's legitimacy.[194] Hannen P. (the older brother of Nicholas Hannen) upheld the marriage and declared that marriages in Japan according to Japanese laws would be recognized by the English courts as 'Japan has taken its place among civilized nations whose forms and laws and ceremonies are not to be treated as on the same footing with those of the Baroloy tribe.'[195]

The case has the hallmarks of a put-up test case for, although the Attorney General was represented to oppose the application, his counsel's only objection was that the fact of the marriage had not been proved whereupon Lowder, who was then on holiday in London, was called as a witness to describe the ceremony and confirm that he knew the signatories of the marriage certificates. An affidavit from Hatoyama Kozo, Chief Professor of Law at the Imperial University, confirmed the monogamous

---

190 A marriage at a British Consulate between a Japanese girl and a Chinese who was born, educated and became a British subject at Singapore; 9 October 1873; NCH.

191 Law Officers to Granville, 28 August 1873; FO83/2299.

192 Ibid.

193 Hornby 1929, pages 292–294.

194 *Brinkley v. Attorney General* (LR XV P&D 76 (1890)).

195 Ibid.

nature of Japanese marriage law.[196] Two years later, Salisbury accepted that a British subject who married a Japanese woman and purported to renounce his British nationality could do so by a simple declaration that he had become a Japanese subject.[197] Thus, in under forty years, the British had come full circle in Japan from fiercely resisting Japanese interference to some switching nationality.

There are 237 marriages involving Britons in Japan during 1860–1899 listed by Pedlar[198] but this figure must be an underestimate as he does not include marriages performed at the Consulates[199]—only the Legation and various Anglican churches in the Treaty Ports. Of the marriages he lists, 11 involved Japanese wives and 30 other Western spouses (16 wives and 14 husbands). Of the 74 marriages celebrated at the Legation between 1862–1890 (after which date, no more are listed), all 15 after October 1887 were conducted by an Anglican minister whereas, before then, most were conducted jointly by the Minister (or *Chargé d'Affaires*) and an Anglican minister with just one by a minister alone and three by the Minister or *Chargé d'Affaires* alone. The earliest marriages listed by Pedlar outside the Legation were church weddings in Kobe from 1876. Of the 36 marriages in a Kobe church, one was noted as having been preceded by a ceremony at the Consulate and another at the German consulate. Elsewhere, church weddings are listed only from 1887 in Yokohama, 1891 in Hakodate and 1892 in Nagasaki and Tokyo.

OC1865[200] reserved jurisdiction over lunatics to the Supreme Court and this jurisdiction passed to HMCJ by OC1878. It was in the nature of a protective jurisdiction over British subjects, not an 'aggressive' one as against

---

196 Wilkinson considered that, had Japanese marriage law and customs been presented accurately to the High Court, it could not be assumed the *Brinkley case* would have been decided the same way for Japanese law allowed concubinage, divorce by mutual consent or by the husband and the marriage ceremony was a 'mere drinking session' (Wilkinson to le Poer Trench, 12 April 1895; FO881/6629). Although the British legal establishment in Japan was on notice of the impending action (for Gubbins had alerted Aston at HMCJ that he had notarized various related documents; 3 November 1888; FO798/46), there is no evidence that it sought to interfere in the English proceedings.

197 Tokyo Vice-Consul to de Bunsen, 5 June 1893, reporting receipt of a letter from the *Chiji* of Tokyo-fu about a British subject who had declared himself a Japanese subject and de Bunsen's reply confirming Salisbury's consideration, and acceptance, of the position the previous year; FO798/51.

198 Neil Pedlar, *An Indexed List of British Marriages Solemnized During Extraterritoriality in Japan 1860–1899* (Newquay: Four Turnings Publications, 1993). See also FO345–34. Pedlar's records are based, in large part, upon the returns in this file.

199 We know from footnotes 189 and 190 that such marriages were solemnized.

200 Section 55.

Japan. The records contain just four examples of this jurisdiction being exercised. In 1868 Frederick Harrison, a clerk employed in Nagasaki, was removed back to Shanghai by his employer who applied to the Supreme Court for permission to return him to England.[201] When, in 1882, George Berwick's partner filed a Petition in Lunacy with HMCJ in respect of him, Robertson was appointed acting Judge to travel on circuit to Hakodate to hear the Petition. Robertson ordered the Consul to supervise the sale of Berwick's property and use the proceeds to buy him and his family a passage to England—because of the perceived improved chances of Berwick's recovery in England and the fear that the government would incur expenses if he remained in Japan.[202]

In 1886, Hannen travelled on circuit to Kobe to hear Whymark's petition that he be appointed the administrator of the affairs of William Lees, a local pilot who had been detained at the international hospital there after his mind had become deranged. Whymark was represented by John Creagh who had drawn up and witnessed the Petition which revealed that Lees had debts of $450 against assets of $1,500. Hannen granted the Petition.[203] Finally, in 1896, the friends of Arthur Norman, the owner and editor of *The Rising Sun and Nagasaki Express*, petitioned that he be restrained as a lunatic incapable of managing his own affairs.[204] Longford heard the initial application and adjudged Norman to be insane[205] but only the Judge had jurisdiction to make an order regarding his affairs so Mowat went to Nagasaki on circuit to hear the Petition. However, Mowat broke down and Wilkinson was summoned from Shanghai to act as Judge. Again, Wilkinson deputed the Consul to administer Norman's affairs and dispose of his assets before transferring him to the Hong Kong Lunatic Asylum as the nearest place acceptable for Western lunatics.[206] Where someone had no assets, it seems that the local Consul would simply take practical steps to remove the individual without any formal proceedings: when Edward Wilson Claud King arrived at Nagasaki from Yantai in a state of unsound mind, Longford kept him under restraint at the Consulate

201 Grooms to Hornby, 23 January 1868; FO656/22.

202 Robertson to Granville, 21 August 1882; FO46/293.

203 4 and 6 December 1886; HN.

204 Nagasaki Consul to Mowat, telegram 19 December 1896; FO796/15.

205 7 April 1897; TRS&NE.

206 Norman died there; Colonial Secretary, Hong Kong to Nagasaki Consul, telegram, 22 November 1897; FO796/15. The *Nagasaki Press* bought Norman's newspaper business, closed it and consolidated all its publications into the *Nagasaki Press*.

whilst seeking to raise, through public subscription, sufficient funds to send him under a carer to Shanghai.[207]

As coroners, Consuls, with a jury of three, held inquests into unexplained deaths of Britons within Japan or Japanese waters.[208] The only official record is the Nagasaki Minute Book for Inquests, 1884 to 1898;[209] otherwise, we are reliant upon newspaper reports, references in correspondence[210] or, very occasionally, other case reports. The earliest reported inquest was held in September 1862 in Yokohama when the jury recorded that C.L. Richards had been 'feloniously, wilfully and of malice aforethought killed and murdered by an unknown Japanese'.[211] Apart from this and two similar killings in Yokohama in 1864—all of which led to British demands upon the *bakufu* to apprehend and punish the malefactors—inquests were uncontroversial. The Nagasaki records all show practical co-operation between the British and the Japanese authorities on a day-to-day working level in relation to Inquests with Japanese police officers and other officials giving evidence frequently concerning the death or the finding of the corpse. The inquest into the death (suicide) of Thomas McBain, 4th Engineer on the *Kobe maru,* was even held on board that ship. Whilst the holding of Inquests other than in a Court or a Consulate was not common, this was not a unique occurrence. The first reported Nagasaki Inquest into the death by drowning of HMS *Rattler*'s doctor had been held on board that ship in 1865.[212]

Of the nine inquests recorded in the Nagasaki Minute Book of Inquests, two deaths were due to natural causes, three to suicide, three to drowning whilst swimming in the harbour (whether deliberate or not was never clear) and one to murder.[213] This pattern broadly mirrors over 50 other inquests reported in the newspapers between 1862 and 1898 (nearly 40 in Yokohama, 10 in Kobe, three in Nagasaki, two in Hakodate and one in each

---

[207] 10 March 1897; TRS&NE. The appeal raised $156 (including donations of $20 from Satow and $10 from Longford). $31.50 was paid for King's passage and $20 was given as a gratuity to his carer and the balance was remitted to the Consul-General in Shanghai for King's benefit.

[208] Deaths on board British vessels outside Japanese waters were investigated under the MSA.

[209] FO796/12.

[210] For example, the report on the Inquest into Noble's death (see page 141).

[211] 11 October 1862; NCH.

[212] Report, 28 November 1865; FO796/25.

[213] James Gerard's death. The inquest, on 21 October 1897, found that Gerard died of stab wounds inflicted by William Cuthbert and Cuthbert was remanded to the Nagasaki consular gaol; FO796/12. Cuthbert was then charged with murder, transferred to Yokohama and tried before HMCJ where a jury convicted him of manslaughter.

of Tokyo and Niigata) where 12 were suicide, six unlawful killings and 24 accidental deaths (which included several drownings in the harbours). John White, a pilot based in Nagasaki, died of exposure and exhaustion when his pilot boat capsized as he went out to a vessel.[214] In 1882, during an operation to re-float the *Mary Tathen* which had run aground off Hakodate, O'Conor and Todd lost their lives when the vessel sank.[215] Robert Elton died of exposure and hunger in 1883 when he tried to make his way from Nagasaki to Kobe in an open boat.[216] The only judicial activity in Niigata was Troup's holding an Inquest on the master and three sailors from the *Textor* who drowned—along with Peter Petersen, the *Runnymede*'s master[217]—when a boat bringing them ashore capsized when trying to cross the river bar. Only a Malay seaman from the *Textor* survived. Troup recorded that he held the Inquest without a jury 'in the absence of any British residents at this place.'[218]

Coroners' juries were not averse to adding comments critical of authorities—both Japanese and British. When returning an open verdict on the death of Joseph Johnson, who died of wounds in Nagasaki, the jury called attention to the 'extraordinary lack of vigilance displayed by the native police stationed at the nearby guardhouse' which had a good view of the place of the attack.[219] When Herbert Truck, a stoker on HMS *Victorious*, drowned, the jury found the accident was caused by an overloaded sampan but the drowning would not have happened if someone on board the ship had enforced the ship's standing orders regarding overcrowding of boats.[220]

---

214 22 March 1884; TRS&NE.

215 4 October 1882; HN.

216 13 March 1883; HN.

217 This incident occurred shortly after Petersen had been convicted of harbouring a deserter in Hakodate. Petersen was Norwegian so no Inquest was held into his death. As the *Runnymede* was returning to Hakodate and its acting master had no funds to hand, Troup asked Eusden to collect from the acting master the proceeds raised from a sale of Petersen's possessions aboard the ship and to collect his wages. However, as the ship had earned nothing on its voyage to Hakodate, the acting master drew an order on Barnard, the lawyer, at Yokohama—the ship's owner—for them. In early January 1870, the *Runnymede* sank near Niigata when returning there but no one in Hakodate heard about this until some time later when the *Behara* touched at Hakodate on route from Niigata to Yokohama. As there was no consul from Sweden and Norway in Japan, Eusden remitted the payment order for Petersen's wages and the monies raised from the sale of Petersen's possessions to Hornby to place into the hands of the consul for Sweden and Norway in Shanghai. Eusden to Hornby, 11 March 1870; FO656/35.

218 Minutes of Inquest attached to Troup to Board of Trade, 8 November 1869; FO262/176.

219 Flowers to Hornby, 12 November 1872; FO656/34.

220 Minutes of Inquest, 28 July 1898; FO796/12.

Probate and Administration

OC1860 gave the Courts jurisdiction in Probate and Administration matters,[221] but OC1865 restricted this to uncontested applications with contested cases being reserved to the Supreme Court or, after OC1878, HMCJ.[222] Upon intestacy, the deceased's property vested in the Judge until Letters of Administration were granted[223] or, where the property was *bona vacantia*, as the Crown's representative until the deceased's affairs were completely wound up.

Estates ranged from reasonably substantial ones of up to £12,000[224] and £18,000[225] to the hopelessly insolvent. Unsurprisingly, wealthier members of the community tended to leave wills (which could be left with a Consul for safe-keeping[226]) with only three Probate applications involving estates, where the figures are available, of below $1,000 against just three intestate estates exceeding this amount. Testate deaths were very much the exception among the British community, so the Supreme Court (or HMCJ) and the Consuls were disproportionately involved in administering the affairs of the poorer members of the community and the consular correspondence files are replete with correspondence on the winding up of their intestate estates.

In early 1871, eight intestate estates were before the Yokohama Court: two were insolvent, three had assets of under $100, two between $200–500 and just one of $5,000.[227] By the year's end, a further 17 intestate estates had been handled but various unclaimed gold and jewellery items remained with the Yokohama Court[228] and unclaimed balances, from under ten shillings to £80, from ten intestate estates from Japan remained on the Supreme Court's books in 1883[229]—in the case of two estates, they had been there since 1866.

---

221 Section XXXVII.

222 The Yokohama Court, initially, dealt with intestate estates and contentious probate and administration matters without reference to the Supreme Court but Hornby, when settling its on-going arrangements, reserved contentious probates to the Supreme Court; Hornby to Hannen 13 September 1872; FO656/39.

223 Section 59 OC1865.

224 Although, we may wonder whether the whole estate of medical doctor, Griffith Richard Jenkins who died in Ceredigion, was situated within Japan.

225 The estate of Charles Sutton, the Nagasaki stevedore; FO796/5.

226 Longford to James, 25 September 1885; FO798/44.

227 Bate to Goodwin, 8 March 1871; FO656/37.

228 Annual returns; FO656/37.

229 Mowat to Granville, 28 August 1883; FO656/53.

Where executors were prepared to execute the Will, matters were, usually, straight-forward and most Probates were granted by the Consuls—although the Tokyo Vice-Consul transferred three cases[230] to HMCJ in 1894. It must be possible that the stated reasons for these transfers were a fiction and were recorded simply so that matters were handled by HMCJ as opposed to the Tokyo Vice-Consul who, by this time was attached to the Legation's Chancery and handled very little pure consular (or judicial) work. The only Nagasaki probate case transferred to HMCJ concerned Charles Sutton's estate.[231] Not only was this a large estate at £18,000 but it was also a complicated one as he left a 'Japanese family' and was executor of several other estates, including that of a Swedish national. Mowat advised that, if Sutton's executrix wished not to act because of these other estates, she must renounce the whole execution and the Consul should refer the Swede's estate to the Swedish authorities.[232]

The case of Mrs Adams' deceased husband highlighted some complications exacerbated by extra-territoriality. Her husband had appointed two USA citizens as his executors but the transfer of his real property to them had not been registered at the Consulate, the US consulate or the *ken-cho*.[233] When Mrs Adams sought to have the property registered in her name, Mowat advised that, given the nationality of the executors, jurisdiction was vested in the USA courts and the Consul could not make the sought vesting order.[234] The final Letters of Probate granted by the Courts were those issued by the Nagasaki Court in respect of W.H. Devine who died days before extra-territoriality's end with an estate estimated at £800.[235] Ringer's affidavit in support of his application for probate claimed an unspecified 'great urgency' for its immediate grant.[236] This was disingenuous for the Consul had advised him to take out probate immediately (and notwithstanding that the other named executor had not joined in the application) given extra-territoriality's impending extinction.[237]

---

230 One due to its claimed complexity; another for practicality because HMCJ's Chief Clerk was the executor's Attorney and the third was that of Hugh Fraser, the late Minister; Longford to Mowat, 23 January 13 March and 11 June 1894; FO 798/51.

231 1893; FO796/15.

232 Mowat to Nagasaki Consul, 8 August 1893; FO796/10.

233 Nagasaki Consul to Mowat, 7 May 1896; FO796/10.

234 Mowat to Nagasaki Consul, 1 June 1896; FO796/10. With the approaching end of extra-territoriality, the need to regularize all land titles gave this issue greater significance.

235 Register of Civil Cases, FO796/5.

236 Nagasaki Court minutes, 14 July 1899; FO796/8.

237 Nagasaki Consul to Wilkinson, 8 July 1899; FO796/10.

Intestacies were equally straightforward when the intestate had next-of-kin in Japan: they would apply to the Court for Letters of Administration; provide a bond to the Court to assure that they would administer the estate properly;[238] obtain Letters of Administration, publicize notices of their appointment and require all debts due to the deceased to be paid by a specified date—by when all claims should also be notified—and administer the estate. Where the next-of-kin were unable (or unwilling) to take out Administration—because, as with Frederick Pyne, a clerk in the Japanese Telegraph Office, the estate was insolvent with assets of $347 against debts of $725,[239] it fell to the Consul to administer the estate.

Where next-of-kin were not resident in Japan, they could appoint an attorney in Japan to take out Administration on their behalf. When John Richeson, a steward on the Mitsubishi steamer *Hiroshima maru*, died in 1877 leaving a widow and two children in Liverpool but Richard Ford, with whom Richeson had had business dealings, declined to take out Administration pursuant to the widow's power of attorney, Flowers realized his personal effects for $56 which he remitted to the Supreme Court. Troup advised Richeson's widow to apply to the Supreme Court for the monies;[240] but it took until late 1879 before she applied to the Supreme Court through solicitors in Liverpool.[241]

In the absence of any next-of-kin, intestate estate administrations commenced with the Consul informing the Judge of the death, describing briefly the deceased's assets and liabilities and either requesting instructions[242] or, occasionally, suggesting how to proceed. The Judge would appoint an Official Administrator[243] to collect in the deceased's assets, pay his debts and account for the balance. Usually, the appointee was the Consul, sometimes the Law Secretary or, very occasionally, a third party. The relevant Consul—or, more often, the consular constable under his

[238] The Courts could dispense with the provision of a bond as *In re Henry Mills dec'd* where the deceased's personal effects were minimal; Nagasaki Court minutes, 18 July 1893; FO796/8.

[239] Flowers to Hornby, 31 January 1874; FO656/42.

[240] Flowers to Goodwin and Troup to Mowat, 30 October and 7 December respectively, 1877; FO656/42.

[241] French to Rennie, 30 December 1879; FO656/39.

[242] Flowers reported the death of William Huddle 'at the Japanese Hospital of smallpox' to Hornby, said he had collected his personal effects and requested instructions: 31 January 1876; FO656/42.

[243] Only the Judge could appoint an Official Administrator in respect of intestate estates; Hornby to Myburgh, 13 February 1867; FO656/18.

direction—would dispose of the deceased's assets, pay his debts and remit the monies to the widow in Britain[244] or, where she was in Japan, pay the net proceeds to her to enable her to buy a passage back to England.[245] It was not uncommon to find no relatives. When K.R. Mackenzie, Glover's old partner, died intestate in 1873 with a rumoured wife in London, a year elapsed whilst the Consul wound up his affairs with no one coming forward to claim his assets; so Ts1,413 were remitted to the Supreme Court's safe-keeping.[246]

Which debts of the deceased were to be allowed could give rise to argument. In 1868, Flowers, before receiving formal instructions from Hornby, was forced to sell the deceased's (Lovell's) clothes because they were becoming damp[247] and realized just $130 against debts of $306. Hornby disallowed claims by the Bellevue Hotel, where Lovell had died, for food provided to Lovell's 'China boys' and for the sheets when the hotel claimed the boys' food was a regular charge when their master ordered food and it was the general custom throughout China and Japan to burn whatever was about people when they died in an hotel.[248]

A balance always needed to be struck between practicality and strict legality. In *In re Estate of Charles C. Clarke*, Hornby advised Myburgh that, as Clarke and his partner, Hooper, were parties to an appeal[249] then before the Supreme Court, nothing could be done pending the issue of Letters of Administration other than to let Clarke's partner wind up the partnership and produce accounts to the Court.[250] This may be contrasted with *In re E.M. Gudgeon* where Hornby advised that, because there was little property, the estate should be wound up and small pressing debts, such as wages and funeral expenses, paid; but larger creditors should stand over until an Administrator was appointed.[251] When Edward Lock of Niuzhuang died in Nagasaki in 1868, with debts there of Ts9,000 against assets there of Ts1,500, Hornby advised dividing the proceeds of sale at Nagasaki amongst

---

244 Flowers to Hornby, 20 August 1873; FO656/42. Andrew Grey, a shipwright, had arrived recently from England, where he had left his wife and family, so Flowers requested permission to wind up the estate and remit the proceeds without more ado.

245 Flowers to Hornby 31 July 1873; FO656/42. Flowers requested Hornby's permission to pay the net balance of the deceased's estate to his widow to enable her to proceed home as she was in poor circumstances.

246 Flowers to Hornby, 18 November 1873, 22 January 1874 and 11 January 1875; FO656/42.

247 Flowers to Hornby, 24 June 1868; FO796/10.

248 Flowers to Hornby, 28 July 1868; FO796/10.

249 *Bavier v. Hooper and Clarke.*

250 Hornby to Myburgh, 20 April 1867; FO656/18.

251 Hornby to Enslie, 21 March 1870; FO656/18.

the creditors there in proportion to their claims rather than consolidating all the assets and liabilities.[252]

Although extra-territoriality imposed its own complexities upon the administration of will trusts, some complexities would exist in any event. Deaths in Japan of British subjects normally resident elsewhere were subject to Probate or Letters of Administration granted in the place of residence. When J.P. McEwen of Shanghai died in the Naval Hospital at Yokohama in 1896, HMCJ simply sent his original will to the Supreme Court with a copy to his executor in London with directions to the named executor to apply to the Supreme Court for Probate.[253] Greater complications arose when the deceased was resident elsewhere but had assets and liabilities in Japan. When Adam Blyth of the Shanghai Customs Service died at Yokohama in 1889, Jamieson collected Blyth's possessions amounting to Ts316, paid the funeral expenses of $264 and suggested he settle the local claims before remitting the balance and effects to the Supreme Court which had jurisdiction as Blyth had been a Shanghai resident.[254] Similarly, when John Young, master and part owner of the *Witch*, died in the Japanese Hospital in Nagasaki in 1873, the vessel's agents defrayed his funeral expenses and Flowers simply collected together his effects and passed them to the new master to hand to Young's wife who was coming out from England to join her husband and expected to arrive shortly in Hong Kong.[255]

Japanese subjects were involved when they were married to or, more often, lived with a British subject or had possession of the deceased's assets. A most heart-rending case was that of William Reed's Japanese widow. Reed was a dairyman who died with net assets of just $18.85 plus a calf which had been seized by another Japanese. Despite lengthy correspondence with the Japanese authorities, the Consul failed to obtain restitution of the calf so Mrs Reed was left to carry her claim for it to a Japanese court.[256]

At this time, residence in the Treaty Ports conferred no separate domicile[257] so the wealthier deceased were subject to UK probate duties on the personalty—but not realty—in their estates. It had been customary to

252 Hornby to Nagasaki Consul, 5 August 1868; FO656/18.
253 Mowat to Jamieson, 4 September 1896; FO656/49.
254 Jamieson to Rennie, 5 September 1889; FO656/49.
255 Flowers to Hornby, 26 September 1873; FO656/42.
256 McClatchie to French, 26 September 1878; FO656/40.
257 *In re Tootal's Trusts* (LR23 (1883) ChD 532). This decision was overturned later by the House of Lords in *Casdagli v. Casdagli*; [1919] AC 145.

pay such duties on the entire estate in China and Japan since the Supreme Court's establishment;[258] but, in 1886, Macdonald's executors challenged the presumption that Japanese leases were personalty. The question was referred by HM Treasury to the Law Officers who opined that, given the terms under which land was held in Japan, it was realty for probate duty purposes and, so, exempt from duty.[259] The surprise is that it took so long for the point to be argued; but the question was raised contemporaneously in Xiamen.[260] Although settled for the future, the Foreign Office volunteered no repayments of probate duty already paid.[261] HM Treasury was more accommodating a decade later when the issue of double payment arose where estate duty was charged in both Japan and England on the same estates. HM Treasury accepted that, where estate duty was charged in the UK on the same property, duty due in Japan would be reduced *pro tanto* and, if already paid, should be refunded.[262] An early beneficiary of this ruling was Enslie's estate.

Enslie may have been legally qualified but questions regarding his will provided HMCJ's final public hearing.[263] His will had been proved and Letters of Probate granted two years earlier but the investment powers of its executor (Brushfield) were unclear and questions had arisen over certain bequests to his Japanese housekeeper and whether Enslie had already made over cash legacies to her during his life-time. The case appears to have been reserved for the honour of being the last one dealt with publicly by HMCJ because Enslie had been a member of the Japan Consular Service, the case was relatively straightforward and it was uncontested by his sisters, his closest living relatives.

Kaleidoscope of Regimes

It is important to appreciate that this focus on the Courts provides a one-sided view of extra-territoriality's workings (i.e. suits against British defendants). Extra-territoriality was exclusive as each nationality's authorities dealt only with claims against its own subjects. The British (as claimants, prosecutors and witnesses) faced a kaleidoscope of jurisdictions

258 Ibid.
259 Report by the Law Officers and Dr Parker Deane, 9 June 1886; FO656/53.
260 Iddesleigh to Rennie, 8 November 1886; FO656/53.
261 Foreign Office to HMCJ, 18 March 1887; FO656/53.
262 Bertie to Hannen, 14 April 1897; FO656/53.
263 *In re J.J. Enslie*, 13 January and 3 February 1900; JWM.

which required considerable mutual co-operation and support between officials of the different countries to make extra-territoriality work.[264] For example, in *Holme Ringer & Co. (agents for American barque Vestor) v. J.K. Taylor*,[265] when the US plaintiffs sought delivery of wrecked parts of their ship from a British defendant, he claimed a lien on the wreckage for salvage. However, the Consul made it clear that the defendant's salvage claims must be taken in the US consul's court for the Court had no jurisdiction in the matter of a claim for salvage on an American ship: it being entirely under U.S. jurisdiction and he had ascertained that the US consul was prepared to hear such a claim.[266] Little has been published in the English language about British claims and prosecutions against Japanese and other foreign defendants and a review of such British claims is outside the scope of this book.

Foreign consuls intermediated suits brought by their nationals in the Courts; but, how involved could they become in a case's determination—especially if they wished to complain about the result? Jurisdictional conflicts also surrounded witnesses appearing before foreign consular courts: could a British subject be compelled to appear as a witness in a foreign court and, if he appeared, what sanctions could that court impose if he refused to answer its questions (issues which applied in reverse with foreign witnesses in the Courts)?

These questions arose first in *Glackmeyer v. McKechnie* and its surrounding cases in 1865.[267] During the original hearing in the Kanagawa Court, the US consul—who was present during the proceedings—sought to interfere in the proceedings and complained subsequently to Hornby who set out the British position and distinguished judicial proceedings and channels of appeal from diplomatic ones. Hornby advised that maladministration of the law could be a proper subject for complaint by a foreign consul, but such a complaint must be pursued through diplomatic channels; such complaints should not be addressed to the Judge. Equally, a Consul should afford a foreign consul the opportunity of hearing any case against a British subject which he may have forwarded to the Consul. Whilst, this could be achieved by seating him near the Judge, it gave the foreign consul no right to interfere in the case.[268]

264 Whilst not all co-operated, the correspondence shows that the British and USA consuls did so in most cases—if only out of mutual interest; e.g. FO656/29.

265 Civil case no. 24 of 1879; FO796/4.

266 Ibid.

267 See page 208. For an overview of this and related cases, see Munson, 2013, chapter 5.

268 Hornby to Flowers, 24 November 1865; FO656/18.

As for witnesses, British subjects could decline to give evidence in a foreign court except under a subpoena issued by a Consul. If the British witness refused to answer questions or committed another contempt in that foreign court, he could be evicted from that court but no Court or Consul would execute a foreign court's judgment against such a British witness by way of penalty; a Consul could only penalize a British subject for his disobedience of a Consul's subpoena.[269] Hornby distinguished between an individual being in another country (and, therefore, under its laws) and in a consular court in Japan where a consul possessed jurisdiction only over his fellow citizens. Searle, a British subject, had consented to be called as a witness in the US court case of *Ricker v. Glackmeyer* but refused to answer certain questions put by the defence whereupon the US consul sought to punish him for contempt and requested the Consul to enforce this punishment. Searle, by consenting to be a witness, was bound to answer all questions put to him in the US consular court; but the US consul could not punish Searle for the contempt—the US consul's only remedy was to eject Searle from his court.[270]

The rarity of similar disputes suggests that, in practice, the system of compelling the attendance of foreign witnesses worked well enough. As between the Japanese and British authorities, there appear to have been no disputes and we see frequent requests both ways to order the attendance of the other's subjects as witnesses. The only known Japanese refusal of a British request was in the *Chishima case* when the Japanese authorities refused to permit the Japanese pilot to give evidence at the Naval Court. Likewise, British and other Western consuls ordered their subjects to appear in each others' courts as when, in the *Green v. Green* matrimonial dispute, Flowers wrote to the French consul asking him to order M. Hyver to attend court as a witness to give evidence.[271]

As Anglo-Japanese commercial relations developed and became ever more mixed, it became impossible for the Courts to ignore proceedings in the Japanese courts; particularly on questions relating to conflicts, the applicability of Japanese courts' decisions on factual matters before them, the provisions of Japanese law itself and the enforcement of Japanese judgments. In the appeal of *George Blakeney (Defendant and Appellant) v. Hirose Sima (Plaintiff and Respondent)*,[272] Blakeney sought to plead a

269 Hornby to Flowers 13 December 1865; FO656/18.
270 Hornby to Flowers (private), 10 January 1866; FO656/18.
271 Flowers to French consul, 14 June 1866; FO796/29.
272 Judgment 21 November 1883; FO656/36.

Japanese judgment in a suit brought by Sima against the person to whom Blakeney had sold Sima's property but the Supreme Court concurred with HMCJ in holding that Blakeney was unable to do so (and no estoppels arose) because Blakeney had not been party to the Japanese proceedings. However, in *Tanaka Ichinosuke & Others v. Whittall,* the Supreme Court upheld HMCJ's judgment that Whittall was estopped from disputing the plaintiffs' ownership of a steamer because a Japanese court had decided the question in a case between Whittall and Tanaka.[273]

Absent any presentation as to Japanese law where relevant, the Courts decided matters on the basis of English law as seen in *Imperial Japanese Government v. Francis Augustus Cope and William Petrie Mitchell* on appeal. No evidence having been tendered as to the Japanese law upon the points involved, Hannen treated the question as one of English law throughout but left open the question of whether such evidence as to the relevant Japanese law could have been properly given.[274] In the *Chishima case*, however, evidence was submitted to HMCJ as to Japanese law on the Emperor's immunity and formed the basis of Mowat's interlocutory decision.

Where Britons brought claims against Japanese in the Japanese courts and those courts made an order against the plaintiff, the Courts would enforce those orders; but, in 1889, the question arose over enforcing Japanese court rules about costs. In *Matsuhira Shogo v. A.T. Watson*, Shogo sought to recover $16.70 costs to which the Japanese court rules entitled him, but Jamieson refused the claim unless he could produce the Japanese court's certificate of those costs.[275] The case was not re-heard; but, in a clear attempt to have Hannen decide the issue, the point was raised again six months later in *Higashiro Toshigiro v. S. Samuel & Co.* Hannen approved Jamieson's judgment and said that, if the Japanese court had awarded costs, it would have been his duty to enforce the award and take the Japanese certificate as conclusive but, absent such certificate, he could not assess what the costs should be under Japanese rules.[276]

OC1859 reflected the Treaty in providing only for jurisdiction over suits between British subjects; but OC1860 extended this jurisdiction to include suits by Japanese or foreigners against British subjects and allowed British subjects to sue Japanese or foreigners in the Courts where the defendant's

273 Judgment 29 October 1886; FO656/36.
274 Judgment, 6 December 1881; FO656/36 and FO1092/364.
275 8 June 1889; JWM.
276 14 December 1889; JWM.

consent was obtained.[277] However, the latter provision was not followed through into OC1865. There is no explanation why this provision allowing suits against foreigners with their consent was dropped and we must speculate that either it had never been used or, when drafting OC1865, Hornby applied his Levantine experience and considered such method of proceeding was not how extra-territoriality should work except in relation to counter-claims for which the Rules made specific provision.

Under the Treaty, a Briton complaining against a Japanese was required to state his grievance to the Consul who should inquire into its merits and arrange it amicably and, if he could not make such an arrangement, request the Japanese authorities' assistance so that they could together examine the merits and decide it equitably.[278] Although we have a report of a joint hearing before Japanese officials and Flowers at the Kanagawa Court in 1865 in cross-actions between Albert Edelman (a foreigner under British protection) and Shibuya Seigoro, a silk merchant,[279] such joint examinations never became institutionalized and the Courts heard cases against Britons whilst the Japanese courts dealt with British claims against Japanese subjects. 'Making the system work' required close, and time-consuming, contact between Consuls and local Japanese authorities: without it, British claims against Japanese could not be pursued effectively and British commercial interests would suffer. The Tokyo correspondence shows this close contact as does Robertson's describing his relations with the *Chikenji* of Kanagawa *ken* as of a 'cordial and satisfactory nature'.[280]

British plaintiffs were required first to file their complaint against a Japanese with the local Consul who, then, presented the case formally to the Japanese authorities (and, in the early days, acted as an advocate and presented the case before Japanese officials)—although, later, it became common for counsel to present the plaintiff's arguments even when the Consul was present.[281] The documentation and terminology used for

---

277 Sections XI and XII.

278 Article VI. In practice, Japanese claims against Britons were processed by the local governor's office (later, the local *saibansho*) and forwarded to the Court which issued the plaint or summons against the defendant concerned—although Robertson said that Japanese sailors serving on British vessels had no hesitation in appealing direct to the Consul for support in disputes against the ships' masters.

279 7 January 1865; TJH. Seigoro was awarded $5,908 due to Edelman's conduct being 'irregular and censurable in the highest degree'.

280 Robertson to Wilkinson, 25 February 1872; FO881/2135.

281 For instance, we see Duncan presenting E.C. Kirby's appeal in a case in the Japanese courts even though Quin was in attendance; 1, 5 and 8 April 1876; HN.

British claims in the Japanese courts would have been familiar to British litigants for they were based largely upon British procedures. In 1877, Wilkinson and the Tokyo Superior Court drew up an agreed procedure and forms—in English—for appeals by Britons in the Japanese courts. In time, many British litigants presented their claims direct to the *saibansho* without the Consul's intermediation, a procedure which was eventually regularized except for claims against the Japanese government which still needed to pass through the Consul.[282]

British consuls often acted as consuls for other Western Powers which did not have as full a consular representation in Japan as Britain. This was particularly the case in the out-ports but there were also instances of such 'doubling up' in Yokohama and we see reports of consuls sitting as judges in other countries' courts. Strictly, the laws applicable in such courts should have been the laws of the relevant country; but it was often the case that the consuls applied English legal principles in deciding such cases—especially where British lawyers represented clients before such courts. However, while there was no objection to British consuls taking on such additional consular activities (and they were allowed to retain any remuneration paid by the foreign country), the Consuls could not enforce the judgments they gave when sitting in foreign courts by virtue of their British consular authority or through the mechanisms of the Courts.[283] This would have required a diplomatic convention between Britain and the country concerned but none was entered into.

Strictly, the Treaty did not displace Japanese jurisdiction over British claims against foreigners; but, as seen in Chapter 1 (British Extraterritoriality), everyone adopted, from the beginning, an exclusive approach whereby foreigners' suits against Britons were heard in the Courts and, in reverse, British suits against foreigners were heard in their own courts. Again, claims were made initially to the Consul who transmitted them to the relevant foreign consul for action. The complexities of this international *mélange* may be seen in *HSBC v. H. Ohl* (*qua Administrator of the estate of E. Seyd & Co.*) before the North German consular court in 1871. HSBC sought to enforce its mortgage over some silk bales which it had financed. It had followed common trade financing practice but had not perfected its mortgage in accordance with German mercantile law so its

[282] Legation Circular to Consuls, 9 June 1877; FO881/4116.
[283] Law Officers to Clarendon, 29 December 1869; FO83/2299.

claim as a secured creditor was rejected, both in that consular court and on appeal to Germany.[284]

Where the relevant foreign country had no representation at all in Japan, a Briton's only recourse was, through the Minister and the Foreign Office, to the foreigner's home authorities—as suggested by Hornby when Duus used his Danish nationality and refused to comply with a Supreme Court judgment.[285] Only where the foreign defendant's country had no extra-territorial treaty with Japan did the Japanese courts exercise jurisdiction.

Extra-territoriality's exclusive nature caused difficulties with mixed partnerships and prevented the formation of local British joint-stock companies. *Murray & Wallworth & Co.* was a partnership of two Britons and a US citizen, Tucker, who, on its liquidation, became its liquidator. Suits against partnerships needed to be served on each individual partner;[286] but, as Tucker was a US citizen, Gower had not served him with notice of the appeal hearing. When Tucker became aware of the appeal, he proceeded to Shanghai and requested a re-hearing;[287] but Goodwin explained to Tucker that none was possible and, although the judgment against the firm must stand as against the other two partners, it could not be enforced against him as a USA citizen.[288]

When, following an unsuccessful attempt by two Kobe British merchants to register a company (the Hiogo Gas Company) in 1873,[289] it was proposed to extend the Companies Act 1867 to Japan and allow the formation of British joint stock companies in Japan, it was suggested that provision should be included to the effect that all members would be British subjects and any transfer to a non-subject would be void.[290] However, the proposed regulations were never implemented as the Law Officers had earlier explained that, even were an Order in Council formulated, the limit on the members' liability would bind only a Court—not another foreign court.[291] When the company's promoters then suggested that the

---

284 22 September 1871, NCH.

285 Hornby to Eusden, December 1869; FO656/18. See also page 227.

286 Rule 252.

287 Gower to Hornby, 9 May 1871; FO656/34.

288 Goodwin to Gower, 2 May 1871; FO656/18.

289 Mowat confirmed that no power to register the company existed and the Minister had no authority under OC1865 to make regulations to permit such registrations as they were not for the 'peace, order or good behaviour' of British subjects; Mowat to Gower of 8 April 1873; FO656/41.

290 Hannen to Hornby, 12 August 1875 with draft Order in Council; FO656/28.

291 Foreign Office to Hornby, 26 October 1868; FO17/502.

company could place itself under Japanese jurisdiction, the Foreign Office raised the question with the Law Officers in view of its importance and its general bearing on foreign jurisdiction in Japan. They replied simply that the proposal 'should not be entertained'.[292] From the liquidation case *In re Hiogo Hotel Limited* before SCHK which concerned solely Japan-based facts,[293] it would appear that investors overcame this difficulty by incorporating companies in Hong Kong.

Inevitably, Britons with claims against non-Britons tried to bring them within the Courts' ambit. The Courts allowed claims against foreigners to be brought into account in two ways: first, through the netting off of amounts due and, second, by allowing counter-claims to suits brought by the foreigners against Britons under Rule 55 which applied to counter-claims generally. Netting off claims appears to have been non-contentious but only operated where clear money claims were due each way. After a three day hearing over a claim for $150 in *Yokoyama Zensuke v. Malcolm, Wilcox & Co.*, the suit was dismissed because, despite the plaintiff's proving his claim, it was shown that he owed the defendants even more – although the Court could not order the plaintiff to pay that amount.[294]

In *Nagao Mohee & Others v. J.H. Wignall*, the plaintiffs sued for the delivery of engines and a boiler for a steamer which Wignall had agreed to deliver to them. There was no dispute as to the contract but Wignall argued that he had other just claims against the plaintiffs and was entitled to retain the engine and boiler until those claims had been settled. The Court ruled that, until those claims were settled, Wignall could retain the engines and boiler.[295] On the other hand, in *Fukuda Heisuke v. Mourilyan, Heimann & Co.*, the defendants admitted their liability for the $106 which Heisuke claimed in respect of goods sold to them but argued that he owed the firm monies on another account which the firm wished to set off. However, the Court found no evidence that Heisuke had agreed to give the firm any rights of set off in respect of the other account and so gave judgment in full for the plaintiff—but, the Court suspended its judgment for four months so as to allow Mourilyan, Heimann & Co. the opportunity to bring an action in the Japanese courts against Heisuke on the other account.[296]

---

[292] Tenterden to Law Officers and Law Officers to Derby, 20 May and 13 June 1876; FO83/2299.

[293] 10 February 1894; JWM.

[294] 10 March 1877; JWM.

[295] 12 August 1871; HN.

[296] 5 February 1876; HN.

By entering a suit in the Court, a foreign plaintiff was deemed to submit to the Courts' jurisdiction (which included compliance with the Rules—which provided for counter-claims) and the Court took care to require such security as to costs and otherwise[297] as would enable it to do justice in the case.[298] As regards non-Japanese foreigners, counter-claims were non-contentious; but, although, the Rules applied equally to Japanese plaintiffs, the Japanese authorities came to resist the Courts hearing counter-claims against Japanese plaintiffs. They viewed this as a breach of the Treaty, which gave the Britain no jurisdiction over claims against Japanese but the point was not ruled upon by the Courts until the *Chishima case.*

Even with foreigners, the matter was not free from complications. When OC1881 was promulgated, section 47 went beyond the Rules and required a foreign plaintiff, as a condition of his suit, to enter both a formal submission to the Court and the written sanction of his own governmental authority to such submission. Foreign reaction was swift. The USA and Chinese consuls in Kobe refused to grant their sanction or to process British claims against their citizens. The Kobe *Kenrei* did likewise but the Kanagawa *Kenrei* gave a qualified consent but, at the same time, he also passed the matter on to the Japanese government which objected to the new procedure and raised the matter with the Minister.[299]

Hornby's draft Order in Council of 1876 had suggested giving the Courts complete discretion over counter-claims against foreigners and no one in East Asia had been consulted on OC1881 or knew what had led to section 47 being included. Wilkinson believed that the Ottoman Empire Order in Council 1873 had been taken as a model for OC1881—and this was subsequently confirmed by Streatfield, the Foreign Office legal adviser.[300] The Ottoman Empire Order in Council 1873 was made in order to overturn the effects of the Privy Council's decision in the *Laconia*[301] (on appeal from Hornby in Constantinople) where it was held that, in cases initiated by a foreigner in the consular courts in the Ottoman Empire, the foreigner could not be said to have submitted to the jurisdiction merely by

297 Security was required because the Courts lacked jurisdiction over foreigners to enforce orders or judgments made during the proceedings—whether or not a counter-claim was raised.

298 HSW 1882 Memorandum.

299 In China, the local *taotai* would affix their personal—not official—chops to the consent but used the section 47 requirement as an additional opportunity for exactions from Chinese plaintiffs before granting their consent whereas there was no suggestion of such behaviour in Japan.

300 See page 30.

301 *Papayanni v. The Russian Steam Navigation Company*; 1862: 2 Moo P.C. 183.

instituting proceedings and that his sovereign's consent was required. The Foreign Office did not address the matter so far as Japan and China were concerned until OC1881. It said that the only object behind section 47 was to ensure that there would be no diplomatic objections to the Courts' exercising jurisdiction over the foreigner concerned and to ensure security for costs. It was not intended to extend jurisdiction but to be a condition to a foreigner's availing himself of the Courts' jurisdiction over British subjects.

However, this was not how it was seen in East Asia and *The Hiogo News* claimed that if the 'genius' who had designed section 47 had deigned to consult officials in Japan 'nothing so ridiculously embarrassing' would have occurred.[302] It was feared that the Japanese authorities might construe any British refusal to hear cases without their consent as either a design to accentuate British jurisdiction or an admission that their consent was necessary in cases involving a Japanese plaintiff.[303] Given the reaction by the USA and Japanese authorities, the Yokohama and Shanghai Bars considered that section 47 should be abrogated[304] and Parkes asked Wilkinson, as Crown Advocate, to find a solution.[305]

Ultimately, OC1886 resolved the issue by amending section 47 to allow suits by foreigners provided the plaintiff first filed his consent to the Court's jurisdiction and, only if required by the Court,[306] filed a certificate of non-objection from his own authorities and provided such security as the Court required. In the meantime, Wilkinson issued a semi-public Opinion that section 47 merely consolidated the already existing provisions relating to suits by foreigners and the formal submission to jurisdiction and he opined that the consent of the plaintiff's national authority gave the Courts no greater power than they acquired by the plaintiff's filing his petition.[307] Importantly, any national authority which gave its consent undertook no responsibility for executing the judgment. He advised that Consuls should, likewise, consent to a British subject submitting as plaintiff to a foreign court's jurisdiction in any civil suit should that consent be required.

---

302 Editorial, 28 June 1882; HN.

303 Wilkinson Memorandum.

304 HSW 1882 Memorandum.

305 Parkes to Wilkinson, 4 September 1882; FO656/31.

306 The *Glamorganshire* showed that these two matters were fully within the Courts' discretion.

307 Wilkinson to Parkes, 6 September 1882; FO656/31.

He disposed of the Japanese authorities' concerns by confirming that nothing in OC1881 suggested any different exercise of the judicial discretion vested in the Courts to allow them to hear counter-claims against Japanese subjects. He also approved the Kanagawa *Kenrei's* qualification that his consent was given on the understanding that the submission extended no further than previous submissions by Japanese plaintiffs in the Courts and entailed no new consequences in derogation of the rights of Japanese subjects to enter the Courts as plaintiffs upon the same footing as British subjects entered Japanese courts.[308]

After Wilkinson issued his Opinion, the USA Minister ordered the USA Kobe consul to comply with the section 47 requirement and stop holding-up British claims against USA citizens.[309] At Wilkinson's suggestion, the Kobe *Kenrei* was informed of the Kanagawa *Kenrei*'s approach and required to follow it. As the Kobe Chinese consul's refusal had been grounded on the precedents of the stances taken by the local *Kenrei* and the USA consul in Kobe, he was informed of their new stance and fell into line.

The whole affair illustrates the lack of thought on the part of London officials who promulgated OC1881 without consulting British officials in Japan or China and assumed that what worked in Ottoman territories would work automatically in Japan without considering the differing political conditions. Wilkinson revealed a thorough grasp of the legal background and a deft touch for the diplomatic sensitivities when he finessed a way through the minefield without triggering a major upset with the Japanese government or other nations over extra-territoriality around the time of the first Tokyo Treaty Revision Conference.

308 Ibid.
309 Parkes to Wilkinson, 19 October 1882; FO656/31.

CHAPTER SIX

APPEALS

Appeals were a feature of the Courts from the very beginning but a greater number of civil suits were appealed than criminal cases. Appeals in criminal cases were, very largely, limited to questions of law as the appellate courts did not seek to re-open determinations of fact made by the lower courts.

Criminal Offences

A defendant's right of appeal in the case of criminal offences was limited and only a handful of criminal cases involved appeals and there is only one report of an appeal in relation to a shipping offence. Before OC1865, a convicted defendant could, within 15 days of the sentence, appeal to the Minister who could confirm, vary or reverse such sentence as he saw fit.[1] After OC1865, appeals were permitted against conviction only upon a point of law—and Rule 332 required the appeal to be lodged within 48 hours of sentencing. Where a defendant, such as Hartley, failed to appeal within the set time limits, the Judge had 'no authority to take cognizance of the case'.[2] When a Consul sat with Assessors, if any Assessor disagreed with him, the Consul was obliged to make a report of the case, within 20 days (unless the defendant had already lodged an appeal), to the Minister (or, after OC1865, the Judge) who had authority to confirm, vary or reverse the sentence.[3] A Consul was also obliged to submit a report of the trial to the Judge in all convictions upon indictment.[4] In practice, the Judge could also, as in the O'Farrell deportation case,[5] review cases where his consent to deportation orders was required.

---

[1] Section VIII, OC1859 and Section IX, OC1860.

[2] French to Wilkinson, 18 July 1878; FO656/39.

[3] Section II OC1861 (which removed the requirement under Section VIII, OC1860 (which replaced Section VII, OC1859) to send a report to the Foreign Secretary who had this power).

[4] Section 80, OC1865.

[5] See page 146.

Appeals lay to the Privy Council from any judgment, order or sentence of the Supreme Court in the exercise of its original or appellate jurisdiction on a point of law provided the Supreme Court declared the case to be a fit one for such an appeal[6] or where the Privy Council, on application, granted a convicted defendant leave to appeal.

Whereas the pre-OC1865 regime, in effect, allowed appeals on grounds of fact, the OC1865 regime followed the customary position in England where no appeal against conviction lay on grounds of fact. A seeming inconsistency was that, where the Assistant Judge presided over a trial in the Supreme Court (or, after OC1878, in HMCJ), OC1865 allowed the defendant an automatic right to a re-hearing before the Judge. Initially, the Press considered that this could allow criminals to escape punishment;[7] but there is no evidence that such a right was exercised in Japan in respect of criminal offences before, or after, OC1878. As most criminal offences were heard by a Consul (and, apart from the initial 18 months from its establishment in 1871 until it was restructured by Hornby in 1872, the Yokohama Court was treated as the Kanagawa consular court—not a branch of the Supreme Court) or the Judge, the provision would only have applied to cases heard by the Assistant Judge in HMCJ after OC1878.

Until 1865, the Minister, in his capacity as Consul-General, provided the immediate supervision of the Consuls' exercise of their judicial functions. When Morrison convicted and sentenced Charles Munsol to prison for 12 months, he sent Alcock a report of the case (whether because Munsol appealed or otherwise is unclear). Alcock reminded Morrison that, in order that he could consider the legality and justice of the whole proceedings and sentence, it was necessary that Morrison should send all the depositions and minutes of the court proceedings to the Minister and not just the summary conclusions.[8]

There is no apparent evidence of case reports having been sent to the Foreign Secretary under OC1859 and OC1860 and the *Moss case* is the only recorded example of a pre-1865 appeal against sentence and the Minister's reviewing and varying a sentence imposed by a Consul. As seen in that case, the Minister's power was construed narrowly. The first recorded Special Case submitted to Hornby on appeal was *Reg.* (*on information of G.T. Terry, Superintendant of Municipal Police at Yokohama*) *v. Morris, Holes* et al.[9] when three defendants appealed against their conviction and

[6] Section 140, OC1865.
[7] 29 July 1865; NCH.
[8] Alcock to Morrison, 13 September 1859; FO796/17.
[9] Hornby to Myburgh, 4 June 1866; FO656/18.

sentence for non-payment of an additional $20 licence fee levied by the Municipal Council to keep a house of entertainment and to sell liquor. Hornby upheld their appeal on the grounds that the Municipal Authority had no power to levy additional fees.[10] It had levied the additional charges solely as a money-raising exercise—as it was in financial difficulties at that time—rather than for the legitimate purposes of regulating such establishments.

The only reported appeal to HMCJ in relation to a criminal offence was the *Nimrod*'s master's appeal from Nagasaki against his conviction, and $5 fine, for shipping crew from Yokohama without doing so before the Yokohama shipping officer. Rennie and Wilkinson rejected the appeal as the papers were irregular and the master was seeking to adduce new evidence whereas HMCJ could not look beyond the case as stated by the Nagasaki Court.[11] During the whole period, no appeals from Japan by defendants in criminal cases were made to the Supreme Court but, in 1897, Edith Carew sought leave direct from the Privy Council to appeal to it against her murder conviction. However, a six member panel rejected her application.[12] She applied on three grounds: that HMCJ had no jurisdiction, that Mowat had misdirected the jury and that there had been an improper admission of evidence. Further, she wished to present additional evidence which had arisen since the trial. As the panel had dismissed her first ground, it refused to consider the application further as '... save in very exceptional cases, leave to appeal in respect of a criminal investigation is not granted...'[13] and her counsel conceded he could not argue that the original proceedings were contrary to natural justice. Her application to the Privy Council was followed in 1899 by that of Charles Emil Leopold who sought leave to appeal against his conviction in HMCJ for fraud in December 1898. Pleading poverty, he approached the Privy Council direct for leave to appeal to it but, in September 1899 in an unreported decision, a three-man panel chaired by the Lord Chancellor dismissed his application.[14]

In criminal matters, the prosecution was unable to appeal against any adverse finding on factual grounds; but, in two cases, the Japanese Customs established a right of appeal on a point of law. First, they established a right to apply from the Yokohama Court direct to the Privy Council

10 Hornby to Myburgh, 17 September 1866; FO656/18.
11 *Reg. v. Howard Clark* (Defendant and appellant); 15 March 1879; JWM.
12 *Ex Parte* Edith Mary Hallowell Carew [1897] AC 719.
13 21 August 30 October and 6 November 1897; KWC.
14 30 September 1899; EW.

for leave to appeal to it—without going first to the Supreme Court. Then, after HMCJ's establishment, the Japanese Customs established, in the *Hiogo treasure case*,[15] that the prosecution could appeal from a Consular Court to HMCJ on a point of law by way of case stated just as the prosecution in England could appeal to the High Court from a magistrates' court by way of case stated.[16]

In the first *Hartley case*, when Wilkinson's decision that the Treaty's prohibition on opium imports did not extend to medicinal opium triggered diplomatic protests against 'so one-sided a view'[17] of the Treaty, the Japanese government wished to appeal against it to the proper authorities.[18] When Lowder, counsel for the Japanese Customs, intimated to Wilkinson after the hearing that he could see no provision in OC1865 or the Rules for an appeal, Wilkinson referred him to precedents in which the Privy Council had allowed appeals under its inherent jurisdiction. The Japanese government's London agents must have moved swiftly for Lowder quickly informed Wilkinson that leave had been granted but requested him not to forward the record of the case to London pending the Japanese government's receipt of advices by post.[19]

Such leave was unusual for Mowat asked Wilkinson 'what authority there is for an appeal going direct from your Court to the Privy Council'[20] and there is nothing to show the basis upon which the Privy Council granted leave. We must assume that it was as a courtesy to the Japanese government. Besides challenging Wilkinson's interpretation of the Treaty, the Japanese government threatened to argue that he was 'not lawfully competent to determine this charge'[21] but indicated to Salisbury that, if Britain accepted that Wilkinson's decision was not binding, this would probably prevent the appeal.[22]

Before that appeal came on, Wilkinson determined the second *Hartley case* and convicted Hartley of importing 'smoking' or 'non-medicinal' opium after requiring the Japanese prosecution to specify the opium as such. The Japanese government objected (as, otherwise, it could be taken as approving Wilkinson's earlier interpretation) and threatened a second

---

[15] *Reg. (on the prosecution of the Superintendent of Customs at Hiogo) v. HSBC;* 24 January 1882; NCHLR.

[16] Ibid.

[17] Terashima Munenori to Parkes, 7 March 1878; FO656/49.

[18] Ibid.

[19] Wilkinson to Parkes, 30 March 1878; FO656/49.

[20] Mowat to Wilkinson, 30 September 1878; FO656/39.

[21] Japanese Legation to Salisbury, 14 June 1878; FO46/360.

[22] Ibid.

appeal to the Privy Council on this point.[23] The Japanese government had found the British weak point for the Foreign Office did not wish either appeal to go ahead as they would 'explore the want of jurisdiction of the court at Kanagawa'[24] and, when the Law Officers advised that Wilkinson's judgments could not be upheld,[25] Salisbury confirmed this to the Japanese[26] who 'decided not to apply for leave to appeal'[27] in the second case and abandoned the appeal in the first case.

In the *Hiogo Treasure case*, HSBC sought to rely on the Austro-Hungarian treaty and the Treaty's 'most favoured nation' provision to resist the forfeiture of three boxes of gold specie which the Japanese Customs claimed HSBC had imported contrary to the Trade Regulations and which the Treaty allowed to be confiscated. When Aston, Kobe Consul, upheld HSBC's contention,[28] the Japanese Customs sought to appeal to HMCJ as the Austro-Hungarian treaty provided a right of appeal but HSBC argued that the Rules allowed no such right. HMCJ allowed that the prosecution could appeal by way of case stated on a point of law but, after remissions to Kobe for correction of the stated case, it found against the Japanese Customs on the appeal and, despite initial threats to appeal to the Privy Council, the Japanese Customs dropped the prosecution.

The only occasion on which there was a suggestion of an appeal in a criminal case from HMCJ to the Supreme Court was the *Normanton* case where, Alfred Robinson—a Shanghai solicitor who would have been used to practising before it—served notice after Drake's conviction that he would apply for a special case to be stated for submission to the Supreme Court.[29] However, there is no evidence that any such appeal was pursued.

Where legal processes would not permit a review of the conviction or sentence, several better-connected litigants had no compunction about resorting to extra-legal pressure. This followed three principal avenues: memorials from a concerned community asking the Judge or Minister to intervene; press coverage; and personal lobbying of the Minister and/or the Judge. Besides publicity, the object of this lobbying was to pressure

23 Japanese Legation to Salisbury, 12 July 1878; FO46/360.

24 Foreign Office to Parkes, 30 November 1878; FO46/360.

25 Law Officers to Salisbury, 17 January 1879; FO46/360.

26 Salisbury to Japanese Legation, 7 February 1879; FO46/360.

27 Kennedy to Salisbury, 21 December 1880; FO46/362.

28 This reflected Wilkinson's ruling in *Imperial Japanese Customs v. Abdul Khym* that British practice was to follow article VII of the Austro-Hungarian treaty and, upon acquittal on a Customs charge, return the property to the defendant; 9 November 1878; JDH.

29 16 December 1886; HN.

the Minister into exercising his power to remit a sentence or grant a pardon.

The power of Pardon was vested in the Minister. Originally an *ad hominem* Power granted to the Governor of Hong Kong and the Minister to Beijing, Letters Patent in 1866 vested the then Minister to Tokyo, his successors and deputies with power to pardon offenders convicted in Japan.[30] The Minister held this power concurrently with the Governor of Hong Kong but Stanley, the Foreign Secretary, instructed Parkes to reach an understanding with the Governor as to their respective exercise of the power and suggested that the Minister exercise the power except in respect of convicts transferred to Hong Kong when the Governor should do so.[31]

When Lowder, during Edith Carew's trial, initiated a prosecution against Jacobs, the nanny—and a key witness in its case against Edith Carew, for Walter Carew's murder and the British authorities wished to halt this move, temporary panic reigned. The Foreign Office had mislaid the 1866 Letters Patent and, therefore, sought to have Jacobs pardoned under the Queen's sign manual before recognizing that pardons applied only to convicted persons and could not be exercised beforehand.[32] By OC1865, the Minister was empowered to commute death sentences; a power which Satow exercised immediately after Edith Carew's conviction when he commuted her death sentence to one of life imprisonment with hard labour—not least because 'no hangman could be got'.[33] There were no other murder convictions or death sentences passed during the period of extra-territoriality so this was the only example of the Minister's power of commutation being exercised.

Formal applications for Pardons required evidence to suggest that the conviction was wrong. One successful appeal supported by a memorial was that of Browning when the British residents of Izmir, Browning's birthplace, addressed a Memorial to Hornby claiming that the whole tenor of the evidence tended to show that he acted in self-defence and the

---

[30] Home Office to Law Officers, 20 December 1865; TS1454. It applied only to people convicted in the Consular Courts and, the following year, was supplemented to cover people convicted in the Supreme Court (Law Officers to Foreign Office, 18 May 1866; TS 25/1480).

[31] Stanley to Parkes, 25 September 1866; FO656/19.

[32] Foreign Office to Home Office, 11 January 1897; FO46/510. The Home Office suggested the Crown Prosecutor assume control of the prosecution and enter a *nolle prosequi* (Home Office to Foreign Office; 19 January 1897) but Lowder withdrew his charge before this became necessary.

[33] Satow to Bertie 24 November 1896; Ruxton 2007, page 58.

jury, convinced of the absence of intent, convicted him only of manslaughter.[34] This must have been one of the first memorials that Hornby received upon arrival in Shanghai and he took up this memorial for, in 1868, Browning wrote thanking him for 'his influence and intercession in … obtaining my pardon and liberation'.[35]

Edith Carew's family used their political connections at Home to lobby on her behalf; first to have her removed from Hong Kong back to the UK[36] and, when her application for leave to appeal to the Privy Council was refused, to seek a Pardon claiming that she had not received a fair trial and the conviction was against the evidence.[37]

The Press could be particularly partisan and Press criticism was part of a Consul's life. In Nagasaki, after the first Norman case,[38] Norman used his ownership of *The Rising Sun and Nagasaki Express* to re-try the case, decide it in his favour and ridicule the Consul. The criticism spread from Nagasaki to Kobe and Yokohama for both *The Hiogo News* and the French *L'Echo du Japon* criticized Hall's decision.[39] In addition, Norman lobbied the Minister at whose instance Hannen required Hall to explain himself.[40] Another example occurred when Nelson, the chief engineer on the *Felbridge*, prosecuted its steward before the Nagasaki Court for assault. When Quin merely fined the steward, Nelson launched into lengthy letter correspondence published in the local and Kobe newspapers complaining about 'consular justice in Nagasaki' and denouncing Quin for actions which he claimed were 'beneath criticism' for believing the steward's account rather than Nelson's—which was supported by the captain and

34 Memorial from the British residents of Izmir to Hornby, 3 July 1865; FO656/22. See also page 147.

35 Browning to Hornby, 2 June 1868; FO796/22.

36 Accompanied by an Inspector of the Hong Kong Police going home on leave, she travelled back to the United Kingdom second class on a steamer and was allowed her liberty on board and dined in the saloon with the other passengers; 6 November 1897; KWC.

37 Petition for Clemency. The Law Officers conceded that Mowat's summing up was unsatisfactory and suggested referring the matter to the Home Office to assess the medical evidence (30 March 1898). The Home Secretary found no new grounds to justify recommending remission and it was another 11 years before Carew was released. FO46/510.

38 See page 124.

39 8 August 1883; HN. See also: 30 June 7 and 28 July 1888; TRS&NE.

40 Hannen's principal complaint was not the conviction but Hall's merely making a judicial order against Norman to cease obstructing the Japanese police rather than imposing a heavy punishment—which Hall explained as resulting from the Japanese authorities' only seeking such an order. Hall to Hannen, 18 July 1883; FO796/3, pages 130–145. He went on to say that Norman's view of the question '…that as a British subject with treaty rights he had no concern whatever with the Japanese authorities and Japanese laws…' was shared by 'a not inconsiderable section of the British residents here'. Hall to Hannen, 31 August 1883; FO796/3.

second officer.[41] That the prosecution could not—generally—appeal against an acquittal did not prevent Barnard (a Yokohama barrister), petitioning Hornby, in 1868, to reverse Consul Fletcher's dismissal of a charge for conspiracy and assault brought by Barnard against several others. Barnard claimed that 'the ridiculous manner in which trials are conducted'[42] by Fletcher showed his 'utter incompetency ... for the judicial duties of judge.'[43] Barnard's Petition suggests yet another example of personal squabbles and vendettas being pursued through the courts with threats to use London-based contacts to raise the matter in Parliament and lobby the government. There is no evidence that Hornby took any action. It was not the only example of lawyers appearing to be unaware of the procedural rules for Dohmen was compelled to explain to Dickins, defence counsel in the *Archibald King case,* that no appeal, other than on a point of law, lay against conviction in criminal cases and that King would need to rely upon Dohmen's being required to submit a report to the Judge following his convicting King with dissenting Assessors.[44]

The notable exception to the Judge's usual support for the Consuls was when Heineman, a Kobe businessman, complained to Parkes against Gower's convicting him for contempt when, in court, he had criticized Gower for turning up late to hear a case where Heineman had been summoned to act as an Assessor. Parkes forwarded the complaint to Hornby[45] who, despite Gower's protestations, overturned the contempt conviction and ordered Gower to remit the $25 fine.

Lobbying the Minister, or raising a matter to the diplomatic plane was another form of extra-legal appeal by lobbyists. Such activity had several potential advantages: first, it could be a cheaper means of proceeding in that no lawyers or expensive court fees needed to be incurred—but successful lobbying required organization and commitment from a number of people and/or support from people with influence. Then, there was always the hope that, when the matter was considered in London, the Foreign Office would seek the Law Officers' opinion—particularly when there were diplomatic overtones as in the *Hartley cases*—or officials would be concerned about the matter being raised in Parliament. This was relevant where there were any legal doubts about the original process. However, lobbying could also be undertaken even if there was no legal

41 12 March and 9 April 1890; TRS&NE.
42 Barnard to Hornby and related Petition, 18 November 1868; FO656/22.
43 Ibid.
44 Dohmen to Hornby 19 June 1875; FO656/40.
45 Parkes to Heineman, 10 December 1874; FO656/19.

basis for any appeal. Here the relevant lobbyists sought simply to apply political pressure to achieve a changed verdict or sentence through action by the Executive.

Barnard had backed up his complaints to Hornby about Fletcher's dismissal of his case with a direct threat to lobby MPs. When both R.G. Watson and Hornby ignored the Memorials in the *Cousens case* to which they were subjected, the newspapers reported loud threats from the British community to raise the matter in Parliament,[46] but there appears to have been no follow-through.[47] The Memorial to Watson claimed the prosecution was brought simply because it was an assault on a consular *scindo* and 'the Japanese prosecutor was an unwilling witness…'[48] and talked in grandiose terms that 'the principles of law and justice have not guided the proceedings of [the Kobe Consular Court], that your Excellency should take such measures as you may deem requisite to prevent any recurrence … and to remove the discredit which appears to us to attach to the British Consulate at Kobe' before claiming that Cousens 'in ignorance, waived his right of appeal'. Watson dismissed the Memorial as a 'not very accurate' description of the facts whilst Hornby simply refused to receive it as it was 'no part of the duty of a judge to receive memorials in respect of judgments passed by a consular tribunal.'[49]

Civil Cases

Whilst OC1859 made no provision for appeals (simply allowing the Consul to amend his judgment or grant a new trial after informing the parties of his initial decision[50]), OC 1860 provided for appeals, within 15 days of the judgment, to the Consul-General where the sum claimed was below $1,000 or, otherwise, to SCHK.[51] A party could not adduce new factual evidence on appeal but could introduce further 'legal evidence' if he had been ignorant of it or unable to produce it at the original trial.[52]

46 7 November 1872; NCH.

47 Granville was unaware of the case; Granville to Hornby, 7 January 1873; FO17/660.

48 Watson to Hornby, 6 October 1872; FO656/19.

49 Hornby to Watson, 30 October 1872; FO656/19.

50 Rule XVII.

51 Sections XI and XIII OC1860. Letters Patent of 6 July 1864 to the Chief Justice of Hong Kong detailed the procedure for filing the appeal and the Consul's duty to provide copy minutes of the Court hearing. They authorized the Consul to require reasonable security from the appellant (including from one or two other sureties satisfactory to the Consul).

52 Section XVI OC1860.

OC1865 removed the involvement of both the Consul-General and SCHK in the process and substituted the Supreme Court as the appellate body for all appeals from Courts in Japan. Appeals were permitted as of right only where the sums in dispute exceeded $250 although a Court could grant leave to appeal in other cases where it seemed 'fit and expedient'.[53] In practice, appeals were allowed in any case where it seemed just—regardless of the sum in dispute.[54] From the Supreme Court, appeals lay to the Privy Council: as of right, where the disputed amount exceeded $2,500[55] and the appeal was lodged within 15 days of the judgment or, otherwise, where the Supreme Court considered it 'just and expedient'.[56] In both cases, the Supreme Court could require the appellant to provide security up to $2,500.[57] Where the Supreme Court refused leave to appeal, an aggrieved party could apply direct to the Privy Council for such leave[58] although nobody appears to have exercised this right. Of potentially great practical importance, all payment or performance judgments were suspended pending any appeal to the Privy Council.[59]

Even where the disputed amount exceeded $250 so that litigants could appeal as of right, Rule 154 required that they act expeditiously within seven days of the original judgment; otherwise, litigants needed the Court's permission to appeal. When the master and owners of the *Cathaya* sought leave out of time to appeal against the Kobe Court's judgment in favour of the Imperial Japanese Railways in relation to a short delivery of cement, the Court refused them permission because they were more than a month late and it would be unfair to this particular plaintiff as no appeal had been made in two similar cases.[60]

Where the Assistant Judge or Law Secretary (as opposed to the Judge or either of them sitting as acting Judge) heard a case under the extraordinary jurisdiction of the Supreme Court or HMCJ, either party could, as of

---

53 Section 119.

54 This was true in Japan; but *Moss v. Alcock* is an example of a case where the trial judge refused leave to appeal. Appeals from SCHK to the Privy Council were allowed as of right only in cases where the amount in dispute exceeded £500—otherwise, leave was required. After the jury had awarded Moss $2,000 damages, both Alcock's counsel and Moss sought leave to appeal against the Chief Justice's decisions as to his jurisdiction to hear the case (see page 118) but the judge said that he would not assist either party to pursue an appeal as there had been too much litigation on the matter already: Smale to Alexander (acting Colonial Secretary in Hong Kong), 31 December 1861; FO46/30.

55 Section 131.

56 Section 137.

57 Section 133.

58 Section 139.

59 Section 132.

60 19 April and 24 May 1876; HN.

right, demand a re-hearing before the Judge.[61] Such re-hearing was not, technically, an appeal but a new hearing. This meant that fresh evidence could be adduced and new legal arguments raised without the restrictions applying upon an appeal. This right was criticized immediately upon OC1865's publication as potentially giving rise to complications[62] and, in practice, the judiciary soon came to try to avoid its use.

When Tombrink (as trustee for Glover's bankrupt estate) applied to the Supreme Court for a re-hearing of *HSBC v. Tombrink*, regarding HSBC's claim to a lien for Ts7,500 over arms and ammunition shipped to Glover, on the grounds of the informality of the original hearing, Rennie opposed him with the 'floodgates' argument. Rennie argued that, were such re-hearing to be granted, this would 'open the door to perpetual re-hearings from Provincial Courts' as the Consuls were not lawyers and most cases were conducted more or less irregularly.[63] Nonetheless, Goodwin ordered a re-hearing in preference to an appeal. In 1872, Hornby held that re-hearings did not apply to the Yokohama Court and Rennie, in a case in Shanghai, curtailed the right further in 1886 by interpreting 're-hearing' as equating to appeal so that re-hearings were held solely upon the evidence presented in the lower court and not *de novo*.[64]

Despite these questions regarding re-hearings, references to re-hearings from, and in, Japan are few. Whilst there is a reference to Gower's remitting the 'appeal fees' of 2% on the filing of the Petition and 2% for the 're-hearing' in *A.S. Lobes (as agent for the China and Japan Trading Company) v. Holmes for the Master and Owner of ss Gordon Castle*[65] in a claim for $872, the case is described in the Judge's Minute Books as an appeal. The practical difference may be slight; but, if it were an appeal, it shows the problems with the correct terminology not always being used in correspondence.

A certain flexibility and discretion was exercised in applying the rules. In a dispute between Felix Beato and P&O over the balance of accounts, Dickins applied for a re-hearing only to be opposed by Ness who said that, as the case had been heard in the Yokohama Court, there could be no re-hearing. Goodwin agreed but, by consent, allowed Dickins to appeal.[66] Rennie, in accordance with usual practice, rejected the defendant's

---

61 Sections 14 and 19.
62 29 July 1865; NCH.
63 *HSBC v. Tombrink (Trustee of Glover, Daw & Co.)*; NCHLR 1871, page 447.
64 Cited by Hannen in *C.G. Wilson v. J.W. Hall*, 19 November 1887; JWM.
65 Gower to Hornby, 2 March 1874; FO656/41.
66 *Beato v. P&O*; 9 December 1876; JWM.

application for a re-hearing in *Polder v. Lewis* because Dohmen had sat as acting Judge (not as acting Assistant Judge) and the defendant had no new evidence;[67] but, in similar circumstances a year later, told the defendant in *Capt. Thomas v. A.J. Clarke* that, as a favour, he would grant a re-hearing—but, nevertheless, he said that he had read the papers and it would be a waste of time and urged the defendant to drop the matter.[68]

One re-hearing which succeeded was *Baron Francis von Stillfried v. W.H. Waggott* where von Stillfried sued Waggott for $16 for photographs of a Japanese woman and child taken at Waggott's request. Dohmen, as acting Assistant Judge, had dismissed the claim because the Yokohama custom was that there was no charge for rejected proof photographs; but, in a re-hearing three weeks later, Rennie upheld von Stillfried's claim as his advertisements had stated clearly his terms of business (which required payment for proofs) and Waggott was aware of these terms of business when commissioning the photographs. However, as von Stillfried was a foreigner and outside the Court's jurisdiction, Rennie ordered that he must produce the 24 copies as ordered and he could only receive the $16 after he had deposited these copies with the Court.[69]

Re-hearings were meant to be within the Supreme Court or HMCJ but, after OC1865, not in other Courts. However, in an example of a practical approach, we find Enslie and two Assessors re-hearing a case in 1875 in Kobe. When Nakamura Shobei sued Lucas & Walters over a short delivery of sugar, the Court ordered Lucas & Walters to deliver the remaining 75 bags of sugar to Shobei against his paying the $300 purchase price. However, a few days later, a re-hearing was granted on the defendants' petition as they claimed they had acted not as principals but as agents and should, therefore, have no liability. Enslie and the two Assessors accepted this and reversed their earlier decision.[70] In 1877, Annersley and two Assessors, after a day's hearing of Kniffler's claim against the *Atholl*'s master for $5,524 for damage to a cargo of brass sheets, said they were dissatisfied with the results of the case's hearing because it had been so hurriedly set down that they directed a new trial where proper scientific evidence should be produced regarding the alleged chloride damage to the brass sheets. Meanwhile, they also suggested that the case that might be 'speedily settled by arbitration'. The parties were unable to agree and, when the

---

67 22 November 1880; JDH.
68 12 November 1880; JDH.
69 11 March and 2 April 1880; JDH.
70 7 and 21 October 1875; HN.

re-hearing came on, the Court said simply that it had considered the new scientific evidence and no further hearing was necessary before it gave judgment for Kniffler in full.[71]

There are no official records relating to appeals from Japan to SCHK prior to 1865 and only a brief newspaper report of one, *Kemptner v. Hoey*, a dispute over a cargo of rags, in which SCHK upheld the Yokohama Consul's finding for the plaintiff.[72] The first record of an appeal to the Consul-General under OC1860 was *In re Barnett v. Hoey* which was a land dispute involving a claim by Barnett against Hoey for falsely leasing land to him in Nagasaki to which Hoey had no right. Alcock upheld Morrison's decision and doubled the costs award against Hoey whose conduct he described as 'unscrupulous, illegal and highly reprehensible'.[73]

Alt & Co. v. Stephens, master of the Ann was the final appeal from Nagasaki to the Consul-General before the OC1865 regime. The claim by Alt & Co for £84 commission for arranging a charter had been heard in the Nagasaki Court with two Assessors on 3 April 1865. The Consul—with the agreement of the Assessors—had found for the defendant and awarded him costs whereupon Alt & Co lodged a Notice of Appeal the next day and the papers were forwarded to Winchester, the acting Consul-General. Winchester recorded that he had reviewed all the papers several times on 1 May before fully confirming the Nagasaki Court's decision and ordering the appellant to pay the costs of the appeal.[74]

From Yokohama, we have only two newspaper reports of civil appeals to the Consul-General under OC1860. Winchester allowed the first appeal in *Cook v. Samuel Rowell* over a partnership dispute,[75] but rejected the second appeal in a claim for $57 paid on account of goods sold but undelivered.[76]

After 1878, appeals from Provincial Courts no longer went direct to the Supreme Court but first to HMCJ. The first appeals to HMCJ in 1879 arose from John Will's bankruptcy in Hakodate and disputes between creditors over priority to his assets[77] and a dispute in Kobe over a claim for $250 demurrage charges when the *Galley of Lorne* delayed its sailing after the

---

[71] 25 August and 15 September 1877; HN.

[72] 3 October 1863; TJH. The original trial had taken place in Yokohama in March 1862 and the appeal was heard before Ball J. in SCHK on 27 August 1863.

[73] Alcock to Morrison, 29 June 1860; FO262/7 and FO796/20.

[74] Winchester to Gower, 3 May 1865; FO796/28.

[75] 20 May 1865; TJH.

[76] *Daniel McKenzie v. Hansard & Co.*, 22 July 1865; TJH.

[77] *Mathew Catlin Adams v. John Will*, 15 November 1879; JDH.

Governor of Hong Kong, Sir John Pope Hennessy, had booked tickets on it from Kobe to Hong Kong only to cancel them before the sailing date.[78] Otherwise, we see few appeals from the out-ports to HMCJ—which supports the view that, after 1879, most significant cases were begun in HMCJ and only the smaller cases were heard at the out-ports' Courts. In only one case did a litigant appeal to the Supreme Court against HMCJ's dismissal of his appeal from a Provincial Court.[79]

Appeals to the Supreme Court began almost as soon as it was established in 1865. From 1865 to 1878, appeals averaged four a year with the bulk coming from Yokohama—particularly prior to the Yokohama Court's establishment in 1871. After that, most came from Kobe (which evidences its growing commercial importance after it opened in 1868). We see seven cases from Nagasaki, five from Hakodate and just two from Tokyo.[80] With HMCJ's establishment, appeals to the Supreme Court dropped off and, apart from six in 1882, averaged just one a year for the remainder of the period until the final appeal in 1896. The 1882 spike in appeals may reflect the judicial hiatus caused by Rennie's absence on leave in 1881 (during which Robertson, an experienced Consul but only recently called to the Bar, and Dohmen, who was also an experienced Consul but unqualified, temporarily ran HMCJ) and procedural manoeuvrings as three of that year's appeals were on interlocutory questions.

Four Supreme Court judgments in 1881 and one in 1882 related to cases heard before the Yokohama Court in 1877 or 1878. These delays were due, in part, to the bankruptcy of a litigant, as in *E.C. Kirby & Mitchell v. Howles*, or attempts by the parties to negotiate matters; but, in a large part also to French's long illness in 1880 and 1881 which caused a backlog of cases—not just from Japan, which Hannen tackled when appointed acting Chief Justice on French's death.

Shipping cases, at over a third of the known cases, formed the largest category of appeals followed by general commercial, trading and debt cases at nearly a third with the subject matter of many of the remainder unknown.[81] Of the others, three were land or boundary disputes and individual claims for defamation, conversion, breach of employment contract and a partnership dispute. Not all appeals related to the substantive case;

---

[78] *John Pitman v. Arthur Groom*, 29 November 1879; JDH.

[79] *Blakiston v. J.H. Duus* heard by the Supreme Court on 25 July 1882 concerned Blakiston's appeal from HMCJ against its dismissal of his suit before the Tokyo Court. Judgment sent by Hannen to Robertson on 26 September 1882; FO656/39.

[80] Table 22.

[81] Table 23.

a quarter of the known cases involved interlocutory points prior to the substantive appeal—or even the substantive case being heard at first instance. As the *Chishima cases* showed, these procedural cases could be no less important than substantive cases.

Many litigants in appeals represented a roll-call of the leading Western traders in Japan and support the view that most appeal cases were shipping or commercially related cases: the trading house of E.C. Kirby & Co. was involved in no fewer than six appeals[82] and Thomas Glover in four.[83] Two-thirds of appeals involved only British litigants against just under a third of cases in the Nagasaki Court whilst Japanese and foreign litigants were involved in 15 cases each.[84] These proportions are unsurprising given the $250 claim minimum for appeals as of right and that most appeals involved shipping and major commercial disputes (both sectors in which the British were dominant). Overall, nearly half as many plaintiffs again than defendants appealed against the lower Courts' decisions.[85] However, if we exclude Japanese and foreign appellant plaintiffs (for none could be a defendant in the Courts), we see that, amongst British litigants, slightly more defendants than plaintiffs (30 to 27) were appellants.

Goodwin said in 1871 that it was 'with much unwillingness'[86] that he received appeals in Anglo-Japanese disputes as such cases were rarely presented satisfactorily. Whilst this may have been the case in earlier days when parties were unrepresented, it cannot have been true for appeals from the Yokohama Court and HMCJ from 1870 onwards as counsel became more involved in arguing cases at first instance.

Appeals were allowed and dismissed almost evenly[87] but it is noticeable that over half of the appeals from HMCJ were dismissed which, simplistically, would suggest that its establishment and staffing (generally) by one or, often, two experienced legally qualified judges improved the

82 *E.C. Kirby v. Hart* in 1872, *Reynell v. E.C. Kirby (as agent for Hall & Holtz)* in 1873 and *Burgoyne, master of Galley of Lorne v. E.C. Kirby* in 1875 (from Kobe), *E.C. Kirby v. Devine* in 1874 and *William Howles v. E.C. Kirby* in 1881 (and again in 1882) (from Yokohama).

83 *Glover & Alt & Co. v. J. Maltby* from Nagasaki in 1867, *Glover v. Duus* from Hakodate in 1868 and two cases involving HSBC's claims in Glover's liquidation from Nagasaki in 1871 (*Tombrink (liquidator of the Glover estate) v. HSBC* and *Prushita v. HSBC*).

84 Although Britons appear to have formed the larger part of the litigants in Yokohama in 1862–1899, this may reflect the newspapers' reporting policies. (Note that these figures do not correlate to Table 24 as that Table ignores those cases where there is insufficient information to complete the Table.)

85 Table 24. (Again, given the absence of relevant information, the figures in the Tables 24 and 25 do not correspond exactly.)

86 Goodwin to Adams, 30 September 1871; FO 656/19.

87 Table 25.

judicial calibre in Japan. This proportion is a reversal of the 12 out of 20 appeals allowed from the Yokohama Court. Only 13 out of 30 appeals were allowed from the Kanagawa Court and the other Provincial Courts. This suggests that the results of appeals do not support arguments that legally untrained or inexperienced Consuls were worse at delivering a just (or legally justifiable) result than the legally trained judges of the Yokohama Court.

The principal ground for allowing an appeal was that the first instance decision was wrong as a matter of law, but there is no evidence that legally untrained Consuls were more likely than legally trained judges to be overturned on this ground. Appeals were allowed on this ground both before, and after, the Yokohama Court's establishment. The Hakodate Consul's (incorrect) refusal to allow money paid on mistake of fact in *Howell v. Creditors of Porter's Bankrupt Estate* was overturned as was Hannen's decision in a convoluted trade dispute in *Edward Whittall v. Yukioke Shobei* involving $35,000 when the Supreme Court held that he had reached the wrong legal conclusion.[88] In two cases involving Beato,[89] the Supreme Court took a different view from the jury as to the evidence and allowed the appeals. In the first, it heard the appeal entirely on papers and criticized Dickins, Beato's counsel, for 'an entire absence of professional feeling' for attributing his loss to the judge's partiality before holding the jury wrong on one aspect and allowing Beato's appeal in part.

Japanese appellants were the most successful category of appellants, being unsuccessful in only one out of their eight appeals and losing only two out of the seven appeals where they were the respondents.[90] British and foreign appellants succeeded in just under half their appeals and, as respondents, won a majority of appeal cases. These figures do not suggest any bias in favour of British litigants at the Supreme Court level.

This quantitative interpretation is supported by a more subjective review of the 15 appeals involving a Japanese litigant; eight as appellant and seven as respondent. The Supreme Court dismissed Japanese appeals in just one case (*Imperial Japanese Government v. Beato* in 1868 of which no details are traceable) but allowed the appeal in the other seven cases. Of these, the Privy Council reinstated HMCJs ruling in the *Tsune Kijima case*. In *Chaya Yakichi v. Mourilyan & Heiman & Co,* Hornby substantially

---

[88] Judgment, 27 May 1884; FO656/36.

[89] *Felix Beato v. James Davison & Co* (a cross-action), 4 September 1875, and *Beato v. Sturrock*; 14 December 1878; NCHLR.

[90] Table 25.

allowed the appellant's claim because the Kobe Consul had misread the charter-party.[91] In the two *Governor of Kanagawa Ken v. Cope & Others* hearings, the first was an interlocutory point (as to production of the title deeds to the land in dispute) while, on the appeal of the substantive decision, the Supreme Court held that, following the jury's verdict on one aspect, HMCJ's decision should be partially varied in the appellant's favour. In *Akita han v. Blakiston Marr & Co*, the correspondence[92] suggests that the Japanese plaintiff had not presented its initial case particularly well and, when it was remitted for a new hearing as to evidence and quantum, the Japanese plaintiff largely succeeded. There is no explanation in the other two (both re-hearings) as to why the original decisions were reversed.[93] Where the Japanese party was the respondent, it lost in only the *Chishima case,*[94] so that, apart, possibly, from this case, none of these appeals supports accusations of an anti-Japanese bias on the part of the Supreme Court.

The greater success of Japanese litigants on appeal, *might* support claims that the lower Courts were biased against Japanese litigants; but, given the small number of cases involving non-British litigants, this risks reading too much into the figures; particularly as the lower Court level figures provide little support for such a view. Even in the *Chaya Yakichi case*, Hornby recognized that the Consul had done his best to do justice between the parties.

Appeal cases could be conducted entirely by written submissions: sometimes, simply the original pleadings plus the Court Minutes of the hearing and the Notice of Appeal together with any Reply that the respondent chose to make (together termed the Record of Appeal); *Rainbow Lewis & Co. (in liquidation) v. Hall & Holtz* on appeal from Nagasaki in 1870 was such an example.[95] In other cases, as with the first interlocutory appeal in the *Glamorganshire*, counsel on both sides prepared the submissions.

Counsel were employed in over half the appeals to the Supreme Court after the Yokohama Bar was established.[96] In nearly a quarter of appeals to the Supreme Court, counsel appeared on both sides and for just one side in almost another quarter—although, here, the unrepresented party

91 14 January 1875; NCHLR.

92 Goodwin to Adams, 30 September 1871; FO656/19.

93 *Komei v William Curtiss* and *Arai Josuka v. William Curtiss*, both 6 October 1877; JWM.

94 The result in *Ichinosuke Sempachi v. Porter* is unclear.

95 24 January 1870, Judge's Minutes Books; FO1092/364.

96 Tables 22 and 26.

may have had counsel settle written submissions to the Supreme Court but we only know this to have been the case in a few cases. There was little difference in terms of result whichever route was adopted and, even where counsel appeared for one side only, the numbers of appeals allowed and those dismissed balanced each other.

Appeals were an expensive business: first, fees payable by the appellant; second, the requirement for the appellant to provide security for costs; third, the legal costs of pursuing the appeal itself. Counsel (usually from Shanghai) were often instructed and, even if not, would often have prepared written submissions; fourth, the general delays and inconvenience of pursuing an appeal in Shanghai; and, fifth, a losing defendant's obligation to pay interest from the day of the initial judgment at, usually, 8%.[97]

Fees were charged on the various processes: $5 for filing a motion to appeal; $10 for a Court Order allowing an appeal; $100 for filing the Appeal Petition; $100 for any hearing in the Court on the Petition; and $5 on the appellant's filing security.[98] In addition, Supreme Court fees were charged at 4% *ad valorem* on the disputed amount.[99] The Rules did not cover all eventualities as seen by the questions regarding the level of fees payable in the libel case of *Goertz v. Cruchley* where the damages would be settled by a jury.[100] Inevitably, litigants quibbled over the fees or sought rebates if they did not obtain the desired result. In *Akita han v. Blakiston Marr & Co*, when the Judge modified the original Hakodate judgment slightly in favour of the appellants, they sought a proportionate rebate of fees.[101] In *Imperial Japanese Government v. Beato*, Hornby fixed the appeal fees at $15 but had no objection to remitting them if they were to come from the Japanese government;[102]—something not done in other cases. This distinction, and the levying of appeal fees on the Japanese government in the *Chishima case*, suggests that, whilst fees were remitted for Japanese plaintiffs in Japan, they were not remitted automatically in appeals.

---

[97] Supreme Court judgment in the *Glamorganshire*. However, in *Groenewort v. Pritchard*, interest at 10% had been allowed (Goodwin to Flowers, 3 October 1866; FO656/7).

[98] See Hornby to Gower, October 1865 in relation to *Sanders v. Alt & Co*; FO656/18.

[99] In *Chaya Yakichi v. Mourilyan & Heiman & Co. (as agents for the ss. Washi)*, where the claim was $2,169, $80.60 fees were paid and remitted to the Supreme Court by a cheque for Ts 62.90; Annersley to Hornby, 1 October 1874; FO656/41.

[100] Annersley to Hornby, 10 July 1875; FO656/41.

[101] Troup to Hornby, 29 August 1872; FO656/35.

[102] Hornby to Kanagawa Consul, 12 May 1868; FO656/18.

Security (usually a bond in the Judge's favour or a cash deposit with the Court) was to be provided within 14 days after filing the application.[103] The Consul had discretion as to amount and provider and Hornby refused to interfere with a Court's discretion regarding security.[104] *Charles Parker v. Henry Cook*, in the Kanagawa Court, was an unusual civil action arising out of a criminal case when Parker sued Cook for damages suffered during an assault on him by Cook and his wife (for which Cook had been fined $75 and his wife $25). When Myburgh dismissed the civil suit, Parker sought leave to appeal which Myburgh granted subject to Parker's providing $250 security or sureties therefor. When Myburgh refused to accept the sureties, Parker petitioned direct to Hornby, who re-affirmed that the sureties must be acceptable to the Consul.[105] $250 was a common level of security,[106] but the amount could be higher and, in *Gaudaubert v. Hart Smedley*, Enslie required Gaudaubert to furnish two sureties of $500 each.[107]

After around 1870, such evidence as we have suggests that only those cases involving a major point of principle or large sums were appealed. In the *Glamorganshire*, the amount claimed was at least $57,000 and, in the *Chishima case*, around £100,000—plus, of even greater importance to the Japanese government, a point of principle. However, before this time, this was not always the case, and it was only after four appeals heard in Yokohama in quick succession in 1869, where Hornby used costs to discourage appeals, that his message was heeded and we see fewer judicial complaints about unmeritorious appeals. In *Esdale v. Bourne*, he declared that it was never intended that 'appeals should be sent up on frivolous grounds'[108] as the parties had incurred considerable expense on a matter where there could not be two opinions. He awarded full costs against the appellant so that, in future, parties might 'pause and consider whether it is worth their while to send in appeals'.[109] He reinforced this disapproval of

---

103 See Hornby to Gower, October 1865 in relation to *Sanders v. Alt & Co*; FO656/18.

104 Hornby to Myburgh 31 August 1867 in relation to *Charles Parker v. Poole*; FO656/18.

105 Petition from Parker to Hornby, 29 March 1867; FO656/22, on which Hornby endorsed 'I have read Petition and agree with finding of Court but if Plaintiff insists on appeal he can appeal but must provide $250 security for costs, $100 for fees or sureties acceptable to the Consular Court.'

106 Flowers to Hornby, 11 June 1866 and 2 November 1867 respectively, regarding *Groenewort v. Pritchard* and *Glover & Co. & Others v. J. Maltby*; FO656/14.

107 Enslie to Goodwin, 23 June 1871; FO565/34.

108 2 July 1869; NCH.

109 Ibid.

litigation involving petty sums when a spirit of fair dealing and compromise would have resolved the matter by refusing the appellant his costs in *James Bell, master of the Evangeline v. Aspinall Soper*—despite overturning the original decision on a technicality.[110]

Some plaintiffs must have continued litigation solely to maintain commercial pressure. In *William Howles v. E.C. Kirby & Others*, Howles sought tortious damages for the alleged conversion of his property. The case, which arose out of a compromise agreement in 1870 between Howles and his creditors, was heard in the Yokohama Court in 1877 by Wilkinson with a jury which found for the defence. Howles appealed claiming that the verdict was against the evidence and that Wilkinson had misdirected the jury. Between his appeal being lodged and its being heard, Howles became bankrupt so the appeal was pursued by his estate which May partly, explain the delay until 1881 before judgment was given in the appeal. Hannen dismissed the appeal with costs as he found the jury decision not contrary to the evidence and the summing up put nothing too strongly against the plaintiff—quite the contrary.[111] Again, costs were used to penalize a perceived unmeritorious appellant.

The actual costs varied from case to case with the details usually confidential to the litigants except when taxed. The records contain few examples of taxation but one example was the Supreme Court's taxing an appellant's costs at $231 in 1875[112] whilst Reynell complained that, despite winning in the Supreme Court, E.C. Kirby required that his costs be taxed so Reynell claimed $80 which he had spent on travelling to Yokohama to consult counsel plus $250 counsel's fees[113] and a $66.25 half-share of the cost of copying relevant Court documents (total $396).[114]

We see only three examples of moneyless appellants appealing *in forma pauperis*. The first was Porter's appeal from Hakodate when Eusden described him as being in a perfect state of impecuniosity surrounded by creditors on all sides.[115] In *Howles v. E.C. Kirby & Ors*, the Yokohama Court

[110] Ibid. The other cases that year were *N.P. Kingdom v. Wilkie & Robinson* and *De Connigh Vernende & Co. v. Hudson, Malcolm and Stott*, 3 June and 5 August respectively, 1869; NCH. Hornby said the latter case seemed to have been litigated purely for the sake of litigation whilst, in the first case, as counsel had not been employed at first instance, the appeal might have been decided easily on papers (i.e. without a hearing involving counsel).

[111] Printed judgment, 12 December 1881; FO656/39.

[112] Letter from Hornby to unidentified addressee, 12 February 1875; FO656/42.

[113] *E.C. Kirby & Co for Hall & Holtz v. Reynell*; Gower to Hornby, 17 March 1873; FO656/41.

[114] Gower to Hornby, 31 March 1873; FO656/41.

[115] Eusden to Hornby, 26 September 1870 in relation to *Ichinosuke Sempachi v. Porter*; FO656/35.

originally granted Howles leave to appeal *in forma pauperis* but the defendant subsequently contested this as Howles was earning over $150 per month whereupon Wilkinson revoked such leave.[116] Similarly, in *Dobbs v. Bunting* on appeal from HMCJ in 1890, when Bunting applied to the Supreme Court to dismiss Dobbs's Petition of Appeal,[117] Dobbs produced security for costs and ceased to act *in forma pauperis*[118] (although he appears not to have prosecuted the appeal for, in December 1890, it was dismissed for want of prosecution[119]).

The Press could be as condemnatory of judges in civil cases as in criminal cases. In 1880 the *Japan Gazette* had faced contempt proceedings for its derogatory comments about Dohmen[120] whilst, in 1897, the *Kobe Weekly Chronicle* complained that Schroeder, the owner and editor of the *Eastern World* who was also its Yokohama correspondent, was unable to obtain redress from—or even a hearing before—Troup on a claim. It went on to compare Troup with Mowat, 'a good and painstaking man', before suggesting that Troup should follow Mowat's example and retire on a pension.[121] As with criminal cases, litigants were not averse to complaining directly, and informally, to the Judge without a formal appeal. In 1869, Angus Topping, a sailor on the *Gaucho*, sought Hornby's assistance with his claim for arrears of wages about which he had consulted Marks who saw the Consul without success and charged Topping $25 for his services.[122] No substance is given for Topping's complaint nor is there any evidence that Hornby was able to assist. Blakiston even complained to French about Eusden's advising him that appeals were to be made to HMCJ after 1878.[123]

The volume of informal complaints was lower with civil than criminal cases—perhaps, because counsel were more likely to have been involved; and, after 1870 by when several lawyers were established in Yokohama, we see few such complaints. However, in 1887, Hugo Kniffler had his counsel, Kirkwood, complain to Hannen about Enslie's conduct in the Nagasaki Court[124] only for Enslie to refute the allegations and demand that they be

---

116 21 July 1877; JWM.
117 Chief Justice's Minute Books, 28 March 1890; FO1092/364.
118 Ibid, 22 April 1890.
119 Ibid, 15 December 1890.
120 See page 39.
121 23 October 1897; KWC.
122 Topping to Hornby, 27 May 1869; FO656/21.
123 Chief Clerk to Blakiston, 3 March 1879; FO656/18.
124 Kirkwood to Hannen, 5 May 1887; FO796/10.

'substantiated or unconditionally withdrawn',[125] which demand Hannen supported as he saw no reason why Kniffler had been unable to obtain justice from the Court and pointed out that Kniffler had abandoned his appeal against Enslie's decisions.[126] Kirkwood withdrew the complaints.

Besides Consuls' general requests for instructions from time to time, they also sought guidance on particular issues. In 1872, Flowers sought Hornby''s advice in *Burkhill v Glover's Estate* where Burkhill had failed to set down the case for hearing within the specified time and it had been dismissed upon the defendant's application. Flowers enquired how and to whom the appeal should be made—and, if to the Nagasaki Court, whether it should be granted.[127] The next year, Gower sought instructions about an executor's application to remove a will from his Court for transmission to England where the executor lived, 'because, as an *ex parte* application, it cannot be taken to you by way of appeal'.[128]

This informality could, of course, create difficulties, for, as seen by Annersley's seeking instructions in the Rainbow Lewis & Co bankruptcy claims, the Judge was in a delicate situation where his advice was being sought yet he might end up deciding the matters judicially. Hornby highlighted this difficulty 'where extra judicial opinions may lead to mischief'[129] when responding to Brandt's complaint about Jamieson and four nautical Assessors deciding against him. Hornby declined to express an opinion as he had not seen the judgment but explained that two barristers were leaving Shanghai for Yokohama by steamer and either would be able to proffer advice 'which my judicial position precludes me from offering'.[130]

Informal appeals or direct complaints to the Minister could bring the Law Officers into play whenever the matter was passed to the Foreign Office. They would also be involved where there was a claim (or the threat of such a claim) against a government department or official. As such, the Law Officers could be seen as an extra-judicial appellate system of sorts. We saw, in Chapter 1 (British Extra-territoriality), how they advised that Moss's conviction and fine be overturned and the extent to which the Minister relied upon their advice in respect of Regulations. When Hoey claimed damages from the Legation itself in respect of a lease of premises

125 Enslie to Hannen, May 17; FO796/10.
126 Hannen to Kirkwood, 25 May 1887; FO796/10.
127 Flowers to Hornby, 25 July 1872; FO656/42.
128 Gower to Hornby, 8 March 1873; FO656/41.
129 Hornby 1929, page 293.
130 Hornby to Brandt, 7 August 1869; FO656/21.

at Yokohama, the Legation referred the matter to the Foreign Office which, in turn, passed the matter on to the Law Officers who advised that Hoey's claims could not be sustained.[131] If he disagreed, his only option was to bring a suit against the Crown.[132]

A more interesting case arose out of the civil war in Japan 1868–1869 when the Tokugawa forces occupied Hakodate. First, the Law Officers said it was a question of fact for the Minister to determine whether or not a state of war existed. If one did, then the Japanese government had belligerent rights as against British subjects and assets caught up in the conflict; but, if there were no state of war, then the Treaty applied and British subjects would have the benefit of extra-territoriality.[133]

In 1869, Robertson questioned the validity of Hornby's award against him of an order personally to refund monies awarded by Robertson when sitting as arbitrator in respect of a collision at sea involving the *Ocean Queen*. When the case had originally come before him as Consul, Robertson had ruled (correctly) that he had no jurisdiction as it was an Admiralty matter. However, the parties requested, and agreed, that Robertson should sit as an arbitrator to hear the case and he had done so together with four nautical assessors. On the case's conclusion, Robertson had awarded the plaintiffs more than the $10,000 they had claimed against the *Ocean Queen* and went on to require payment of his award by virtue of his consular office. The defendants appealed to Hornby against the damages award. Hornby, rightly in the view of the Law Officers, held that the case and proceedings were full of irregularities and that it was outside the power of any arbitrator to award more than the amount claimed. However, they advised that when Hornby ordered Robertson personally to repay the money to the *Ocean Queen's* owners, Hornby himself was acting *ultra vires*. Hornby had ordered Robertson to repay the money by claiming that the Supreme Court had authority over its own officers. The Law Officers did not dispute this in relation to Robertson's activities in Court but advised that, as the arbitration was a private arrangement with the parties, Robertson was not sitting in an official capacity as Consul but had been acting privately. As such, Hornby had no such authority over him and could not order Robertson to repay the award. In conclusion, the Law Officers' advice to Robertson was that he should protest against Hornby's provisional order and his authority to grant it—but, they went on to advise that if Robertson

131 Hammond to Law Officers, 31 August 1867; FO96/308.
132 Law Officers to Stanley, 28 August 1868; FO83/2299.
133 Law Officers to Clarendon, 19 April 1869; FO83/2299.

were sued by the *Ocean Queen*'s owners, he would need to obtain his own legal advice.[134]

It was not uncommon, in appeals, for the Supreme Court to require further evidence or information before it would proceed to a full hearing. In *Groenewort v. Pritchard & owners of the steamer Hiogo*, the plaintiff sued for $3,000 contained in a treasure box which the *Hiogo*'s crew had dropped into the water whilst carrying it on board the vessel. The plaint was filed in April 1866 and the Nagasaki Court heard it on 1 May 1866 with two Assessors wherefrom it was appealed to the Supreme Court which, on 30 June referred it back to Nagasaki for further evidence as to the ownership of the money: whether it belonged to the plaintiff or his employers.[135] After this further evidence had been taken in Nagasaki on 17 July the appeal was finally heard on 23 August when judgment was given in favour of the plaintiff. In 1871, the Supreme Court remitted *Akita han v. Blakiston Marr & Co* to Hakodate not just for additional evidence but for a complete re-hearing as the plaintiff's evidence was deficient regarding the precise arrangements for the chartering of the vessel concerned.

Appeals to the Privy Council involved even greater delay and expense and substantial security was required.[136] All appeals from the Supreme Court—even Admiralty appeals—were governed by the rules applicable to colonial appeals.[137] Leave was sought to appeal to the Privy Council in seven cases but, although granted in all of them, it was not pursued in the first three cases. Hornby, when re-hearing *De Connigh Vernede & Co. v. Hudson, Malcolm & Co.* in Yokohama, upheld the Consul's decision but granted the plaintiff appellant's application to appeal to the Privy Council. However, the appeal was never pursued—either because it was regarded as hopeless or, more likely, because a settlement was reached.[138] In *Clark v. Hall*, the plaintiff paid the $15 fee to apply for the Supreme Court's leave to appeal,[139] but there is no evidence that the application was pursued.

---

[134] Law Officers and Travers Twiss to Clarendon, 18 December 1869; FO83/2299. The files do not reveal the ultimate outcome.

[135] Flowers to Hornby, 11 June 1866; FO656/14. Schuit & Co deposed that, although it was their property, they had made Groenewort responsible for the money.

[136] In the *Chishima cases*, the Japanese government and P&O put up $2,500 and $1,000 for their respective appeals.

[137] Admiralty appellate procedures applied only to appeals from Admiralty Courts within HM Possessions. Registrar Privy Council to Registrar Supreme Court, 28 March 1882 in relation to *Hochung v. Lapwing*, on appeal from China; FO656/65.

[138] 9 and 28 October 1869; JTOM.

[139] Mowat to Wilkinson, 30 September 1878 enclosing the appeal application and fee; FO656/39.

Similarly, in the long-running *Howles v. Kirby* case, no steps were taken to pursue Howles's application for leave to appeal to the Privy Council[140] so, at a formal hearing in March 1882 with no one appearing, the Supreme Court dismissed the application.[141] The first case from Japan heard by the Privy Council—technically two cases with different plaintiffs, but the substantive trials were heard together as they had the same defendants and arose out of the same facts—was the *Glamorganshire* in 1887.[142] The *Chishima cases* were also shipping cases and arose out of the same facts but went to appeal on preliminary, but unrelated, questions. For practical purposes, it is easiest to treat these four cases as just two.

All defendants are able to slow cases down, but the distance and delays introduced by Privy Council appeals acted in a defendant's interests. However, the *Glamorganshire* is the only case from Japan where the Privy Council was involved as a delaying tactic whereas, from 1882 onwards, we see increasing numbers of appeals from the Supreme Court in China-originated cases which were not pursued. One must believe that these appeals were lodged solely to benefit from the rule that enforcement of judgments was suspended pending an appeal to the Privy Council which appeal would be dismissed for want of prosecution only after six months from the date it was lodged with the Privy Council Office.[143]

Besides illustrating the procedural tactics used by defendants to drag out a case and delay a final decision in an attempt to avoid payment or to compel the other side to compromise its claim, the *Glamorganshire* but also shows the Courts' unwillingness to allow section 47 of OC1881 to be used prevent a meritorious case being heard. The case also provides a snapshot of contemporary commercial life on the China Coast with evidence of finance, banks' interest rate policy and proof that, even then,

---

140 Robertson to Hannen, 24 January 1882; FO656/49.

141 Chief Justice's Minute Book; FO1092/364.

142 *The Owners of the British Steamship 'Glamorganshire' v. The Master, Owners and Crew of the American Ship 'Clarissa B. Carver,'* and *The Owners of the 'Glamorganshire' v. S.D. Warren & Co.* (together, **the *Glamorganshire***); [1888] AC 454.

143 Order in Council, 13 June 1853. The first case was *Morris & Anor v. The Union Insurance Society of Canton* lodged with the Privy Council Office (**PCO**) on 7 March 1882 and dismissed on 30 October 1882 (see correspondence on those dates from PCO to the Supreme Court Registrar). This characteristic was also seen in early nineteenth century appeals from Australia where 'those who could most afford the cost and delay of appeals to England were in a strong position to obtain a favourable outcome even from cases they had apparently lost' by lodging an appeal to the Privy Council which was, subsequently, unpursued: Bruce Kercher, *Debt, Seduction and Other disasters: the birth of civil law in convict New South Wales* (Sydney: Federation Press, 1966), page 16.

commerce was exposed to exchange rate fluctuations whilst also reminding us just how common shipping accidents were.

The defendants went to the Supreme Court on three occasions: first, on a preliminary interlocutory point before the substantive hearing in HMCJ; second, in relation to the substantive decision (and, when they lost that appeal, they went to the Privy Council); before, third, appealing against HMCJ's assessment of damages. It took barely four months between the collision and HMCJ's judgment in the initial proceedings—despite the interlocutory appeal to Shanghai, and only a further six months before the Supreme Court heard the appeal on HMCJ's substantive decision; but, significant delays were produced by the Privy Council appeal when eighteen months elapsed before the case was heard by the Privy Council. Then, the plaintiffs drew out matters for a further year by arguments over quantum.

When the *ss. Glamorganshire* collided with the *Clarissa B. Carver*, an American sailing vessel off Kobe on 7 June 1885 the latter sank with the loss of its cargo of rags. When its owners and the cargo owners sought to recover their losses[144] in two separate actions brought in HMCJ sitting in Admiralty, the *Glamorganshire*'s owners counter-claimed and alleged the *Clarissa B. Carver* was responsible for the accident. One action involved the *Clarissa B. Carver*'s owners claiming for the loss of their vessel whilst the second action was brought by the owners of its cargo of rags in respect of their loss.

The case was set down quickly before HMCJ, but, even before the substantive case, the *Glamorganshire*'s owners demanded that HMCJ exercise its powers under OC1881 and OC1886 to require the *Clarissa B. Carver*'s owners to provide security in respect of their counter-claim. When HMCJ dismissed this motion on 7 July they appealed to the Supreme Court[145] where they were represented by Wilkinson whilst the plaintiffs relied upon written submissions.[146] The hearing of this interlocutory appeal commenced on 29 August before the full court of Rennie and Mowat but was adjourned in order to obtain Hannen's statement of his reasons for dismissing the defendants' motion.[147]

---

144 The cargo was valued at $22,000. The amount of the ship claim is not given but must have exceeded $35,000 for the defendants claimed the *Clarissa B. Carver* was worth only this amount.

145 Mowat to Hannen 8 August 1885 acknowledged receipt of the appeal on this motion; FO656/39.

146 Chief Judge's Minute Book for the hearing on 12 September 1885; FO1092/364.

147 In his judgment, Rennie admonished Hannen for considering that he was not obliged to submit his reasons along with the motion for appeal and minutes of the HMCJ hearing; Printed judgment delivered on 16 September 1885; FO656/39.

Hannen stated that his main reason for not ordering security to be given was that he was convinced it would practically amount to a denial of justice as it would be impossible for the plaintiffs to raise the amount of security required and he considered that, whether the motion was refused or granted, the *Glamorganshire*'s owners would not obtain any redress even if they were blameless.[148] When Supreme Court reconvened on 12 September Mowat was unavoidably absent[149] so Rennie proceeded to deal with the appeal alone. He held that, as he would not be justified in interfering with HMCJ's decision, the appeal must be dismissed.[150]

Both substantive actions were then heard together before Hannen in HMCJ who found in favour of the plaintiffs on all points in both actions on 12 and 20 October 1885 and he dismissed the *Glamorganshire*'s owners' counter-claim. In the cargo case, the defendants had attempted two lines of attack over and above challenging the facts claimed by the *Clarissa B. Carver*'s owners in the ship action: first, that the cargo-owners had no *locus* to bring their claim as they could not demonstrate unimpeachable title to the cargo as they had previously endorsed the bills of lading over to Baring Brothers, Hong Kong as security for related trade finance. When finding for the cargo owners on this point, Hannen offered to qualify his judgment by suspending payment until it was clear that payment would provide an absolute discharge of liability in respect of the cargo but the defendants rejected this offer.

The *Glamorganshire*'s owners' second technical attack was to attempt to non-suit the cargo-owners by claiming that their action should have been brought *in personam* and not *in rem* in Admiralty (i.e. against the *Glamorganshire*'s owners personally and with no right to attach the vessel itself). Hannen rejected this because the plaintiff's claim had been started in the ordinary way as an action *in rem*—by a threat of the arrest of the ship—and, by consent, bail was put in.[151]

Unsurprisingly, the defendants appealed both cases (including their counter-claims) to the Supreme Court. The grounds for appeal in the ship case were almost entirely factual (i.e that the *Clarissa B. Carver* was responsible for the accident—not the *Glamorganshire*); but, in the cargo case, two additional points were raised: first, that the respondents had not submitted to the Courts' jurisdiction as required by section 47 OC1881 and,

148 Hannen to Rennie, 1 September 1885; FO656/49.
149 Chief Judge's Minute Book for the hearing; FO1092/364.
150 Ibid.
151 Hannen to Rennie, 5 May 1886; FO656/49.

second, that HMCJ had improperly found that the respondents had proved their title to recover damages. The full Supreme Court (plus two merchant navy captains as nautical assessors) heard the appeals on 5 and 16 April 1886 when the appellants were represented by two counsel and the plaintiffs by one.[152]

The Supreme Court dismissed the appeals in two judgments on 10 April and 31 May 1886. The Supreme Court held that the appeal was totally unnecessary and ordered the Appellant to pay the costs of the appeal.[153] With regard to the argument that the American plaintiffs had not submitted to the Courts' jurisdiction, the Supreme Court held that the matter had been sufficiently dealt with by the Assistant Judge of HMCJ on summons and, no steps having been taken to have the order set aside or rescinded, no appeal to the Supreme Court could then be sustained on the point.[154] The case report does not explain the Supreme Court's reasoning for dismissing the other grounds for appeal but the Supreme Court did add a restriction to its decree in relation to the cargo claim to ensure that payment was not due until the various interests in, and claims on, the cargo were settled.[155]

Still resisting the inevitable, the *Glamorganshire*'s owners appealed to the Privy Council[156] on three grounds: first (and in relation to both claims), that both HMCJ and the Supreme Court had come to the wrong conclusions as to factual responsibility for the collision; and (in relation only to the cargo claim), second, that, because of the endorsed bill of lading, the cargo owners had not shown sufficient title to the cargo; and third, that HMCJ was not an Admiralty Court and, even if it were, it could not enter a reservation that the $22,000 damages on the cargo case were not payable until it was clear that payment was a complete discharge of the *Glamorganshire*'s owners from all liability regarding the cargo.[157]

The Privy Council appeal did not come on until 21 and 22 March 1888 when both sides were represented by leading counsel[158] before a four-man panel which gave an extempore judgment on 22 March. The Privy

152 Chief Judge's Minute Book for the hearing; FO1092/364.

153 Ibid.

154 Newspaper report included with FO656/39.

155 [1888] AC 454, pages 466/467.

156 The appeal papers were received by the Privy Council Office in September 1886; PCO to Supreme Court Registrar, 6 September 1886; FO656/65.

157 6.Asp.Mar.Law Cas.344, page 345.

158 Sir Walter Phillimore QC and H. Stokes for the appellants and Myburgh QC and Melsheimer for the respondents.

Council held that the questions regarding the ships' handling had been settled by the concurrent decisions of the lower Courts so that the *Glamorganshire*'s counsel felt unable to dispute the finding.[159] When the appellants' counsel attempted to argue that the *Clarissa B. Carver* had breached Maritime Regulations in the positioning of its starboard bow light, the Privy Council took the opinion of its nautical assessors and rejected these contentions.[160] As to the cargo action, the Privy Council held that the Supreme Court's restriction met exactly 'the justice of the case'[161] and so dismissed the appeal with costs against the appellant.

The Privy Council did not address the issue of HMCJ's jurisdiction and there is no evidence the point was even argued before the Privy Council.[162] It is difficult to avoid the impression that the appeal was entirely unmeritorious and the plaintiffs, who instructed the more well-known counsel and solicitors, had formulated a lengthy appeal petition simply to prolong the matter and even their counsel felt unable to argue many of its enumerated points.

The printed judgment was sent to Shanghai on 16 May 1888[163] but even this did not end the matter for the defendants then disputed the assessment of the damages. The HMCJ Registrar had held an enquiry in July 1886 into the question but it was objected to by the defendants who appealed first to the Judge who, with only one modification, affirmed it in October 1886 before again appealing to the Supreme Court. However, this appeal was not prosecuted until the outcome of the Privy Council appeal whereupon they petitioned the Supreme Court to vary the Registrar's Report first, to reduce the value of the *Clarissa B. Carver* to $35,000; second, to reduce the interest rate allowed from the date of HMCJ's original decision from 8% to 4%; and, third, to set the exchange rate between (silver-based) Dollars and (gold-based) US Dollars at 80 instead of 76.

The Supreme Court received this appeal in September 1888 but the case was not heard until 9 April 1889.[164] Yet again, the appellants lost when the Supreme Court held that a ship's value is 'always a difficult question'[165]

---

159 [1888]AC454, page 462.

160 Ibid.

161 Ibid, page 466.

162 Without further explanation of the appellant's reasoning for this point, it is difficult to comment given that OC1865 and OC1878 clearly constituted HMCJ as a Vice-Admiralty court.

163 PCO to Supreme Court; FO656/65.

164 See printed judgment in FO656/39.

165 Ibid.

but, as it was a factual question, the decision of the Registrar and the Judge would be upheld. As for the second point, the Judge had found that banks charged Europeans 8% whilst paying 5% on deposits and, despite the *Glamorganshire*'s owners arguing that 4% was the statutory rate in England, the Registrar had allowed 8% which was confirmed by the Judge as 'The practice in Asia has always been 8%'[166] whilst the third point, which had been argued strenuously on the first day, was not pursued.

The last, and most famous, appeal from Japan heard by the Privy Council also arose from a shipping collision and sinking. However, unlike the *Glamorganshire*, all the appeals to the Supreme Court and the Privy Council in the *Chishima cases* concerned interlocutory points and there was no hearing at all on the substantive facts.

166 Ibid.

CHAPTER SEVEN

THE *CHISHIMA—RAVENNA* COLLISION

The Shimonoseki Straits, scene of the Western Powers' bombardment of the *Choshu* rebels in 1864, were the setting, in 1892, for the incident which triggered the climax of the Japanese government's long-running battle to restrict and end British extra-territoriality in Japan.[1] The *Chishima kan*, a Japanese light cruiser of 741 tons,[2] was on the home-leg of its journey from Saint-Nazaire, where it had been constructed and handed over to the Imperial Japanese Navy, when, on 29 November 1892 off Matsuyama in Ehime *ken*, it collided with the *Ravenna*, a P&O steamer of 3,257 tons out of Kobe bound for Hong Kong, and sank immediately with the loss of 74 sailors out of a complement of 90 whilst the damaged *Ravenna* limped into Nagasaki. With echoes of the *Normanton* incident, the loss of the *Chishima* and so many lives was felt deeply in Japan, all the more so as its fleet consisted of only some 30 ships—many of which were unsea-worthy.

There was never any judicial determination of the facts surrounding the collision and the interlocutory proceedings of the ensuing court cases[3] overlapped with—if they did not encourage—the final moves in the minuet danced by the two governments to end extra-territoriality. After the preliminary hearings in the *Chishima cases*, Mutsu Munemitsu, approached Maurice de Bunsen, the *Chargé d'Affaires*, in the Summer of 1893 about re-opening the treaty re-negotiations and the court case went into a state of suspension whilst Aoki Shuzo negotiated the 1894 Treaty. Abolition of extra-territoriality and the Treaty's renegotiation had been discussed on and off for over ten years and would have occurred almost certainly at some stage during the 1890s even without this dispute; but it is

[1] Appendix VII provides a timeline of the events.

[2] The *Chishima kan* was designed by Louis-Émile Bertin, the French naval architect and, from 1886 to 1890, special foreign adviser to the Imperial Japanese Navy. It carried 11 guns and three torpedo tubes. Although completed at Saint-Nazaire on 1 April 1892 it had been commissioned formally into the Imperial Japanese Navy only on 24 November at Nagasaki.

[3] *The Imperial Japanese Government v. P&O* [1895] AC 644 (***IJG v. P&O***) (the ***Chishima case***) and *Tsune Kijima & Others v. P&O* (reported as *P&O v. Tsune Kijima & Others* [1895] AC661 (***P&O v. TK&O***) (the ***Tsune Kijima case***; together, the ***Chishima cases***).

conceivable that the eruption of this very public litigation helped to precipitate the final negotiations and concentrate both governments' minds on the need to settle the main question.

There was no agreement as to the precise events surrounding, or responsibility for, the collision so a somewhat straitened Japanese government, which had spent some 'seven to eight hundred thousand yen (£100,000–£115,000)'[4] on the *Chishima*'s construction, looked for compensation from P&O which, in turn, denied responsibility for the collision and claimed reimbursement for the *Ravenna*'s repairs. In a dispatch sent via Vancouver, de Bunsen saw immediately the makings of a major diplomatic problem.[5] From then, the matter escalated until the preliminary points reached the Privy Council which reviewed the foundations of Britain's extra-territorial regime in Japan.

The incident and the ensuing cases exemplify many practical aspects of the operation of British extra-territoriality in Japan and how the two authorities balanced mutual co-operation to make the system work whilst defending their own interests amidst the emotion of the British community in Japan (and on the China Coast) and equally nationalistic Japanese elements.

The Naval Court

The first stage, on the British side, was the holding of a Naval Court. The *Ravenna*'s captain applied formally to the Consul in Nagasaki for such a Naval Court upon the vessel's arrival there; but, from the beginning, it was considered more likely that the Naval Court would be held at Yokohama.[6] Its function was to enquire into the *Ravenna*'s part in the accident and the role of its officers. The four man Naval Court, held over five days in December 1892,[7] was presided over by HMS *Leander*'s captain and included Troup, a Lieutenant from HMS *Leander* and the master of a merchant vessel then in port. It acquitted the *Ravenna*'s master, chief officer and others on duty at the time 'of any blame for the collision but stated

[4] De Bunsen to Rosebery, 1 December 1892; FO46/480.

[5] Ibid. Regular mail to London went via Suez whereas urgent dispatches too long to be sent by telegram went via Vancouver, the Trans-Canadian Railway and the Atlantic.

[6] 7 December 1892; TRS&NE. Naval Courts were usually held in the nearest port (in this case, either Kobe from which the *Ravenna* had sailed, or Nagasaki into which it put for repairs) but, given the immense public—and governmental—interest, Yokohama was more convenient.

[7] 20–23 and 28 December 1892.

that, had the *Ravenna*'s engines been instantly stopped and reversed ... the effects of the collision might have been modified'.[8]

The Japanese government and local authorities traditionally co-operated with the British authorities and had always been helpful in similar enquiries in the past. In this case, the Japanese authorities were only partially co-operative. Lt. Kaburaki, the *Chishima*'s commander, and the other survivors were allowed to attend, and give evidence to, the Naval Court but the Japanese government refused to allow the *Ravenna*'s Japanese pilot (Kitano Yoshibei), who was navigating the ship at the time, to attend; instead, he was detained at Nagasaki where *The Rising Sun and Nagasaki Express* reported that he was being 'subjected to almost daily examination'.[9] Ultimately, he was prosecuted for manslaughter. The account of the incident and its aftermath given to the Naval Court makes gripping reading; but, the collision's cause all came down to the *Chishima*'s claim that it could not see the *Ravenna*'s navigation lights against the *Ravenna*'s claim that the *Chishima* was too far over in a very narrow shoaled passage and, when spotted by the *Ravenna*, continued to apply (and increased) a starboard helm despite the *Ravenna*'s signaling, correctly in accordance with the rules for approaching vessels, that it was turning to port. With both boats turning towards each other, the inevitable happened and they collided.

The Naval Court's principal focus was upon the British officers' competence, their conduct of the *Ravenna*'s navigation and their immediate actions to assist the sinking *Chishima*, and whether the *Ravenna* had complied with Board of Trade regulations in terms of lifeboats and other equipment. Its role was not to determine civil liability for the collision as between the two vessels. However, its importance to all may be seen by P&O's instructing Lowder to represent the *Ravenna*'s master and officers whilst several Japanese government officials and the Ministry of Justice's foreign legal adviser, Kirkwood, were in court to watch the proceedings. De Bunsen and Longford, then Tokyo Vice-Consul, were present at the Naval Court proceedings as a mark of respect to the host government's sensitivity to the incident. We also see the beginnings of the later manouevrings. When Lowder sought to question Kaburaki, the latter challenged Lowder's right to examine him and said he was there to assist the

---

8 De Bunsen to Rosebery, 2 January 1893; FO46/480. He enclosed the *Japan Weekly Gazette*'s account of the hearing, which is pasted into FO46/480. Unless otherwise indicated, references to the Naval Court proceedings are taken from this account.

9 21 December 1892.

Naval Court—not to be cross-examined. Troup explained that, when approached to allow the Japanese sailors to give evidence, the Prefect of Kanagawa had placed no restrictions on their being required to answer questions in the same way as other witnesses. A compromise was reached whereby the President ruled whether or not each of Lowder's questions was appropriate before Kaburaki responded to the President and not to Lowder.

The Japanese Press accused the *Ravenna* of bad seamanship and inhuman conduct in relation to the survivors from the *Chishima kan.*[10] In response to this criticism, Lowder challenged anyone to come forward with claims of lack of care for the survivors. The day after his principal evidence, Kaburaki returned to the witness stand to complain that he and the others had received poor treatment and went on to allege failures on the *Ravenna*'s master's part by detailed reference to Board of Trade Regulations. We must suspect that, overnight, Kaburaki had been briefed on these regulations—as how many Japanese naval officers would be familiar with their detailed sub-sections? This was early evidence of 'spin' to detract from possible Japanese seamanship failings highlighted in the earlier evidence and pressaged the legal battle to follow. There was little evidence for any general lack of care and the substance of Kaburaki's claims amounted to complaints that he was not placed immediately in a first class cabin as befitted his status as an officer and that the *Ravenna*'s master failed to give details of his port of registry and ports from and to which he was bound. Given the number of Japanese officials who came on board the *Ravenna* immediately after the accident (including the local prosecutor to interview the Japanese pilot), the master's failings could hardly be regarded as major defaults.

The only grounds for alleging a lack of even-handedness in the Naval Court proceedings was, as several Japanese newspapers complained, that Japanese witnesses were excluded from the courtroom while Kaburaki was giving evidence—a course which had not been followed with British witnesses. It is not clear from the accounts why the Naval Court took this step—which it took only part way through Kaburaki's evidence.[11]

When called as a witness, Kaburaki said that, although he spoke English, he wished to speak through an interpreter and the interpretation was done by 'Mr Kenny, the court interpreter.' The only dispute about

[10] 14 December 1892; TRS&NE.

[11] De Bunsen to Rosebery, 2 January 1893; FO46/480.

interpretation arose when the *Chishima*'s helmsman admitted hearing the *Ravenna*'s whistle and understanding its meaning (namely, that the *Ravenna* was turning to port). Kaburaki interjected that the translation was wrong, so Kenny put the question again and received the same answer and assured the court that there had been 'no mistake in translating.' Of course, there was no simultaneous translation for the benefit of the many Japanese Naval and governmental officials in the courtroom; but, Kirkwood was present and intervened twice during Kaburaki's examination by Lowder. Given the near verbatim newspaper accounts, we may assume that the Japanese side was fully briefed after each day's proceedings: a view supported by Kaburaki's return to the witness stand to complain about his treatment. There is no evidence that language created a great difficulty for the Japanese side. The only interpretation problems encountered were in finding an interpreter for one of the *Ravenna*'s Lascar sailors;[12] but, this would be no different in a court in Britain or in a Japanese court.

Contemporaneously, a Japanese Committee of Inquiry sat at the Marine Department in Tokyo. Initial Japanese newspaper reports suggested that, although of the view that the catastrophe was not due to the negligence or carelessness of the *Chishima*'s captain, officers or crew, they were not altogether without responsibility and the Committee was inclined to inflict certain disciplinary punishment on the captain and one or two of his subordinates for negligence of duty.[13] However, when the Committee's final findings were published, it found no proof of negligence by Kaburaki.[14] The *Ravenna*'s Japanese pilot was not so lucky for he was convicted of manslaughter by a Japanese criminal court in Nagasaki, away from the glare of Yokohama's foreign community, and fined the maximum penalty of $200 plus costs.[15] After this, we hear no more about him or who paid his fine and it is impossible to tell if he was simply the 'fall-guy' for the Japanese in this incident or whether his career was adversely affected by this incident and ruling.

---

12 It took three attempts to find someone in Yokohama who could perform an adequate job.

13 Translation of report in the *Nichi Nichi Shimbun* (described by de Bunsen as 'a Government organ' and transmitted by de Bunsen to Rosebery, 2 January 1893; FO46/480).

14 Translation of findings transmitted by de Bunsen to Rosebery, 6 February 1893; FO46/480.

15 22 February and 1 March 1893; TRS&NE and confirmed in De Bunsen to Rosebery, 6 March 1893; FO40/480.

The Legal Battle

Given this background, it is unsurprising that the Japanese government and P&O failed to reach any compromise on their respective claims. The emotional political background was heightened by the existence, since 1890, of an elected Diet in which many members clamoured for the abolition of all extra-territorial rights. Late 1880s Japan, with Bertin as its foreign adviser, had looked to France for its naval construction and espoused the *Jeune Ecole's* ideas of a *guerre de course* so, by the early 1890s, its naval forces consisted largely of small guard and coastal vessels. However, the Imperial Japanese Navy was beginning to look to increase its role, shape and size within the Japanese military and such new directions led to increasing budgetary disputes with the Diet. The loss of prestige which the Imperial Japanese Navy suffered as a result of the *Chishima kan*'s loss came on top of its cost overruns and poor performance—for which the French government had been obliged to compensate Japan. Designed to reach 22 knots, the *Chishima kan* could achieve only 19 knots and, despite being delivered a year late, it had sustained a number of unplanned repair stops on its delivery trip from France so that its original cost of ¥675,000 had increased to over ¥1 million. As Schencking said, the loss of the *Chishima kan* provided opposition members of the Diet with further ammunition with which to criticize the Japanese government.[16]

It was with this background that the Japanese government had an unenviable choice: to compromise its claim against P&O in any immediate settlement, to forego any chance of any recovery from P&O or to submit its claim to British courts sitting in Japan. If it pursued P&O, the Japanese government would be compelled to sue in the Courts as P&O was a British company. The Japanese authorities, at both a central and local level, had initiated litigation in the Courts before; but, this case emphasized more than any other the humiliation of extra-territoriality. Previous civil cases had been relatively routine or mundane and involved routine debt collection or smaller commercial disputes whereas this dispute involved a key instrument of state, namely a warship, and the drowning of many Japanese sailors.

The Japanese government chose to commence proceedings in Admiralty against P&O in HMCJ and, on 25 May 1893, in the name of The

[16] See David C. Evans and Mark R. Peattie, *Kaigun* (Annapolis, Naval Institute Press, 1997) chapter 1 and J. Charles Schencking, *Making Waves* (Stanford, Stanford University Press, 2005) pages 66 to 68.

Imperial Japanese Government, issued a writ claiming $850,000 damages for the *Chishima*'s loss. P&O sought to use every legal and procedural weapon at its disposal as it defended the claim. Apart from denying any responsibility on the part of the *Ravenna* and its officers—and arguing the *Chishima*'s responsibility—for the collision, P&O sought to counter-claim $100,000 for the *Ravenna*'s repairs. It is unlikely that, absent the Japanese suit, P&O would have made this claim, which it would have needed to pursue in the Japanese courts; but, given P&O's commercial interests in Japan, it must be doubtful. P&O's counter-claim must be seen, therefore, as part of the general cut and thrust of litigation.

The judicial hearings never addressed responsibility for the collision and all revolved around a preliminary procedural matter 'of considerable international interest'[17] which would test the limits of British extra-territoriality. Could P&O counter-claim in the Courts for the *Ravenna*'s repairs or must it commence a separate action in the Japanese courts? This seemingly minor procedural point was, to the Japanese government and all interested observers, the key question. If P&O succeeded in having the Courts hear its counter-claim, it would mean an extension of the extra-territorial regime and a lessening of Japan's own jurisdiction and sovereignty for a foreign court sitting in Japan would be able to adjudicate on claims against Japanese litigants—a result which all would construe as an opening towards a form of 'mixed court'.

Despite the extra-territorial regime's existence for over thirty years, the issue had never been decided in a Court; and the Japanese government had no intention of surrendering the point without a fight. By the late 1880s, the practice was that the Courts did not entertain counter-claims against Japanese plaintiffs for, if they were allowed, counter-claims might equally be allowed in Japanese courts—a result which British officialdom considered undesirable. Chapter 5 (Civil Jurisdiction) examined the broader background to counter-claims but, despite this late 1880s practice, it is unclear exactly when, or why, it was adopted for, despite the Legation's Second Secretary, Cecil Spring-Rice, instancing only the Blockley counter-claim against a Japanese defendant,[18] the records show the Courts had not always followed this line.

---

[17] De Bunsen to Rosebery, 4 July 1893; FO46/480.

[18] Memorandum prepared, in 1893, by Spring-Rice on the Courts' jurisdiction over counter-claims and enclosed with de Bunsen to Rosebery, 13 July 1893; FO46/480 (**Spring-Rice Memorandum**).

In 1873, Dohmen, when notifying the Japanese authorities that he had set down a Japanese plaintiff's claim, explained that he would hear the defendant's counter-claim at the same time as the Japanese plaintiff's claim[19] and, while there is no report of such a hearing, there is also no evidence that the Japanese authorities responded adversely to this way of proceeding. In 1877, *Kusumoto Matsutaka Gonchiji of Tokio Fu v. Arthur Blockley and Bridget Blockley* involved the Tokyo government's claim before Wilkinson in the Tokyo Court for $618 ground rent in respect of the Blockleys' Yedo Hotel in Tsukiji.[20] The Blockleys defended the claim, and counter-claimed for $5,000 damages, arguing that the Japanese government had violated their lease and injured their trade by allowing foreigners to reside elsewhere than in Tsukiji. At no point did the Japanese, who were represented by Lowder, argue that the Blockleys' counter-claim was inadmissible before the Court. The arguments on the Japanese side were twofold: technical and political. First, as a matter of privity of contract, the agreements as to foreigners' residence in Tokyo were between the Japanese government and the foreign Ministers and, as the Blockleys were not parties to the agreements, they could not enforce them. Second, the Japanese government's actions were an act of state for which it could not be sued; and it was on this second ground that Wilkinson found for the Japanese. He did not address the issue of the Blockley's ability to institute a counter-claim; but, in explaining the delay in his giving judgment, said that, although he thought the case an easy one, the US court at Yokohama had decided a similar case differently and that the US court's decision, whilst not binding, was entitled to respect. In 1880, the Kobe Court refused to entertain a counter-claim only because it arose from an entirely different matter;[21] with no suggestion that, otherwise, it could not have been brought.

Come 1883 and *Yukioke Shobei v. Whittall*, Hannen found for the plaintiff in HMCJ and explained that the defendant had brought no cross-action pursuant to which he could claim a set-off.[22] The Supreme Court, when allowing Whittall's appeal, re-iterated that he would have been entitled to a cross-action against the plaintiff for breach of contract; but, as there was none, it could not address the point.[23] The change in British practice

[19] Dohmen to Honda Takahonda, 31 December 1873; FO798/1.

[20] 3 and 17 February 31 March and 1 September 1877; JWM. By coincidence, counsel in that case had been Kirkwood and Lowder; but, now, in a reversal of their positions, Kirkwood advised the Japanese government whilst Lowder was for P&O.

[21] *Motono Shobei v. James Blackmore*, 7 October 1880; JDH.

[22] 8 December 1883; JWM.

[23] *Whittall v Yukioke Shobei*, 16 May 1884; NCHLR. Rennie's comments—which were *obiter*—could only have been made had he assumed that a counter-claim could lie.

between 1880 and 1883 may have been the result of the point being raised through the greater focus on the legal minutiae surrounding extra-territoriality at the contemporaneous Treaty revision discussions. However, even in 1889, we see a British defendant in Kobe seeking to raise a counter-claim against a Japanese plaintiff—which Longford refused because the defendant had already commenced an action in the Japanese courts.[24] Ambrose Berry Walford, for the Japanese government, in his submissions to HMCJ in the *Chishima case*, argued that this Kobe case was a precedent for rejecting counter-claims against Japanese plaintiffs; but, Mowat held that, on a proper construction of Longford's ruling, the counter-claim had been rejected because the defendant had already instituted proceedings in the local Japanese court.[25]

Against this, practice in other consular courts in Japan was different: a French consular court had recently permitted a counter-claim against a Japanese subject[26] and the Dutch and German legations supported this view;[27] but the USA, despite the case referred to earlier by Wilkinson, now favoured the Japanese interpretation of the *Ansei* treaties. Even among British practitioners in Japan and China, there was no unanimity of view on the question's legal merits. Spring-Rice (and Jamieson, the Assistant Judge, in his judgment in the Supreme Court) referred to Hornby and Rennie's conflicting views: where Hornby considered that such counter-claims did not lie whereas Rennie thought they were admissible. By the 1890s, practice in British courts in China was also different for counter-claims against Chinese plaintiffs were entertained.[28]

Why had the Courts not decided this issue during the preceding 35 years of extra-territorial jurisdiction? First, as the Privy Council recognized,[29] counter-claims were a relatively recent innovation in English court procedure.[30] Second, there seem to have been few instances where

[24] *Oshimaya & Co. v. H.E. Reynell & Co.*, 17 August 1889; JWM.

[25] The *Japan Weekly Advertiser* report referred to in footnote 32.

[26] Spring-Rice Memorandum. The result was much diplomatic correspondence and ongoing discrimination by the Japanese government against the successful individual.

[27] De Bunsen to Rosebery, 13 July 1893; FO46/480.

[28] An NCH editorial claimed that 'the established practice of the Supreme Court in Shanghai has always been to allow such counter-claims' when commenting upon Supreme Court proceedings in *Yuan Tse-yuan v. Major Bros. Ltd* after the Privy Council's judgment in the *Chishima case*. The plaintiff withdrew his claim and Wilkinson, for the defendant, withdrew its counter-claim so the Supreme Court was not compelled to decide the issue for China going forward; 20 September 1895; NCH.

[29] *IJG v. P&O*, page 655.

[30] The Admiralty Courts Act 1861 provided for counter-claims in the Admiralty courts after 1861 and the Judicature Act, 1873 provided for counter-claims generally after 1873.

the issue arose and, after, around 1880 at least, the Courts seem to have operated on the basis that all claims against Japanese defendants should be referred to the Japanese courts—an approach supported by both Parkes and Plunkett when they had assured successive Japanese Foreign Ministers that neither OC1881 nor OC1886 was intended to extend British jurisdiction beyond the previously existing limits. Although each qualified his assurances as being subject to reference to the government back home, neither reference had elicited any response from London.[31]

The question was only raised now because P&O—not the Japanese government—raised it and it was P&O that initiated the appellate process when HMCJ rejected its attempt to bring the counter-claim. After the Supreme Court decision in P&O's favour, the Japanese government could hardly fail to take the matter on appeal. It had started the litigation and, whilst it might have preferred to tackle the question on an inter-governmental basis (by seeking the Foreign Secretary's ruling under section 4 of Foreign Jurisdiction Act 1890 which required him to determine disputes as to jurisdiction), it had little option but to follow through the legal process to its conclusion and turn to diplomacy only if it failed in the legal processes.

The costs and inconvenience involved in any appeal to the Supreme Court—let alone the Privy Council—were enough to deter all but the most deep-pocketed of litigants: and, even then, the dispute needed to justify the appeal. At over £100,000, the Japanese claim was the largest brought before the Courts and P&O's would-be counter-claim for £10,000 one of the larger other claims. Given the lack of any binding decision and the absence of agreement amongst British legal practitioners on the question, it would have been surprising had P&O not raised a counter-claim as part of its defence. On the other hand, the Japanese government saw immediately that, were HMCJ to allow a counter-claim, it could lead to a wider mixed court regime and, having received assurances from two successive British Ministers that OC1881 and OC1886 were not intended to extend the Treaty, it would inevitably treat any decision to permit the counter-claim as an exercise in bad faith.

The near verbatim report in the *Japan Weekly Advertiser* provides a good description of the proceedings in HMCJ.[32] P&O's first procedural

[31] De Bunsen to Rosebery, 4 July 1893; FO 46/480.

[32] Sent by de Bunsen to Rosebery on 4 July 1893 and pasted into the file; FO46/480. Unless otherwise indicated, descriptions of, and quotes from, the proceedings in HMCJ are taken from this.

point was that the plaintiff, 'The Imperial Japanese Government', was such a 'vague and ill defined body' that it had no standing to bring any claim and its claim should be dismissed.[33] After discussion, P&O's counsel accepted that this was simply a means of identifying the Emperor, who, as sovereign, owned the warship.

Lowder, for P&O, next argued that, as a foreigner, the Emperor should enter a formal submission to the Court's jurisdiction and provide security for costs and damages as required by Article 47 of OC1881, and, unless this were done, the case should be dismissed. In response, Kirkwood argued that Article 3 of OC1881 defined 'foreigner' as 'a subject of the Mikado of Japan' and, as the Emperor was clearly not a subject, it could not apply to him. In support, he referred to Salisbury's confirmation to Count Inouye (Japanese Foreign Minister), in April 1887, that 'foreigner' in OC1881 and OC1886 did not include the Japanese government and there was no intention to require the Japanese government to submit formally to the Courts' jurisdiction;[34] but Lowder dismissed this confirmation, and the assurances from Parkes and Plunkett to the Japanese government in relation to OC1881 and OC1886, as 'merely the opinion of a Government ... not a decision of a Court of Law'. Mowat again overruled P&O's arguments and held that the Emperor was not a 'foreigner' for the purposes of OC1881 and, therefore, need not enter a formal submission or provide security.

After these initial points were dealt with in the early sittings, most of the discussion revolved around the Treaty, the Orders in Council and the Rules and concerned the Courts' jurisdiction to consider counter-claims against Japanese plaintiffs and whether, if such counter-claims were permissible, the Courts could—or should—be ordered to provide security under the Rules.

P&O relied on two principal arguments: first that Rennie had decided that the Courts could not enquire behind, but were bound by, the Orders in Council[35]—and must, therefore, order such a formal submission and provision of security. In the alternative, English law provided that, where a foreign sovereign voluntarily entered the British courts as a plaintiff, he waived his sovereign immunity and submitted to the court's jurisdiction. The Japanese response was that the Emperor was in a different position as

---

33 Precedents existed for the Japanese government suing under such nomenclature: e.g. *The Imperial Japanese Government v. Francis August Cope and William Petrine Mitchell*, a dispute over land title which went on appeal from HMCJ to the Supreme Court in 1881; FO1092/364.

34 Spring-Rice Memorandum.

35 *Tai Wan Wah v. Adamson Bell*, 16 August 1884; NCH.

he was compelled, by the Treaty, to bring his claim in the Courts. Further, a counter-claim was admissible only where an original action could be brought and, again by the Treaty, no original action could be brought by P&O in the Courts; only in the Japanese courts. Rather as an afterthought, on the final day of argument, Walford argued that, as the collision occurred within Japanese territorial waters, Japanese law must apply—even in a dispute heard before a British court. Under Japanese law, the Emperor could do no wrong and was immune from suit. Thus, even if a counter-claim were possible, it could not be brought in this case because the Emperor could not, as a matter of Japanese law, be held liable.

Whatever he decided, Mowat would incur the odium of either the Japanese (with all its negative political, commercial and diplomatic consequences) or the majority of the British community in Japan (which backed extra-territoriality); so, he avoided the question. On 3 July 1893, in a reserved judgment after four days' of hearing spread over the previous month, he dismissed P&O's application to institute a counter-claim by seizing upon Walford's last point to extricate himself from his unenviable position. He held that, as the disaster occurred within Japanese territorial waters, Japanese law applied and, as, by Japanese law, the Emperor was above that law and unactionable, no original action (and, therefore, no counter-claim) could be brought. This left the admissibility of counter-claims against Japanese plaintiffs as an open question. By describing Walford's final point as 'the only valid argument', Mowat implicitly accepted that counter-claims could be brought against Japanese plaintiffs but had sought to avoid diplomatic friction by not deciding the point.

Lowder announced immediately P&O's intention to appeal to the Supreme Court. Meanwhile, de Bunsen wrote again to Rosebery repeating the history of the question and warned that Rosebery would be compelled to decide the point politically if the Japanese raised it under the Foreign Jurisdiction Act 1890.

Both parties strengthened their teams for the appeal. For P&O, Lowder was joined by Francis Q.C. and A.P. Stokes (both from Hong Kong) and the Japanese government instructed Wilkinson and his son to join Kirkwood. The appeal was heard over four days (10–14 October 1893) before the Supreme Court adjourned to consider its judgment which was handed down on 25 October. The Chief Justice's notebook provides only skimpy details of the arguments and simply notes the 'appeal motion granted with costs here and in the court below'[36] whilst the Assistant Judge's

[36] Chief Justice's notebook entry, 25 October 1893; FO1092/364.

notebook is briefer still with just a list of cases cited in argument;[37] but a near verbatim *North China Daily News* report of proceedings is pasted into the Foreign Office file.[38]

There was much argument as to the construction of the Orders in Council and whether they took precedence over the Treaty and, in view of Mowat's *ratio decidendi*,[39] whether the Inland Sea constituted part of the High Seas and, so, was amenable to Admiralty jurisdiction. On this final point, Francis Q.C. claimed that Mowat himself had raised the point and Lowder had not been prepared for it and so had not argued it. He compared the Inland Sea with the Solent where, notwithstanding that it was English territorial water, Admiralty jurisdiction applied because it was a public highway. Both parties re-iterated their earlier points with Kirkwood stressing the Treaty to suggest that the Emperor's appearance before a Court was not the same as a foreign sovereign appearing before a court in England whereas Francis Q.C. relied upon Rennie's decision that Orders in Council prevailed over the Treaty and, finally, the general principle that a sovereign who entered an English court was deemed to submit to its jurisdiction.

During argument, both judges conceded that the issue of whether counter-claims could lie against Japanese (or Chinese) plaintiffs had never been decided specifically in the Supreme Court. While Hannen adverted to the *Blockley case*, Jamieson addressed the *Fusing v. Ocean*[40] and *Hochung v. Lapwing*,[41] which were the two relevant Supreme Court cases. In the former, Hornby had refused an attempt by the defendant (whose counsel had been Hannen) to file a counter-claim due to its being out of time—although Hornby had expressed doubts as to whether any counter-claim could lie against a Chinese plaintiff. In *Hochung v. Lapwing*, the Supreme Court had allowed a counter-claim against the Chinese plaintiff (and required the plaintiff to provide security)—but the plaintiff had not argued the point. When the Privy Council had then considered the case on other points, the plaintiff had, again, not taken the point and neither had the Privy Council itself suggested that the counter-claim could not lie.

---

[37] Assistant Judge's notebook entry, 10 October 1893; FO1092/365.

[38] Sent by de Bunsen to Rosebery, 8 November 1893; FO46/480. Unless otherwise indicated descriptions of, and quotes from, the Supreme Court proceedings are based on this.

[39] For precedent purposes, a court's judgments are analysed into *ratio decidendi*—the reason for the decision—which constitutes binding precedent, and *obiter dicta* which, being commentary, are not.

[40] 29 May NCHLR.

[41] (1883) LR 7 App 512.

De Bunsen's earlier warning of potential diplomatic difficulties was timely for Hannen held that the Inland Sea was the highway of nations and, therefore, HMCJ had jurisdiction in Admiralty where maritime law made the Emperor responsible for the actions of his servants on board his vessels. Further, as Japan had initiated the proceedings, it could be taken to have submitted to the HMCJ's jurisdiction and, accordingly, was amenable to counter-suit. HMCJ's rules of procedure and OC1881 and OC1886 warranted giving leave for a counter-claim and ordering that security be given and, although without explaining himself, said that 'those rules and orders did not exceed the provisions of the treaties'. Further, the court had an inherent jurisdiction to allow the counter-claim to be heard and to order that security be given. Jamieson reached the same end conclusion but for different reasons. In essence, he conceded that the Inland Sea was Japanese territorial water but said it was also a public highway and, therefore, subject to Admiralty law and jurisdiction. He also held that, until it was overruled, the Supreme Court was bound by its practice in *Hochung v. Lapwing* of allowing counter-claims against Chinese plaintiffs. Whilst he accepted that the Emperor was not a subject for the purposes of OC1881, it must be the case that either the Rules or the rules of the higher courts in England applied to the current proceedings (he thought the latter) and, so, agreed that the Emperor, having submitted to the jurisdiction, was amenable to counter-claim.

Japanese reaction was swift and, the next day, the Japanese government sought the Supreme Court's leave to appeal to the Privy Council which was granted on 6 November upon its paying $2,500 into court by way of security.[42] De Bunsen informed Rosebery that the Japanese would regard a final decision of a counter-claim against them as constituting a violation of the Treaty[43] before forwarding Japan's protest against Hannen's judgment that the Inland Sea is the Highway of Nations.[44]

In London, realization of the diplomatic problems dawned and the Foreign Office sought advice from the Law Officers and Sir Edward Hertslet—Librarian and Keeper of Foreign Papers within the Foreign Office and a leading international law specialist. The Law Officers adopted a narrow, interpretative view of the Treaty and, in backing the Japanese government's interpretation, opined that OC1881 and OC1886 extended

[42] No appeal lay as of right in respect of preliminary points—only certain final decisions. Therefore, a disappointed party needed to apply to the Supreme Court for permission to appeal its decision to the Privy Council.

[43] De Bunsen to Rosebery, 8 November 1893; FO46/480.

[44] De Bunsen to Rosebery, 13 November 1893; FO46/480.

the Courts' jurisdiction in Japan beyond what could be justified by the Treaty and all British claims against a Japanese should be prosecuted in the Japanese courts.[45] Hertslet advised that the Inland Sea was Japanese inland territorial water.[46]

While the case rumbled on in the background as a political and diplomatic headache for both parties, Aoki was negotiating the 1894 Treaty with Rosebery and Kimberley. It was signed on 16 July 1894 and, *inter alia*, abolished British extra-territoriality in Japan as from 1899. After the 1894 Treaty had been settled (but not signed), the Privy Council Office informed the Foreign Office that the appeal papers had been received and a hearing was expected in November 1894.[47] In fact, the hearing took place only in May 1895. There is nothing in the files to explain the delay to May 1895; it may have been due simply to P&O's need to prepare its appeal against the Supreme Court's decision in the *Tsune Kijima case* and a general wish to await the House of Lords' decision in *Smurthwaite v. Hannay* on the principal point in that appeal (which decision was not handed down until 3 August 1894[48]) and, with court vacations, the consequent knock-on effects.

In November 1894, the Foreign Office asked the Treasury Solicitor to instruct the Law Officers to appear, as *amici curiae*, before the Privy Council 'to watch the case on behalf of HMG' in view of the questions it raised with regard to the Inland Sea and construction of the Orders in Council.[49]

The Privy Council heard the appeal over four days in May 1895. Its importance to all concerned is reflected in a seven man Committee (including the Lord Chancellor (Herschell)) hearing the case[50] and the attendance of both Law Officers supported by a Junior as *amici curiae* on behalf of the Crown and each of IJG and P&O fielding two Leaders and two Juniors.

---

45 Law Officers to Rosebery, 12 December; 1893 FO46/480. This advice was given notwithstanding that their predecessors as Law Officers in 1881 had approved the draft of OC1881—see pages 29–30.

46 Hertslet to Rosebery, 16 December 1893; FO46/480.

47 PCO to Foreign Office, 5 July 1894; FO46/480. The PCO had received the Supreme Court transcript in January 1894 (PCO to Supreme Court Registrar, 9 January 1894; FO656/65) but nothing explains why it took a further six months before formally notifying the Foreign Office.

48 See page 301.

49 Foreign Office to Treasury Solicitor, 24 November 1894; FO46/480.

50 The more usual composition was a five or six man committee. Of the 31 reported Privy Council cases in [1895] AC, only seven had a seven man committee (two had eight). Whilst the Lord Chancellor sat on 20 appeals, he delivered the judgment in only eight, including *IJG v. P&O*.

The Japanese argument was the familiar one that HMCJ was, ultimately, a creation of the Treaty and the Treaty's precise terms gave it no jurisdiction to hear any case against a Japanese; albeit that Japan conceded that facts which might support a counter-claim could be adduced by P&O to defend its claim. Furthermore, as the sovereign, the Emperor—like the Crown in the UK—was immune from suit in Japan. Then, for the first time in the three hearings, we see the 'threat' argument; namely, if, under the Treaty, any discretion were vested in the Courts to hear a counter-claim against Japanese plaintiffs, it must follow that a similar discretion was vested in the Japanese courts to entertain counter-claims by Japanese defendants in actions brought by British plaintiffs. Consequently, British subjects might find themselves rendered amenable to the jurisdiction of the Japanese courts to an extent not contemplated by the Treaty.

In all the controversy surrounding the case one must recognize that P&O's position was not without justification. Its essential point was that, by entering a suit in HMCJ, Japan had submitted to HMCJ's jurisdiction for the purposes of that case and all matters arising out of it. This would be the position in England—even where the plaintiff was a sovereign. P&O argued that it would be unfair and inconvenient if the same incident gave rise to claims in two separate courts in different jurisdictions; the relevant Orders in Council were clear and, following Rennie in *Tai Wan Wah v. Adamson Bell*, the Courts could not go behind them and HMCJ was obliged to allow the counter-claim. Even if the Japanese interpretation of the Treaty were right, it dealt only with claims by Japanese subjects and as, patently, the Emperor was not a subject, the normal English procedural rules applied.

Herschell delivered the Privy Council's reserved judgment on 3 July and, whilst dressed up in legal argument and analysis, one can see the wider political considerations behind it. In its opening paragraph, the Privy Council looked beyond Japan (where, for practical purposes, any decision was of time limited value) to China by describing the 'appeal ... of considerable importance in relation to ... British Consular Courts in China and Japan'.[51] If P&O's contention were well founded, 'it must apply equally where a British subject brings an action in a Japanese or Chinese Court against a Japanese or Chinese subject ... the effect would be to deny the British subject any redress in the local Court except upon terms of his submitting to its arbitrament a dispute which under the treaty was

[51] *IJG v. P&O*, page 650.

reserved exclusively for the determination of the British Consular Court. Such a proceeding would be ... clearly inconsistent with treaty rights.'[52] The Privy Council described Hannen's propositions on the Inland Sea as 'obviously open to serious controversy',[53] and said that, while it was unnecessary to decide the question, they should not be regarded as being sanctioned.[54]

IJG v. P&O is the only reported case which examines the origins and reasons behind extra-territorial jurisdiction in Japan. The Privy Council observed that 'The considerations which led to ... the extra-territorial jurisdiction of the Courts of the defendants' own nation are not in doubt. Such treaties with Eastern nations were well known, and ... had their origin in a distrust of the local tribunals and of the systems of law administered by them. Eastern ideas in these respects were completely out of harmony with the views of Western civilization' before recognizing the changes in Japan and the recent 1894 Treaty by conceding that 'During recent years a great change has been wrought in Japan. The circumstances which gave rise to the desire for extra-territorial jurisdiction are ceasing or have ceased.'[55]

Were P&O's claim not set up by way of counter-claim, the Courts would have no jurisdiction and the proper forum would be a Japanese court.[56] Whilst the Treaty gave the Courts exclusive jurisdiction over complaints against British subjects so 'with claims against a Japanese subject, the Courts ... of that country are ... alone competent to deal'.[57] It dismissed P&O's argument that, by bringing his claim in the Courts, the Emperor had elected his tribunal and must take the consequences of that election as 'altogether a false view of the situation. It is not a matter of election ... He has no choice'.[58]

The Privy Council accepted that, by dis-allowing counter-claims, it might cause hardship and inconvenience to British defendants, but it was the price that they must pay for immunity from suit in the Japanese courts. Britons could not claim the advantage of the Courts' exclusive jurisdiction and, concurrently, object to their limited jurisdiction. The Privy Council dismissed P&O's claim that the Treaty did not apply to the Emperor as a

52 Ibid, page 657.
53 Ibid, page 652.
54 Ibid, page 651.
55 Ibid, page 654.
56 Ibid, page 655.
57 Ibid.
58 Ibid, page 656.

plaintiff for 'the treaties must be interpreted according to their manifest spirit and intention'.[59]

Despite so much argument before all courts having been expended on the terms of the Orders in Council and the Rules, the Privy Council expressed no opinion upon them as it was clear that they could not confer upon the Courts a wider jurisdiction than that conferred by the Treaty.[60]

Having vindicated the Japanese government in its interpretation and application of the Treaty, the Privy Council flagged the law in Admiralty whereby, if the *Chishima* were partly to blame for the collision, it would succeed in recovering only one half of the damage it had suffered before saying it was unnecessary to decide now how the law would be applied to this case. It is difficult to read these remarks, which are clearly *obiter dicta*, as anything other than a warning to the Japanese government as to the likelihood of ultimate success for its full claim and an encouragement to consider its position as regards the substantive claim.

The Drowned Sailors

Whilst the Chishima case has received considerable attention over the years, the claims by relatives of the drowned sailors—Tsune Kijima (and 61 other plaintiffs or groups of plaintiffs)—for damages against P&O have received no attention. None of the literature on the *Chishima case* refers to the *Tsune Kijima case* but it also reached the Privy Council and it illuminates aspects of the system and completes the context of the decisions in the *Chishima case*. As with *IJG v. P&O*, no hearing addressed the question of responsibility for the collision. All the hearings concerned a procedural point: namely, whether or not the Rules (and, to the extent they were silent on the question, the rules of procedure in the English courts) permitted the joinder in one suit of different and distinct causes of action not being causes of action by and against the same parties.

Some twelve months after the collision, on 23 November 1893—and after the Supreme Court's decision in the *Chishima case*—the plaintiffs issued proceedings in HMCJ and joined their claims together in a single suit. P&O applied immediately for the suit's dismissal with costs arguing that distinct causes of action were joined improperly in the petition. Whilst each of the representatives of the drowned sailors might have a

[59] Ibid, pages 657 and 658.
[60] Ibid, page 658.

separate cause of action against P&O (albeit arising from the same facts), the Rules did not allow a group of plaintiffs with separate causes of action to be joined together as co-plaintiffs in one action; they should each have brought a separate action.[61]

HMCJ granted P&O's application whereupon the plaintiffs appealed to the Supreme Court which heard their appeal on 16 April 1894. Although P&O was represented at the appeal, the plaintiffs were unrepresented.[62] In a reserved judgment on 23 April 1894, the Supreme Court, applying the recent judgment of the Court of Appeal in England in *Hannay v. Smurthwaite*,[63] granted the appeal saying the Court had a discretion and 'under all the circumstances of the case that discretion should be exercised in favour of the plaintiffs'.[64] On 28 April 1894, P&O applied *ex parte* for leave to appeal to the Privy Council. The application was adjourned twice until 30 May 1894 (presumably, to give the plaintiffs notice of the application) when it was granted against P&O's depositing $1,000 as security for costs.[65]

P&O's Privy Council appeal in this case was heard immediately upon the conclusion of the hearing in *IJG v. P&O* on 28 May 1895; but its lesser importance can be seen immediately by Lord Hobhouse withdrawing thereby reducing the court to six judges whilst P&O was represented by only a Leader and Junior and the British government was unrepresented. As in the Supreme Court, the Respondents 'were not represented at the bar, but their case was very fully and very ably stated in a written argument addressed to the Supreme Court'.[66] On 20 July 1895 (17 days after the *IJG v. P&O* judgment), the reserved judgment was delivered by Lord MacNaghten—not Lord Herschell (who had heard the case as Lord Chancellor, but no longer held that office due to the fall of Rosebery's administration). The Privy Council followed the House of Lords' recent judgment in *Smurthwaite v. Hannay*,[67] which had reversed the Court of

---

[61] Different causes of action could be joined only where the plaintiff and defendant were the same—not where there was a common set of facts giving rise to separate causes of action by different plaintiffs.

[62] The Assistant Judge's notebook records that: 'The Appellants have filed a written argument'; FO1092/365.

[63] [1893] 2QB 412.

[64] *P&O v. TK&O*, page 662. Neither the Chief Justice nor the Assistant Judge's notebook (FO1092/366 and FO1092/365 respectively) explains why the Supreme Court decided to exercise its discretion.

[65] Chief Justice's notebook; FO1092/366. The PCO acknowledged receipt of the appeal on 8 August 1894; PCO to Supreme Court Registrar; FO656/65.

[66] *P&O v. TK&O*, page 663.

[67] [1894] AC 494.

Appeal judgment upon which the Supreme Court had relied, and held that 'it is clear that such a suit as the present is not and never was maintainable in England'.[68] Consequently, the appeal was allowed with costs.

Settlement

The road was now clear for HMCJ to hear the substantive action in the *Chishima case* which had been set down for hearing in October 1895. For commercial reasons, however, P&O had no wish to engage in lengthy litigation with the Japanese government and requested Viscount Selborne, a director of P&O who was Salisbury's son-in-law and had been appointed recently as Under-Secretary of State in the Colonial Office, to seek Salisbury's assistance in sounding out the Japanese Minister in London with a view to a settlement on the basis of P&O's paying a maximum of £10,000 (a mere 10% of the Japanese claim).[69] After a period of haggling over the amount, the Japanese government agreed, in September 1895, to a settlement whereby P&O paid £10,000 compensation plus the Japanese government's costs in relation to the counter-claim.[70] On 1 October 1895, both parties applied to the Supreme Court for the release of their respective security deposits, which release was ordered.[71] The settlement occasioned 'some surprise'[72] in Japan and the perceived disadvantageous terms were used as a stick by the opposition with which to beat the government.

---

[68] *P&O v. TK&O*, page 665.

[69] Freshfields & Williams (P&O's solicitors) to Selborne (2 August 1895; FO46/480) enclosing two drafts of a memorandum (**P&O Memorandum**) outlining the background and legal position regarding P&O's potential liabilities and P&O's thinking about a possible settlement. The first draft had been prepared internally by P&O, but the second (a variant on this) had been prepared by its London counsel.

[70] Correspondence between Foreign Office, Selborne, P&O and Salisbury, August and September 1895; FO46/480. Although the Foreign Office memorandum from Sir Thomas Henry Sanderson (Permanent Under-Secretary of State at the Foreign Office) to Sir F. Sutherland of P&O (3 September 1895; FO46/480) refers to 'the costs of the recent suit' (implying all the Japanese government's costs), P&O clarified quickly that it was limited to the 'costs arising out of the proceedings in the matter of the counter-claim' (P&O to Salisbury, 4 September 1895; FO46/480). Japanese nationalists criticized the Japanese government when they realized the limited nature of the costs reimbursement—a point that the Japanese government had tried to cloak; Chang 1984, page 101.

[71] Chief Justice's notebook; FO1092/366.

[72] A copy of the *Japan Gazette* (date uncertain) enclosed with Satow to Salisbury, 24 September 1895; FO46/480.

What the Chishima Cases *Show*

The *Chishima cases* are not representative of the usual day to day proceedings in the Courts or the administration of British justice in Japan. Nevertheless, they provide a number of insights into British legal practice in Japan and *IJG v. P&O* provides our only judicial insight into the reasons and basis for British extra-territoriality in Japan; but despite suggesting, at all levels, that external influences played a part in the Courts' decisions, neither case gives substantial support for the contemporary Japanese views that the whole system was riddled with an anti-Japanese, pro-British bias. The parties' sophisticated tactics and legal arguments show that British legal practice in Japan, which could not be divorced from that in China, was not a low calibre affair.

By the 1890s both British and Japanese authorities knew that extra-territoriality's days were numbered in Japan but both needed to make the system work. Practical co-operation and assistance with respect shown by each authority to the other was balanced, on both sides, by the need to attend to their respective community pressures. On the Japanese side, this meant being sensitive to any possibility that the existing regime's boundaries would be extended. The Japanese government allowed the *Chishima*'s officers and crew to appear before the Naval Court—but prevented the *Ravenna*'s pilot from giving evidence (and prosecuted him). Although one can understand why domestic pressures constrained the Japanese government to pursue P&O for compensation, it is not clear why it litigated as opposed to using diplomatic/commercial pressure.

Even though nothing suggests that it would have initiated a claim against Japan for the *Ravenna*'s repairs,[73] once the court battle was commenced, P&O had little option but to mount an aggressive defence and, as part of such defence, to raise a counter-claim which could only improve the ultimate outcome for it. Unlike the great majority of defendants in the Courts, P&O could fund the legal costs involved and was sufficiently important that the British government would have been obliged to support it against any unfair pressure from the Japanese government (unlike the successful French counter-claimant[74]).

---

[73] In thanking Salisbury for his influence in obtaining a settlement, P&O said that it would have been willing to settle long ago 'if the magnitude of [the] claim had not been such as to render any other course impracticable than to fight that claim *á l'outrance*'. P&O to Salisbury, 4 September 1895; FO46/480.

[74] See footnote 26.

For the Japanese government, defeat on its substantive claim could always be put down (justifiably or not) to bias and unfairness on the Courts' part; but, the right of foreign defendants to raise counter-claims against them by Japanese plaintiffs in the Courts went to the heart of extra-territoriality and no Japanese government could allow this point to pass without a fight.

Only the *Hartley cases* compare with *IJG v. P&O* in terms of legal significance for the extra-territorial regime. Although raising an equally critical issue, they were 'smaller' in substance whereas this dispute was a 'big' case in financial terms and the point of principle was as—if not more—important than the sums involved. Its importance and legal complexity are shown by the Legation having Spring-Rice prepare his memorandum, which covered the entire history of counter-claims in Japan, whilst, in London, the Law Officers, Hertslet and Streatfield advised the British government.

The alertness of the legal community in Japan to English legal developments is demonstrated by the *Tsune Kijima case* being brought so soon after the Court of Appeal's decision in *Hannay v. Smurthwaite*. It is, however, difficult to view the *Tsune Kijima case* as anything other than a tactical device by the Japanese government to pressurize P&O in pursuit of its own claim. It is unlikely that the relatives of the drowned sailors would have united to pursue a claim (let alone pursue, and fund, an appeal to the Supreme Court or enter a defence to P&O's appeal in the Privy Council) on their own initiative or without the acquiescence (if not positive encouragement) of the Japanese government. The case's timing supports this view. Proceedings were issued in HMCJ in November 1893 just days after the Supreme Court had granted IJG permission to appeal to the Privy Council in *IJG v. P&O* and some three months after the Court of Appeal's decision in *Hannay v. Smurthwaite* allowing joinder in similar cases[75] (i.e. shortly after details of the judgment would have reached Japan in the normal course).

Had the *Tsune Kijima case* not been merely a tactic in the Japanese government's armoury, one must ask why Tsune Kijima and the other plaintiffs had not issued separate proceedings before this time or, even, why they did not do so immediately upon HMCJ's granting P&O's application to dismiss the joinder. Either course would have been a more certain route to bring P&O to account for their claims had the action been genuine and

[75] 11 August 1893; [1893] 2QB 412.

not tactical. However, one must wonder why, if the aim were to apply the maximum legal pressure on P&O, 60 separate actions had not been instituted—either contemporaneously with the Japanese government's own action or immediately upon the Supreme Court's decision. Was it a question of cost? There is no explanation; but, the launching of a multiplicity of actions would have created an administrative headache for P&O (and, perhaps, also for the Japanese government's legal team). This reinforces the idea that the claim by the drowned sailors' relatives was never intended as a serious claim but only ever as a tactical distraction for P&O.[76]

Each party played the litigation game aggressively and involved leading legal players in their fight and, in November 1893, the Ministry of Marine established a six man committee headed by Hozumi Nobushige[77] to advise it on the Privy Council appeal. Both *Chishima cases* give the lie to general criticisms of the competence and calibre of the administration of justice in the Courts and cast a favourable light on HMCJ for its decisions in both cases were upheld by the Privy Council—albeit, in *IJG v. P&O*, on different grounds—whilst those of the Supreme Court were overturned.

The tactics employed by both sides would not have been out of place in the most sophisticated legal arena thus demonstrating that legal practice in the Courts and on the China Coast was not a backward, low grade affair. Given the Courts' practice of not taking counter-claims against Japanese defendants, P&O's raising one—and arguing that OC1881 and OC1886 superseded the Treaty—does not suggest a low calibre or untrained legal community; quite the reverse. The sophistication can be seen by the number (and comparative obscurity) of the cases cited, particularly by P&O's counsel, in the Supreme Court on submission to the jurisdiction (particularly by sovereigns), Admiralty law, the definition of the high seas, and the area of counter-claims and by the fact that P&O raised no new lines of argument before the Privy Council.

P&O took every point that it could before HMCJ to have the *Chishima case* dismissed before applying the tactical and wider political pressure of the counter-claim. It was brave for P&O first to seek to strike out the Japanese claim on the basis that IJG was a 'vague and ill defined body' and to suggest that the Emperor should sign personally a submission to HMCJ's jurisdiction. Legal ingenuity was also shown by making the point that, as

76 This view that the *Tsune Kijima case* was merely a tactical adjunct to the *Chishima case* may explain why it has received no coverage in the commentaries.

77 Hozumi, Professor of Law at Imperial University, had been called to the Bar by Middle Temple in 1879 and was an expert in Western laws.

the Emperor was not a subject, he was outside the terms of the Treaty and, therefore, within the general rules regarding submission by sovereigns to the jurisdiction. It would have been acceptable to make these points in a British context; but, in 1890s Japan with its reverence of the person of the Emperor, we must admire Lowder's courage in taking such points.

Although the Japanese also argued the minutiae of the Orders in Council and the Rules, their simple point all along was reliance upon the Treaty's precise wording—and it was upon this point that the Privy Council found for them. Against this, it is surprising that the Japanese only raised the 'threat' argument before the Privy Council and not earlier in either HMCJ or the Supreme Court where the local British communities might have been more concerned by it. We have no explanation for this failure, especially as the reason given for the practice of not allowing counter-claims against Japanese plaintiffs was that British subjects would find themselves amenable to Japanese courts. Perhaps it was that, after the 1894 Treaty, the real threat was Britons being subject to Chinese courts.

The *Chishima cases* remind us that even apparently well-heeled litigants look to save on costs. P&O applied for a refund of fees after its successful appeal to the Supreme Court in the *Chishima case*—but Kimberley rejected their application as P&O had not objected at the time of payment.[78] In the *Tsune Kijima case*, the plaintiffs saved by relying solely upon written submissions for both appeal hearings and argued the appeal fees payable in respect of the Supreme Court appeal should be the fixed $20 fee payable 'where judicial relief or assistance is sought but not the recovery of money'[79] as it was an interlocutory matter; were the appeal to bear the costs of the principal action, it would add a further $380 *ad valorem*. Mowat refused to process the appeal pending Hannen's decision on the point. We must assume that Hannen accepted the fixed fee as Mowat forwarded the appeal papers some six weeks later[80]—another sign, perhaps, of Hannen seeking to dispel any suggestions of bias on the Supreme Court's part.

Despite the prominence accorded the question of counter-claims by the *Chishima case*, we must question how great a practical problem the inability to bring counter-claims against Japanese plaintiffs really was given that, as the Privy Council made clear, defendants could use all the facts which might give rise to a counter-claim as a shield in defence of the

[78] Hannen to A.P. Stokes, 9 September 1894; FO656/76.
[79] Mowat to Hannen, 30 January 1894; FO656/49.
[80] Mowat to Hannen, 14 March 1894; FO656/49.

action. In practice, the exercise of set-off rights substantially eliminated the adverse consequences of the bar on counter-claims against Japanese subjects because it was only in those rare cases where the defendant's claim exceeded the plaintiff's that the bar would be a problem. Japanese plaintiffs made up around a third of civil plaintiffs and, it is unlikely that, in the debt, supply of goods and services and wage claims, which made up around two-thirds of all Japanese claims, a defendant's counter-claim would exceed the plaintiff's claim because, had it done so, the defendant would probably have pursued his larger claim in the Japanese courts beforehand. It may have been more of an issue in shipping and the larger commercial dispute cases—but with only one Nagasaki case referring to claims against a Japanese plaintiff (and here a set-off was effected)[81]—it is more likely that the inability to bring counter-claims was an irritation rather than a real obstacle. Also, Britons resorted regularly to the Japanese courts and, as the dispute between Whittall and Tanaka showed, it was not impossible for claims arising out of the same facts to be brought under both systems. Therefore, the inconvenience and hardship factor alluded to by P&O could be over-emphasized.

Japanese—at the time and subsequently—alleged prejudice and bias on the Courts' part and cite the *Chishima case* as an example due to the perceived unfairness of the settlement where the Japanese government recovered barely a tenth of its original claim and its legal costs; although, for Chang, most criticism of the settlement stemmed from domestic politics and he explains why the settlement was not unfair to the Japanese in the context of Admiralty law at the time.[82] The settlement was reached ahead of the substantive trial and must be taken as having been acceptable to both parties in the light of all the circumstances—even if, as is often the case in litigation, one or other party might have wanted more. It is also unclear whether those opposition voices who criticized the Japanese government for agreeing the settlement had ever fully considered its position as a litigant.

Whilst both parties had reasons for wanting a settlement to what was now purely a commercial dispute, the Japanese government cannot have been under such financial or other pressure (and there is no suggestion that the British government applied any pressure) to settle that, had it been wholly confident of the *Ravenna*'s responsibility (even were the *Chishima* also partially responsible), it would not have continued the

81 *Yoshimoto Kebichi and Shinsuke v. Boyd & Co.*; civil case 2 of 1878; FO796/4.

82 Chang 1984, chapter 5.

substantive action. More broadly, Japan was being pressured by Russia, with support from France and Germany, to surrender most of its gains under the Treaty of Shimonoseki which ended the Sino-Japanese War, 1894–1895 and wanted British diplomatic support to resist such pressure (or, at a minimum, non-intervention on the side of Russia). Given the Imperial Japanese Navy's change of focus away from the ideas of the *Jeune Ecole*, Japan was also looking to Britain increasingly for its advanced warship construction. Although none of the files evidences any linkage, the decision-makers cannot have been unaware of the wider diplomatic situation. Accordingly, having established the point of principle and negotiated the ending of extra-territoriality, the Japanese government must have taken the view that, commercially (and diplomatically), the level of costs incurred to date (over ¥120,000) and likely to be incurred in the future and the risks that any recovery might be limited, outweighed all possible gains—especially as the Japanese government could claim that P&O's payment was 'equivalent to an admission that the blame for the collision did not rest with the *Chishima*'.[83]

Any assessment of the Courts' even-handedness involves a subjective assessment of the various decisions. The Naval Court was the only British official body that considered the substantive facts and, although its purpose was investigative—not judicial, one senses that its conclusion that the *Ravenna* was not responsible for the collision resonated with the Privy Council which spent the later part of its judgment, *obiter*, indirectly warning the Japanese that they were unlikely to recover their full claim; a finding and warning that, as indicated above, the Japanese government seemed to accept. Had each vessel been in any way partly responsible, the damages to each would have been split equally and the Japanese government's net recovery would have approximated at most £45–50,000—and only half this amount if one took account of the statutory limit on liability under the Merchant Shipping Act 1894.[84] Had the Japanese case been constrained truly by this statutory limit, Japanese criticism of the settlement would have had greater justification; but, this statutory limit never became an issue in the contemporary public discussion.

With the Naval Court, its only apparent lack of even-handedness was in clearing the court of future Japanese witnesses during Kaburaki's

[83] Satow to Salisbury, 18 March 1896; MT9/548.

[84] Chang explains why both sides assumed that the MSA1894 limitation on liability spoke to procedural matters and not substantive rights and, so, applied to the Japanese claim despite MSA1894 post-dating the accident; Chang 1984, pages 109–110.

testimony without any explanation when similar steps had not been taken in respect of the British witnesses. This created a perception of unfairness and discrimination, even if none actually resulted in its findings. As shown by the squabble over Kenny's translation, the Japanese sailors were quite capable of disagreeing with each other. Any imputation of unreliability on the part of Japanese witnesses would have been unfair for the *Ravenna*'s mate confessed subsequently that he had not spoken the truth to the Naval Court about the *Chishima*'s lights as he was colour-blind and had merely repeated what the *Ravenna*'s other witnesses had said.[85]

The contemporaneous holdings of British and Japanese enquiries into the collision illustrates the point about Naval Courts that, usually, they heard only part of the overall picture and could well reach different conclusions based upon only a partial picture. Although perhaps more adversarial than most Naval Court hearings, that into *Ravenna*'s role and conduct in this case could still look only to the British vessel and would not have had complete insight into the factors affecting the *Chishima kan*. Accusations of bias against the Naval Court must bear this situation in mind. The Naval Court in this case also highlights three other differences from the norm: first, unlike in the case of the *Normanton*, Kirkwood attended the Naval Court to watch over the interests of the Japanese government—despite its having no formal role in the proceedings. Second, the Naval Court was able to hear witnesses from the Japanese side—something which had not been possible in the case of the *Normanton*. Finally, the *Ravenna* had a pilot on board—and a Japanese one at that—so that it would have been difficult to have accused the master of any navigational errors: it was a case of looking to the *Ravenna*'s immediate actions before, and reactions to, the collision.

No Japanese was justified in disputing HMCJ's decisions in the *Chishima case* for they all went Japan's way except for needing to accept that the description 'The Imperial Japanese Government' was synonymous with the Emperor. Here, the Japanese government was merely following precedent and the choice of party and description lay wholly with it. It could have elected to sue in the name of the Minister of Marine—but that was not HMCJ's election and, so, no ground for accusing HMCJ of any anti-Japanese bias. Admittedly, HMCJ's decision in the *Tsune Kijima case* went against the Japanese side; but, it involved a highly technical matter of procedure and interpretation of the Rules and was, ultimately, upheld by the

---

85 Ernest Browne (chief officer, *Ravenna*) to Capt. Castle (Naval Court President), 23 October 1895; MT9/548.

Privy Council to be correct. There does not appear to have been any suggestion that, despite HMCJ's not following the Court of Appeal in *Hannay v. Smurthwaite* (which was only of persuasive—not binding—authority), its decision was biased or made other than on technical grounds.

It is difficult to see any anti-Japanese bias in the Supreme Court's handling of the *Tsune Kijima case*, where it considered fully the plaintiffs' written submissions, followed the Court of Appeal decision in *Hannay v. Smurthwaite* and exercised its discretion to allow the co-plaintiffs' appeal and claim. Japanese complaints about the Supreme Court's handing of the *Chishima case* may appear to be more justified. Counter-claims against Japanese plaintiffs were a grey area (and legal grounds could be found for deciding the matter either way), but Hannen was tactless (and may have given an impression of an anti-Japanese bias) in alluding to the Shimonoseki Incident when holding that the Inland Sea was part of the highway of nations. In drawing comparisons between the Inland Sea and the Solent, Jamieson, although reaching the same end result, was more tactful. It is quite possible that the Supreme Court was influenced by the background views of the Shanghai community in reaching the decision it did. Certainly, it operated in an environment where counter-claims against Chinese plaintiffs were an accepted way of proceeding. Nevertheless, the Supreme Court's ruling was overturned by the Privy Council which vindicated Japan on all points relating to the Treaty.

As a creature of treaty, extra-territoriality and its operation could never be removed from the shadow of politics and international diplomacy. The Japanese government's approach to the *Chishima cases* cannot be divorced from the overall context of the time. Abolition of extra-territoriality had been a key policy goal of all Japanese governments from the Iwakura Mission onwards and was backed enthusiastically by nationalist elements whose enthusiasm was matched only by the determination of the bulk of the British community to defend its privileged position. Each group was suspicious of its own government's approach to the issue.

The Japanese governments' various attempts during the 1880s to negotiate the end of extra-territoriality had been aborted under pressures from the nationalist wing of Japanese politicians, who pressed for immediate abolition with no transitional arrangements whereas the British community in Japan doubted the British authorities' commitment to what the community saw as its interests: doubts that had been confirmed by Salisbury's concessions after the *Hartley cases* and the negotiations during the 1880s for the abolition, or tempering, of British extra-territorial rights. This political background—and the views of the local communities—cannot have been absent from the minds of the judges in either case.

Whereas the Japanese government was subject to the political pressures raised by the clamour over the sinking, within its territorial waters, of one of its warships and the drowning of 74 sailors at a time of general political stress within Japan, there is no evidence that the British government took any 'view' on whether a counter-claim should lie or sought to use the case to expand the scope of extra-territoriality. Quite the reverse, it had long conceded the principle of extra-territoriality's abolition in Japan and British diplomats in Tokyo were more concerned about the damage to Anglo-Japanese relations generally which might flow from the incident and the related legal disputes. This concern was a real one in the contemporary diplomatic context where Britain was competing with France, Germany and the USA for influence over, and commercial contracts with, Japan and watchful of Russia's expansion in East Asia. Despite this concern and close governmental links with P&O, a mainstay of imperial communications, the British government could take no direct part in the litigation and needed to await its outcome before facilitating a settlement.

British concerns can be seen from the beginning when de Bunsen was present throughout the Naval Court hearings. Mowat, although relatively new to the position of Judge for Japan, cannot have been unaware of the British diplomats' sensitivities as to the adverse diplomatic consequences should he allow the counter-claim. This sensitivity is demonstrated by his handling of the initial procedural points in the *Chishima case*: accepting that Japanese attitudes would not permit claims to be brought in the name of the Emperor, he dismissed the argument that the plaintiff was misnamed and encouraged the defendants to accept that the plaintiff's description as 'The Imperial Government of Japan'. Likewise, his rejection of P&O's demand that the Emperor enter a formal submission to HMCJ's jurisdiction.

However, the British trading and resident community, with its somewhat high-handed view of the Japanese legal system and the need to comply with Japanese laws, felt it natural that they should be entitled to bring counter-claims against Japanese in the Courts. Therefore, it is hard not to believe that Mowat's judgment was influenced by the immediate external situation when, navigating between the Scylla and Charybdis of the opposing communities' views, he dodged the issue. Walford's contention that the collision occurred within Japanese territorial waters so that Japanese law must apply as regards liability on the Emperor's part, allowed

Mowat to dismiss the counter-claim—thereby satisfying the Japanese constituency in the immediate case whilst not irreversibly removing the possibility of counter-claims from the British community.

Similarly, it is impossible to believe that Hannen and Jamieson were not tempered in their judgment by the views of the British community in Shanghai which was, generally, vocal in its resistance to any form of Chinese interference and recent Supreme Court practice which had been to allow counter-claims against Chinese plaintiffs. Hannen, from his past experience in Japan—not least in relation to discussions on Treaty revision, must have been aware of Japanese sensitivities on the point; but, on the ground in Shanghai, there was no countervailing influence of the weight of the Japanese government.

Had the Privy Council wished, it could have found grounds to reach a different decision for the question was not clear-cut as evidenced by the divergent views expressed by the French, Dutch, German and American governments. The appellate committee contained the Lord Chancellor, a senior member of the government, who, although sitting in a judicial capacity, cannot have been unaware of the government's wish to deepen relations with Japan—at both a diplomatic and commercial level: a policy common to all late nineteenth century Administrations. The hearing's timing, after the recent 1894 Treaty, must have been significant. Again, it must be conceivable that the Privy Council was no less influenced by the surrounding politics than the two lower courts. It took a wider perspective than either of the lower courts and made clear that the effects of any decision could not be confined to Japan but would extend also to China. As abolition of extra-territoriality had been conceded already to Japan, there could be no reason to reach a decision which would antagonize Japan and, concurrently, give Chinese courts grounds to assume jurisdiction over British subjects. Thus, its decision on the question of counter-claims must have seemed inevitable after the 1894 Treaty.[86] However, in making it clear that the Japanese government was unlikely to succeed in full in its claim, the Privy Council, no less than Mowat, sought to strike a balance and accommodate both parties.

The courts, at all levels, showed great courtesy to the Japanese government and its representatives: at the HMCJ hearing, two of its higher officials sat within the bar of the court whilst, in the Supreme Court, the

[86] Then, Privy Council judgments were, by convention, unanimous. The court's voting records were destroyed in the Blitz, so it is impossible to ascertain whether any judges dissented.

Japanese acting Consul-General in Shanghai sat on the Bench with the presiding judges.[87] The Privy Council's judgment was courteous to Japan by recognizing the advances in its legal system—so distinguishing Japan from other countries where extra-territoriality would continue. This courtesy is emphasized by various distinctions between the *Chishima case* and the *Tsune Kijima case* where, ostensibly, the Japanese government had no interest: the judicial panel's reduction from seven to six members between the two cases; the Law Officers appearing as *amici curiae* and Herschell's delivering the judgment in the former but not the latter and the 17 day gap between the two judgments.

Generally, the Privy Council's strict interpretation of the Treaty's language was a continuation of the approach taken by the Law Officers and Foreign Office advisers over the years of giving effect to the exact terms of the Treaty whereas officials and practitioners on the ground in East Asia all too often attempted to operate the Treaty as they wished it had been written.

87 10 October 1893; *North China Daily News*.

CHAPTER EIGHT

THE END OF EXTRA-TERRITORIALITY

The *Chishima cases* overlapped with the final negotiations surrounding the 1894 Treaty which brought British extra-territoriality to an end; but the road to this treaty had been long and tortuous, pitted with potholes and lined with many a diversionary cul-de-sac. While Parkes suggested that 'there was no surprise on the one hand and no concession on the other when extra-territoriality was established by the treaties of 1858',[1] the subject was to form a backdrop to all Japan's foreign dealings from the late 1860s until the nineteenth century's end.

Although just one of several countries with extra-territorial rights, Britain was 'the only Power which ... made entirely adequate provision for the discharge of the duties imposed upon foreign nations by the necessity of exercising Consular jurisdiction'.[2] Nevertheless, as the *Ansei*—and most subsequent—treaties included 'most favoured nation' clauses, it would be necessary for Japan to re-negotiate all these treaties in order to secure the complete abolition of Western extra-territorial rights.[3] However, given Britain's contemporary predominance amongst the foreign nations in Japan, it looked first to secure British agreement before negotiating the surrender of other countries' extra-territorial rights and it is upon the Anglo-Japanese discussions that this chapter focuses—principally from the standpoint of the British records.

There are no references in the British diplomatic files before the late-1860s of any Japanese wish to end extra-territoriality—or, even, complaints about it—but, with the Meiji Restoration, the subject came to hover in the background of all Japan's overseas dealings. Japan concluded treaties with Spain, the North German Confederation and Sweden and Norway along the lines of the *Ansei* treaties immediately after the Meiji

[1] Per Cassell, *Grounds of Judgment* (Oxford: Oxford University Press, 2012) page 92.

[2] Plunkett to Granville, 2 July 1884; FO881/5072.

[3] A point emphasized in 1873 when Japan negotiated a new treaty with Italy which abolished Italian extra-territoriality and provided Italians with rights of access to Japan's interior. The other Powers, led by Parkes, simply claimed similar rights of access by virtue of the Treaty's 'most favoured nation' article whilst not yielding their extra-territorial rights. This meant that Japan would not implement the Italian treaty. See Jones, 1931 page 86.

Restoration and the Japanese government and Parkes negotiated the Austro-Hungarian treaty (which clarified and extended aspects of the older treaties)[4] but the Japanese government was soon looking to re-negotiate the Treaty's extra-territorial aspects.[5]

The Iwakura Mission

The Treaty provided that, upon twelve months' notice, either Japan or Britain could demand its revision after 1 July 1872[6] and one of the Iwakura Mission's aims was to raise the subject with the Western Powers.[7] Iwakura and Granville discussed the question on 27 November 1872 when the two countries' fundamental position was set out. Iwakura stated that 'if ... foreigners were amenable to Japanese law ... [there was] no reason why the same facilities for trade and intercourse should not be granted as existed in England...'[8] whilst Granville responded that 'as soon as Japan had a proper code of laws administered by tribunals upon which the British government could rely, a great change would take place in the feelings entertained in regard to this matter ... In all such cases, the policy of the British government was to yield the local authority jurisdiction over British subjects in precise proportion to their advancement in enlightenment and civilization.'[9] In short, Japan would open up fully to trade provided extra-territoriality was abolished—which the British would only concede when a transparent and effective legal system existed in Japan.

Another aspect of the *Ansei* treaties which Japan considered a restriction on its sovereignty was their tariff regime: Japan was subject to the tariff regime provided in those treaties and was not free to set its own tariffs. Although not linked intrinsically to extra-territoriality, tariffs and extra-territoriality quickly became linked for negotiating purposes. John Harrington Gubbins, the Japanophile Japanese Secretary at the Legation, made clear this linkage in 1887 in a Memorandum on the history of recent treaty revision negotiations:[10] the foreign Powers would only grant tariff

---

4 See page 9.

5 See Auslin, 2004, chapter 6 and also Cassell, 2012 chapter 6.

6 Article XXII.

7 For a discussion of the Iwakura Mission, see Nish, 1998.

8 Memorandum prepared by W.G. Aston, who acted as interpreter at the meeting; FO881/2138.

9 Ibid.

10 Gubbins was also the English Secretary to the 1882 Revision Conference. Memorandum prepared 30 February 1887; FO881/5773 (**Gubbins Memorandum**).

autonomy in return for opening up of the country which Japan would only grant in return for the abolition of extra-territorial jurisdiction.

Ahead of Iwakura's visit to London, the British Legation had sought the British community's views on treaty revision. Flowers and Gower submitted to Adams various memoranda from traders in Nagasaki and Kobe.[11] The memoranda highlighted the severe nature of Japanese criminal law and complained of the difficulty of obtaining effective redress against Japanese defendants (criminal and civil)—although the Nagasaki traders seemed more concerned about the level of duties and rents and the lack of access to the interior.[12] However, none envisaged Britain's surrendering any of its extra-territorial rights at that time and Granville told Parkes after the Iwakura meeting that the British government was not prepared to expose British subjects to the risks of abolishing extra-territoriality at a time when Japan seemed unable to discharge the responsibilities which it would assume as a result of abolition.[13]

Nonetheless, Japanese politicians continued to argue that the treaties 'caused people to remark that Japan was under a "foreign yoke"'.[14] Parkes accepted that the higher classes considered the treaties to be one-sided and conceded that their bitterness in this regard was exacerbated by 'the attitudes of Europeans in Japan ... [which have] ... been, with few exceptions, aggressive...'[15] Nevertheless, he considered that much of the discontent was stirred up by the politicians themselves. He suggested that Japanese politicians pushed for revision because of their need to justify '... the somewhat grandiloquent phrases used by them ... on the subject of Treaty Revision. Such expressions as Sovereign Rights, by repeated repetition in the local Japanese press ... have gratified the national vanity and have raised expectations...'[16]

Japan pursued three courses in its campaign to achieve the abolition of extra-territoriality: first, a campaign to apply the Treaty strictly;[17] second,

---

[11] Flowers to Adams, 30 December 1871 and Gower to Adams, 31 January 1872; FO881/2135.

[12] None of Holme Ringer & Co., Gribble & Co., Maltby & Co., Glover & Co. and Dohmeney complained of any problems concerning legal cases against Japanese defendants.

[13] Granville to Parkes, 13 January 1873; FO881/2159.

[14] Parkes to Derby, 27 January 1877 recounting discussion with Sameshima; FO46/263.

[15] Memorandum from Frederic Marshall (an employee of the Japanese Legation in Paris) to Derby, 6 May 1874; FO46/263.

[16] Parkes to Salisbury, 27 October 1879; FO46/267.

[17] Strict enforcement of the Treaty was wider than just extra-territoriality. In 1883, Plunkett noted that 'If ... England should refuse to admit terminability under any

as we saw in Chapter 3 (Criminal Jurisdiction), a concerted attempt to have the Courts give effect to Japanese domestic and municipal laws and regulations; and, third, diplomatic negotiations. Of course, none was mutually exclusive and each had a reinforcing effect upon the others. Each course was applied with different emphases from time to time—largely depending upon the inclinations of the relevant Japanese governmental officials and the exigencies of Japanese domestic politics at the time. In 1874, Parkes lamented that '...the unfriendliness which is now so universally complained of is the work of the last twelve months and is probably, therefore, the result of the policy pursued by the present government...'[18]

An early instance of Japan's strict application of the Treaty occurred in 1874 when it suddenly stopped coaches which carried Westerners from running between Yokohama and Odawara, which was outside the Treaty limits, despite coaches having run for several years previously. Concurrently, it adopted a more aggressive attitude towards infractions of the Treaty limits and demanded that the British authorities impose penalties upon those subjects who breached them. Parkes conceded that the Japanese government was within its rights to stop the coaches and excursions beyond the Treaty limits but, given its previous practice in permitting them, suggested that its new actions were 'unreasonable and vexatious'.[19] Adding to this vexation, the Japanese authorities now argued that the limits should be measured by the route taken as opposed to a straight-line basis as the British contended.

Japan also favoured visiting British politicians and officials whom it thought amenable to its cause. Two particular *bêtes-noires* of Parkes in this regard were John Pope Hennessy, Governor of Hong Kong, and Sir Edward James Reed, the Liberal MP and naval architect. Both were feted on their visits to Japan in the late 1870s—in the hope, Parkes claimed, it would help Japan in regard to the forthcoming Treaty revision discussions.[20]

circumstances, Japan proposes to drop Treaty revision altogether, and to revert to the strict letter of the existing Treaty ... [and] ... withdraw all those extra privileges which she has granted of later years to foreigners but which are not expressly secured ... by the existing Treaty; for instance, ... travel in the interior for health and science, the toleration accorded to Christian missionaries in the interior, the possibility of sepulture of foreigners in the Japanese cemeteries, etc;' Plunkett memorandum, 31 October 1883; FO881/4870.

[18] Parkes to Derby, 12 May 1874; FO881/2495.

[19] Parkes to Derby, 28 April 1874; FO881/2494 and FO881/2496.

[20] Parkes to Tenterden, 12 August 1879; FO363/2. See also Hugh Cortazzi 'Sir Edward Reed (1830–1906): Naval Architect' in *Biographical Portraits Vol VII*, ed. Hugh Cortazzi

The Tokyo Treaty Revision Conferences

In 1878, Sameshima (Japanese Minister for Foreign Affairs) admitted that the Japanese government had no current intention of demanding that jurisdiction over foreigners should be ceded to them,[21] but Japan did request a conference with the Western Powers to discuss revision of the existing treaties: not just their extra-territorial aspects but also tariffs. When Japan made its request, Austria-Hungary, Italy, France and Germany all asked Britain for its views but the Foreign Office said that the subject could not be considered until Salisbury had returned from the Congress of Berlin which was then ongoing.[22] Subsequently, Salisbury insisted that Britain would not agree to waiving Article XXII of the Treaty's requirement for twelve months' notice to terminate the Treaty and deprecated Japan's desire to increase its tariffs.[23] Here, one must remember that, at the time, Britain was the leading exponent of free trade.

Meanwhile in 1878, the Japanese Minister in Washington and the USA had negotiated a treaty whereby the USA renounced its rights to extra-territoriality and to restrict Japan's tariff autonomy—but the treaty was never implemented because its final provision stipulated that it would only come into effect when all other Powers had concluded similar agreements with Japan. Many Europeans considered that the USA had agreed the provisions in the hope of engendering Japanese goodwill whilst knowing full well that they would never be implemented because the European Powers would never make similar renunciations.

Originally, Japan had suggested that the revision Conference take place in London but, after much time had been spent in discussions between the Western Powers themselves and in agreeing the Conference's practical arrangements, it was not convened until January 1882 when it was held in Tokyo. Ahead of this Conference, the Legation had, again, sought the British community's views. The Yokohama General Chamber of Commerce's response was concerned principally with tariffs but also complained of the unsatisfactory manner in which claims against Japanese subjects were handled by the Japanese courts—a position exacerbated by Japanese bankruptcy laws which it considered operated to the detriment

(Global Oriental, Folkstone, 2010), pages 44–57 for a description of Reed's visit to Japan and the public correspondence between him and Parkes in *The Times*.

21 Adams to Derby, 2 April 1878; FO881/3744.

22 Internal memorandum by H. Hervey (a Foreign Office official), 1 July 1878; FO46/264.

23 Salisbury to Wooyeno Kagenori, 2 November 1878; FO881/3765.

of foreigners. It also raised the need for Japan to protect foreigners' intellectual property rights.[24]

Ahead of the Conference, Japan tabled a revised draft treaty which would replace the Treaty's extra-territorial provisions by a far more limited extra-territoriality. This would subject British subjects to a concurrent dual system of Japanese and British jurisdiction—depending, principally, upon the potential level of punishment which a crime would attract (in criminal matters) and provide that, generally, the defendant's courts should have jurisdiction in civil matters (including the right to hear counter-claims arising on the action). Parkes criticized the proposals which he said would 'inevitably cause confusion and a conflict of authority'[25] and Britain indicated that it was unwilling to agree to the abolition of extra-territoriality until new courts had been established and new Japanese laws and rules of court procedure had been completed and translated.[26]

This first Conference ended inconclusively and a second Conference was convened in Tokyo from 1886 to 1887. By the time this second Conference convened, Western governments had all conceded the principle of extra-territoriality's abolition and Granville instructed Plunkett, the British Minister and Delegate to the Conference, that 'HMG have no desire to perpetuate their Consular jurisdiction in Japan ... any longer than is necessary for the legitimate protection of British interests.'[27] The questions at this second Conference concerned the timing, transitional arrangements and the *quid pro quo* to be extracted from Japan in terms of commercial advantages for the abolition of extra-territoriality.

Lengthy multilateral discussions took place in Tokyo ahead of the second Conference to try to find a way forward. However, by the end of 1885, these had become bogged down—partly due to deaths and changes amongst the foreign Minsters based in Tokyo but also due to dissensions within the Japanese Cabinet.[28] When the Second Conference finally

---

[24] Yokohama General Chamber of Commerce to Parkes, 8 July 1879; FO881/3992, and Kennedy to Salisbury, 22 October 1879; FO881/4220.

[25] Parkes memorandum, January 1881; FO881/4380.

[26] Foreign Office memorandum, 4 April 1883; FO881/4778.

[27] Granville to Plunkett, 11 January 1884; FO881/5072. This merely confirmed the Protocol to the Korean treaty of 1883 whereby Britain agreed to release its extra-territorial rights in Korea 'when ... the laws and legal procedures of Corea shall have been ... modified and reformed ... to remove the objections which now exist to British subjects being placed under Corean jurisdiction and Corean judges shall have attained similar legal qualifications and a similar independent position to those of British judges.' Francis Taylor Piggott, *Extra-territoriality* (London, 1892), page 237.

[28] Plunkett to Granville, 17 October 1885; FO881/5380.

convened in May 1886, its work was divided between one committee which focused upon trade and tariff questions and a second committee which concentrated upon jurisdiction and extra-territoriality. Hannen was heavily involved in the Conference's work—particularly in relation to this second committee—and was appointed formally as a second British Delegate at the end of 1886.

Rennie said that, prior to this second Conference, Japan had put forward such unduly large demands that Britain could not agree the abolition of extra-territoriality but, now, Japan appeared 'ready to accept more moderate concessions' and he foresaw no objection to the opening of Japan's interior where foreigners would be subject to a limited Japanese jurisdiction.[29] The jurisdiction committee considered various arrangements for handling cases involving foreigners (all based upon the assumption that British subjects in Japan should observe and obey Japanese laws and regulations)—from Mixed Courts on the Egyptian model, through having some cases heard in Japanese Courts and some (more contentious civil cases or those criminal cases involving heavier penalties) still heard in consular courts to having foreign judges sitting in Japanese courts in all cases concerning foreigners.[30] However, no resolution was ever reached which could command total Japanese acceptance.

All the discussions were bedevilled, on the Japanese side, by disputes and positional stances taken by the various domestic political factions and, on the Western side, by rivalries between the Western Powers themselves. Initially, all foreign Powers had been negotiating together but, by 1885, Plunkett, at least, was urging that co-operation with the other European Powers was no longer useful, but detrimental, to British policy and commercial interests in Japan: '...foreigners are no longer "*solidaires*" and ... Great Britain could make a better bargain if she had only to consult English and Japanese convenience'.[31] Both Salisbury[32] and Rosebery[33]

29 Memorandum by Rennie dated 26 September 1884 enclosed with Plunkett to Granville, 17 October 1884; FO881/5072.

30 See draft treaty in FO881/5235. Takaaki Hattori presents an interesting perspective on the proposal for foreign judges in Japanese courts when arguing that it 'could not have been proposed if Japan's leaders, so sensitive to infringements upon national sovereignty in other spheres, had considered the administration of justice an essential part of that national sovereignty'; Takaaki Hattori, 'The legal profession in Japan: its Historical Development and Present State' in Arthur Taylor von Mehren ed. *Law in Japan: The Legal Order in a Changing Society* (Harvard University Press, Cambridge Mass., 1963), pages 116 *et seq*.

31 Plunkett to Granville, 18 June 1885; FO881/5235.

32 Salisbury to Plunkett, 2 August 1885; FO881/5235.

33 Rosebery to Plunkett, 7 July 1886; FO881/5380.

accepted his recommendation that Britain would be better off consulting its own interests rather than trying to co-ordinate with the other Powers.

The history of these Conferences, and Britain's role in them, is worthy of a study in terms of changing international relations, diplomatic manoeuvrings and intrigue and also domestic Japanese politics, but such a study is, in the end, fruitless as nothing came of the Conferences themselves.[34] Discussions at the second Conference involved much to-ing and fro-ing over proposals[35] which, broadly, would have confined British jurisdiction to Yokohama, Kobe, Nagasaki and Hakodate for the next three years but the Courts would have applied Japanese laws. Elsewhere in Japan, Britons would have been subject to Japanese jurisdiction but in certain criminal cases and all civil claims above a certain amount, foreign judges would have been included on the judicial panel and on appeal. Meanwhile, Japan would re-organize the constitution of the Japanese courts and establish, in consultation with the Western Powers, a public legal code in accordance with Western legal principles.[36]

Disputes simmered between the Western Powers over the number and nationality of the foreign judges to be included on the Japanese judicial panels. Britain argued for at least half to be British or American but British and American judges were more expensive than continental judges and the British demands would impose considerable additional expense on the Japanese Ministry of Justice. Bismarck suggested that France was being difficult on the issue and, whilst Germany would prefer to limit British and American judges to a third of all foreign judges, he was prepared to allow Britain to decide and insist upon a half.[37] Keswick of Jardine Matheson, on the other hand, recognized that Japan was entitled to a change in the system of extra-territoriality and was broadly happy with the proposals but wished to see at least one British judge in all cases involving British subjects—even if not in a majority in the court—because he mistrusted foreign judges of other nationalities.[38]

[34] Certain solutions which found favour from time to time such as the admission of foreign lawyers to practise before the Japanese courts, the use of the English language in all court cases involving foreign interests and the inclusion of foreign judges make interesting reading in the context of the late twentieth century discussions to open-up the Japanese legal market to international participation.

[35] See proposals listed in FO881/5380.

[36] Plunkett to Rosebery, 11 June 1886; FO881/5380.

[37] Sir Edward Malet (British Ambassador to Berlin) to Iddesleigh, 3 January 1887; FO881/5631.

[38] Memorandum dated 29 September 1886 by Sir Philip Currie of a meeting with Keswick on behalf of the Japan Merchants in London; FO881/5380.

By the end of 1886 a crisis had been reached in the deliberations as, besides continuing arguments over the foreign judges, France objected to English being the sole language to be used in the Japanese courts where foreigners were involved and the Conference was adjourned until January 1887.[39] When the Conference resumed, Plunkett complained that the German Minister in Tokyo was 'working actively against England and practically controls the Japanese Foreign Office through the Vice-Minister for Foreign Affairs'[40] and he suspected that Germany was having separate negotiations with Japan for a new treaty.

Despite these crises and manoeuvrings, a draft treaty regarding extra-territoriality had been practically agreed apart from one or two minor matters by June 1887 and the Conference waited only upon the results of the tariff committee.[41] This soon completed its work and a complete draft treaty was sent to London in July and the Conference stood adjourned until 1 December 1887.[42]

However, internal dissensions broke out quickly on the Japanese side and wrecked any chance of further progress when the French legal adviser to the Ministry of Justice attacked Inouye (the Foreign Minister) personally for alleged mismanagement of the negotiations and for conceding the involvement of so many foreign judges. Some Japanese Cabinet members argued that the new arrangements reduced Japan to the level of Egypt and no change would be better than to accept the proposals. To British eyes, this Cabinet dissension was complicated further by German rivalry and intrigues.[43] As a result, the Japanese government asked, initially, for revisions to the only recently settled draft treaty before, at the end of July it decided to complete the re-drafting of the new legal Codes before finalizing any new treaty as it did not wish to submit the new Codes to foreign governments for comment. Japan recognized that this 'put an end to treaty revision in its present shape'[44] as producing the Codes would take at least two years.

The Japanese Prime Minister admitted to Plunkett 'that Treaty revision was really little more than the stick that had been made use of to attack Count Inouye: the causes of dissatisfaction felt by some members of the cabinet were partly personal and partly political'.[45] Even Gubbins opined

39 Plunkett to Iddesleigh, 10 October 1886; FO881/5380.
40 Plunkett to Salisbury, telegram 13 February 1887; FO881/5631.
41 Plunkett and Hannen to Salisbury, 2 June 1887; FO881/5631.
42 Plunkett to Salisbury, 18, July 1887; FO881/5631.
43 Ibid and telegram 25 July 1887; FO881/5631.
44 Plunkett to Salisbury, 30 July 1887; FO881/5631.
45 Plunkett to Salisbury, 30 July 1887; FO881/5631.

that 'It may fairly be said ... that Japan must accept full responsibility for the abortive results of Treaty revision negotiations...'[46] because agreement had almost been reached when Japan needed to revisit the basic elements afresh. As a result, the Japanese government began to acquire the reputation of changing the question whenever an answer hove in sight. Sir Thomas Sanderson,[47] whilst accepting that the Japanese considered 'Consular extra-territoriality ... an offence to their national dignity and inconsistent with their present state of civilization,'[48] opined that, in the Treaty revision negotiations, 'their method of negotiation is to discuss an arrangement at great length and when they have extracted a certain number of concessions to throw the whole over and begin afresh, withdrawing their previous offers...'[49]

Gubbins explained[50] that, whereas many outsiders assumed that that Treaty revision was a question simply between the Japanese government and the Treaty Powers, this was far from the case. There were '...two difficulties:

1. Internal politics;
2. Japan's Treaty with China.[51]

... on the broad issue of Treaty revision, the Japanese nation is not of one mind, and partly from ... the unsettled condition of Japanese politics ... the Japanese government have persistently put foreign politics in the foreground, and in this was the revision of Japan's Treaty ... have been invested with an importance which never ought to have been given to it ... Japanese Ministers have to deal with forces which are largely beyond their control,

[46] Gubbins Memorandum. Gubbins was a Japanophile so his analysis cannot be dismissed as an anti-Japanese view. His view was shared by Bismarck who remarked that 'the Japanese Government appeared to be completely at sixes and sevens among themselves and the Cabinet seemed to be a house divided against itself,' Malet to Salisbury recounting a discussion with Count Berchem (Under Secretary of State for Foreign Affairs in Germany), 7 December 1889; FO881/5933.

[47] Then, Assistant Permanent Under-Secretary in the Foreign Office.

[48] Internal Foreign Office Memorandum by Sanderson, 14 August 1893; FO881/6417.

[49] Ibid.

[50] Gubbins Memorandum.

[51] Japan wished to deal with China separately whereas the Sino-Japanese treaty of Tianjin, 1871 contained a 'most favoured nation' provision whereby China would obtain all the benefits the Western Powers gained from their negotiations without being obliged to make any concessions. Gubbins considered, 'it is quite impossible for [Japan] to come to an understanding with China on a basis of reciprocity' but, at the Conference, China had rejected all Japanese proposals to it which had contained no reciprocal element. Ultimately, the Sino-Japanese War of 1894–1895 and the treaty of Yantai resolved the issue.

and which may at any moment swell ... [and] overturn a cabinet...' [because of internal rivalries]. Gubbins concluded that, in practice, everyone was content with the *status quo.*

Given the disarray on the Japanese side, official minds appeared to move towards Plunkett's view, expressed as early as 1885, that unless one Power took the lead in cutting the Gordian knot, there was 'no prospect of any arrangement being arrived at during the lifetime of any of the present Delegates' and that outright abolition of extra-territoriality was the only workable solution.[52] Japan also abandoned the idea of multilateral discussions in favour of one-on-one discussions with the foreign Powers and, towards the end of 1888, in a proposal which, as Satow pointed out, went against its earlier declared intention to await the drafting of the new legal Codes before recommencing treaty re-negotiations,[53] suggested separate negotiations with Britain alone. The Japanese government proposed a new treaty which would continue the current arrangements for five years after which all consular jurisdiction would cease. It also proposed to appoint foreign judges to the Japanese supreme court and extend the right of appeal to that court in criminal and civil cases. The British Minister, le Poer Trench, considered the proposals to be the best that Britain could hope to obtain.[54]

Clearly, once Japan had reached an agreement with Britain, it hoped that the other Powers would conclude similar agreements—the implicit threat if they did not being that it would denounce its treaties with them. A new round of to-ing and fro-ing over drafts of a new treaty ensued between not just Japan and Britain but also with the other Powers. However, all was brought to a halt in November as a result of an attack in which Okuma, the Foreign Minister, was injured.[55] Gubbins had no doubt that the attack was the outcome of the excitement surrounding the revised treaty negotiations.[56]

Even as the discussions were under way, Hannen had suggested that 'sooner than agree to the present proposed draft ... extra-territoriality should be abolished absolutely at the end of 10 years, if, in the meantime, the *status quo* were maintained'.[57] When the discussions terminated,

---

[52] Plunkett to Salisbury, 30 July 1885; FO881/5235.

[53] Satow to Foreign Office, 2 February 1889; FO881/5933.

[54] Le Poer Trench to Salisbury, telegram 29 December 1888 and letter 16 January 1889; FO881/5933.

[55] Fraser to Salisbury, 14 November 1889; FO881/5933.

[56] Gubbins memorandum 21 October 1889; FO881/5933.

[57] Hannen memorandum, 31 January 1889; FO881/5933.

Francis Taylor Piggott, British legal adviser to the Japanese Prime Minister in relation to the new constitution, suggested to Hugh Fraser, the Minister, that he could see no half-way house between foreign judges and Japanese judges. To him the solution appeared 'to be:

1. The continuation of the status quo for a certain number of years, after which Consular jurisdiction is to cease, and Japan to assume her judicial autonomy;
2. The creation of a ... Judicial College, graduates of which are to be raised to the Bench.'[58]

The purpose of the delay was to allow time for Japan to establish a trained independent judiciary and complete work on drafting, and publishing, a comprehensive set of law Codes based upon Western legal principles—thereby meeting the basic Western requirements of publicized laws enforced by an independent body.

Salisbury took the cue and advised the British Cabinet that he proposed to submit to Japan the draft of a new treaty prepared by Hannen. This draft dropped earlier proposals for provision to be made for interpreters and advocates in the Japanese courts to be conversant in English; for foreign advocates to be admitted to the Japanese bar and for foreigners to be included amongst Japanese prosecutors. Salisbury recommended that Britain should recognize Japan's modernization and highlighted the desire of British traders in Japan for access to the whole country.[59] In the middle of 1890, Salisbury proposed to Japan that 'a Treaty should at once be signed, containing all those provisions on which the British and Japanese negotiators have already been able to come to an agreement, and that by a Protocol ... the extension of Japanese jurisdiction over British subjects, and all those concessions which the Japanese Government make dependent upon it, should be postponed for a period of not less than five years, and until the new Courts and Codes have been in operation for at least 12 months'.[60] Japan was also invited to join the international conventions on the protection of intellectual property.

Fraser described the Japanese government as being so '...surprised at receiving proposals of such unprecedented liberality exactly from Great Britain...' that it was 'racking their brains to find out what snare might be

[58] Piggott to Fraser, 30 December 1889; FO881/6056.
[59] Foreign Office memorandum, 19 June 1889; FO881/5861.
[60] Salisbury to Fraser, 5 June 1890; FO881/6056.

lying under the conditions...' However, whilst Aoki Shuzo, the Foreign Minister, was anxious to conclude a treaty, the Japanese Cabinet was vacillating between the fear of opening Japan and the shame of hesitating to do so.[61] Nothing, however, came of Salisbury's initiative for Count Ito told Fraser that, since Japan was passing through another crisis in home affairs, Treaty revision was a matter on which a Japanese government could not risk another failure and it would 'be wisest to defer the negotiation a little longer and then secure it somewhere in Europe'.[62]

Meanwhile, Japan promulgated its new Codes in 1890—apart from that part of the Civil Code which related to personal status. Whilst this was a major step in achieving the Western Powers' demand for a publicized law, another development was to cause further hesitations on the part of Japanese Cabinets. 1890 also saw the first nationally elected Diet which revealed that a great portion of the Japanese political class was vehemently opposed to opening Japan to foreigners—even in return for abolition of extra-territoriality. So great was the opposition that Gubbins suggested that the Japanese government's position was not favourable to the successful conclusion of a new treaty because it continued to be weakened by divided counsels and was embarrassed by the hostility of a Diet which it struggled to control.[63] In February 1893, an amendment to the Address to the Throne seeking to prohibit the residence of foreigners in the interior was only defeated after a hard struggle[64] whilst, on the eve of the Diet's re-assembly in November that year, de Bunsen still considered that '... the movement in opposition to the mixed residence of foreigners in Japan ... shows a great want of unanimity in the country as to the basis on which alone a revision of the Treaty is possible'.[65] The Japanese government's position was not made any easier by the *Chishima-Ravenna* collision in November 1892 and the ensuing domestic furore.

W.E. Davison, the Foreign Office's legal adviser, suggested that Britain had '...already agreed ... that so soon as Japan shall have adopted a legal system based broadly on the general principles which are common to the legal systems of civilization, we will surrender our extra-territorial jurisdiction...'[66] To British eyes, the continued delays in negotiating a new treaty were all down to Japan's unwillingness to re-open discussions.

---

[61] Fraser to Salisbury, 10 November 1890; FO881/6056.
[62] Fraser to Salisbury, 27 January 1892; FO881/6317.
[63] Gubbins memorandum, 5 December 1892; FO881/6417.
[64] De Bunsen to Rosebery, 17 February 1893; FO881/6488.
[65] De Bunsen to Rosebery, 23 November 1893; FO881/6488.
[66] 10 April 1893; FO881/6417.

Discussions in London

At last, in August 1893, Mutsu Munemitsu, then Foreign Minister, asked de Bunsen if negotiations on Treaty revision could re-open in London with Aoki, now Ambassador to Berlin, in place of Kawase, Ambassador to London, as negotiator in view of his specialized knowledge of the subject. Mutsu also requested that Fraser, the British Minister to Tokyo, remain in London to conduct the negotiations with Aoki[67] who tabled a draft treaty where 'much was taken verbatim from the draft treaty of Lord Salisbury's proposals of 1890'.[68] Aoki, Fraser and Gubbins discussed the matter informally in London. By October 1893, Fraser could inform Aoki that, in principle, there was a deal to be done on a new treaty whereby Japan could, after five years, give a year's notice to bring the treaty into force but with a protocol whereby Japan agreed not to give such notice until the new Codes were all in operation.[69]

Mutsu now requested that the negotiations be conducted formally[70] but Rosebery hesitated because of recent anti-foreigner agitation in Japan[71] (which was also linked to the Japanese government's bringing its suit before HMCJ in *IJG v. P&O*) and asked de Bunsen whether he should withdraw his *non possumus*.[72] De Bunsen recommended 'conducting negotiations with a strong and friendly Government like the present ... [and that] ... if we are to wait till the anti-foreign spirit has entirely died out, Treaty revision must be indefinitely postponed...'[73]

Internal Foreign Office thinking was reflected by Francis Leveson Bertie[74] who adopted a *realpolitik* position and warned that 'If we refuse to negotiate or leave unanswered the Japanese proposals a strong anti-English movement ... may ensue. It is possible that no Government may be strong enough to demand the Treaty with foreign powers. On the other hand the exigencies of party warfare may drive whatever party may be in

---

67 De Bunsen to Rosebery, 18 August 1893 (telegram and letter); FO881/6488. For a discussion of the Japanese perspective of the final round of negotiations of the 1894 Treaty and Mutsu's role, see Louis G. Perez, *Japan Comes of Age: Mutsu Munemitsu and the Revision of the Unequal Treaties* (Fairleigh Dickinson University Press, Madison, 1999).

68 Gubbins to Bergue (a Foreign Office official), 19 February 1894; FO881/6582.

69 Fraser to Aoki, 10 October 1893; FO881/6488.

70 Mutsu to de Bunsen, 6 December 1893, FO881/6582.

71 The agitation was sufficiently concerning for Vice-Admiral Freemantle, commanding the China Station, to order HMS *Caroline* from Shanghai to Yokohama (Freemantle to Admiralty, 17 January 1894; FO881/6582).

72 Rosebery to de Bunsen, 11 January 1894.

73 De Bunsen to Rosebery, 12 January 1894; FO881/6582.

74 Then, Assistant Under-Secretary of State.

power into a denunciation[75] leaving us with no trade advantages and without extra-territorial jurisdiction. In such a case, we are not locally in a position to enforce our existing Treaty rights. The Japanese have a navy nearly as strong as that of China. Their coast defences are nearly finished and will be formidable and their army consists of 70,000 well-armed and well-drilled troops ... The great interest which Japan and China have in common, and which is also an English interest, is to keep Russia out of Corea...'[76] Sanderson endorsed on the Memorandum that 'we shall do wisely to move in a leisurely manner in the direction of negotiation',[77] a view which Rosebery noted seemed 'to sum up our policy at this moment'.[78]

Informal discussions continued in London between Fraser, Gubbins and Aoki over the draft Treaty and the Protocols' precise wording before, finally, Kimberley—who had replaced Rosebery as Foreign Secretary when Rosebery formed a government upon Gladstone's retirement—informed Fraser that Britain would agree to formal negotiations but the opening up of Japan to trade and the right of foreigners to possess land were non-negotiable requirements of any new treaty. After further haggling over these issues and the protection of copyright, the 1894 Treaty was agreed and signed by Kimberley and Aoki on 16 July 1894 together with two Protocols relating to coasting trade and Japan's joining the international conventions in relation to the protection of intellectual property.

The 1894 Treaty provided that the Treaty '...and all Arrangements and Agreements subsidiary thereto ... shall cease to be binding, and, in consequence, the jurisdiction then exercised by British Courts in Japan ... shall ... cease and determine, and thereafter all such jurisdiction shall be assumed and exercised by Japanese Courts'[79] but that the 1894 Treaty should 'not take effect until at least five years after its signature ... after ... [the Japanese government] ... shall have given notice ... to have the same brought into operation'[80] which notice could be given any time after four years. The Japanese government undertook, in a formal letter from Aoki,

[75] Japan had denounced the Portuguese treaty in 1892 on the grounds that, despite repeated requests over many years, Portugal had failed to maintain a consular representative in Japan to exercise any jurisdiction over its subjects.

[76] Memorandum of 12 January 1894; FO881/6582.

[77] Ibid.

[78] Ibid.

[79] Article XX.

[80] Article XXI.

not to give notice until the new Codes were fully operative. The 1894 Treaty and its associated Protocols and letters reflected the basic positions set out by Iwakura and Granville at their meeting some 22 years earlier: Japan recovered its jurisdiction over foreigners within its territory but, in return, allowed foreigners access to its interior for trade and residence and adopted public legal codes based on Western principles. Japan had not recovered the full sovereignty which it had lost by the *Ansei* treaties in respect of tariffs but the 1894 Treaty was to last only 12 years from its coming into effect at which time there would be nothing to prevent Japan addressing this issue. Britain in surrendering extra-territoriality but retaining the tariff regime for a further 12 years had looked to commercial advantage over the protections which extra-territoriality gave its subjects—protections which, with a modernizing Japan, were of decreasing practical value.

When news of the 1894 Treaty reached Asia, the *North China Herald* described it as 'incredible, but ... true'[81] and reflected the feelings of many in the Western community in Japan—and China—when it claimed that the 1894 Treaty represented 'a complete surrender on the part of Great Britain'.[82] Despite fulminations by sections of the foreign press in Japan, the British government took no notice. Neither would it satisfy the London based China Association which complained about having been kept in the dark about the negotiations.[83] When the *Star in the East* Lodge worried that Japanese law forbade meetings of secret societies and wondered what protections the 1894 Treaty would afford Lodges, the Foreign Office said the matter could not be made a treaty stipulation and merely advised a 'wait and see' attitude.[84]

Gubbins accepted that the British community in Japan largely considered that the British government had abandoned its interests; but, he suggested that much of the community's concern arose from the mystery in which the treaty negotiations had been shrouded for so many years—a shroud which he complained was not at the behest of the British government. That said, he suggested that the community was well aware of the weakness of Britain's negotiating position.[85] Many of the British trading houses were more realistic and accepted the loss of extra-territoriality in return for access to the interior and the continuation of the favourable

[81] Editorial; 31 August 1894, NCH.
[82] 14 September 1894, NCH.
[83] Memorandum in FO881/6582.
[84] Bertie to Sir C. Dalrymple MP, 13 December 1894; FO881/6582.
[85] Gubbins memorandum, 26 February 1894; FO881/6582.

tariff regime. The diplomats were also concerned that if Britain failed to satisfy Japan then it would seek to negotiate arrangements with Germany—Britain's commercial rival—or even Washington where Gubbins considered that 'the question is so little understood that [Japan] might get terms which we should find it difficult to accept'.[86]

It was not only the British community that the Foreign Office kept in the dark: it was also somewhat disingenuous towards other countries. When the Italian Ambassador questioned Sir Thomas Sanderson in May 1894 about possible discussions between Britain and Japan, the Foreign Office simply said that Japan had submitted a draft new treaty which it was examining—but the draft would require considerable modifications before it could be accepted.[87] Just two months later Kimberley informed the Italian Ambassador (and the German *Chargé*) who had been invited to the Foreign Office, that the 1894 Treaty was about to be concluded.[88]

Signature of the 1894 Treaty did not end the process for there were numerous details to be completed and Satow, during his time as Minister from 1895 to 1900, was much engaged in matters ranging from the adherence of India and various British colonies to the 1894 Treaty to resolution of the land titles in respect of leasehold interests in the Treaty Ports and matters dealing with intellectual property. In this last area, Britain renounced extra-territoriality, with effect from 1897, for the 'hearing and determination ... insofar as it applies to patents, trademarks and designs'[89] so that British subjects could benefit from the 'most favoured nation' provisions arising from the German treaty revisions which had given immediate protection to Germany in the area of intellectual property but had provided that the Japanese courts were to determine such intellectual property matters.

In 1897, Satow negotiated a consular convention with Okuma to allow Consuls to continue to act judicially in relation to shipping offences (except those which involved a disturbance of the peace in Japan) and to allow the heirs of deceased British subjects in Japan to take possession of the deceased's property if the heirs were also British subjects. These provisions were reciprocal.[90]

---

86 Gubbins to Foreign Office, 12 March 1894; FO881/6582.
87 Kimberley to Sir Clare Ford (Ambassador to Rome), 16 May 1894; FO881/6582.
88 Kimberley to Paget, 13 July 1894; FO881/6582.
89 FO881/7033.
90 FO881/7033 and FO881/7539.

Discussions surrounding revision of the Treaty had brought to the surface many debatable points connected with extra-territoriality.[91] One involved the extradition of British subjects from Japan and it was an area where Japanese governments adopted a narrow interpretation of the Treaty. Questions surrounding extradition rumbled on alongside the Treaty revision talks but were always deferred due to the greater importance attached to these talks.

Extradition of foreigners was not a numerous problem in Japan and, until the late 1880s, Britain had simply exercised the powers under the Fugitive Offenders Act, 1881 (and its precursors) as extended by OC1884 to extradite British subjects back to face prosecution in other British possessions[92]—although it had long been recognized that no power existed to extradite British subjects to third countries; but, this was because the Extradition Act, 1870 applied only to British possessions.[93] However, in 1885 in a case involving an American citizen, the Japanese adopted the view that the *Ansei* treaties applied only to crimes committed within Japan; and it had not surrendered its territorial jurisdiction over foreigners within Japan in respect of crimes committed in third countries. This was, undoubtedly, correct on a strict interpretation of the Treaty: presumably, the drafters had never considered such details and had proceeded on the basis that British subjects were subject to British consular jurisdiction in all aspects. The USA acquiesced in the Japanese view on practical grounds when the Japanese authorities undertook to arrest the wanted suspect and deliver him to the American authorities for extradition.

The British authorities adopted the same approach in 1889 when Campos, a Hong Kong born British subject of Macanese extraction, fled from Hong Kong, where he was wanted on forgery charges, to Kobe. The Consul arrested him but the Japanese authorities complained immediately so a similar approach to the earlier US case was adopted whereby the British released Campos from the Consular gaol at Kobe, the Japanese arrested him and, as an act of state, extradited him to Hong Kong at the request of the British.[94] However, when, in 1890, the Nagasaki local authorities allowed the Consul to return to Hong Kong some British

[91] See Piggott 1892, page 1.

[92] James E. Hoare, 'Japan undermines extra-territoriality: extradition in Japan 1885–1899', Ian Nish and Charles Dunn eds. *European Studies on Japan*, (Tenterden, Kent, 1979), pages 125–129.

[93] Legal Opinion from Law Officers and Dr Deane, 6 June 1873; FO17/660.

[94] See Hoare 1979 for a fuller description of the incident.

military deserters by the traditional methods, the Japanese government sought an extradition treaty with the British to regularize matters.

Substantial agreement had been reached by Autumn 1892 on a rendition agreement when a new Japanese government sought, instead, a formal extradition treaty as 'Count Mutsu is an emphatic supporter of the doctrine that extra-territoriality in Japan is limited to jurisdiction in respect of offences committed within the country ... [and] ... in no case can a fugitive ... from abroad be arrested and held on the warrant of the Court of his own nation established in Japan.'[95] Fraser supported the Japanese request for an extradition treaty after the case of the Spaniard, Nieves[96]—who had been held at the instance of the Spanish authorities in the British Gaol at Yokohama and had 'caused that establishment to be watched by Japanese detectives and blockaded for months'.[97] However, he was instructed not to pursue the question because Treaty revision discussions were ongoing. When Fraser returned to the issue in 1893, the Foreign Office still doubted 'the expediency of making any fresh treaty with Japan while the question of the revision of the old one is in suspense' as 'no serious harm will be done by leaving matters as they are at present'.[98]

So matters rested until after the conclusion of the 1894 Treaty when Satow, at the Singapore government's request, asked the Japanese to follow the earlier precedents and have the Japanese police arrest Kam Quen Sean who was believed to have fled to Japan following his charge with embezzling $100,000. The Japanese government agreed but stated that 'in the absence of an Extradition Treaty ... [it] ... must be regarded as an Act of State, and ... should [not] be considered as a precedent...'[99]

The British government reconsidered the need for an extradition treaty but its legal advisers identified a number of technical problems in having any such treaty prior to the ending of extra-territoriality. Furthermore, it did not wish to create a precedent which might cause Turkey, Persia and China to request similar treaties.[100] So, the British government, again, concluded that an extradition treaty with Japan 'would at present not

95 De Bunsen to Rosebery, 7 October 1892; FO881/6417.

96 See Hoare 1979.

97 Fraser memorandum, 28 November 1892; FO881/6417.

98 Internal note by Currie endorsed by Rosebery, 17 and 20 respectively, August 1893; FO881/6417.

99 Satow to Salisbury, 5 December 1895; FO881/7912.

100 Internal Foreign Office memorandum by C.B. Robertson, 22 October 1896; FO881/7912.

serve any useful end' but volunteered that 'as soon, however, as the 1894 Treaty shall come into force [it] will be prepared to re-examine the question with a view ... of meeting the wishes of the Japanese government for a permanent arrangement'.[101] Okuma initially 'quite understood the point ... [and] ... saw no objection to acting on the same plan as hitherto, of dealing with such cases as might arise on the grounds of international comity'[102] but, when the Nagasaki Consul sought the co-operation of the local police later that year to arrest a suspect fleeing from Hong Kong, the Japanese government reversed itself and said a treaty was now needed.[103] When the suspect did not appear in Nagasaki, the matter was dropped.

Implementation of the 1894 Treaty

In July 1898, the Japanese government gave notice to Britain that the 1894 Treaty would come into force on 17 July 1899—but there remained a small technical problem as regards extra-territoriality. Whilst the 1894 Treaty became operative generally on 17 July 1899, the Austro-Hungarian and French treaties abolishing the extra-territorial rights of their subjects and citizens only became operational on 4 August and, under the 'most favoured nation' provisions of the 1894 Treaty, British subjects were entitled to claim the same rights. Practical questions also arose as to the status of matters of which the Courts were seised on the date when extra-territoriality lapsed.

Satow and Aoki (again Foreign Minister) agreed that the 1894 Treaty's 'operation as regards Her Majesty's Consular jurisdiction should be suspended until 4 August 1899 ... [and] ... as regards any judicial matters pending in any ... [Courts] ...on the day above-mentioned'.[104] Thus, besides extending the date for the abolition of extra-territoriality to 4 August the agreement also provided for the Courts to continue to exercise jurisdiction over all cases before them prior to that date. In explaining the deferral to 4 August to the Consuls, Satow instructed them that it was 'to be hoped ... there will be no troublesome cases between 17 July and August 4 and we may perhaps anticipate ... that they will be the usual refusals of duty or police cases...' and the Consuls should '...do whatever seems to you desirable to discourage people from bringing actions during

[101] Salisbury to Satow, 13 November 1896; FO881/7912.
[102] Satow to Salisbury, 8 January 1897; FO881/7912.
[103] Lowther to Salisbury, 2 June 1897; FO881/7912.
[104] Villiers to Hannen, 19 August 1899; FO656/58.

this transitional period'.[105] Aoki told the Kobe Governor '...to wink at any small offences that could ... be passed over till 4 August...'[106] but, otherwise, failed to give clear instructions to judicial and police authorities in the ports.

No publicity was given to this agreement between Satow and Aoki and the foreign Press in Japan stirred up confusion over the precise date for extra-territoriality's end. The *Eastern World* complained that British subjects were 'quite in the dark as to what jurisdiction they were under' after 17 July until Satow confirmed publicly, on 18 July that British subjects could still bring actions in the Courts up to 4 August.[107] On that date, British jurisdiction ceased formally and the Governor of Kanagawa *ken* and the Mayor of Yokohama held garden parties at the Cricket Ground celebrating the ending of extra-territoriality or, in the words of the *Eastern World*, 'making us forget the funeral of consular jurisdiction'.[108]

The Suspension of Jurisdiction in Japan Order in Council of 7 October 1899 (**OC1899**) gave retrospective effect to extra-territoriality's end and provided that 'as regards all such matters and cases as come within the jurisdiction of the Japanese Courts, the operation of the Orders in Council regulating Her Majesty's jurisdiction in ... Japan shall cease to be in force and operation ... as from 4 August 1899 except as regards any judicial matters pending ... on the day above-mentioned'. This left a number of untidy loose-ends as one could not just eliminate all references to Japan in the earlier (and still extant) Orders in Council relating to British jurisdiction in China and Korea because OC1884 dealt with Korea by incorporating provisions in them which referred to Japan.[109] One important detail which remained unchanged was the Supreme Court's name. This continued as the 'Supreme Court for China and Japan' until it became the 'Supreme Court for China and Korea' by the China and Korea (Supreme Court) Order in Council 1900. The continued use of this title triggered complaints from the Japanese Consul-General in Shanghai but the Foreign Office considered that as 'the Japanese government have not complained, I should take no notice of the Japanese Consul'[110] and advised that the name would be dealt with in a future consolidating Order in Council.

---

105 Satow to Kobe, Yokohama and Nagasaki Consuls, 16 June 1897; Ruxton 2005, page 415.

106 Hall to Satow, 1 August 1899; Ruxton 2005, 425.

107 22 July 1899; EW.

108 29 July 1899; EW.

109 W.E. Davidson to Hannen, 23 March 1900; FO17/1432.

110 Bertie's endorsement on Hannen to Salisbury, 5 October 1899; FO17/1394.

Winding up the administrative loose ends of extra-territoriality largely fell to Wilkinson. It involved not only the conclusion of all pending cases but registration of new titles for the old leases in the concessions and the transfer of the affairs of the old foreign municipalities' affairs in Kobe and Osaka (being the only ones which still ran themselves) to the Japanese authorities. The last contentious case 'not only in the British Court but as regards any remnants of foreign jurisdiction'[111] was a civil suit against Reynell brought on 30 July 1899 in Kobe. It was still pending in November 1899 when the Japanese government expressed its wish '...to wipe it [the case and all remnants of foreign jurisdiction] out of existence...'[112] and encouraged Satow to influence Wilkinson to accede to the defendant's application for it to be either struck out for want of prosecution or transferred to the Japanese courts—but this was a judicial matter in which Satow could not interfere.[113]

The Foreign Office also expressed concern that the winding up of HMCJ's affairs seemed 'to take a very long time'[114] and would be '...be glad to see the doors shut...'[115] It should not have been surprised at the time taken because, as early as February 1899, Satow had anticipated that Wilkinson would take until the end of the year to finish all the civil and criminal cases, leaving just one bankruptcy case outstanding which he proposed should be handled by appointing Bonar as acting Assistant Judge.[116] This timetable was largely adhered to because Wilkinson had wound up most business at HMCJ by early 1900 when he and Bonar sat on the Bench at the beginning of February for the final public hearing before HMCJ when Wilkinson delivered his reserved judgment in *In re Enslie*.[117]

The courtroom was packed with members of the public for this occasion. The current Yokohama and Kobe bars—apart from Kirkwood—were also present at the barristers' table along with Hiram Parkes Wilkinson, the Crown Advocate for China, and Ideoru, a Japanese barrister who, although not admitted to HMCJ, was given a seat at the barristers' table. After Wilkinson's judgment, Litchfield made a concluding speech in honour of the court before C.D. Moss, the Court Clerk, uttered the final

[111] Whitehead to Satow, 29 November 1899; Ruxton 2005, page 219.

[112] Ibid.

[113] In the event, Wilkinson heard the case as arbitrator, thus satisfying all parties; ibid. See page 226.

[114] Villiers to Satow, 6 February 1900; Ruxton 2005, page 31.

[115] Ibid.

[116] Satow to Gosselin, 22 February 1899; Ruxton 2007, pages 153 and 154.

[117] See page 241.

words spoken in HMCJ when he declared 'Know all men, this Court stands adjourned. God Save the Queen.'[118] After rounds of several farewell dinners and presentations, Wilkinson left Yokohama on home leave from 23 February 1900 for three months and left Bonar in charge of HMCJ as acting Judge in his absence.[119]

On his return, Wilkinson dealt with the final administrative details involved in closing HMCJ. The court's own monies were transferred to the Legation's account whilst unclaimed amounts in respect of deceased estates were remitted to HM Treasury, and amounts held on trust for particular persons were transferred to the Yokohama Consulate and the Consul-General and Vice-Consul in Yokohama were appointed the judicial trustees of such monies.[120] The archives of HMCJ and its predecessor courts in Yokohama were also transferred to the Consulate-General. On 1 June 1900, Wilkinson issued his final Circular as Judge to all the Consuls informing them of HMCJ's formal closure.[121]

---

118 3 February 1900; JWM and EW.
119 Wilkinson to Salisbury, 31 January and 23 February 1900; FO46/534.
120 Wilkinson to Salisbury, 29 May 1900; FO46/534.
121 Circular of 1 June 1900 enclosed with Wilkinson to Salisbury, 2 June 1900; FO46/534.

CHAPTER NINE

CONCLUSION

Extra-territoriality is sometimes regarded as being synonymous with the Western settlements and Treaty Port life: it should not be. It was just one aspect of the wider Treaty and foreign settlement regime. Whilst, from a modern perspective, there can be no counterpoint to the Japanese view that extra-territoriality was offensive to its sovereignty and status, it is possible to demonstrate that the prejudices which gave rise to the original demands for extra-territoriality did not translate into an institutional bias on the Courts' part. This study has focused on how the British Courts operated in Japan from 1859 to 1899 and has examined the large bedrock of cases in the Courts and the individuals who operated the system to re-assess criticisms of the British extra-territorial system made by earlier studies. It does not support earlier criticisms that Japanese litigants 'might meet with downright bias and injustice',[1] or support those complaints which have revolved around the Courts' structure with its appeals process involving Shanghai and London (and alleged attendant delays and expense) and a restricted original jurisdiction besides a general questioning of the legal competence of the judicial officers who ran the system. Apart from Chang,[2] previous writers have not considered these criticisms in the context of the Courts' wider case-load.

The initial structure was instituted somewhat hurriedly in 1859 and 1860 but, alive to its problems (and those in China), the British authorities sought to remedy them and, over the forty years of extra-territoriality, the Courts evolved from legally untrained Consuls trying under 50 cases or so annually into a system, involving several hundreds of cases a year, supervised by an experienced Judge, who heard all the important cases, and a Bar to represent litigants. Physical security was the Western settlements' principal concern for their first five years, so the principal focus of any examination of the Courts—and any deficiencies—should be on the comprehensive system established by OC1865. This was implemented just

[1] Jones 1931, page 70.

[2] Chang 1984.

as the Courts' work-load increased significantly until it appears to have plateau-ed (or, in some ports, declined after) around 1880.

Consuls continued to hold Courts in their own Provinces but under judicial supervision. OC1865 simplified the appellate process so all appeals—in civil cases and (in theory, but not in practice) in criminal cases—went to the Supreme Court and thence to the Privy Council. Criticisms of this structure must be considered in the context of an average of just three appeals annually to the Supreme Court before 1878 and just one a year from HMCJ afterwards, with even fewer appeals within Japan from the Courts to HMCJ. Until 1877, nearly a fifth of the appeals were heard within Japan and, only afterwards, did all appeals go to Shanghai (save only for the few post-OC1878 appeals from the Provincial Courts to HMCJ). Claims of undue delay due to distance between Japan and Shanghai are not borne out by the cases. Even in the *Glamorganshire*, where it would appear that the defendants played the system to drag out the case, it took only six months from HMCJ's initial decision to the Supreme Court's deciding the appeal. In litigation, this is not a long period and one cannot always blame the structure for actions of the litigants. The greatest delays in appeals to the Supreme Court occurred around 1877–1881 but these were due to the Courts' workload, the parties' own circumstances or the Chief Justice's illness—not distance from Shanghai.

Appeals to the Privy Council would, obviously, engender greater delays, but such appeals were only ever intended to be the exception; and the delays that occurred were no different from colonial appeals and even litigation in England. In reality, complaints about Privy Council appeals were more theoretical than substantive as only the defendants in the *Glamorganshire* used a Privy Council appeal as a delaying tactic—unlike losing defendants in China. Jones' complaint that expense alone precluded Japanese litigants from appealing to the Supreme Court[3] is not supported by the cases. Six Japanese litigants appealed to the Supreme Court—all but one successfully—and, at about a tenth of all appellants, the proportion of Japanese appellants matched the proportion of Japanese plaintiffs in civil cases reported in Yokohama. Further, it was perfectly possible for litigants to have their appeals heard entirely on papers—in both the Supreme Court and the Privy Council.

OC1865 is criticized for reserving Admiralty and matrimonial jurisdiction to the Supreme Court. Given the legal complexities surrounding both

[3] Jones 1931, page 70.

jurisdictions, it is difficult to see what other course could have been adopted prior to the introduction of a legally qualified judiciary into the Courts. The lack of Admiralty jurisdiction was a valid concern given the number of shipping related disputes that came before the Courts; but, even this criticism can be over-stated. Hornby and Goodwin heard Admiralty cases on circuit in Japan up until 1870 and, with the Yokohama Court's establishment in 1871, the problem went away—except in the outports, where few Admiralty cases were ever initiated. The Courts' lack of matrimonial jurisdiction before OC1878 conferred it upon HMCJ was not a practical issue as contemporary mores meant that few people brought matrimonial disputes to court: they simply adjusted their lifestyles and living arrangements. The only reported matrimonial case before 1878 was compromised under Hornby's aegis and none was reported after 1878.

A more practical concern for many residents—but one which has not been raised previously—was the reservation of jurisdiction to the Supreme Court in the case of Letters of Administration until 1878. This resulted in delays in handling intestacies whilst the Consuls communicated with Shanghai. By and large, this drawback did not affect the Japanese and could be argued to be a small price for the British community to pay for extra-territoriality. In practice, it affected more the poorer members of the community as the wealthier members tended to leave Wills where Probates could be granted by the Consuls except in contested cases (of which there are no reports).

An obvious defect of the wider extra-territorial regime was the absence of any procedure for handling cases where multiple nationalities were involved. This concern applied to both civil and criminal matters. In 1877, when Bennet, William and Hansen were arrested by the Japanese police for trying to pass off counterfeit $500 HSBC notes in Yokohama, all were tried separately: Bennet before the Danish consul, Williams before the US consul and Hansen, a naturalized British subject, before the Consul.[4] The absence of a combined criminal jurisdiction might mean that, as in this case, a prosecution had to be run several times with concomitant additional costs but it appears not to have been a major problem—at least so far as the British authorities were concerned. The concern was more for the Japanese authorities and the wider community for, as seen in Chapter 4 (The Sea), some countries' consuls were not prepared to exercise their jurisdiction and the Japanese could not. Again, as discussed in Chapter 5

[4] 1 March 1877; NCH.

(Civil Jurisdiction) with civil matters, it might necessitate Britons taking separate proceedings in the Japanese courts but, as the Privy Council recognized in *IJG v. P&O*, this was simply a practical price the British community needed to pay for the benefits it saw in having extra-territoriality.

Letters written by Hornby to justify the Yokohama Court's establishment have been cited by others as evidence for the deficiencies of legally untrained Consuls;[5] however, they should be read with care for his other correspondence shows a tendency to exaggerate a position in order to make a point. The problem can also be overstated. We must be realistic about the Consuls' case-load: most criminal offences involved minor public order offences of a type generally handled by lay magistrates in Britain who, at that time, would not necessarily have been attended by legally qualified clerks for hearings. Further, half or more of criminal offence cases involved shipping offences where jurisdiction arose not because of extra-territoriality but international shipping practice as codified for British vessels by the Merchant Shipping Acts. With just over 20 Yokohama residents over the entire 40 year period being gaoled for over a month—and just seven for a year or longer, it is difficult to argue that the Courts' criminal jurisdiction drove the need to professionalize the service. Professionalization was driven by civil cases: whilst many civil cases were relatively straightforward debt recovery cases, a third of civil cases in Yokohama and Kobe—and a tenth in Nagasaki[6]—involved claims of over $250. Shipping disputes, which tended to be more complex, involved 15% or more of those Ports' civil cases.[7]

Criticism is sometimes voiced of Student Interpreters acting as locums in charge of consulates—with the implication that they were involved in the discharge of judicial functions. Certainly, they acted as locums; but, to extrapolate from this to suggest that they acted as consul judges would be wrong. There is no evidence that they did so—in fact, to the contrary. They had no jurisdiction and could not, therefore, have presided over any judicial proceedings. Where junior locums were in place, it was necessary to appoint formally more senior consuls to act with jurisdiction—as when Robertson was attached to Tokyo to deal with legal proceedings because Hall, a junior locum, lacked such jurisdiction.

None can deny that, initially, the Consuls lacked legal training; however, they mostly did their best to do justice between the parties before

[5] Platt 1971, page 191; Hoare 1994, page 58.

[6] Table 20.

[7] Table 19.

them and the deficiency was appreciated and addressed. First, OC1865 gave the Judge, in place of a legally unqualified Consul-General, exclusive supervisory responsibility for the Consuls' judicial duties and an essential part of the Judge's role was to advise and support them. Second, Hornby realized rapidly that Japan required its own dedicated judicial officer and, from 1871, Yokohama had its own resident judge. Third, Consuls were allowed to read for the Bar during their furloughs and, in time, a basic legal knowledge became part of the Student Interpreter-ship examinations.

Apart from Troup, after 1878, the Yokohama Consul was a lawyer as he was, *ex officio*, Assistant Judge so, absences apart (when, occasionally, a legally unqualified official might hold an acting position), there were two legally trained judges handling the majority of all cases in Japan. With the Kobe Consul, who had the next highest legal work-load, also usually legally qualified after this time, it left only Nagasaki and Hakodate with only the occasional legally qualified Consul; but, both ports' legal case-load dropped after 1880 and, at all times, the Consuls there were able to call upon the Judge for advice in cases of difficulty. The Tokyo Vice-Consulate's legal work-load dropped away to almost nothing after 1880 so it was really moot whether or not its Vice-Consul was legally qualified—not least because HMCJ was so close by in Yokohama.

From 1872, when Hornby settled the Yokohama' Court's status, until the end of extra-territoriality, the system was dominated by a handful of individuals, all of whom were pretty much of the same generation: Hannen, Wilkinson and Mowat, as judges; Enslie, Robertson and Troup as increasingly senior Consuls and Kirkwood, Litchfield and Lowder as barristers.[8] That the first two, along with Rennie, became Chief Justice, attests to the high calibre of HMCJ's judges.

Unlike at home and in most colonies, the Judges were all appointed 'at Her Majesty's pleasure' and, like the Consuls, were Crown servants under the Foreign Office. Whether due to this lack of tenure or to their individual professionalism,[9] we see none of the occasional squabbles between individual members of the judiciary and the Executive that occurred in the early years of SCHK or the Australian colonies. Similarly, judicial orders were implemented by other governmental officials—unlike the USA's

---

[8] In its obituary of Lowder, the *Eastern World* said that he and Kirkwood had 'practically monopolized the forensic practice' in the Courts for much of their time in Japan; 1 February 1902; EW.

[9] Apart from Vyse (whose role in the Ainu Bones affair led to his resignation), none was removed for his handling of cases.

Yokohama naval commander who ignored its Yokohama consul's fine on McCondville. A similar harmony was evident in the policies of successive British governments towards Japan in relation to the Courts. Apart from Derby's tenure of the Foreign Office from 1874–1878, British foreign policy was dominated by just three men—Granville, Salisbury and Rosebery, as Foreign Secretary or Prime Minister—from 1870 until the ending of extra-territoriality. Policy did not change as governments changed but displayed a bi-partisan gradual but consistent move towards recognizing Japan's aspirations to end extra-territoriality and the role of the Courts.

Jones's claim that 'there were not usually many lawyers' to assist litigants[10] is not borne out generally after the early 1870s by when a thriving Bar existed in Yokohama. Except, perhaps, in a couple of cases in the last two or three years, all litigants were able to access the legal advice they needed. The only defendant in a criminal case who was recorded as having claimed he could not obtain legal advice was Captain Drake at his committal proceedings in Kobe; but, his claim was challenged by the prosecution counsel—and as the prosecution had come from Yokohama, one must wonder why Drake had been unable to obtain advice from there. Whilst lawyer numbers dropped, and stabilized, from 1880 onwards, many counsel stayed substantial periods in Japan and became part of the community's social and commercial fabric and were well able to provide legal advice. The *Glamorganshire* and the *Chishima cases* show high levels of legal sophistication and an awareness of current legal developments in England. Although practicalities, cost or a perception of higher standards meant that Shanghai counsel were usually instructed for appeals, this was not always the case and Yokohama-based counsel appeared occasionally before the Supreme Court in Shanghai—as they had when it sat in Japan before 1877—besides settling the terms of many appeals heard entirely on papers.

From the beginning, the British authorities recognized the implicit corollary of extra-territoriality was that Britain would control its subjects and provide effective remedies for Japanese claimants and the Judges and most Consuls were concerned that there should be no criticism of the Courts. To this end, there was a close relationship between most Consuls and local Japanese officials to ensure that the system worked. Although Japanese litigants were obliged to conduct cases through the medium of English and English jurisprudence reflected different cultural norms and involved novel concepts and the practices and procedures of the Courts

[10] Jones 1931, page 69.

were, in many ways, alien to what the Japanese would have known before 1859, the Courts provided interpreters and most Consuls spoke Japanese besides taking time to explain procedural requirements and treating Japanese litigants sympathetically. If anything, many in the British community considered that the authorities leant over too far backwards to accommodate Japanese concerns about British behaviour. Even the Japanese government accepted that the British system was comprehensive for, even though pressing for Japanese regulations to be enforced automatically, its Minister for Foreign Affairs conceded that 'no Treaty Power excepting Great Britain possessed the means of enforcing such regulations by the infliction of penalties in its own Courts'.[11] He compared the situation with the USA, which accepted Japanese municipal regulations as binding upon its citizens, but where '...there is no case recorded in which an American citizen has been punished for infraction of Japanese law'.[12]

Inevitably, individual Japanese litigants could be dissatisfied with the results of individual cases; but, the judicial officers' concern to demonstrate their independence shows through in the cases and it is difficult to justify claims of bias by the Courts against Japanese litigants. Chang demonstrated this by looking at just five well-known cases.[13] This book has reviewed a much wider range of cases and goes deeper and wider than previous writings to show that there were no consistent patterns which would prove an institutional bias—although there are suggestions that individual Britons may have sought to shelter behind the Courts to avoid legitimate liabilities to 'smaller' Japanese traders and individuals. This tended not to happen with larger Japanese businesses or the Japanese authorities and, even with 'smaller' traders and individuals, it availed the defendants naught. Where a quantitative analysis of the case results shows Japanese litigants' results as out of line with other groups (thereby raising questions of possible bias), a detailed consideration of the individual cases usually explains the discrepancies away. This was true even in jury trials where one might expect jurors to favour their fellow citizens. Against this, two cases involving Japanese prosecutors heard by Consuls with Assessors would suggest that Assessors could be prejudiced in favour of their fellow subjects—particularly in the earlier days;[14] but, this conclusion is not

[11] Parkes to Salisbury, 24 January 1880; FO46/267.
[12] Ibid.
[13] Chang 1984.
[14] The Moss and Archibald King cases.

applicable to all cases heard with Assessors. Even in the two cases concerned, the Consuls—whose decision was final in such cases—acted independently of such pressures.

Despite this, Consuls were not prepared to convict in a number of cases arising from breach of the Customs' Regulations where they considered a conviction would be 'unjust' or 'unfair' to the defendant. This often led to their re-interpreting the Treaty as they wished it had read. Here, a prejudice was clearly operating; but it was more a prejudice against perceived inflexibility by the Japanese Customs and in favour of a perception of 'fairness' than an inherent anti-Japanese bias for the Courts imposed the Treaty's penalties wherever they considered the defendant had acted wrongly. Where the Japanese authorities complained of these re-readings of the Treaty or other attempts to extend the boundaries of extra-territoriality beyond the Treaty's strict terms, the Foreign Office, its internal legal advisers and the Law Officers always adopted a narrow constructionist approach to the Treaty, which favoured Japan. This was a consistent feature of British governments of both political hues so there was little of the expansion of British rights and power that 'men on the spot' so often achieved elsewhere in British imperial history.

Overall, Gubbins concluded that the Treaty provisions had, over time, 'worked out their own salvation' and, despite occasional conflicts of jurisdiction and mistakes of detail, justice was, in practice, secured. Britain's position was unique in that no other Treaty Power matched the efficiency or extent of the Courts. Japanese suitors had confidence in the Courts and British residents had little about which to complain as justice was prompt, on the whole satisfactory and nearly costless (to them, if not to the British taxpayer).[15]

This impression of a generally professionally run and even-handed system which operated without bias to dispense substantial justice to all-comers, who had access to a competent, independent Bar suggests two broader conclusions about the operation of British extra-territoriality in Japan. First, the Japanese authorities were able to use the Treaty's language in order to counter any expansionist tendencies exhibited by local British officials (and as an active tool in their battle to end extra-territoriality). This highlights the distinction between Japan and China where the Mixed Court was established in Shanghai, counter-claims

[15] Gubbins memoranda, 30 February 1887; FO881/5773; and 26 February 1894; FO881/6582.

against Chinese subjects were permitted in the Supreme Court, extradition to British territories continued and all sailors on British warships benefitted from British protection. Even in smaller matters, we see differences from practice in China with the remission of court fees for Japanese plaintiffs and the waiver of their need to provide security in certain cases. Few Japanese sought to use British extra-territorial rights to avoid Japanese government control and Japan's standing is shown by Britain giving no support or encouragement to such few attempts as were made.

Perhaps paradoxically, it is through cases and incidents involving extra-territoriality that we can see Britain's recognition of Japan's growing power and independence from foreign tutelage until it reached a position of equality. Several cases and incidents stood as a proxy for direct diplomacy and allowed both countries to adjust their relationship gradually without formal agreements or declarations. In each of the *Hartley cases*, the Campos extradition case and the *Chishima cases*, the 'men on the spot' all inclined to a wider interpretation of Britain's rights than the Treaty justified (and interpretations supported by practice in China); but, in each, the authorities in London adopted a narrow interpretation which accommodated Japan. The ultimate recognition of Japan's being on a par with Western powers came with the 1897 Hakodate incident when Britain was compelled to accept that, absent treaties, sailors on its warships had no greater protection in Japan than in Western countries.

Although extra-territoriality was clearly a 'Big Issue' in late Nineteenth century Japan, it is difficult to avoid the suspicion that its impact on Anglo-Japanese relations was out of all proportion to the numbers of British subjects in Japan at that time. In 1880, foreign residents numbered just above 6,000, of whom just over 1,000 were British (with over 3,600 being Chinese).[16] Even looking at sailors on board British vessels trading with Japan, we see that (on the basis of the available reports) just some 20 a year out of some 25,000 were prosecuted for criminal offences committed onshore Japan—as distinct from shipping offences.[17] Extra-territoriality may have engendered a secure feeling or atmosphere amongst Britons in Japan but its biggest practical benefit may have been—at least in the early

---

[16] Appendix IV.

[17] Table 3 and Plunkett to Granville, 22 July 1884; FO881/5072. In 1883, a total of 37,371 sailors on ships of all nationalities visited Japan. Even recognizing that not all the sailors on board the British vessels would have been British subjects and that the newspaper reports may have under-reported criminal offences in Yokohama and Kobe, this was not a high proportion.

years after Japan's opening—as a means of avoiding 'Don Pacifico' type incidents to the detriment of Britain's overall relations with Japan. Granville, in his discussions with Iwakura and afterwards, had certainly been aware of the risks that incidents arising out of perceptions of abuse of Japanese jurisdiction could trigger demands for a more active or interventionist response than any British government would wish to take.

This study recognizes that the British courts did not operate in isolation and that all the Western Powers had their own consular courts in Japan at that time. Thus, it is perhaps appropriate to consider related areas of interest to historians of the period which this study does not cover. Where Britons had claims against other foreigners, they needed to interact with those courts but that interaction is outside the scope of this book—as are what were the increasing numbers of claims by Britons against Japanese individuals and businesses during the period. Strictly, such latter claims had nothing to do with extra-territoriality but were an ordinary function of Japan's territorial jurisdiction. However, their handling did colour the views of Britons—and officialdom—about the need or otherwise for British extra-territoriality and the discussions for revision of the Treaty. A study of such claims—and particularly the handling of Anglo-Japanese disputes and actions in the immediate period after extra-territoriality's ending would be necessary to show whether or not the British community's fears surrounding extra-territoriality's end were justified or not.

Apart from Johannes Berchtold's work on the British courts in the Ottoman Empire,[18] there are no recent in depth studies of the workings of British extra-territoriality elsewhere. Thus, there is scope to compare the British system in Japan with how British extra-territoriality worked elsewhere in addition to comparing the work of the Courts with the work of the consular courts of other countries in Japan to see whether the conclusions drawn here are equally applicable to those courts of other countries.

[18] Johannes Berchtold, *Recht und Gerichtigkeit in der Konsulargerichtsbarkeit* (Oldenbourg Wissenschaftsverlag GmbH, Munich, 2009).

EPILOGUE

With the ending of the extra-territoriality and the Courts, the structures and personnel which they had sustained for the last forty years melted away. In Yokohama, the British gaol—empty of all its inmates—was acquired by the Japanese government which had made separate arrangements to accommodate foreign prisoners under a special regime in the Sugamo gaol. HMCJ's courtroom and facilities, which were part of the consulate-general, simply reverted to consular use and all that remains of that Court is the Royal Coat of Arms which now hangs in the Yokohama Archives of History—itself housed in the post-1923 British consulate-general. In the other consulates, the courtrooms which had never been distinct parts of the consulate also reverted to general use—as did the consular gaols which had been merely outbuildings within the consulate compound. Nothing now remains of them as, for one reason or another, all the consulates were replaced during the twentieth century. Of HMCJ's last personnel, Wilkinson transferred to Shanghai where he succeeded Hannen as Chief Justice whilst Bonar became fully subsumed in his consular work. The Clerk and acting Registrar, C.D. Moss, established himself in Yokohama towards the end of 1900 as an Estate and Commission Agent and Insurance Broker but died two years later whilst George Hodges, the Usher, retired.[1] For the other Consuls, judicial work ceased to form part of their work save in relation to the Merchant Shipping Acts where they continued to determine cases of shipping offences and to hold Naval Courts and Inquiries. However, punishments ceased to include fines and terms of imprisonment but were confined to deductions from wages.

The ending of extra-territoriality meant that British lawyers in Japan lost their court functions and faced reduced work opportunities. Among the lawyers present at the last public session of HMCJ, Lowder continued to practise in Yokohama in association with Japanese lawyers and patent attorneys before dying in 1902, aged 59.[2] Litchfield initially returned to Shanghai but seems not to have stayed there long for he soon returned to Yokohama where he worked in partnership with Japanese attorneys until his death, aged 64, in 1907.[3] Crosse also left Japan after HMCJ closed but

1 6 October 1900 and 6 June 1902; EW.
2 Obituary, 1 February 1902; EW.
3 Obituary, 14 September 1907; EW.

returned to Kobe in 1905 where he worked in association with a Japanese lawyer until his death some 15 years later.[4] His most famous subsequent trial was when he defended Bethell before the Supreme Court on circuit in Seoul in 1908 on a charge instigated by the Japanese authorities who then controlled the Korean government. George Hawthorne Scidmore, the sole US lawyer at that hearing, returned to work in the US consular service—principally in Japan—until he died in 1922. Kirkwood continued to act as legal adviser to the Ministry of Justice until 1901 when he retired to England where he lived in retirement in London and Bath until 1926.

Ahead of extra-territoriality's ending, Duncan McNeill had left Japan in 1895 for Hong Kong before moving to Shanghai in October 1895.[5] From Kobe, Brushfield also left for Shanghai after 1899. Here, he supervised and ran Hiram Parkes Wilkinson's practice whilst the latter was away from Shanghai during his father's Chief Justice-ship until 1905.[6] Walford was the only lawyer to return to practice in England where he practised on the Midlands and Oxford Circuit[7] until he died in 1920. These departures were part of a general drift of foreigners from Japan to Hong Kong and Shanghai; but, whereas, there was no obvious ongoing role for foreign lawyers in Japan once extra-territoriality had ended, there were disputes as to the cause of the wider drift away. Some suggested that abolition of extra-territoriality was the cause but the *Eastern World* argued that it had more to do with a general rise in price levels and a decline in the foreigners' standards of living and business opportunities in Japan after the Sino-Japanese War.

Law reports continued to be published in the English language Press but, of course, these now covered only cases in the Japanese courts—although, unsurprisingly, there was a focus on cases involving foreigners. Whilst cases between Japanese and British litigants continued, one gets a sense from the level of reports in the decade immediately after the end of extra-territoriality that cases between British litigants alone dropped off dramatically—although, the make up of those cases that were reported appears to have remained unchanged. It is unclear whether other civil disputes between British subjects were settled by arbitration or were litigated elsewhere—e.g. Hong Kong, Shanghai or Britain. In the immediate aftermath of the ending of extra-territoriality, the Press was full of

[4] See Directories.

[5] 4 October 1895; NCHLR.

[6] See Directories. Hiram Parkes Wilkinson was required to absent himself from Shanghai: first, as British Commissioner for claims arising from the Boxer Rising and then as acting Judge in Bangkok.

[7] Whittington-Egan, 1996, page 214.

criticisms for the Japanese judges: for their lack of expertise, slow handling of cases with frequent adjournments and, even, for a lack of knowledge of Latin![8] Many cases went on appeal where the appeal court tended to re-hear the whole case. The Press suggested that the low calibre of the Japanese judges was attributable to low judicial salaries which meant that the better judges quickly left the Bench for private practice once they had obtained some experience.

The Press was critical of seemingly harsh sentences passed in criminal cases against British subjects—particularly in cases arising out of disputes with coolies but the *Eastern World* praised the Japanese police, whose future behaviour had caused the foreign community much nervousness before the 1894 Treaty came into force, for having 'behaved with great tact and discretion' so that foreigners now looked upon them with respect.[9]

Remnants of Treaty and the abolition of extra-territoriality continued to cause problems in the first decade of the Twentieth century. That the British community continued, in some ways, to proceed as though the end of extra-territoriality had changed nothing for them was shown in a 1908 divorce case in England.[10] The case decided that marriages entered into in Anglican churches in Japan after the abolition of extra-territoriality were null and void so far as English law was concerned. As they did not constitute a marriage under Japanese law, they would not be recognized in England. In future, Britons who wished to marry in Japan needed to ensure that either their marriages were recognized by Japanese law or they married before a British official in accordance with the Foreign Marriage Act 1891. Some 35 to 50 marriages were affected. The decision affected not just the marriages themselves but also the legitimacy of any offspring and, potentially, inheritance rights. Bishop Awdry, the Anglican bishop for Japan, recognized that the Church was at fault for not having addressed the issue—whereas both Satow and Hall had been clear from the beginning of the problems of such marriages.[11]

Within Japan, British subjects were no longer required to register with the consulates and were allowed to travel, and own land, throughout Japan. However, a problem arose in respect of the perpetual leases which had been granted to foreigners under the Treaty in respect of land in the

8 19 January 1901; EW.

9 2 May 1903; EW.

10 *Marshall v. Marshall*, (1908) unreported.

11 See 15 and 22 February and 30 May 1908; EW and 20 February and 9 April; JWC for a general discussion of the issues.

Western settlements in Yokohama, Kobe, Nagasaki and Osaka.[12] The new Japanese Civil Codes did not recognize the concept of a perpetual lease: the closest being a perpetual *superficies* (or rights to the buildings on the land—but not rights to the land itself). Without legal recognition of their perpetual leases, the foreigners could not transfer their interests in them. After lengthy discussions on the subject between the diplomats and also in the English language Press—which printed learned discourses on the position of *superficies* under Roman law from Gaius onwards—the Diet passed primary legislation to recognize the existing perpetual leases.

Another land related issue arose in respect of the Japanese buildings tax. The extra-territorial regime had not provided any mechanism for the Japanese government to collect this tax—or any other tax—from Westerners who benefitted from extra-territoriality. With the abolition of extra-territoriality, the Japanese government sought to collect taxation—including this buildings tax—from all foreigners in Japan; but the Western residents objected that this particular tax was not permitted by the new treaties. Eventually, the matter went to international arbitration at The Hague in 1904 where the question was decided in favour of the foreign landowners. Walford was the British government's counsel at this arbitration and Bonar the arbitrator nominated by Britain to the arbitration tribunal. Both questions were resolved when the building tax was permitted by the Anglo-Japanese Treaty of 1911 which replaced the 1894 Treaty and allowed British subjects to own land in Japan on the same basis as Japanese subjects. The Japanese government then announced that it would negotiate individually with the perpetual leaseholders to buy out their leases.

Extra-territoriality and British courts continued to intrude upon Anglo-Japanese relations for the remainder of the decade: this time in Korea where Japan assumed an increasingly dominant position as the decade progressed until Korea was annexed in August 1910 when all Korea's other treaties were annulled—including Britain's 1883 Treaty of Amity and Commerce with Korea. All British extra-territoriality in Japanese territories had now expired and, with the 1911 Anglo-Japanese Treaty, Japan regained its tariff autonomy thus ending the final 'unfair' vestige of the *Ansei* treaties.

---

[12] There were no distinct Settlement areas in Hakodate, Niigata, Tokyo or Taiwan.

APPENDIX I

LEGAL OFFICERS, MINISTERS AND FOREIGN SECRETARIES, 1859–1899

Her Britannic Majesty's Supreme Court for China and Japan, 1865–1900

Judge/Chief Justice
Sir Edmund Hornby, 1865–1877
Sir George French, 1878–1881
Sir Richard Temple Rennie, 1881–1891
Sir Nicholas John Hannen, 1891–1900
Sir Hiram Shaw Wilkinson, 1900–1905

Law Secretary
John Fraser, 1865–1868
Robert Anderson Mowat, 1868–1878

Assistant Judge
Charles Wycliffe Goodwin, 1865–77
Robert Anderson Mowat, 1879–1891
George Jamieson, 1891–1897
Frederick Samuel Augustus Bourne 1898–1916

Crown Advocate, 1878–1899
Nicholas John Hannen, 1878–1881
Hiram Shaw Wilkinson, 1882–1897
Hiram Parkes Wilkinson, 1897–1924

Yokohama Court, 1870–1878

Nicholas John Hannen, 1871–1874 (acting Assistant Judge)
Charles Wycliffe Goodwin, 1874–1877 (Assistant Judge)
Hiram Shaw Wilkinson, 1877–1878 (acting Law Secretary)

Her Britannic Majesty's Court for Japan, 1879–1899

Judge
Richard Temple Rennie, 1879–1881
Nicholas John Hannen, 1881–1891
Robert Anderson Mowat, 1891–1897
Hiram Shaw Wilkinson, 1897–1899

Crown Advocate
Montague Kirkwood, 1882–1885

Crown Prosecutor
Henry Charles Litchfield, 1885–1899

British Ministers in Tokyo

Ministers

Sir Rutherford Alcock, 1859–1865
Sir Harry Parkes, 1865–1883
Sir Francis Plunkett, 1884–1887
Hugh Fraser, 1889–1894
Power Henry Le Poer Trench, 1894–95
Sir Ernest Mason Satow, 1895–1900

Chargés d'Affaires[1]

F.G. Myburgh, 1861
Lt.Col. E.St.J. Neale, 1862–64
F.O. Adams, 1871–1872
R.G. Watson, 1872–73
J.G. Kennedy, 1879–1882
Maurice de Bunsen, 1892–94
G.A. Lowther, 1895

Foreign Secretaries

Earl of Clarendon, 1855–1858
Earl of Malmesbury, 1858–1859
Earl Russell, 1859–1865
Earl of Clarendon, 1865–1866
Lord Stanley, 1866–1868
Earl of Clarendon, 1868–1870
Earl Granville, 1870–1874
Earl of Derby, 1874–1878
Marquis of Salisbury, 1878–1880
Earl Granville, 1880–1885
Marquis of Salisbury, 1885–1886
Earl of Rosebery, 1886
Earl of Iddesleigh, 1886–1887
Marquis of Salisbury, 1887–1892
Earl of Rosebery, 1892–1894
Earl of Kimberley, 1894–1895
Marquis of Salisbury, 1895–1900

[1] Only those holding the post for a substantial period of time or mentioned in the text are listed.

APPENDIX II

ORDERS IN COUNCIL APPLICABLE TO JAPAN

Japan Order in Council, 1859
Japan Order in Council, 1860
Japan Order in Council, 1861
Japan Order in Council, 1863
Japan Order in Council, 1864
China and Japan Order in Council, 1865
China and Japan Order in Council, 1869
China and Japan Maritime Order, 1874
Orders in Council regulating Consular Fees of 19 June 1868 and 21 July 1876
China and Japan Order in Council, 1877
China and Japan Order in Council, 1878
China and Japan Order in Council, 1881
The China, Japan and Corea Order in Council, 1884
The China, Japan and Corea Order in Council, 1884 (Supplemental)
The China, Japan and Corea Order in Council, 1886
The China, Japan and Corea Order in Council, 1886 (no. 2)
The Consular Fees (China, Japan and Corea) Order, 1892
The China and Japan Order in Council, 1898
The China, Japan and Corea (Supreme Court) Order in Council, 1899
The Suspension of Jurisdiction in Japan Order in Council, 1899

APPENDIX III

BRITISH LAWYERS IN JAPAN

Part I—Independent Practitioners

Name	First reference in Japan
Francis Walker Marks	1867
Frederick James Barnard	1867
H. Ross Johnson	1870
Douglas Cooper	1871
Frederick Victor Dickins	1871
John Frederick Lowder	1872
John Richard Davidson	1872
Gavin Parker Ness	1873
Albert Gibson	1874
William Montague Hammett Kirkwood	1874
Andrew Duncan	1874
Robert John Beadon	1877
Henry Charles Litchfield	1878
Herbert Bellasis	1878
John Creagh	1881
Ambrose Berry Walford	1888
Francis Taylor Piggott	1888
H.J. Pearce	1890
Duncan McNeill	1891
Charles Neville Crosse	1893
H.A.C. Brushfield	1893
P. Mackenzie Skinner	1897

Part II—Legally Qualified Consuls

Name	Qualification date
Hiram Shaw Wilkinson	1872
John Frederick Lowder	1872
James Joseph Enslie	1877
Russell Robertson	1880
John Carey Hall	1881
Ernest Mason Satow	1887
Joseph Henry Longford	1889
Henry Alfred Constant Bonar	1894
William Joseph Kenny	1896

Part III—Other Lawyers referred to as practising before the Courts

Name	Nationality	First reference in Japan
G.W. Hill	USA	1874
Gross	French	1875
Henry Willard Denison	USA	1878
George Hawthorne Scidmore	USA	1890
Professor Alexander Tison	USA	1890
Professor Henry Terry	USA	1890

APPENDIX IV

FOREIGN POPULATION IN JAPAN[1]

Part I—Total numbers of individual residents and firms

Year	British	Other Westerners	Chinese	Total	British	Other Westerners	Chinese	Total
	Individuals				Firms			
1879	1,035	1,363	3,649	**6,047**	90	141	89	**320**
1880	1,057	1,302	3,584	**5,943**	108	150	102	**360**
1881	1,127	1,426	3,553	**6,106**	109	159	78	**346**

Part II—Breakdown of numbers of individuals between the Ports in 1881

Port	Yokohama	Tokyo	Kobe & Osaka[2]	Nagasaki	Hakodate	Total[3]
British	594	158	248	98	29	**1,127**
Other Westerners	904	189	238	135	20	**1,426**
Chinese	2,245		623	599	26	**3,553**
Total	**3,743**	**347**	**1,109**	**832**	**75**	**6,106**

[1] Based upon Memorandum by Plunkett, 31 October 1883; FO881/4870.

[2] Plunkett advised that the foreign community in Osaka was made up entirely of missionaries.

[3] There appears to have been a mis-allocation of 60 between Chinese and other Westerners.

APPENDIX V

TABLES RELATING TO CASES

Note on Sources

These Tables have been compiled from the following sources:

Yokohama[1]	1867–1872	semi-annual returns: FO 656/29;
	1859–1869	Lowder's report to Parkes;[2]
	1862–1899	references to figures based on newspaper reports are to case reports in various English language newspapers published in Japan 1859–1899, and listed in the Sources and Bibliography.
Nagasaki	1859	reports in FO262/6;
	1860	newspaper reports (as above);
	1863–1866	reports in FO796/20, FO796/25, FO796/28 and FO796/29;
	1866–1874	semi-annual returns: FO656/14, FO656/34 and FO656/42;
	1875–1899	court records/ minute books: FO796/2, FO796/4, FO796/7, FO796/8 and FO796/14 (which, for 1878–1899, reflect the Register of Civil Cases, for the period in FO796/5);
	Fees	Register of Civil Cases and Register of Criminal Cases, FO796/5 and FO796/6 respectively.
Hakodate	1863–1878	semi-annual returns: FO 656/34, FO656/35 and FO656/49. There are no semi-annual returns for 1864. The first case, in 1863, is listed as no. 32, which suggests 31 prior cases (civil cases, criminal cases and shipping offences).
Kobe and Osaka	1870–1875	semi-annual returns: FO656/34 and FO656/41;
	1869–1899	references to figures based on newspaper reports are to case reports in various English language newspapers published in Kobe 1869–1871, 1876–1888 and 1897–1899, and listed in the Sources and Bibliography.
Tokyo	1871–1891	semi-annual returns: FO798/10, FO798/14, FO798/17, FO798/20, FO656/40, FO798/45, FO656/49 and FO798/51.
Appeals to:	Consul-General and SCHK	newspaper reports and, from Nagasaki, 1859–1865, FO796/20;

(*Continued*)

(Cont.)

Supreme Court	the Minute Books of the Judge/Chief Justice and the Assistant Judge (FO1092/ 364, /365 and /366); various correspondence files; the NCHLR; and, for the Yokohama asterisked column in Table 22, the figures come from Lowder's report referred to above, which lists the totals without providing any details.
Naval Courts of Enquiry	FO796/11, FO796/26; and reports in the various newspapers listed in the Sources and Bibliography.

Notes: Not all sources are consistent with each other. For instance, in 1866, FO796/29 mentions two cases (Loureiro prosecuting Stachbury for assault and a Dutch subject prosecuting three sailors for burglary) which are not listed in the semi-annual returns of cases in FO656/14 for that year. The 1867, 1868 and 1869 Yokohama figures in Parts I of Tables 3 and 17 are taken from the semi-annual returns; however, the information provided in Lowder's report (referred to above) suggests a total number of 153, 163 and 277 criminal offences and 106, 99 and 106 civil cases in those years (against 105, 212 and 181 criminal offences and 56, 97 and 51 civil cases) respectively listed in the semi-annual returns. An official report from Tokyo suggests that the civil cases for 1874 and 1875 in Table 17 totalled 41 and 48 cases (against 48 and 28 reported in the semi-annual returns) respectively.[3] Similarly with Kobe, a report from Gower (arguing for additional consular staff) suggests the criminal figures should be 47, 9 and 86 for 1870, 1871 and 1872 (against 54, 8 and 81 shown in Part I of Table 3 taken from the semi-annual returns) and 36 and 62 civil cases in 1871 and 1872 (against 54 and 106 respectively shown in Part I of Table 17).[4]

There are discrepancies between the figures where there is insufficient information to breakdown the case details. In these situations, the detailed breakdowns will not always match the total numbers of cases in any particular port.

With criminal offences, defendants occasionally faced a number of different charges. Thus, the totals for the breakdowns of the charges can even exceed the total number of defendants.

[1] References in these Tables to Yokohama encompass the Kanagawa Court, the Yokohama Court and HMCJ.

[2] Lowder to Parkes, 17 November 1869 constituting Inclosure No. 4 with Parkes to Clarendon dated 5 November 1869; FO881/1750 (dates *sic*).

[3] Dohmen to Parkes, 23 Jaunuary, 1876; FO798/25 and FO262/508.

[4] Gower to Parkes, 28 May 1873; FO262/246.

Table 1. Japan–wide, 1859–1899. Summary of Court case-load by year.

Year	Privy Council appeals	Appeal cases	Total cases	Civil cases	Total criminal offences	Criminal offences	Shipping offences	Sailors as defendants in criminal cases	Total sailors and shipping offences
1859			2	1	1	1		1	1
1860		2	16	7	9				
1861			8	4	4				
1862			24	12	12	4			
1863			32	12	20	9		2	2
1864		3	102	31	71	3		2	2
1865		4	206	52	154	15	3	10	13
1866		2	323	112	211	53	32	24	56
1867		5	225	77	148	89	59	1	60
1868		5	369	126	243	189	54		54
1869		4	312	71	241	113	112	18	130
1870		3	479	111	368	215	153	5	158
1871		7	562	175	387	237	150	6	156
1872		3	561	222	339	97	128	35	163
1873		1	359	176	183	109	74	34	108
1874		5	431	166	265	166	99	61	160
1875		4	188	87	111	76	35	29	64
1876		7	254	87	167	72	95	34	129
1877		2	195	72	123	37	86	22	108
1878	2	4	323	75	248	106	142	22	108
1879		1	213	78	135	52	83	31	124
1880			130	56	74	46	28	23	51
1881		8	109	39	70	28	42	11	53
1882		5	86	16	70	3	67	2	69
1883		1	45	12	33	13	20	5	25
1884		3	53	6	47	9	38	6	44
1885		1	99	19	80	26	54	12	66
1886		1	56	13	43	20	23	15	38
1887			38	12	26	8	18	5	23
1888	2		56	12	44	10	34	4	38
1889		2	101	26	75	42	33	33	66
1890		1	36	10	26	4	22	2	24
1891			30	5	25	3	22	2	24
1892			24	5	19	7	12	6	18
1893		2	26	6	20	8	12	4	16
1894	2	1	20	2	18	6	12	5	17
1895			56	9	47	13	34	9	43
1896		1	46	11	35	15	20	9	29
1897	1		56	5	51	23	28	13	41

(*Continued*)

Table 1. (*Cont.*)

Year	Privy Council appeals	Appeal cases	Total cases	Civil cases	Total criminal offences	Criminal offences	Shipping offences	Sailors as defendants in criminal cases	Total sailors and shipping offences
1898			87	7	80	33	47	21	68
1899	1		40	8	32	4	28	1	29

Notes: Civil cases are enumerated by numbers of civil cases.

Criminal Offences are enumerated by numbers of defendants.

Privy Council appeals include appeals from the Supreme Court together with applications to the Privy Council for leave to appeal to it (whether or not such leave was granted).

Where overlapping details from official records and newspapers are available for any year, the higher of the two figures has been taken. This Table summarizes information that is available in more detail in Tables 3, 17 and 22.

This Table should not be taken as exhaustive as to the actual numbers of cases but reflects only those of which there is a record—either in official records or in newspaper reports.

The figures for 'Sailors' is, almost certainly, an under-estimate—and significantly so for the earlier years—as it is not always possible to identify sailors in criminal cases.

The principal purpose of this Table is to give the reader a sense of the numbers of cases with which the Courts dealt, the proportionate breakdown between civil and criminal offences and, within the latter, to show the numbers of shipping offences—which, strictly, had nothing to do with extra-territoriality. It also puts the numbers of cases taken on appeal—both to the Supreme Court and to the Privy Council—into the perspective of the Courts' total case-load in Japan.

Table 2. All Ports, 1859–1899. Criminal Offences–shipping offences and criminal cases: summary case-load.

Port	Adjusted years	Defendants		Shipping offences	Criminal cases	Sailors/ visitors	Residents
		No.	Annual average				
Nagasaki							
1866–74	8.5	411	48	274	137	32	100
1875–80	6	304	51	215	89	61	28
1881–90	10	222	22	165	57	33	24
1891–99	8.5	233	27	162	71	53	18
1875–99	**24.5**	**759**	**31**	**542**	**217**	**147**	**70**
Annual average		*31*		*22*	*9*	*6*	*3*
1866–99	**33**	**1,170**	**35**	**816**	**354**	**184**	**170**
Annual average		*35*		*22*	*11*	*6*	*5*
Yokohama (based on semi-annual returns)							
1860–66 + 1872	8	616	77				
1867–71	5	1,047	209	311	736		
1860–72++	**13**	**1,866**	**143**	**311**	**736**		
Yokohama (based on newspaper reports)							
1862–70	7	91	13	18	73	36	37
1871–80	10	655	65	320	335	185	150
1881–90	10	198	20	130	68	41	27
1891–99	8.5	42	5	20	22	9	13
1862–99	**35.5**	**986**	**28**	**488**	**498**	**271**	**227**
Annual average		*28*		*14*	*14*	*8*	*6*
Kobe & Osaka, 1870–1875 (based on semi-annual returns)							
1870–75	5.5	347	63	140	207	46	161
Annual average		*63*		*25*	*38*	*8*	*29*
Kobe, 1869–1899 (based on newspaper reports)							
1869–80	8	110	14	42	68	42	26
1881–90	8	88	11	56	32	21	11
1891–99	2.5	53	21	31	22	10	12
1869–99	**18.5**	**251**	**14**	**129**	**122**	**73**	**49**
Annual average		*14*		*7*	*7*	*4*	*3*

(*Continued*)

Table 2. (*Cont.*)

Port	Adjusted years	Defendants		Shipping offences	Criminal cases	Sailors/ visitors	Residents
		No.	Annual average				
Hakodate							
1863–65	2	2	1		2		2
1866–70	5	36	7	23	13	5	8
1871–78	7	30	4	6	24	9	15
1863–78	**14**	**68**	**5**	**29**	**39**	**14**	**25**
Annual average		*5*		*2*	*3*	*1*	*2*
Tokyo							
1871–75	5	45	9				
1876–90	15	16	1				
1871–90	**20**	**61**	**3**				

Notes: Defendants include all criminal offences, both criminal cases and shipping offences. Criminal cases include all sailors and residents.

++ These figures are based on Inclosure No. 4—see footnote 2 at the beginning of this Appendix—and semi-annual returns, 1870–1872 and using the higher figure from the two sources, where relevant.

Table 3. All Ports, 1859–1899. Criminal Offences—shipping offences and criminal cases: annual case-load.

Part I—All ports, 1859–1899
(based on semi-annual returns and other official reports)

Port	Nagasaki				Yokohama+		
Year	*Defendants*	*Shipping offences*	*Criminal cases*	*Sailors*	*Defendants*	*Shipping offences*	*Criminal cases*
1859	1		1	1			
1860					9		
1861					4		
1862					12		
1863	4		4	2	15		
1864	1		1	1	70		
1865	1		1	1	152		
1866	55	26	29	14	146		
1867	41	32	9		105	26	79
1868	28	10	18		212	41	171
1869	31	25	6	1	181	76	105
1870	89	75	14		217	46	171
1871	40	27	13	5	332	122	210
1872	42	24	18	9	208		
1873	44	34	10	2			
1874	34	21	13	1			
1875	23	11	12	10			
1876	54	41	13	4			
1877	57	43	14	7			
1878	87	58	29	27			
1879	53	41	12	8			
1880	30	21	9	5			
1881	22	14	8	4			
1882	8	7	1	1			
1883	26	18	8	4			
1884	34	27	7	4			
1885	45	30	15	8			
1886	5	1	4	2			
1887	20	17	3	3			
1888	16	10	6	4			
1889	26	21	5	3			
1890	20	20					
1891	24	20	4	3			
1892	18	12	6	6			
1893	17	12	5	2			
1894	17	12	5	5			
1895	46	33	13	9			
1896	31	20	11	6			
1897	33	22	11	10			
1898	27	14	13	11			
1899	20	17	3	1			

+This Table excludes results which are based solely upon newspaper reports (see Parts II and III)

Hakodate				Kobe & Osaka+				Tokyo
Defendants	*Shipping offences*	*Criminal cases*	*Sailors*	*Defendants*	*Shipping offences*	*Criminal cases*	*Sailors*	*Defendants*
1		1						
1		1						
10	5	5						
2	1	1	1					
3	3							
13	11	2	1	16				
8	3	5	3	54	29	25	2	
4	1	3	1	8		8		3
3	2	1	1	81	35	46	13	5
7	1	6	1	94	35	59	20	6
				88	37	51	11	19
7	1	6	4	22	4	18		12
1		1						3
3		3	2					2
5	1	4						2
								2
								2
								1
								3
								1

Part II—Yokohama, 1862–1899
(based on newspaper reports)

Year	Defendants	Shipping offences	Criminal cases	Sailors/ visitors	Residents
1862	4		4		4
1863	4		4		4
1864	2		2	1	1
1865	16	3	13	9	4
1866	20	1	19	10	9
1869	42	14	28	16	12
1870	3		3		3
1871	9	2	7		7
1872	94	67	27	12	15
1873	32	4	28	11	17
1874	124	41	83	49	34
1875	47	19	28	15	13
1876	59	35	24	9	15
1877	59	43	16	11	5
1878	115	60	55	40	15
1879	77	42	35	20	15
1880	39	7	32	18	14
1881	45	28	17	7	10
1882	61	60	1	1	
1883					
1884					
1885	10	4	6		6
1886	2		2	1	1
1887					
1888	27	24	3		3
1889	48	12	36	30	6
1890	5	2	3	2	1
1891	2		2	1	1
1892	1		1		1
1893	3		3	2	1
1894	1		1		1
1895	1	1			
1896	4		4	3	1
1897	4		4	2	2
1898	24	17	7	1	6
1899	2	2			
Total	986	488	498	271	227

Note: No newspaper reports are available for 1867 and 1868. No cases were reported in the newspapers in years: 1883, 1884 and 1887.

Part III—Kobe, 1869–1899 (available years)
(based on newspaper reports)

Year	Defendants	Shipping offences	Criminal cases	Sailors/ visitors	Residents
1869	1		1		1
1870	8		8	4	4
1871	4		4		4
1876	50	19	31	21	10
1877	2		2	2	
1878	39	23	16	12	4
1879	3		3	3	
1880	3		3		3
1881	3		3		3
1882					
1883	4	2	2	1	1
1884	13	11	2	2	
1885	25	20	5	4	1
1886	36	22	14	12	2
1887	6	1	5	2	3
1888	1		1		1
1897	14	6	8	1	7
1898	29	16	13	9	4
1899	10	9	1		1
Total	251	129	122	73	49

Note: No newspaper reports are available for 1872–1875 and 1889–1896. No cases were reported in the newspapers in 1882.

Table 4. Criminal Cases, 1862–1899: Offences classified by defendants.

Part I—Numbers

Port	Public Order					
	Assault & Battery			Drunk & disorderly, Criminal damage etc		
	Defendants	Residents	Sailors	Defendants	Residents	Sailors
Nagasaki (1875–1899)	94	35	59	71	15	56
Yokohama (1862–1899) (based on newspaper reports)	179	93	86	180	41	139
Kobe & Osaka (1870–1875) (based on semi-annual returns)	95	79	16	44	26	18
Kobe (1869–1899) (based on newspaper reports)	63	29	34	37	4	33
Hakodate (1863–1878)	16	12	4	8	3	5

Note: Assault and Battery includes all offences against the person, including grievous bodily harm, murder, manslaughter and rape.

Theft			Miscellaneous		
Defendants	Residents	Sailors	Defendants	Residents	Sailors
22	7	15	30	13	17
61	38	23	47	33	14
15	15		53	41	12
13	7	6	19	9	10
4	1	3	11	9	2

Part II—Percentages
(The numbers from Part I expressed as percentages)

Port	Public Order					
	Assault & Battery, etc			Drunk & disorderly, Criminal damage, etc		
	Total as % of defendants in port	Residents as % of defendants charged with offence	Sailors as % of defendants charged with offence	Total as % of defendants in port	Residents as % of defendants charged with offence	Sailors as % of defendants charged with offence
Nagasaki (1875–1899)	43	37	63	33	21	79
Yokohama (1862–1899) (based on newspaper reports)	38	52	48	39	23	77
Kobe & Osaka (1870–1875) (based on semi-annual returns)	46	83	17	21	59	41
Kobe (1869–1899) (based on newspaper reports)	48	46	54	28	11	89
Hakodate (1863–1878)	41	75	25	21	38	62

Theft			Miscellaneous		
Total as % of defendants in port	Residents as % of defendants charged with offence	Sailors as % of defendants charged with offence	Total as % of defendants in port	Residents as % of defendants charged with offence	Sailors as % of defendants charged with offence
10	32	68	14	43	57
13	62	38	10	70	30
7	100		26	77	23
10	54	46	14	47	53
10	25	75	28	82	18

Part III—Totals (numbers and percentages)
(The numbers from Part I expressed as percentages)

Port	Defendants			*Percentages*	
	Total	Total Residents	Total Sailor/ Visitors	*Residents*	*Sailors/ Visitors*
Nagasaki					
1866–74	137	100	37	73	27
1875–99	217	70	147	32	68
Yokohama (based on newspaper reports)					
1862–99	467	205	262	44	56
Kobe & Osaka					
1870–75 (based on semi-annual returns)	207	161	46	78	22
1869–99 (based on newspaper reports)	132	49	83	37	63
Hakodate					
1863–78	39	25	14	64	36

Table 5. Criminal Cases, 1862–1899: Prosecutors.

Port	Prosecutor										Total
	British		Japanese				Municipal Police		Foreigner		
			Authorities		Individual						
	No.	%	No.	%	No.	%	No.	%	No.	%	No.
(Percentages are given in relation to the known prosecutors)											
Nagasaki											
1866–74	95	*69*	17	*12*	15	*11*			10	*7*	137
1875–80	32	*36*	20	*22*	21	*24*			16	*18*	89
1881–90	18	*32*	16	*29*	18	*28*			5	*9*	57
1891–99	14	*20*	37	*52*	13	*18*			7	*10*	
1866–99	159	*45*	90	*25*	67	*19*			38	*11*	354
Yokohama											
(based on semi-annual returns)											
1867–72	41	*8*			43	*8*	391	*74*	51	*10*	526
1862–1899											
(based on newspaper reports)											
1862–70	48	*72*	3	*4*	11	*16*			5	*7*	67
1871–80	69	*32*	48	*22*	71	*33*			28	*13*	216
1881–90	17	*26*	11	*17*	24	*36*			14	*21*	66
1891–99	10	*53*	3	*16*	4	*21*			2	*11*	19
1862–99	144	*39*	65	*18*	110	*30*			49	*13*	368
Kobe											
(based on newspaper reports for available years)											
1869–71	1	*8*	3	*23*	4	*31*	2	*15*	3	*23*	13
1876–88	25	*29*	29	*33*	17	*20*	12	*14*	4	*5*	87
1897–99	3	*14*	2	*9*	17	*77*					22
1869–99	29	*24*	34	*28*	38	*31*	14	*11*	7	*6*	122
Hakodate											
1863–78	7	*19*	20	*56*	9	*25*					36

Notes: The Nagasaki 1875–1899 figures, together with those based on the Yokohama and Kobe newspapers, are based upon a reading of the Minutes and newspaper reports to determine at whose behest the prosecution was principally undertaken. The Nagasaki 1866–74 figures and the Yokohama 1867–1872 figures are based upon the semi-annual returns where it is impossible to look behind the returns to ascertain this whereas, with Hakodate, this information, although not in the semi-annual returns, is, usually, available from a reading of the correspondence records.

The figures in the 'Total' column are for the known prosecutors or, if not available, the total of criminal cases, as the case may be.

Table 6. Nagasaki, 1866–1899. Criminal Cases: Prosecutors.

Prosecutor/ Year	British	Japanese		Foreigner	Total Defendants	Charges
		Authorities	Individuals			
1859	1				1	
1863		2	2		4	
1864		1			1	
1865		1			1	
1866	22			7	29	
1867	9				9	
1868	15		1	2	18	
1869	5	1			6	
1870	9	3	1	1	14	
1871	4	8	1		13	
1872	10		8		18	
1873 (H1)	8		2		10	
1874	12	1			13	
1875	3	7	2		12	16
1876	5	4	4		13	13
1877	3	1	4	6	14	14
1878	10	3	6	10	29	33
1879	6	1	5		12	13
1880	5	4			9	11
1881	5	1	2		8	12
1882	1				1	1
1883	4	1		3	8	8
1884	1	4	1	1	7	11
1885	2	5	7	1	15	20
1886	1		3		4	5
1887	1	2			3	7
1888	2	1	3		6	6
1889	1	2	2		5	9
1890			(*no cases reported*)			
1891		2	1	1	4	4
1892		6			6	11
1893	5				5	15
1894		5			5	9
1895	4	2	7		13	17
1896	3	4	1	3	11	13
1897	1	9		1	11	19
1898		8	4	1	13	19
1899	1	1		1	3	4
Totals						
1859–1874	**95**	**17**	**15**	**10**	**137**	
1875–1899	**64**	**73**	**52**	**28**	**217**	**289**
1859–1899	**159**	**90**	**67**	**38**	**354**	

(*Continued*)

Table 6. (*Cont.*)

Prosecutor/ Year	British	Japanese		Foreigner	Total Defendants	Charges
		Authorities	Individuals			
Percentage of Defendants						
1859–1874	*69*	*12*	*11*	*7*		
1875–1899	*29*	*34*	*24*	*13*		
1859–1899	*45*	*25*	*19*	*11*		
Annual average of Defendants						
1859–1874	8	1	1	1	11	
1875–1899	3	3	2	1	9	
1859–1899	4	2	2	1	9	

Note: No breakdown of individual charges against the same defendant is possible from the reports from 1859–1865 or the semi-annual returns from 1866–1874.

Table 7. Criminal Cases, 1862–1899: Prosecutors and defendants' residence.

Part I—Nagasaki, 1875–1899

Prosecutor	Total Defendants	Japan Resident		Sailors		Other Visitors	
		No.	%	No.	%	No.	%
British							
1875–80	43	20	*47*	20	*47*	3	*7*
1881–90	11	6	*55*	5	*45*		
1891–99	13	4	*31*	8	*62*	1	*8*
Total	67	30	*45*	33	*50*	4	*6*
Japanese							
1875–80	43	7	*16*	35	*81*	1	*2*
1881–90	36	17	*47*	17	*47*	2	*6*
1891–99	49	9	*18*	37	*76*	3	*6*
Total	128	33	*26*	89	*70*	6	*5*
Foreigners							
1875–80	1	1	*100*				
1881–90	5	2	*40*	3	*60*		
1891–99	9	7	*77*	2	*23*		
Total	15	10	*67*	5	*33*		
Total 1875–99	217	70	*35*	137	*60*	10	*5*

Part II—Yokohama, 1862–1899
(based on newspaper reports)

Prosecutor	Total Defendants	Japan Resident		Sailors	
		No.	%	No.	%
British	146	89	*61*	57	*39*
Japanese Authorities	64	22	*34*	42	*66*
Japanese individuals	102	47	*46*	55	*54*
Foreigners	44	28	*64*	16	*36*
Total	356	176	*51*	170	*49*

Note: Percentages are given as proportion of defendants where the nationality of the prosecutor is known. Almost certainly, the figures over-estimate the proportion of residents as it is not always possible to identify sailors or other transient visitors.

Part III—Kobe, 1866–1899
(based on newspaper reports)

Prosecutor	Total Defendants	Japan Resident		Sailors	
		No.	%	No.	%
British	29	13	45	16	55
Municipal Police	14	1	7	13	93
Japanese Authorities	34	10	29	24	71
Japanese individuals	38	20	53	18	47
Foreigners	7	5	71	2	29
Total	122	49	40	73	60

Table 8. Criminal Cases, 1862–1899. Breakdown of offences by prosecutor.

Part I—Nagasaki, 1875–1899

Prosecutor	Public Order							Theft		Other		Totals	
	Assault & Battery		Drunk & disorderly		Criminal damage		Total						
	No.	%	No.	%	No.	%	%	No.	%	No.	%	No.	%
British	26	35	15	20	8	11	66	11	15	14	19	74	26
Japanese Authorities	37	31	29	25	23	19	85	11	9	18	15	118	42
Japanese Individuals	35	57	8	13	5	8	78	7	11	6	10	61	22
Foreigner	15	54	11	39	1	4	97					27	10
Total	113	40	63	22	37	13	75	29	10	38	14	280	

Part II—Yokohama, 1862–1899 (based on newspaper reports)

Prosecutor	Public Order							Theft		Other		Totals	
	Assault & Battery		Drunk & disorderly		Criminal damage		Total						
	No.	%	No.	%	No.	%	%	No.	%	No.	%	No.	%
British	51	35	27	18	1	1	54	34	23	33	23	146	41
Japanese Authorities	29	45	20	31	3	5	81			12	19	64	18
Japanese Individuals	49	48	28	27	5	5	80	16	16	4	4	102	29
Foreigner	31	70	2	5	1	2	77	8	18	2	5	44	12
Total	160	45	77	22	10	3	69	58	16	51	14	356	

Part III—Kobe, 1869–1899 (based on newspaper reports)

Prosecutor	Public Order							Theft		Other		Totals	
	Assault & Battery		Drunk & disorderly		Criminal damage		Total						
	No.	%	No.	%	No.	%	%	No.	%	No.	%	No.	%
British	13	38	4	12	4	12	62	9	26	4	12	34	12
Municipal Police	2	14	9	64			78	2	14	1	7	14	10
Japanese Authorities	18	45	7	17	6	15	77			9	23	40	28
Japanese Individual	27	60	6	13	5	11	84	2	4	6	13	46	33
Foreigner	6	86	1	14			100					7	5
Total	66	53	27	19	15	11	29	13	9	20	14	141	

Table 9. Criminal Cases, 1862–1899: Acquittals.

Port	Defendants (as per Tables 2 and 3)	Pleaded: Guilty	Pleaded: Not Guilty to one or more charges	Found: Guilty of one or more charges	Found: Not Guilty of all charges	*Acquittals as a percentage of all defendants %*
Nagasaki, 1875–99	210	56	154	100	54	*26*
Yokohama						
1867–72 (based on semi-annual returns)	944			798	146	*15*
1862–99 (based on newspaper reports)	506	230	264	159	90	*18*
Kobe & Osaka, 1870–75 (based on semi-annual returns)	207			136	71	*34*
Kobe, 1869–99 (based on newspaper reports)	120	41	79	54	25	*21*
Hakodate, 1863–78	39			31	8	*21*
Tokyo, 1871–97	61			42	19	*31*

Notes: The Yokohama 1867–1872, Kobe & Osaka, Hakodate and Tokyo figures do not enable us to determine how defendants pleaded.

The Nagasaki columns do not add up horizontally as several defendants faced multiple charges and split their pleas or were acquitted of only one of several charges and pleaded (or were found) guilty to others.

Table 10. Criminal Cases, 1862–1899: Pleas and acquittals by prosecutor.

Part I—Nagasaki, 1875–1899

Prosecutor	Defendants	Pleaded Guilty to one or more charges		Acquitted of all charges	
		No.	%	No.	%
British	64	21	*34*	11	*18*
Japanese Authorities	72	26	*36*	14	*19*
Japanese Individuals	50	6	*12*	16	*32*
Foreigner	27	3	*11*	13	*48*
Total	**213**	**56**	***26***	**54**	***25***

Part II—Yokohama, 1862–1899

Prosecutor	Defendants	Pleaded Guilty to one or more charges	Acquitted of all charges	
			No.	%
British	146	22	23	*16*
Japanese Authorities	64	28	9	*14*
Japanese Individuals	102	32	17	*17*
Foreigner	44	7	19	*43*
Unknown	142	34	5	*4*
Total	**498**	**123**	**73**	***15***

Notes: Acquittals also includes all cases where the charges were withdrawn.

Often, the reports do not enable us to know how a defendant pleaded; or, occasionally, if we know this information, we do not know the result of the trial.

Part III—Kobe, 1869–1899

Prosecutor	Defendants	Pleaded Guilty to one or more charges		Acquitted of all charges	
		No.	%	No.	%
British	26	8	*31*	11	*23*
Municipal Police	14	11	*79*		
Japanese Authorities	33	11	*33*	9	*27*
Japanese Individuals	35	9	*26*	8	*12*
Foreigner	7	1	*14*	2	*29*
Total	**115**	**40**	***35***	**30**	***26***

Table 11. Nagasaki, 1875–1899. Criminal Cases Acquittals: time-sliced by numbers and percentages.

Prosecutor	British			Japanese						Foreigners			All
				Authorities			Individuals						
Years	Def	Acq	%	Def	Acq	%	Def	Acq	%	Def	Acq	%	%
1875–77	11	1	*10*	12	3	*25*	10	1	*10*	6	5	*83*	*25*
1878	9	4	*45*	3	1	*33*	6	1	*17*	10	7	*70*	*57*
1879–84	20	2	*10*	11	2	*18*	7	3	*43*	3			*17*
1885–89	8	2	*25*	9	2	*22*	14	6	*43*				*32*
1890–94	5			13	1	*8*	1	1	*100*	1			*10*
1895–99	8	2	*25*	24	5	*21*	12	4	*33*	7	1	*14*	*23*
1875–99	**61**	**11**	***18***	**72**	**14**	***20***	**50**	**16**	***32***	**27**	**13**	***48***	***26***

Def : number of defendants.
Acq : number acquitted of all charges.
All : percentage of all defendants acquitted of all charges

Table 12. Hakodate, 1863–1878. Criminal Cases: Convictions.

Prosecutor	Residents			Sailors			All		
	Total	Guilty	Not guilty	Total	Guilty	Not guilty	Total	Guilty	Not guilty
British	5	1	4	4	4		9	5	4
Japanese Authorities	14	12	2	7	6	1	21	18	3
Japanese Individuals	6	6		3	2	1	9	8	1
Total	**25**	**19**	**6**	**14**	**12**	**2**	**39**	**31**	**8**

Table 13. Criminal Cases, 1862–1899: Punishments.

Port	Warning, etc	Fines $			Prison (**Bold** indicates sentences to be served with Hard Labour) Days				Years	
		<6	6–20	20>	<7	7–14	15–28	29–364	1 year	1 year>
Nagasaki (1875–1899)										
Prosecutor										
British	7	16	4	3	7	1, **1**	5, **1**	3, **1**		
Japanese	17	42	7	4	7	5, **1**	9, **7**	1		
Foreigner	1	6	5	1				1, **1**		
	25	64	16	8	14	6, **2**	14, **8**	5, **2**		
Yokohama (1862–1899) (based on newspaper reports)										
Prosecutor										
British	12	22	6	1	2	7, **2**	1	5, **9**	**3**	6
Japanese Authorities	8	27	1	6	1, **3**	3, **1**	3, **3**	4, **3**		1
Japanese Individuals	10	31	6	2	6	6, **2**	1, **3**	5, **9**		
Foreigner	2	7	2		2	2	4, **2**	2, **3**	1	1
Unknown	24	40	2		12	6, **2**	5, **2**	6, **1**	1	2 2
	56	127	17	9	23, **3**	24, **7**	14, **10**	22, **25**	1, **4**	2, **10**
Kobe & Osaka (1870–1875) (based on semi-annual returns)	18	41	17	1	11	10	4	7		

(*Continued*)

Table 13. (*Cont.*)

Port	Warning, etc	Fines $			Prison **Bold** indicates sentences to be served with Hard Labour Days				Years	
		<6	6–20	20>	<7	7–14	15–28	29–364	1 year	1 year>
Kobe (1869–1899) (based on newspaper reports)										
Prosecutor										
British	5			1	1	2	**3**	6, **3**		
Municipal Police	6	3				1				
Japanese Authorities	17	7	1	7		1		1		
Japanese Individuals	14	11	3	2	1			1, 1		
Foreigner	1	1	3	1			1, 1			
	43	22	7	11	1, 1	4	1, 4	7, 5		
Hakodate (1863–1878)	3				6	2	2	2	**3**	

Notes: 'Warning' includes defendants being given a warning (even if acquitted), being bound over to keep the Peace, being ordered to be deported, being ordered to pay the costs of the trial and/or—whether alone or in addition to another such punishment—to pay damages to the individual at whose behest the prosecution had been brought.

Of those imprisoned for over one year in Yokohama, one sailor was sentenced to five years, three residents and three sailors to two years each, and one resident to 18 months. Edith Carew's death sentence was commuted to life imprisonment.

Table 14. Shipping Offences, 1862–1899: Nationality, charges and results.

Port/Years	Total	British	Japanese	Foreign	AB	DD
		Defendants			Charges	
Nagasaki						
1866–1874	264	205	9	60	8	
1875–1878	153	126	11	16	22	6
1896–1899	73	60		13	2	1
	500	**391**	**20**	**89**	**32**	**7**
Percentages		*78*	*4*	*18*	*11*	*3*
		(*percentages of Total Defendants*)			(*as percentage*	
Yokohama						
(based on newspaper reports)						
1862–70	18	14		4	1	
1871–80	320	290		30	61	21
1881–90	130	118		12	23	
1891–99	20	20			6	3
	488	**432**		**56**	**91**	**24**
Percentages		*89*		*11*	*21*	*6*
		(*percentages of Total Defendants*)			(*as percentage*	
Kobe						
(based on semi-annual returns)						
1870–75	140				8	27
Percentages					*6*	*19*
					(*as percentage*	
(based on newspaper reports)						
1869–99	129				16	11
Percentages					*15*	*10*
					(*as percentage*	
Hakodate						
1866–78	29				6	11
Percentages					*15*	*28*
					(*as percentage*	

Notes: AB principally, assault and battery; but also includes other offences against the person such as murder and manslaughter
AWOL absent without leave, including desertion
DD drunk and disorderly
Ref Duty refusal of duty.
Defendants were often charged with more than one offence—especially where drunkenness and/or refusal of duty were concerned.
Equally, the offence is often not clear from either the records or the newspaper reports.

It is very difficult to identify the nationality of the defendants in Hakodate and Kobe, 1870–1875. In Kobe, 1870–1875, there was only one Japanese defendant, and, perhaps, some 22 defendants of other non-British nationality.

			Pleaded Not Guilty to at least one charge		Acquitted of all charges	
Ref Duty	AWOL	Other	No.	%	No.	%
			of Defendants		of Defendants	
14	3				19	*7*
112	29	3	40	*26*	15	*10*
20	57	3	15	*21*	5	*7*
146	**89**	**6**	**55**	***10***	**39**	***8***
52	*32*	*2*				
of known offences)						
13	1	3	11	*61*	4	*22*
132	83	23	151	*47*	56	*18*
19	16	12	40	*31*	10	*8*
5	5	1	4	*20*	4	*20*
169	**105**	**39**	**206**	***42***	**74**	***15***
39	*25*	*19*				
of known offences)						
56	49				15	*11*
40	*35*					
of known offences)						
51	20	12	27	*21*	9	*7*
46	*18*	*11*				
of known offences)						
5	12	5			5	*17*
13	*31*	*13*				
of known offences)						

Table 15. Shipping Offences, 1862–1899: Punishments.

Port/Years	Warning, etc	Fines			Prison until departure	Prison					
		$				Days					1 year
		<6	6–20	20>		<7	7–14	15–28	29–42	43–364	
Nagasaki											
1866–74	1	43	58	10	60	64, 1	21	13	1	1	
1875–78		17	10		27	9	7	4	31	4	
1896–99	2	19	2	2	1	4, 10	1, 8	7, 8	1, 7	1	
Yokohama (based on newspaper reports)											
1862–99	39	66	7	8	3	40, 12	24, 11	10, 22	8, 14	7, 22	1
Kobe											
1870–75 (based on semi-annual returns)	33	23	10		1	18	5	17	2	13	
1869–99 (based on newspaper reports)	16	17	6		1	4, 2	24, 8	5, 5	16, 9	8, 1	
Hakodate											
1866–78	5	6	2	1	1	5	2				

Notes: 'Warning, etc.' includes defendants being given a warning (even if acquitted), ordered (or agreeing) to go back on board and work normally, being ordered to pay the costs of the trial and (only very occasionally)—whether alone or in addition to another punishment—to pay damages to the individual at whose behest the prosecution has been brought.

The fines were usually expressed in Dollars. Very occasionally, the fine was expressed as the number of days' pay a sailor was fined; in this case, very roughly, it approximated $1 per day.

Only a selection of the available years for Nagasaki has been taken so as to give an illustration of the proportional breakdown of sentences.

Table 16. Naval Courts of Enquiry, 1864–1899.

Summary

Port	Ground for holding a Naval Court					Result (where known)		
	Loss/ collision	Discipline	MSA	Other	Total	No blame	Censure	Suspension of Certificate
Yokohama	22	10	3	5	40	13	22	3
Nagasaki	19			3	22	8	11	6
Kobe	10	1	1		12	5	4	1
Hakodate	3		1		4	4		
	54	11	5	8	78	30	37	10

Notes: Occasionally, several officers were the subject of an investigation and each could be subject to a different result.

'MSA' means an enquiry held in relation to a breach of the obligations of an officer (usually, the master) under the Merchant Shipping Acts.

Table 17. All Ports, 1859–1899. Civil Cases: case-load.
Part I (Based on semi-annual returns)

Port	Nagasaki				Yokohama			
Plaintiff	Total	Br	Jap	For	Total	Br	Jap	For
Year								
1859					1			
1860	1	1			6			
1861	2		1	1	2			
1862					12			
1863					12			
1864					31			
1865	5	3		2	47			
1866	20	12	2	7	91			
1867	20	19		1	56	51	4	1
1868	29	25	1	3	97	66	17	14
1869	18	13	1	4	51	36	7	8
1870	21	17	2	2	65	40	5	20
1871	3	3			107	75	8	24
1872	4	2		2	93	61	10	22
1873	5	4		1				
1874	12	4	6	2				
1875	14	4	6	4				
1876	9	2	3	4				
1877	4	1	3					
1878	9		3	6				
1879	31	10	12	9				
1880	22	7	12	3				
1881	4	1	2	1				
1882	7	1	2	4				
1883	4	1	2	1				
1884	2	1	1					
1885	4	2	2					
1886	8	5	1	2				
1887	5	2	2	1				
1888	2		2					
1889	2	2						
1890	2	1		1				
1891	1		1					
1892	1		1					
1893	2		2					
1894		*(none were recorded)*						
1895	5	2	2	1				
1896	5	1	2	2				
1897		*(none were recorded)*						
1898	1	1						
1899	1	1						
Total	286	148	74	64	671	329	51	89

Note: Br means British; Jap means Japanese; For means a Foreigner.

Hakodate				Tokyo				Kobe & Osaka			
Total	Br	Jap	For	Total	Br	Jap	For	Total	Br	Jap	For
1	1										
1	1										
1	1										
2	2										
7	4	3						18	14	1	3
7	2	1	4	4	4			54	35	6	13
2		2		17	6	6	5	106	56	18	32
5		1	4	22	9	8	5	117	53	23	41
3	1	2		48	22	12	14	62	28	19	15
2	1	1		28	14	8	6	16	9	7	
1		1		25	18	2	5				
				19	5	9	5				
1		1		5	2	2	1				
				2		2					
				2		2					
				2		2					
				1	1						
				1		1					
				1			1				
				3	1	2					
33	13	12	8	148	82	56	42	373	195	74	104

Part II—Yokohama and Kobe, 1862–1899
(based on newspaper reports)

Port	Yokohama				Kobe			
Plaintiff	Total	British	Japanese	Foreigner	Total	British	Japanese	Foreigner
Year								
1862	2	2						
1863	2	1		1				
1864	4	3	1					
1865	11	7	1	3				
1866	2	1	1					
1867								
1868	1		1		3	2	1	
1869	7	6		1	2	1		1
1870					8	6		2
1871	18	15		3	6	3	2	1
1872	33	22	4	7				
1873	27	15	10	2				
1874	41	31	3	7	1	1		
1875	27	3	2	22	1	1		
1876	38	24	6	8	14	6	6	2
1877	46	25	13	8	3	1		2
1878	49	32	10	7	11	6	3	2
1879	44	26	8	10	1	1		
1880	27	14	7	6	5		3	2
1881	26	14	12		7	3	1	3
1882	7	5	1	1	1	1		
1883	5	4	1		2	1		1
1884	4	2		2				
1885	14	12	2		1			1
1886	5	5						
1887	5	4	1		1		1	
1888	9	5	2	2	1	1		
1889	20	14	3	3	1		1	
1890	8	3	1	4				
1891	4	3		1				
1892	4	3	1					
1893	4	2	2					
1894	2	1	1					
1895	4	3		1				
1896	5	4		1	1	1		
1897	1	1			4	4		
1898	4	4			2		1	1
1899	4	3		1	3	2	1	
Total	514	319	94	101	79	41	20	18

Table 18. Civil Cases, 1859–1899. Summary and annual averages.

Plaintiff/ Year	Adjusted Years	Total suits		British		Japanese		Foreigner	
		No.	*Annual average*	No.	*Annual average*	No.	*Annual average*	No.	*Annual average*
Nagasaki									
1860–74	12	141	12	103	9	13	1	25	3
1875–78	4	36	9	7	2	15	4	14	4
1879–80	2	53	27	17	9	24	12	12	6
1881–99	18.5	56	3	21	1	22	1	13	1
1875–99	**24.5**	**145**	**6**	**45**	**2**	**61**	**2**	**39**	**1**
1860–99	**36.5**	**286**	**8**	**148**	**4**	**74**	**2**	**64**	**1**
Yokhohama (based on semi-annual returns)									
1859–72	14	671	48						
1867–72	6	469	78	329	55	51	9	89	15
Yokohama (based on newspaper reports)									
1862–99	37.5	514	14	319	9	94	3	101	3
Kobe (based on semi-annual returns)									
1870–75	6	373	62	195	33	74	12	104	17
Kobe (based on newspaper reports)									
1868–71	4	19	5	12	3	3	1	4	1
1874–89	16	50	3	22	1	15	1	13	1
1896–99	3.5	10	3	7	2	2	1	1	0
1868–99	**23.5**	**79**	**3**	**41**	**2**	**20**	**1**	**18**	**1**
Hakodate									
1865–78	14	33	2	13	1	12	1	8	1

Notes: Annual Averages calculated on the basis of adjusted years (i.e. excluding those years for which there are no records or reports—i.e. as opposed to where there are records but no cases are recorded.)

The Tokyo figures are distorted by the surge in cases between 1872–1877 so annual averages for the whole period would be misleading.

Table 19. Civil Cases, 1862–1899. Classification.

Port/Plaintiff	Total claims	Debt	Goods & Services	Wages/ employment	Shipping	Others
Nagasaki 1860–74						
British	103	48	9			16
Japanese Authorities	3	2				1
Japanese Individuals	10	1	1			
Chinese	4			1	3	
Other Foreigners	21	11	6			1
Total	**141**	**62**	**16**	**1**		**21**
Nagasaki 1875–99						
British	45	17	17	1	5	5
Japanese Authorities	12	8				4
Japanese Individuals	49	4	17	6	8	14
Chinese	22	4	15		2	1
Other Foreigners	17	5	4	1	5	2
Total	**145**	**38**	**53**	**8**	**20**	**26**
Yokohama 1862–99						
(based on newspaper reports)						
British	319	61	73	24	43	56
Japanese Authorities	5	3			1	1
Japanese Individuals	89	12	49	15	7	6
Chinese	19	4	11	2	1	1
Other Foreigners	82	19	28	3	16	10
Total	**514**	**99**	**161**	**44**	**68**	**74**
Kobe 1868–99						
(based on newspaper reports)						
British	41	6	13		10	9
Japanese	20	5	10		3	2
Foreigners	18	1	4		7	6
Total	**79**	**12**	**27**		**20**	**17**
Hakodate 1865–78						
British	13	3	5		1	4
Japanese Authorities	5	3				1
Japanese Individuals	7	2			1	1
Foreigners	8	1		3 (sailors)		2
Total	**33**	**9**	**5**	**3**	**2**	**8**

Notes: The breakdown of claims in Tables 19, 20 and 21 ignores probate and interlocutory applications and claims where details are not known. Thus the figures will not necessarily tally with the total claims brought in any Court as shown in Table 17 (or in the column headed 'Total Claims' in this Table).

Table 20. Civil Cases, 1862–1899. Amounts of claims (where available).

Port/Plaintiffs	No.	$					
		<5	5–10	11–25	26–100	101–250	250>
Nagasaki, 1866–74							
British	103		6	2	9	3	14
Japanese Authorities	3						
Japanese Individuals	10						
Chinese	4			1			
Other Foreigners	21				3		2
Total	**141**		**6**	**3**	**12**	**3**	**16**
Nagasaki, 1875–99							
British	45		7	4	17	3	5
Japanese Authorities	12				9		
Japanese Individuals	49	13	4	8	12	2	8
Chinese	22		1	7	10	4	
Other Foreigners	17		1	1	6	2	5
Total	**145**	**13**	**13**	**20**	**54**	**11**	**18**
Yokohama, 1862–99 (based on newspaper reports)							
British	319	5	8	29	82	27	88
Japanese Authorities	5				1		4
Japanese Individuals	89	5	8	7	30	9	24
Chinese	19		2	4	5	2	3
Other Foreigners	82	3	4	13	19	9	32
Total	**514**	**13**	**22**	**53**	**137**	**47**	**151**
Kobe, 1868–99 (based on newspaper reports)							
British	41			1	13	5	14
Japanese	20			1	3	4	7
Foreigners	18		2		3	2	7
Total	**79**		**2**	**2**	**23**	**11**	**28**

(Continued)

Table 20. (*Cont.*)

Breakdown of claims over $250 in Yokohama and Kobe

	Yokohama, 1862–1899			Kobe, 1868–1899		
Dollars ($)	250–1,000	1,000–5,000	5,000>	250–1,000	1,000–2,000	2,000>
British	43	28	17	7	3	4
Japanese Authorities	3		1	4	3	
Japanese Individuals	15	5	4			
Chinese	2		1			
Other Foreigners	14	8	10	3		4
Total	77	41	33	14	6	8

Notes: The Kobe claims over $2,000 included an insurance claim for $45,000.
Nagasaki: To determine the value of claims:
(i) for 1875–1877, the Nagasaki Court Minute Book is used;
(ii) for 1878–1899, the Register of Civil Claims is used.

Table 21. Civil Cases, 1862–1899. Results.

Port/ Plaintiff	Total cases	Settled	Fought No.	Fought %	Result for Plaintiff No.	Plaintiff Percentage of all cases	Plaintiff Percentage of fought cases	Result for Defendant No.	Defendant Percentage of all cases	Defendant Percentage of fought cases
Nagasaki, 1860–1874										
British	103	21	77	74	69	87	90	8	8	10
Japanese Authorities	3		3	100	2	67	67	1	33	33
Japanese Individuals	10	1	9	90	6	70	67	3	30	33
Chinese	4	1	3	75	2	75	67	1	33	25
Other Foreigners	21	6	12	67	8	67	67	4	19	50
Total	**141**	**29**	**104**	**74**	**87**	**62**	**84**	**17**	**12**	**16**
Nagasaki, 1875–1899										
British	45	15	30	67	22	49	73	8	18	36
Japanese Authorities	12	8	4	33	4	100	100			
Japanese Individuals	49	7	42	86	24	63	57	18	37	43
Chinese	22	8	14	64	10	82	71	4	18	29
Other Foreigners	17	4	13	76	6	59	46	7	41	54
Total	**145**	**42**	**103**	**71**	**66**	**74**	**64**	**37**	**26**	**36**
Yokohama, 1867–1872 (based on semi-annual returns)										
British	329	50	279	85	224	83	80	55	17	20
Japanese	51	10	41	80	28	75	68	13	25	32
Foreigners	89	14	75	84	54	76	72	21	24	28
Total	**469**	**74**	**395**	**84**	**306**	**81**	**77**	**89**	**19**	**23**
Yokohama, 1862–1899 (based on newspaper reports)										
British	319	14	272	85	188	63	69	84	26	31
Japanese Authorities	5		5	100	3	60	60	2	40	40
Japanese Individuals	89	7	81	91	51	65	63	30	30	40
Chinese	19		16	84	13	68	81	3	16	19
Other Foreigners	82	2	80	98	56	71	70	24	29	30
Total	**514**	**23**	**454**	**88**	**314**	**66**	**69**	**145**	**28**	**32**

(*Continued*)

Table 21. (*Cont.*)

Port/ Plaintiff	Total cases	Settled	Fought No.	Fought %	Result for Plaintiff No.	Plaintiff Percentage of all cases	Plaintiff Percentage of fought cases	Result for Defendant No.	Defendant Percentage of all cases	Defendant Percentage of fought cases
Kobe & Osaka, 1870–1875										
(based on semi-annual returns)										
British	195	54	116	*59*	96	*77*	*83*	20	*10*	*17*
Japanese	74	11	47	*64*	26	*50*	*55*	21	*28*	*45*
Chinese	37		37	*100*	26	*70*	*70*	11	*30*	*30*
Other Foreigners	67	22	41	*61*	27	*73*	*66*	14	*21*	*34*
Total	**373**	**87**	**241**	***65***	**175**	***70***	***73***	**66**	***18***	***27***
Kobe, 1868–1899										
(based on newspaper reports)										
British	41	1	33	*80*	18	*46*	*55*	15	*37*	*45*
Japanese	20	2	18	*90*	8	*50*	*44*	9	*45*	*50*
Foreigners	18	1	17	*94*	14	*83*	*82*	2	*11*	*12*
Total	**74**	**4**	**68**	***92***	**40**	***59***	***59***	**26**	***35***	***38***
Hakodate, 1865–1878										
British	13	3	10	*77*	4	*54*	*40*	6	*46*	*60*
Japanese Authorities	5	1	4	*80*	4	*100*	*100*			
Japanese Individuals	7	2	5	*71*	3	*71*	*60*	2	*29*	*40*
Foreigners	8	1	7	*88*	3	*50*	*43*	4	*50*	*57*
Total	**33**	**7**	**26**	***79***	**14**	***64***	***54***	**12**	***36***	***46***
Tokyo, 1871–1899										
British	82	13	69	*84*	62	*91*	*90*	7	*9*	*10*
Japanese	56	8	48	*86*	42	*89*	*88*	6	*11*	*13*
Foreigners	41	10	31	*76*	30	*98*	*97*	1	*2*	*3*
Total	**179**	**31**	**148**	***83***	**134**	***92***	***91***	**14**	***8***	***5***

Notes: Bankruptcy and Probate cases are ignored for the purposes of this table.

For Nagasaki, a judgment has been made on the basis of the Court Minute Books—so as to allow for partial successes rather than following the Register of Civil Claims' records.

Results are not always known. Thus, the figures for the results will not always equal the number of cases.

The percentages of 'Results for Plaintiff' also takes account of cases which settled or where the Defendant admitted the plaintiff's claim.

Table 22. Appeals, 1859–1899.

Case-load
(by year judgment given)

Part I—Appeals in Civil Cases from the Provincial Courts

From/Year	Total number of appeals	Yokohama	Nagasaki	Hakodate	Kobe	Tokyo
Section A. To the Supreme Court of Hong Kong, 1859–1865						
1863	1	1				
Total	1	1				
Section B. To the Consul-General, 1859–1865						
1859		(-)				
1860	2	(1)	1			
1861		(-)				
1862		(-)				
1863		(-)				
1864	3	(3)				
1865	3	1 (2)	1			
Total	8	1 (6)	2			
Section C. To the Supreme Court, 1865–1878						
1865	2	1	1			
1866	2	(1)	1			
1867	5	4 (1)	1			
1868	5	1 (4)		1		
1869	4	4 (4)				
1870	3	1	1	1		
1871	7	1	2	2	2	
1872	3	1			2	
1873	1				1	
1874	5	1	1	1	2	
1875	4	2			1	1
1876	9	6			2	1
1877	2	2				
1878	4	3			1	
1881	4	4				
1882	1	1				
Total	61	32 (10)	7	5	11	2

(Continued)

Table 22. (*Cont.*)

From/Year	Total number of appeals	Yokohama	Nagasaki	Hakodate	Kobe	Tokyo
			Section D. To HMCJ, 1879–1899			
1879	4	1		2	1	
1880	3	2		1		
1881	2				1	1
Total	9	3		3	2	1

Notes: The bracketed figures under Yokohama in Sections B and C are those referred to in Lowder's report mentioned in the Note on Sources at the beginning of this Appendix V. The 'Total' column takes the larger figure for Yokohama.

Appeals listed in Section C of Part I from Yokohama in 1881 and 1882 were in relation to cases heard by the Yokohama Court prior to the implementation of OC1878.

The 'appeals' listed from Yokohama to HMCJ in 1879 and 1880 in Section D of were, technically, rehearings within HMCJ.

Part II—Appeals in Civil Cases from HMCJ

Section A. To the Supreme Court, 1879–1899

1881	1882	1883	1884	1885	1886	1889	1890	1893	1894	1896	**Total**
3	6	1	3	2	1	2	1	2	1	1	23

Section B. From the Supreme Court to the Privy Council

1888	1894	Total
2	2	4

Note: Years in which no appeals were reported have been ignored.

Table 22. (*Cont.*)

Part III—Appeals in Criminal Cases from the Provincial Courts

From/Year	Total	Yokohama	Nagasaki	Kobe
	Section A. To the Consul-General, 1859–1865			
1859	1		1	
1860	1	1		
	Section B. To the Supreme Court, 1865–1878			
1866	1	1		
1868	1	1		
	Section C. To HMCJ, 1879–1899			
1879	2		1	1
Total	6	3	2	1

Note: There were no appeals in criminal matters from either the Hakodate or the Tokyo Courts.

Part IV—Applications for leave to appeal in Criminal Cases made direct to the Privy Council

Year/ Appeal from	Yokohama	HMCJ
1878	2	
1897		1
1899		1
Total	2	2

Note: No civil appeals went direct from Courts in Japan to the Privy Council.

Table 23. Appeals in Civil Cases: Classification.

Appeal from	Total	Debt, etc	Shipping	Land	Procedural	Other
Yokohama	37	6	7	2	8	7
Kobe	13	2	4		1	1
Nagasaki	9	4	3	1		1
Hakodate	8	4	2			1
Tokyo	3	1				
HMCJ	23	3	8		7	
Total	**93**	**20**	**24**	**3**	**16**	**10**
Percentage of known cases		*32%*	*38%*	*5%*	*25%*	*16%*

Notes: Only those cases where sufficient details are known about the nature of the case are included.

'Debt, etc' includes claims for debt, bankruptcy matters and trade and commercial disputes.

Table 24. Appellants in Civil Cases: Identities.

Appeal from	Appellant		Respondent
	Plaintiff	Defendant	
Yokohama			
British	8	11	23
Japanese	5		1
Foreigner	2		2
Nagasaki			
British	2	4	5
Foreigner			1
Kobe			
British	2	4	7
Japanese	1		1
Foreigner	1		
Hakodate			
British	6	1	6
Japanese	1		1
Foreigner			1
Tokyo			
British	1	1	2
HMCJ			
British	8	9	16
Japanese	1		4
Foreigner	5		3
Totals	**43**	**30**	**73**
British	27	30	59
Japanese	8		7
Foreigner	8		7

Table 25. Appeals in Civil Cases: Results.

Part I—by appellant

Litigant	Appellant		Respondent	
	Allowed	Dismissed	Allowed	Dismissed
British	22	28	21	27
Japanese	7	1	2	5
Foreigner	2	3	1	4
Total	31	32	24	36

Part II—by Port and identity of appellant

Appeals from	Total appeals	Plaintiff as appellant		Defendant as appellant	
		Allowed	Dismissed	Allowed	Dismissed
Yokohama	37	4	5	8	3
Kobe	13	2	1	1	3
Nagasaki	9		2	2	2
Hakodate	8	4		1	
Tokyo	3		1		1
HMCJ	23	6	7	3	5
Total	93 (102)	16	16	15	14

Note: The breakdown ignores those cases where insufficient information is available.

Table 26. Use of counsel in appeals and results (civil cases).

Appeal from	Both parties represented by Counsel	Appellant only represented by Counsel	Respondent only represented by Counsel	Written submissions prepared by Counsel
Yokohama	1 Allowed	3 Allowed		2 joint notes: Both allowed
	1 Dimissed	1 Dismissed		2 separate notes prepared: 1 Allowed; 1 Dismissed
	1 Not known	1 Settled		
Nagasaki	2 Allowed			
Kobe	3 Dismissed	1 Dismissed	1 Allowed	
Hakodate	1 Allowed 1 Settled			
HMCJ	2 Allowed	3 Dismissed (in one, the opposing side made written submissions)	1 Allowed (the opposing side made written submissions)	3 separate notes prepared: 1 Allowed 2 Dismissed
	2 Dismissed		1 Dismissed (the opposing side made written submissions)	

Table 27. Nagasaki, 1878–1899. Fees in civil and criminal cases.

Year	Fees		Combined total fees
	Civil	Criminal	
		$	
1878	29	136	165
1879	175	104	279
1880	79	24	103
1881	6	34	40
1882	69	10	79
1883	10	25	35
1884	100	21	121
1885	32	37	69
1886	36	10	46
1887	14	25	39
1888	23	15	38
1889	6	31	37
1890	68	29	97
1891	Nil	19	19
1892	Nil	24	24
1893	Nil	22	22
1894	Nil	21	21
1895	24	42	66
1896	37	45	82
1897	Nil	22	22
1898	3	29	32
1899	87	24	111
Total	798	749	1,547
Annual average	*36*	*34*	*70*

Note: These annual fees are just in relation to the laying of the suits themselves. There may have been additional fees for service of petitions etc.

APPENDIX VI

LIST OF DEPORTATIONS FROM JAPAN, 1866–1899

Year	No.	From	Deportee	To	Grounds
1860	1	Yokohama	Michael Moss	England	Assault, etc (the *Moss case*)
1866	3	Hakodate	Trone, Renish and Whiteley	Hong Kong	Convictions in the Ainu Bones affair
1870	6	Yokohama	Christopher Gaunt	"	
			John Davis	"	
			Charles Stenson	"	
			David Duncan	"	
			John Andrews	Madras	Drunk & disorderly
			Henry Sanderson		Fourth offence of drunkenness
1871	13	Yokohama	Dunn		Incorrigible rogue and vagabond
			Charles Harvey		Threatening arson
			Lawrance		Theft
			William Harris	Hong Kong	Larceny
			Henry Sheppard	"	Robbery
			James Kelly	"	Incorrigible vagrant
			William McAllister	"	
			Muston	"	No ostensible means of livelihood
			Prinjam	"	
			Ah-Man	"	
			Sallun	"	Failure to provide sureties
			John Williams	"	
			James Cochrane	"	Theft and Assault
1872	4	Yokohama	Frederick Summerville	"	Theft
			Ah-Sim	"	
			George Purvis	"	Assault on a Japanese and Drunkenness
			William Barnes		Assault

(*Continued*)

Appendix VI. (*Cont.*)

Year	No.	From	Deportee	To	Grounds
	2	Kobe	Westmoreland	England	Inebriate and dismissed from Japanese service
			Pedro	"	Trying to drown a fellow sailor
1873	2	Yokohama			
	1	Nagasaki	F. Macmain	Shanghai	
1874	10		William Lawrance		
			Amatsa		Theft of boots
			George Frier		Assault on a Japanese and criminal damage
			Daniel Roberts		Drunkenness and Theft
			John Fitzherbert		Drunkenness
			Richard Manicu		"
			Vera Lami		Drunkenness and Disorderly conduct
			William Collins		Wandering about without any visible means of subsistence
			W. A. Smyth		
			Tracey		
1875	1	Kobe	Henry Trone	Hong Kong	Persistent offender
1876	1		William McBeth		Drunkenness, rogue and vagabond
1877	None				
1878	1	Yokohama	John Gazen		Malicious assault and destroying blanket belonging to the Japanese police
1879	2	Nagasaki	Koh Tek Lok	Hong Kong	Stealing bones from the cemetery for Japanese soldiers who died in the Taiwan campaign

(*Continued*)

Appendix VI. (*Cont.*)

			William Samuel Common	Hong Kong	Returned in breach of section 113 OC1865
1880	1	Yokohama	Ahmet (alias Batchoo)		Wounding with intent to commit GBH and being unable to find sureties upon release from two years' hard labour
1888	1	Nagasaki	John Davis	Hong Kong or England	Breach of the Peace
1892	1	Yokohama	C.H.A. Welch	England	Convicted of felonies before the Supreme Court
1895	1	Nagasaki	Joseph White		Theft
1898	1		W.H. Cource	Hong Kong	
1899	1		D. Ballantyne		

Note: This list has been prepared from a variety of sources; but, it should be noted that the sources are not always consistent with each other and, also, the Table should not be taken as being comprehensive. It also includes individuals where there is no other record of their offence. The sources are:

a. Nagasaki case reports: (FO796/2, FO796/3,FO796/7, FO76/14);
b. Correspondence files where we find the Warrants of deportation being sent from Shanghai to Yokohama or, sometimes, copies of those issued by the Yokohama Court: (FO656/18, FO656/19 FO656/37 FO656/39, FO656/4, FO656/42, FO656/50 and FO7/791); and
c. List of Deportees prepared by the Supreme Court. In 1878, Mowat responded to a request from Parkes for a list of all deportations but admitted that he could not produce details before 1870 due to the loss of records in the fire which destroyed the Supreme Court building; (Mowat to Parkes, 10 October 1878; FO656/50).

APPENDIX VII

CHISHIMA CASES: TIME-LINE OF EVENTS

Date	*Chishima v. Ravenna*	External
1890		Parliamentary democracy introduced into Japan
1892		
August		Count Ito becomes Prime Minister and Mutsu Munemitsu Foreign Minister
November		
29/30	The collision	
December		
20–29	British Naval Court Japanese Committee of Inquiry	
1893		
January	Japanese Inquiry clears Kaburaki (the *Chishima*'s captain)	
March	Japanese pilot of *Ravenna* convicted of manslaughter	
May		
25	Japanese government commences proceedings against P&O in HMCJ in *IJG v. P&O*	
31		
June	HMCJ preliminary hearings	
3, 5, 12 and 13		
29	HMCJ hearing refuses permission for P&O's counter-claim	
30	P&O appeals to Supreme Court	
August		Mutsu Munemitsu approaches de Bunsen to re-open Treaty revision negotiations
11	Court of Appeal, in *Hannay v. Smurthwaite*, permits joinder between plaintiffs with different causes of action	

(*Continued*)

Appendix VII. (*Cont.*)

Date	*Chishima v. Ravenna*	External
October		
10–14	Supreme Court hearing of appeal in the *Chishima case*	
25	Supreme Court judgment allowing P&O's counter-claim	
26	Japanese government seeks leave from Supreme Court to appeal to Privy Council	
November		
6	Supreme Court grants the Japanese government leave to appeal to the Privy Council	
23	Tsune Kijima and Others issue proceedings against P&O, by way of joinder, in HMCJ	
December	P&O seeks dismissal of these proceedings arguing that such joinder is not permitted. P&O's application granted and joinder action by Tsune Kijima and Others is dismissed by HMCJ	Aoki Shuzo travels to London for Treaty re-negotiations
		Diet dismissed due to extreme nationalist moves on the extra-territoriality question
1894		
March		
3		Rosebery becomes Prime Minister and Kimberley Foreign Secretary
April		
16	Supreme Court hears appeal in *Tsune Kijima* case	
23	Supreme Court allows appeal of Tsune Kijima and Others and reinstates their action	
28	P&O seeks leave to appeal to the Privy Council	
May		
30	Supreme Court grants P&O leave to appeal to the Privy Council in *Tsune Kijima* case	

(*Continued*)

Appendix VII. (*Cont.*)

Date	*Chishima v. Ravenna*	External
June		Sino-Japanese War commences
July	Privy Council Office notifies Foreign Office that appeal in *IJG v. P&O* ready to proceed	
16		1894 Treaty signed by Aoki Shuzo and Kimberley
August		
3	House of Lords delivers judgment in *Smurthwaite v Hannay* reversing Court of Appeal and disallows joinder between plaintiffs with different causes of action	
1895		
April		Treaty of Shimonoseki ends Sino-Japanese War Triple Intervention leading to concession by Japan (formalized in the Treaty of Yantai in November, 1895)
May		
21, 22, 24, 28	Privy Council hears Japanese government's appeal in *IJG v. P&O*	
28	Privy Council hears P&O's appeal in *Tsune Kijima*	
June		
23		Rosebery resigns and is replaced as Prime Minister by Salisbury who is also Foreign Secretary
July		
3	Privy Council allows Japanese government's appeal in *IJG v. P&O*	
20	Privy Council allows P&O's appeal in *Tsune Kijima case* (case of Tsune Kijima and Others thereby lapses)	

(*Continued*)

Appendix VII. (*Cont.*)

Date	*Chishima v. Ravenna*	External
August		
2	P&O requests Selborne's assistance to seek Salisbury's intervention with Japanese government to settle *IJG v. P&O* dispute	
September		
3	Settlement reached	
October		
1	Supreme Court releases the parties' security deposits in both cases	

SOURCES AND BIBLIOGRAPHY

Primary Sources

Statutes

Behring Sea Award Act, 1894.
The Consular Marriage Act, 1868.
Foreign Jurisdiction Act, 1843.
Foreign Jurisdiction Act, 1890.
The Foreign Marriage Act, 1891.
Fugitive Offenders Act, 1881.
The Merchant Shipping Act, 1894.
Seal Fishery (Behring's Sea) Act, 1891.
Seal Fishery (North Pacific) Act, 1893.

Orders in Council

Japan Order in Council, 1859.
Japan Order in Council, 1860.
Japan Order in Council, 1861.
Japan Order in Council, 1863.
Japan Order in Council, 1864.
China and Japan Order in Council, 1865.
China and Japan Order in Council, 1869.
China and Japan Maritime Order, 1874.
Orders in Council regulating Consular Fees of 19 June 1868 and 21 July 1876.
China and Japan Order in Council, 1877.
China and Japan Order in Council, 1878.
China and Japan Order in Council, 1881.
The China, Japan and Corea Order in Council, 1884.
The China, Japan and Corea Order in Council, 1884 (Supplemental).
The China, Japan and Corea Order in Council, 1886.
The China, Japan and Corea Order in Council, 1886 (no.2).
The Consular Fees (China, Japan and Corea) Order, 1892.
The China and Japan Order in Council, 1898.
The China, Japan and Corea (Supreme Court) Order in Council, 1899.
Suspension of Jurisdiction in Japan Order in Council, 1899.
China and Corea (Supreme Court) Order in Council 1900.
The China and Corea Order in Council, 1904.

Official Records

All the Official Records in the British National Archives which are cited in the main body of this book.

Collections of Primary Sources

Digest of British Orders in Council relating to China and Japan (London: Biblio Life LLC, 2012).

Pedlar, Neil, *An Indexed List of British Marriages Solemnized During Extraterritoriality in Japan 1860–1899* (Newquay: Four Turnings Publications, 1993).
Ruxton, Ian ed., *The Correspondence of Sir Ernest Mason Satow, British Minister in Japan, 1895–1900* Vol. One (Ian Ruxton: 2005).
Ruxton, Ian ed., *The Semi-Official Letters of British Envoy Sir Ernest Satow from Japan and China (1895–1906)* (North Carolina: Lulu Press Inc., 2007).
Steeds, David and Nish, Ian, *China, Japan and 19th Century Britain* (Dublin: Irish University Press, 1977).

Law Reports

Barber v. Lamb (1860) 8 C.B. (N.S.) 95.
Brinkley v. Attorney General (1890) LR XV P&D 76.
Ex Parte Edith Mary Hallowell Carew [1897] AC 719.
China Merchants Steam Navigation Company v. W.L. Bignold (aka *Hochung v. Lapwing*) (1883) LR 7 App 512.
The Steamer *Fusing* v. The Steamer *Ocean*; 29 May 1875; NCHLR.
The *Glamorganshire* [1888] AC 454 and 6 Asp. Mar. Law Cas. 344.
Grant v. Easton (1883) LR 13 QBD 302.
The *Griefswald* (1859) 166 Eng Rep 1200 (Swabey 430).
Hannay v. Smurthwaite [1893] 2 QB 412.
Hart v. Gampuch (1872) 4 L.R.P.C. 439.
The Imperial Japanese Government v. Peninsular and Oriental Steam Navigation Company [1895] AC 644.
Ince v. Thorburn (1886) LR 11 App 180.
R. v. Keyn (The *Franconia*) (1876) 2 Exch 63.
Oxford v. Provand (1888) LR 2 PC 135.
Papayanni v. The Russian Steam Navigation Company 2 Moo. P.C. (N.S.) 1863 (15 Eng Rep 862) (*The Laconia*).
Smurthwaite v. Hannay [1894] AC 494.
Swire v. Francis (1877) LR 3 App 106.
Tapp v. Jones (1874) LR 9 CP 413.
Tamvaco v. Simpson (1866) 34 LJCP 268, affirmed LR1 CP 363.
In re Tootal's Trusts (1883) LR 23 ChD 532.
Tsune Kijima & Others v. Peninsular and Oriental Steam Navigation Company [1895] AC 661.
All the Law Reports relating to Japan in *North China Herald* and *Supreme Court and Consular Gazette*, 1860–1899.
All the Law Reports in the *Japan Weekly Mail*, 1862–1900.

Secondary Sources

Newspapers

Canton Friends of China: 1861
The Eastern World: February–December 1900.
The Friends of China and Hong Kong Gazette: 1858; October–December 1860.
Hiogo and Osaka Herald: January 1878–March 1870.
The Hiogo News: April 1868; April–December 1870; January–December 1876; July 1877–December 1888.
The Hiogo Shipping List and General Advertiser: January 1870; January 1875–June 1876, July 1877–December 1879.

The Japan Commercial Times: 1864.
Japan Daily Herald: January 1874–February 1875; 1876–1877; October 1878–June 1881.
The Japan Gazette: November 1875; September 1878; July–November 1881; December 1886; 1889.
The Japan Herald: November 1861–1865; January-August 1878.
The Japan Mail: January and February 1874.
Japan Times: September 1865–June 1866.
Japan Times Overland Mail: May 1868–December 1869.
Japan Weekly Mail: 1870–1879; March 1880–March 1900.
The Kobe Advertiser and Shipping Register: January–June 1879.
The Kobe Chronicle: July 1897–December 1900.
Nagasaki Shipping Advertiser: July–October 1861.
North China Herald: 1860–March 1900 (except 1866–August 1868 and 1873).
The Tokio Times: 1878.

Bibliography

Alcock, Sir Rutherford, *The Capital of the Tycoon* (London: Longman, Green and Co., 1863).

Alcock, Sir Rutherford, *The Capital of the Tycoon: A Narrative of Three years' Residence in Japan Volume 2* (London: Longman, Green, Longman, Roberts & Green, 1863; reprinted ULAN Press).

Allen, B.M., *The Rt. Hon. Sir Ernest Satow: A Memoir* (London: Keegan Paul, Trubner, Trench and Co., 1933).

Auslin, Michael Robert, 'Negotiating with Imperialism: Japan and the Unequal treaty regime 1858–72' (PhD diss., University of Illinois 2000) (subsequently published as *Negotiating with Imperialism: The Unequal Treaties and the Culture of Japanese Diplomacy* (Harvard: Harvard University Press, 2004)).

Beasley, W.G., *Great Britain and the Opening of Japan 1834–1858* (London: Luzac, 1951).

Beasley, W.G., *The Basis of Japanese Foreign Policy in the Nineteenth Century* (London: SOAS, 1955).

Beasley, W.G. and Pulleybank, E.G. eds., *Historians of China and Japan* (London: 1961).

Beasley, W.G., *The Meiji Restoration* (London: Oxford University Press, 1973).

Beasley, W.G., *Japanese Imperialism 1894–1945* (Oxford: Oxford University Press, 1978).

Beasley, W.G., *The Rise of Modern Japan* (London: Weidenfeld and Nicolson, 1990).

Benton, Laura, *Law and Colonial Cultures* (New York: Cambridge University Press, 2002).

Black, J.R., *Young Japan, Yokohama and Yedo 1858–1879* (New York, 1883; reprinted Oxford: Oxford University Press, 1968) (two volumes).

Blacker, Carmen, '*Laurence Oliphant and Japan, 1858–88*' in *Biographical Portraits vol. II*, ed. Ian Nish (Japan Library, 1997), 35.

Cary, Otis, *Japan and its Regeneration* (New York: Volunteer League Library, 1899).

Cassel, Pär Kristoffer, *Grounds of Judgment: Extraterritoriality and Imperial Power in Nineteenth Century China and Japan* (New York: Oxford University Press, 2012).

Chang, Richard T., *The Justice of the Western Consular Courts in Nineteenth Century Japan* (Connecticut and London: Greenwood Press, 1984).

Checkland, Olive, *Britain's Encounter with Meiji Japan, 1868–1912* (London: Macmillan, 1989).

Ch'en, Paul H., 'The Treaty System and European law in China: A Study on the Exercise of British Jurisdiction in Late Imperial China' (paper presented at Conference on European Expansion and Law, Bad Homburg, 1988).

Coates, P.D., *The China Consuls* (Hong Kong: Oxford University Press, 1988).

Cobbing, Andrew, '*Iwakura Tomomi (1825–1883)*' in *Biographical Portraits vol. VIII*, ed. Hugh Cortazzi (Leiden-Boston: Global Oriental, 2013), 1.

Cortazzi, Hugh, 'Dr. Willis (1837–1894),' *Monumenta Nipponica* Vol. 39 (1984), 147–161.

Cortazzi, Hugh, 'The First British Legation in Japan (1859–1874),' *PJS* 102 (1984), 25.

Cortazzi, Hugh, *Mitford's Japan: Memories and Recollections 1866–1906* (London: The Athlone Press, 1985).

Cortazzi, Hugh, *Dr. Willis in Japan* (London: The Athlone Press, 1985).

Cortazzi, Hugh, 'Dr. John Batchelor,' *PJS* 105 (1986), 20.

Cortazzi, Hugh, 'Yokohama 'Frontier Town' 1859–1866,' *PJS* 105 (1986), 33.

Cortazzi, Hugh, 'Britain and Japan: A Personal View,' *PJS* 118 (1991), 32.

Cortazzi, Hugh and Daniels, Gordon, *Britain and Japan 1859–1991 Themes and Personalities* (London: Routledge, 1991).

Cortazzi, Hugh, '*Sir Harry Parkes, 1828–1885*' in *Biographical Portraits vol. I*, ed. Ian Nish (Japan Library, 1994), 1.

Cortazzi, Hugh, '*Sir Rutherford Alcock, 1809–1897*' in *Biographical Portraits vol. II*, ed. Ian Nish (Japan Library, 1997), 20.

Cortazzi, Hugh, '*John Batchelor, Missionary and Friend of the Ainu, 1855–1945*' in *Biographical Portraits vol. II*, ed. Ian Nish (Japan Library, 1997), 216.

Cortazzi, Hugh, '*Thomas Wright Blakiston (1832–91)*' in *Biographical Portraits vol. III*, ed. J.E. Hoare (Japan Library, 1999), 52.

Cortazzi, Hugh, '*Sir Francis Plunkett, 1835–1907: British Minister at Tokyo, 1884–87*' in *Biographical Portraits vol. IV*, ed. Hugh Cortazzi (Japan Library, 2002), 28.

Cortazzi, Hugh, '*Hugh Fraser, 1837–1894, British Minister at Tokyo, 1889–94*' in *Biographical Portraits vol. IV*, ed. Hugh Cortazzi (Japan Library, 2002), 41.

Cortazzi, Hugh ed., *British Envoys in Japan 1859–1972* (London: Global Oriental, 2004).

Cortazzi, Hugh, *Britain and the 'Re-opening' of Japan* (London: Japan Society Publications, 2008).

Cortazzi, Hugh, '*Sir Edward Reed (1830–1906): Naval Architect*' in *Biographical Portraits vol. VII*, ed. Hugh Cortazzi (Folkestone: Global Oriental, 2010), 44.

Cortazzi, Hugh, '*Sir Francis Ottiwell Adams, KCMG, CB, British Diplomat (1826–89)*' in *Biographical Portraits vol. VII*, ed. Hugh Cortazzi (Folkestone: Global Oriental, 2010), 96.

Cortazzi, Hugh, '*The Times and Japan in the Nineteenth Century*' in *Biographical Portraits vol. VIII*, ed. Hugh Cortazzi (Leiden-Boston: Global Oriental, 2013), 663.

Daniels, Gordon, 'Sir Harry Parkes and the Meiji Settlement 1868–1883,' *PJS* 115 (1990), 17.

Daniels, Gordon, *Sir Harry Parkes, British Representative in Japan 1865–83* (Richmond: Japan Library, 1996).

Dickins, F.V. and Lane-Poole, Stanley, *The Life of Sir Harry Parkes* (London: Macmillan and Co., 1891) (two volumes).

Dudden, Alexis, *Japanese Colonization of Korea* (Honolulu: University of Hawai'i Press, 2005).

Duus, Peter, *The Abacus and the Sword* (London: University of California Press, 1995).

Earns, Lane, 'British Influence in the Foreign Settlement of Nagasaki,' *PJS* 125 (1995), 48.

Evans, David C. and Peattie, Mark R., *Kaigun* (Annapolis: Naval Institute Press, 1997).

Field, Irene Darden, 'Thomas Glover of Nagasaki,' *PJS* 88 (1979), 10.

Fox, Grace, *Britain and Japan 1858–1883* (Oxford: Oxford University Press, 1969).

Gubbins, J.H., *The Civil Code of Japan* (translation) Volume I and Volume II (Tokyo, 1897 and 1899 respectively).

Hall, W.E.A., *A Treatise on the Foreign Powers and Jurisdiction of the British Crown* (Oxford: The Clarendon Press, 1894).

Hammer, Joshua, *Yokohama Burning* (New York: Free Press, 2006).

Hinckley, Frank E., *American Consular Jurisdiction in the Orient* (Washington DC: W.H. Loudermilk, 1906).

Hoare, J.E., 'The Japanese Treaty Ports' (PhD diss., Queen Mary College London, 1971. (subsequently published as *Japan's Treaty Ports and Foreign Settlements* (Folkestone, Kent: Japan Library, 1994)).

Hoare, J.E., 'The 'Bankoku Shimbun' Affair: Foreigners, the Japanese Press and Extraterritoriality in Early Meiji Japan', *Modern Asian Studies*, Vol. 9, No.3 (Cambridge University Press, 1975).

Hoare, J.E., 'Mr. Enslie's Grievance: the Consul, the Ainu and the Bones,' *PJS* 78 (1976), 14.

Hoare, J.E., 'The Chinese in the Japanese Treaty Ports, 1858–1899: The Unknown Majority', *Proceedings of the British Association for Japanese Studies*, Vol. II (1977), Part I.

Hoare, J.E., 'Japan undermines extraterritoriality: extradition in Japan 1885–1899' in Ian Nish and Charles Dunn eds., *European Studies on Japan* (Tenterden: Paul Norbury Publications, 1979), 125.

Hoare, James E., 'Extraterritoriality in Japan, 1858–1899', *The Transactions of the Asiatic Society of Japan*, Third Series, Vol. XVIII (Tokyo, 1983).

Hoare, James, *'British Journalists in Meiji Japan'* in *Biographical Portraits vol. I*, ed. Ian Nish (Japan Library, 1994), 20.

Hoare, J.E., 'The Tokyo Embassy, 1871–1945,' *PJS* 129 (1997), 24.

Hoare, J.E., *'Britain's Japan Consular Service, 1859–1941'* in *Biographical Portraits vol. II*, ed. Ian Nish (Japan Library, 1997), 94.

Hoare, J.E., *Embassies in the East* (Richmond: Curzon, 1999).

Hoare, J.E., *'Korea, Taiwan and Manchuria: Britain's Consular Service in the Japanese Empire, 1883–1941'* in *Biographical Portraits vol. VIII*, ed. Hugh Cortazzi (Leiden-Boston: Global Oriental, 2013), 130.

Honjo, Yuki Allyson, *Japan's Early Experience of Contract Management in the Treaty Ports* (London: Japan Library, 2003).

Hornby, Sir Edmund, *An Autobiography* (London: Constable & Co. Ltd., 1929).

Howland, Douglas, *Translating the West: Language and Political Reason in Nineteenth Century Japan* (Honolulu: University of Hawai'i Press, 2002).

Howland, Douglas and White, Luise eds., *The State of Sovereignty* (Bloomington: Indiana University Press, 2009).

Jansen, Marius ed., *The Cambridge History of Japan, Volume V* (Cambridge: Cambridge University Press, 1989).

Jones, F.C., *Extraterritoriality in Japan* (Yale and Oxford: Yale University Press, 1931).

Kayaoğlu, Turan, *Legal Imperialism, Sovereignty and Extraterritoriality in Japan, the Ottoman Empire, and China* (New York: Cambridge University Press, 2010).

Keeton, G.W., *The Development of Extraterritoriality in China* (2 volumes) (London: Longmans, Green and Co., 1928).

Kercher, Bruce, *Debt, Seduction and Other Disasters: the birth of civil law in convict New South Wales* (Sydney: The Federation Press, 1966).

Kornicki, Peter, *Bibliography of Japanese History to 1912* (Cambridge: Cambridge University Press, 1996).

Kornicki, Peter Francis, *'Frederick Victor Dickins (1838–1915)'* in *Biographical Portraits vol. III*, ed. J.E. Hoare (Japan Library, 1999), 66.

Kotenov, A.M., *Shanghai Mixed Court: Its Mixed Court and Council* (Shanghai: North-China Daily News and Herald Limited, 1925).

Lynn, Martin, 'British Policy, Trade, and Informal Empire in the Mid-nineteenth Century', in *Oxford History of the British Empire Volume III*, ed. Andrew Porter (Oxford: Oxford University Press, 1999), 101.

McMaster, John, 'British Trade and Traders in Japan, 1859–69' (PhD diss., SOAS, 1962).

McOmie, William, *The Opening of Japan 1853–1855* (Folkestone: Global Oriental, 2006).

Minear, Richard H., *Japanese Tradition and Western Law* (Harvard: Harvard University Press, 1970).

Morse, E.S., *Japan Day by Day 1877* (Boston and New York: Houghton Mifflin & Company, 1917).

Morton, Robert, *'A.B. Mitford (1837–1916)'* in *Biographical Portraits vol. VIII*, ed. Hugh Cortazzi (Leiden-Boston: Global Oriental, 2013), 117.

Munson, Todd S., *The Periodical Press in Treaty Port Japan* (Leiden: Global Oriental, 2013).

Munn, Christopher, *Anglo-China: Chinese People and British Rule in Hong Kong, 1841–1880* (Richmond: Curzon Press, 2001).

Munn, Christopher, 'Hong Kong, 1841–1870: All the Servants in Prison and Nobody to Take Care of the House' in *Masters, Servants, and Magistrates in Britain & the Empire, 1562–1955*, eds. Douglas Hay and Paul Craven (Chapel Hill and London: The University of North Carolina Press, 2004).

Newbury, Colin, 'The Semantics of International Influence: Informal empires reconsidered' in *Imperialism, the State and the Third World*, ed. Michael Twaddle (London: British Academic Press, 1992).

Nish, Ian, *The Anglo-Japanese Alliance: The Diplomacy of Two Island Empires 1894–1907* (London: University of London Athlone Press, 1966).

Nish, Ian, *Japanese Foreign Policy 1869–1942* (London: Routledge and Kegan Paul, 1977).

Nish, Ian, '*John Harrington Gubbins, 1852–1932*' in *Biographical Portraits vol. II*, ed. Ian Nish (Japan Library, 1997), 107.

Nish, Ian, ed., *The Iwakura Mission in America and Europe: A new Assessment* (Richmond: Japan Library, 1998).

Nish, Ian, '*Lord Rosebery (1847–1929) and Japan*' in *Biographical Portraits vol. VII*, ed. Hugh Cortazzi (Folkestone: Global Oriental, 2010), 58.

Nish, Ian, '*Sir Cecil Spring Rice (1861–1918) and Japan*' in *Biographical Portraits vol. VII*, ed. Hugh Cortazzi (Folkestone: Global Oriental, 2010), 112.

Norton-Kyshe, James William, *History of the Laws and Courts of Hong Kong, Tracing Consular Jurisdiction in China and Japan* (London and Hong Kong, 1898; reprinted Hong Kong: Vetch and Lee, 1971).

Okamura, T., 'The Progress of the Judicial System of Japan,' *PJS* vol. iii (1894), 103.

Oliphant, Laurence, *Narrative of the Earl of Elgin's Mission to China and Japan* (New York: Harper and Brothers, 1860).

Osterhammel, Jurgen, 'Britain and China', in *Oxford History of the British Empire, Volume III*, ed. Andrew Porter (Oxford: Oxford University Press, 1999), 146.

Otte, T.G., '*Lord Salisbury (1830–1903)*' in *Biographical Portraits vol. VIII*, ed. Hugh Cortazzi (Leiden-Boston: Global Oriental, 2013), 57.

Paine, S.C.M., *The Sino-Japanese War of 1894–1895* (New York: Cambridge University Press, 2005).

Perez, Louis G., *Japan Comes of Age: Mutsu Munemitsu and the Revision of the Unequal Treaties* (Madison: Fairleigh Dickinson University Press, 1999).

Piggott, F.S.G., *Broken Thread: An Autobiography* (Aldershot: Gale and Polden, 1950).

Piggott, Sir Francis (Chief Justice, Hong Kong), *Extraterritoriality, The Law relating to the Consular Jurisdiction and to Residence in Oriental Countries* (London: William Clowes & Sons Ltd, first edition 1892; second edition 1907).

Platt, D.C.M., *Finance, Trade, and Politics in British Foreign Policy 1815–1914* (Oxford: The Clarendon Press, 1968) (chapter 5 and Conclusion), 262 and 353.

Platt, D.C.M., *The Cinderella Service* (London: Longman, 1971) (chapter 5), 180.

Rogala, Jozef, *The Genius of Mr. Punch: Life in Yokohama's Foreign Settlement, Charles Wirgman and the Japan Punch 1862–1887* (Yokohama: Yurindo Press, Ltd., 2004).

Ruxton, Ian, 'The Ending of Extra-territoriality in Japan' in *Turning Points in Japanese History*, ed. Bert Edstrom (Japan Library: 2002), 84.

Ruxton, Ian, 'Sir Ernest Satow (1843–1929) in Tokyo, 1895–1900' in *Biographical Portraits vol. IV*, ed. Hugh Cortazzi (Japan Library, 2002), 53.

Ruxton, Ian, 'Joseph Henry Longford (1849–1925), Consul and Scholar' in *Biographical Portraits vol. VI*, ed. Hugh Cortazzi (Folkestone: Global Oriental Limited, 2007), 53.

Safford, Frank and Wheeler, George, *Practice of the Privy Council in Judicial Matters* (London: Sweet and Maxwell Limited, 1901).

Satow, Sir Ernest, *A Diplomat in Japan* (Oxford: Oxford University Press, 1968).

Savaliev, Igor R., 'Rescuing the Prisoners of the Maria Luz: The Meiji Government and the 'Coolie Trade', 1868–1875' in *Turning Points in Japanese History*, ed. Bert Edstrom (Japan Library: 2002), 71.

Schencking, J. Charles, *Making Waves* (Stanford: Stanford University Press, 2005).

Scully, Eileen P., *Bargaining with the State from Afar: American Citizenship in Treaty Port China, 1844–1942* (New York: Columbia University Press, 2001).
Storry, G.R., 'Some Victorians in Japan,' *PJS* 24 (1958), 26.
Takahashi, Sakiye, 'Application of International Law during the Chinese-Japanese War,' *PJS* vol. v (1897), 2.
Tarring, Charles James, *British Consular Jurisdiction in the East* (London: Stevens and Haynes 1887).
Wall, Rachel F., *Japan's Century* (London: Historical Association, 1964).
Whittington-Egan, Molly, *Murder on the Bluff* (Glasgow: Neil Wilson Publishing, 1996)

INDEX

a. Vessels
b. Legislation
c. Cases
d. Newspapers, etc
e. General

a. Vessels

Abbey Cowper 174
Airlie 179
Ann 265
Annie Muriel 170
Annie W. Weston 101
Arctic 166, 171n, 177
Ardgowan 179n
HMS Argus 132
Argyll 180, 181
Atholl 264
HMS Audacious 206

Belgic 182
Birker 137n
Bolivar 23
Bombay 182
Borneo 185
Bullion 157

Cadiz 205
Caleban 171
HMS Caroline 328n
Carrier Dove 170
Castle Rock 179n
Cathaya 18, 206, 262
HMS Champion 104
Chanticleer 173
Ching Too 212
Chiri maru 206
Chishima kan see *Chishima cases*
Clarissa B. Carver see the *Glamorganshire*
Columbia 169
Cosmao 125
Cyclops 110
Cyprus 173

HMS Daphne 130
Dilsberg 180
Dorothy 171n, 179n

Ella Beatrice 181
Evangeline 272

Fair Leander 206
Felbridge 259
Forward Ho 123
HMS Frolic 130

Gaelic 164
Galley of Lorne 204, 265, 267n
Gaosheng see Kowshing
Gaucho 123, 149, 273
ss Glamorganshire see the *Glamorganshire*
Gordon Castle 263
Grasmere 175

Hedwig 158
Helen Black 116
Hellespont 136
Hideyoshimaru 178
Hildon 102
Hing Sang 94
Hiogo 276
Hiroshima maru 238
Hopewell 122n
HMS Hunt 112

Immortalité 41
Imogen 175
Induna 122n
HMS Iphigenia 181
Island Queen 192

John Milton 125
Jolly 159
Julie 24

Kiinokuni maru 184
Kinipponmaru 158

Kobe maru 234
Kokonoye maru 91, 130, 188
Kowshing 164
Kumamoto maru 134n

Lady Belona 169, 178
HMS Leander 129n, 166, 284
HMS Lily 107n, 108n
Lord Wolseley 168

Macedon 183
Marcia 183
Mary Mildred 144
Mary Tathen 235
Maud 167
Morvern 175
Mount Lebanon 183

Naniwa 164
HMS Narcissus 107, 108
Nemo 101n, 165, 170
Nepaul 192
New York 223
Nimrod 255
Norfolk 205
Normanton see *Normanton* case

HMS Ocean 150
Oceana 170
Ocean Gem 207n
Omi maru 177n
USS Oneida 182
Oneiza 180n
Orphan 219
Osaka 178
Otento Sama 217
Oxfordshire 17

Pathan 130
Pembrokeshire 104
Plainsmeller 184

Queen Elizabeth 182

HMS Rattler 234
ss Ravenna see *Chishima cases*
Riversdale 174
Runnymede 159, 235
Rupek 177

Saikyo maru 102
Sakata maru 139, 184
Satsuma 179n, 182
Sekiro maru 184
Serpent 169n, 177
Siam 181
Sinkolga 104, 183
Sir Charles Napier 173n, 175n
Snap 182, 224
Snowflake 171n
Staley 169n
Star of Peace 182
Strathleven 172
Sunbeam 123, 149
Sydney 164

Teviot 172
Textor 235
Thales 164
Theseus 184
Thibet 185
Thomas Perry 173, 182
Thompson 159, 175
Tsukuba kan 165

Undine 204

Vestor 242
Viceroy 207
Victoria 207
HMS Victorious 235
HMS Vulcan 175

Wanja 101, 171n
G.H. Wappens 158n
Washi 176n, 177, 270n
Witch 240
Woyomaru 185

Yazeyama 164
Yetchiu maru 180, 181
Yiksang 165
Yuzao 175

b. Legislation (primary and secondary)

Amalgamation/Legal Practitioners Ordinance, 1862 cap.13 58n

Bankruptcy Act 1883 202
Behring Sea Award Act 1894 166

Clandestine Marriage Act, 1754 230
Consular Marriage Act, 1849 230
Consular Marriage Act, 1868 30, 230

Extradition Act 1870 332

Foreign Jurisdiction Act, 1843 10, 11, 19n
Foreign Jurisdiction Act 1890 292, 294
Foreign Marriage Act, 1891 230, 351
Fugitive Offenders Act 1881 332

Marriage Confirmation Act, 1825 230
Married Women's Property Act 1882 210
Married Women's Property Act 1870 210

Orders in Council
- China and Corea Order in Council, 1904 20, 39
- China and Japan Order in Council, 1865 (**OC1865**) 10, 16, 18–26, 28, 31–33, 35n, 36n, 39, 41–43, 48–50, 58, 60n, 73, 75, 89, 93n, 116n, 144n, 147, 152, 153, 163n, 192, 208, 223, 227–229, 232, 236, 245, 247n, 253, 254, 256, 258, 262–265, 281n, 339, 340, 343
- China and Japan Order in Council, 1869 20, 35n
- China and Japan Order in Council, 1878 (**OC1878**) 26–30, 48, 49, 53, 54, 58n, 74, 79, 93, 94, 142, 143, 191, 205, 209, 232, 236, 254, 281n, 340, 341
- China and Japan Order in Council, 1881 (**OC1881**) 29, 33n, 34, 228, 249–251, 277–279, 292, 293, 296, 297n, 305
- China, Japan and Corea Order in Council, 1884 (**OC1884**) 29, 155, 332, 335
- China, Japan and Corea Order in Council, 1886 (**OC1886**) 29, 250, 278, 292, 293, 296, 305
- China, Japan and Corea (Supreme Court) Order in Council, 1899 (**OC1899**) 335
- Japan Order in Council, 1859 (**OC 1859**) 10–12, 106, 118, 191, 244, 253n, 254, 261
- Japan Order in Council, 1860 (**OC1860**) 12, 13, 19, 31, 36, 93n, 109, 118, 144n, 152, 191, 192n, 227n, 236, 244, 253n, 254, 261n, 265
- Japan Order in Council, 1861 (**OC1861**) 13, 14, 41, 253n
- Japan Order in Council, 1863 14
- Japan Order in Council, 1864 14
- Ottoman Empire Order in Council 1873 29, 249
- The Suspension of Jurisdiction in Japan Order in Council, 1899 335

Seal Fishery (Behring's Sea) Act 1891 166
Seal Fishery (North Pacific) Act 1893 166

c. Cases

Note: case names are not always referred to consistently in the records: references in the text and footnotes reflect the records concerned.

Edgar Abbott v. John Baikie, master of *Ching Too* 212
Mathew Catlin Adams v. John Will 265n
Akita han v. Blakiston Marr & Co 198, 216n, 217n, 269, 270, 276
Alt & Co. v Stephens, master of the *Ann* 265
Antimony case 225
Apcar v. Martin 229
Arai Josuka v. William Curtiss 269n
Mrs D'Arcy v. S. Reich 198n
Kate Banff v. James Stuart Clark 193
Barber v. Lamb 39n
Barnard v. Wilkin 212
in re Barnett v. Hoey 265
Bassett v. Charles Munroe 97
Bavier v. Hooper & Clarke 239n
Felix Beato v. James Davison & Co. 268n
Beato v. Rickett as agent for P&O 212, 263
Beato v. Sturrock 268n

James Bell, master of the *Evangeline* v. Aspinall Soper 272
Benjiro v. Houseal 217
Berwick v. J.P. Connor 209n
Master ss *Birker* v. Edward Edmond 137n
Peter Bishop v. Macarthur 72n
Bankruptcy of J.R. Black and Alex McKechnie 202n
George Blakeney v. Hirose Sima 243
Blakiston v. J.H. Duus 266n
Blockley v. Staffordshire Fire Insurance Company 197n
Board of Trade v. Thomas Berwick 171n
Mary C. Bohm v. Abbott 72
Filomeno Braga v. Watkins & Hammond 204n
Brinkley v. Attorney General 231n, 232n
Mary Oastler Burdiss v. James Johnstone (ex'or George Burdiss) 197n
Burgoyne, master of the *Galley of Lorne* v. E.C. Kirby 267n
Burkhill v. Glover's Estate 274
Busch Schraub & Co. v. C. Hyver 61n

Campbell v. Davison (*qua* Administrator of the estate of R.B. Scotland) 70, 244
Campseang v. W.I. Graham 201n
ex parte Edith Mary Hallowell Carew 43n, 255,
Casdagli v. Casdagli 240n
Chaya Yakichi v. Mourilyan, Heimann & Co. 61, 268–270
Chief engineer of *Osaka* v. Fletcher, master of *Osaka* 178
Chinese Consul v. Wong Pun Dzu 155
Ah Chong v. J. Grigor and J. Pitman (ex'ors of Rangan) 228
Clark v. Hall 276
in re the estate of Charles C. Clarke 239
Henry Clarke v. The Northern Pacific Steamship Company 207n
De Connigh Vernede & Co. v. Hudson, Malcolm & Co. 272n, 276
Cook v. Frey 60n
Cook v. Samuel Rowell 265
C.H. Coster v. W.H. Tapp 176n
The Coventry Machinists Company v. S. Cocking 72n
Curtis & Carey v. W.E. Pyne 166n
Custom House v. Peterson 121
Custom House v. Oscar Vidre 121

Louis de Daeker v. Cereno Johnson 173n
James Davison & Co. v. Oriental Banking Corporation 213, 222n
Deguchi v. Carter 110n
Dening v. *Japan Gazette* 204n
Messrs. Dessandier & Cie. v. HSBC 195n
Elizabeth Diack v. John Diack 210n
James W. Dixon v. James R. Anglin 208n
Dobbs v. Bunting 273
Andrew Duncan and N.N. Nordenfeldt v. C.J. Strome 64n

in re J. J. Enslie 241n, 336
Esdale v. Bourne 271
in re Esplen 207

Ruth Farnsworth v. C.W. White and F.E. White 197n
Findlay Richardson & Co. v. Pitman & Co. 25
Fukuda Heisuke v. Mourilyan Heimann & Co. 248
Fusing v. Ocean 295

Gaudaubert v. Hart Smedley 271
Glackmeyer v. McKechnie 208, 242
The owners of the British Steamship "*Glamorganshire*" v. The master, owners and crew of the American Ship "*Clarissa B. Carver*" see the *Glamorganshire*
The owners of the "*Glamorganshire*" v. S.D. Warren & Co. see *The Glamorganshire*
Glover v. Duus 267n
Glover & Co. & Ors v. J. Maltby (also referred to as Glover & Alt & Co. v Maltby) 267n, 271n
Goertz v. Cruchley 208, 270
Green v. Green 192, 209, 243
Groenewort v. Pritchard and the owners of the steamship *Hiogo* 85n, 89n, 270n, 271n, 276
in re E.M. Gudgeon 239

J.W. Hall v. Frischling 225
Hall & Holtz v. Rainbow Lewis & Co. 203, 269
Hanjiro v. Jaquemot 221n
Hannay v. Smurthwaite see Smurthwaite v. Hannay
Henson v. Porter 64
Higashiro Toshigiro v. S. Samuel & Co. 244
Hiogo Hotel case 65, 193, 212
in re Hiogo Hotel Limited 248
Hirose Sima v. Blakeney 221n
Hirota Omakichi v. John Woodward 129n
Hochung v. *Lapwing* 276n, 295, 296
Hodnett v. Butler (master *Cyclops*) 110n

Holme Ringer & Co. (agents for American barque *Vestor*) v. J.K. Taylor 242
Horie Giske v. L. Horsley 207
Howell v. Creditors of Porter's Bankrupt Estate 268
William Howles v. E.C. Kirby & Ors 267n, 272, 277
HSBC v. H. Ohl (*qua* Administrator of the estate of E. Seyd & Co.) 246
HSBC v. Tombrink (trustee of Glover, Daw Co.) 263

Ianguro v. William Cotton 178
Ichinosuke Sempachi v. Alexander Porter 198, 269n, 272n
Ikushima Gohei v. Mourilyan, Heimann & Co. 216
Imperial Japanese Customs v. Captain Crighton 123n
Imperial Japanese Customs v. Abdul Khym 257n
Imperial Japanese Customs v. Edward Ward 123n
Imperial Japanese Government v. Beato 268, 270
Imperial Japanese Government v. Francis Augustus Cope and William Petrie Mitchell 244, 293n
The Imperial Japanese Government v. Peninsular and Oriental Steam Navigation Company (***IJGvP&O***) see *Chishima cases*
Inouye Mankichi of the Yaomi Hotel v. Edward Allan Wallace Mackay 143n
Messrs Isaacs Bros v. Northern Pacific Steamship Company 222n
Ishi Senzo v. Cocking & Singleton 222
Iwasaki Yatoro v. Capt. Philip Colomb RN 206

G. Jaffray v. J. Wickers & J.J. Keswick 209
Japanese Customs v. James K. Taylor 122n
Japanese Customs House v. Dobson, master of *Sunbeam* 123
The Japanese Government v. George Anderson 217
Japanese Government v. master and owner of *Helen Black* 116n
Japanese Government v. Mansfield 124
Japanese Government on behalf of Yasutoya Sayoske v. Pai-Yokusan 112
Japanese Government v. John Marshall Scott 116n
Japanese Police v. Barber Field 131, 132
Japanese Police v. H.C. Gullard 40n, 131n
Japanese Police v. Hardnett 139n

Governor of Kanagawa ken v. Cope & Ors. 269
Kaneko Suikichi v. James F. Mitchell 102, 218
Katashiro v. James John Budd 139n
Katsuki v. Richard A. Ford 102
Kawaguchi and Kamakitchi v. W. Wallace 221n
Kemptner v. Hoey 265
N.P. Kingdom v. Wilkie & Robinson 272n
Kirby v. China Fire Insurance 211n
E.C. Kirby v. Devine 267n
E.C. Kirby v. Hart 267n
E.C. Kirby & Mitchell v. Howles 67, 266
E.C. Kirby (as agent for Hall & Holtz) v. Reynell 267n, 272n
Carl Beato Klante v. Capt James 177n
Kniffler v. Ringer 193, 212, 222
Kniffler v. Stoddart 193, 273, 274
Komei v. William Curtiss 269n
Kumitaro Yataro v. Mathews & Scott 130n
Kusumoto Matsutaka Gonchiji of Tokio Fu v. Arthur Blockley and Bridget Blockley 290, 295

The *Laconia* 3, 249
Lancing v. Young 173
Lane Crawford v. Charles Gabriel 72
Lasschuit v. Hansard 210n
S.F. Lawrence v. master of ss *Morvern* 175n
Livingston v. Lewis 208
A.S. Lobes (as agent for the China and Japan Trading Company) v. Holmes for the master and owners of the ss *Gordon Castle* 263

McKechnie v. Glackmeyer 74
Marshall v. Marshall 351
Matsushira Shogo v. A.T. Watson 244
in re Henry Mills dec'd 238n
Mitsumizo Teizo v. J.F. Mitchell 210n
Moggs v. master and owners of *Norfolk* 205
Albert Morris v. James Norton Lock 61n
Morris & Anor v. The Union Insurance Society of Canton 277n
Moss v. Alcock see main index
Motono Shobei v. James Blackmore 290n
Murakami Shujiro and Okano Otomatsu v. George MacArthur RN, commanding *HMS Daphne* 130n

Nagao Mohee & Others v. J.H. Wignall 248
Nakao Masahiro officer of the Nagasaki Kencho on behalf of the Japanese Government v. Alfred Glover 214n
New York v. *Ocean Queen* 223
Nickel & Co. v. Frederick da Sylva 94n
Nomaguchi Kenichi v. Arthur Norman 124
Nomi Daisuki v. J.W. Sutherland 212
Nutall v. Anglin 204n

Oka Jutaro v. William Cox 108n
Oki Mohei v. Taylor 226
Oshimaya & Co. v. H.E. Reynell & Co. 291n

Ah Qui v. Hescroft 177n

P&O v. John Scott 205
The Pacific Mail Steamship Company by Walter Thompson v. Henry Gribble & Co. 192
Papayanni v. The Russian Steam Navigation Company See the *Laconia*
Charles Parker v. Henry Cook 271
Charles Parker v. Poole 271n
Remegio Perez v. Imperial Insurance Company of London 66n, 213n
John Pitman v. Arthur Groom 266n
Polder v. Lewis 264
Alexander Porter v. Duus 192, 208
Prushita v. HSBC 267n

Rainbow Lewis & Co. (in liquidation) v. Hall & Holtz 203, 269
Reg. v. Adds 102n
Reg. v. Mariano Blanco 132n
Reg. v. Bolton, Moor & Hobbs 133
Reg. v. Thomas Bozer 136n
Reg. v. Browning 106, 147
Reg. ats J. Tannenbaum v. A.F. Augustus Walsh Bush 110
Reg. (ats Yu Sow Chow) v. Carozzi 170
Reg. v. Carter 110n
Reg. v. Chun Pat 133
Reg. v. Howard Clark 255n
Reg. v. Cocking and Singleton 171n
Reg. v. Cooper and Jenkins 129n
Reg. v. Cousens see *Cousens case*
Reg. ats Playfair v. Angus Croal 171n
Reg. v. Cuthbert see Cuthbert, William
Reg. ats Japanese Police v. G. Davey 110n
Reg. v. Edwards 131
Reg. v. Ekins and Verrall 110n
Reg. ats Okada Sakichi v. William Harris 107n
Reg. (ats T. Lenz representing the Police Committee of the Hiogo Municipal Council) v. Alvum Hazlett 103n
Reg. v. Captain of *Hopewell* 122n
Reg (on the prosecution of the Superintendent of the Customs at Hiogo) v. HSBC see *Hiogo Treasure case*
Reg. v. Capt. Hutchison 171
Reg. at instance of Japanese Authorities v. master of *Induna* 122n
Reg. ats Japanese Authorities v. William Ramsey Kennedy 121
Reg. v. Archibald King see King, Archibald
Reg. ats Japanese Police v. Eli Knowles 108n
Reg. v. C.E. Leopold 102
Reg. (ats Arima Gunzi) v. John Luke 130n
Reg. v. Lyne 150n
Reg. v. McLure and Mason 227n
Reg. v. James Mackintosh 136n
Reg. ats Ward v. W.J. Masefield 102n
Reg. (ats H.I.R.M.) v. The *Maud* 167
Reg. (on information of G.T. Terry, Superintendent of Municipal Police At Yokohama) v. Morris, Holes et al. 254
Reg. v. Albert Morris 128n, 135n
Reg. (ats Governor of Kanagawa) v. Moss see *Moss affair*
Reg. on the prosecution of the Japanese Authorities v. Arthur Norman 124
Reg. v. Oastler & Mighton 134
Reg. ats Cereno Johnson v. Adam Olsen and Louis de Daeker 173
Reg. ats Kawada Usaburo through the Japanese Police v. Perkins 107n
Reg. (ats Nippon Yusen Kaisha) v. Ryder 102n
Reg. v. F.H. Sanders 129
Reg. ats Japanese Government v. John Scott 108
Reg. v. Smith 102n
Reg. v. Smyth 133
Reg. v. Suliman 132n
Reg. v. Talbot & Anglin 39
Reg. ats Governor of Kanagawa v. Tatham, Davies and Davies 134n
Reg. ats Rebecca Reich v. Rosa Zanzulicht 101n
Reynell v. Cameron 84, 193

Reynell v. E.C. Kirby for Hall & Holtz 64, 267n
Ricker v. Glackmeyer 208, 243
Roderic v. Wheeler 204n
E. Rothmund v. T.W. Mercer 221n
H.I.R.M. Consul v. Howard (aka Keily) 160n

Saadkia case 9n
Sakai Takakichi and Suzuki Matsugoro v. Mrs. Blockley 204n
Sanders v. Alt & Co. 63, 270n, 271n
Schoyer v. Hope, Ashing & Asow 77
Carl Seitz v. H. McArthur 204
Henry Seymour v. Walter F. Page 61n
Shimidzu Chiubi v. William Warburton 217n
Shoya Johichi v. James F. Mitchell 222
Smith v. Escombe 207
Smurthwaite v. Hannay 297, 301, 304, 310
Sono v. Daniel Robertson 133
Misses Sowter v. Mr & Mrs Rowe 197n, 225, 226
Baron Francis von Stillfried v. W.H. Waggott 264
F. Store acting for the Japanese Government v. J.F. Mitchell 223n
Joseph August Sylva v. Henry Lucas & Co as agents for Union Assurance Society 214n

Tai Wan Wah v. Adamson Bell 293n, 298
Tanaka Ichinosuke & Others v. Whittall 244
Joseph Tannenbaum v. Anne Grand and Adele Schwartz 101n
Captain Thomas v. A.J. Clarke 264
Tombrink (liquidator of the Glover estate) v. HSBC 267n
in re Tootal's Trusts 240n

Tsune Kijima & Others v. Peninsular and Oriental Steam Navigation Company (***P&OvTK&O***) see *Chishima cases*
US Court v. Searle 208

Master of *G.H. Wappens* v. Hashimoto Yokichi and Matsumoto Nijiro 158n
John Wareham, first mate of Japanese barque *Kinippponmaru* charged by Macfarlane, master 158
John Waters v. Wallworth & Co. 219n
Louise Wehrun v. Ellen Walker 85n
Edward Whittall v. Yukioke Shobei 268, 290n
Wilkie & Laufenberg v. E.C. Kirby 224
Estate of Frederick Wilkie v. A.P. Porter 220n, 224n
Owners of *William H. Macy* v. Owners of the *Isis* 67, 68
C.G. Wilson v. J.W. Hall 263n
Sophie Witt v. Greenberg 201n
Won-Sing t/a Campseang v. John Davis 194n

Yamamoto Hempei v. Lucas & Walters 64n
Yatsugoro v. Denny 112
Yokoyama Zensuke v. Malcolm, Wilcox & Co. 248
Yoshimoto Kebichi and Shinsuke v. Boyd & Co. 307n
Yuan Tse-yuan v. Major Bros. Ltd 291n

d. Newspapers, etc.

Directories 60, 62–65, 74n
Eastern World xxvi, 62, 195, 273, 335, 350, 351
L'Echo du Japon 259
Hiogo & Osaka Herald xxvii, 60, 61n, 208
The Hiogo News xxvii, 65, 69 81, 99, 137, 168, 225, 250, 259
Japan Daily Herald xxvi
Japan Daily Mail 187
Japan Gazette xxvi, 39, 70, 204, 208, 273
Japan Herald xxvi, 71, 77, 188
Japan Mail 204, 208
Japan Punch 39n, 71, 206, 227
Japan Weekly Advertiser 292
Japan Weekly Mail xxvi, xxvii, 43, 98, 115
Kobe Weekly Chronicle 64, 65, 168, 214, 226, 273
Nagasaki Shipping List and Advertiser xxvi
North China Daily News 295
North China Herald xxvii, 106, 330
Supreme Court and Consular Gazette 50, 202n
The Times 14n, 19

e. General

Note: no reference is included to an individual in respect of source citations in the footnotes.

Abbott 206
Adams 237
Adams, Francis Ottiwell 80, 86, 220, 221, 317
Adds 139
Adminstration of estates see Probate and Administration
Admiralty Advocate see Law Officers
Admiralty jurisdiction 12, 22–26, 28, 29, 166, 177, 191, 192, 205, 275, 276, 278–281, 295, 296, 340, 341
Ainu bones affair 73, 77, 83, 100, 112, 113, 143, 146n, 343n
Alcock, Sir Rutherford 11, 13–16, 31–36, 47, 54n, 73, 75n, 77, 106, 117–119, 136, 138, 143n, 159, 177, 227, 254, 262n, 265
Anderson, Captain 113, 114
Andrews, John 145
Annersley, Adolphus A. 18, 77n, 81, 116, 123, 132, 146, 203, 264, 274
Anping xxii
Aoki, Shuzo 283, 297, 327–329, 334, 335
Apcar 229
Appeals 12, 13, 18, 22, 24, 25, 26, 28, 29, 42, 43n, 48, 53, 71, 74, 76, 77, 188, 199
  Civil cases 261–282
  Costs 72, 219, 292
  Criminal cases 253–261
  Records xxv, xxvii, xxviii, 11, 12, 18, 50, 89
Arbitration 53, 204, 213, 223–226, 264, 275, 336, 350
D'Arcy 197
Arichi, Admiral 164n
Asan 164
Assessors 12, 41, 42, 152,
  Bias: in civil cases 219
    in criminal cases 131, 134, 135, 149, 345, 346
  Cases: civil 70, 213, 214, 264, 265, 276
    criminal 95–97, 103, 110, 115, 118, 129, 135, 143, 260
  Jurisdictional role:
    in civil cases 26, 191, 192, 213
    criminal cases 13, 24, 93–95, 253
  Japanese proceedings 2, 3, 184
  Nautical assessors 274, 275, 280, 281
Assistant Judge
  of HMCJ 27, 28, 30, 39, 45, 55, 56, 64, 79, 80, 83, 84, 94, 132, 153, 254, 262, 264, 280, 336, 343
  of the Supreme Court xxvii, 16–18, 20, 28, 48, 51, 54, 55, 57, 87, 88, 90, 142, 254, 262, 291, 294, 301
  and the Yokohama Court 20, 21–26, 48–53, 69, 87, 212, 254, 268
Aston, William George 76, 130, 134n, 156, 173, 232n, 257
Attorney General of England see Law Officers
Attorney General of Hong Kong 14, 31, 33, 47, 73, 147, 177
Auslin, Michael Robert 2, 6, 9
Austria-Hungary 9, 10, 38, 161, 257, 316, 319, 334
Awdry, Bishop 351
Aymonin 204

Bail 94–96, 139, 188; see also Sureties in criminal cases
Bakufu 2, 5, 6, 9, 35, 75, 115, 116, 120, 124, 234, 275; see also Tycoon
Banff, Kate 193n; 212n
Bangkok 19n, 350n
Bankoku Shimbun 38n, 119
Bankruptcy proceedings 5, 16, 19, 71, 194, 200, 202, 203, 211, 212, 226, 265, 266, 274, 319, 336
Barnard, Frederick James 62, 63, 69, 70, 235n, 260, 261
Barnes, Frederick 156
Barrie 72
Barristers see Lawyers
Bassett 97
Batchelor, John 117, 125
Bate, Clifford 40, 45, 85, 91, 212
Baudouin 207, 208
Beadon, Robert John 61, 69
Beato, Felix/Felice 212, 213n, 263, 268
Behring Sea/Strait 165, 166
Beijing 4n, 11n, 16, 258
Bell, Thomas 210
Bellevue Hotel 239
Belligerent's rights 162–165, 275
Beltram 103
Berchtold, Johannes 348

Bertie, Francis Leveson 66n, 328
Bertin, Louis-Émile 283n, 288
Berwick, George 100, 107, 193, 209n, 233
Bethell, Ernest Thomas 350
Bias in results see Prejudice
Bishop, clerk of HMCJ 85, 91
Bismarck, Prince 322, 324n
Black, John Reddie 38n, 119, 120, 201n, 202n
Blackmore, J 103
Blakiston, Thomas Wright 100, 196, 220, 266n, 273
  Assault on Kiroku 113–115, 117, 150
Blockley, Arthur and Blockley, Bridget 101n, 197, 209, 210, 218, 289, 290
Blyth, Adam 240
Board of Trade 136, 151, 179–181, 202, 285, 286
Bonar, Henry Alfred Constant 30n, 56, 336, 337, 349, 352
Bourne, Frederick Samuel Augustus 57
Braga, Filomeno 204
von Brandt, (Prussian Minister) 23n, 274
Brinkley, Captain 231, 232n
British Naval Mission to Japan 227
British Prize Court 162
British Regulations and Japanese laws and regulations 12–14, 18, 31–39, 48, 73, 93, 102, 110, 116, 117, 119, 120, 138n, 149, 207, 247, 274, 318, 321, 345
  Attorney General of Hong Kong's input 14, 31, 33, 73, 177
Brown, Alfred 108
Browne, Ernest 309n
Browning case 15, 147, 258, 259
Brushfield, H.A.C. 62, 65, 66, 69, 94n, 181, 213, 214, 241, 350
Budd, James 139
Buildings tax 352
Bungay, George 104
de Bunsen, Maurice 117, 232n, 283–285, 294, 296, 311, 327, 328
Burkhill 274
Butterfield & Swire 204

Cabeldu, Philip S. 199
Campbell 70, 224
Campbell oil exchange affair 82, 120
Cape Omaezaki 181, 182, 186
Cardiff 101
Carew case 19n, 42, 43n, 54, 66, 68, 72, 84, 101, 106, 132, 139, 143, 144n, 255, 258, 259
Carew, Edith Mary Hallowell see *Carew case*
Carew, Walter see *Carew case*
Carlson, Gustave 179n
Caroe 156
Carozzi 101n, 170
Carrea, Wilhelmina 197
Carter 110
Chang, Kai 169
Chang, Richard T. xxiii, 65n, 115, 307, 308n, 339, 345
Chesterman, Robert 224
Chief Justice
  of Hong Kong 12n, 19, 118, 119, 261n, 262,
  of the Supreme Court xxvii, 15–19, 22–25, 27, 28, 31, 34n, 39, 48, 49, 53–59, 73, 87, 88, 90, 91, 113, 132, 142, 144, 145, 147, 192, 199, 206n, 253, 262, 266, 270, 294, 301, 313, 340, 343, 349, 350; see also Deputy Judge
China xxvii, 119, 159, 189, 198, 239, 324, 329, 333
  China-Japan War 1894–1895 see Sino-Japanese War, 1894–1895
  Consular courts and extra-territoriality xxii, xxiv, 3, 4, 6, 14–16, 19, 22, 28, 33, 34, 39, 48, 50, 51, 54, 57, 73, 96, 152, 154, 159, 161, 219, 220, 241, 249–251, 276n, 277, 291, 295, 296, 298, 303, 306, 312, 335, 339, 340, 346, 347
  Consular and court staff in 74–76, 83, 87, 336
  Transfer of prisoners to 142, 143
  Western traders in 11, 50, 118, 194, 277, 284, 330
Chinese extra-territoriality in Japan 155, 156, 160, 162, 172, 249, 251
Chishima cases xxiv, xxv, xxvii, xxviii, 54, 67, 68, 180, 181, 183, 185, 188, 243, 244, 249, 267, 269–271, 276n, 277, 282, 283–315, 327, 344, 347
Clarendon, Earl of 52, 154
Clarke, Charles C. 239
Clarke, Edward 118n
Clataud 199n
Clifton, S. 201n
Collins, A.R. 201n
Colomb, Capt. Philip RN 206
Commander Islands 166
Committal proceedings 62, 65, 94, 110, 117n, 125, 147, 187, 188, 344
Company, formation of British company in Japan 247, 248
Comptoir d'Escompte de Paris 102, 139
Connor 100, 107, 209n
O'Conor 235

Constantinople 3, 15, 39n, 49, 50, 249
Consular assistance following the 1894 Treaty's coming into force 7
Consular constables 45, 66, 82, 84, 86, 88, 95, 102, 103, 105, 111, 113, 114n, 139, 140n, 141, 146n, 169, 171, 176, 197, 208, 212, 238
Contempt of court 39, 106, 128, 132, 226, 243, 260, 273
Cook 206, 271
Copper Island 165
Cortazzi, Sir Hugh 1n
Coster, C.H. 176n
Counsel see Lawyers
Counter-claims 245, 248, 249, 251, 278, 279, 289–299, 302–307, 310–312, 320, 346
Cousens, Alfred and *Cousens case* 112, 119, 131, 138, 140n, 150, 261
Creagh, John 64–66, 69, 96, 103, 233
Cross, Henry 218
Crosse, Charles Neville 65, 66, 69, 94n, 130n, 131n, 213, 225, 229, 349
Crown Advocate 72, 73, 94, 132
  China 55, 90, 250, 336
  China and Japan 53, 71, 74, 89
  Japan 66, 69, 74, 75, 83, 94, 96, 132, 133, 188, 258n
Crown Prosecutor see Crown Advocate: Japan
Cruchley, William 60–62, 64n, 69, 135, 204, 208
Currie, Sir Philip 202
Customs seals, breach of regulations see Trade Regulations
Cuthbert, William 41, 72, 106, 139, 144, 234n

de Daeker, Louis 173
Dagu 164, 165
Danenberg 213
Davidson, John Richard 62, 63n, 67
Davis, John 145, 146
Davison, James 213n, 224
Davison, W.E. 58, 327
Deane, J. Parker 2n, 160
Dening 204, 205
Denison, Henry Willard 59
Dent & Co. 201n
Deportation 11, 14, 70, 82, 97, 106, 113, 118, 119, 125, 135, 136, 143–147, 174, 253
Deputy Judge 17, 23, 51, 53
Derby, Earl of 18, 37, 38, 77n, 153, 154, 156, 160, 258, 344
Desaunais, Aristide Victorin Eugene 125
Deshima 6
Dessandier, Messrs. & Cie. 195
Devine, W.H. 237
Diack, Elizabeth 210
Dickins, Frederick Victor 25, 62, 63, 67, 69, 81, 83, 86, 133, 228, 260, 263, 268
Discipline on merchant vessels see Offences against discipline
Divorce see Matrimonial jurisdiction
Dixon, James W. 208
Doel, Peter 111n
Dohmen, Martin 4, 39, 55, 79–83, 85n, 101n, 115, 119, 129, 150, 217, 218, 220, 221, 260, 264, 266, 273, 290
Drake, Captain see the *Normanton* case
Duman-Vence, Commander 125
Duncan, Andrew 63n, 64, 67n, 208, 245n
Duus, John 208, 227, 247

Ebisu Minato xxiin
Edelman, Albert 245
Ehime ken 283
Elton, Robert 235
Enslie, James Joseph 56n, 57, 74, 79, 80, 83–85, 88, 95, 104, 193, 219, 241, 264, 271, 273, 274, 343
Esplen 207n
Eusden, Richard 75, 77, 78, 83, 90n, 100n, 220, 228n, 235n, 272, 273
Extradition 39, 332–334, 347
Extra-territoriality
  Background and meaning xxi–xxv, xxviii, 1–10, 30, 76, 80, 85, 112, 114, 149, 151–153, 227–230, 284, 299, 303, 304, 310, 339–348
  Japan's policy to end extra-territoriality 9, 10, 37, 39, 63, 100, 115, 123, 149, 150, 160, 196, 283, 288, 297, 312, 315–338
  Kaleidoscope of regimes 153, 155, 158, 159, 162, 241–251

O'Farrell, Daniel 146, 253
Faulds 124, 150
Fawcett 140n
Fines
  for criminal offences xv, 11, 13, 14, 18, 21, 24, 36–38, 42–45, 93, 106–108, 110–112, 114–119, 121, 123, 124, 128, 134–138, 148, 255, 259, 260, 271, 274, 287, 344, 349
  for failure to register 228
  for non-appearance as a juror 42, 213
  for shipping offences 158–160, 169n, 171–175, 178, 183
Firearms offences, etc 33, 35–38, 102, 104, 117–119, 123–125, 136, 138n

Fletcher, Consul 21, 23, 260, 261
Fletcher, master of *Osaka* 178
Flowers, Marcus 17, 75, 90n, 125, 126, 202n, 208n, 209, 217, 224, 238–240, 243, 245, 274, 317
Ford, Richard 102, 199, 238
Foreign Minister (of Japan) 6, 109n, 158n, 189, 220, 292, 293, 319, 323, 325, 327, 328, 334, 345
France 41, 125, 126, 162, 163n, 164, 195, 196, 243, 283n, 288, 291, 308, 311, 312, 319, 322, 323, 334
Francis, Q.C. 66n, 67, 294, 295
Fraser, Hugh 142, 166, 237n, 326–329, 333
Fraser, John 51, 54
French, Sir George 49, 51, 53, 54, 57, 71, 72, 83, 84, 87, 146, 266, 273
Fujita, Hiro 104
Furious riding 33, 108, 110, 150
Gaols 139–144
  British gaol at Yokohama 73, 88, 94, 113, 137, 139, 140, 143, 144, 170, 333, 349,
  Consular gaols 86, 94, 102, 106, 126, 137, 140n, 143, 144, 349
  Gaol terms see Prison sentences
  Japanese gaols 136n, 137, 139, 140–142, 349
  Transfer of prisoners within Japan 142
  Victoria gaol, Hong Kong 13, 19, 118, 139, 142–144, 258, 259
Gaudaubert 271
Gen-ga-so 155
Gerard, James 234n
Germany 23, 41, 62, 163, 232, 246, 247, 291, 308, 311, 312, 315, 319, 322–324, 331
Gilbert 150
Giske 207
the *Glamorganshire* 185, 188, 222, 250n, 269–271, 277–282, 340, 344
Glover & Co. see Glover, Thomas
Glover, Alfred 214
Glover, Thomas (and bankruptcy) 106, 201n, 203, 211, 224, 239, 263, 267, 271, 274, 317
Goertz 208, 270
Gohei, Ikushima 216
Goodwin, Charles Wycliffe 48, 49, 54, 59, 70, 78, 83, 217n
  Assistant Judge
    and Appeals 18, 25n, 71, 198, 199, 263, 267
    on circuit in Japan 23n, 53, 192, 341
    in Shanghai 16, 18, 43, 51, 55, 77n, 178, 247
    and the Yokohama Court 23, 24, 40, 42, 45, 48, 51–53, 58n, 63, 87–89, 145, 208, 221
Gower, Abel 63, 129, 135, 136, 138, 141, 142, 144, 228, 229, 247, 260, 263, 274, 317
Granville, Earl 6, 79, 89n, 94n, 202, 227, 261n, 316, 317, 320, 330, 344, 348
Greenberg 201
Grey, Andrew 239n
Gribble, Henry 199, 317n
Grigor 201n
Gross, P. 68
Gubbins, John Harrington 81, 82, 232n, 316, 323–325, 327–331, 346
Gye 201n, 202n

Hakodate xxi, 32, 43, 47, 64, 83, 98, 110n, 177, 188, 227n, 228, 232, 233, 235n, 275, 322, 352n
Hakodate cases
  Appeals 198, 199, 227, 265–268, 270, 272, 276
  Civil cases 194–196, 200, 208, 215, 216, 219, 224
  Criminal cases 100–102, 107, 113, 114n, 125, 128, 146n, 227
  Inquests 234, 235
  Naval Courts 181, 182
  Shipping and shipping offences 98, 155, 159, 168, 169, 175, 178, 179
Hakodate Consul 77, 78, 81, 83, 88, 113, 227, 343
Hakodate Court (including records) xxv, xxvi, 43, 64, 81, 91, 97–100, 155n, 171n, 209n
Hakodate, Governor of 113, 114
Hakodate Incident, 1897 161, 165, 347
Hall 124, 199
Hall & Holtz 203, 269
Hall, John Carey 57, 66, 78, 80, 85, 108, 130, 131, 142, 143, 197, 198n, 213, 214, 225, 226, 229, 259n, 342, 351
Hannen, Lord 52, 231
Hannen, Sir Nicholas John 34, 49, 56, 80, 86, 89, 343
  Barrister 42, 51, 61, 178
  Chief Justice (and as acting Chief Justice) xxvii, 48, 49n, 53–56, 87, 90, 266, 272, 295, 296, 299, 306, 310, 312, 349
  Crown Advocate 55, 74, 89
  Judge of HMCJ 48, 53, 56, 57, 74, 75, 94, 96, 158, 177n, 188, 202, 205, 207, 208, 217, 233, 244, 259, 268, 273, 274, 278, 279, 290

Judge of Yokohama Court 23–26, 40, 42, 45, 48, 51–53, 58, 70, 77, 80, 83, 86, 87, 90, 114n, 122, 133, 145, 220, 221, 224, 231
Treaty Revision 53, 54, 321, 325, 326
Hardnett 139, 184
Harris, Townsend 6
Harrison, Edward 106
Harrison, Frederick 233
Hart, J.W. 199n, 204
Hartley cases 27, 29, 30, 38, 121, 123, 128, 149, 253, 256, 260, 304, 310, 347
Hartley, John see *Hartley cases*
Hatoyama, Kozo 231
Hatten, Alfred 145
Hawai'i xxiin
Hazlett, Alvum 103n
Hennessy, Sir John Pope 266, 318
Her Britannic Majesty's Court for Japan (**HMCJ**) see HMCJ
Her Britannic Majesty's Supreme Court for China and Japan (**Supreme Court**) see Supreme Court
Herschell, Lord 297, 298, 301, 313
Hertslet, Sir Edward 296, 297, 304
Hewett, Capt. RN 132
Hill, Captain 206
Hill, G.W. 63n, 67, 68
Hinckley, Frank 3, 6
Hiogo Gas Company 247
Hiogo Hotel case 65, 193, 212
Hiogo ken, Governor of 65, 104, 187
Hiogo Treasure case 10n, 64, 256, 257
HMCJ 10n, 40, 82, 232n, 340, 341
Closure of 57, 226, 241, 328, 336, 337, 349
Costs, fees and procedures of 39, 44, 45, 71, 72
Establishment and jurisdiction 27–30, 39, 48, 142, 153, 166, 167, 205, 209, 211, 232
Extraordinary jurisdiction 17, 28n, 39, 192, 193, 262
Judges 16n, 28n, 30n, 34n, 48, 54–57, 71, 73, 78, 88, 343, 349
Lawyers practising in see Lawyers
Other officials 86, 88, 89, 96, 237, 349
Records of xxv, xxvii
Registrars 83, 84, 88, 202, 206, 281, 349
HMCJ cases
Appeals 28, 29, 81, 244, 254–257, 262, 264–269, 273, 278–281
Chishima cases 244, 268, 288, 290–293, 296, 298, 300–302, 304–306, 309–312
Civil cases 110, 166, 177, 191–194, 202, 206, 211, 212, 217
Criminal cases 41, 93–95, 110, 115, 124, 126, 138, 142, 145, 146n, 186n, 188, 234n
Lunacy 233, 343, 349
Probate and Administration 236, 237, 240
HM Treasury 11, 72, 87–90, 241, 337
Hoare, James E. xxiv, 9, 113
Hobart-Hampden 131n, 213
Hobhouse, Lord 301
Hodges, George 86, 349
Hodgson, Pemberton 11, 114n
Hodnett 110
Hoey 265, 274, 275
Hokkaido 113, 125, 181
Hollman 199
Holme, Ringer & Co. 242, 317n
Hong Kong 19, 113, 118, 174, 176, 177, 185, 233, 240, 248, 262, 279, 283, 332, 334, 350; see also *Moss v. Alcock*
Attorney General see Attorney General of Hong Kong
Chief Justice see Chief Justice of Hong Kong
Deportation from Japan to 113, 144, 146
Government (and officials) 44, 45, 103, 118, 143, 144, 258
Governor 147, 258, 266, 318
Lawyers 15, 52n, 58, 62, 66n, 67, 70, 147, 294, 350
Prize Court 162
Supreme Court of Hong Kong see SCHK
Transfers from Japan to gaol in see Gaols: Victoria gaol, Hong Kong
Transfers from Japan for trial in
of criminal cases 13, 15, 19, 147, 148
of shipping offences 155, 156
Hong Kong and Shanghai Banking Corporation (**HSBC**) see HSBC
Honjo, Allyson 5
Hornby, Sir Edmund Grimani 30, 33, 39, 40, 49, 73, 74, 77, 78, 81, 83n, 86–88, 91, 147, 243, 247, 249
Arbitration 223, 224, 275, 276
Belligerent rights 164
Cases
Appeals 25n, 77, 147n, 192, 242, 254, 255, 258–260, 261, 263, 268–276
in China 49, 87, 291, 295
Civil 193, 202, 203, 208, 209, 212, 213, 218
Criminal 95, 113–116, 122, 123, 128, 138, 147

Probate and Administration 89, 235n, 236n, 238, 239
Shipping offences 154, 176
on circuit in Japan 20n, 23, 40n, 49, 50, 54, 66, 192, 193, 341
Court costs and fees 43, 72, 220, 270
Deportation 145, 146
Gaols 140–143
Lawyers 58–61, 66, 67, 69–71
Marriages 230, 231, 341
OC1865 and associated Rules 16, 42, 48, 245
OC 1878 26, 29, 249
Registration of British Subjects 228, 229
Retirement 29, 45, 49, 53, 84, 87
Turkey 14, 15
Yokohama Court 20–29, 45, 51, 52, 236n, 254, 263, 342, 343
House of Lords 240n, 297, 301,
Hozumi, Nobushige 305
HSBC 84, 195, 203, 246, 256, 257, 263, 267n, 341
Huddle, William 238n
Hyver, C 243

Ichinoka Antimony Mining Corporation 225
Imperial Japanese Government see Japanese government
Imperial Japanese Navy 283, 288, 308
Imperial Japanese Railways see Japanese Railways
Imperial University 63, 68, 231, 305n
Indictable offences 24, 26, 41, 93–96, 103, 104, 110, 115, 125, 126, 147, 171, 188, 253
Inland Sea 32, 110, 207, 295–297, 299, 310
Inouye, Kaoru Count 158n, 189, 293, 323
Inquests 41, 42, 66, 115, 141, 179, 234, 235
Inquiries into Deaths at Sea (Inquiries) 151, 152, 179, 180, 349
Instructions to Consuls 50
Interpreters and Interpretation 4, 66, 68, 84, 85, 125n, 129, 141n, 213, 286, 287, 316n, 326, 345; see also Student Interpreters
Intestacy see Probate and Administration
Iran 333
Isaacs, Messrs Bros. 222
Istanbul See Constantinople
Italy 196, 315n, 319, 331
Ito, Hirobumi 327
Iwakura Mission 4n, 6, 198, 310, 316, 317, 330, 348
Iwakura, Tomomi see Iwakura Mission
Iwasaki, Yatoro see Mitsubishi Shipping
Izmir 51, 258

Jacobs, Ernest 104
Jacobs, Mary Esther 258
Jaffray 209
Jamieson, George 48, 49n, 57, 76, 78, 132, 240, 244, 274, 291, 295, 296, 310, 312
Japan, Emperor of 20, 35, 163n, 208, 244
see also *Chishima cases*
Japanese civil war, 1868/69 162, 163, 275
Japanese government xxiv, 2, 5–10, 26, 27, 30n, 32, 35–38, 65, 67–69, 74, 75, 111, 114–120, 122, 124, 135, 136, 154, 161, 164–166, 181, 187, 189, 196, 198, 199, 220, 221, 223, 224, 227, 228, 231, 234, 246, 249, 251, 256, 257, 270, 271, 275, 276n, 315, 316, 318, 319, 323–329, 332–336, 345, 347, 349, 352; see also *Chishima cases*; Foreign Minister; Ministry of Justice; and Ministry of Marine
Japanese Lawyers 62, 68, 133n, 165, 305, 336, 349, 350
Japanese Pilotage Regulations 110, 207
Japanese Prize Court 162–165
Japanese Railways 36, 61, 63n, 69n, 125, 146, 204, 262
Jardine Matheson 17, 162, 164, 165, 212n, 322
Jenkins, Griffith Richard 236n
Jinrikisha coolies 45, 104, 107, 109, 111, 129, 217
Johnson (defendant) 139
Johnson, Cereno 173
Johnson, H. Ross 59, 70
Johnson, Joseph 235
Jones, C.P. 17
Jones, F.C. xxiv, 340, 344
Judge (including acting Judge) xxv, 18, 28n, 236, 238, 242, 253, 254, 257, 260–263, 271, 273, 274, 301n, 339, 343, 344
of HMCJ 4, 25, 27, 28, 30, 39, 40, 45, 47–58, 71–75, 78, 84, 87, 88, 90, 91, 94, 132, 140, 142, 144, 145, 153, 212, 233, 264, 267, 268, 281, 282, 311, 337, 343, 344
of Supreme Court see Chief Justice; and Deputy Judge
of Yokohama Court see also Assistant Judge of HMCJ; and Yokohama Court: Judges
Jury 42, 43, 118, 119, 147, 180, 262, 345
civil cases 26, 71, 197, 206–209, 212, 213, 218, 268–270, 272
criminal cases 42, 93–96, 115, 126, 131–133, 149, 186, 188, 234n, 255, 259

inquests see Inquests
jurors and jury lists 41, 42, 106, 134, 213

Kaburaki, Lieutenant 285–287, 308
Kader, Abdul 17
Kakichi 17
Kam Quen Sean 333
Kanagawa 32, 43, 82, 208, 254, 257
Kanagawa Consul see Yokohama Consul
Kanagawa Court xxvii, 10n, 23, 27, 40, 44, 55, 60, 77, 118, 147, 153, 192, 201n, 205, 208, 211, 213, 242, 245, 268, 271
Kanagawa, Governor of (and other Japanese officials) 67, 111, 117, 118, 161, 220, 245, 249, 251, 286, 335
Kaohsiung xxii
Kawase (ambassador to London) 328
Kelly, John 174
Kennedy, J.G. 82
Kenny, William Joseph 286, 287, 309
Kerr 140
Kettle, Constable 86
Kimberley, Earl of 90, 297, 306, 329, 331
King, Archibald (and *Reg. v Archibald King*) 63, 68, 110, 115, 131, 134, 260
King, Edward Wilson Claud 233, 234n
Kirby, E.C. 245n, 267, 272
Kirkwood, William Montague Hammett 63, 64, 67–69, 72, 74, 75, 84, 103, 181, 189, 209, 273, 274, 285, 287, 290n, 293–295, 309, 336, 343, 350
Kitano, Yoshibei 285
Kniffler, Louis and Hugo 23n, 193, 212n, 222, 264, 265, 273, 274
Kobe xxi, xxii, 17, 41, 61, 66, 82, 176n, 204, 229, 232, 247, 249, 251, 257, 259, 278, 317, 322, 332, 336, 352 see also Gaols: Consular gaols; and Lawyers
Kobe cases
Appeals 257, 260–262, 264–266, 269
Chishima cases 283, 284n, 290, 291
Civil 84, 193–197, 199–201, 205, 211–217, 219, 221, 225, 226, 336, 342
Criminal cases 93–103, 105, 106, 108, 115, 116, 122, 123, 125–130, 134, 135, 137–140, 143, 146, 148, 187, 228, 344, 347n
Inquests 234, 235
Inquiries into deaths at sea 179
Lunacy 64, 233
Naval Courts 115, 181–183, 186, 187
Shipping offences 156, 167–170, 173, 175,
Kobe Consul 18, 40, 55, 80, 82, 83, 88, 96, 125, 130, 138, 343
Kobe Consulate 56, 85
Kobe, Governor of 129, 249, 251, 335; see also Hiogo ken, Governor of
Kobe newspapers and records xxvi, xxvii, 61, 65, 69, 97, 204, 259
Kobe, Regulations affecting 33
Korea 39, 57, 219, 320n, 329, 335, 350, 352
Kwok, Ching 179

Lami, Bang 183
Laufenberg 64, 65
Law Officers 2, 3n, 10–15, 20, 23, 26, 27, 30–38, 47, 72–74, 114, 119, 160, 161–163, 194, 231, 241, 247, 248, 257, 259n, 260, 274, 275, 296, 297, 304, 313, 346
Law Secretary 16, 24–26, 48n, 51, 54, 55, 73, 74, 78, 94, 95, 132, 202, 238, 262
Lawrence, Edward 63
Lawyers xxi, 9, 10, 15, 21, 22, 25, 34, 39, 40, 47, 50–55, 57–72, 78, 83, 84, 87, 94, 96, 103, 133, 148, 151, 180, 186, 188, 194, 208, 209, 221, 222, 228, 231, 235n, 238, 245, 246, 250, 255–257, 260, 267–270, 272–274, 280, 281, 290n, 291–295, 302n, 305, 313, 322n, 336, 343, 344, 349, 350, 352; see also: Hong Kong Lawyers; Japanese Lawyers ; and Shanghai lawyers
Layard, Consul 161
Lee, Fong 179
Lees, William 193, 206, 233
Leopold, Charles Emil 102, 144, 201, 255
Letters of Administration see Probate and Administration
Lewis, Rainbow & Co. 201n, 203, 274
Lewis, Richard 199
Linstroom 156
Litchfield, Henry Charles 59, 62, 63, 66, 69, 72, 75, 96, 133, 188, 336, 343, 349
Liverpool 238
Livingston 208
Lock, Edward 221, 222
Lock, Edward (of Niuzhuang) 239
Longford, Joseph Henry xxiin, 5, 82, 84–86, 139, 233, 234n, 285, 291
Lowder, John Frederick xxiin, 59, 63n, 65, 67–69, 75n, 117n, 123, 145, 180, 181, 187, 188, 231, 256, 258, 285–287, 290, 293–295, 306, 343, 349
Lowther, Gerald 161, 165
Lovell 239
Lucas & Walters 204, 264
Lunacy jurisdiction xxiv, 64, 84, 193, 232, 233

Lurgan, Lord 76
Lushington 3

McBain, Thomas 234
McClatchie 81
McEwen, J.P. 240
McGregor, H. 66, 95, 96
McKechnie, A.R. 201n, 202n, 208
McMaster, John 5
McNeill, Duncan 350
Macdonald, John 89, 241
Mackay, Edward 143
MacKenzie, K.R 97, 203, 239
Mackintosh, James 136
MacNagthen, Lord 301
Macpherson (Assessor in *Reg. v. Moss*) 118n
Macpherson, Alexander 103
Malcolmsen 201n
Malmesbury, Earl of 11
Maria Luz affair 52, 67, 68, 74
Marine Court of Inquiry (Japanese) 183–185, 287
Marks, Francis Walker 63, 70, 221, 273
Marriages xxiv, 230–232, 351
Martin 229
Masefield, John 94, 102, 125, 126, 143
Matrimonial jurisdiction 12, 191, 192, 209, 223, 340, 341
Matsuyama 283
Meiji government see Japanese government
Melsheimer 280n
Merchant Shipping Acts (MSA) xxviii, 151–153, 159, 167, 169, 171, 173, 175, 177–180, 234n, 308, 342, 349
Merchant Shipping Act 1854 (MSA1854) 152n, 155, 159, 172n, 176, 178
Merchant Shipping Act 1894 (MSA1894) 152, 178n, 179n, 308n
Mikado see Japan, Emperor of
Miller, Robert 111
Ministry of Justice 189, 285, 322, 323, 350
Ministry of Marine 305
Mitchell, James F. 102, 199, 210, 218, 222, 223
Mitsubishi Shipping 184, 206, 226, 238
Montaltado de Jesus, J.A. 197
Mooney, Joseph 136
Morf 225
Morimoto, Yoshimatsu 104
Moritani, Denzaburo 201n
Morris, Albert 128, 135, 221
Morrison, George 86, 89, 106, 254, 265
Moss affair (*Reg. v. Moss*) 19, 32, 35, 36, 47, 62, 117–119, 131, 134, 138n, 143, 150, 254, 274, 345n; see also *Moss v. Alcock*
Moss v. Alcock 11, 12n, 14, 15, 19, 77, 118, 119, 262n
Moss, C.D. 85, 91, 96, 188, 336, 349
Moss, Michael see *Moss affair* and *Moss v. Alcock*
Most favoured nation 8–10, 257, 315, 324n, 331, 334
Mowat, Robert Anderson 49, 51, 54, 76, 79, 273, 343
  Assistant Judge of Supreme Court 49, 50, 55, 57, 88, 278, 279
  Carew case 54n, 66, 255, 259n
  Chishima cases 244, 291, 293–295, 306, 311, 312
  Judge of HMCJ 30, 48, 53, 55, 56, 65, 84, 90, 166, 167, 193, 212, 233, 237
  Law Secretary 24, 49, 51n, 53, 54, 78, 176, 205n, 229n, 247n, 256
  Retirement 54, 56, 84, 233, 273
Muller, Albert 147
Munroe, Charles 97
Murray, George 219
Muta, Masajiro 104
Mutsu, Munemitsu 6, 161, 283, 328, 333
Myburgh Q.C. 280n
Myburgh, F.G. 17, 47, 61, 89, 121, 136, 143, 202n, 239, 271

Nagasaki xxi, 66, 105, 111, 114, 140, 144, 177, 189, 203, 207, 232, 237, 317, 322, 332, 334, 352; see also Gaols: Consular gaols
Nagasaki cases
  Appeals 255, 265–267, 269, 274, 276
  Chishima cases 283–285, 287
  Civil cases 17, 84, 107, 112, 177, 193–197, 199–203, 205, 209–211, 214–217, 222, 224, 233, 236n, 307, 342
  Criminal cases 41, 97–102, 104–107, 111, 121, 122, 124, 126, 127, 129, 135–137, 139, 146, 149, 150, 155
  Inquests 234, 235
  Inquiries into deaths at sea 179
  Naval Court 164n, 182, 284
  Probate and Administration 237, 239, 240
  Shipping offences 158, 167–172, 174, 175
Nagasaki Consul 11, 14n, 17, 47, 63, 80, 83, 86, 88, 106, 114, 125, 164, 165, 209, 227, 228, 273, 343
  Regulations issued by 33
Nagasaki Consulate 141n, 230n

Nagasaki Court 132
Costs and fees 43, 44
Hornby on circuit 20, 51n, 192, 209, 217
Records xxv–xxviii, 64, 97, 99, 103, 104, 148, 158, 167, 174, 182, 193n, 210–212, 234
Nagasaki, Governor of 1n, 113, 129, 218
Nagasaki newspapers xxvi, 64, 99, 182, 233n, 259
Nakamura, Shimsuke 218
Nakamura, Shobei 264
Naval blockades 162, 163, 165n
Naval Court of Enquiry xxviii, 115, 151, 152, 164, 165, 172, 179–188, 224, 243, 349
Naval Court and the *Chishima cases* 284–286, 303, 308, 309, 311
Neale, Lt. Col. St. J. 32, 47
Ness, Gavin Parker 62, 63n, 263
The Netherlands 6, 52, 160, 203, 291, 312
Netting off see set-off
Niigata xxi, xxii, 88, 235, 352n
Niuzhuang 239
Noble 141, 234n
Norman, Arthur 84, 124, 193, 233, 259
Normanton case 65, 66, 104, 115, 175, 185–189, 257, 283, 309, 344
Norris, Captain 206
North German Confederation see Germany
Norton-Kyshe, James William 76
Norway see Sweden and Norway

Occidental Hotel, Kobe 197
Offences against discipline 152–155, 157, 158, 169, 170, 172, 173
Olsen, Adam 173
Okamura, Teruhiko 68
Okuma, Count 325, 331, 334
Opium 27n, 38, 123, 128, 135n, 149, 256; see also *Hartley cases*
Orders in Council see b. Legislation
Oriental Banking Corporation 45
Osaka xxi, xxii, 33, 82, 88, 111n, 141, 142, 167, 199, 200, 205, 207, 336, 352
Osborn 229
Ottoman Empire see Turkey

P&O 145, 182, 185, 192, 205, 263, 276; see also *Chishima cases*
Pardon, Minister's power of 19, 258, 259
Paris, Joseph 174
Parkes, Sir Harry 20n, 52, 73, 74, 77, 83, 111, 113, 114, 120, 133, 147, 158, 176n, 198, 199, 229, 258, 260
Austro-Hungarian treaty, negotiations for 9, 10, 316
Consular and judicial establishment 77, 78n, 82, 86, 220, 221
Consul-General in Shanghai 15n, 207
Extra-territoriality and Japanese attempts to end it 4, 36–38, 315, 317, 318–320
Korea 57
Regulations, promulgation of 33, 36–38, 116, 120, 163
Section 47, OC1881 250, 292, 293
Yokohama Court: establishment and jurisdiction 21–23, 26, 27n, 29, 51, 52, 69
Pauncefote, Julian (Lord Pauncefote) 27n, 202
Peacock, Peter 86n, 89
Pearce, H.J. 64, 65
Pedlar, Neil 232
Peninsular and Oriental Steam Navigation Company (**P&O**) see P&O
Perez, Remegio 66, 213, 225
Persia see Iran
Peru xxiin, 52
Petersen, Peter 159, 235
Philadelphia 183
Phillimore, Sir Robert Joseph 2n, 3n, 162
Phillimore, Sir Walter 280n
Phillips, Charles 204
Piggott, Sir Francis Taylor 69, 326
Playfair, Frank 84, 94n, 130, 213, 225, 226
Plunkett, Sir Francis 53, 105, 189, 292, 293, 317n, 320, 321, 323, 325
Pollard (Attorney General in Hong Kong) 147
Port of Registry 176, 177, 286
Porter, Alexander 64, 208, 219, 224, 272
Portugal 160n, 329n,
Prejudice xxiii, xxviii, 120, 303, 304, 307, 309, 310, 339, 345, 346
appeals 268, 269, 306
civil cases 191, 207, 214–219
criminal cases 112, 115, 120, 126–135, 149
Naval Courts 184, 185, 188, 309
shipping offences 156, 173
Prison sentences see also Gaols
Criminal cases 13, 14, 18, 36, 65, 77n, 93, 97, 99, 102, 108, 110n, 115, 118, 119, 126, 130, 132, 134n, 135–139, 144, 174, 175, 188, 221, 234n, 254, 258, 342
for contempt 226
Shipping offences 152, 158, 169–171, 173–176

to be served outside Japan 142, 143
Privy Council xxivn, 3, 18, 24–26, 28n, 29, 42, 43n, 54, 202, 249, 254–257, 259, 262, 268, 276–278, 280–282, 284, 291, 292, 295–301, 304–306, 308, 310, 312, 313, 340, 342
Privy Council Office (**PCO**) 277, 280n, 297, 301n
Prize Court see British prize Court; and Japanese Prize Court
Probate and Administration 11, 40, 89, 197, 236–241, 274, 341
Protection and protective jurisdiction xxiv, 13, 153, 159, 177, 228, 229, 232, 245, 347
Prussia see Germany
Punitive jurisdiction (as distinguished from protective jurisdiction) 151, 153, 154, 173
Pyne, Frederick 171n, 238

Quarantine regulations see British Regulations
Queen's Advocate see Law Officers
Qui, Ah 177
Quin, John James 80, 126, 164n, 165, 245n, 259

ss *Ravenna* see *Chishima cases*
Reed, Sir Edward James 318
Reed, William 240
Registrar of:
  HMCJ (and Yokohama Court) 83–85, 88, 91, 202, 206, 212, 281, 282, 349
  Supreme Court 16
Registration of British Subjects 13, 86, 100, 106, 110n, 128, 148, 196, 227–229, 351
Regulations see British Regulations
Reich, S. 197
Reilly, Sir Francis Savage 16, 34
Rennie, Sir Richard Temple 53, 81, 87
  Barrister in Shanghai 49, 52, 66, 71, 74, 263
  Chief Justice 48, 50, 87, 90, 263, 278, 279, 290n, 291, 293, 295, 298, 343
  Ending of extra-territoriality 4, 321
  Judge of HMCJ 39, 48, 53–55, 88, 207, 210, 255, 264, 266
  Shipping offences 152n, 156
Reynell 193, 226, 272, 336
Rice, Cecil Spring 289, 291, 304
Richards, C.L. 234
Richeson, John 238
Ricker 208
Robben Island 166, 171n
Robertson, Russell 40, 45, 57, 77, 83, 245, 343
  Arbitration 223, 275
  Circuit to Hakodate 64, 91, 188, 233
  Consul in Kanagawa/Yokohama 5, 21, 25, 53, 55, 80, 98, 217, 266, 342
  Qualification as barrister 79, 266
  Shipping offences 158, 172, 180, 181, 245n
Robinson, Alfred 66, 188, 257
Robinson, Edward 66, 96
Roderic 204
Rosebery, Earl of 227, 294, 296, 297, 301, 321, 328, 329, 344
Ross, Alexander 199
Ross, John (Assessor in *Reg. v. Moss*) 118n
Ross, John (sailor on *Bullion*) 157
Rowe, Mr & Mrs 65, 225, 226
Royal Navy 116n, 161, 163, 168, 180
Rules of procedure in the Courts (Rules) 12, 14, 16, 23, 24, 26, 58, 60, 61, 74, 94, 191, 219, 220, 228, 245, 247–249, 253, 256, 257, 260–263, 270, 293, 296, 300, 301, 306, 309
Russell, Earl 13, 20, 32–34, 50, 73
Russell, Lord John see Earl Russell
Russia 1n, 6, 30, 106, 163, 165–167, 171, 308, 311, 329
Ryutara, Koide 62

Sailors xxii, xxviii, 57, 84, 85, 97–102, 104, 107, 108, 110, 111, 125, 130, 132, 137, 138, 145, 147, 148, 151–179, 183, 186, 189, 195, 196, 235, 245n, 273, 283, 286–288, 300, 304, 305, 309, 311, 347
Salisbury, Marquis of 38, 71, 90, 166, 232, 256, 257, 293, 302, 310, 319, 321, 326–328, 344
da Salvo, George 174
Sameshima 317n, 319
Sanders, F.H. 129
Sanderson, Sir Thomas 54n, 302n, 324, 329, 331
Sanski 113
Saris agreement 1
Saris, Captain 169
Sasaki, Otajiro 104
Sasebo 164, 165
Satow, Sir Ernest Mason 5n, 7, 19n, 30, 45, 56, 66, 69, 75, 79–82, 84, 86, 120, 133, 234n, 258, 325, 331, 333–336, 351
Satsuma daimyo 162
Sawa 220
Scarfield, Elizabeth 101, 144n
SCHK 14, 15, 248, 343
  Moss v. Alcock 11, 12n, 14, 19, 118, 119, 262

OC1865 17, 19, 192, 262
pre-1865 jurisdiction 12, 13, 47, 93n, 147, 191, 192
pre-1865 Appeals 11, 12n, 261, 265
Schroeder, F. 62, 69, 273
Scidmore, George Hawthorne 68, 350
Sclavo 159
Scotland, R.B. 224
Scott, John Marshall 108, 116, 204
Scully, Eileen xxiv
Seal fishing 30, 101, 106, 165, 166, 170, 171
Searle 243
Security, provision of
in Appeals 262, 270, 271, 273, 276
in *Chishima cases* 293, 295, 296, 301, 302
in civil cases 23n, 221, 228, 249, 250, 261n, 271, 278, 279, 347
for Letters of Administration 238
Seitz, Carl 204
Selborne, Viscount 302
Selby, Prideaux 207
Sentake, Seijiro 104
Set off 248, 290, 307
Shanghai 66, 67, 84, 86, 89, 96, 142, 146, 152, 157, 165, 176, 202n, 205, 219, 233, 240, 310, 312, 346, 347, 350
Consul-General 15n, 27, 78, 207, 234, 235
Consul-General and Chief Justice positions unified 49n, 53, 57, 87
Shanghai Customs Service 240
Shanghai Lawyers 49–55, 62, 63, 65–67, 70–72, 87, 90, 96, 178, 250, 257, 270, 274, 295, 344, 349, 350
Shanghai Returns 95n, 194n, 201
Shibuya, Seigoro 245
Shimonoseki 32, 182; see also Treaty of Shimoneski
Incident 310
Straits 283
Shipping, civil disputes 23, 24, 72, 177, 192, 195, 197, 200, 205, 307, 341, 342; see also *Chishima cases*; and the *Glamorganshire*
Appeals 267, 277, 282
Shipping, registration 76, 86, 159, 169, 171, 173, 177, 255
Shipping offences xxviii, 43, 93, 96, 97, 99, 137, 148, 151, 167–176, 255, 266, 342, 347, 349
Appeals 253
Classification of offences 99, 170
Jurisdiction 152, 153, 156, 159, 331; see also Offences against discipline
Punishments 137, 174, 175
Shogun see Tycoon
Singapore 19n, 58, 177, 231n, 333
Sino-Japanese War, 1894–1895 xxii, 154, 161–163, 165, 308, 324n, 350
Skinner, P. Mackenzie 65, 66, 69, 225
Smale, John 14n, 34
Smyth, N.A. 125, 133
Snow, Captain 165
Solicitor General see Law Officers
Solicitors see Lawyers
Sowter, Misses 65, 197, 225, 226
Spain 315, 333
Stanley, Lord see Derby, Earl of
Star in the East Lodge 330
Stillfried, Baron Francis von 264
Stirling, Admiral 1, 6, 35
Stokes, A.P. 67, 294
Stokes, H. 280n
Streatfield, Francis Henry Thomas 29, 249, 304
Student Interpreters 7n, 55, 75, 76, 78, 80, 84, 85, 88, 90, 131n, 342, 343
Superficies 352
Sublime Porte see Turkey
Supreme Court 10n, 22, 24, 25, 29, 39, 50, 78, 115, 145, 199, 202n, 241, 291, 312, 339–341, 350 (*note Shanghai is often used synonymously with Supreme Court*)
Cases arising from Japan-based facts 176–179, 202n
Costs 43, 44, 71, 263, 270, 272
Establishment and jurisdiction 15–20, 23, 27–29, 39, 42, 48, 57, 73, 93, 153, 191n, 205, 209, 218, 223, 232, 236, 254, 262, 263, 335, 340, 341
Records xxvii, 24n, 58n, 67, 96, 236
Supreme Court of Hong Kong (**SCHK**) see SCHK
Sureties in criminal cases 32, 122n, 132, 145, 146, 209; see also Bail
Sutton, Charles 236n, 237
Swabey 119, 138n
Sweden and Norway 41, 156, 235n, 237, 315
da Sylva, Frederick 94n, 130n
Sylva, Joseph 214

Tabor 209
Tainan xxii
Taiwan xxii, 41n, 69, 86n, 102, 164, 352
Takahashi, Professor Sakai 165n
Tamsui xxii
Tanaka 244, 307
Tannenbaum, Joseph 110
Taylor, James K. 122
Temperance Hall, Yokohama 210

Tenterden, Charles Abbott (Lord Tenterden) 160
Terashima, Munenori 220
Terry, Professor Henry 63
Thailand 11, 76
Thompson, Victor 130n
Thornton, Sir Edward 160
Tison, Professor Alexander 65, 67
Todd 235
Togo, Hachihiro 164
Tokugawa see *Bakufu*
Tokyo xxi, xxv, xxvii, 17, 23, 31, 63, 82, 98, 115, 133n, 197n, 198, 245, 352n
Tokyo Court (and its proceedings and results) 44, 45, 64, 80, 81, 86, 97, 98, 101, 115, 124, 140, 167, 194–196, 199, 200, 216, 222, 235, 237, 266, 290, 343; see also *Campbell Oil exchange affair*; and King, Archibald
Tokyo Legation (including Minister to Tokyo) 4, 7n, 11n, 56, 84, 89, 144, 258, 311, 328
Tokyo Superior Court 246
Tokyo Vice-Consul 17, 43, 55, 80–82, 86, 88, 209
Tombrink 203, 224, 263
Topping, Angus 273
Torikusa 129
Trade Regulations (and Japanese Customs regulations) 7, 13, 37, 115, 120–123, 127, 128, 131, 135, 227, 257, 346
Transient visitors to Japan xxii, 99, 148, 149
Treaty limits 99, 116, 117, 125, 229, 318
Treaty of Commerce and Navigation, 1894 (**1894 Treaty**) xxviii, xxix, 7, 162, 283, 297, 299, 306, 312, 315, 328–331, 333, 334, 351, 352
Treaty of Humen, 1843 3, 4n
Treaty of Nanjing, 1842 4n, 31
Treaty of Shimonoseki, 1895 162, 163n, 308
Treaty of Tianjin 1858 1, 4, 6
Treaty of Tianjin, 1871 324n
Treaty of Yantai, 1895 163n, 324n
Treaty of Yedo 1858 (**Treaty**) xxi, xxii, xxiv, 1, 3, 6–13, 18, 22n, 27, 31–35, 37–39, 42, 93, 99, 115–117, 119–123, 128, 135, 148, 149, 151, 154, 160, 161, 191, 198, 200, 221, 227, 231, 244–246, 249, 256, 257, 275, 292–300, 305, 306, 310, 313, 315–320, 327 329, 332, 339, 346–348, 351
Treaty Revision 4, 38, 53, 54, 154, 188, 189, 251, 283, 291, 312, 315–337
Trench, Power Henry le Poer 165, 325
Trent Incident 164
Trone, Henry 146
Troup, James 81, 84, 343
  Chishima cases 284, 286
  Consul (other than Yokohama) xxii, 96, 103, 113–115, 131, 142, 143n, 146, 156, 186–188, 235, 238
  Consul/Consul-General at Yokohama (and Assistant Judge) 28, 30, 55, 56, 80, 81, 84, 94, 229, 273, 343
Truck, Herbert 235
Tsune, Kijima 268, 283, 297, 300, 304–306, 309, 310, 313; see also *Chishima cases*
Tucker 247
Turkey 9n, 14, 30n, 229, 249, 251, 333, 348
Turner, Cooper 62
Twiss, Sir Travers 2n, 162n
Tycoon 2, 16, 20, 35, 116, 117, 163n; see also *Bakufu*

United States of America 4, 6n, 35, 54, 59, 61, 153, 154, 157, 160–162, 164, 196, 237, 242n, 247, 249–251, 291, 311, 312, 319, 332, 343, 345; see also Washington

Vyse, Francis Howard 32, 35, 36, 62, 77, 83, 113, 117n, 118, 192, 208, 343n

Waggott, W.H. 264
Walford, Ambrose Berry 291, 294, 311, 350, 352
Walker, Ellen 110
Washington 157, 160, 319, 331
Wates, Captain 183
Watson, R.G. 36, 52, 89, 138, 229, 261
Wehrun, Louise 110
Westmoreland 125, 146
White, Constable 212
White, John 235
Whittall 244, 290, 307
Whymark, George Harvey 64, 225, 233
Wignall, J.H. 199, 224, 248
Wileman, Alfred Ernest 179, 181
Wilkie, Frederick 219, 224
Wilkins, John H. 59
Wilkinson, Hiram Parkes 67, 336, 350
Wilkinson, Sir Hiram Shaw 45, 49, 50, 57, 58, 232n, 343
  Acting Assistant Judge of HMCJ 94, 255
  Acting Assistant Judge of Supreme Court 57, 142, 143n
  Acting Law Secretary 26, 27, 30, 45, 48, 78, 140, 222, 246, 257, 272, 290
  Cases: Appeals 273, 276
    Carew case 30, 66, 72

Chishima cases 67, 291, 294
Civil cases 206, 213, 225, 228, 336
Criminal cases 126, 131, 146, 172
Hartley cases 27, 123, 253, 256, 257
Shanghai cases 278, 291n
Chief Justice 48, 56, 57, 87, 349, 350
Consular official in Kobe 122, 126, 138, 143, 171, 172
Crown Advocate for China 55, 74, 75, 90, 249, 250, 251
End of Extra-territoriality 226, 336, 337
Judge of HMCJ 48, 55–57, 71, 75, 84, 90, 143, 193, 233
Prosecutor in Japan 133
Qualification as lawyer 63, 79
Retirement 84, 87n
Shipping offences and jurisdiction 153–157, 161, 172, 249
Student Interpreter 54, 55, 76
Tokyo Vice-Consular Court 45
Yokohama Court see Acting Law Secretary
Will, John 100, 265
Willis 49
Wills see Probate and Administration
Wilson, George 142, 143n
Winchester, Charles Alexander
acting Consul-General 2, 15, 134, 135, 265
Consul Nagasaki 106
Witnesses 21, 41, 45, 61, 70, 77, 84, 131, 218, 221, 222, 225, 229, 231, 243
British in foreign and Japanese courts 4, 241–243
Japanese witnesses in Courts 15, 84, 85, 130, 133, 147, 149, 150, 217, 243, 286, 287, 308, 309
Specific cases 108, 128–130, 133, 134, 139, 147, 148, 183, 187, 208, 258, 286, 309
Witt, Sophie 201
Woodward, Edward Daniel 66, 84, 95, 96
Wooton, T. 204

Yeijuchi Minseki 104
Yiksang Incident 165
Yokohama xxi, xxvii, 4, 17, 21, 33, 39n, 41, 43, 52, 53, 56, 62, 64, 66, 74, 84, 86, 105, 114n, 115, 125, 126, 138, 147, 157, 164, 166, 167, 173, 178, 186, 187, 208, 223, 232, 235n, 255, 272, 318–320, 322, 328, 335, 337, 344, 349, 352; see also Gaols
Yokohama Bar (and barristers) see Lawyers
Yokohama British Garrison 106, 148, 150, 163
Yokohama cases 17, 20, 21n, 89, 95
Appeals 264–268, 271, 275
Chishima cases 284, 287, 290
Civil cases 177, 178, 194, 196, 197, 200, 201, 204, 205, 208, 209, 211–213, 215, 221, 222, 224, 264, 265, 272, 273, 340, 342
Criminal cases 95, 97–102, 106, 108, 110, 117n, 122, 123, 132, 138–140, 145, 148, 160
Inquests 234
Inquiries into deaths at sea 179
Naval Courts 182, 184, 185
Probate and Administration 236, 240
Shipping offences 158, 167–172, 175
Yokohama Consul (and Consul-General) xxv, xxvi, 5, 17, 18, 21, 25, 27, 28, 30, 32, 33, 35, 45, 47, 53, 55, 56, 69, 77, 79–81, 83, 88, 118, 153; see also Robertson, Russell; and Troup, James
Yokohama Consulate (and Consulate-General) 23, 40, 51, 85, 86
Yokohama Court 10n, 40, 45, 48n, 59, 66, 84, 91, 94
Costs of and fees in 43–45, 220
Establishment, jurisdiction and procedures xxvii, 20–27, 29, 34n, 40, 42, 47, 48, 50, 51, 74, 77, 85, 93, 145, 146n, 191, 193, 205, 206, 223, 224, 255, 263, 341–343
Judges 48, 52, 53, 55, 63, 78, 83n, 87, 89;
Records xxvi, xxvii, 52, 105, 192, 194, 195, 216, 337
Yokohama General Chamber of Commerce 226, 319
Yokohama, Governor of 5, 161; see also Kanagawa, Governor of
Yokohama newspapers xxvi, 62, 69, 98, 105, 162, 167, 168, 194, 195, 204, 212, 259
Yokohama Race Club 209
Yoshida, Mitsu 104
Young, John 240

Xiamen 164, 241

www.ingramcontent.com/pod-product-compliance
Lightning Source LLC
LaVergne TN
LVHW020650300926
849161LV00004B/878
* 9 7 8 9 0 0 4 2 5 7 5 6 6 *